THE PRINCIPLE OF LEGALITY IN INTERNATIONAL AND COMPARATIVE CRIMINAL LAW

This book fills a major gap in the scholarly literature concerning international criminal law, comparative criminal law, and human rights law. The principle of legality (non-retroactivity of crimes and punishments and related doctrines) is fundamental to criminal law and human rights law. Yet this is the first book-length study of the status of legality in international law – in international criminal law, international human rights law, and international humanitarian law. This is also the first book to survey legality and non-retroactivity in all national constitutions, developing the patterns of implementation of legality in the various legal systems (e.g., common law, civil law, Islamic law, Asian law) around the world. This is a necessary book for any scholar, practitioner, and library in the area of international, criminal, comparative, human rights, or international humanitarian law.

Kenneth S. Gallant is a professor at the University of Arkansas at Little Rock William H. Bowen School of Law. His previous positions include professor at the University of Idaho, prosecutor with the district attorney of Philadelphia, and clerk for the Hon. Louis H. Pollak of the U.S. District Court, Eastern District of Pennsylvania and for the Hon. Samuel J. Roberts of the Supreme Court of Pennsylvania. He has been a Fulbright Scholar at the National Law School of India University and Tribhuvan University in Nepal. He was elected as the first representative of counsel on the Advisory Committee on Legal Texts of the International Criminal Court, was a founding member of the International Criminal Bar, and was on its first governing council.

CAMBRIDGE STUDIES IN INTERNATIONAL AND COMPARATIVE LAW

Established in 1946, this series produces high-quality scholarship in the fields of public and private international law and comparative law. Although these are distinct legal sub-disciplines, developments since 1946 confirm their interrelation.

Comparative law is increasingly used as a tool in the making of law at national, regional, and international levels. Private international law is now often affected by international conventions, and the issues faced by classical conflict rules are frequently dealt with by substantive harmonization of law under international auspices. Mixed international arbitrations, especially those involving state economic activity, raise mixed questions of public and private international law, while in many fields (such as the protection of human rights and democratic standards, investment guarantees, and international criminal law) international and national systems interact. National constitutional arrangements relating to "foreign affairs," and to the implementation of international norms, are a focus of attention.

The Board welcomes works of a theoretical or interdisciplinary character, and those focusing on the new approaches to international or comparative law or conflicts of law. Studies of particular institutions or problems are equally welcome, as are translations of the best work published in other languages.

A list of books in the series can be found at the end of this volume.

The Principle of Legality in International and Comparative Criminal Law

KENNETH S. GALLANT
University of Arkansas at Little Rock

CAMBRIDGE UNIVERSITY PRESS
Cambridge, New York, Melbourne, Madrid, Cape Town, Singapore, São Paulo, Delhi, Dubai, Tokyo, Mexico City

Cambridge University Press
32 Avenue of the Americas, New York, NY 10013-2473, USA

www.cambridge.org
Information on this title: www.cambridge.org/9780521187602

First published 2009
First paperback edition 2010

A catalog record for this publication is available from the British Library

Library of Congress Cataloging in Publication data

Gallant, Kenneth S., 1951–
The principle of legality in international and comparative criminal law / Kenneth S. Gallant.
p. cm.
Includes bibliographical references and index.
ISBN 978-0-521-88648-2 (hardback)
1. Criminal jurisdiction. 2. International offenses. 3. Human rights. 4. International criminal courts. 5. Criminal law. I. Title.
K5165.G35 2008
345–dc22 2008037413

ISBN 978-0-521-88648-2 Hardback
ISBN 978-0-521-18760-2 Paperback

To the rule of law as a just and certain guide to human conduct

Brief Contents

Explanatory Note on Spelling — *page* xix
Acknowledgments — xxi
Introduction — 1
1 Legality in Criminal Law, Its Purposes, and Its Competitors — 11
2 A Partial History to World War II — 46
3 Nuremberg, Tokyo, and Other Postwar Cases — 67
4 Modern Development of International Human Rights Law: Practice Involving Multilateral Treaties and the Universal Declaration of Human Rights — 156
5 Modern Comparative Law Development: National Provisions Concerning Legality — 231
6 Legality in the Modern International and Internationalized Criminal Courts and in the UN Trust Territories — 303
7 Legality in Customary International Law Today — 352
Conclusion: The Endurance of Legality in National and International Criminal Law — 404
Appendix A: Chart of Non-retroactivity Provisions in Criminal Law by Nations — 411
Appendix B: Legality and Non-retroactivity Provisions as of 1946–47 — 425
Appendix C: Constitutional and Other National Provisions Implementing the Principle of Legality Today — 438
Bibliography — 541
Table of Authorities — 553
Index — 579
Afterword and Update — 599

Contents

Explanatory Note on Spelling *page* xix
Acknowledgments xxi

Introduction 1
0.a. Retroactivity, Justice, and Sovereignty 1
0.b. Plan of This Book 4
0.b.i. Outline of Chapters 4
0.b.ii. Principles and Rules: Two Key Definitions 6
0.c. The Arguments of This Book 8
0.c.i. The Argument: Non-retroactivity of Crimes and Punishments 8
0.c.ii. Some Sub-arguments 9
0.c.iii. The Meta-argument: Law as Created by International Criminal Courts and International Organizations in Light of Claims Made by Individuals 10

1 Legality in Criminal Law, Its Purposes, and Its Competitors 11
1.a. Legality in Criminal Law and the Rule of Law Generally 14
1.b. Purposes of Legality in Criminal Law 19
1.b.i. Human Rights Protective Purposes 20
1.b.ii. Legality and Legitimacy 23
1.b.iii. Separation of Powers, Democracy, and Legality in National and International Law 24
1.b.iv. Legality and the Purposes of Criminalization 26
1.b.iv.A. Accountability, Restorative Justice, and Reconciliation: Purposes of Criminal Law Applying Specifically, but Not

Exclusively, to International Criminal Law and Post-conflict Societies 30
1.c. Competitors to Strict Legality as a Principle of Law 31
1.c.i. Indeterminacy of Language and Impossibility of Pure Non-retroactivity 31
1.c.i.A. Statutory Interpretation as Eroding Legality 33
1.c.i.B. Common Law Development of Criminal Law 35
1.c.ii. Crime Creation by Analogy in Civil Law 36
1.c.iii. Legality as an Optional Principle of Law or Justice 38
1.c.iv. Legality as a Principle with Limited or No Binding Effect in International Criminal Law 38
1.c.v. Legality as Binding in Normal Circumstances, with Exceptions in Extraordinary or Transitional Times 39
1.c.vi. Defenses That Do Not Go to Whether an Act Is Criminal 39
1.c.vii. Legality and Prior Establishment of Court Systems 40
1.c.viii. Change of Name, Character, or Jurisdiction of Offenses 40
1.c.viii.A. In International Courts 41
1.c.viii.B. In National Courts: Domesticating International Crimes and the Problem of Representation Jurisdiction 42
1.c.ix. Collective Punishment or Punishment of Hostages 42
1.c.x. Authoritarianism and Anti-Legality 44

2 A Partial History to World War II 46
2.a. Overview 47
2.a.i. Civil Law and Common Law 47
2.a.ii. Islamic Law 51
2.a.iii. A Note on Japan and China 54
2.b. Literacy and Accessibility of Criminal Law 55
2.c. Between the Two World Wars 56
2.c.i. The Versailles Settlement and Criminal Law Legality 56
2.c.ii. Fascist and Communist Attacks on Legality between the Wars 59
2.c.ii.A. The End of Legality in the Weimar Republic's Laws 59

2.c.ii.B. Danzig's Abandonment of Legality and the Permanent Court of International Justice Response 62
2.c.ii.C. Other Dictatorships: The Soviet Union and Italy 64

3 Nuremberg, Tokyo, and Other Postwar Cases 67
3.a. Violations of the Laws and Customs of War as Criminal before Nuremberg: Atrocities and Other Crimes 69
3.a.i. Beyond Traditional War-Crime Atrocities 72
3.b. Nuremberg: Searching for Consensus 73
3.b.i. Anti-legality: Churchill and Morgenthau Favor Summary Executions 73
3.b.ii. The London Conference: The French Oppose Ex Post Facto Crime Creation; the Americans, Soviets, and British Favor Plenary Power to Define Crimes 76
3.b.ii.A. Negotiating the Ex Post Facto Issue at London 87
3.b.iii. The Major Nuremberg Trial: Ex Post Facto in the Indictment and Arguments 91
3.b.iii.A. The Indictment and Preliminary Defense Motion 91
3.b.iii.B. Arguments of the Prosecutors 93
3.b.iii.C. The Defense Arguments 99
3.b.iii.C.I. Authority of the Charter versus the Principle of Legality 100
3.b.iii.C.II. Crimes against Peace (Aggressive War) and Conspiracy 102
3.b.iii.C.III. War Crimes and Crimes against Humanity 104
3.b.iv. The Nuremberg Judgment 110
3.b.iv.A. The Crime against Peace (Aggressive War and War in Breach of Treaties) and Conspiracy 115
3.b.iv.B. War Crimes 117
3.b.iv.C. Crimes against Humanity 119
3.b.iv.D. Summary of the Main Nuremberg Judgment 125

3.b.iv.E. Divisions within the Nuremberg Tribunal? Judges Nikitchenko and Donnedieu de Vabres 126
3.c. Legality in Other Postwar Cases (Mostly from Europe) 129
3.c.i Recognition That an Act Is Criminal under Some Applicable Law When Committed as the Key to Legality of Crimes 130
3.c.ii. Against Legality: Retroactive Criminalization of Moral Wrongs and Non-criminal Legal Violations 134
3.c.iii. Retrospective Expansion of Jurisdiction in the Post–World War II National Courts 135
3.c.iv. Members of Criminal Organizations in the Nuremberg Charter and Control Council Law No. 10: Retroactivity and Collective Punishment 136
3.d. Legality in the IMTFE (Tokyo Tribunal): Dissensus Revealed 139
3.d.i. The IMTFE Charter 139
3.d.ii. The Majority IMTFE Judgment: Based in Existing International Law? 142
3.d.iii. The Separate IMTFE Opinions 143
3.d.iii.A. Justice Jaranilla (Philippines): Retroactivity Permissible in International Criminal Law 143
3.d.iii.B. President Webb (Australia): Retroactivity May Be Permissible 144
3.d.iii.C. Justice Röling (Netherlands): Retroactivity Permissible in International Criminal Law as Alternative to "Political" Disposition; *Nullum Crimen* Not a Principle of Justice 144
3.d.iii.D. Justice Bernard (France): Natural Law Is Not Retroactive Law 147
3.d.iii.E. Justice Pal (India): Against Retroactive Creation of Crimes; Admitting Retrospective Creation of Tribunals 150
3.e. If the Nuremberg and Tokyo Judgments Violated the Principle of Legality, Can They Nonetheless Form the Basis of Legitimate Law? Justice Pal Answers 152
3.f. Conclusion 155

4 Modern Development of International Human Rights Law: Practice Involving Multilateral Treaties and the Universal Declaration of Human Rights 156
4.a. The Universal Declaration of Human Rights 158
4.a.i. The Text 158
4.a.ii. History and *Travaux Préparatoires* of the UDHR Non-retroactivity Provision (and Beginnings of the ICCPR Provision) 160
4.b. The ICCPR 175
4.b.i. The Text 175
4.b.ii. History and *Travaux Préparatoires* of the ICCPR Non-Retroactivity Provision 178
4.b.ii.A. Beginnings, through Spring 1950 (Sixth Session of the Commission on Human Rights) 178
4.b.ii.B. 1952 and Beyond 188
4.b.ii.C. General Principles of Law: No Exception to Legality Intended 191
4.c. The Convention on the Rights of the Child: Universality of *Nullum crimen* and Prohibiting Even Accusations of Retroactive Crime 201
4.d. The Regional Human Rights Treaties: European, American, African, Arab 202
4.d.i. European Convention for the Protection of Human Rights and Fundamental Freedoms 203
4.d.ii. American Convention on Human Rights: Broadening of Procedural Protections 203
4.d.iii. African Charter of Human and Peoples' Rights: Against Collective Punishment 205
4.d.iv. Revised Arab Charter on Human Rights 205
4.d.v. Charter of Fundamental Rights of the European Union: Legality Controlling an International Organization? 206
4.e. Non-Derogability of Legality in the Treaties 206
4.f. Legality in the International Humanitarian Law System: Application to International and Internal Conflicts and Occupation 207
4.f.i. Non-retroactivity 207
4.f.ii. Against Collective Punishments and Hostage Taking to Ensure Good Behavior 211

4.g. Reservations to Provisions on Legality by Parties to the Worldwide Treaties 213
4.g.i. Lack of Reservations in the Treaties for *Ta'azir* Crimes in Islamic Law and Lack of Persistent Objection 214
4.h. Limits to Rule of Legality in Modern Treaties: Statutory Interpretation, Common Law Case Development, and Civil Law Analogy 217
4.i. Patterns of Treaty Nonparticipation 224
4.j. Individual, State, and International Organization Ability to Raise Legality in Criminal Proceedings as an International Law Claim under the Treaties 225
4.k. Status of Actions Discussed in This Chapter under International Law 228

5 Modern Comparative Law Development: National Provisions Concerning Legality 231
5.a. Content and Limitations of the Material in This Chapter and the Appendices on National Law 231
5.b. Legality in Constitutions of the World in 1946–47 237
5.c. Non-Retroactivity of Crimes and Punishments in National Legal Systems Today: At Least a General Principle of Law 241
5.c.i. Sources of the Requirement of Non-retroactivity of Crimes and Punishments in National Law 243
5.c.ii. Non-retroactivity in the Constitutional Texts: Act Focus and Law Focus 251
5.c.iii. Crimes According to International Law and General Principles of Law in the Constitutional Non-retroactivity Provisions and in National Judicial Practice 261
5.c.iv. Modern Adoption or Readoption of Legality by Major States That Had Rejected It 265
5.c.v. Other Legality Issues in the Constitutional Texts 271
5.c.v.A. *Lex mitior*, and the Issue of Mixing *Nullum crimen, Nulla poena* and *Lex mitior* 271
5.c.v.B. Legality and Freedom in the Modern Constitutions 274
5.c.v.C. *Lex certa* in the Constitutions 274

5.c.v.D. Narrow Interpretation and Analogy in the Constitutions 275
5.c.v.E. Retroactive Expansion of National Jurisdiction: Domestic Incorporation of Crimes under the Law of Another State or Crimes under International Law – A Current Version of Retroactive Re-characterization? 276
5.c.vi. Exceptions and Possible Exceptions to Non-retroactivity of Crimes and Punishments 278
5.c.vii. Representation (or Vicarious) Jurisdiction: A Challenge for Legality 282
5.c.viii. What Is Punishment for Purposes of Invoking the Non-retroactivity Rules of Criminal Law? A Brief Note 287
5.d. Non-retroactivity of Court Creation and Prohibitions of Special Courts 290
5.e. Personal Punishment and Rejection of Collective Punishment: Also General Principles of Law 293
5.f. The Status of National Constitutions and Other Internal Legal Acts of States as State Practice for Constituting Customary International Human Rights Law 299
5.g. The Transformation of Legality in National Law since World War II 301

6 Legality in the Modern International and Internationalized Criminal Courts and in the UN Trust Territories 303
6.a. Legality in the ICTY, ICTR, and SCSL (and the Nascent Lebanon Tribunal) 304
6.a.i. Non-retroactivity (*Nullum crimen, nulla poena sine lege*) in These Courts Generally 305
6.a.i.A. The Special Case of Contempt in the ICTY 309
6.a.ii. Legality as a Jurisdictional and Substantive Issue, Right of the Individual to Complain, and the International Legal Personality of the Individual 311
6.a.ii.A. Claim of Violation of Non-retroactivity as Issue Individuals May Raise and Court Must Consider 312
6.a.ii.B. Argument That Court Created by an International Organization Should Not

Examine Whether a Prosecution Is Prohibited by Rule of *Nullum crimen*, so Long as the Crime Is Named in the Organic Documents of the Court 314
6.a.iii. Legality of Courts 316
6.a.iii.A. Claims That These Courts Are Not Established by Law: Powers of International Organizations, the International Legal Personality of Individuals, and the Issue of Special Courts 316
6.a.iii.B. Creating New Jurisdictions Retrospectively 318
6.a.iv. Retroactive Re-characterization of Crime in These Tribunals? 320
6.a.v. Note on Legality in the Special Tribunal for Lebanon 324
6.b. Legality in the Internationalized Tribunals and a Note on Legality in Internationally Supervised Trust Territories 325
6.b.i. The Internationalized Tribunals 325
6.b.ii. A Note on Legality in UN Trust Territories as Another Example of International Organization and National Practice 330
6.c. The ICC and the Principle of Legality 331
6.c.i. Situations Involving Only States Parties to the ICC Statute at All Relevant Times 333
6.c.ii. Security Council Referrals of Situations Involving Nonparty States and Retroactive Acceptances of Jurisdiction by States 337
6.c.iii. Legality as a Jurisdictional Issue in the ICC 343
6.d. Status of Actions of the Security Council, Other UN Bodies, and the Recent International Criminal Courts and Tribunals under International Law 344
6.d.i. Practice and *Opinio juris* of International Organizations, Including International Tribunals, as Contributing to Customary International Law and General Principles of Law 347

7 Legality in Customary International Law Today 352
7.a. The Core Rules of Legality in Customary International Law 352
7.b. Elaboration of the Core Rules: *Nullum crimen* 357
7.b.i. Foreseeability 359
7.b.i.A. Indeterminacy of Language and the Necessity of a Foreseeability Doctrine 359

7.b.i.B. Foreseeability and the Development of Criminal Law by Judicial Decision, Statutory Interpretation, and Analogy 360
7.b.i.C. Foreseeability, *Lex certa*, and the Void-for-Vagueness Doctrine 362
7.b.i.D. Foreseeability and Accessibility 363
7.b.i.E. Dangers of the Foreseeability Doctrine and Limitations on the Doctrine 364
7.b.ii. Re-characterization in International and National Courts 367
7.b.ii.A. Retroactive Re-characterization of a Crime as International, or as a Different Type of International Crime, in National or International Courts 367
7.b.ii.B. Legality and the Debate over Direct Application of International Criminal Law in National Courts 369
7.b.ii.C. Universal Jurisdiction over International Law Crimes 370
7.b.ii.D. Representation (Vicarious) Jurisdiction and Legality 371
7.b.ii.E. Purely National Re-characterization 372
7.b.iii. General Principles of Law as a Source of Applicable Criminal Law 373
7.b.iv. Criticism of International Criminal Law as Generally Violating Principles of Legality 374
7.b.v. Defenses 375
7.b.vi. The Right Not to Be Prosecuted 376
7.c. Elaboration and Discussion of the Core Rules: *Nulla poena* 378
7.c.i. *Nulla poena* as Applicable to Crimes under International Law 379
7.c.ii. Criticism of *Nulla poena* as Inapplicable to International Criminal Law 383
7.c.iii. *Nulla poena* and Re-characterization 389
7.c.iii.A. *Nulla poena* Where There Has Been a Retroactive Re-Characterization of a National Crime into an International Crime 389
7.c.iii.B. *Nulla poena* and Re-characterization of Crimes in National Courts: Universal Jurisdiction over International Law Crimes 390

7.c.iv. *Nulla poena* and Representation (Vicarious) Jurisdiction 391
7.c.v. *Nulla poena* and General Principles of Law 391
7.c.vi. *Nulla poena* as Applying to Punishments Only, and Not to Other Sanctions 392
7.d. *Nullum crimen, Nulla poena* as Binding International Organizations and International Courts 393
7.e. Legality and Jurisdiction of Courts 394
7.e.i. Creation of New Courts or Expansion of Jurisdiction of Existing Courts 394
7.e.ii. Requirement that Court Be Established by Law 395
7.f. Personality of Punishment and Prohibition of Collective Punishments 395
7.g. Right of the Individual to Raise Claim of Violation of Legality as a Matter of International Law, and the International Legal Personality of Individuals 397
7.h. International Law Legality, National Law Legality, and the Prosecution of Core International Law Crimes in National Courts 398
7.i. *Jus cogens* Status for Non-retroactivity of Crimes and Punishments? 399
7.j. International Organizations as Participants in the Process of Creating Customary and Other Binding International Law 402

Conclusion: The Endurance of Legality in National and International Criminal Law 404

Appendix A: Chart of Non-retroactivity Provisions in Criminal Law by Nations 411
Appendix B: Legality and Non-retroactivity Provisions as of 1946–47 425
Appendix C: Constitutional and Other National Provisions Implementing the Principle of Legality Today 438
Bibliography 541
Table of Authorities 553
Index 579
Afterword and Update 599

Explanatory Note on Spelling

In this book a number of inconsistencies of spelling, capitalization, and typeface appear. Where quoting from or citing to written sources, it uses the spelling of the original source. This being the case, one may well find *judgment* and *judgement*, *offense* and *offence*, *defense* and *defence*, *recognize* and *recognise*, *Quran* and *Koran*, *crimes against humanity*, *Crimes against Humanity* and *Crimes Against Humanity*, and other inconsistencies scattered throughout this book.

Many of these inconsistencies arise from differences between American English and spelling elsewhere in the English-speaking world. I am an American, but most UN sources, the Statute of the International Criminal Court, and many other documents related to international human rights law, international humanitarian law, and international criminal law use British spellings in their English-language texts. Other inconsistencies, such as the fact that a single place in Germany is called *Nuremberg*, *Nuernberg*, *Nürnberg*, and *Nurnberg*, arise from the use of these different spellings and transliterations in the sources. As suggested by the Cambridge University Press editors, I use the popular English spelling *Nuremberg*, except in quotes and names of documents. Indeed, I generally use the style suggested by the Cambridge University Press editors, except for quotes and names of documents, for capitalization, typeface, diacritical marks, and similar matters.

The citations in this book involve documents from almost two hundred countries and several international organizations and treaty systems. Secondary sources are from many countries and include internal references to books in several languages and books that are long out of print. I have not eliminated all inconsistency in the form of citations.

To paraphrase Mark Twain, I make this explanation for the reason that without it the reader might suppose that my sources and I were attempting to spell words consistently and not succeeding.

– The Author

Acknowledgments

I appreciate the help and encouragement that I have received in working on this book. Chief among those are people who encouraged me first to start doing it, and then to declare it finished and stop doing it. These include Mary Beth Lagenaur, Mark Drumbl, Tom Sullivan, and Gene Mullins. My friends and colleagues at the International Criminal Bar, especially its founding President, Elise Groulx, have helped me develop an understanding of the challenges of international criminal law in practice.

Other people who have given me especially useful feedback on one stage or another of the drafts include (in alphabetical order) Diane Marie Amann, Hans Bevers, Neils Blokker, Roger Clark, Lynn C. Foster, Haider Ala Hamoudi, Leila N. Sadat, and Joshua M. Silverstein. I have also received a hearing and support from the rest of the faculty at the University of Arkansas at Little Rock William H. Bowen School of Law.

Kathryn Fitzhugh, Professor of Law Librarianship at the University of Arkansas at Little Rock William H. Bowen School of Law; Melissa Serfass, Professor of Law Librarianship, also at UALR Bowen School of Law; and Jeff Woodmansee helped with finding and obtaining sources. Prof. Fitzhugh was especially important in finding many of the international statutes cited. Student research assistants who worked on this, especially on cite and fact checking and gathering the constitutional provisions in Appendix C, included Aarol Tyler Broyles, Mosemarie D. Boyd, Christine M. Hendrickson, Timothy E. Semotan, Samuel P. Trenchi, Joseph D. Tobler, Lawrence E. Moore III, and Adam G. Weeks.

All of the people listed above have contributed to this book, though many of them disagree with a few or many of its points. None of them can be blamed for any of its remaining errors.

I also gratefully acknowledge financial support including research grants and support for student assistance from the University of Arkansas at Little Rock William H. Bowen School of Law.

Introduction

0.a. RETROACTIVITY, JUSTICE, AND SOVEREIGNTY

The English-language version of the Nuremberg Judgment observes,

> [T]he maxim *nullum crimen sine lege* is not a limitation of sovereignty, but is in general a principle of justice.[1]

This statement – that "nothing is criminal except by law [existing at the time of the act]" is a mere nonbinding principle of justice – has a cynical ring to it. It implies that judges can and should ignore principles of justice in service of the sovereign powers that created their court. This was pointed out rather explicitly in the dissent to the Tokyo Judgment by Justice Radhabinod Pal of India, who argued that the International Military Tribunal for the Far East should not create crimes that did not exist at the time a defendant acted: "for otherwise the Tribunal will not be a 'judicial tribunal' but a mere tool for the manifestation of power."[2] The depth of the disagreement over the issue of retroactivity might be judged by Justice Pal's use of this statement. It refers to – and perhaps parodies – a similar passage by Lord Wright. Wright had argued that all the crimes in the Nuremberg Charter (and hence in

[1] *United States v. Göring*, Judgment of 30 September 1946, 1 TRIAL OF THE MAJOR WAR CRIMINALS BEFORE THE INTERNATIONAL MILITARY TRIBUNAL: NUREMBERG 14 NOVEMBER 1945–1 OCTOBER 1946 171, 219 (Nuremberg: International Military Tribunal 1947) [hereinafter IMT, TRIAL].

[2] *United States v. Araki*, Dissenting Opinion of Radhabinod Pal at 36, 109 THE TOKYO MAJOR WAR CRIMES TRIAL: THE JUDGMENT, SEPARATE OPINIONS, PROCEEDINGS IN CHAMBERS, APPEALS AND REVIEWS OF THE INTERNATIONAL MILITARY TRIBUNAL FOR THE FAR EAST (John R. Pritchard, ed., Robert M. W. Kemper Collegium & Edwin Mellen Press 1998) (November 1948) [hereinafter IMTFE RECORDS] (the pagination of the separate opinions in this case is problematic, as they are not consecutive with the rest of the trial or each other).

the Tokyo Charter) were, at the time, crimes under international law,[3] a position with which Justice Pal violently disagreed.

In the French version of the Nuremberg Judgment, even the reference to justice disappeared: "[N]ullum crimen sine lege *ne limite pas la souveraineté des États; elle ne formule qu'une règle généralement suivie.*"[4] The French version could be rendered into English as "*[n]ullum crimen sine lege* does not limit the sovereignty of States; it only formulates a rule that is generally followed."[5]

The Nuremberg statement carries with it the implication that individual human rights (especially of the evil) fade in the face of the collective powers that make up sovereignty. In the French version, it is a statement that might have been made by the Nazi leaders themselves[6] or the leaders of the former

[3] [Lord] Wright [of Dursley], *War Crimes under International Law*, 62 L.Q. Rev. 40, 41 (1946).

[4] Quoted in Henri Felix August Donnedieu de Vabres, *Le procès de Nuremberg devant les principes modernes du droit pénal international*, 70(I) Recueil des Cours 477, 503 (1947) [hereinafter Donnedieu de Vabres, *Le procès*] (Henri Donnedieu de Vabres was the principal French judge at the Nuremberg Trial of the Major War Criminals). Accord, A. Cassese, *Crimes Against Humanity: Comments on Some Problematical Aspects* [hereinafter Cassese, *CAH*], in The international legal system in quest of equity and universality: L'ordre juridique international, un système en quête d'équité et d'universalité: Liber Amicorum G. Abi-Saab 429, 433–35 (Laurence Boisson de Chazournes & Vera Gowlland-Debbas eds., Martinus Nijhoff 2001) (also pointing out that the clause in the English of the Nuremberg Judgment, "on this view of the case alone, it would appear that the maxim has no application to the present facts" does not appear at all in the French text; and arguing that Donnedieu de Vabres and original French chief prosecutor François de Menthon at Nuremberg believed that the acts constituting crimes against humanity prosecuted there were war crimes in any event, and therefore there was no *nullum crimen* problem as to them), citing Donnedieu de Vabres, *Le procès*, as well as Henri Felix August Donnedieu de Vabres, *Le jugement de Nuremberg et le principe de légalité des délits et des peines*, 27 Revue de droit penal et de criminologie 813, 826–27 (1946–47); Susan Lamb, *Nullum crimen, nulla poena sine lege* in International Criminal Law, in 1 The Rome Statute of the International Criminal Court: A Commentary 733, 737 n.13 (Antonio Cassese, Paola Gaeta & John R. W. D. Jones eds. 2002).

[5] Cassese, *CAH* at 433–34 attributes the difference between the two authoritative texts as due to the fact that the Nuremberg Tribunal was "reticent and vague" on the ex post facto issue.

[6] See Law of 28 June 1935 Amending the German Criminal (Penal) Code § I, published in 1935 Reichgesetzblatt, pt. I, p. 839 (Germany), translated and reprinted in United States v. Alstoetter (*Justice Case*), 3 Trials of War Criminals before the Nuernberg Military Tribunals under Control Council Law No. 10 [hereinafter T.W.C.] 176–7 (USMT, 4 December 1947), amending German Penal Code art. 2; Law of 28 June 1935, Code of Criminal Procedure and Judicature Act §I, published in 1935 Reichgesetzblatt, pt. I, p. 844 (Germany), translated and reprinted in *Justice Case*, 3 T.W.C. at 177–80, adding German Code of Criminal Procedure arts. 170a & 267a, and allowing the Reich Supreme Court to ignore precedent where inconsistent with "the change of ideology and of legal concepts

Soviet Union,[7] for they had no use for the restraint of legality as a matter of justice. Each of them, however, would have far different views on the identity of evildoers whose rights are to be ignored.

Bernard Victor Aloysius Röling, justice from the Netherlands at the Tokyo War Crimes Tribunal, agreed with the French version at Nuremberg. His statement, an attempt to face down the cynicism with which either version of the Nuremberg statement might be read, was even more remarkable:

> If the principle of "nullum crimen sine praevia lege" were a principle of *justice*,... the Tribunal would be bound to exclude for that very reason every crime created in the Charter ex post facto, it being the first duty of the Tribunal to mete out justice. However, this maxim is not a principle of justice but a rule of policy, valid only if expressly adopted, so as to protect citizens against arbitrariness of courts (nullum crimen, nulla poena sine lege), as well as against arbitrariness of legislators (nullum crimen, nulla poena sine praevia lege).[8]

Today, *nullum crimen, nulla poena sine lege* is not only a principle of justice. It embodies an internationally recognized human right. One of the most respected international law commentators and judges, Theodore Meron, has gone so far as to state, "The prohibition of retroactive penal measures is a fundamental principle of criminal justice, and a customary, even peremptory, norm of international law that must in all circumstances be observed in all circumstances by national and international tribunals."[9] The transformation of the principle of legality into rules of law has led to fundamental and continuing changes in how international criminal law is made and applied.

Consideration of the Nuremberg statement, its correctness at the time, its justice, and how it has been superseded by the growth of international human rights law, led to this book.

which the new state has brought about." Law of 28 June 1935 Code of Criminal Procedure and Judicature Act §II, translated and reprinted in 3 T.W.C. at 178–79. See Chap. 2.c.ii.A (on how these laws effectively abolished the legality principle in criminal law in the Third Reich).

[7] See Chap. 2.c.ii.C on the absence of the legality principle from the law of the USSR at this time.

[8] Separate Opinion of Röling, J., at 44–45, 109 IMTFE Records (italics substitute for underlining in typewritten original).

[9] Theodore Meron, War Crimes Law Comes of Age 244 (Oxford Univ. Press 1998) [hereinafter Meron] (discussed further in Ch. 7.i).

0.b. PLAN OF THIS BOOK

0.b.i. *Outline of Chapters*

Chapter 1 introduces the issues raised by the principles of *nullum crimen sine lege* and *nulla poena sine lege*, which are the core of the principle of legality in criminal law. It also raises a few other issues of legality in criminal law. It discusses the relationship of legality and retroactivity in criminal law to issues of the rule of law more generally. It discusses both the human rights and the criminal law purposes of legality. The emphasis is on the prior existence of not only a criminal law but also a criminal law that was applicable to the actor at the time of the alleged crime. The chapter also introduces two other issues connected to legality. The first concerns creation of courts and court systems according to law (including retrospectivity of court creation). The second is the requirement of individual criminal responsibility and the concomitant prohibition of collective punishment. Finally, this chapter addresses several doctrines and views that could cause erosion or rejection of various aspects of the principle of legality, including judicial crime creation, expansive interpretation of criminal statutes, analogy, the view that language – and hence criminal law – is always indeterminate, and the lure of authoritarianism.

Chapter 2 briefly reviews the history of the principle of legality in criminal law up to World War I, drawing material from common law, civil law, Islamic law, and a few other sources. It then covers interwar events, focusing on the German abandonment of the principle in the 1930s and the international legal reaction.

Chapter 3 covers World War II and the Nuremberg, Tokyo, and other postwar trials. It emphasizes the issues of legality and retroactivity that were raised during the war concerning war crimes and international prosecutions, in the negotiations leading up to the London Charter, and in the judgments of the Nuremberg and Tokyo Tribunals. This chapter also focuses particularly on the French view of legality in the London negotiations and at Nuremberg and Tokyo – which has been far more influential than it has been given credit for being. The chapter also covers legality as dealt with by a number of different nations in the aftermath of World War II. Rather than rehash the debates of the past sixty years over whether the Nuremberg Judgment was proper, the discussion of the judgment focuses on its claim that *nullum crimen* was not a limitation of sovereignty or lawmaking authority at the time. The section on the Tokyo Tribunal deals with the open debate on issues of legality in the different opinions. The chapter concludes that the claim that *nullum crimen* was not a limitation on sovereignty was correct at the end of World War II. One of the points of the book is that this is no longer so.

Chapter 4 covers the international activities of states concerning legality in criminal law in the modern period. It begins with the Universal Declaration of Human Rights (UDHR) and the drafting history of its non-retroactivity provisions. It discusses the major international human rights treaties requiring non-retroactivity in criminal law, including the International Covenant on Civil and Political Rights (ICCPR) (including the *travaux préparatoires* of the non-retroactivity provisions); the regional human rights conventions; and the Convention on the Rights of the Child. It also covers the international humanitarian law (IHL) treaties demanding legality in criminal proceedings, including the Third and Fourth Geneva Conventions of 1949 and the two Additional Protocols of 1977. Concerning the regional human rights treaties and the IHL treaties, it examines the requirement of individual criminal responsibility – including the ban on collective punishment – as well as non-retroactivity issues. In the IHL material, the chapter gives special attention to Common Article 3 of the 1949 Conventions and Additional Protocol II of 1977, because these involve the obligations that states have taken on themselves even during the stresses of civil war. The chapter examines the reservations that states have made to both the human rights and humanitarian law treaties to determine the effect on their obligations concerning non-retroactivity in criminal law. It also considers some of the jurisprudence from international tribunals and commissions interpreting the legality provisions of these documents.

Chapter 5 examines the constitutional and other legal provisions of the various states around the world to the extent that they deal with legality in criminal law. In those states with no constitutional provision, other applicable law is considered. This chapter examines prohibitions of retroactivity of crime creation, increases in punishment, and creation of new and special courts. It also considers the issue of individual responsibility and collective punishment and the issue of general liberty to do everything that is not forbidden by law. Three appendices collect and classify these provisions from nations worldwide. Appendix A indicates the existence and source of non-retroactivity provisions worldwide. Appendix B collects legality provisions current as of 1946–47, when the United Nations first studied the matter. Appendix C collects legality provisions as they exist around the world today.

Chapter 6 examines the principle of legality in the international and internationalized courts and tribunals from the International Criminal Tribunal for the Former Yugoslavia (ICTY) through the International Criminal Court (ICC) and the new tribunals such as Sierra Leone, Kosovo, East Timor, and Cambodia. It examines both legal texts of the courts and practice for those courts where there is practice. The ICC provisions particularly are more complex than they are sometimes given credit for being, and limit the jurisdiction of the court, including in some cases of referrals by the UN Security Council. The ad hoc and internationalized tribunal materials will discuss how the principle of legality in criminal law binds international organizations as well as states in the process of lawmaking.

Chapter 7 shows that both *nullum crimen* and *nulla poena* (in reasonably strong – though not the strongest – forms) have become rules of customary international law that bind both states and international organizations. They apply as binding customary and treaty international human rights protections to prosecutions brought under both national and international criminal law, and in both national and international tribunals. It shows how the principles of notice, foreseeability, and accessibility of law can provide a working definition of non-retroactivity of crimes and punishments, even though language itself always has some indeterminacy. This chapter demonstrates, contrary to views popular in some circles, that *nullum crimen* and *nulla poena* (the prohibitions of retroactive crime creation or increases in punishments) truly apply in international criminal law. It also demonstrates that the requirement of some sort of individual criminal responsibility and the prohibition of collective criminal punishment are rules of customary international law, binding both states and international organizations.

0.b.ii. *Principles and Rules: Two Key Definitions*

This book is about the principles of legality and non-retroactivity, as well as specific rules of legality and non-retroactivity in different legal systems. Principles and rules cannot be completely separated. Notice, for example, the usage of *principle* in the English version of the Nuremberg Judgment excerpt herein, and the use of *règle* ("rule") in the French version. Nonetheless, it is useful to adopt usages of the terms that are as clear as possible.

To the extent possible, the term *rules* will apply to rules of law. That is, it will refer to normative statements that are binding on relevant actors and may be enforced through the use of government coercion. For example, a constitution might provide, "No person may be convicted of a crime for an act which was not a crime when committed." This states a rule of non-retroactivity of criminal definition that is applicable in the legal system controlled by the constitution. If necessary, it may be enforced by the courts, through a refusal to convict or punish a person pursuant to a retroactively defined crime. A rule of treaty law or customary international law may bind states or other actors.

H. L. A. Hart distinguished between first- and second-order rules (primary rules of conduct and rules of recognition and adjudication).[10] This book will include both types in the usage of *rules.* For example, the prohibition of robbery is, in Hart's terms, a first-order rule controlling the conduct of each of us. The rule mentioned in the preceding paragraph on the non-retroactivity of criminal definition is, for Hart, a second-order rule. It determines when and to which acts a first-order criminal definition might apply. In some cases, a rule may come into conflict with another rule, and a choice may have to be made between them (or, in a system allowing for use of judicial precedent, one or both rules may be modified).[11]

In contrast, the term *principles* will apply to normative concepts or statements that may or may not have hardened into rules of law. They may or may not be reflected in the legal system of particular states. A principle may articulate a norm or other idea distilled from examination of specific rules of law or may state a formulation of an idea that is normatively preferred by the speaker. Principles may play a role in the determination of specific cases.[12] For most purposes of this book, what matters is that a principle may be instantiated in various different legal systems by differently articulated rules. To some extent, the rules instantiating principles may actually have different content.

Principles will also be used in the technical phrase "general principles of law," one of the canonical sources of international law listed in the Statute of the International Court of Justice and the earlier Statute of the Permanent Court of International Justice which can be used in international adjudication.[13] In this usage, a general principle may operate as one rule that is used to decide a case. Indeed, a "general principle of law recognized by the community of nations" may provide a rule that makes an act criminal.[14]

[10] H. L. A. Hart, The Concept of Law 94–99 (2d ed., Clarendon Press 1994) (1st ed., 1961).
[11] Cf. *id.* at 261–63 (in the second-edition postscript).
[12] Cf. *id.* (agreeing with Ronald Dworkin and other critics of Hart's work that legal principles exist and play this type of role).
[13] Statute of the International Court of Justice art. 38(1); Statute of the Permanent Court of International Justice art. 38.
[14] See, e.g., International Covenant on Civil and Political Rights art. 15(2); Prosecutor v. Tadic (Appeal of Vujin), Judgment on Allegations of Contempt against Prior Counsel, Milan

This is just one example of the ways in which lawmakers, translators, and others frequently fail to distinguish between *rule* and *principle* in a consistent way.[15] It is therefore vital that the reader and advocate consider how these words, like all other words, are actually being used by the speaker or writer.

The first two chapters of this book consider the principle of legality in criminal law, its purposes, and its development into rules of law, mostly in national systems. Chapter 3 shows how varying views of the principle of legality influenced the post–World War II prosecutions of the German and Japanese war criminals, even though, as indicated in the Nuremberg Judgment, it had not at that time hardened into a rule of international law. Chapter 4 shows how the principle of legality became articulated into related rules in various modern human rights and humanitarian law treaties. Chapter 5 examines the scope of implementation of the principle of legality as rules of law among the countries of the world, and Chapter 6 does the same for the modern (i.e., post-Nuremberg and Tokyo) international and mixed international and national criminal tribunals. Finally, Chapter 7 brings together the materials in Chapters 4 through 6 to show that there is now a rule of legality in customary international criminal law. (However, as already pointed out, legality is also a "general principle of law" in the technical international law sense.)

0.C. THE ARGUMENTS OF THIS BOOK

This book is generally written in what Europeans call the "scientific" style of writing about law – or at least some of the author's European friends and colleagues tell him so. That involves a good bit of collection, description, classification, and characterization of sources. Yet writing about law almost always involves an argument of one sort or another. To the extent that this book makes arguments, they are as follows.

0.c.i. *The Argument: Non-retroactivity of Crimes and Punishments*

Legality in criminal law, especially its most important constituent, the non-retroactivity of crimes and punishments, applies in both national and international criminal law, as a matter of customary international human rights

Vujin, Case No. IT-94-1-A-R77 (ICTY App. Ch., 27 February 2001) (general principles of law provide law under which contempt of the Tribunal may be punished).

[15] See, e.g., Finland Const., ch. 2, § 8.

law. These rules are also general principles of law recognized by the community of nations. No one may be convicted for an act that was not criminal at the time done under some applicable law. No one may be subjected to a punishment that was not authorized for the act at the time done under some applicable law. At present, international law applies this rule of non-retroactivity. Claims that these principles do not apply as rules of international law are no longer correct.

The requirement of individual criminal responsibility and the prohibition of collective punishments are other elements of legality that have become part of customary international human rights law. They are also general principles of law recognized by the community of nations.

There is diversity in the national treatments of legality in criminal law. These include many versions stronger than that found in customary international law. These versions may require crime and punishment definition by prior statute (rather than allowing for case law or customary international law development as well), require something resembling a tariff of punishments for each crime, prohibit special courts or the retroactive creation of new courts, or prohibit the retroactive expansion of criminal jurisdiction. There are some patterns in the distribution of these rules by type of legal system but not strict consistency. These stronger versions are binding in their respective national legal systems but have not passed into requirements of customary international law.

Because there is such diversity of legal systems worldwide, specific rules of international law developed from national systems must work for each of the major systems of law. Thus, the rule developed here is stated in terms that will make sense in the civil law, common law, and Islamic law systems, as well as the international human rights system of treaties and organizations for monitoring and enforcing the treaties.

o.c.ii. *Some Sub-arguments*

In reaching its major conclusions, naturally this book reaches additional conclusions. A few of them are set forth here because they address controversial issues or simply because the author finds them interesting.

As of World War II, the conclusion of the Nuremberg Tribunal that non-retroactivity of crimes and punishments was a principle of justice (or, as in French, a rule that is generally followed), but was not a limitation on sovereignty, was correct.[16]

[16] See generally Chap. 3.

At the London Conference, which drafted the Charter of the International Military Tribunal, and at Nuremberg, the views of the French participants on legality in criminal law were very important.[17]

Very few persons or states involved in the drafting of the International Covenant on Civil and Political Rights (ICCPR) held the view that "general principles of law," which may be the basis of criminalization in Article 15(2) of the ICCPR, are anything other than a subset of international law, which may be a basis of criminalization in Article 15(1) of the ICCPR.[18]

Since Nuremberg, there has been a tremendous increase in the acceptance of non-retroactivity of crimes and punishments in national constitutions[19] and in international treaties and other legal documents.[20]

0.c.iii. *The Meta-argument: Law as Created by International Criminal Courts and International Organizations in Light of Claims Made by Individuals*

This book deals with customary international criminal law and customary international human rights law related to criminal proceedings. It makes at least one claim about changes in how such law is made.

Customary international criminal law and international human rights law related to such proceedings are now made in substantial part through the acts and *opinio juris* of international organizations as well as states. The acts of international organizations described here are principally, though not exclusively, judgments and other acts of international criminal courts and tribunals. Other relevant acts of international organizations include judgments and other acts of regional human rights tribunals; views stated by worldwide and regional human rights treaty commissions; and acts of organs of international organizations doing such things as establishing and operating tribunals and defining or making other statements about international criminal law and international human rights law. The judgments of the international criminal courts and tribunals and the judgments and views of the human rights courts and commissions are almost always made in response to claims of right made by individuals.

This indicates a growth of the international legal personality both of international organizations and of individuals.

[17] See generally Chap. 3.b.ii.
[18] See generally Chap. 4.b.ii.C.
[19] See generally Chap. 5.b–c.
[20] See generally Chap. 4.

1

Legality in Criminal Law, Its Purposes, and Its Competitors

The creation of international criminal law, especially in international criminal tribunals, frequently raises questions concerning "the principle of legality of crimes and punishments (*le principe de légalité des délits et des peines*)."[1] Many rules have made up the principle of legality in criminal law, although not all of them apply in all societies that accept the principle:

1. No act that was not criminal under a law applicable to the actor (pursuant to a previously promulgated statute)[2] at the time of the act may be punished as a crime.
2. No act may be punished by a penalty that was not authorized by a law applicable to the actor (pursuant to a previously promulgated statute)[3] at the time of the act.
3. No act may be punished by a court whose jurisdiction was not established at the time of the act.
4. No act may be punished on the basis of lesser or different evidence from that which could have been used at the time of the act.[4]
5. No act may be punished except by a law that is sufficiently clear to provide notice that the act was prohibited at the time it was committed.
6. Interpretation and application of the law should be done on the basis of consistent principles.

[1] Henri Felix August Donnedieu de Vabres, *Le procès de Nuremberg devant les principes modernes du droit pénal international*, *in* 70 RECUEIL DES COURS DE L'ACADÉMIE DE DROIT INTERNATIONAL 477, 501, *passim* (1947).

[2] The phrase in parentheses applies only to some nations and legal systems that follow this rule.

[3] The phrase in parentheses applies only to some nations and legal systems that follow this rule.

[4] *See* Calder v. Bull, 3 U.S. (3 Dallas) 386, 390 (1798).

7. Punishment is personal to the wrongdoer. Collective punishments may not be imposed for individual crime.
8. Everything not prohibited by law is permitted.[5]

These rules have been implemented in a variety of versions, with different articulations or slogans. In international and comparative law, the two articulations most frequently associated with the principle are *nullum crimen sine lege* and *nulla poena sine lege* – which in English mean, roughly, nothing is a crime except as provided by law, and no punishment may be imposed except as provided by law, respectively.[6] These are often equated with *nullum crimen sine praevia lege* (nothing is a crime except under previously existing law) and *nulla poena sine praevia lege* (no punishment may be imposed except under previously existing law) – and indeed, this book will treat these pairs of slogans as equivalent. Other formulations and articulations of the principle of legality in its various aspects include, for example, *nullum crimen, nulla poena sine lege scripta* (nothing is a crime and no punishment may be imposed except by a written law),[7] *nullum crimen, nulla poena sine praevia lege scripta* (nothing is a crime and no punishment may be imposed except by a previously declared written law), *nulla poena sine crimine* (no punishment may be imposed except for crime), and *nullum crimen sine poena legali* (nothing is a crime without a legal penalty).

One of the most famous formulations of legality in criminal law was set out by Paul Johann Anselm Ritter von Feuerbach at the beginning of the nineteenth century. He brought together three of the phrases above, *nulla poena sine lege*, *nulla poena sine crimine*, and *nullum crimen sine poena legali* as stating the heart of the idea.[8]

[5] This last item is a quotation from the Draft Outline of an International Bill of Human Rights, art. 25, U.N. Doc. E/CN.4/21/Annex A, p. 17 (1 July 1947), which is discussed in greater detail in Chap. 4.a.ii.

[6] The choice not to use the translations of George P. Fletcher, 1 The Grammar of Criminal Law: American, Comparative, and International (Foundations) 81 (Oxford Univ. Press 2007), and Jerome Hall, *Nulla Poena Sine Lege*, 47 Yale L.J. 165 (1938) is deliberate. Fletcher, at 81, says, "*Nullum crimen, nulla poena sine lege* (No crime, no punishment, without prior legislative definition)," and Hall, at 165, is to the same effect. I use Fletcher's English as the rough translation of *nullum crimen, nulla poena sine praevia lege scripta*. As will be seen throughout this book, *lege* or *lex* in the general sense of law can include both common law and some forms of non-treaty international law, as well as statutory or treaty texts.

[7] Antonio Cassese, International Criminal Law 141 (Oxford Univ. Press 2003); Ilias Bantekas & Susan Nash, International Criminal Law 127–28 (2d ed., Cavendish Publishing Ltd 2003).

[8] Paul Johann Anselm Ritter von Feuerbach, Lehrbuch des gemeinen in Deutschland geltenden Peinlichen Rechts ¶ 24, p. 20 (Georg Friedrich Heyer 1801), discussed in Hall, at 169–70.

Some names for parts or all of the principle of legality in criminal law in various systems include "the rule against *ex post facto* laws,"[9] "the principle of non-retroactivity of crimes and punishments," "the requirement of *lex certa* (that the law be clear or certain)," "the requirement of *lex stricta* (that the law be narrowly construed)," "the requirement that a court be (previously) established by law," and "the rule *jus de non evocando* (against removal of trial to special, rather than regularly existing, criminal courts)."[10] A related doctrine, that punishment is personal, forbids collective punishment of those who are innocent of a particular act because they belong to the same family, clan, village, or other group as do the actual culprits.

These different statements reflect different versions of the principle of legality that have been applied in the law of the past two centuries or so. This book addresses versions that have been an important part of the debate over international criminal law and international human rights law. These include the strong view, prevalent in many civil law countries, that nothing is a crime and that no punishment may be imposed except by a previously proclaimed statute (*nullum crimen, nulla poena sine praevia lege scripta*). This may require that specific penalties be set out for specific crimes. Some common law traditions have prohibited the retroactive application of new statutory crimes and newly increased punishments (e.g., the rule against ex post facto laws in American constitutional law[11]) but have not prohibited the development of criminal law by the case law method. In such states, it is particularly important that legality limits the unforeseeable retroactive expansion of criminal liability by judicial decision, as well as prohibits retroactive crime creation and statutory penalty increases.[12] As to penalties,

[9] 1 William Blackstone, Commentaries on the Laws of England *46 (Univ. of Chicago Press 1979) (1765); U.S. Const. art. I, §§9–10.

[10] *See generally* Prosecutor v. Kanyabashi, Decision on Defence Motion for Jurisdiction, Case No. ICTR-96-15-T, ¶¶ 30–32 (ICTR Tr. Ch., 18 June 1997); Prosecutor v. Tadic, Decision on Defence Motion for Interlocutory Appeal on Jurisdiction, Case No. IT-94-1-A, ¶¶ 45–48, 61–64 (ICTY App. Ch., 2 October 1995).

[11] U.S. Const. art. I, §§ 9–10, discussed extensively for the first time and limited to criminal law in *Calder*, 3 U.S. (3 Dallas) at 390.

[12] This is now current in Europe under the European Convention on Human Rights (4 November 1950; entered into force 3 September 1953) and in the United States under the combination of its constitutional ex post facto and due process provisions. For European cases in the European Court of Human Rights, see Kokkinakis v. Greece, Judgment, ¶ 40, Eur. Ct. H.R., Application No. 14307/88 (25 May 1993); G. v. France, Judgment, Eur. Ct. H.R., Case No. 29/1994/476/557, Application No. 15312/89 (27 September 1995); Baskaya v. Turkey, Judgment, ¶ 39, Eur. Ct. H.R., Application Nos. 23536/94 and 24408/94 (8 July 1999). For the United States, see Bouie v. City of Columbia, 378 U.S. 347 (1964); Rogers v. Tennessee, 532 U.S. 451 (2001), both of which interpret U.S. Const. art. I, §§9–10 (ex post facto clauses) and amends. V and XIV (1) (due process clauses).

many states do not have a specific tariff of penalties for various crimes but merely require that the law specify the maximum penalty an offender may suffer for committing a given crime.

One other formulation is very useful to consider. Some scholars have suggested using *nullum crimen, nulla poena sine iure* (instead of *lege*) to indicate that both written statutory law and uncodified (but binding) law, such as common law and customary international law, can be used to meet the strictures of legality.[13] Perhaps unfortunately, this usage has not caught on in the jurisprudence or general literature. This book uses *nullum crimen, nulla poena sine lege* to include written statutory law, common law, customary international law, and other forms of binding law. Where written statutory or treaty law is required, this book uses *lege scripta* instead of simply *lege.*

Most of this book is about the non-retroactivity of criminal law worldwide. The other aspects of the principle of legality and the rule of law in the criminal sphere will be discussed more briefly.

This book does not address the issues concerning whether changes in evidence or general procedural law may be retroactively applied to allow convictions of crime. The non-retroactivity of crimes and punishments discussed in this book is separate from the debates, common in American law, over the retroactivity of decisions concerning criminal procedure and collateral protections of individual rights (e.g., the right to be free from unreasonable searches and seizures for criminal evidence) in criminal cases. The one arguably procedural aspect that will be addressed in some detail here is the retrospective creation or expansion of criminal jurisdiction of courts to address events that have already occurred.

1.a. LEGALITY IN CRIMINAL LAW AND THE RULE OF LAW GENERALLY

We might usefully change the name of the principle of legality to the *principle of illegality*, as it requires that an act be illegal in the criminal law before it

[13] E.g., Stefan Glaser, *La méthode d'interpretation en droit international pénal*, 9 Revista Italiana di Diritto e Procedura Penale Nuova Serie 757, 766 (1966) (in French, indicating that *iure* meant law in the wider sense of *droit*, in contrast to the narrower usage of "*lois au sens strict de ce terme*" – what English speakers would limit to "statutes" – and applying the phrase particularly to international criminal law); M. Cherif Bassiouni, Crimes against Humanity in International Criminal Law 144, 162 (2d ed., Transnational Publishers, 1999); Ward N. Ferdinandusse, Direct Application of International Criminal Law in National Courts 232–36 (TMC Asser Press 2006); Geert-Jan Knoops, Defenses in Contemporary International Criminal Law 156–57 (Transnational Publishers 2001).

can be punished. This change might make learning the criminal law easier for students and would make the non-retroactivity aspects of the principle clearer to the general public.

Yet the name *legality* shows a deep connection with the rule of law: legality is a requirement that the specific crimes, punishments, and courts be established legally – within the prevailing legal system. The recent U.S. Supreme Court decision invalidating the use of military commissions that had not been established according to the applicable rules of law[14] exemplifies how legality in this broad sense remains at the heart of criminal law issues, especially when unusual questions of jurisdiction arise.

Legality in criminal law is one manifestation of the more general notion of the rule of law in society.[15] The principles of advance notice and prospective application of crimes and punishments might fairly be considered the minimum requirement for the rule of law.

Some have suggested that solely prospective application is one of the defining characteristics of any legal rule within the rule of law.[16] This view has not been generally accepted as a matter of law, although several countries, mostly from the civil law tradition, have adopted it as part of their constitutional order.[17] Others may allow retroactivity only if "no acquired rights are infringed,"[18] or a similar formulation. Various thinkers and politicians have argued that prospectivity should extend beyond the purely criminal law. Philosophers and others have suggested that the principle of advance notice ought to be general, if not to all law, then at least to all public law in which the state limits the life, liberty, property, or other rights of the citizen. For example, John Locke believed that the principle of advance notice of

[14] Hamden v. Rumsfeld, 548 U.S. 557 (2006) (in part IV of the opinion, a majority agreed that any military commission must be created according to the "constitution and laws").

[15] For some twentieth- and twenty-first-century views, *see, e.g.*, Charles Sampford, Retrospectivity and the Rule of Law (Oxford Univ. Press 2006); Brian C. Tamanaha, On the Rule of Law: History, Politics, Theory 97–98, 139 (Cambridge Univ. Press 2004); Muhammad Salim al-'Awwa, *The Basis of Islamic Penal Legislation, in* The Islamic Criminal Justice System 127, 135, 139–40 (M. Cherif Bassiouni ed., Oceana Publications 1982); Joseph Raz, *The Rule of Law and Its Virtue*, 93 L.Q. Rev. 195 (1977); Lon L. Fuller, The Morality of Law (rev. ed., Yale Univ. Press 1969); Friedrich A. Hayek, The Road to Serfdom 72 (Univ. of Chicago Press 1975) (1944).

[16] Tamanaha, *supra* note 15; Geoffrey de Q. Walker, The Rule of Law: Foundation of Constitutional Democracy 322 (Melbourne Univ. Press 1988), quoted and criticized in Sampford, *supra* note 15, at 65–68.

[17] *See, e.g.*, Costa Rica Const. art. 34; Croatia Const. art. 89; Haiti Const. art. 51; Macedonia Const. art. 52; Mexico Const. art. 14; Morocco Const. art. 4; Niger Const., art. 16; Norway Const. art. 97; Paraguay Const. art. 14; Peru Const. art. 103; Tonga Const. art. 20.

[18] Slovenia Const. art. 155.

law should apply to property rights as well as to penal law, at least where citizens or subjects of the concerned state are involved.[19] He admitted that advance notice of law may not always be possible in dealings with foreigners or foreign powers. The connection of English criminal law to the doctrine of forfeiture of property means that one cannot necessarily conclude that Locke would have applied the principle of advance notice to the entire law of private dealings in property. He does not appear to require it in the law of private contracts either.

At the time of the adoption of the American Constitution, many people understood its ex post facto clauses to prohibit "all retrospective laws, or laws governing or controlling past transactions, whether . . . of a civil or a criminal nature."[20] Yet soon after adoption, these clauses (on their face unlimited) were defined judicially to cover only criminal statutes.[21] More recently, liberal thinkers such as John Rawls have viewed legality as a key element of just societal arrangements.[22] During the post-Communist period of European history, prospectivity of rules securing property rights and the obligation of contracts has been considered important both to rule of law and to economic development. There remain those who question the value of strict prospectivity of all rules of law, and they have been making efforts to set out on a rational basis the types of matters to which it should not apply.[23]

Prospectivity is not the only value connected to the rule of law, though it is one of the most important to the criminal law. Why is it so important in the criminal law in particular? First, "of all branches of law, criminal law is most obviously and directly concerned with shaping and controlling human conduct."[24] Second, the criminal law enforces the most important behavioral values imposed by a state.[25] Third, the criminal law expresses the highest legal condemnation of acts in a society. Perhaps most important,

[19] JOHN LOCKE, *Second Treatise of Government* §§136-37, 147, *in* TWO TREATISES OF GOVERNMENT 270–73, 279–80 (Classics of Liberty Library 1992) (1689–90).

[20] *See* 2 JOSEPH STORY, COMMENTARIES ON THE CONSTITUTION OF THE UNITED STATES §1345, p. 199 (Lawbook Exchange 2005) (2d ed., Charles C. Little and James Brown 1851), discussing U.S. Const. art. I(9, 10).

[21] *Calder*, 3 U.S. (3 Dallas) at 391, 396.

[22] JOHN RAWLS, JUSTICE AS FAIRNESS 238 (Belknap Press/Harvard Univ. Press 1971).

[23] *E.g.*, SAMPFORD, *supra* note 15, *passim*; FULLER, *supra* note 15, at 51–63. For a review of recent retrospective taxation law (affecting dealings between the state and the citizen concerning property rights) in representative common law jurisdictions, *see* SAMPFORD, *supra* note 15, at 147–56, 159–64.

[24] FULLER, *supra* note 15, at 59.

[25] The values imposed by the state may not be all of the most important values of a society. Others may come from nonlegal tradition, religion, or other sources.

the criminal law applies the highest legal sanctions available to a society: deprivation of freedom, confiscation of property, and in some societies, death. As a result, the need for fairness of both substantive and procedural rules is at its greatest here.

Among the other important values of the rule of law is the generality of enactments. In the criminal law this is dealt with by the rules against bills of attainder, the device by which specific individuals or groups are targeted for conviction by statutes. Another value is the fairness of the tribunal in which matters are heard. In criminal law, this is addressed by the requirement that a tribunal be fair, impartial, and established by law. It is also addressed by many rules of fairness in the criminal proceeding itself, which are not the subject of this book.

Another value connected to modern understandings of the rule of law is the individual responsibility of the actor and the rejection of arbitrariness in choosing whom to punish. Thus, punishments are personal to actors and may not be either based merely on guilt by association or imposed collectively on family, village, or religious group.

Personality of punishment – and the elimination of collective punishment – is deeply connected to the growth of the state as a replacement for private vengeance. It is the opposite of the blood feud, in which the family of the victim takes revenge on the family of the perpetrator of an offense. Personality of punishment does not require the state to become the prosecutor,[26] but it does require the state to limit the persons who may be held personally accountable for crime to those with some connection to the act or fault in the act. The principle of legality requires that there be some law that a person – not merely someone related to the person by blood, marriage, place of residence, nationality, race, religion, or a similar factor – has violated before being declared a criminal or punished as a criminal.

Individuality of guilt and punishment is also connected to the modern liberal notion of individuals as the primary "units of action in the world."[27] If it is the individual who acts and who makes choices concerning which actions to take, then criminal liability without individual responsibility for acts or omissions makes little sense.

[26] In traditional Islamic law, the victim or a relative of the victim must seek retribution against the offender in many cases of homicide or battery (*quesas* crimes). M. Cherif Bassiouni, *Quesas Crimes*, *in* BASSIOUNI, *supra* note 15, at 203, 207–09.

[27] George P. Fletcher, *Collective Guilt and Collective Punishment*, 5 THEORETICAL INQUIRIES IN LAW 163 (2004), quoted by MARK A. DRUMBL, ATROCITY, PUNISHMENT, AND INTERNATIONAL LAW 35–6 (Cambridge Univ. Press 2007).

This does not prohibit the notion of joint criminal responsibility for acts, whether defined by accomplice liability (as in most jurisdictions), conspiracy (as in many common law countries), criminal organizations (as in many civil law countries) or corrupt enterprises (as in the United States), corporate criminal liability (though criminal liability of a corporation does not by itself justify death or imprisonment for persons associated with the corporation), or other forms of group criminality.[28] Nor does it prohibit requirements to inform authorities about one's knowledge of crime. It does, however, require that each criminally liable natural person have some individual criminal responsibility.[29]

The general responsibility of the individual for action has not prohibited the growth of defenses based on pressures external or factors internal to the actor. Thus, the defense of duress appears in both national and international systems and is based upon the way certain threats from other persons limit the realistic freedom of actors to conform their behavior to the law. Similarly, the insanity defense recognizes that certain persons are too mentally incapacitated to make choices that carry with them individual criminal responsibility. However, the notion of individuality of responsibility (and hence punishment) limits some of these defenses, especially the defense of superior orders.[30] The argument against collective punishment does have another side. Without collective punishment, pressure increases to ensure individual criminal liability.

The principle of legality, in at least one of its expressions, is a declaration of the underlying freedom of the individual: "Everything that is not prohibited by law is permitted."[31] Regardless of the form of government and the political theories that control it, underlying all societal constraint is the notion that

[28] For one form of group criminality, described by the International Criminal Tribunal for the Former Yugoslavia (ICTY) as "joint criminal enterprise," see Prosecutor v. Milutinovic, Decision on Dragoljub Ojdanic's Motion Challenging Jurisdiction: Joint Criminal Enterprise, ¶ 10, Case No. IT-99-37-AR72 (ICTY App. Ch., 21 May 2003), available at http://www.un.org/icty/milutinovic/appeal/decision-e/030521.pdf. This is particularly controversial because of claims that it was created retroactively. See Chaps. 6.a.i, 7.b.

[29] See Chaps. 5.f, 7.f. In cases of corporate criminal liability, there may or may not also be individual liability of natural persons. Corporate criminal liability does not exist in all jurisdictions.

[30] See, e.g., Rome Statute of the International Criminal Court art. 33 (17 July 1998; entered into force 1 July 2002) [hereinafter ICC Statute].

[31] Draft Outline of an International Bill of Human Rights art. 25, U.N. Doc. E/CN.4/21/Annex A, p. 17 (1 July 1947), discussed in greater detail in Ch. 4.b. The Documentation to the Draft Outline, U.N. Doc. E/CN.4/3/Add.1, pp. 314–18 (2 June 1947), shows that, by 1947, many nations had constitutions embodying this principle. See also Appendix B.

each of us is free.[32] Limitations may be imposed – indeed, to all but the most thoroughgoing anarchist, they must be imposed – and the principle of legality does not by itself say what those limitations can be. Nonetheless, the point of legality is that these limitations must themselves be specified and knowable. Beyond the specified legal limitations, the range of human freedom is limited only by our imaginations, our wills, our abilities, and the physical limitations imposed by nature.

The principle of legality in criminal law challenges many of the current process-based notions of law itself, such as the description of the law as "a process of authoritative decisionmaking."[33] Certainly the law is partly that. Yet the vitality of the principle of legality means that law must also be what the general public thinks it is: a set of reasonably certain rules by which we all must conduct our lives.[34]

Criminal law legality is also opposed to another current strain of international law thought. Much of international law is said to be "soft" law, made of policy statements that indicate a direction in which to proceed without being formally or factually binding. Certainly this concept has generally enriched the international law discourse. Criminal law, however, results in persons being arrested and imprisoned. It forbids or compels; it does not indicate a direction. The principle of legality ensures that the things that are forbidden or compelled can be known to those who must act on the basis of international criminal law.

1.b. PURPOSES OF LEGALITY IN CRIMINAL LAW

The purposes of the principle of legality in criminal law can be divided into four sets. The first set includes the protection of individual human rights. The second promotes legitimacy of governance. These reasons justify including legality in the fundamental structure of government and of the international human rights system as an integral part of public international law. A third set suggests that legality in criminal law protects the

[32] See U.N. Doc. A/C.3/SR.1007, ¶¶ 3–4 (meeting of 31 October 1960) (statement of Argentine representative). See also Chaps. 4.a.ii (on libertarianism in U.N. discussions) & 5.c.v.B (in national constitutions).

[33] This is a favorite phrase of the New Haven school of international jurisprudence, associated with the late Myres S. McDougal.

[34] Cf. H. L. A. HART, THE CONCEPT OF LAW 79–99 (2d ed., Clarendon Press 1994) (1st ed., 1961), which sees both rules of conduct and second-order rules for deciding among rules of conduct as characteristic of the developed rule of law.

structure of democratic (or even nondemocratic) governance by assigning lawmaking authority to the correct organ of government. This works differently in national and international criminal law. The fourth set pertains to promotion of the purposes of criminalization. These suggest that practicality aligns with morality on this issue, although counterarguments exist. To some extent, these purposes overlap, though, as we will see, not completely.

1.b.i. *Human Rights Protective Purposes*

The importance of the principle of legality as a protection of the individual in criminal law is at least threefold. Legality first ensures that one who wishes to avoid criminal liability may do so by providing notice of what acts the state or other lawmaking and law enforcement entity will consider criminal and what the available penalties will be.[35] It promotes predictability in judging the legal consequences of one's actions. These purposes are also obviously connected to the rule against collective punishments of nonparticipants in crime and to the prohibition of retroactive crimes and punishments.

Notice requires not only that a law has been in existence but also that it has been applicable to the actor at the time of the act.[36] If the law was not applicable to the actor, then the actor had no notice of the requirement to conform his or her behavior to the standard set out in the law. The law must also be accessible to those who are bound by it.[37] Indeed, accessibility of law through publication is the chief feature of the principle of criminal law legality as implemented in almost all current societies. A person need not actually have received notice of a criminal law. This is one point of the rule, common to most systems, that ignorance of the criminal law is no excuse for crime. Few citizens of any state read all of the criminal law, and yet most citizens know the law well enough to avoid serious criminal activity

[35] See, e.g., C.R. v. United Kingdom, Judgment, ¶¶ 34, 60, 62, Eur. Ct. H.R. Case No. 48/1994/495/577, Application No. 20190/92 (27 October 1995); Cantoni v. France, Judgment, ¶¶ 33, 35, Eur. Ct. H.R., Case No. 45/1995/551/637, Application No. 17862/91 (15 November 1996); Advisory Opinion on the Consistency of Certain Danzig Legislative Decrees with the Constitution of the Free City, 1935 P.C.I.J. (ser. A/B) No. 65, at 53–6 (4 December); CASSESE, *supra* note 7, at 145–52; SALVATORE ZAPPALÀ, HUMAN RIGHTS IN INTERNATIONAL CRIMINAL PROCEEDINGS 195 (Oxford Univ. Press 2003).

[36] Castillo Petruzzi v. Peru, Judgement, ¶ 121, Inter-Am. Ct. H.R., Petition No. 11,319 (30 May 1999), applying American Convention on Human Rights art. 9, 1114 U.N.T.S. 123 (22 November 1969; entered into force 18 July 1978). Accord, International Covenant on Civil and Political Rights art. 15(1), 999 UNTS 171 (concluded, 16 December 1966; entered into force 23 March 1976); Universal Declaration of Human Rights, art. 11(2), UNGA Res. 217 (III), U.N. GAOR, 3d Sess., 1st plen. mtg., U.N. Doc A/810 (10 December 1948).

[37] *See* Lambert v. California, 355 U.S. 225 (1957).

most of the time. It is sometimes said that, in this aspect, legality acts as a procedural protection, because a criminal law prohibition must be appropriately announced (whether by statute or, in the common law tradition, by judicial decision) before it may be enforced against an individual. When the individual takes advantage of the procedure of notice, he or she can avoid acting criminally.

Legality also protects the individual against the arbitrary power of the political, the prosecutorial, or the judicial departments[38] to punish through the substantive creation of new crimes or the increase in punishments after an act is done,[39] and it protects individuals from the fear that their acts may be so judged. It protects individuals from punishment (e.g., fines, imprisonment, execution, and other penalties) where there was no punishment (or a lighter punishment) provided at the time an act was done. Through the rules against bills of attainder,[40] legality prevents legislative targeting or conviction of specific persons without the stating of general rules in advance. It thus substantively protects life, liberty, and property, and provides the procedural protection of prior notice. Legality in criminal law is necessary to the historical conception of rule of law that seeks to restrain tyranny that arises from the arbitrary application of coercive force.[41]

The liberty-favoring maxim that everything not forbidden is permitted, discussed previously, shows a third purpose of legality in criminal law. It protects the underlying freedom of the human being, no matter how the law is made. When limited to the criminal law, the principle of legality does not perfectly protect liberty to commit non-criminalized acts. In virtually all legal systems there are non-criminal limitations on individual action. These may come in the form of rules of private law or non-criminal government regulations. Nonetheless, legality remains an important protection for the reservoir of freedom that remains after the criminalization of specific acts

[38] Cesare Beccaria, On Crimes and Punishments (Dei Delitti e delle Pene) 13-7 (Henry Paolucci tr., MacMillan 1963) (1764) (especially Chaps. 3–4). See also Bassiouni, *supra* note 13, at 127–30.

[39] See, e.g., United States v. Araki, Separate Opinion of Bernard Victor Aloysius Röling at 44–45, 109 The Tokyo Major War Crimes Trial: The Judgment, Separate Opinions, Proceedings in Chambers, Appeals and Reviews of the International Military Tribunal for the Far East (John R. Pritchard ed.; Robert M. W. Kemper Collegium and Edwin Mellen Press 1998) (1948) (protection from arbitrariness of both legislatures and courts; asserts that this is a matter of policy, not justice); *Rogers*, 532 U.S. at 460 (accepting both notice and protection from arbitrariness reasons for non-retroactivity).

[40] See, e.g., U.S. Const. art. I(9, 10).

[41] See Tamanaha, *supra* note 15, at 97–98, 139; cf. U.N. Doc. A/C.3/SR.1009, ¶¶ 9–10 (meeting of 2 November 1960; Argentina emphasizes importance of legality to liberty).

in any given society. Even when a dictator makes the law, as in Fascist Italy,[42] legality can provide a bare minimum of protection against arbitrariness in the exercise of state power.

A corollary to the protection of freedom is the protection of innocence. An action that was innocent (i.e., might freely be committed without incurring criminal liability) when done should not be punished by the state. This appeared early in the case law[43] and is now part of the doctrine.

This third purpose has not been historically prominent among lawyers' and jurists' justifications for the principle of legality. It can become so to the extent that the protection of liberty is considered a fundamental purpose of government.[44]

The notice justification for the doctrine has often been most prominent. Yet the average citizen does not generally read or understand the details of the criminal code; and most legal systems adhere to some version of the notion that ignorance of the law is no excuse for crime. The principle of notice guarantees persons the opportunity to gain notice of the criminal law, which requires some sort of accessibility of the law rather than a requirement of actual receipt of notice.[45]

[42] See Chap. 2.c.ii.C.

[43] *Calder*, 3 U.S. (3 Dallas) at 390, 396.

[44] Glaser, *supra* note 13, at 762–64.

[45] In American law, cf. Lambert v. California, 355 U.S. 225 (1957). Some systems do define some crimes that are committed only when a person violates a known legal duty to do or omit an act, as where a person can be convicted of knowingly failing to file a tax return only if the person knew of the duty to file the return.

Hans Kelsen has a peculiar passage in which he states that *nullum crimen sine lege* may conflict with the principle that ignorance of the law is no excuse. Hans Kelsen, *Will the Judgment in the Nuremberg Trial Constitute a Precedent in International Law?*, 1 INT'L L.Q. 153, 164–65 (1947). "If knowledge of a non-retroactive law is actually impossible – which is sometimes the case since the assumption that everybody knows the existing law is a fiction – then there is, psychologically, no difference between the application of this non-retroactive law and the application of retroactive law which is considered to be objectionable because it applies to persons who did not and could not know it." *Id.* Kelsen argues that this is a reason not to apply *nullum crimen* in international criminal law. However, the mere fact that not everyone knows the entire law does not mean that it is impossible for persons to know the essence of the law. The fact that most persons would not be able to pass a test on the detailed law of murder in any given legal system does not imply that they do not have a fundamental notion that deliberate killing is wrong and illegal, absent some very limited circumstances such as self-defense.

Recent news reports from Uganda have, however, suggested a tragic example where Kelsen may have a point. Leaders of the Lord's Resistance Army (LRA), under investigation by the prosecutor of the International Criminal Court, have justified LRA attacks against civilians through a claimed right to punish people who speak against them. The LRA has also been involved in the recruitment and abduction of children to become soldiers. One might say it is impossible for such brainwashed persons (i.e., the recruited children) to

Thus, the primary benefit of the principle of legality as a matter of human rights may actually be the limitation of arbitrary governmental power over persons.[46] Whether a person actually knew the details of the law he or she is accused of violating, that person and the public can ascertain whether such a law existed at the time of the offense and what punishment was attached to the offense. This naturally feeds into the legitimacy protection purpose of legality.

1.b.ii. *Legality and Legitimacy*

Legality promotes the legitimacy of the rule of criminal law and the rule of law as a whole. The legitimate deterrent effect of criminal law for an individual who is a "rational and autonomous legal subject" – that is, "its power to influence the decision-making of individuals in a socially constructive way" – is a product of its "rational and knowable" character.[47] One who does not break the law as it stood, and yet is punished ex post facto, is likely to see the law as less legitimate, and "the administration of justice is accordingly brought into disrepute."[48] Similarly, those who do not break the law can observe that, in fact, those who do have the opportunity to know that their conduct was forbidden.[49] This encourages respect for the law – that is, it encourages those bound by it to see it as legitimate and to obey it for reasons other than sheer fear of punishment. The same things can be said about retroactive increases in punishment for an act that was criminal when done.

know the international law against systematic attacks on civilian populations, even after that person reaches adulthood.

This suggests a reason to wonder whether the principle that ignorance of the law is no excuse, or the abolition of the defense of superior orders, might themselves justly have exceptions, rather than to suggest that it is acceptable to apply newly created crimes retroactively.

[46] *Castillo Petruzzi*, Judgement, ¶ 121, quoted in 2 JEAN-MARIE HENCKAERTS & LOUISE DOSWALD-BECK, CUSTOMARY INTERNATIONAL HUMANITARIAN LAW (PRACTICE) ¶ 3714, p. 2500 (Cambridge Univ. Press 2005) (study published by the International Committee of the Red Cross).

[47] Bruce Broomhall, *Article 22: Nullum crimen sine lege*, *in* COMMENTARY ON THE ROME STATUTE OF THE INTERNATIONAL CRIMINAL COURT: OBSERVERS' NOTES, ARTICLE BY ARTICLE ¶ 9, pp. 447, 450 (Otto Triffterer, ed., Nomos-Verlagsgesellschaft, 1999) (hereinafter OBSERVERS' NOTES).

[48] Broomhall, *supra* note 47, at 450 (citing John Calvin Jeffries, Jr., *Legality, Vagueness, and the Construction of Penal Statutes*, 71 VA. L. REV. 189, 205–10 (1985); FERDINANDUSSE, *supra* note 13, at 236–8.

[49] Cf. ANDREW ASHWORTH, PRINCIPLES OF CRIMINAL LAW 69–70 (5th ed., Oxford Univ. Press 2006).

Legality also encourages confidence that acts that do not violate the law as it stands will not be punished, decreasing fear of illegitimacy in lawmaking and law enforcement. Legality also promotes legitimacy to the extent that it encourages the legislature to write clear laws, which can be applied predictably, rather than allow the judiciary to usurp the legislature's position by applying unclear laws.[50] Such applications will, nearly by definition, be unpredictable, at least until the judicial clarifications take hold. Unpredictability (at least unpredictability that goes against the accused) could be avoided if courts always applied the most restrictive interpretation available. Despite the general rule that penal statutes be strictly applied, in many legal systems, doubt concerning interpretation of the criminal definition is not always resolved for the defendant.

Here again, the law must have been applicable to the actor at the time of the act, as well as merely having been in existence.[51] If not, no legitimate authority – or authority that would be seen as legitimate by the actor – bound the actor to the standard of conduct required by the law. This requirement of legitimacy of application (including the point in the section above that if a law is not applicable to an actor, there is no notice that the actor is bound by it) is one of the themes throughout this book.

Legitimacy is a strong underpinning for the requirement that courts be independent, impartial, and created by law. Without such guarantees, it is difficult for many (whether or not accused of crime) to respect criminal proceedings as legitimate or as likely to lead to correct and reliable results.

1.b.iii. *Separation of Powers, Democracy, and Legality in National and International Law*

Criminal law legality helps preserve the functions of governance to their proper organs. It protects separation of powers. In doing so, it protects the legitimacy of criminal law. Legality operates slightly differently in most national governments and in international law to protect this interest.[52]

The principle of legality in national criminal law, especially in its versions requiring written enactments (*nullum crimen, nulla poena sine lege scripta*), may protect separation of powers in national constitutional regimes. In

[50] See Ferdinandusse, *supra* note 13, at 222–23.

[51] *Castillo Petruzzi*, Judgement, ¶ 121, applying ACHR art. 9. Accord, ICCPR art. 15(1); UDHR art. 11(2).

[52] For a discussion of this issue in the context of the international criminal court, see Dominic Raab & Hans Bevers, *The International Criminal Court and the Separation of Powers*, 3 Int'l Orgs. L. Rev. 93 (2006).

these versions, it requires legislatures to act to create new crimes rather than allow executive fiat or judicial decision to determine, perhaps retroactively, what acts will be criminal. This is considered to protect democracy, by protecting the power of the democratically elected legislature to define crime.[53] As discussed previously with respect to legitimacy, legality encourages the legislature to exercise its functions properly, by writing clear laws that can be applied predictably.

In common law systems, non-retroactivity promotes, not merely protects, the separation of powers. Non-retroactivity deprives the courts of their antique function of developing new crimes out of whole cloth in specific cases. It therefore throws this function onto the legislature, where it belongs.

The legislature is the branch of government worldwide most generally subject to popular election.[54] Thus, whether or not a particular system requires a statutory definition of crimes and punishments, legality promotes democracy. It promotes the definition of crimes and punishments by the democratic organ of government. It is thus appropriate that international human rights documents such as the International Covenant on Civil and Political Rights protect both legality in criminal law and democratic governance.[55]

Several rules of legality other than the non-retroactivity rules are also connected to separation-of-powers issues. These include the rule against legislative convictions (bills of attainder) and the rule that courts must be independent, impartial, and established by law.

Some believe that this separation of powers is necessary to the protection of liberty. They argue that "if it was to guarantee the liberty of the individual, criminal law could be based only on legislation."[56] This view has had great

[53] See MACHTELD BOOT, GENOCIDE, CRIMES AGAINST HUMANITY, WAR CRIMES: NULLUM CRIMEN SINE LEGE AND THE SUBJECT MATTER JURISDICTION OF THE INTERNATIONAL CRIMINAL COURT ¶ 80, p. 95 (Intersentia 2002), relying on Entscheidungen des Bundesverfassungsgerichts [BVerfGE] 49, 89, 125 (German Constitutional Court) (no parties or date given) and VOLKER KREY, STUDIEN ZUM GESETZESVORBEHALT IM STRAFRECHT: EINE EINFÜHRUNG IN DIE PROBLEMATIK DES ANALOGIEVERBOTS 211 (Duncker & Humblot 1977).

[54] In most parliamentary systems, the lower house of the legislature is usually directly elected and chooses the executive leadership (the prime minister and government). In presidential systems, both the executive (president) and legislature may be popularly elected. In some systems, such as that of France, there may be both an elected president and a government chosen by the elected legislature.

[55] ICCPR, arts. 15 (legality) and 25 (free elections).

[56] UN Doc. A/C.3/SR.1009, ¶ 10 (meeting of 2 November 1960) (Argentina) (note that this is a direct quote from the UN Summary Record, which does not purport to be a verbatim transcript of the meeting).

influence even among common law thinkers,[57] although as we will see, it is not currently customary international law that binds states and international organizations.[58]

The principle of legality has functions that apply specifically to the criminal aspects of public international law. It prevents international organizations (particularly international criminal tribunals and courts) from exceeding their jurisdiction by providing clear limitations on what is criminal.[59] This presents an analogue to the function of preserving the separation of powers in national courts that apply national law.

Legality in international criminal law also notifies states of their duties (even if, at present, international criminal law prescribes punishment only for individuals). These duties include both the duty to prevent the atrocities prohibited by international criminal law and the duty to bring alleged perpetrators to trial.

1.b.iv. *Legality and the Purposes of Criminalization*

The purposes of criminal law are frequently listed as deterrence (general and specific), retribution, incapacitation, and rehabilitation. To this list, one might add accountability, restorative justice and restitution, and reconciliation. This last group is often not addressed in general criminal law literature, except for the literature on international criminal law and some recent writing on domestic restorative justice. Although these purposes are particularly apparent in post-conflict societies to which international criminal law applies, they might well be considered in terms of domestic criminal law as well.

The legitimacy-protecting purpose of legality links directly to the general purposes of criminal law, most prominently to general and specific deterrence. That is, both the public as a whole and the would-be criminal are deterred from committing crimes that have previously been forbidden. Nearly by definition, it is difficult to be deterred from "criminal activity" that has not been forbidden.[60] Indeed, economic theory suggests that punishing persons for non-forbidden acts reduces the deterrent effect of the criminal law, because it reduces the difference between the costs of doing

[57] Alfred P. Rubin, The Law of Piracy 343 (Naval War College Press 1988); Paul H. Robinson, *Fair Notice and Fair Adjudication: Two Kinds of Legality*, 154 U. Pa. L. Rev. 335, 337–45 (2005); Fletcher, *supra* note 6, at 80–87.

[58] See Chaps. 5.c.ii, 7.a.

[59] Ferdinandusse, *supra* note 13, at 222–23; Broomhall, *supra* note 47, at 450–51.

[60] See Robinson, *supra* note 57, at 365.

what has been criminalized and what has not been criminalized.[61] This is a strong criminological reason for criminal law to follow the doctrine of legality. Without the human rights basis for legality, however, it would not be enough to suggest that criminal law be compelled always to comply with this principle.

Care has to be taken with this argument. One can imagine effective threats of punishment by administrative or executive officials who deterred conduct that had not been forbidden by law – that is, by the act of the appropriate lawmaking body. Nonetheless, in this case, the legitimacy of the prohibition might be in question, but the efficacy of the deterrent depends on the warning being accessible to those whom it is intended to deter before they act. Retroactive punishment in this system might work in deterring conduct, but only to the extent that it indicated a continuing intent to punish the same behavior prospectively.

Perceived legitimacy of criminal law promotes compliance separately from the fear of punishment that deters violation. To the extent this is true, legality has an additional compliance-related purpose. Although evidence does suggest that the legitimacy of criminal justice systems promotes compliance, it is not clear how much of this effect is due to the degree of legitimacy gained by advance warning (non-retroactivity) of crimes and punishments.[62]

There are some arguments, however, that suggest that legality does not necessarily promote crime prevention. One might claim that expansive interpretation of criminal statutes or creation of new crimes by analogy to old crimes forces the populace to avoid morally or legally dubious practices, lest the doubt be resolved against the actor. The practical problem with this theory is that it assumes that persons could predict which currently legal acts will be considered illegal in the near future. The theoretical and moral problem with this theory is that it proposes arbitrary government action as a means of promoting compliance and is utterly against the spirit of liberty that underlies modern human rights law, whether arising from national constitutions and other internal law or from international law.[63]

[61] Cf. Raymond Dacey & Kenneth S. Gallant, *Crime Control and the Harassment of the Innocent*, 25 J. of Crim. Justice 325 (1997).

[62] Cf. Tom R. Tyler, Why People Obey the Law (2d ed., Princeton Univ. Press, 2006) (argues from social science evidence – empirical studies in a U.S. city – that perceived legitimacy is an important factor in promoting compliance; however, non-retroactivity was not one of the specific indicators of legitimacy studied; whether this can be generalized to other societies remains to be studied).

[63] See Robinson, *supra* note 57, at 365.

The suggestion that this is a problem only in a few cases, such as the chilling of free speech,[64] understates the danger of this doctrine. It is here, then, that a difference in quality arises concerning the human rights rationales for legality and the criminological reasons that might support or oppose legality.

The goal of incapacitation of wrongdoers through the criminal law is also promoted by the principle of legality, at least as far as the definition of the crime. Here, however, the target audience is not the prospective criminal but law enforcement. Legality (*nullum crimen*) informs the police and courts which acts society wants prevented and, thus, which wrongdoers need to be incapacitated. *Nulla poena*, however, is sometimes seen as preventing incapacitation of dangerous persons who have not been reformed by imprisonment. Some societies are again beginning to accept "non-criminal law" devices to incapacitate dangerous persons for periods longer than those authorized by criminal law, even where those devices have not been specified in advance of the criminal act.[65] This was one point of the now-discredited Soviet practice of using incarceration and other measures against "socially dangerous" persons who had not violated criminal law.[66] Therefore, the issue of what constitutes criminal punishment becomes an important issue, and the expansion of so-called non-criminal sanctions – especially those that restrict liberty – remains a potentially grave danger. Except for the danger connected with retroactivity, this issue will be beyond the scope of this book – though not because it is unimportant.

The notion of retribution is also connected to an idea of legality. Retribution, as to both existence and amount of punishment, is in most versions of the theory based upon the fact and degree of wrongfulness of an act. Such wrongfulness demands punishment as a matter of fairness and justice. It depends upon a stated morality. More than that, it depends upon a general understanding of the quality of wrongfulness and the punishment

[64] See *id.*

[65] See Kansas v. Hendricks, 521 U.S. 346, 361 (1997) (retroactive application of post-incarceration confinement of certain sex offenders permitted as "civil commitment scheme"); Germany Strafgesetzbuch [StGB] [Penal Code] § 2(6); Lithuania Penal Code, art. 3(4), discussed in Chap. 5.c.viii.

[66] See, e.g., 1926 RSFSR Crim. Code art. 7, quoted in Harold J. Berman, Soviet Criminal Law and Procedure: The RSFSR Codes 25 (Harvard Univ. Press 1966) (all translations from this book are by Berman & James W. Spindler). John N. Hazard & Isaac Shapiro, The Soviet Legal System: Post-Stalin Documentation and Historical Commentary 4 n. 3 (Oceana Publishers for Parker School of Foreign & Comparative Law 1962), document the 1926 RSFSR Criminal Code as Decree of 22 November 1926, effective 1 January 1927, [1926] I Sov. Uzak. RSFSR, No. 80, Item 600. *See generally* Ch. 2.c.ii.B.

deserved for it. This would lead naturally to the legal statement of crimes and punishments.

Retribution for moral wrongdoing – or non-criminal legal wrongdoing – has occasionally been used as a reason for evading the requirement of prior criminalization before punishment.[67] A claim that punishment has been earned for an act that the actor knew was wrong might come from a natural law theory, as well as from positive law criminalization. Thus, even though retributive theory might best be implemented by prior announcement of criminal law, some versions of it would appear to tolerate exceptions to the rule.

Retributive theory can also be said to challenge the split between criminal and non-criminal law. A moral wrong, under most modern versions of retributive theory, must be knowable to actors in advance. A moral wrong may deserve severe punishment, whether or not the specifics of criminal punishment have previously been decreed for it, as with the wrongfulness of aggressive war, denounced by treaty without specific criminalization before World War II.[68] A wrong may also deserve severe punishment under various versions of natural law theory, in which case, the advance knowability might come from nature rather than government. Yet, if the moral rule is known in advance, this version of legality would allow for its punishment. If generalized, this version of legality could be considered essentially to do away with *nulla poena*. So long as the moral wrongfulness of an activity was clear under the prevailing moral system, specific announcement of penalties would be unnecessary. As will be seen, this version of legality was articulated in some post–World War II cases. It has, for good reason, generally been expunged from modern law.[69]

The deterrent, incapacitating, and retributive goals of criminal law are general, sociological, and (in the case of retribution) philosophical, and, to some, religious. They are not tied to the existence of any particular type of state. Therefore, the form in which legality might appear in a given system is not solely predetermined by these purposes. So, the criminal prohibitions and punishments to which persons are bound might come, for example, from a legislature, as in many civil law and other societies; from a combination of legislative and judicial decrees, as in many common law

[67] *E.g.*, United States v. Göring, Judgment of 30 September 1946, 1 TRIAL OF THE MAJOR WAR CRIMINALS BEFORE THE INTERNATIONAL MILITARY TRIBUNAL: NUREMBERG 14 NOVEMBER 1945–OCTOBER 1946 171, 219 (International Military Tribunal 1947).

[68] E.g., Kellogg-Briand Pact ("Pact of Paris") arts. 1–2, 46 Stat. 2343, 2345–46, 94 U.N.T.S. 57, 59–63 (27 August 1928; entered into force 24 July 1929).

[69] For discussion of some competing views after World War II, see Chap. 3.c.ii.

jurisdictions[70]; from administrative decrees, as in both democratic and dictatorial states; or directly from religious edicts, as in some Islamic states and other societies.

1.b.iv.A. Accountability, Restorative Justice, and Reconciliation: Purposes of Criminal Law Applying Specifically, but Not Exclusively, to International Criminal Law and Post-conflict Societies

Accountability, restorative justice (including restitution and reparations), and reconciliation are three purposes of criminal law, and of the rule of law in general, in the wake of mass violence. Thus, they are particularly suitable for consideration as purposes of international criminal law.

These purposes are not limited to international crime, however. Accountability is prominent among the reasons given for prosecutions of public domestic crimes such as bribery and other forms of government and business corruption. It is related to notions both of retribution and of restoring that which was taken by crime. Restorative justice and restitution are very important to criminal law in many civil law countries, which use the *partie civile* system to allow for restitution and other forms of compensation for crime victimization. Crime victim restitution is becoming an important part of the criminal justice system even in some common law jurisdictions that do not have the *partie civile* tradition. Finally, so-called victim-offender mediation claims to approach crime from the point of view of reconciliation. Reconciliation is also a purpose of some traditional justice systems.

Accountability is related to retribution. It is often referred to as the goal of the battle against impunity of leaders who promote violence. Legality promotes accountability in that it requires clear standards (*lex certa*) against which the conduct of leaders and other actors can be measured. However, in a few cases, the non-retroactivity aspect of the legality principle may delay imposition of accountability. For example, the Rome Statute of the International Criminal Court (ICC), the treaty that is the organic document of the ICC, does not allow the court to exercise jurisdiction over the crime of aggression until a definition is adopted as part of the ICC Statute. The ICC will be able to handle cases of aggression only as to acts taking place after the adoption of the definition, meaning that it will not be able to hold leaders accountable for prior acts, even if they clearly fall within any ordinary language definition of *aggression*.

[70] *Pace* Robinson, *supra* note 56, at 337–45.

Restorative justice and reconciliation are perhaps less affected by the doctrine of legality. Restorative justice, at least, is affected, in that legality may set limits on who can be required to provide restitution and reparation through the criminal justice system, and on the amount of restitution and reparation that can be provided through that system. Persons who seek to limit the use of criminal justice in restoring war-torn societies sometimes argue that legality in criminal law prevents the criminal justice system from identifying and working with all of those who may be complicit in the preceding mass violence.[71]

1.C. COMPETITORS TO STRICT LEGALITY AS A PRINCIPLE OF LAW

Several competitors to the strict notion of legality exist. They have different degrees of generality. Some are attacks on the notion of the neutral rule of law in general. Others attack the notion of absolute non-retroactivity of crimes and punishment or other aspects of the principle of legality. Others are specific to the applicability of non-retroactivity rules to international criminal law. A few of them will be addressed here. Except for the radical attacks of authoritarianism, most of these critiques lead to a general rule of non-retroactivity in criminal law, but there are different views of how flexible the pre-announced definition of a crime may be, who may exert jurisdiction over crimes, and what to do about possible exceptions to the principle.

1.c.i. *Indeterminacy of Language and Impossibility of Pure Non-retroactivity*

One competing idea is that, in practice, not all rules can be set out in advance, even in the limited area of criminal law. This was made clear by Jerome Hall: "In a sense, all case law – and that includes jurisprudence interpretive of statutes or codes – operates retroactively. For only fictitiously can it be said that all acts found to be criminal upon trial were criminal when committed."[72] This is true in the civil law system, which requires statutory interpretation, and in the common law system.

Language is indeterminate. No set of words, devised by either legislators or judges, will place a clearly and completely defined set of possible acts

[71] E.g., Mark A. Drumbl, *Punishment, Postgenocide: From Guilt to Shame to* Civis *in Rwanda*, 75 N.Y.U. L. Rev. 1221 (2000).

[72] Hall, *supra* note 6, at 171. See also Sampford, *supra* note 15, at 16–17, *passim*.

within the definition of a crime while clearly defining all other acts to be outside the definition.[73] There may well be many acts clearly within the hard core of a definition of crime as well as a multitude of acts clearly outside of the definition (think of all acts one can commit that are not assault).[74] Yet there will always be some indeterminacy of meaning at the edges of the definition. Many of the close cases, where there is uncertainty as to the meaning of the law, will themselves be identifiable. Thus, there may be some understanding of the risk of violating the law even in the areas of uncertainty.

For Hall, *nullum crimen sine lege* and *nulla poena sine lege* are of necessity pragmatic rules requiring some judgment in application. He believed they could not absolutely and always be applied to prevent any possible retroactive application of new criminal law and new punishments. Hall concluded that the principle of legality should nonetheless be part of the criminal law: "A plausible rationalization of deliberate retroactivity cannot be made."[75] Thus, this type of critique of legality goes to ways to limit the unfairness of retroactive crime creation in light of the limitations of language.

The indeterminacy of language at the boundaries is an issue for legislators who write statutes and for judges in all systems who interpret them. It is especially an issue for those judges who apply criminal law in a common law system, in which at least some rules exist that are stated in court decisions rather than statutes. Even with principles of narrow interpretation, a statute might be applied to cases that are not within the narrowest possible meaning that a citizen might reasonably give it – that is, they may apply to cases not within the smallest core of meaning to which all would agree that the text of the statute applies. On the other hand, the common law process of judicial development of crimes can produce a stable, predictable definition of crime, even though defined – to some extent – after the facts.[76] Either can work well, and each has difficulties, as pointed out by the legal philosopher H. L. A. Hart:

> Much of the jurisprudence of this century [the twentieth] has consisted of the progressive realization (and sometimes the exaggeration) of the important fact that the distinction between the uncertainties of communication by authoritative example (precedent), and the certainties of

[73] See Hart, *supra* note 34, at 123–29 (a classic discussion). One recent study of the problem of language indeterminacy in the context of comparative law (including the issue of criminal law formation) is Sharron Gu, The Boundaries of Meaning and the Formation of Law: Legal Concepts and Reasoning in the English, Arabic, and Chinese Traditions (McGill-Queen's Univ. Press 2006).

[74] This example is from my colleague Joshua Silverstein.

[75] Hall, *supra* note 6 at 172. Sampford, *supra* note 15, argues that there are some cases in which retroactivity is justifiable in many areas of the law, including criminal law.

[76] Hall, *supra* note 6, at 171.

> communication by authoritative general language (legislation) is far less firm than [a] naïve contrast suggests.[77]

Indeterminacy of language is one reason criminal law can never be completely clear and certain. The ideal of *lex certa* can never be absolute as a rule of legality in criminal law. The issue here will always be whether the law is certain enough, and what warning to potential offenders is sufficiently clear to guide the populace to avoid crime.[78]

One commentator, Matthew H. Kramer, has recently argued that strict legality is possible, and desirable, in criminal law, even in the face of indeterminacy:

> [U]navoidable retroactivity is not . . . present in the small number of criminal law cases that hinge on questions to which there are no determinately correct answers. In any benignly liberal democratic system of law, a background norm – a rule of closure – prescribes that no one is to incur criminal penalties for conduct that was not determinately unlawful at the time of its occurrence. Hence, when a court decides that a thitherto indeterminate question about the culpability or permissibility of a certain kind of conduct should be resolved through the classification of such conduct as criminally culpable, the norm articulated by that decision will be applied only prospectively.[79]

Would that it were so! It might be conceivable that, even with the unavoidable uncertainties of language, the world imagined by Kramer could exist. Unfortunately, the rule of lenity – that where it is unclear whether the legal definition of a crime covers the act charged, the accused should be acquitted – generally does not work this perfectly. In most common law jurisdictions, it is not the practice to use cases to announce wholly prospective rules of law that are not applied to the case being decided. As we will see throughout this book, Hall's description of the way criminal litigation actually works in both the civil and the common law worlds is more accurate than Kramer's.

1.c.i.A. Statutory Interpretation as Eroding Legality

The indeterminacy (within limits) of all human language guarantees that criminal statutes require interpretation. In promoting the aims of legality, narrow interpretation of criminal liability in statutes is to be preferred to

[77] Hart, *supra* note 34, at 126.
[78] See Chap. 7.b.i.C.
[79] Matthew H. Kramer, Objectivity and the Rule of Law 120 (Cambridge Univ. Press 2007).

expansive interpretation.[80] In this way, the application of criminal statutes is limited to the hard core of meaning that almost any reader would derive from a statute. This ensures that statutes truly give notice of what acts are criminal, and prevents abuse of power by retroactive expansion of meaning. Consistent application of appropriate interpretive techniques can limit the area of indeterminacy of statutes and common law definitions but will not eliminate it.

Realistically, narrow interpretation is not always applied in most systems. It is thus important that expansive (sometimes called "extensive") interpretation be limited in a way that protects individuals from retroactive creation of new crimes. This can be done. So long as an act is within a reasonable interpretation of a statutory definition, the actor is warned that the act might be criminal – whether or not that act has previously been held to be criminal: "[E]xtensive interpretation is limited by the broadest actual denotation which the words [of a statute] symbolize. The standard is an objective one and may be contrasted with the derivation of factual referents resulting from imaginative expansion of a statute into an all-embracing 'principle.'"[81] So long as this limit is actually applied, legality can be made consistent with various versions of extensive interpretation of criminal statutes.

Extensive interpretation does have three potential problems for legality that are not associated with narrow interpretation. The first is simply that interpretation might not be limited by the reasonable meanings of the words of a statute and will, in fact, expand criminal liability retroactively. In a system that allows expansive statutory interpretation, courts must exercise care to reject attempts to do this.[82]

The second problem is that the risk of being wrong about whether an act is criminal within the meaning of a statute is generally assigned, in an expansive interpretation system, to the individual actor. A narrow interpretation system seeks to avoid this as much as reasonably possible, though it cannot be avoided completely.

The third problem is that the area of possible over-deterrence of activity that is not meant to be criminalized becomes larger in an expansive interpretation system. This results in a bias against the rule that there is liberty to act unless an action is specifically and clearly prohibited. Some might argue that this is, in itself, a rejection of the principle of legality. Fortunately, legality can be preserved, so long as applications are kept within the reasonable

[80] See, e.g., ICC Statute art. 22.
[81] Hall, *supra* note 6, at 174.
[82] *Bouie*, 378 U.S. at 347 (rejecting, as inconsistent with due process of law, an effort to interpret a statute prohibiting unlawful "entry" onto land to include unlawfully remaining on land after a lawful entry).

set of meanings that the words of a statute might have. This problem does, however, demonstrate that the requirement of *lex certa* (that the law be clear or certain) is a vital part of the principle of legality. A law that is so vague that it does not have limited contours that the populace can make out cannot provide adequate warning of what may be determined to be criminal.

An unexpected expansion of interpretive method in defining crime can also have the effect of retroactively creating crime. If actors come to depend upon narrow interpretation of criminal statutes, they may be surprised if a later, expansive interpretation is applied to criminalize some of their acts.

These over-deterrence arguments demonstrate the connection of legality and liberty. Without the principle of legality to protect against retroactive criminalization of acts, the liberty to do all of those things that are not prohibited is undermined.

1.c.i.B. Common Law Development of Criminal Law

Those who accept the civil law notion that only a previously proclaimed statute can provide adequate notice of what is a crime naturally attack the common law process as incompatible with legality. Recently, some authors from the common law tradition have agreed.[83] Development of legality in the common law system will be discussed further in the next chapter.[84] Nonetheless, a few points can be made here.

Within the common law system as a whole, the era of wholesale crime creation, in which courts rather than legislatures created the major common law felonies (e.g., murder, robbery, rape), is over. Today, the task of the common law court is generally statutory interpretation, as well as development of residual common law principles, which are often very important. In common law systems, these principles often make up what in civil law countries would be called the "general part" of criminal law, such as definitions of the notion of acts, culpable mental states, general defenses, and so on.

In important ways, common law articulations of rules of criminal law are like statutory articulations. They can be more or less clear. They can be applied narrowly – so that only acts clearly within their scope are construed as criminal – or they can be applied broadly. For purposes of implementing legality, narrow interpretation is more effective than broad interpretation.

[83] See Rubin, *supra* note 57 at 343; Robinson, *supra* note 57, at 337–45; Ashworth, *supra* note 49, at 68–73.

[84] See Chap. 2.a.i.

Nonetheless, not every common law court interprets case law as narrowly as possible.

So long as an act can reasonably be construed as within the ambit of a common law definition of crime, the actor is warned, in the same way that an actor is warned by a statute. This can be true even if the act was not specifically held to be criminal in a prior case. The same principles and caveats apply here as in the case of statutory interpretation. This is why, as a matter of theory, the problems raised by statutory interpretation and common law criminal development are so closely related and are dealt with together here.

Hall's view of both common law lawmaking and statutory interpretation responded to the civilian view, such as in the French Declaration of the Rights of Man and of the Citizen, that only specific statements of law in statute could provide the *lege* which gives notice of what is criminal[85] – *nullum crimen, nulla poena sine praevia lege scripta.*[86] Hall's type of argument showed that the essence of the modern common law of crimes, as well as of the civil law, was, in fact, based in legality.[87]

This view also demonstrates the importance of foreseeability to the analysis of legality in the common law world. Common law rules, like statutory rules, have areas of uncertainty at their boundaries. As noted previously, the actor must have fair warning that a common law rule can be reasonably interpreted to criminalize his or her act or the principle of legality is violated.

1.c.ii. *Crime Creation by Analogy in Civil Law*

Analogy is a practice of crime creation used in some civil law societies. It declares some acts actually outside the coverage of a statute to be criminal because they are like acts that are covered by the statute, in ways that are relevant to preventing the evil addressed by the statute. In the traditional use of crime creation by analogy to a statutory text, one looks to see whether the act involved bears close resemblance to an already forbidden act.[88]

[85] FEUERBACH, *supra* note 8, at ¶ 24, p. 20; France Declaration of the Rights of Man and of the Citizen art. 8 (1789); France Code Pénal art. 4 (this provision entered the penal code in 1810), all discussed in Hall, *supra* note 6, at 168–70 (also referring to France Const. (1791)).

[86] See BANTEKAS & NASH, *supra* note 7, at 127–28.

[87] See Hall, *supra* note 6, at 167–68; Chap. 2.a.i, on the limitations of common law crime creation in the modern period; Chap. 4.h on European Court of Human Rights cases dealing with legality in common law context.

[88] See A. H. Campbell, *Fascism and Legality*, 62 L.Q. REV. 141, 150–51 (1946).

The common law criticized the practice of crime creation by analogy. Some cases before World War II (and even much earlier) interpreted *nullum crimen* as prohibiting analogy,[89] because analogy criminalizes acts plainly outside the text of a statute. Indeed, that is the purpose of the doctrine's existence.[90] However, before World War II, many civil law countries had not generally prohibited the practice.

Analogy is inconsistent with the strictest civil law interpretation of legality, which requires a previously announced criminal statute covering the act in question. Whether or not one requires narrow statutory interpretation, analogy goes beyond statutory interpretation in that it explicitly recognizes criminality outside of a statute. Its civil law critics characterize analogy as a source of criminal law that is independent of statute and therefore illegitimate. Nonetheless, civil lawyers have recognized that there is a connection between problems of expansive interpretation and analogy, in that both create the possibility of retroactive crime creation.[91]

In this sense, analogy resembles the earlier practice of the common law that indeed resulted in the creation of new crimes.[92] Civil law analogy is, however, unlike common law crime creation, in that the civil law system in which it operated did not recognize precedent in the same way as the common law. Thus, a decision that retroactively creates a crime by analogy would not necessarily be followed in similar cases in the future. And if a similar decision were made in the future, it would once again appear as a retroactive creation of a crime not in the statute books. The civil law's refusal to use precedent generally has the disadvantage of making this type of decision seem arbitrary, but it also prevents a bad decision from being repeated just because it has once been made.

Recently, a Turkish court applied a criminal sentencing law by analogy. The law on its face applied to editors, but the court used analogy to apply it to a publisher. This creative use of analogy was rejected by the European Court of Human Rights as inconsistent with *nulla poena sine lege* as embodied in Article 7 of the European Convention on Human Rights.[93]

Civil law crime creation by analogy to statute applies to different matters from the current common law decision-making tool called "reasoning by analogy." In the common law, a case is examined to determine whether it is

[89] See United States v. Wiltberger, 18 U.S. (5 Wheat.) 76, 96 (1820); Hall, *supra* note 6, at 172, *passim*.
[90] Boot, *supra* note 53, at ¶¶ 84–85, at pp. 101–02.
[91] Cf. *id.*, at ¶ 90, at pp. 106–09.
[92] See Chap. 2.a.i.
[93] *Baskaya*, Judgment.

sufficiently like a prior case in relevant ways that it can be said that the prior case controls it as precedent. Common law analogy thus works only if there are genuine, relevant similarities between cases that create a reason to hold that a rule (whether statutory or otherwise) applies to both. By contrast, civil law analogy only applies if the current case falls outside the language of the statute involved.[94]

1.c.iii. *Legality as an Optional Principle of Law or Justice*

A third challenge to legality comes from the language of the Nuremberg Judgment: legality is a principle of criminal law that is optional for states ("generally adopted," in the French version; "a principle of justice" in the English version), but it is not a binding matter of international human rights law for either states or international institutions. Much of this book is devoted to showing how this statement came to be made and how the rule it enunciates has changed.

1.c.iv. *Legality as a Principle with Limited or No Binding Effect in International Criminal Law*

A fourth challenge, related to the third but specific to international criminal law, states that, in this field, legality has been treated by states and national and international courts as less important and less enforceable than in domestic criminal law. Some scholars, such as M. Cherif Bassiouni, find that *nullum crimen* has played a limited role in international criminal law, and that *nulla poena* is either absent from international criminal law or applicable only "by analogy."[95] This arose from the Nuremberg treatment of legality as a matter that could be discarded. It remains popular today among supporters of international criminal law as a means to control and punish the worst of the worst in human behavior. Addressing this challenge is also central to the task of this book, which concludes that reasonably strong versions of both *nullum crimen* and *nulla poena* are part of customary international criminal law today.[96]

[94] For a civilian commentator's discussion of the difference between the two types of analogy, see BOOT, *supra* note 53, at ¶¶ 84–85, 95, at pp. 101–02, 112–13.

[95] See BASSIOUNI, *supra* note 13, at 158–59, 162, 176; ZAPPALÀ, *supra* note 35, at 196; GUÉNAËL METTRAUX, INTERNATIONAL CRIMES AND THE *AD HOC* TRIBUNALS 356–57 (Oxford Univ. Press 2005); Hubert Rottleuthner & Matthias Mahlmann, *Models of Transition: Old Theories and Recent Developments*, *in* RETHINKING THE RULE OF LAW AFTER COMMUNISM 191 (Adam Czarnota, Martin Krygier & Wojciech Sadurski, eds., Central European Univ. Press 2005).

[96] See Chap. 7.

1.c.v. *Legality as Binding in Normal Circumstances, with Exceptions in Extraordinary or Transitional Times*

A view that the principle of legality in criminal law, strictly followed, is "coherent, if slightly unrealistic" has persisted.[97] Radical evil needs to be punished. The nature of such evil may not be fully predictable in advance, this view holds. Thus, criminal law may have some retroactive aspects, but in the rare instances in which this is the case, the system should be clear about what it is doing and why.[98] This issue remains important for transitional justice – the set of criminal and other legal issues arising from the transition from some form of tyranny or violent societal disintegration to democracy and rule of law.[99]

Transitional justice can also be abused by new authoritarian regimes. During the debates that led to the International Covenant on Civil and Political Rights (ICCPR), both the right-wing Spanish regime of Francisco Franco and the left-wing Cuban regime of Fidel Castro spoke about the possibility of retroactive criminal law in transitional periods.[100]

1.c.vi. *Defenses That Do Not Go to Whether an Act Is Criminal*

Certain matters in substantive criminal law do not go to whether an act is criminal, and thus do not affect the fairness of the warning given to an actor at the time of his or her act. Thus, some argue that matters involving excuse defenses (e.g., insanity) should not be dealt with as matters of non-retroactive crime definition: the act remains criminal even though the actor might later be judged to be not guilty by reason of insanity.[101]

One cannot simply say that "culpability" determinations are not about what we criminalize.[102] In fact, crimes are often defined in terms of culpability levels exactly because it is the doing of the act culpably that makes it criminal (or criminal at a certain level). Thus, these matters do, in fact, go to whether the warning given was fair.[103] Retroactively increasing the degree of a grossly negligent homicide from manslaughter to murder would certainly

[97] Jeffries, *supra* note 48.

[98] See Hart, *supra* note 34, at 208–12; Sampford, *supra* note 15, *passim*.

[99] See, e.g., Rottleuthner & Mahlmann, *supra* note 95.

[100] UN Doc. A/C.3/SR.1008, ¶ 9 (Cuba) (meeting of 1 November 1960); UN Doc. A/C.3/SR.1011, ¶ 26 (Spain) (meeting of 3 November 1960); both discussed in Chap. 4.b.ii.C.

[101] See Robinson, *supra* note 57, at 387–92.

[102] *Id.* at 379–81 (arguing acceptablity of determining matters of culpability law ex post facto).

[103] Cf. Hart, *supra* note 34, at 132–33 (on how it is possible to develop a fairly clear definition of a phrase such as "due care" in civil and criminal law).

impinge on the fairness of notice given to an accused person. Driving too fast and accidentally killing someone is different from deliberately shooting someone to death. Retroactively conflating these actions would be unfair.

Even those who accept this reasoning, however, would generally limit it to matters that do not change whether the act was wrongful. Justification defenses, such as self-defense, indicate that an act was rightful.[104] Thus, they may not, under this theory, be limited or eliminated ex post facto.[105]

1.c.vii. *Legality and Prior Establishment of Court Systems*

Some see the erection of a new or special court or jurisdiction to try crimes as violating the principle of legality, even if there were already courts in existing jurisdictions that could try the crimes.[106] This principle is "originally derived from constitutional law in civil law jurisdictions."[107] Some modern human rights thought and law continue to maintain this,[108] because newly erected special courts have often been used as instruments of repression, by targeting specific persons, often for political reasons,[109] and by retroactively creating criminal law.

1.c.viii. *Change of Name, Character, or Jurisdiction of Offenses*

Little attention has been paid to legality in situations where the law that was applied to the actor at the time of the crime may not have been the law of the forum trying the case. This is because of the standard view that "criminal courts do not apply foreign penal law."[110] Nonetheless, there are a number of cases in which law of another jurisdiction may become part of the process of determining whether a person has committed a crime.

In international criminal courts and tribunals, this includes cases where the court holds that acts were crimes under national law when committed.

[104] See Robinson, *supra* note 57, at 382–84.

[105] But see FLETCHER, *supra* note 6, at 147–48, cited in Chaps. 4.h, 7.b.v.

[106] See Robert Lansing & James Brown Scott, *Memorandum of Reservations Presented by the Representatives of the United States to the Report of the Commission on Responsibilities (April 4, 1919), Annex II to Commission on the Responsibility of the Authors of the War and on Enforcement of Penalties, Report Presented to the Preliminary Peace Conference (Versailles, March 29, 1919), in* 1 THE LAW OF WAR: A DOCUMENTARY HISTORY 842, 860, 865 (Leon Friedman, ed., Random House 1972).

[107] See *Kanyabashi*, Case No. ICTR-96-15-T, at ¶ 31.

[108] See ACHR art. 8(1) (requirement in criminal cases of "competent, independent, and impartial tribunal, previously established by law").

[109] See *Kanyabashi*, Case No. ICTR-96-15-T, at ¶ 31.

[110] LUC REYDAMS, UNIVERSAL JURISDICTION: INTERNATIONAL AND MUNICIPAL LEGAL PERSPECTIVES 5 n. 31 (Oxford Univ. Press 2003) (collecting sources).

Under this theory, it is acceptable to punish them later as international crimes in international tribunals.[111]

In national courts, this arises in cases of what is called representation or vicarious jurisdiction. This arises when a person alleged to have committed a crime elsewhere cannot, for some reason usually unrelated to the nature of the offense, be extradited to the place of the crime or some other place appropriate for trial of the case. In this situation, some states try the person in their own courts, generally using their own law as the base law for the prosecution.[112] It may also occur in cases where states claim universal jurisdiction over customary international law crimes but claim to use their own domestic law in the prosecution.[113]

The seldom-addressed question is this: when, consistent with the principle of legality, can a person be tried for violation of a different law, or law from a different jurisdiction, from the law that applied at the time of the act? This is an additional theme addressed throughout this book.

Where criminal law from a different jurisdiction is used, and the lawmaking jurisdiction is not involved at all, one premise becomes very important to this argument. The evil of the act makes one liable, and conviction is justifiable if some entity other than the lawmaker prosecutes the actor, so long as the act was criminal under law that was applicable to the actor when the act was done. This suggests that what might be called "retroactive re-characterization" of national crimes to international crimes should be limited to crimes that are evil in themselves, or in the language of the criminal law, *malum in se.*

1.c.viii.A. In International Courts

As we will see,[114] the post–World War II prosecutions introduced three related views into the discussion of legality. One view argued that aggressive war was morally and (for states) legally wrong before World War II, and thus it was acceptable to make it an individual crime following the war. A second view was that crimes against humanity merely brought into international criminal law acts that were already criminal under national law, and thus could be punished internationally without violating the principle of *nullum crimen.* A third view was that crimes against humanity (or at least many of them) were already war crimes under international criminal law, and the

[111] This is discussed in Chaps. 3.b.iv.C, 3.c.i, 6.a.iv, 7.b.ii, 7.c.iii.
[112] See Chaps. 5.c.vii, 7.b.ii.D.
[113] See Chaps. 5.c.v.E, 7.b.ii.C.
[114] See Chap. 3.

designation of the crime could be changed without violating the principle of *nullum crimen*. Since the postwar prosecutions, the first of these three views has been abandoned as a general technique for crime creation, but the other two have had some continuing vitality.[115]

Certainly, the transformation of national crimes into crimes against humanity meets the criterion set out previously. These crimes, involving slaughter, rape, and other inhumane conduct, are malum in se, or evil in themselves. The transformation of war crimes into crimes against humanity does not involve a change of prescriptive jurisdiction in the same way (because it can fairly be stated that war crimes were already prohibited by international law). But in any case, war crimes defined by atrocity (as opposed to crimes such as spying or fighting out of uniform) are evil in themselves in ways similar to crimes against humanity.

1.c.viii.B. In National Courts: Domesticating International Crimes and the Problem of Representation Jurisdiction

Two issues arise with changing the name, character, or jurisdiction of offenses in national courts with regard to legality. First, the issues of defining international crimes discussed just previously persist along with an additional problem. That is, when an international crime is prosecuted in a national court, is the law under which the prosecution occurs national or international? For purposes of legality, which law must be in place at the time of the act?

Second, some states will prosecute persons for acts committed elsewhere solely because they cannot extradite the accused to a more appropriate forum. This is generally known as the exercise of representation jurisdiction. The questions then arise: For purposes of legality, which law must have been in place at the time of the act? Suppose the two states authorize different levels of penalty for the act?[116] Finally, is it just for one country to enforce another's criminal law on a person, where that person's acts were illegal but not necessarily evil in themselves (i.e., *malum prohibitum*)?

1.c.ix. *Collective Punishment or Punishment of Hostages*

At least one theory supports collective punishment or execution of innocent hostages for the acts of another. This is the view that crime can be prevented

[115] See Chaps. 6.a.iv, 7.b.ii, 7.c.iii.
[116] See Chaps. 5.c.vii, 7.c.iv.

if a criminal's entire family, village, or other social unit can be punished or threatened with punishment to a member. Some argue that these social units will then require their members to conform to the law or to otherwise exhibit appropriate behavior.[117]

Even in the case of collective responsibility, pre-announcement of law and penalties would seem to be required. It is difficult for the community to know what to enforce against its members without such knowledge. Once again, this demonstrates that non-retroactivity alone is insufficient to completely protect the community from tyranny. This theory provides another example of how the general purposes of crime prevention cannot be used, consistently with human rights, to override the principle of legality. Collective punishment cannot legally be implemented today under the Geneva Convention (No. IV), protecting civilians in cases of war and occupation (where the desire of an outside authoritarian force to gain community compliance might be the greatest),[118] or other human rights treaties prohibiting collective punishment.[119] Moreover, some national constitutions define crime as individual and prohibit collective punishment.[120]

Where modern policing does not exist as a state function, collective punishments privately imposed may serve needed functions. Compensation by a wrongdoer's family to a victim or victim's family or even a practice such as the blood feud may be a social means to limit violence. Privately enforced compensation schemes may provide some measure of restorative justice as well. Unfortunately, outside of the existence of some form of state or other control, these systems may depend heavily on the ability of the victim's social unit to threaten or use force.

[117] For a relatively recent legal example of collective punishment, see Judicial Regs. of Somaliland, arts. 23, 24 ("collective penalty of special contribution" imposed on a group where one of its members commited an offense in this UN Trust Territory), suspended for two years by Somaliland Ord. No. 14 (2 August 1954), Bulletino Officiale No. 8 (16 August 1954), all noted in 1954 UNYBHR 321; cf. Bassiouni, *supra* note 15, *Quesas Crimes* at 206–09; Ahmad Abd al-Aziz al-Alfi, *Punishment in Islamic Criminal Law* 227, 230, *in* Bassiouni, *supra* note 15 (both discussing the use of local community pressure to limit crimes, but pointing out that, in Islam, only restitution can be imposed collectively, not punitive sanctions such as execution); see also Richard Posner, Law and Literature 52 (rev. ed., Harvard Univ. Press, 1998). One of the great novels of the twentieth century, Chinua Achebe, Things Fall Apart (Astor-Honor 1959), centers on Ibo society during the period of decline of a version of hostage taking.

[118] Geneva Convention (No. IV), art. 33 (12 Aug. 1949; entered into force, 21 October 1950).

[119] E.g., African Charter of Human and Peoples Rights art. 7(2), 21 I.L.M. 59 (1982); ACHR art. 5(3).

[120] See Chap. 5.e.

Collective punishment may also have a more sinister purpose, especially in situations of armed conflict or occupation. Such punishment may be used as a cover for ethnic or other cleansing or even genocide, as where a village is destroyed and its people killed or moved out. When used in this way, it may be a part of what has been called "utilitarian genocide," the killing of a group essentially to steal its wealth.[121]

This book argues that the norm forbidding collective criminal punishment or criminal punishment of individual non-criminals has become part of international human rights law.[122] However, groups (or at least a large percentage of members of groups), and not just a few leading individuals, may share responsibility for mass atrocity in ways that are best dealt with non-criminally – as when some Hutus who did not participate in the Rwandan genocide nonetheless occupied land previously owned by murdered Tutsis. As Mark Drumbl has recently argued, developing subtle ways to understand this responsibility and realizing its importance may help develop better responses to the problems of mass violence.[123]

1.c.x. *Authoritarianism and Anti-legality*

A last competing idea is that the entire notion of legality and the rule of law according to so-called neutral principles is deeply flawed. Legality embodies the idea of the "legislative" state, governed by "impersonal, that is, general and preestablished norms" that are applied with as little discretion as possible.[124] This unrealistically reduces, and indeed attempts to eliminate, the will, along with personal power and decision, as a driving force of government and statecraft.[125] Instead, contrary to the principle of legality, "[t]he

[121] See Vahakn N. Dadrian, *A Typology of Genocide*, 5 International Review of Modern Sociology 201 (1975).

[122] See Chaps. 4.d.iii, 4.f.ii, 5.e, brought together in Chap. 7.f.

[123] See Drumbl, *supra* note 27.

[124] Carl Schmidt, Legality and Legitimacy 3–4 [*7–8] (Jeffrey Seitzer trans. & ed., John P. McCormick intro., Duke Univ. Press 2004) (1932; republished with an Afterword by Schmidt in 1958) (page citations to 2004 edition, followed by that edition's reference to the 1932 German edition, starred in brackets). The focus of this work is on the legitimacy of the lawmaker in the rule of law. The issue of prospectivity as part of legality is mentioned, as in the quoted phrase here, but is not the main focus. Interestingly, the issue of legality in criminal law is not a major theme of the book.

In his introduction, McCormick calls Schmidt "the last century's foremost reactionary thinker." McCormick, *in id.*, xiii. Originally a German conservative, Schmidt eventually threw his lot in with the Nazis, and even before joining the party assisted with "the legal details of the Nazi coordination of power." McCormick, *id.*, xxi-xxii.

[125] *Id.* at 4, 9, 86 [*8, 14, 88].

best thing in the world is a command."[126] This view not only admits the acceptability of retroactive criminalization but also suggests the acceptability of political authorities "convicting" persons without judicial trial, which impugns the notion that independent, impartial courts are necessary.

At least one prominent proponent of this view claimed to have advanced it between the world wars as "a despairing attempt to safeguard the last hope of the Weimar Constitution, the presidential system"[127] (i.e., executive decrees avoiding the lawmaking system of Parliament, apparently as an alternative both to the perceived vacuous value-neutrality of the parliamentary legislative state and the anticonstitutional Fascist state). However, the notion of command as a principal feature of government turned out to be congenial to the National Socialists when they seized power,[128] and it was certainly consistent with Adolf Hitler's version of Friedrich Nietzsche's philosophy. When brought into the Nazi system, this type of thinker could argue that "the bold and imaginatively endowed criminal" could use "the phrase *nulla poena sine lege*" to make "the *Rechtsstaat* a laughingstock."[129]

The two major Communist states, the Soviet Union and the People's Republic of China also rejected legality, and especially legality in the criminal law. For their theories, legality impaired the ability of the ruling class (specifically in their cases the proletariat) to use law as an instrument of class struggle.[130] Non-retroactivity in criminal law has now become part of the constitution of Russia and the statutory law of the People's Republic of China.[131]

[126] *Id.* at 9 [*13].
[127] Afterword in *id.* at 95.
[128] See Chap. 2.c.ii.A on the Nazi destruction of legality.
[129] Carl Schmidt, On the Three Types of Juristic Thought 93 (Joseph W. Bendersky trans., Praeger 2004) (1934).
[130] See Chap. 2.c.ii.C on the rejection of legality by the Soviet Union.
[131] See Chap. 5.c.iv.

2

A Partial History to World War II

The principle of legality has a long and checkered history in Western and other systems of jurisprudence. It appears in some form in many legal systems but also was subject to many exceptions and violations in those systems.[1] For example, various implementations of legality, in both the criminal and non-criminal law, appeared in Justinian's compilations of laws.[2] One of the most famous sections of the Magna Carta guarantees that no free man should be deprived of liberty, property, protection of the laws, or life, except according to law.[3] This has been read by moderns as an embodiment of the principle of legality, in the sense of prohibiting retroactive criminalization or punishment. However, it is unclear whether it would have been understood to mean that the substantive law must have been proclaimed in advance of the criminal act or merely that the procedural law must be obeyed, or something of both.[4] Indeed, as with many provisions of documents or statements of general principle from many ages that we moderns would call "open texture[d],"[5] it is not clear

[1] Charles Sampford, Retrospectivity and the Rule of Law 9–12 (Oxford: Oxford Univ. Press 2006) (touching on Greek, Roman, Christian, Muslim, and Jewish views).

[2] Jerome Hall, *Nulla Poena Sine Lege*, 47 Yale L.J. 165, 166 (1938) (citing Digest 15.16.131 and related provisions).

[3] England Magna Carta art. 39 (1215).

[4] See Hall, *supra* note 2, at 167 (taking the view that both meanings, procedural and substantive law, inhere in the phrase *lex terrae* in Magna Carta art. 39, but that one cannot reliably read that article as an implementation of "*nulla poena* in its present significance"); cf. F. M. Powicke, *Per Iudicium Parium vel per Legem Terrae*, in Magna Carta Commemoration Essays 96, 103 (The Lawbook Exchange 2005) (Henry Elliot Malden ed., Royal Historical Society 1917) ("phrase 'lex terrae' suggests . . . many varieties of law and procedure"); Paul Vinogradoff, *Magna Carta, C. 39*, in *id.* 78, 83–89, 95.

[5] See Oscar Schachter, *Interpretation of the Charter in the Political Organs of the United Nations*, in Law, State, and International Legal Order: Essays in Honor of Hans Kelsen 270, 274 (Salo Engel ed., Univ. of Tennessee Press 1964), cited in José E. Alvarez,

that there would have been consensus at the time, if anyone had asked the question.[6]

2.a. OVERVIEW

2.a.i. *Civil Law and Common Law*

Conventional wisdom, which is often conventional because it has a great deal of support in the evidence, credits the Enlightenment and eighteenth- and nineteenth-century positivism for the growth and spread of the principle of legality into a fundamental element of criminal law in many nations worldwide.[7] Among the Western philosophers and jurists credited with fostering the movement are Charles de S. Montesquieu, Cesare Beccaria, William Blackstone, and Paul Anselm Feuerbach.[8] As Christopher L. Blakesley has pointed out, the principle of legality in criminal law is supported by natural law as well as by positivist theorists.[9] Major political and legal documents in which the principle was implemented included the Austrian Penal Code

INTERNATIONAL ORGANIZATIONS AS LAW-MAKERS 85 (Oxford Univ. Press 2005) (for use of "open texture" to describe the UN Charter); see H. L. A. HART, THE CONCEPT OF LAW 127–28 (2d ed., Clarendon Press 1994) (1st ed., 1961) (description of most or all legal standards of behavior as having "what has been termed *open texture*").

[6] For an example of this sort of problem in international law, see, e.g., ALFRED P. RUBIN, THE LAW OF PIRACY 104–13 (Naval War College Press 1988) (demonstrating disagreement as to the source of law of "crimes against the law of nations" in the eighteenth century). An example in domestic constitutional law is the demonstration that there was no agreed-upon meaning of "establishment [of religion]" in U.S. law at the time of the adoption of the U.S. Bill of Rights, in LEONARD LEVY, *No Establishment of Religion: The Original Understanding*, in JUDGMENTS: ESSAYS ON AMERICAN CONSTITUTIONAL HISTORY 169 (Quadrangle Books 1972).

[7] E.g., Hall, *supra* note 2, at 165, 168–69; Stefan Glaser, *Nullum Crimen Sine Lege*, 24 J. COMP. LEGIS. & INT'L L., 3d ser., 29, 30 (1942); M. CHERIF BASSIOUNI, CRIMES AGAINST HUMANITY IN INTERNATIONAL CRIMINAL LAW 127 (2d rev. ed., Kluwer Law Int'l 1999).

[8] See Charles de S. Montesquieu, L'ESPIRIT DES LOIS (1748); CESARE BECCARIA, ON CRIMES AND PUNISHMENTS (DEI DELITTI E DELLE PENE) 13–20 (Henry Paolucci trans., Macmillan Publishing 1963) (1764) (chaps. 3–4); 1 WILLIAM BLACKSTONE, COMMENTARIES *46 (1765); PAUL JOHANN ANSELM RITTER VON FEUERBACH, LEHRBUCH DES GEMEINEN IN DEUTSCHLAND GELTENDEN PEINLICHEN RECHTS, ¶ 24, p. 20 (Georg Friedrich Heyer 1801).

[9] Christopher L. Blakesley, *Extraterritorial Jurisdiction*, in 2 INTERNATIONAL CRIMINAL LAW 33, 93 n.328 (M. Cherif Bassiouni, ed., 2d ed., Transnational Publishers 1999), relying on HUGO GROTIUS, TREATING OF THE RIGHTS OF WAR AND PEACE 384, 385 (Evats trans., 1945), and EMERICH DE VATTEL, THE LAW OF NATIONS: OR THE PRINCIPLES OF THE LAW OF NATURE, APPLIED TO THE CONDUCT AND AFFAIRS OF NATIONS AND SOVEREIGNS (Pomeroy trans., 1805). SAMPFORD, *supra* note 1, at 11–12, discusses some of the philosophical difficulties natural law theory might cause for the concept of notice.

of 1787, the United States Constitution (1787), the French Declaration of the Rights of Man (1789), and other constitutions and statutes.[10]

The goals of notice and limitation of arbitrariness are similar in varying legal systems. However, because of different traditions of lawmaking, the notion of a law is different in the common law system than in the civil law and some other legal traditions.[11]

In one version of the non-retroactivity doctrine, notice requires only that the act have been criminal at the time done. It need not be punished under the same statute or other rule of law that was in effect at the time the act was committed. The first time this doctrine entered into a legal text may have been in 1780, in Massachusetts: "Laws made to punish for actions done before the existence of such laws, *and which have not been declared crimes by preceding laws*, are unjust, oppressive, and inconsistent with the fundamental principles of a free government."[12] This provision only requires non-retroactivity of crime creation. Doctrine from case law would soon specifically require non-retroactivity of increased punishments as well.[13]

Post–French Revolution implementations of the principle of legality in the civil law system often emphasize the statement of the law previously promulgated in a specific statutory form, *nullum crimen sine praevia lege scripta*. This requires that a legitimate legislative authority promulgate a positive statement of law before the allegedly criminal act.[14] In the French Declaration of the Rights of Man and of the Citizen, both the fact

[10] E.g., Delaware [U.S.] Declaration of Rights and Fundamental Rules, art. 3 (1776) ("retrospective Laws, punishing Offenses committed before the Existence of such Laws, are oppressive and unjust and ought not to be made"), discussed in SAMPFORD, *supra* note 1, at 13; Austria Penal Code ¶ 1 (1787), quoted in Glaser, *supra* note 7, at 29; U.S. Const. art. I, §§9–10 (ex post facto clauses) (1787, effective 1789), discussed extensively for the first time and limited to criminal law in Calder v. Bull, 3 U.S. (3 Dallas) 386, 391, 396 (1798); German Criminal (Penal) Code of 1871, art. 2, translated and reprinted in *Justice Case*, 3 TRIALS OF WAR CRIMINALS BEFORE THE NUERNBERG MILITARY TRIBUNALS UNDER CONTROL COUNCIL LAW NO. 10 (T.W.C.), 1, 177n (USMT, 4 December 1947) (1948). See also the pre–World War II Italian Criminal Code, arts. 1–2, discussed in A. H. Campbell, *Fascism and Legality*, 62 L.Q. REV. 141, 143 (1946).

[11] See, e.g., Stefan Glaser, *La méthode d'interpretation en droit international pénal*, 9 REVISTA ITALIANA DI DIRITTO E PROCEDURA PENALE 757, 762–64 (1966).

[12] Massachusetts [U.S.] Bill of Rights art. XXIV (1780) (emphasis added), reprinted in DOCUMENTS OF AMERICAN HISTORY 107, 109 (Henry Steele Commager, ed., 4th ed., Appleton-Century-Crofts, 1948).

[13] Calder v. Bull, 3 U.S. (3 Dallas) at 396.

[14] Rubin, *supra* note 6, at 343 (suggesting that the common law world has accepted this proposition, or at least ought to accept it).

that an act is criminal and the specific law under which a person may be charged must have been knowable at the time of an alleged crime.[15]

The most controversial and important exception to this formulation of the principle of legality in the civil law tradition is the principle of analogy,[16] a civilian technique of criminalizing acts not covered by a statute if they are within the reason of the statute.[17] An act that bears a close, relevant resemblance to a statutorily forbidden act may, under this principle, be punished under the statute. One can view the requirement that the act be within the reason of the statute as providing some notice that the act may be criminal and as providing a significant limitation on the arbitrary expansion of the criminal law. Nonetheless, unlike the interpretation of statutes, which is designed in both civil and common law systems to discover the meaning of the statute, analogy in this sense specifically goes beyond the meaning of a statute.

The common law system from its inception did not depend upon specific statutory articulations to define crimes. Judges originally defined the major common law felonies, such as murder, rape, and burglary, through case law. Today in most common law jurisdictions, statutory definitions of crimes exist. These definitions often depend, however, on an understanding of the concepts developed through case law: for example, many jurisdictions define murder in terms of a killing with "malice aforethought." That phrase does not have the ordinary-language meaning of those words but is a technical term defined by a long history of case law. Yet in almost all cases, the ordinary person in countries that follow case law understands what is necessary not to become a murderer.

Concern for legality constrained executive and legislative power at an earlier time in England than in continental Europe.[18] There were, however, important exceptions. Common law felonies continued to evolve in the English and other courts, and in retrospect, one can see that case law sometimes expanded them.[19] Larceny, for example, grew by case law into a set of crimes that are now known, both in ordinary language and the law of many jurisdictions, as theft.[20] It is unclear whether, early on, there was a

[15] See, e.g., France Declaration of the Rights of Man and the Citizen art. 8 (1789).

[16] Discussed extensively in Bassiouni, *supra* note 7, at 130–37; Hall, *supra* note 2, at 172–80.

[17] See Chap. 1.c.ii.

[18] Hall, *supra* note 2, at 167–68.

[19] *Id.* at 170–71.

[20] See Rex v. Chisser, (1678) T. Raym. 275, 83 Eng. Rep. 142 (K.B.) (creating doctrine that person examining goods for purchase constructively takes them from possession of owner-seller for purposes of wrongful-taking element of larceny); Rex v. Pear, (1779) 1 Leach 212, 168 Eng.

consciousness of this occurring or whether this was considered retroactive application of new law. There were major and controversial innovations in England and elsewhere in the common law world that clearly created retrospective criminal law. The statutorily created court of criminal equity known as the Star Chamber was one of these. By the early nineteenth century, it appears to have been accepted that the British Parliament had authority to enact ex post facto criminal laws, though these carried an "odium" with the public.[21]

Well into the twentieth century, misdemeanors – minor crimes – could, in various common law jurisdictions, be created after the fact, essentially by arguing that the act charged was against public morality.[22] The British House of Lords more recently abolished the doctrine of a residual judicial power to create new common law crimes.[23] Even the European Court of Human Rights recently accepted a common law court's destruction of the marital defense to rape (a felony) after the commission of the act, on the ground that it was foreseeable that the defense might no longer be considered good law.[24]

Rep. 208 (Cent. Crim. Ct.) (creating crime that came to be known as "larceny by trick"); Regina v. Hall, (1868) 169 Eng. Rep. 291 (intent to take wrongfully for purpose of "selling" back to true owner equated to intent to permanently deprive as element of larceny). Compare Statute, 39 Geo. III, c. 85 (An Act to protect Masters and others against Embezzlement, by their Clerks or Servants) (creating crime of embezzlement). See generally JOSHUA DRESSLER, UNDERSTANDING CRIMINAL LAW 591–614 (4th ed., LexisNexis 2006) (discussing common law and statutory development of larceny and related doctrines).

[21] R. A. MELIKAN, *Pains and Penalties Procedure: How the House of Lords 'Tried' Queen Caroline*, in 2 DOMESTIC AND INTERNATIONAL TRIALS, 1700–2000: THE TRIAL IN HISTORY, VOLUME II 54, 57 (Manchester Univ. Press 2003).

[22] See, e.g., Shaw v. DPP, [1962] AC 220 (H.L.); Commonwealth v. Mochan, 177 Pa. Super. 454, 110 A.2d 788 (1955). Common law "misdemeanours" still exist in Brunei, Laws of Brunei, Ch. 4 § 37 (Rev. 2001), at http://www.agc.gov.bn/pdf/Cap4.pdf, but it is not clear that this includes the continuing authority of courts retroactively to create new common law misdemeanours.

[23] Knuller (Publishing, Printing and Promotions), Ltd. v. DPP, [1973] AC 435 (H.L.), discussed in RICHARD CLAYTON ET AL., THE LAW OF HUMAN RIGHTS ¶ 11.147, at p. 619–20 (Oxford Univ. Press 2000). But cf. ANDREW ASHWORTH, PRINCIPLES OF CRIMINAL LAW 70 (5th ed., Oxford Univ. Press 2006) (criticizing *Knuller* as actually allowing some common law crime creation).

[24] See C.R. v. United Kingdom, Judgment, Eur. Ct. H.R. (27 October 1995) (in fairness to the British and European Courts, there is an argument in this case that the statute in question had already abolished the defense at the time of the alleged crime); cf. Rogers v. Tennessee, 532 U.S. 451 (2001) (accepting case law "eliminating" rule that a death must occur within a year and day of the act causing it to constitute murder, but Tennessee had never actually applied that rule in its law). The European Court of Human Rights also held that East German policies allowing use of force against persons illegally leaving the German Democratic Republic (in effect at the time of the acts in question) could not be

The marital-rape case demonstrates why the civil law's emphasis on the prior existence of a statute (*praevia lege scripta*) is not always the whole story. In that case, a previously enacted statute defined rape.[25] The question was whether the judicial decision in the case unpredictably and retroactively broadened the scope of criminal liability under the statute. Broadening of application of statutes by interpretation is not unique to the common law system. It can occur in almost any existing legal system.

Despite the early absence of statutory definitions, the common law system produced a reasonably stable, reasonably predictable set of felonies generally knowable by the populace. The definitions of crimes such as murder, robbery, rape, and burglary appear to have been as well understood by the populace in the common law world as by their counterparts in the civil law world, even without promulgation of specific statutory articulations. As to criminal law, this idea can be traced back at least to Bracton, who relied on both long usage and ties to the natural justice of the Creator for the clarity of common law.[26] The fact that this law is tied to natural justice does not mean that authorities have not also declared it. More recently, in the work of Hans Kelsen, one may properly find common law or customary law described as positive law so long as it operates to restrain conduct through notice and enforcement in the same way that statutes do.[27]

2.a.ii. *Islamic Law*[28]

The Islamic legal system has a different conception of crime and public prosecution than does the civil or common law system. However, the legality

used to justify or excuse killing persons crossing the Berlin Wall. See Streletz v. Germany, Judgment, Applications Nos. 34044/96, 35532/97, & 44801/98, Eur. Ct. H.R. (22 March 2001) (but there was an argument that the policy did not invalidate the German Democratic Republic law as it applied to the defendants at the time of their acts).

[25] See *C.R.*, Eur. Ct. H.R., at ¶¶ 16–18.

[26] 2 H. Bracton, De legibus et consuetudinibus Angliae 22 (G. E. Woodbine, ed.; reprint, S. E. Throne trans., Harvard Univ. Press 1968), discussed in Sharron Gu, The Boundaries of Meaning and the Formation of Law: Legal Concepts and Reasoning in the English, Arabic, and Chinese Traditions 124–25 (McGill-Queen's Univ. Press 2006).

[27] See Hans Kelsen, General Theory of Law and State 113–15 (Anders Wedberg trans., Russell & Russell 1961) (1945). Kelsen was not, however, an unbending critic of retroactivity in criminal law. See Hans Kelsen, *Will the Judgment in the Nuremberg Trial Constitute a Precedent in International Law?*, 1 Int'l L.Q. 153, 164–65 (1947), discussed in Bassiouni, *supra* note 7, at 163–65.

[28] The current author is not a scholar of Islam, and thus this section relies principally on secondary sources in English.

principle has been traced to the Quran itself.[29] The Quran and practices of the Prophet contain examples of criminal law made non-retroactive, such as prohibition of marriage of a man with his sister, acts of usury, and crimes of "blood-guilt" committed before the Islamic revelation,[30] though questions have been raised about whether there are counterexamples as well.[31]

Islamic law defines both the forbidden acts and the penalties for *hudud* crimes in advance.[32] *Quesas* and *diyya* crimes, principally homicide and battery, punished by retribution and/or compensation also have their substance and punishment defined in advance.[33] These categories of crimes and punishments are therefore defined according to methods that embody legality as understood in other legal systems.[34] The model of prosecution here is different from that in the common law system, as it is the victim or the victim's family who, in general, pursues retaliation or compensation.

Ta'azir crimes can be punished at the discretion of Islamic judges. The types of punishment that can be given and the principles on which discretion may be exercised are based in Islamic and community standards. These, it is argued by many Islamic scholars, provide appropriate limitations of legality.[35] For example, Hisham M. Ramadan argues that these crimes can be defined by the Islamic legislature of the appropriate country and time, but that "[k]nowledge of the prohibition is an indispensable punishment requirement."[36] Muhammad Salim al-'Awwa emphasizes that in "the system

[29] Quran, Surat 17:15 (stating that God does not punish "until we have sent a Messenger"), Surat 35:25 (stating that "Every nation had its Messenger raised up to warn them"), translated and discussed in Jafar Habibzadeh, *The Legality Principle of Crimes and Punishments in the Iranian Legal System*, 5 Global Jurist Topics 9 (2005), at http://www.bepress.com/gj.

[30] Taymour Kamel, *The Principle of Legality and Its Application in Islamic Criminal Justice*, in The Islamic Criminal Justice System 149, 158–59 (M. Cherif Bassiouni ed., Oceana Publications 1982), relying on the Quran, Surat 4:23 (marriage with sisters). The source of the non-retroactivity of usury law and crimes of blood guilt is the Hadith of the farewell pilgrimage discourse of the Prophet translated and quoted in Muhammad Salim al-'Awwa, *The Basis of Islamic Penal Legislation*, in *id.* at 127, 134.

[31] Al-'Awwa, *supra* note 30, at 136–39 (arguing that four claimed examples of retroactive criminal law from the time of the Prophet did not in fact involve retroactive application of revealed or other law).

[32] Aly Aly Mansour, *Hudud Crimes*, in Bassiouni, ed., *supra* note 30, at 195, 197–201.

[33] See M. Cherif Bassiouni, *Quesas Crimes*, in Bassiouni, ed., *supra* note 30, at 203–09.

[34] Kamel, *supra* note 30, at 157–59 (also noting that some Westerners do not see the crimes of *quesas* and *diyya* as following principles of legality).

[35] *Id.* at 166–68; Habibzadeh, *supra* note 29, at 12.

[36] Hisham M. Ramadan, *On Islamic Punishment*, in Understanding Islamic Law: From Classical to Contemporary 43, 51 (AltaMira Press 2006) (footnote omitted). See also Kamel, *supra* note 30, at 168 ("The representatives of the community know that they are expected to warn fairly before punishment").

of *Ta'azir*," legislative authorities in Islamic states have the "duty of protecting social interests and prescribing appropriate penalties."[37] He continues: "All jurists agree... that the authorities may not impose such penalties retroactively, nor inflict penalties for previously non-criminalized acts or without giving notice of the punishment."[38] Al-'Awwa ties the principle of legality in criminal law to the principle of "rule of law which... prevents all branches of government from behaving arbitrarily."[39] In most Islamic countries today, discretionary punishments are specified by statute, meeting the *nulla poena* requirement of a maximum preexisting penalty.[40]

However, some Islamic scholars argue that the principle of legality applies somewhat differently to *ta'azir* crimes than to *hudud* or *quesas* crimes. For example, a technique similar to civil law analogy has been approved by some authorities in dealing with *ta'azir* crimes and punishments, dating back to the tenth century C.E. (far earlier than the modern civil law doctrine).[41] Although the types of penalties a judge may give are limited, the judge has wide discretion in choosing among them and imposing them.[42] In Afghanistan in the early twentieth century, there was opposition to the statutory introduction of non-retroactivity of punishment, on the ground that this voided the discretion of judges in cases of *ta'azir* crimes.[43]

If one does not accept the argument that *ta'azir* crimes are consistent with the principle of legality, the persistence of these crimes across a substantial portion of the Islamic world could pose a challenge to the principle as a *jus cogens* rule of international law and would raise the issue of persistent objection to *nulla poena* as a norm of customary international law applicable to these states. However, Islamic law countries today generally do not object to international law obligations concerning non-retroactivity of criminal law.[44]

Two reasons can be advanced here for the Islamic community's acceptance of the principle of legality as a statement of law. First, this acceptance could be based on the Islamic religious idea that God is the sole ultimate source

[37] Al-'Awwa, *supra* note 30, at 135.
[38] *Id.*
[39] *Id.*
[40] Habibzadeh, *supra* note 29, at 12; cf. al-'Awwa, *supra* note 30, at 135.
[41] Ghaouti Benmelha, *Ta'azir Crimes*, in Bassiouni, ed., *supra* note 30, at 211, 216–17 & n15, relying on Abu 'Abd Allah al-Zubayr (d. 939 C.E.) of the Sahfi'i school of Islamic jurisprudence (who set forth maximum discretionary punishments for various crimes related to or analogous to fornication and to theft of an object of "at least the minimum legal value").
[42] *Id. passim.*
[43] Glaser, *supra* note 7, at 32.
[44] See Chaps. 4.g.i & 7.i.

of law,[45] combined with the belief that the Quran is God's final prophetic word to humanity. Thus, all law, in the largest sense of the word, has already been given. Second, the authority of the Quran, the Sunna, and the Hadith has persisted in the face of the will of individual rulers. In practice, they have provided for some sense of a rule of law in criminal matters from the early years of the Islamic era, which, it is argued, was not matched in the West until the French Revolution.[46]

It is difficult to argue that, in the classical period, an Islamic ruler was bound in application of *ta'azir* law to anything like the modern articulations of the principle of legality.[47] The ruler was allowed to punish acts that had not been previously defined as criminal. In the modern period, however, Islamic religious states have codified *ta'azir* crimes and punishment sufficiently such that they meet the principle of legality as articulated by many societies around the world, and they have accepted the non-retroactivity of crimes and punishments explicitly in their constitutions, statutes, and treaty law.[48] Many secular states with majority Islamic populations have done so as well.[49]

Without question, the preceding paragraphs emphasize the legalist aspects of the Islamic tradition. It was not so long ago that a prominent Western arbitrator stated that an Islamic state might have no law but "a purely discretionary justice [administered] with the assistance of the Koran."[50] The reason for emphasizing the legalist tradition in Islam, other than the tradition's existence and intrinsic importance, is that, as will be seen, it has been vitally important in both the modern international[51] and internal[52] decisions regarding legality made by almost all Islamic law states.

2.a.iii. *A Note on Japan and China*

Japan also had a much different notion of crime and public prosecution from that of Western countries for much of its history. The principle of

[45] Kamel, *supra* note 30, at 151 & n.8, relying on the Quran, Surat 6:57.

[46] Cf. Gu, *supra* note 29, at 151.

[47] See Haidar Ala Hamoudi, *The Muezzin's Call and the Dow Jones Bell: On the Necessity of Realism in the Study of Islamic Law*, 56:2 Am. J. Comp. L. (forthcoming) (sec. II.A).

[48] *Id.* For discussion and quotation of the modern provisions implementing legality in these states, see Chap. 5.c.i, ii, iii, viii, 5.e & Appendix C.

[49] See Chap. 5.c.i, ii, iii, viii, 5.e & Appendix C.

[50] *Arbitration between Petroleum Development (Trucial Coast) Ltd. and the Sheikh of Abu Dhabi*, 1 I.C.L.Q. 247, 250–51 (1952) (Lord Asquith of Bishopstone, Arbitrator).

[51] See Chap. 4.g.i.

[52] See Chap. 5.c.i, ii, iii, viii & 5.e.

nullum crimen sine lege was introduced into the Criminal Code of 1880.[53] Both *nullum crimen* and *nulla poena* have existed in Japanese law since the emergence of post–World War II Japan.[54]

During the Qing dynasty, China had a highly bureaucratized legal system, with an extensive code setting out acts to be punished. Even so, the Qing Code had a provision for using analogy to decide cases not precisely covered by the code.[55] The constitution of the nationalist Republic of China, which succeeded the Qing dynasty, and currently governs Taiwan, to this day does not have a constitutional provision on the retroactivity of criminal law.[56] As will be discussed later, the People's Republic of China recently prohibited the retroactivity of crimes and punishments by statute.[57]

2.b. LITERACY AND ACCESSIBILITY OF CRIMINAL LAW

One reason non-statutory development might have worked as well as statutory development to promote notice to the populace of what is criminal is the issue of literacy. For most of human history, most of us have been unable to read or write. Indeed, this would include the nonclerical European governing classes well into the early-modern period. Thus, intelligible basic prohibitions that emerged from the common law system may have provided as much or more notice to citizens as statutory formulations. In the Islamic world, the memorization and recitation of the Quran and related writings may have played a similar role. In the economically developed world today, no one but a criminal lawyer or judge is likely to be familiar with the majority of specifics of a nation's criminal code or case law, and yet most of us avoid criminality most of the time.

Literacy and written law have not, by themselves, been guarantors against mass atrocity. The Holocaust against the Jews, Gypsies, and others by the

[53] CARL F. GOODMAN, THE RULE OF LAW IN JAPAN: A COMPARATIVE ANALYSIS 273–75 (Kluwer Law Int'l 2003).

[54] Japan Const. art. 39 (*nullum crimen*); Japan Crim. Code art. 6. See also Goodman, *supra* note 53, at 283 (arguing that analogy is prohibited in Japan but liberal statutory interpretation is not).

[55] THE GREAT QING CODE art. 44, p. 74 (William C. Jones trans., Clarendon Press 1994). This edition does not indicate when this provision entered Chinese law, but the translation uses language that would be familiar to modern civil lawyers, at least those who read about civil law in English.

[56] See Chap. 5.c.iv & Appendix C.

[57] See Criminal Law of the People's Republic of China arts. 3 & 12; Legislation Law of the People's Republic of China arts. 9 & 84; all discussed in Chap. 5.c.iv & Appendix C.

Germans is a prime example. More recently, Yugoslavia was a literate society before descending into mass violence in the 1990s.

Literacy and related issues of knowledge remain important today. Many of the worst atrocities of the past thirty-five years have occurred in places where illiteracy was high, such as Cambodia, Afghanistan, the Sudan, Rwanda,[58] and the Democratic Republic of the Congo. Many of those involved in fighting are unlikely to have access to a copy of international criminal law texts that they can read. Most of us who are literate do not. Yet is it too much to expect and insist that – literate or not – we all understand that genocide by mass murder, the crime against humanity of extermination and mass murder as part of a systematic attack on a civilian population, and the war crime of murder are both wrong and criminal?

2.C. BETWEEN THE TWO WORLD WARS

The period preceding World War II was of great importance for modern international criminal law. It saw the development of a number of proposals for international criminal law and an international criminal court.[59] It also saw the Nazi and Soviet destruction of the principle of legality of criminal law in their own systems.

2.c.i. *The Versailles Settlement and Criminal Law Legality*

There was a proposal for a high tribunal of the Allied nations at the Paris Peace Conference, at Versailles, after World War I, which would have been an international criminal court. The discussion surrounding this proposal dealt with a number of issues of legality, including the *nullum crimen, nulla poena* issue and the problem of creating new criminal jurisdictions.

On the issue of sentencing, the Allies' Commission on the Responsibility of the Authors of the War and on Enforcement of Penalties proposed that the sentence for "violations of the laws and customs of war" (i.e., war crimes) or "violations of . . . the laws of humanity" (an early formulation of "crimes against humanity") could be "such punishment or punishments as may

[58] See UNESCO Institute for Statistics (2007), http://stats.uis.unesco.org/unesco/TableViewer/document.aspx?ReportId=124&IF_Language=eng&BR_Country=6460 (reporting that as of 2000, 41.2 percent of Rwandan women over fifteen years of age and 28.6 percent of Rwandan men were not literate).

[59] See 1 Benjamin Ferencz, An International Criminal Court: A Step towards World Peace: A Documentary History and Analysis (Half a Century of Hope) 36–65 (Oceana 1980) (also reprinting major documents of the effort).

be imposed for such an offense or offenses by any court in any country represented on the tribunal or in the country of the convicted person."[60] Admittedly, one could characterize this as a weak endorsement of *nulla poena*, because it is difficult to imagine a person understanding in advance that the harshest law of any number of states might apply to him or her, much less to imagine that person knowing what that harshest law might be. At the very least, however, the public of the relevant societies could see that a retroactively increased punishment would not be imposed – that is, the public could determine that the harshest punishment had not itself been increased retroactively. There is, however, a possible interpretation friendlier to *nulla poena*. One could view the lawmaking authority here as the international community, through its creation of the laws and customs of war. One could also find, given the practice of armies throughout history, that violations of the laws and customs of war were punishable by penalties including death (as were many other military offenses). The greatest national penalty would here be within the penalty permitted under international law.

Another important strand of thought argued that a new jurisdiction may not be created to try crimes that had been committed previously. Thus, following World War I, the United States objected to the creation of a truly international criminal tribunal to try individuals for war crimes, because it would be "the creation of a new tribunal, of a new law, of a new penalty, which would be *ex post facto*."[61] The United States had no objection to a state trying enemy soldiers for war crimes under its own law in its own military courts or commissions when the victims were nationals of the state

[60] Commission on the Responsibility of the Authors of the War and on Enforcement of Penalties, Report Presented to the Preliminary Peace Conference (Versailles, 29 March 1919), published at 14 A.J.I.L. 95 (1920), reprinted in 1 THE LAW OF WAR: A DOCUMENTARY HISTORY, 842, 856, 857 (Leon Friedman, ed., Random House 1972). But cf. Reservations by the Japanese Delegation [to the Report of the Commission on Responsibilities], 14 A.J.I.L. at 151–52 (stating "many crimes have been committed by the enemy [Germany and its allies] in the course of the present war in violation of the fundamental principles of international law," but expressing reservations about whether belligerents could try offenders for war crimes "after the war is over," and questioning "whether international law recognizes a penal law applicable to those who are guilty"), reprinted in JOHN C. WATKINS, JR., & JOHN PAUL WEBER, WAR CRIMES AND WAR CRIME TRIALS: FROM LEIPZIG TO THE ICC AND BEYOND: CASES, MATERIALS AND COMMENTS 37 (Carolina Academic Press 2006).

[61] Robert Lansing & James Brown Scott, Memorandum of Reservations Presented by the Representatives of the United States to the Report of the Commission on Responsibilities (4 April 1919), Annex II to Commission on the Responsibility of the Authors of the War and on Enforcement of Penalties, Report Presented to the Preliminary Peace Conference (Versailles, 29 March 1919), published at 14 A.J.I.L. 95 (1920), reprinted in 1 THE LAW OF WAR, *supra* note 60, at 842, 860, 865. See also, e.g., P. D., *Note on the Nuremberg Trials*, 62 L.Q. REV. 229, 231 (1946) (discussing this issue at Nuremberg).

in question; nor did it object to two or more states whose nationals were victims of the same acts combining their military courts or commissions into a single entity for trial pursuant to the laws of the states.[62]

Either of these solutions would involve a jurisdiction that had been previously defined, created by sovereigns existing at the time of the crimes, and with the authority to prescribe limits to the behavior of the actor at the time of the alleged crime. Although, in general, a state has no authority to prescribe limits to behavior of another state's soldiers, all these solutions require is that a state has the authority to prohibit them from committing war crimes – as defined in international law – on its own territory or against its nationals. There has been a long debate as to whether domestic law or international law actually provides the substance of the law under which war criminals are prosecuted. Even if the substantive law is conceptualized as national law, the conduct punished by such law must be such as is permitted by international law definitions to be punished by the law of the state trying the crime.[63]

The high tribunal was never formed. The Treaty of Versailles included provisions by which Germany recognized the right of the Allies to try persons "accused of having committed acts in violation of the laws and customs of war," who would, if found guilty, "be sentenced to punishments laid down by law."[64] The courts to try these persons would be "the military tribunals of [the] Power" whose nationals were victims of the crimes; if nationals of more than one power were involved, the courts would be "military tribunals composed of members of the military tribunals of the Powers concerned."[65] These provisions reflected the American view that jurisdiction, as well as criminal definition, should not be retroactive. Prosecutions, however, were not brought in these tribunals.

There were a few prosecutions for war crimes that resulted in convictions and short sentences in a German court at Leipzig.[66] Nonetheless, these were truly convictions and sentences for war crimes.

[62] Lansing & Scott, Memorandum of Reservations *supra* note 61, at 842, 860, 864.

[63] Cf. Kenneth S. Gallant, *Jurisdiction to Adjudicate and Jurisdiction to Prescribe in International Criminal Courts*, 48 Villanova L. Rev. 763, 774–75 (2003), citing Restatement (Third) of Foreign Relations Law of the United States §404, Rptr's n.1 (Am. L. Inst. 1987), and Kenneth C. Randall, *Universal Jurisdiction under International Law*, 66 Tex. L. Rev. 785, 795–97 (1988).

[64] Treaty of Versailles art. 228 (28 June 1919; entered into force 10 January 1920).

[65] *Id.* at art. 229.

[66] Some of the judgments were translated and printed in English at *Current Notes*, 16 A.J.I.L. 628ff. (1922), excerpted in Watkins & Weber, *supra* note 60, at 52–67. The post–World War I events were prominent in the thinking of Henri Donnedieu de Vabres, the principal French judge at Nuremberg, concerning the lawfulness of aggressive war. See Chap. 3.b.iv.E; Henri

The Treaty of Versailles had a provision by which "[t]he Allied and Associated Powers [would] publicly arraign William II of Hohenzollern, former German Emperor, for a supreme offense against international morality and the sanctity of treaties."[67] This trial never took place, as the kaiser had taken refuge in the Netherlands and the Netherlands refused to extradite him. One of the reasons that the Netherlands gave for refusing was that the acts for which he was to be tried were not defined under any international statute – that is, the principle of legality was being violated.[68]

2.c.ii. *Fascist and Communist Attacks on Legality between the Wars*

Concern for legality just before and after World War II – a period of great importance for international criminal law – was largely a reaction to Germany's destruction of the principle in 1935. Destruction of the principle in the new Soviet Union gained less attention in the world at large, though its effects lingered well beyond the end of World War II.

2.c.ii.A. The End of Legality in the Weimar Republic's Laws

The Weimar Republic had a version of the principle of legality in its constitution, allowing punishment only for acts that the law "had declared punishable before commission," an implementation of *nullum crimen sine lege*.[69] This followed Germany's 1871 criminal code, which prohibited punishment unless such punishment had been "prescribed by statute before the act [was] committed," an implementation of *nulla poena sine lege* that appears to incorporate *nullum crimen* as well.[70] Observers before World War II noted that the loosening of principles of statutory interpretation had weakened the principle in Germany several years before the rise of National Socialism.[71] Then, a fire at the Reichstag prompted passage of a 1933 statute

Felix August Donnedieu de Vabres, *Le procès de Nuremberg devant les principes modernes du droit pénal international*, 70(I) Recueil des Cours 477, 574 (1947).

[67] Treaty of Versailles art. 227.

[68] Howard Ball, Prosecuting War Crimes and Genocide: The Twentieth-Century Experience 22 (Univ. Press of Kansas 1999).

[69] Germany Const. ("Weimar Constitution") art. 116 (1919), trans. attrib. to Joseph Gollomb, in Bassiouni, *supra* note 7, at 132–33 n.25.

[70] German Criminal (Penal) Code of 1871, art. 2, translated and reprinted in *Justice Case*, 3 T.W.C. at 177n.

[71] Hall, *supra* note 2, at 175 n.43, citing Dahm, Special Report for the International Congress of Comparative Law at 3, 4 (date not given). See also Machteld Boot, Genocide, Crimes against Humanity, War Crimes: Nullum Crimen Sine Lege and the Subject Matter Jurisdiction of the International Criminal Court ¶ 76, p. 86 (Intersentia 2002).

retroactively imposing the death penalty for arson in connection with that act.[72]

Nonetheless, the wholesale abandonment of the principle of legality in 1935 by the Nazi government caused both a political and a legal shock. A law of 28 June 1935, proclaimed for the German Government by Adolf Hitler as führer and Reich chancellor and by the Reich minister of justice, stated:

> Whoever commits an act which the law declares as punishable or which deserves punishment according to the fundamental idea of a penal law or the sound sentiment of the people, shall be punished. If no specific penal law can be directly applied to the act, it shall be punished according to the law whose underlying principle can be most readily applied to the act.[73]

This was one of the laws necessary for the implementation of the *Führerprinzip* (leadership principle) by the Nazi government.[74] That it was meant to destroy the principle of legality in criminal law was emphasized shortly after its proclamation by Hans Frank, president of the Academy of German Law and Nazi Party *Reichsleiter*:

> By means of... [this law], the liberal foundation of the old penal code "no penalty without a law" was definitely abandoned and replaced by the postulate, "no crime without punishment," which corresponds to our conception of the law.
>
> In the future, criminal behavior, even if it does not fall under formal penal precepts, will receive the deserved punishment if such behavior is considered punishable according to the healthy feelings of the people.[75]

It was also one of the laws cited in the *Justice Case* as demonstrating that the operation of the Nazi justice system during World War II was integral to the crimes against humanity perpetrated by the regime and by those participating in it.[76] Under the worst interpretation of the legality of the Nuremberg main trial, the defendants would be punishable under Hans

[72] Statute "*Lex van der Lubbe*," RGBl. I, 151 (Germany, 29 March 1933) (retroactively allowing death penalty for arson in the Reichstag fire), discussed in Boot, ¶ 76, p. 86 & n.19 (noting that other laws retroactively imposing the death penalty followed in 1936 and 1938).

[73] Law of 28 June 1935, Amending the Criminal (Penal) Code § I, published in 1935 Reichsgesetzblatt, part I, p. 839 (Germany), translated and reprinted in *Justice Case*, 3 T.W.C. at 176–77, amending German Penal Code art. 2.

[74] See quotations of German officials on Adolf Hitler's role as supreme judge of criminal law in Opinion and Judgment, *Justice Case*, 3 T.W.C. at 1011–14 (4 December 1947).

[75] Statement of Hans Frank, 14 September 1935, translated and printed in *Justice Case*, 3 T.W.C. at 1022; accord, Speech of Franz Schlegelberger, 10 March 1936, University of Rostock, translated and printed in *Justice Case*, 3 T.W.C. at 1082.

[76] Opinion and Judgment of *Justice Case*, 3 T.W.C. at 979, 990–91, 1022, 1082–83 (the law "destroyed the feeling of legal security and created an atmosphere of terrorism").

Frank's theories, as the healthy feelings of the Allied peoples condemned the Nazi brutalities against both their own citizens and others, as well as the aggressive war the Nazi leaders brought to Europe.[77]

The 1935 law has a peculiarity that appears to take it out of more moderate interpretive traditions. Although it appears to rely on analogy as the means for creating new crimes, in fact the law distorts that conception. In a moderate use of analogy, one looks to see whether the act involved bears close resemblance to an already-forbidden act.[78] Under the Law of 28 June 1935, an act that is perceived to be "deserving of penalty according to the fundamental conceptions of a penal law and sound popular feeling"[79] will be punished. Analogy is to be used only to determine which law will be used to punish the act. It is also worth pointing out that the law does not limit itself to the creation of minor crimes, as with the common law rule permitting misdemeanor punishment of acts against public morals.[80] This law was not, however, utterly novel, in that the Soviet Union had dealt with legality in a similar way in the 1920s.[81]

Another law of the same date, proclaimed by the same authorities, on criminal procedure does appear to treat reasoning by analogy as requiring examination of whether an act bears resemblance to an already-forbidden act, though it is not clear whether this is meant to limit the previously quoted text.[82] The interpretation given by Hans Frank contains no such

[77] Cf. Nuremberg Judgment, 1 IMT, TRIAL at 219 (it would be "unjust" if the defendants' wrongs were "allowed to go unpunished"); Comments of André Gros, in Minutes of Conference Session, 25 July 1945 [Doc. LI], published in REPORT OF ROBERT H. JACKSON UNITED STATES REPRESENTATIVE TO THE INTERNATIONAL CONFERENCE ON MILITARY TRIALS: LONDON, 1945, 381–82 (rep. AMS Press 1971) (U.S. Gov't Printing Off. 1949 [submitted by Jackson to the Secretary of State 15 December 1947]) ("the French people and other people of the occupied countries just want to show that the Nazis were bandits. It is not very difficult to show. There has been an organized banditry in Europe for many years. The result was crimes").

[78] See Campbell, *supra* note 10, at 150.

[79] Law of 28 June 1935, Amending the Criminal (Penal) Code § I, published in 1935 Reichsgesetzblatt, part I, p. 839 (Germany), translated and reprinted in *Justice Case*, 3 T.W.C. at 176–77, amending German Penal Code art. 2.

[80] Cf., e.g., *Mochan*, 110 A.2d 788.

[81] Cf. JOHN N. HAZARD & ISAAC SHAPIRO, THE SOVIET LEGAL SYSTEM: POST-STALIN DOCUMENTATION AND HISTORICAL COMMENTARY, I–4 & n.3 (Oceana Publications 1962), discussing 1926 RSFSR Crim. Code art. 16, reenacting 1922 RSFSR Crim. Code art. 10, [1922] 1 Sob. Uzak. RSFSR, No. 15, item 153 (effective 1 June 1922).

[82] Law of 28 June 1935, Code of Criminal Procedure and Judicature Act § I, published in 1935 Reichsgesetzblatt, part I, p. 844 (Germany), translated and reprinted in *Justice Case*, 3 T.W.C. at 177–80, adding German Code of Criminal Procedure arts. 170a & 267a (allowing the Reich Supreme Court to ignore precedent where inconsistent with "the change of ideology and of legal concepts which the new state has brought about"); Law of 28 June, Code of Criminal Procedure and Judicature Act §II.

limitation.[83] A debate over this issue appears to have existed in Germany at the time.[84]

2.c.ii.B. Danzig's Abandonment of Legality and the Permanent Court of International Justice Response

The National Socialist majority in the Senate of the Free City of Danzig quickly adopted a decree similar to the new German law.[85] At the request of minority parties in the Danzig Senate, the Council of the League of Nations requested an advisory opinion from the Permanent Court of International Justice (PCIJ) on whether this decree was consistent with the constitution of the Free City.

How PCIJ decided that this matter was within its advisory jurisdiction does not directly implicate the principle of legality in criminal law. It does involve a related concern, the role of international organizations in defining law for individuals, which is connected to rule of law in the modern world more generally. It is therefore worth brief consideration here.

The Free City of Danzig was a political entity created by the Treaty of Versailles as part of the territorial adjustments between Poland and Germany after World War I.[86] The Treaty of Versailles stipulated that Danzig would be under the protection of the League of Nations, and the constitution of the Free City of Danzig would be adopted by the people of Danzig, subject to the approval of a high commissioner appointed by the League of Nations.[87]

[83] Accord Speech of Franz Schlegelberger, *supra* note 75, at 1082.

[84] See Boot, ¶ 76, at pp. 86–87, citing H.-L. Schreiber, Gesetz und Richter: Zur geschichtlichen Entwicklung des Satzes "nullum crimen, nulla poena sine lege" 198 (Metzner 1976).

[85] Senate of the Free City of Danzig, Decree of 29 August 1935 to Amend Certain Provisions of the Penal Code arts. 1 & 2, amending Penal Code of the Free City of Danzig arts. 2 & 2a, original in German, Verordung zur Änderung einiger Bestimmungen des Strafgesetzbuches. Vom 29. August 1935, *Gesetzblatt für die Freie Stadt Danzig*, No. 91, 31 August 1935, reprinted in the record of *Consistency of Certain Danzig Legislative Decrees with the Constitution of the Free City*, P.C.I.J (Ser. C) No. 77 at 28ff., available at http://www.icj-cij.org, relevant portions translated into English as part of the petition of the minority parties of the Danzig Senate, *id.* at 18, 20–21 (emphasizing the Nazi origins of the amendment). See also Ole Spiermann, International Legal Argument in the Permanent Court of International Justice: The Rise of the International Judiciary 360 (Cambridge Univ. Press 2005).

[86] Treaty of Versailles arts. 100–08.

[87] Treaty of Versailles art. 103; Constitution of the Free City of Danzig, reprinted in German as Verfassung der Freien Stadt Danzig, arts. 71–75 in the record of *Treatment of Polish Nationals and other Persons of Polish Origin or Speech in the Danzig Territory*, P.C.I.J. (ser. C), No. 56 at 49, 61–62, available at http://www.icj-cij.org.

The Treaty of Versailles did not refer to Danzig as a "state" for purposes of international law, but by 1935, the PCIJ, through its president, treated Danzig as a state eligible to appear before it.[88]

The PCIJ did not treat the issue of the principle of legality as a matter of international human rights – that is, as a question of international law concerning the rights of individuals against state or government authority generally. Rather, it looked at the special role of the League of Nations in protecting Danzig and its constitution. This role grew out of the Treaty of Versailles compromise over the status of Danzig,[89] which had a majority German population, and great economic importance to the newly restored state of Poland. Thus, the League of Nations found itself in the position of being an international organization required by treaty to make and interpret law to be applied internally to an otherwise statelike entity and its citizens. The PCIJ was required to advise on the constitutionality of a particular internal law of Danzig.

On the substance of the legality issue, the PCIJ declared that applying this decree to Danzig violated the constitution of Danzig. The constitution gave Danzig its "character as a State governed by the rule of law (*Rechtsstaat*)."[90] The court held that the Danzig constitution

[88] *Advisory Opinion on the Consistency of Certain Danzig Legislative Decrees with the Constitution of the Free City*, 4 December 1935, P.C.I.J. (ser. A/B) No. 65 at 43–44; there is no reference to statehood of Danzig in the *Advisory Opinion on the Jurisdiction of the Courts of Danzig (Polish Railways)*, 3 March 1928, P.C.I.J. (ser. B) No. 15; *Advisory Opinion on the Polish Postal Service in Danzig*, 16 May 1925, P.C.I.J. (ser. B) No. 11; and the burden of the *Advisory Opinion on the Free City of Danzig and the International Labour Organization*, 26 August 1930, P.C.I.J. (ser. B) No. 18, is to reject the notion that the Free City is a state, because it does not have the right to an independent foreign policy. But see *Advisory Opinion on Treatment of Polish National in Danzig*, 24 February 1932, P.C.I.J. (ser. A/B) No. 44 at 23–24, 25, where Poland is required to treat Danzig, with some exceptions defined in treaties, according to the "ordinary rules governing relations between States." At page 17 of the Polish Railways case, the court gives the traditional rule that "an international agreement, cannot, as such, create direct rights and obligations for private individuals." The ambiguous status of Danzig in the eyes of the PCIJ goes back at least until 1922, according to 1922–1925 P.C.I.J. YEARBOOK (ser. E) No. 1. On 17 May 1922, the Council of the League of Nations passed a Resolution describing how a state that is not a member of the League (or mentioned in the Annex to the League's constituent document) could submit itself to the jurisdiction of the PCIJ. *Id.*, 139–40. On 28 June, the PCIJ decided to transmit the Resolution to "Poland (for transmission to the Free City of Danzig)." *Id.*, 140–41, 251–52. See also Spiermann, *supra* note 84, at 333.

[89] *Advisory Opinion on the Consistency of Certain Danzig Legislative Decrees with the Constitution of the Free City* at 49–50.

[90] *Id.* at 53–56, relying on Constitution of the Free City of Danzig arts. 74, 75 & 79, reprinted in German, Verfassung der Freien Stadt Danzig, in the record of *Treatment of Polish Nationals in Danzig* at 49.

> takes as its starting-point the fundamental rights of the individual; these rights may be restricted . . . in the general public interest, but only in virtue of a law which must itself specify the conditions of such restriction, and, in particular, determine the limit beyond which an act can no longer be justified as an exercise of a fundamental liberty and becomes a punishable offense. It must be possible for the individual to know, beforehand, whether his acts are lawful or liable to punishment.[91]

This shows the PCIJ connecting the principle of legality in criminal law to the rule of law as a more general foundation of government.[92]

The opinion admits that there are matters of interpretation and application of criminal law that are necessarily left to judges, and that it is sometimes "not easy to solve" the question when the need to interpret a law "comes in conflict with the principle that fundamental rights may not be restricted except by law."[93] In this case, however, "the discretionary power left to the judge is too wide to allow of any doubt but that it exceeds these limits."[94]

As mentioned, the PCIJ treated this as a matter of the proper interpretation of the Danzig constitution rather than as a matter of international human rights law. One might, if one wished, see this as a foreshadowing of the Nuremberg idea that *nullum crimen* is a principle of justice but not (yet) as a limitation on sovereignty of states generally. One might also see the claim that persons must be able to tell what is lawful, but that there will always be a need for interpretation, as a foreshadowing of modern doctrines of foreseeability.[95]

2.c.ii.C. Other Dictatorships: The Soviet Union and Italy

Germany was not the only major power to abandon the principle of legality in criminal law. The new Soviet Union did not accept it until about 1960, and then with some apparent exceptions.[96]

Legality in criminal law was part of the 1864 judicial reforms of Czar Alexander II of Russia, though with "gap[s]."[97] Crime creation by analogy

[91] *Advisory Opinion on the Consistency of Certain Danzig Legislative Decrees with the Constitution of the Free City* at 57.

[92] Cf. Chap. 1.a.

[93] *Advisory Opinion on the Consistency of Certain Danzig Legislative Decrees with the Constitution of the Free City* at 56.

[94] *Id.*

[95] Cf. Chap. 1.c.i, Chaps. 4.h & 7.b.i.

[96] For the reinstitution of legality, see Chap. 5.c.iv.

[97] See Samuel Kucherov, Courts, Lawyers and Trials under the Last Three Tsars 36 (Greenwood Press 1974) (Frederick A. Praeger 1953), citing Code of Criminal Procedure

was part of czarist tradition from 1864 to 1903, when it was abolished.[98] This changed again after the Russian Revolution. "By the earliest [Communist] decrees on the courts, the judges were left free to define as criminal whatever their consciences suggested, as guided by Marxist political thought and a residue of the imperial criminal code not found disconsonant with the new life."[99] The principle of legality in criminal law, like most individual rights, was missing from the first Russian Soviet constitution of 1918,[100] as well as the USSR constitutions of 1924[101] and 1936.[102] In 1922, during Vladimir I. Lenin's lifetime, and again in 1926, new criminal codes were adopted that permitted crime creation by analogy, and even more, essentially permitted the criminalization of any "socially dangerous acts":

> With regard to persons who have committed socially dangerous acts or who represent a danger because of their connection with a criminal environment or because of their past activity, measures of social defense of a judicial-correctional, medical, or medico-educational character shall be applied. . . . [103]
>
> If any socially dangerous act is not directly provided for by the present Code, the basis and limits of responsibility for it shall be determined by application of those articles of the Code which provide for crimes most similar to it in nature.[104]

These provisions were an even more thoroughgoing destruction of the principle of legality than were the later Nazi German decrees. The first quoted provision essentially allows for freedom in defining socially dangerous acts or persons without regard to established laws, and for freedom in correcting, including by punishment, such behavior. These provisions

art. 1 & n. (20 November 1864). Kucherov, at 305, notes that, even after the reforms of 1864, "*the legislative and executive powers remained completely autocratic.*"

98 Hazard & Shapiro, *supra* note 80, at I–133, citing N. S. Timasheff, *The Impact of the Penal Law of Imperial Russia on Soviet Penal Law*, 12 Am. Slavic & E. European Rev. 441 (1953).

99 Hazard & Shapiro, at I–131.

100 RSFSR Const. (Fundamental Law) (10 July 1918) (trans. Aryeh L. Unger), in Aryeh L. Unger, Constitutional Development in the USSR 25 (Pica Press 1981).

101 USSR Const. (Fundamental Law) (31 January 1924) (trans. Unger), in *id.* at 59.

102 USSR Const. (Fundamental Law) (5 December 1936) (trans. Unger) in *id.* at 140.

103 1926 RSFSR Crim. Code art. 7, quoted in Harold J. Berman, Soviet Criminal Law and Procedure: The RSFSR Codes 21 (Harvard Univ. Press, 1966) (all translations from this book are by Berman and James W. Spindler). Hazard & Shapiro, *supra* note 80, at I–4 n.3, document the 1926 RSFSR Crim. Code as Decree of 22 November 1926, [1926] I Sov. Uzak. RSFSR, No. 80, Item 600 (effective 1 January 1927). Similar laws existed in the other Soviet Republics. Berman, at 20.

104 1926 RSFSR Crim. Code art. 16, quoted in Berman, *supra* note 103, at 22. Hazard & Shapiro, *supra* note 80, at p. I–4n.3, point out that this was a reenactment of 1922 RSFSR Crim. Code art. 10, [1922] 1 Sob. Uzak. RSFSR, No. 15, item 153 (effective 1 June 1922).

were, unfortunately, widely used. Nonetheless, they did not create as much immediate widespread criticism and controversy outside the Soviet Union as did the changes introduced by the Nazis.

Marxism–Leninism viewed law instrumentally, as a tool of the ruling class to promote its interests. The code provisions quoted previously are quite specific in placing the interest of "social defense" of the dictatorship of the proletariat above the interest of individual human rights. Indeed, some sought to place social defense against dangerous persons on an equal footing with, or even as a replacement for, the idea of punishment for criminal acts: "The system of material *protection* of basic law and the state is defined in the criminal law; this contains the methods of struggle by means of measures of social defense (previously punishments) against persons socially dangerous to this structure and their actions. This category also includes so-called administrative law."[105] This type of thinking became important in the negotiations for what eventually became the Nuremberg Charter.[106]

Other pre–World War II experience demonstrated that the principle of legality in criminal law is not by itself a guarantor against tyranny. Conversely, the experience demonstrated that even tyranny may be controlled in very limited but important ways by legality. Italy never abolished legality in its criminal code. Its Fascist regime even reenacted the principle in the criminal code of 1931.[107]

[105] P. I. STUCHKA, *Law*, in SELECTED WRITINGS ON SOVIET LAW AND MARXISM 143, 153 (Robert Sharlet, Peter B. Maggs & Piers Beirne trans. & eds., M. E. Sharpe 1988). The piece quoted here is a translation of Pravo, 3 ENTSIKLOPEDIIA GOSUDARSTVA I PRAVA [ENCYCLOPEDIA OF STATE AND LAW] 415–30 (Moscow 1925–27).

[106] See Chap. 3.b.ii.

[107] BASSIOUNI, *supra* note 7, at 130–31, citing to Italy Criminal Code of 1931 art. 1; Campbell, *supra* note 10, at 143, discussing Italy Criminal Code arts. 1–2.

3

Nuremberg, Tokyo, and Other Postwar Cases

The Nuremberg Judgment correctly stated then-current law: *nullum crimen sine lege* was not a limitation of sovereignty.[1] Specifically, *nullum crimen sine lege* did not state an international law-based human right that could be asserted by an individual against a state, group of states, or international organization. It was correct at least partly because, at the time, there was little interference by international law in the internal arrangements by which governments ruled their people, and the Nuremberg Judgment itself did not announce the violation of the principle of legality as one of the crimes against humanity and war crimes of which the accused might be convicted.[2] Substantive international human rights and humanitarian law had not evolved to make this a right of individuals enforceable against states (or other prosecuting authorities, such as international organizations – should they come to exist).[3]

[1] See Antonio Cassese, *Crimes against Humanity*, in 1 THE ROME STATUTE OF THE INTERNATIONAL CRIMINAL COURT: A COMMENTARY 353, 354–55 (Antonio Cassese, Paola Gaeta & John R. W. D. Jones, eds., Oxford Univ. Press 2002).

[2] But see United States v. Alstoetter (*Justice Case*), 3 TRIALS OF WAR CRIMINALS BEFORE THE NUERNBERG MILITARY TRIBUNALS UNDER CONTROL COUNCIL LAW NO. 10 [hereinafter T.W.C.] 954, 990 (USMT, 4 December 1947) (where Nazi repudiation of the principle of legality was at least a small part of the basis for condemnation of defendants).

[3] See, e.g., *Advisory Opinion on the Consistency of Certain Danzig Legislative Decrees with the Constitution of the Free City*, 4 December 1935, P.C.I.J. (ser. A/B) No. 65 at 53–56 (relying on Constitution of the Free City of Danzig arts. 74, 75, 79 for the principle of legality in criminal law); *Advisory Opinion on the Jurisdiction of the Courts of Danzig (Polish Railways)*, 3 March 1928, P.C.I.J. (ser. B) No. 15 at 17 (stating traditional doctrine that treaties affect rights between parties to them and do not confer rights and responsibilities directly upon individuals). See also Serge Krylov, *Les notions principales du droit des gens (La doctrine soviétique du droit international)*, 70(I) RECUEIL DES COURS 407, 446–48, 450–51 (1947) (refusal to give individuals direct rights under international law and noninterference in internal affairs of states continued to be the Soviet view of international law after the war) (Judge Krylov was a member of the International Court of Justice).

The English version of the Nuremberg Judgment was also correct in stating that *nullum crimen sine lege* is a principle of justice. At least it was recognized as a fundamental principle of criminal justice by many persons and nations by the time of World War II, including the principal French judge Henri Donnedieu de Vabres.[4]

The drafters of what became the Charter of the International Military Tribunal (IMT), which known as the Nuremberg Charter, struggled over the issue of legality and ex post facto legislation, and whether the issue could be defined out of existence simply by including criminal definitions in the text of the Charter.[5] Because the Nuremberg Charter failed to provide a definitive principle of legality (or to rule out such a principle) in its text, the Nuremberg Tribunal was forced to address the issue.

Despite its denial in the Nuremberg Judgment that the rules of legality were binding, the IMT made extensive, though not fully convincing, efforts to demonstrate that the charter and judgment complied with the rule of *nullum crimen.* At the very least, it is difficult to justify the claim that aggressive war (crimes against peace) or conspiracy to wage aggressive war was a crime in customary international law for which there was individual responsibility at the time the Nazi leaders committed their acts.[6] It is also questionable whether all of the acts denominated crimes against humanity were crimes under international law under another name (e.g., war crimes) at the time they were committed. This is especially questionable for the crimes committed by Germans against German nationals in Germany. In general, no acts had clearly been denoted crimes against humanity, bearing individual criminal responsibility, before the war.

Some extended narrative may be worthwhile here. It will be limited as much as possible to the discussion of legality, and other issues surrounding lawmaking authority in international criminal law will be left for another time.

[4] See *Advisory Opinion on the Consistency of Certain Danzig Legislative Decrees with the Constitution of the Free City*, December 4, 1935, P.C.I.J. (ser. A/B) No. 65 at 53–56 (the principle of legality in criminal law as central to Danzig's "character as a State governed by the rule of law (*Rechtsstaat*)" [translation in English text of judgment]); H. Donnedieu de Vabres, *Le procès de Nuremberg devant les principes modernes du droit pénal international*, 70(I) Recueil des Cours 477, 574 (1947).

[5] See more extensive discussions in Chap. 3.b.ii.

[6] But see Polish Criminal Code art. 113 (1932) (criminalizing incitement to aggressive war in certain circumstances), quoted in translation in 7 UNWCC, Law Reports of Trials of War Criminals, at 91; Henri Felix August Donnedieu de Vabres, Les principes modernes de droit pénal international 414–15 (Librairie du Recueil Sirey 1928).

3.a. VIOLATIONS OF THE LAWS AND CUSTOMS OF WAR AS CRIMINAL BEFORE NUREMBERG: ATROCITIES AND OTHER CRIMES

Before and during World War II, practice and *opinio juris* demonstrated that the laws and customs of war provided a law, *lege*, pursuant to which war-crime atrocities could be prosecuted and punished. A bit of this background needs to be explained here, as popular discussion does not always distinguish among war crimes, crimes against humanity, and aggressive war at Nuremberg and later.

As mentioned in the prior chapter, the settlement that ended World War I provided for trials of Germans for violations of the laws and customs of war in German courts. Some of these trials occurred and resulted in a few convictions.[7]

During World War II, the Soviet Union, the United Kingdom, and the United States all accepted that at least persons who violated the "laws and customs of war" – war crimes in a traditional and restricted sense, controlled by the so-called *jus in bello* – could be tried and punished if they were captured. This law presumed the existence of armed conflict between two states. The state trying the captives could use its civilian or military court systems. However, agreement did not extend past those defendants who had violated then-current international law – the laws and customs of war – and the right to try and punish war crimes was said to end with the reestablishment of peace.[8] Specifically, agreement did not extend to the criminality of violations of international law in beginning wars – *jus ad bellum*. Nor did agreement extend to internal atrocities, which were generally not covered by the law of international armed conflict.

The United States captured, tried, and punished several German saboteurs (and one American national) who landed in the United States.[9] The Soviet Union tried three Germans (and one Soviet national) accused of mass execution of Soviet citizens by gas and other atrocities at the so-called Kharkov trial.[10] To avoid the perceived threat of trials of American prisoners

[7] See Chap. 2.c.i.

[8] On the issue of a peace treaty extinguishing the right to try for war crimes, see generally, e.g., Ex parte Yamashita, 327 U.S. 1 (1946).

[9] Ex parte Quirin, 317 U.S. 1 (1942) (some defendants were executed following the proceeding).

[10] ARIEH J. KOCHAVI, PRELUDE TO NUREMBERG: ALLIED WAR CRIMES POLICY AND THE QUESTION OF PUNISHMENT 66–70 (Univ. of N.C. Press 1998) (these defendants were executed as well), based on the transcripts in THE PEOPLE'S VERDICT: A FULL REPORT OF THE PROCEEDINGS AT THE KRASNODAR AND KHARKOV GERMAN ATROCITY TRIALS

of war, the United States backed off its position somewhat, informing Germany, through Swiss intermediaries, that it would not follow the Soviet example as far as trying German prisoners of war, and that it would observe the Geneva Convention of 1929.[11] The British Foreign Office maintained that the Allies had the right to try German nationals for war crimes. Indeed, they protested German punishment of British soldiers on special operations (presumably out of uniform, and thus in violation of the laws of war) because the punishment was without trial.[12]

At the least, these examples show that there was current during World War II, a notion of individual criminal violation of the laws and customs of war, defined by the community of nations through the process of customary international lawmaking, influenced by the Hague and Geneva treaties on the laws of war.[13] In some cases, this law was imported by reference into the statutory law of the state trying the case. This is explicit in the American judicial cases.[14]

The Allies, calling themselves the United Nations, established a United Nations War Crimes Commission (UNWCC) to investigate allegations of atrocities committed by the Axis powers. The UNWCC accepted the notion that violations of the laws and customs of war existed, and that the Allies could punish them as criminal offenses when committed by nationals of the Axis powers against the Allies or their citizens. It was reluctant to read its mandate more broadly. Whether it would be legal to prosecute non-war-crime atrocities, such as German atrocities against their own nationals, and what the source of law for such crimes could be, were extremely controversial questions in the UNWCC and elsewhere.[15] The issue of individual criminal

(London 1944). Kochavi suggests that one reason the Soviets publicized this trial was to avoid criticism for similar, but extrajudicial, hangings of those alleged to be involved in war crimes.

[11] Kochavi, *supra* note 10, at 72–73; see Geneva Convention Relative to Prisoners of War (27 July 1929; entered into force 19 June 1931), 118 LNTS 343.

[12] Kochavi, *supra* note 10, at 71, 72–73.

[13] Hague Conventions (Nos. I–X) (18 October 1907); Geneva Convention for the Amelioration of the Condition of the Wounded and Sick in Armies in the Field (27 July 1929; entered into force 19 June 1931), 118 LNTS 303; Geneva Convention Relative to Prisoners of War (27 July 1929).

[14] In re Yamashita, 371 U.S. 1, 362 (1946); Ex parte Quirin, 317 U.S. 1 (1942); cf. United States v. Smith, 18 U.S. 153, 162–63 (1820) (international law of piracy taken into U.S. statutory law).

[15] See History of the United Nations War Crimes Commission and the Development of the Laws of War 173, 175–77 (UNWCC comp., H. M. Stationery Office for the United Nations War Crimes Commission 1948) (British, Greek, Norwegian representatives against expansion of UNWCC investigations to include German atrocities against Germans and nationals of their Axis allies; American, Czechoslovak, Netherlands representatives in

responsibility for aggressive war was also controversial at the UNWCC.[16] In the end, it did not go beyond investigating traditionally defined war crimes.

There is a distinction between those who violate the laws and customs of war by fighting (or spying) out of uniform, thus forfeiting the protections that they might otherwise have as prisoners of war, and those who violate the laws and customs of war by attacking civilians or other impermissible targets, committing mass rapes, and so on. The latter are those who perpetrate atrocity and have become the target of prosecution for war crimes, and in some cases crimes against humanity and genocide. However, it is important to note that much of the law of crimes against the laws and customs of war comes from examples of spies and saboteurs who might not have committed atrocities against civilians. Indeed, François de Menthon, the first French chief prosecutor at Nuremberg, admitted that members of the French resistance who fought out of uniform were subject to trial and execution by the Germans (but not to torture and execution without trial).[17] Non-atrocity violations of the laws and customs of war continue to be important.

The definition of traditional war crimes could be interpreted to encompass a large percentage of the German mass atrocity of World War II. At least some British thought held that atrocities committed against German nationals or stateless persons in Allied territory were war crimes punishable by the Allies.[18] For example, the mass murder of German Jews deported to Poland could be brought within traditional doctrines of territorial jurisdiction to prescribe because the killings occurred in the territory of an Allied nation. This activity can thus be brought within the traditional view of mass murder of civilians by occupying forces in an occupied country as a war crime, as well as within traditional views of international jurisdiction.

One also needs to consider who the lawmaker is here. The laws and customs of war are international law, whether treated as customary international law or as the treaty law of the Hague or Geneva process of the past century. Some theorists, however, treat international criminal law as

favor), 177 (World Jewish Congress proposed investigation of crimes against German Jews and nationals of other Axis powers); Kochavi, *supra* note 10, at 144.

[16] See HISTORY, *supra* note 15, at 180–85.

[17] François de Menthon, Opening Speech, 17 January 1946, in THE TRIAL OF THE GERMAN MAJOR WAR CRIMINALS BY THE INTERNATIONAL MILITARY TRIBUNAL SITTING AT NUREMBERG GERMANY COMMENCING 20TH NOVEMBER, 1945, OPENING SPEECHES 89, 117 (H. M. Attorney-General by H. M. Stationery Office 1946).

[18] Kochavi, *supra* note 10, at 152–53.

jurisdictional law authorizing states to prosecute; actual prosecutions in this theory occur pursuant to national law.[19] However, to comply with the non-retroactivity principle of legality, international law must, in some sense, be viewed as defining criminal acts in a way that binds individuals. Otherwise, the only way to bind soldiers in a way that satisfies non-retroactivity would be to find that they are subject to at least some of the internal laws of the states against which they are fighting, merely because of their status as fighters; this peculiar theory is not even considered in the sources.

3.a.i. *Beyond Traditional War-Crime Atrocities*

As mentioned, whether it would be legal to prosecute non-war-crime atrocities and the source of law to prosecute such crimes were extremely controversial issues.[20] In 1915, the governments of France, Great Britain, and Russia had used the phrase "nouveaux crimes de la Turquie contre l'humanité et la civilization" ("new crimes of Turkey against humanity and civilization") to describe the mass murder of ethnic Armenian and Greek-speaking subjects of the Ottoman Empire.[21] These crimes were covered in the Treaty of Sèvres, intended as the peace treaty of the Allies with Turkey, but this treaty never came into effect. The subsequent Treaty of Lausanne and its accompanying Declaration of Amnesty, which replaced the Treaty of Sèvres as the actual peace treaty with Turkey, did not provide for the prosecution of the massacres and provided for a general amnesty for offenses during World War I.[22] Little occurring between this failure to prosecute and World War II would have suggested that crimes against humanity (at least those in one's own territory against one's own co-nationals and against stateless persons) were well established in international law by the time the latter conflict began. From the inception of the UNWCC in 1943 through the time of the London Conference in 1945, the UNWCC was unable to agree to expand its investigations to include these atrocities.[23]

[19] See Luc Reydams, Universal Jurisdiction: International and Municipal Legal Perspectives 22 & n.55 (Oxford Univ. Press 2003) (citing sources); Alfred P. Rubin, The Law of Piracy (Naval War College Press 1988); Harvard Research in International Law, Draft Convention on Piracy with Comments, 26 A.J.I.L. 749, 759–60 (1932).

[20] See History, *supra* note 15, at 173, 175–77; Kochavi, *supra* note 10, at 144.

[21] Declaration of France, Great Britain and Russia, 28 May 1915, quoted and discussed in History, *supra* note 15, at 35, 45.

[22] Treaty of Sèvres arts. 226–28, 230 (10 August 1920; never came into effect); Treaty of Lausanne (24 July 1923), and Declaration of Amnesty (24 July 1923).

[23] History, *supra* note 15, at 173, 175–77.

3.b. NUREMBERG: SEARCHING FOR CONSENSUS

3.b.i. *Anti-legality: Churchill and Morgenthau Favor Summary Executions*

That the UNWCC was worried about the issue of legality in dealing with the Axis leaders does not mean that everyone was. British Prime Minister Winston Churchill and others considered a plan that would avoid all or almost all law. It was a political solution, like Emperor Napoleon's exile, but without the exile.

By the end of 1943, Churchill had formulated a plan to create a list of about fifty to one hundred leaders of Germany, Italy, and Japan who would be declared outlaws by the United Nations. Anyone who found one of these leaders could kill him. If one of them were captured by the armed forces of any member of the United Nations, he would be brought before a court of inquiry only for a determination of identity; if his identity were confirmed, he would be shot.[24] Churchill had developed some of these ideas as early as 1942 and persisted in them until April 1945.[25]

By September 1944, at a meeting in Quebec, at least partly at the urging of U.S. Secretary of the Treasury Henry Morgenthau, Jr., U.S. President Franklin Delano Roosevelt agreed with Churchill that the highest German leaders should be dealt with politically, that is shot without trial.[26] Soviet leader Joseph Stalin wished to try the German leaders, but one suspects that he wanted a show trial, particularly as he also considered the summary execution or long-term imprisonment without trial of thousands of lower-ranking German officers.[27]

[24] Kochavi, *supra* note 10, at 73–75.

[25] Recently released records from Britain's War Cabinet confirm that Churchill argued for execution of Hitler in 1942 (the notes suggest without stating that this would be without trial) and argued for summary execution of Hitler and other leaders as late as April 1945. Remarks from War Cabinet shorthand notes W. M. (42) 86th Mtg., 6 July 1942; W. M. (45) 43d Mtg., 12 April 1945, transcribed, summarized, and released at http://www.nationalarchives.gov.uk/releases/2006/january/january1/war_crimes.htm [hereinafter War Cabinet notes].

[26] Kochavi, *supra* note 10, at 80, 87–89, relying on notes and memoranda of Churchill, Roosevelt, Anthony Eden, Viscount Simon, and Henry L. Stimson; BRADLEY F. SMITH, REACHING JUDGMENT AT NUREMBERG 29 (Basic Books 1977); see M. CHERIF BASSIOUNI, CRIMES AGAINST HUMANITY IN INTERNATIONAL CRIMINAL LAW 4–5 (2d ed., Transnational Publishers 1999).

[27] Kochavi, *supra* note 10, at 41–42, 63–64, 90–91, 220, relying on correspondence between Churchill and Roosevelt for Stalin's opposition to summary execution of the leaders; HENRY KISSINGER, DIPLOMACY 411 (Simon & Schuster 1994) (for Stalin's suggestion at late 1943 Teheran Conference that fifty thousand German officers be executed, his retraction of the statement as a joke after Churchill walked out, and reason to believe it was not a joke); Bassiouni, *supra* note 26, at 5 (suggesting that Stalin sought trials "as a means of re-writing history, and cleansing himself of his own crimes").

Churchill and Roosevelt's view implies that international law places little or no restriction on the political authority of victors to deal with the political leadership of a nation they have vanquished in war. The two leaders did not see the need for an exercise of criminal jurisdiction over the enemy leadership before dealing with them. No specific crime needed to be defined (by an exercise of prescriptive jurisdiction) or proved (by an exercise of adjudicative jurisdiction) against them. Interestingly, though, Churchill held on to some semblance of legal process, in apparently wishing to resurrect the English legal status of outlaw while using process to ensure that the correct persons were identified as outlaws before being executed.[28]

Roosevelt backed off from the summary execution plan because of opposition within his cabinet, and possibly for political reasons.[29] Churchill also refrained from acting on this plan, probably because of fear of German retaliation against British prisoners of war.[30] As the Allies came closer to winning the war, the British government returned to its view that

> Hitler and a number of arch-criminals associated with him (including Mussolini) must, so far as they fall into Allied hands, suffer the penalty of death for their conduct leading up to the war and for the wickedness with which they have either themselves perpetrated or have authorized in the conduct of the war.[31]

The United States, however, did not return to the summary execution view, at least as a political matter of what ought to be done to the leading Nazis. A memo initialed by three U.S. cabinet officers argued that summary execution would "be violative of the most fundamental principles of justice, common

[28] "P. M." (i.e., Churchill) quoted as saying the Nazi leaders should be "treated as outlaws." War Cabinet notes, W. M. (45)43d Mtg., 12 April 1945; for use of phrase "world outlaws" for top German leaders by British cabinet ministers, see Kochavi, *supra* note 10, at 215.

[29] Kochavi, *supra* note 10, at 88–89; Telford Taylor, The Anatomy of the Nuremberg Trials: A Personal Memoir 34, 38 (Alfred A. Knopf 1992) (Taylor was a major American figure in the post–World War II prosecution of the Nazi war criminals, especially as chief prosecutor for the American trials under Control Council Law No. 10 which followed the main Nuremberg Trial – in 1946, he became brigadier general but had not reached that rank at the time covered here).

[30] Kochavi, *supra* note 10, at 89–90.

[31] Aide-mémoire from the United Kingdom [to the United States], 23 April 1945 [Doc. II], published in Report of Robert H. Jackson United States Representative to the International Conference on Military Trials: London 1945, 18 (U.S. Gov't Printing Off. 1949 [submitted by Justice Jackson to the Secretary of State 15 December 1947]) [hereinafter Rep. of Jackson].

to all of the United Nations" and might make the executed leaders "into martyrs."[32]

The Churchill plan avoided the doctrine of legality in criminal law by avoiding criminal law altogether. Many, however, believed this plan to have been legal under the substantive international law doctrines of the time. Even the three U.S. cabinet members who argued against it did not claim it was illegal. They stated: "After Germany's unconditional surrender, the United Nations could, if they elected, put to death the most notorious Nazi criminals, such as Hitler or Himmler, without trial or hearing."[33] Positivist legal theory had infiltrated the highest level of U.S. government, at least to the extent that the legality and justice (or morality or political wisdom) of summary executions, without prescription of or conviction for crime, were treated as different matters.

At a War Cabinet meeting on 3 May 1945, the British government came around to the American view that trials, rather than politically decreed executions, were the best way to deal with the Nazi leadership, but it did not admit that executions without trial would be illegal in international law.[34] This change led to the International Conference on Military Trials (the London Conference), held by the Four Powers (Great Britain, the Soviet Union, the United States, and the Provisional Government of France) from 26 June to 8 August 1945.

Two final notes on the political solution: first, the lawfulness of extrajudicial executions was limited, in the eyes of at least the Western powers, to top enemy leaders. The Americans, British, and French did not believe that soldiers, or even persons fighting or spying out of uniform, could lawfully face execution without trial. Stalin's view was another matter.[35]

Second, the apparent lawfulness of extrajudicial executions of top leaders was eventually cited in a separate opinion in the International Military Tribunal for the Far East (IMTFE or Tokyo Tribunal) justifying the trial of

[32] Memorandum for the President [initialed by Secretary of War Henry L. Stimson, Secretary of State Edward R. Stettinus, Jr., and Attorney General Francis Biddle], 22 January 1945, ("Yalta memorandum" or "Crimean proposal") [Doc. I] published in REP. OF JACKSON at 3, 6 (provided to Jackson as a briefing paper to prepare him for negotiating). This document is also known as the "Three Secretaries Memorandum" and was drafted by Lieutenant Colonel Murray C. Bernays and Major General John M. Weir as a result of intra-U.S. negotiations and compromise on war crimes policy. BRADLEY F. SMITH, THE AMERICAN ROAD TO NUREMBERG 55, 117 (Hoover Institution Press 1982).

[33] Memorandum for the President, 22 January 1945 [Doc. I], published in REP. OF JACKSON at 3, 6.

[34] War Cabinet notes, W. M. (45) 57th Mtg., 3 May 1945; Kochavi, *supra* note 10, at 219.

[35] Cf. Kochavi, *supra* note 10, at 41–42, 63–64, 90–91, 220; Bassiouni, *supra* note 26, at 5.

the leaders of the Japanese aggressive war for crimes against peace, even though these crimes were, as a juridical matter, created ex post facto.[36] Another justice indicated that trying rather than summarily executing the Tokyo defendants was "sufficient proof of the good will of the Allies" to overcome any suggestion that trying them in a court of Allied judges would be unfair.[37] This appears to assume the legality of summary executions as well. Only the separate opinion of the IMTFE President contains a hint that trial before execution was required by international law before World War II.[38]

3.b.ii. *The London Conference: The French Oppose Ex Post Facto Crime Creation; the Americans, Soviets, and British Favor Plenary Power to Define Crimes*

Legality, and specifically the issue of retroactivity of crime definition, did in fact come up in negotiations at the London Conference. It was at the heart of a major disagreement in the negotiations and another issue that had been controversial outside of the conference. The first of these concerned the authority of the conference to define aggressive war and conspiracy to wage aggressive war or to set them forth as crimes in the charter of an international military tribunal. In addition to retroactivity, this discussion was about whether the London Conference or the judges of the international tribunal to be created was the appropriate authority to state whether aggressive war was an international crime, and particularly whether the conference could bind the judges to a definition of this crime. The second issue, highly controversial elsewhere but not so controversial at the conference, was whether atrocities of the Axis leaders against their own citizens or stateless persons (especially those committed on German soil) could be international crimes,[39] even though they were not war crimes in the traditional sense.

This section will show how the debate on legality was framed at the London Conference and what ideas were raised in the negotiation. It will not reproduce all the various texts that were introduced to address the issue,

[36] *United States v. Araki*, Separate Opinion of Justice Bernard Victor Aloysius Röling, 12 November 1948, at 4, 109 The Tokyo Major War Crimes Trial: The Judgment, Separate Opinions, Proceedings in Chambers, Appeals and Reviews of the International Military Tribunal for the Far East (Robert M.W. Kemper Collegium and Edwin Mellen Press 1998) (1948) [hereinafter IMTFE Records].

[37] Separate Opinion of Justice Henri Bernard, 12 November 1948, at 2–3, 105 IMTFE Records.

[38] Separate Opinion of William Webb, President, 1 November 1948, at 14, 109 IMTFE Records.

[39] See, e.g., History, *supra* note 15, at 173, 175–77; Kochavi, *supra* note 10, at 141–71.

nor all the comments made in the formal sessions referring to it.[40] Nor will it address all the other issues concerning lawmaking authority that came up in London, except as necessary to understand the debate on legality.[41]

The easy legal issues for the negotiators were the authority to create an international criminal tribunal and the tribunal's authority to punish traditional war crimes – violations of the laws and customs of war. The American position at the end of World War I that the creation of a new tribunal, with a new jurisdiction, would be impermissibly ex post facto[42] was abandoned by all participants at London.[43] The question of creating a new tribunal had become essentially political. Traditional war crimes were generally defined by treaties such as the 1907 Hague Conventions[44] and the 1929 Geneva Conventions.[45] Despite the argument that these might not apply to some or all of World War II in Europe, because not all the nations were signatories to these pacts, there was general agreement among the Western Allies that the terms of the pacts had become customary international law.[46] Despite the argument that these were not crimes in international law that could be enforced against individuals, there was general agreement among the Western Allies that the history of prosecutions of these acts as crimes in national military and civil courts had demonstrated that they could be treated as crimes under both national and international law.[47] As these crimes had

[40] The American delegation kept and later published a record of the London Conference, REP. OF JACKSON. Translations from French or Russian speakers in REP. OF JACKSON are all from Elsie L. Douglas's stenographic transcriptions of the oral translations by the interpreters at the London Conference and were not checked by the speakers or translators. See Elsie L. Douglas, *Foreword*, in REP. OF JACKSON at xiii. The account here relies heavily on this document.

[41] The author hopes to consider these issues in future work.

[42] See Robert Lansing & James Brown Scott, Memorandum of Reservations Presented by the Representatives of the United States to the Report of the Commission on Responsibilities (4 April 1919), Annex II to Commission on the Responsibility of the Authors of the War and on Enforcement of Penalties, Report Presented to the Preliminary Peace Conference (Versailles, 29 March 1919), published at 14 A.J.I.L. 95 (1920), reprinted in 1 THE LAW OF WAR: A DOCUMENTARY HISTORY, 842, 860, 865 (Leon Friedman, ed., Random House 1972). This objection was also raised to the Nuremberg Tribunal. See, e.g., P. D., *Note on the Nuremberg Trials*, 62 L.Q. REV. 229, 231 (1946).

[43] See REP. OF JACKSON, *passim*.

[44] See especially Hague Convention (No. IV) Respecting the Laws and Customs of War on Land (19 October 1907, entered into force 26 January 1910).

[45] See especially Geneva Convention Relative to Prisoners of War (27 July 1929).

[46] See Comments of Gros, in Minutes of Conference Session, 19 July 1945 [Doc. XXXVII], explaining Draft Article on Definition of Crimes, Submitted by French Delegation, 19 July 1945 [Doc. XXXV] (English text of Draft Article provided by French Delegation), published in REP. OF JACKSON at 295, 293; HISTORY, *supra* note 15, at 186. See also Taylor, *supra* note 29, at 65–67.

[47] See examples of practice in Chap. 2.c.i.

previously been defined, there was no problem in applying them to soldiers and commanders in World War II. Criminalizing them in the charter would therefore not be ex post facto. Nonetheless, difficult issues of legality remained.

The American delegation sought to draft a charter for what became the IMT in a way that avoided any question of prospectivity. Before the London Conference began, the United States circulated a draft (actually a revision of a document presented to the British and Soviet delegations in San Francisco) in which the tribunal would be "bound by the declaration of the parties" that aggression, invasion, war crimes, and other atrocities were criminal.[48] The Four Powers and any others who acceded to the agreement (i.e., "the parties to this Agreement"[49]) would be either making the substantive criminal law of aggression and the other stated crimes or conclusively declaring their view of the international law of these crimes.[50] The tribunal would not be allowed to determine whether they had stated the law correctly. The defense could not make arguments that the alleged acts were not crimes when committed (i.e., it could not argue that ex post facto crime creation was illegal).

The reason for this proposal was that the American team wanted to establish a generally defined crime of aggressive war, applicable to individuals. The generality of the prohibition of aggressive war was, for Justice Robert H.

[48] Revision of American Draft of Proposed Agreement, 14 June 1945, art. 12 [Doc. IX], published in Rep. of Jackson at 55, 57–58:

> In any trial before the International Military Tribunal, the tribunal shall be bound by the declaration of the parties to this Agreement that the following acts are criminal:
>
> (a) Atrocities and offenses against persons or property constituting violations of international law, including the laws, rules and customs of land and naval warfare.
> (b) Atrocities and offenses, including atrocities and persecutions on racial or religious grounds, committed since 1 January 1933 in violation of any applicable provision of the domestic law of the country in which committed.
> (c) Invasion of another country by force or threat of force, or the initiation of war, in violation of international law.
> (d) Launching a war of aggression.
> (e) "International law" shall be taken to include treaties between nations and the principles of the law of nations as they result from the usages established among civilized peoples, from the laws of humanity, and the dictates of the public conscience.

This revision surprised the Soviet and French delegates, who felt they needed time to study it. Smith, *supra* note 26, at 50.

[49] Revision of American Draft of Proposed Agreement, 14 June 1945, art. 3 [Doc. IX] (contemplating that the other Allies, the United Nations, would be invited to accede to the agreement), published in Rep. of Jackson at 56.

[50] The difference between these two ways of viewing the named crimes is worthy of extensive discussion but is not strictly relevant here.

Jackson, head of the American delegation, a key issue of the negotiation.[51] He argued with force: "The definition of a crime cannot be made to depend on which nation commits the act. I am not willing to charge as a crime against a German official acts which would not be crimes if committed by officials of the United States."[52] Aggression as a crime was also vital to the United States because the illegality of Nazi aggression was the United States' political and legal basis for supporting the Allies, especially before the formal U.S. entry into World War II at the end of 1941.[53] For Justice Jackson, at this point, legality meant generality of criminal law. He had less concern for issues of ex post facto law creation.

Without speaking specifically about the principle of legality, the Soviet Union took positions in opposition to it. First, the Soviet attitude, stated by General I. T. Nikitchenko, head of the Soviet delegation, was that the Moscow and Crimea (Yalta) Declarations of the heads of governments of the Big Three had already convicted the principal Hitlerites of crimes.[54] Thus, "the object of [the] trial is, of course, the punishment of the criminals."[55] In the language of some countries, the heads of government had already "attainted" the Nazi leaders, and such a bill of attainder was acceptable. The general went on to oppose the inclusion of organizations such as the Gestapo and SS as defendants, at least partly because the organizations had already been

> declared criminal by authorities higher than the Tribunal itself, both in the Moscow and the Crimea Declarations and the fact of their criminality has definitely been established. We cannot imagine any position in which the Tribunal might possibly bring out a verdict that any one of these organizations was not criminal when it has most definitely been labeled so by the governments.[56]

[51] Comment of Mr. Justice Jackson, Minutes of Conference Session, 25 July 1945 [Doc. LI], Robert H. Jackson, *Preface*, in Rep. of Jackson at 384–85, vii–viii.

[52] Robert H. Jackson, Notes on Proposed Definition of Crimes, Submitted by American Delegation, 31 July 1945 [Doc. LV], published in Rep. of Jackson at 394.

[53] Comment of Mr. Justice Jackson, *supra* note 51, 25 July 1945, in Rep. of Jackson at 383–85.

[54] Comments of General Nikitchenko, 29 June 1945 [Doc. XVII], explaining comments and proposals of Soviet delegation on American draft, 28 June 1945 [Doc. XVI], published in Rep. of Jackson at 104–05, 92.

[55] *Id.* at 105–06.

[56] *Id.* at 107. The Nuremberg Judgment did, in the end, declare that certain organizations had not been proved criminal – a finding from which then-Judge Nikitchenko dissented. See Nuremberg Judgment, 1 IMT Trial at 342; Opinion of Judge Nikitchenko, 1 IMT Trial at 356–64.

Second, A. N. Trainin, Nikitchenko's co-representative, emphasized the authority of the conquering nations to make law applicable to individuals without apparent need for reference to international criminal law generally: "the four countries may, for the purposes of this trial, declare certain acts to be criminal; and for the purposes of this trial the laws declared by the Four Powers should be sufficient."[57] Finally, without giving any reason, Nikitchenko made clear that a "general definition [of aggression] . . . would not be agreeable."[58] Taylor suggests that the Soviets wished to avoid criticism for their part in the destruction of the Polish state and their attack against Finland.[59] It is also possible that they wished to preserve the Soviet Union's freedom of action in the postwar world, which a specific, forward-looking, and generally applicable definition of aggression could inhibit.

All of these statements reflect "the Soviet conception of law as the servant of the political leadership,"[60] or as the Soviet theory put it, as expressing through the intermediary of the state the will of the dominant economic class.[61] This meant that explicit international agreements (rather than custom, which might not reflect current class interests) were the key prescriptive elements of international law, that individuals could not be "direct (*immediats*)" subjects of international law, and that interference of international law into the internal affairs of states was absolutely forbidden.[62] For the purpose of the London Conference, the substantive criminal lawmakers were Stalin, Churchill, and Roosevelt, acting as heads of state or government in making the Moscow Declaration.[63] The leaders, and their representatives at the London Conference, were no more bound by the principle of

[57] Comments of A.N. Trainin, in Minutes of Conference Session, 23 July 1945 [Doc. XLIV], published in REP. OF JACKSON at 335. For a draft Soviet text to this effect, see Redraft of Definition of Crimes, Submitted by Soviet Delegation, 25 July 1945 [Doc. XLVIII], published in REP. OF JACKSON at 373.

[58] Comment of Nikitchenko, Minutes of Conference Session, 25 July 1945 [Doc. LI], published in REP. OF JACKSON at 387.

[59] Taylor, *supra* note 29, at 66.

[60] *Id.* at 59. Accord *Preface*, REP. OF JACKSON at VI. Cf. FRANCIS BIDDLE, IN BRIEF AUTHORITY 472–73 (Greenwood Press 1962).

[61] See Krylov, *supra* note 3, at 415.

[62] *Id.* at 437–43 (treaty and custom), 445 (Soviet law rejects the "Anglo-American" view that "international law is 'part of domestic law' (*le droit international est une «partie du droit interne»*)"), 446–47 (individuals not direct subjects), 450–51 (absolute sovereignty of state in internal matters).

[63] Moscow Declaration (30 October 1943) (Concerning Responsibility of Hitlerites for Committed Atrocities). On its status in international law, cf. BURNS H. WESTON ET AL., INTERNATIONAL LAW AND WORLD ORDER: A PROBLEM-ORIENTED COURSEBOOK 172 (3d ed., West 1997) (describing other major power declarations during and just after World War II as "presumptively non-legal intergovernmental declarations outside the framework of

legality than was the Soviet government when it rejected the principle internally.[64] The political leaders could make retroactive criminal law, they could make this law to cover only the European Axis aggressors, and they could "convict" persons and organizations politically. The Soviets thus reached a result on retroactivity similar to the Americans, but for much different reasons.

Professor André Gros, assistant to the French representative and intellectual spokesperson of the delegation,[65] articulated a very different perspective on legality. Gros agreed with the proposition that the victorious powers could punish German leaders for violations of the traditional international law of war, the laws and customs of war.[66] He certainly believed that international crimes – war crimes – had been committed against the French and others, and that it was vital to start from that perspective.[67] Thus, he accepted criminal prescription through customary international law, even though he came from a civil law system in which statutory statement of criminal offenses is vital to their existence – indeed, from the nation that more or less initiated the modern trend toward this view.[68] Gros apparently understood the need to convince the American and English representatives of the French view, and he understood that the English-language text would probably wind up as the most important. At one point, he stated of his view on lawmaking, "It is difficult for me to discuss this very delicate point in

an international organization . . . [that] settle disputes and chart the course for future relations"), discussing OSCAR SCHACHTER, INTERNATIONAL LAW IN THEORY AND PRACTICE 129–30 (Kluwer 1991) (describing these declarations as "official State acts" from which "it is appropriate to draw inferences that the States concerned have recognized the principles, rules, status and rights acknowledged"). Compare, however, Chap. 3.d.i (on status of Potsdam Declaration as integrated into Japanese instrument of surrender).

[64] See USSR Const. (Fundamental Law) (1936), in ARYEH L. UNGER, CONSTITUTIONAL DEVELOPMENT IN THE USSR 140 (Pica Press 1981); 1926 RSFSR Crim. Code arts. 7 & 16, quoted in HAROLD J. BERMAN, SOVIET CRIMINAL LAW AND PROCEDURE: THE RSFSR CODES 25–26 (Harvard Univ. Press 1966) (all translations from this book are by Berman and James W. Spindler); discussed in Chap. 2.c.ii.C.

[65] For Gros's status as assistant to Judge Robert Falco, see Roster of Representatives and Assistants, International Conference on Military Trials, London, 1945, in REP. OF JACKSON at 441. A reading of the whole conference record indicates that he was the intellectual spokesman, at least, of the French delegation. He was absent in Paris for consultation at the climactic conference meeting 2 August 1945. Minutes of Conference Session, 2 August 1945, published in REP. OF JACKSON at 399.

[66] Comments of Gros, in Minutes of Conference Session, 19 July 1945 [Doc. XXXVII], explaining Draft Article on Definition of "Crimes," Submitted by French Delegation, 19 July 1945 [Doc. XXXV] (English text of Draft Article provided by French Delegation), published in REP. OF JACKSON at 295, 293. See also Taylor, *supra* note 29, at 65–67.

[67] Comments of Gros, *supra* note 66, at 296.

[68] See Declaration of the Rights of Man and of the Citizen art. 8 (France 1789).

another language."[69] Because of the delicacy and importance of the subject and the subtlety of Gros's thoughts, it is worth following them at some length, as they appear in the published record in English.

Gros opposed creating individual criminal responsibility for new crimes, such as aggression and, later, conspiracy to commit aggressive war, because this would be "*ex post facto* legislation."[70] In the French view, the mere act of aggression did not carry individual responsibility in international law before World War II.[71] Thus, "[w]here a state would launch a war of aggression and not conduct that war according to rules of international law, it would be desirable to punish them as criminals, but it would not be criminal only for launching a war of aggression."[72] Gros set out a standard for determining when a crime was being defined ex post facto. Legislating a criminal sanction for an individual is the actual act of creating individual criminal liability: "We think it will turn out that nobody can say that launching a war of aggression is an international crime – you are actually inventing the sanction."[73] In theory, Feuerbach's statement *nullum crimen sine poena legali* (nothing is a crime until a legal penalty is attached to it) is, for Gros, the core of the principle of legality in criminal law.[74]

By the time of World War II, Gros argued, aggressive war was becoming an international crime, but only in the sense of state responsibility for it:

> The subject was often up for discussion in the League of Nations. It is said very often that a war of aggression is an international crime, a consequence of which it is the obligation of the aggressor to repair the damages caused by

[69] Comments of Gros, *supra* note 66, at 296. This moment in the negotiations might be noted as one of the landmarks in the ascendancy of English as a language of diplomacy.

[70] Comments of Gros, 25 July 1945, in Rep. of Jackson at 335.

[71] Comments of Gros, 19 July 1945 and 23 July 1945, in Rep. of Jackson at 295, 328 & 335; Taylor, *supra* note 29, at 65–67. Earlier, however, as a member of the UNWCC representing the French government in exile, Gros had been willing to consider internment without trial for members of Germany's Gestapo and SS, and an expansive definition of war crimes. See Kochavi, *supra* note 10, at 101–02, 112.

[72] Comments of Gros, *supra* note 71, at 295, 296, 381–82.

[73] Comments of Gros, 19 July 1945, in Rep. of Jackson at 295. He appealed to the authority of the academician in the Soviet team, A. N. Trainin, professor of law and member of the Soviet Academy of Sciences. In his previous writings, Trainin had tried to construct the idea of an international crime. He recognized that international law, as it then stood, did not make it punishable. The effort to make war of aggression an international crime was still tentative. See *id.*, at 295–96.

[74] Paul Johann Anselm Ritter von Feuerbach, Lehrbuch des gemeinen in Deutschland geltenden Peinlichen Rechts ¶ 24, p. 20 (Georg Friedrich Heyer 1801), discussed in Jerome Hall, *Nulla Poena Sine Lege*, 47 Yale L.J. 165, 169–70 (1938).

> his actions. But there is no criminal sanction. It implies only an obligation to repair damage....
>
> It may be a crime to launch a war of aggression on the part of a state that does so, but that does not imply the commission of criminal acts by individual people who have launched a war. When you say that a state which launches a war has committed a crime, you do not imply that the members of that state are criminals.[75]

Gros wished that, in the future, planning and waging aggressive war would be considered an individual crime. Sir David Maxwell Fyfe, attorney general and British representative, who chaired most of the London Conference, pushed him to admit that if one called launching an aggressive war a criminal act of a state, then those people who launched the war committed a crime. He responded: "We think that would be morally and politically desirable, but that is not international law."[76]

Gros believed the charter should contain a statement of the subject matter jurisdiction of the court rather than a set of crime definitions.[77] For Gros, this was a means to enforce the principle of legality, because the tribunal would actually determine which acts were criminal at the time they were done. The French Draft Article on the Definition of Crimes, of 19 July 1945,[78] defined what acts come within the subject-matter jurisdiction of the court, including the policy of aggression, but the draft does not purport

[75] Comments of Gros, *supra* note 66, at 295, 297.

[76] *Id.* at 297.

[77] Comments of Gros, Minutes of Conference Session 25 July 1945 [Doc. LI], in Rep. of Jackson at 377–78.

[78] Draft Article on the Definition of Crimes, Submitted by the French Delegation, 19 July 1945 [Doc. XXXV], in Rep. of Jackson at 293 (English translation provided by the French delegation):

> The Tribunal will have jurisdiction to try any person who has, in any capacity whatsoever, directed the preparation and conduct of:
>
> (i) the policy of aggression against, and of domination over, other nations, carried out by the European Axis Powers in breach of treaties and in violation of international law;
> (ii) the policy of atrocities and persecutions against civilian populations;
> (iii) the war, launched and waged contrary to the laws and customs of international law;
>
> and who is responsible for the violations of international law, the laws of humanity and the dictates of the public conscience, committed by the armed forces and civilian authorities in the service of those enemy Powers.

The translation (or possibly drafting) of this article has some technical issues, as, for example, the failure to indicate whether the phrases following the three small Roman numerals are disjunctive (*or* – most likely) or conjunctive (*and*). However, the conjunctive

to set out the substantive criminal law. It would be for the tribunal to determine whether the German defendants' actions were criminal, pursuant to international law.

The French never explicitly said that the rule against ex post facto criminal liability is a limitation of sovereignty in international law or a limitation on criminal jurisdiction of tribunals. Yet they fought vigorously for the view that preexisting international law must provide the substantive law of the tribunal to be created by the London Conference. This view reappeared in some of the opinions of the Tokyo Tribunal and, much later, in the International Criminal Tribunals for the Former Yugoslavia and for Rwanda, as well as in other modern courts.

The French addressed two issues of legality other than retroactive crime definition. First, the French proposal certainly indicates their acceptance of the authority of occupying powers to establish a tribunal after the fact and to give it jurisdiction over international crimes. Second, Gros had a concern similar to the bill-of-attainder issue (though he did not use that phrase) – that is, that a legislative authority, not a court, was in fact convicting specific defendants:

> We [the London Conference members] just have to say what crimes will go before the court. This article says that and only that. The American draft [stating that certain acts, including waging a war of aggression "shall be deemed criminal violations of International Law"] would be a perfect article if we were charged with the duty of making a codification of rules of international law for the punishment of international war criminals, which we are not charged to do.... We must leave the law to the judge to decide.... On the contrary, if you put in a declaration deeming something to be international law, and saying that launching a war of aggression is a violation, you will be criticized, and not by lawyers but by people who will make accusations that the result of the trial was made beforehand.[79]

He thought that no such criticism could be leveled if the judges impartially decided what the law is.[80]

and where the text resumes after the Roman numerals definitely appears to be what the French drafters intended, and that is one of the points of the discussion in the text.

[79] Comments of Gros, *supra* note 77, discussing Redraft of Definition of Crimes, Submitted by Soviet Delegation, 25 July 1945 [Doc. XLVIII] (material in brackets not in original), and explaining Draft Article on the Definition of Crimes, Submitted by the French Delegation, 19 July 1945 [Doc. XXXV], published in Rep. of Jackson at 377–78, 373, 293.

[80] Comments of Gros, *supra* note 77, at 378–79.

Note a particular oddity here: the professor from the civil law jurisdiction is applying a theory much like the traditional common law view that judges discover, rather than make, law in the course of determining cases. For Gros, this was a bold and creative position to take.

It will be difficult for some readers to accept the French explanation for including aggression in the draft. After all, they would be placing within the jurisdiction of a criminal tribunal acts that they asserted were not criminal, and for which none of the Axis defendants – whoever they might be – could be convicted. This is certainly a counterintuitive way to draft a statute for a permanent domestic tribunal. However, given that the other three powers – the three governments that had actually remained in power during the war against the Axis – intended to have the tribunal try the crime of aggression, the most that the French could hope for was to put the decision of whether the crime existed into the hands of the judiciary.

It might also be difficult for some readers to accept that this French draft prohibits new criminal law. A person who directed the preparation and conduct of the war or its atrocities must be "responsible for the violations of international law, the laws of humanity and the dictates of the public conscience"[81] before that person can be convicted. Because international law, the laws of humanity, and the dictates of the public conscience are not defined in this draft, judges are to determine them. The phrase "the dictates of the public conscience" could conceivably be used to allow for ex post facto criminalization. There is not much to be said about this issue except that this phrase disappeared in later drafts, and the French consistently made the argument that aggressive war should not be criminalized after the fact.

Perhaps more significant, neither the French nor any other party raised objections in the formal negotiations to the inclusion of atrocities that did not easily fit into the category of traditional war crimes – especially atrocities committed in Germany against Germans or stateless persons. Gros argued that even internal atrocities were already crimes: "nobody can say [they] are not criminal violations of international law."[82] The source of this view is not wholly clear. At one point, he discusses state practice, which is traditionally the vital factor in creating customary international

[81] Draft Article on the Definition of Crimes, Submitted by the French Delegation, 19 July 1945 [Doc. XXXV], published in Rep. of Jackson at 293 (English translation provided by the French delegation, reproduced in *supra* note 78).

[82] Comment of Gros, Minutes of Conference Session, 23 July 1945 [Doc. XLIV]; Comment of Gros, Minutes of Conference Session, 24 July 1945 [Doc. XLVII] published in Rep. of Jackson at 328, 334–35, 360.

law:[83] "for the last century, there have been many interventions for humanitarian reasons. All countries have interfered in the affairs of other countries to defend minorities who were being persecuted."[84] This statement may be an exaggeration of the scope of humanitarian intervention, but this is forgivable in the heat of discussion. Gros does not, however, argue that there have been criminal prosecutions of individuals for these atrocities, a fact that he found fatal to the claim that aggressive war was an individual crime in international law. One can speculate that this view of atrocity might come from the natural law view of international law – these sorts of atrocities are condemned by natural law, which forms the basis for international law, and (contrary to the views of the Anglo-Saxon state-centric positivists) this law can be applied to individuals and to states. This thought appears in the Opinion of Justice Henri Bernard (France) in the IMTFE.[85] Otherwise, it is difficult to see how the French negotiators could find aggressive war to be ex post facto with regard to the Axis leaders but permit prosecution of non-war-crime atrocities that were not crimes directly under the law of places where the defendants acted or their acts had effects. These non-war-crime atrocities were included in the category that eventually became crimes against humanity in the final Nuremberg Charter.

The United Kingdom delegation held the chair of the London Conference and worked to bridge differences among the other three parties. Yet the delegation did squarely come down on the side of the Americans and Soviets that the charter should define crimes that would bind the proposed tribunal, so that the ex post facto issue could not be raised. At one point, the Americans presented a draft based on a British proposal: "The Tribunal shall be bound by this declaration of the Signatories that the following acts are criminal violations of international law."[86] On 23 July 1945, as the negotiations approached their climax, British conference chairman David Maxwell Fyfe stated:

> I want to make clear in this document [the Charter of the International Military Tribunal] what are the things for which the Tribunal can punish

[83] Later in this book, it will be argued that, in international criminal law at least, the practice of international organizations, including international criminal courts and tribunals, has become an important factor as well. See Chaps. 4, 6 & 7.

[84] Comment of Gros, *supra* note 82, at 360.

[85] Separate opinion of Bernard at 1–2, 105 IMTFE Records.

[86] See Revised Draft of Agreement and Memorandum Submitted by American Delegation, 30 June 1945, Annex para. 5 [Doc. XVIII], adopting point 3 of Amendments Proposed by the United Kingdom, 28 June 1945 [Doc. XIV], published in Rep. of Jackson at 119–21, 86–87.

> the defendants. I don't want it to be left to the Tribunal to interpret what are the principles of international law that it should apply. I should like to know where there is general agreement on that, clearly stated – for what things the Tribunal can punish the defendants. It should not be left to the Tribunal to say what is or is not a violation of international law.[87]

Gros disagreed, saying that this would amount to "a creation [of crimes] by four people who are just four individuals – defined by those four people as criminal violations of international law.... It is *ex post facto* legislation."[88]

Gros was willing to admit that the tribunal would deal only with atrocities connected to the Nazi plan for aggressive war. He wanted, however, to ensure that this limitation was of a jurisdictional type – limiting the subject matter jurisdiction of the tribunal rather than the definition of crimes against humanity to those atrocities committed in connection with this aggressive war.[89] To this extent, he agreed with Justice Jackson that rule of law required that crime definition must be general.

3.b.ii.A. Negotiating the Ex Post Facto Issue at London

The delegations had deep disagreements on the notions of legality and non-retroactivity. There were also deep disagreements on the reasons for these positions.

Two days after the exchange in which Gros refused to give up the ex post facto argument, the French and the Soviets agreed on a text that dealt with the issue of legality without explicitly mentioning it; but they did not agree on an underlying theory of legality. On 25 July 1945, the Soviet delegation proposed a redraft of the definition of crimes, beginning with the *chapeau* (introduction): "The following acts, designs or attempts at any of them shall be deemed crimes and shall come within the jurisdiction of the Tribunal: [definitions of crimes follow]."[90] In that day's meeting, Gros suggested that the *chapeau* be changed from "shall be deemed crimes and shall come within

[87] Comment of Sir David Maxwell Fyfe, 23 July 1945, in REP. OF JACKSON at 328 (materials in brackets added).

[88] Comment of Gros, 23 July 1945, in REP. OF JACKSON at 335.

[89] Comment of Gros, *supra* note 82, at 360.

[90] Redraft of Definition of Crimes, Submitted by Soviet Delegation, 25 July 1945 [Doc. XLVIII], published in REP. OF JACKSON at 373. The full text of the draft article:

> The following acts, designs or attempts at any of them shall be deemed crimes and shall come within the jurisdiction of the Tribunal:
>
> (a) Aggression against or domination over other nations carried out by the European Axis Powers in violation of treaties, agreements, and assurances;

the jurisdiction of the Tribunal" to "shall be deemed to be crimes coming within the jurisdiction of the Tribunal."[91]

He stated that this was merely a formal modification of the Soviet text. It was not. In his next comment, he discussed why this change was so important to his view, making the remark quoted previously, to the effect that the charter must determine what crimes will come before the court, and the judges will decide the law.[92] He also stated that, by leaving the determination of law to the judges, the nations would be less open to a charge that the result of the trial had been predetermined.[93] Under the Soviet text, the tribunal could not examine the crimes as defined to determine whether they were actually violations of existing international law. Gros's amendment was, according to him, designed essentially to make Article 6 jurisdictional: the tribunal shall have jurisdiction to determine whether these acts are crimes under the relevant (international) law. Thus, this amendment was intended to allow the tribunal to address the issue of whether a given crime was ex post facto.

For reasons that he did not state, except to indicate that the draft was full of compromises already, Nikitchenko was ready to accept the French suggestion.[94] Possibly the Soviets believed that the French suggestion could

(b) Atrocities against civilian populations including murder and ill-treatment of civilians and deportation of civilians to slave labour, and persecutions on racial or religious grounds inflicted in pursuance of the aggression or domination referred to in paragraph (*a*) above;
(c) Violations of the laws, rules and customs of war. Such violations shall include murder and ill-treatment of prisoners of war, atrocities, wanton destruction of towns and villages, and plunder.

Any person who is proved to have in any capacity whatever directed or participated in the preparation for or carrying out of any of the above-mentioned acts shall be personally answerable therefore and for each and every violation of international law, of the laws of humanity and of the dictates of the public conscience committed in the course of carrying out the said acts, designs or attempts or any of them by the forces and authorities whether armed, civilian or otherwise in the service of any of the European Axis Powers.

[91] Comments of Gros, 25 July 1945 [Doc. LI], addressing Redraft of Definition of "Crimes," Submitted by Soviet Delegation, 25 July 1945 [Doc. XLVIII], published in REP. OF JACKSON at 377–78, 373. Comments of Nikitchenko, 25 July 1945 [Doc. LI], published in REP. OF JACKSON at 378, that Gros was addressing "the English text" rather than "the Soviet text" appears to mean that Gros was addressing the English translation of the Soviet text rather than the Russian original. The then-current British text did not have the wording Gros was seeking to change.

[92] Comments of Gros, *supra* note 91 at 378–79.

[93] *Id.*

[94] Comments of Nikitchenko, *supra* note 91, at 382.

be interpreted as they preferred: it could reasonably be read to mean that, once the acts set out in the substance of Article 6 were established against a defendant, that defendant had committed a crime. Gros had not suggested changing the language that followed the listing of crimes after the *chapeau*: "Any person who is proved to have... directed or participated in... any of the above-mentioned acts shall be personally answerable therefor."[95] This seems to direct the tribunal to accept the criminality of the acts listed in Clauses a–c of Article 6 without regard to an independent investigation of international law.

This sort of ambiguity eventually prevailed. An American draft introduced on 31 July 1945 began:

> The Tribunal established by the [London] Agreement... shall have power and jurisdiction to try and determine charges of crime against individuals who and organizations which acted in aid of the European Axis Powers and to impose punishments on those found guilty.
>
> The following acts, or any of them, are crimes coming within its jurisdiction for which there shall be individual responsibility: [definitions of crimes follow].[96]

Here, the first sentence follows the notion of Gros that the charter would define the jurisdiction of the tribunal, leaving it to the judges to say what was the relevant substantive (international) criminal law at the time a defendant acted. Indeed, some of the judges at Tokyo read a nearly identical article of the Charter of the IMTFE as merely jurisdictional.[97] In contrast, one could also interpret the language in the second sentence that there "shall" be individual responsibility for these acts as binding the court to view the acts listed (the crime against peace, war crimes, and crimes against humanity) as punishable crimes. Yet that sentence can also reasonably be read as providing definitions of crimes "within the jurisdiction of the court," which would still allow defendants to raise defenses, including the defense that the crimes were created ex post facto.

[95] Redraft of Definition of Crimes, *supra* note 90, at 373.

[96] Revision of Definition of Crimes, Submitted by American Delegation, 31 July 1945 [Doc. LVI], published in REP. OF JACKSON at 395 (bracketed material added). This was also the draft in which the title "CRIMES AGAINST HUMANITY" first appears.

[97] See Separate Opinion of Bernard Victor Aloysius Röling, at 5, 109 IMTFE RECORDS; Dissenting Opinion of Henri Bernard at 9–10, 105 IMTFE RECORDS; Dissenting Opinion of Radhabinod Pal at 33–34, 105 IMTFE RECORDS, all interpreting Charter of the IMTFE art. 5.

The *chapeau* to the famous final version of the article on crime definition in the Charter of the IMT is similar:

> *Article 6.* The Tribunal established by the Agreement referred to in Article 1 hereof for the trial and punishment of the major war criminals of the European Axis countries shall have the power to try and punish persons who, acting in the interests of the European Axis countries, whether as individuals or as members of organizations, committed any of the following crimes.
>
> The following acts, or any of them, are crimes coming within the jurisdiction of the Tribunal for which there shall be individual responsibility: [definitions of crimes follow].[98]

[98] Charter of the IMT [hereinafter Nuremberg Charter] art. 6, appended to the London Agreement, 8 August 1945. The entire article in its final English version as in *United States v. Göring*, 1 TRIAL OF THE MAJOR WAR CRIMINALS BEFORE THE INTERNATIONAL MILITARY TRIBUNAL: NUREMBERG 14 NOVEMBER 1945–1 OCTOBER 1946 11 (International Military Tribunal 1947) [hereinafter IMT, TRIAL], except that the original semicolon in art. 6(c) is left in here:

> *Article 6.* The Tribunal established by the Agreement referred to in Article 1 hereof for the trial and punishment of the major war criminals of the European Axis countries shall have the power to try and punish persons who, acting in the interests of the European Axis countries, whether as individuals or as members of organizations, committed any of the following crimes.
>
> The following acts, or any of them, are crimes coming within the jurisdiction of the Tribunal for which there shall be individual responsibility:
>
> (a) *CRIMES AGAINST PEACE:* namely, planning, preparation, initiation or waging of a war of aggression, or a war in violation of international treaties, agreements or assurances, or participation in a Common Plan or Conspiracy for the accomplishment of any of the foregoing;
>
> (b) *WAR CRIMES:* namely, violations of the laws or customs of war. Such violations shall include, but not be limited to, murder, ill-treatment or deportation to slave labor or for any other purpose of civilian population of or in occupied territory, murder or ill-treatment of prisoners of war or persons on the seas, killing of hostages, plunder of public or private property, wanton destruction of cities, towns, or villages, or devastation not justified by military necessity;
>
> (c) *CRIMES AGAINST HUMANITY:* namely, murder, extermination, enslavement, deportation and other inhumane acts committed against any civilian population, before or during the war; or persecutions on political, racial, or religious grounds in execution of or in connection with any crime within the jurisdiction of the Tribunal, whether or not in violation of the domestic law of the country where perpetrated.
>
> Leaders, organizers, instigators, and accomplices participating in the formulations or execution of a Common Plan or Conspiracy to commit any of the foregoing crimes are responsible for all acts performed by any persons in execution of such plan.

In short, the text of the charter is ambiguous on the status of the principle of legality as a rule of law in the tribunal. It is difficult to escape the conclusion that this ambiguity was deliberate.[99] The ambiguity was obvious enough that the defense seized upon it in making its argument, as will be seen.[100]

3.b.iii. *The Major Nuremberg Trial: Ex Post Facto in the Indictment and Arguments*

When the IMT met, first at Berlin and then for the Trial of the Major War Criminals at Nuremberg, it had a charter open to many interpretations concerning international criminal prescriptive authority, including the authority to define crime ex post facto. Counsel had the opportunity to use these possible theories. The IMT faced the task of reconciling or choosing among these theories.

The differences in views of legality that existed among the nations at the London Conference continued into the trial, along with other views introduced by the defense. The fact that all parties were now arguing from a single text – the charter – did not blunt their differences very much.

3.b.iii.A. The Indictment and Preliminary Defense Motion

The indictment uses different sources of law for the different types of substantive crimes charged against individuals: crimes against peace, war crimes, and crimes against humanity. In the case of each crime, the indictment alleges a violation of the charter and a violation of some other substantive law that the indictment claims existed at the time of the crime. The way these characterizations of sources of law were used in the debate over legality will be discussed later.[101] The three substantive crimes charged against individuals, rather than the charge of conspiracy or the charges against organizations, will be the focus of this discussion.

Protocol Rectifying Discrepancy in Text of Charter, 6 October 1945 [hereinafter October Protocol] (amending Nuremberg Charter, art. 6(c)), reprinted in 1 IMT, TRIAL at 17 changed the semicolon in paragraph c into a comma, at the request of the Soviet Union.

[99] The authority to make law ex post facto was not the only issue of lawmaking power that arose at the London Conference. The author hopes to deal with some of the others in future work.

[100] Otto Stahmer, *Legal Argument*, 17 IMT, TRIAL at 498, 507, discussed in Chap. 3.b.iii.C.

[101] See Chap. 3.b.iv.

Count two on crimes against peace referred to an appendix of treaties and international assurances that were violated.[102] The appendix generally stated that Germany violated each of these treaties and assurances, and it did not claim that individuals had direct criminal liability under the treaties.[103] However, the text charges that the German wars against the various victim nations were "wars of aggression on the part of the defendants," and that the violations of these treaties and assurances were "caused by the defendants"; another appendix generally charges which defendants participated in planning to breach treaties, though without specific reference to which persons were involved with the breach of specific treaties.[104] Only the heading to count two refers to crimes against peace in the charter.[105]

Count three on war crimes had several sections. Each typically referred to treaty provisions, customary law, general principles of law, and the Nuremberg Charter itself. This example, from the portion of the indictment setting out charges of murder and ill treatment of prisoners of war, other members of the Allied armed forces, and persons on the high seas, said that these murders and ill treatment were

> contrary to International Conventions, particularly Articles 4, 5, 6, and 7 of the Hague Regulations, 1907, and to Articles 2, 3, 4 and 6 of the Prisoners of War Convention (Geneva 1929), the laws and customs of war, the general principles of criminal law as derived from the criminal laws of all civilized nations, the internal penal laws of the countries in which the crimes were committed, and Article 6(b) of the Charter.[106]

As discussed previously, there was a great deal of support for the proposition that war crimes were customary international law crimes before World War II.[107] Note, however, that the theory is also advanced that a violation of the penal laws of the countries where the crimes were committed could be re-characterized as a war crime.

[102] Indictment, 6 October 1945, as corrected by the court, 7 June 1946, Count Two – Crimes against Peace § VI, 1 IMT, TRIAL at 27, 42.

[103] Indictment, Appendix C, 1 IMT, TRIAL at 84–92 (twenty-six treaties and assurances listed).

[104] Indictment, Count Two & Appendix A, 1 IMT, TRIAL at 42, 68–79.

[105] Indictment, Count Two, 1 IMT, TRIAL at 42.

[106] Indictment, Count Three – War Crimes § VIII(C), 1 IMT, TRIAL at 42, 52–53. Of course, sufficiently pleading crimes does not guarantee factual accuracy or guilt – this was the section of the indictment that charged the Katyn Forest massacre of Polish officers to the German defendants, *id.* at 54, though it has since been revealed that it was committed by Soviets.

[107] Chap. 3.a.

Count four on crimes against humanity left out the claim of violation of customary international law and reference to specific treaties. It alleged "violations of international conventions, of internal penal laws, of the general principles of criminal law as derived from the criminal law of all civilized nations.... The said acts were contrary to Article 6 of the Charter."[108] The count also advanced the theory that the facts making out war crimes could be re-characterized as crimes against humanity: "The Prosecution will rely upon the facts pleaded under Count Three as also constituting Crimes against Humanity."[109]

The defendants charged with aggressive war filed a pretrial motion claiming that the crime against peace (i.e., aggressive war) had been created ex post facto to apply to them.[110] They also claimed, though without argument, "that other principles of a penal character contained in the Charter are in contradiction with the maxim, '*Nulla Poena Sine Lege.*'"[111] They also objected to a tribunal made up solely of jurists from the victor nations and requested that "the Tribunal direct that an opinion be submitted by internationally recognized authorities on international law on the legal elements of this Trial under the Charter of the Tribunal."[112] In a ruling the same day as the first opening speech, the tribunal refused the motion, at least in part on the ground that Article 3 of the Nuremberg Charter prohibited challenges to the jurisdiction of the tribunal.[113] However, as will be seen, the judgment at the end of the trial wavered on this ground of decision. Moreover, from the opening speeches, it seems obvious that the prosecutors considered the issue of ex post facto lawmaking to be still alive.

3.b.iii.B. Arguments of the Prosecutors

A complete analysis of the prosecution arguments is not necessary here. For our purposes, it is enough to indicate a few points of interest concerning the arguments made by the prosecutors concerning legality. They were

[108] Indictment, Count Four – Crimes Against Humanity § X, 1 IMT, Trial at 65.

[109] *Id.*

[110] Motion Adopted by All Defense Counsel, 19 November 1945, 1 IMT, Trial at 168-70. At the main Nuremberg Trial, translations were provided by the IMT's own translation service. Thus, the source of translations will not be given in each subsequent citation.

[111] *Id.* at 169.

[112] *Id.* at 169–70.

[113] *Id.* at 168–70n., rejected by tribunal, Decision, 21 November 1945, 2 IMT, Trial at 95 ("insofar as [the motion] is a plea to the jurisdiction of the Tribunal, it conflicts with Article 3 of the Charter and will not be entertained. Insofar as it may contain other arguments which may be open to the defendants, they may be heard at a later stage.").

representing their governments in this proceeding and doing so in public. Thus, their statements might have some value as *opinio juris* of the states that they represented.

Justice Jackson's opening for the United States, 21 November 1945, contains the ideas, permeating the eventual judgment, both that the charter states binding law for the tribunal and that the crimes stated in the charter were already crimes in international law before the Nazi leaders acted.[114] The British prosecutor, Sir Hartley Shawcross, opened for the United Kingdom on 4 December 1945 and agreed with Justice Jackson on these positions.[115] These orators appear to have accepted that the Nuremberg Charter was at least potentially ambiguous on whether the charter allowed the tribunal to examine the legality issues, and therefore they argued from both positions.

Justice Jackson also needed to take both of these positions to achieve the aims he had set for himself. He needed to argue that the charter bound the tribunal because he did not want the tribunal to reject the crime of against peace or the crime of conspiracy to wage aggressive war. He needed to argue that the charter crimes were international law crimes before World War II because he wanted the tribunal to declare aggressive war and conspiracy to wage it to be individual crimes in general international law, not crimes that apply just to the leaders of the European Axis.

The French prosecutor, François de Menthon, argued on 17 January 1946 that the Nuremberg crimes against humanity were also "common law crimes such as theft, looting, ill-treatment, enslavement, murders and assassinations, crimes provided for and punishable under the penal laws of all civilised States,"[116] including the then-existing German Penal Code.[117] ("Common law" here is not limited to the technical sense of crimes originally defined by the judiciary of England and other common law countries; it appears to refer to their characteristic of appearing in "the penal laws of all civilised States.") This finds some support in the Nuremberg indictment, in that the count alleging crimes against humanity alleges that the acts involved were "violations of . . . internal penal laws" and of international conventions and general principles of law.[118] (In the view of many, "general principles of law," a phrase

[114] Jackson, Opening, 2 IMT, Trial at 143–47.

[115] Hartley Shawcross, Opening, 3 IMT, Trial at 93–106.

[116] De Menthon, Opening, 3 IMT, Trial at 92.

[117] See de Menthon, Opening, 3 IMT, Trial at 128. This idea has persisted into later thought. See Paul K. Ryu & Helen Silving, *International Criminal Law: A Search for Meaning*, in 1 M. Cherif Bassiouni & Ved P. Nanda, A Treatise on International Criminal Law 22, 29 n.23 (Charles C. Thomas 1973).

[118] Nuremberg Indictment, Count Four § X, 1 IMT, Trial at 65.

taken from the Statute of the Permanent Court of International Justice,[119] and repeated in the Statute of the International Court of Justice,[120] refers to provisions or principles of law present in all or almost all national legal systems.[121]) De Menthon seemed to use certain orders of the Reich, particularly with regard to forced labor, in ways that suggest that they may have overridden the prior German laws against enslavement,[122] which would mean that he must rely either on international law or general principles of law for prescription. Yet elsewhere he points out that German law even during the war did not generally allow a defense of superior orders to justify a violation of German law,[123] suggesting that these laws were never in fact overridden.

Judge Antonio Cassese recently suggested that de Menthon attempted to avoid *nullum crimen* problems by arguing that the crimes against humanity involved in the main Nuremberg trial were also on their facts war crimes.[124] The claim that every crime against humanity was also a war crime does not appear explicitly in de Menthon's opening argument at Nuremberg, but Cassese's inference is reasonable. The notion that every crime against humanity was some kind of a crime, whether a war crime or a common crime under national law, does clearly appear.

De Menthon's opening speech echoed the French view at London that the text of Article 6 of the charter is only jurisdictional and that the tribunal must determine what the law is, particularly whether certain crimes exist under international law:

> France sees fit to ask the Tribunal to qualify juridically as crimes, both the war of aggression itself and those acts in violation of the morality and of the laws of all civilized countries which have been committed by

[119] Statute of the Permanent Court of International Justice art. 38.

[120] Statute of the International Court of Justice art. 38.

[121] Cf. ICCPR art. 15(2) (stating that general principles of law can be a source of law for purposes of determining whether the principle of legality is met); ICC Statute art. 21.

[122] De Menthon, Opening at 107–10, relying on Hague Convention art. 52 and international law for criminality of these acts.

[123] See de Menthon, Opening, 3 IMT, TRIAL at 128.

[124] See A. Cassese, *Crimes Against Humanity: Comments on Some Problematical Aspects*, in THE INTERNATIONAL LEGAL SYSTEM IN QUEST OF EQUITY AND UNIVERSALITY: L'ORDRE JURIDIQUE INTERNATIONAL, UN SYSTÈME EN QUÊTE D'ÉQUITÉ ET D'UNIVERSALITÉ: LIBER AMICORUM G. ABI-SAAB 429, 433–35 (Laurence Boisson de Chazournes & Vera Gowlland-Debbas eds., Martinus Nijhoff 2001) (for the proposition that both the French judge Donnedieu de Vabres and original French chief prosecutor François de Menthon at Nuremberg believed that the acts constituting crimes against humanity prosecuted there were war crimes in any event, and therefore there was no *nullum crimen* problem as to them). Cassese himself believes that crimes against humanity were new at Nuremberg. Antonio Cassese, *Crimes against Humanity*, in 1 CASSESE ET AL., *supra* note 1, at 353, 354–55.

> Germany in the conduct of the war, to condemn those who are chiefly responsible, and to declare criminal the members of the various groups and organizations which were the principal perpetrators of the crimes of Nazi Germany.[125]

On the substantive law, this view reflects a change from the French position at London, which was against the existence of aggressive war as a crime in international law at the time the Nazis acted. It also accepts the notion of declaring certain groups to be criminal for the later purpose of prosecuting their members. It does not, however, reflect a change in the French view that the tribunal, not the charter, must declare what acts are crimes under international law.

The Soviet prosecutor, General Roman Andreevich Rudenko, opened on 8 February 1946, more than two months after Justice Jackson. He repeated the view of Nikitchenko at the London Conference that the charter was absolutely binding on the tribunal and contained the substantive law binding the tribunal. He made explicit the Soviet view: "In the international field, the basic source of law and the only legislative act is a treaty, an agreement between states."[126] Thus, he argued, any rules of law, such as *nullum crimen sine lege*, not found in the Nuremberg text simply have no force in the law governing the tribunal.[127] General human rights principles could not control, or even provide guidance for the interpretation of, the charter.

Interestingly, Rudenko came the closest to calling the IMT an international organization in the modern sense. First, he referred to the trial as being the "first one in history where justice is being done through an agency of an international legal system – the International Military Tribunal."[128] He essentially argued that, by treaty, states could establish international organizations with broad powers: "an international treaty is an absolute and sufficient legal basis for the implementation and the activities of agencies of international justice created by the signatories."[129] Some non-Leninists might infer from the treatment of the IMT as an international organization, combined with the extremely broad powers of states to affect rights negatively through treaties, that a time might come when individuals would need their individual human rights protected against invasion by international organizations, as well as by states.

[125] See de Menthon, Opening, 5 IMT, TRIAL at 370.
[126] Roman Andreevich Rudenko, Opening, 7 IMT, TRIAL at 147–48.
[127] *Id.* at 148.
[128] *Id.* at 147.
[129] *Id.* at 147–48.

Also interesting is that Rudenko's closing argument on 29 July 1946 echoed the ambiguity of the Nuremberg Charter, claiming both that legality was inapplicable in the tribunal and that its strictures were met anyway:

> [F]rom the legal point of view, sentence can be pronounced and carried out without requiring that the deeds which incriminate the defendants be foreseen by the criminal law at the time of their perpetration. Nevertheless, there is no doubt that the deeds of the defendants, at the time when they were being committed, were actual criminal acts from the standpoint of the then existing criminal law.[130]

Shawcross made most of the legal argument for the prosecution, especially on closing. He argued in his closing on 26–27 July 1946 that the defendants were "charged... as common murderers. That charge alone merits the imposition of the supreme penalty and the joinder in the Indictment of this Crime Against Peace can add nothing to the penalty which may be imposed on these individuals."[131] He linked "the Crimes Against Humanity, the War Crimes, the common murders" together,[132] though murders were never charged in the indictment, except as elements of the crimes against humanity and war crimes. This suggests that he believed that what was a crime under national law at the time committed could be re-characterized as a crime under a different name under international law in the tribunal. Yet he also made an argument in contrast to the French view that laws against murder and similar crimes were never repealed or modified in the German Criminal Code. He argued that "[m]urder, extermination, enslavement, persecution on political, racial or economic grounds... done against belligerent nationals, or for that matter, done against German nationals in belligerent occupied territory, would be ordinary War Crimes the prosecution of which would form no novelty."[133] They were also "in their very enormity Crimes Against Humanity."[134] However, he admitted that "German law, departing from all the canons of civilised procedure, may have authorised them to be done by the State or by persons acting on behalf of the State."[135] Yet, to the contrary, he seemed to admit that making new international crimes against humanity of these acts here

[130] Rudenko, Closing, 19 IMT, Trial at 575.
[131] Shawcross, Closing, 19 IMT, Trial at 433, 448, quoted and discussed in Taylor, *supra* note 29, at 495.
[132] Shawcross, Closing, 19 IMT, Trial at 448.
[133] *Id.* at 471.
[134] *Id.* at 470.
[135] *Id.* at 471.

was acceptable because it did "not in any way place those defendants in greater jeopardy than they would otherwise be";[136] this appears to confuse the argument that the acts were ordinary murders when committed with the argument that the acts were war crimes when committed whether or not Germany purported to remove them from the category of ordinary murders.

Shawcross used the commission of war crimes to make a creative argument regarding crimes against peace and conspiracy. A major point of the proceedings, he said (echoing the point Justice Jackson and others had been making since before the London Conference), was "to establish for all time that International Law has the power, inherent in its very nature, both to declare that a war is criminal and to deal with those who aid and abet their States in its commission."[137] Earlier, however, he had used the existence of "piracy, breach of blockade, . . . the case of spies . . . [and] [w]ar crimes" in international law as evidence that international law applies to individuals as well as states.[138] In other words, the proceedings met the requirement of *nulla poena sine lege* because the defendants would be justly condemned to death for war crimes, which were capital offenses in applicable law at the time of their acts. Even if crimes against peace and conspiracy to commit them were not previously in existence, the violation of *nullum crimen sine lege* with respect to them did not matter. The Nuremberg Tribunal could (something like an authoritative common law court) declare such crimes for the future. (Note that the Nuremberg Judgment is not wholly consistent with the argument that all those convicted of aggression and conspiracy were also war criminals in the traditional sense. The tribunal convicted defendant Rudolf Hess of conspiracy and crimes against peace, but not of war crimes or crimes against humanity, and sentenced him to life imprisonment.[139])

Shawcross also argued that crimes against peace were not created retroactively in the charter.[140] He used the jurisdictional connection of crimes against humanity in the charter to crimes against peace[141] to argue that even where they were not war crimes (e.g., oppression of Jews who were German nationals in Germany), they could still be brought without offending

[136] *Id.*
[137] *Id.* at 433, 448.
[138] *Id.* at 464.
[139] See Taylor, *supra* note 29, at 635 (using this as clinching proof that some law at Nuremberg was truly applied ex post facto).
[140] Shawcross, Closing, 19 IMT, Trial at 464.
[141] Nuremberg Charter art. 6.

principles of legality.[142] He also argued that this use of crimes against humanity

> gives warning for the future, to dictators and tyrants masquerading as a State that if, in order to strengthen or further their crimes against the community of nations they debase the sanctity of man in their own countries, they act at their peril, for they affront the International Law of Mankind.[143]

He went so far as to suggest that crimes against humanity might justify judicial action even when committed only internally.[144]

Shawcross argued for the equivalence of illegality and criminality in this case. In arguing for the existence of the crime of aggressive war, especially in violation of treaties, he stated, "[T]here is no difference between illegality and criminality in a breach of law involving the deaths of millions and a direct attack on the very foundations of civilized life."[145]

Shawcross had made another interesting argument in his opening: that the application of international criminal law to individuals was in one way better than its application to states. Applying it to individuals avoids the problem of collective punishment that arises if states are held to be criminal.[146]

3.b.iii.C. The Defense Arguments

A few comments on the defense closing arguments are also worthwhile. Only the arguments bearing on the issues of legality will be covered here, so not all defense speeches will be discussed.[147] To the extent practicable, the topics concerning legality have been grouped together by subject, rather than chronologically or by groups of defendants. Where one counsel essentially followed a similar line, this is indicated in notes, though this may result in an imbalance concerning the factual issue of whose argument was heard most clearly by the tribunal.

One thing that is interesting about the defense arguments is how little argument was made that the prosecution for crimes against humanity were ex post facto as to these defendants. Although there were some claims that

[142] See Shawcross, Closing, 19 IMT, Trial at 470–71.
[143] *Id.* at 472.
[144] *Id.*
[145] *Id.* at 460.
[146] Shawcross, Opening, 3 IMT, Trial at 105.
[147] Additionally, because of its sole focus on legality, this discussion will look very different from more general discussions of the defense, such as Taylor, *supra* note 29, Chap. 17.

war-crimes prosecutions were ex post facto, one might have expected more of these.

First, these were claims made on behalf of individuals under international law and pursuant to an international agreement, the London Agreement and Nuremberg Charter. Non-retroactivity or legality of criminal law was not listed in the charter as a substantive or procedural right of the defendant. Thus, the willingness of the tribunal to hear the arguments represents a step forward in recognizing the right of individuals, the defendants, to make claims under international law.

3.B.III.C.I. AUTHORITY OF THE CHARTER VERSUS THE PRINCIPLE OF LEGALITY

As to the question of whether the principle of legality should be binding on (or even available to) the tribunal, two speeches stand out, those of Otto Stahmer, for defendant Hermann Göring, and Otto Pannenbecker, for defendant Wilhelm Frick. Hermann Jahrreiss, speaking for all defendants on the issue of aggressive war, also raised an issue that indirectly suggested that legality should be binding on the tribunal.

Stahmer argued that Article 6 of the charter was "a mere regulation of competence,"[148] and that the tribunal need not accept the crimes stated in the article if they were not crimes applying to the defendants at the time of the defendants' acts.[149] He recognized the facial ambiguity of the article and argued that it should be construed "in favor of the defendants according to the established legal principle *in dubio pro re*."[150] He argued that, where one interpretation of Article 6 was consistent with a general principle of law, such as *nullum crimen*, and another is not, the interpretation consistent with it should be followed "as corresponding to the author's will."[151]

Pannenbecker expanded on the jurisdictional role of Article 6 of the charter. He relied specifically on the heading of Part II of the charter, which begins with Article 6: "Jurisdiction and General Principles."[152] This bears obvious resemblance to the arguments of the French delegation at the London Conference.[153]

Pannenbecker argued that the tribunal should be bound by the principle of legality. He claimed that "the prohibition of retroaction of penal laws

[148] Otto Stahmer, Argument, 17 IMT, TRIAL at 498, 507.
[149] *Id.* at 507.
[150] *Id.*
[151] *Id.* at 512.
[152] Otto Pannenbecker, Argument, 18 IMT, TRIAL at 164.
[153] See Chap. 3.b.ii. The author knows of no evidence suggesting that Drs. Stahmer and Pannenbecker knew of the debate at the London Conference over this issue.

is a . . . legal principle [that has] found general recognition in all civilized countries as a prerequisite and basic precept of justice"[154] and that it is one of the "legal principles of international custom."[155] In other words, prohibition of criminal retroactivity is both a customary international law and a general principle of law.

Stahmer also made a political-jurisprudential argument that "the legal thesis *nulla poena sine lege* should be especially sacred" to the tribunal.[156] He argued that "no fixed ideological basis for the Charter is discernable . . . [s]ince its signatories stand on very different ideological ground we will have to proceed, as in the international law valid hitherto, from the liberal idea of freedom of ideology."[157] The idea seems to be that, where there is a fixed ideological basis for law, as in the Nazi Reich, the citizen can use that basis to infer from a facially vague law to the result that a court will announce, thus providing protection equivalent to *nulla poena sine lege praevia*.[158] Thus, contrary to codefendant Frank's statements at the time,[159] Stahmer argued that the 1935 statutes and the implementation of the Leadership Principle did not "renounce outright the principle nulla poena sine lege praevia."[160] By contrast, he quoted the Swiss professor Hans Fehr: "Without ideology, law floats in a vacuum. . . . Whoever has no ideology can have no sense of right and wrong."[161] International law had no fixed ideology, apparently because it must mediate between states with different legal ideologies; liberal states had no fixed legal ideology because they chose that condition. In such a condition, only *lege praevia*, a previously established

[154] Pannenbecker, Argument, 18 IMT, Trial at 164. Accord Gustav Steinbauer, Argument for Arthur Seyss-Inquart, 19 IMT, Trial at 46, 52–53 ("this principle *nullum crimen nulla poena sine lege* [is] firmly rooted in almost all law books" – a claim that it is a general principle of law, though the text relies most heavily on the place of the principle in the law of Germany's enemy, and his client's prosecutor, France). Cf. Otto Freiherr von Lüdinghausen for defendant Constantin von Neurath, 19 IMT, Trial at 216, 219 ("in sharp contrast to the principles of law of all democratic states, of every democratic-liberal principle of law [the tribunal] proposes to pass judgment and inflict punishment for actions which at the time they were committed were not governed by law" – not including all civilized states, but only democratic ones, as the source of general principles of law).

[155] Pannenbecker, Argument, 18 IMT, Trial at 165.

[156] Stahmer, Argument, 17 IMT, Trial at 505.

[157] *Id.*

[158] *Id.* at 504–05.

[159] See Chap. 2.c.ii.A, quoting Statement of Hans Frank, 14 September 1935, translated and printed in *Justice Case*, 3 T.W.C. at 1022.

[160] Stahmer, Argument, 17 IMT, Trial at 504 (much of this argument is in small type, indicating it was submitted to the tribunal in writing but not read, and the Latin phrase has spaces between the letters in the original).

[161] *Id.*, quoting Hans Fehr, Recht und Wirklichkeit; Einblick in Werden und Vergehen der Rechtsformen (1927) [page and publisher not cited].

legal text with clear legal meaning, can provide a person with warning as to what the law prohibits.

Robert Servatius, for defendant Fritz Sauckel, briefly touched on a reason to prohibit creation of new crimes in the charter that appears to be based in the structure of international law. He argued that the charter "cannot prohibit what international law permits."[162] Heinz Fritz, for the propagandist Hans Fritzsche, may be said to have instantiated this, arguing that under then existing international law, propaganda was neither a crime against peace nor a war crime but an accepted and generally used means to advance the interests of the state.[163]

Hermann Jahrreiss made a creative argument allied to the notice argument on legality generally, suggesting that the tribunal ought to recognize the principle of legality, even if it interprets the charter as binding. He argued that a person punished under such a law cannot be aware of the illegality or wrongfulness of the act, which he claims is a key aspect of "the European continental conception of penal law,"[164] and that a common lawyer might say is related to the requirement of mens rea: "It is then quite possible for the defendant to be not guilty in the sense that he was aware of the wrongfulness of his commissions and omissions."[165] The sense of this passage is that awareness of the wrongfulness of an act from the existing law (or at least the ability to be aware of it) is a substantive criminal law requirement that should be applied even if the charter is held to be binding.

3.B.III.C.II. CRIMES AGAINST PEACE (AGGRESSIVE WAR) AND CONSPIRACY

Whether aggressive war and conspiracy to wage it were crimes in international law at the time the defendants acted was the most serious legality question that the defense raised. The defendants entrusted Hermann Jahrreiss, a professor of law and associate counsel for defendant Alfred Jodl, with making the legal argument for all defendants on aggressive war as a crime.[166] He recognized the argument of the prosecution that the charter

[162] Robert Servatius, Argument, 18 IMT, TRIAL at 469.

[163] Heinz Fritz, Argument, 19 IMT, TRIAL at 312, 320–24, relying on Hague Rules [Regulations] of Land Warfare art. 24.

[164] Hermann Jahrreiss, Legal Argument, 17 IMT, TRIAL at 460. Taylor, *supra* note 29, at 475 recognizes the strength and importance of this argument.

[165] Jahrreiss, Legal Argument, 17 IMT, TRIAL at 460. Accord, von Lüdinghausen for defendant Constantin von Neurath, 19 IMT, TRIAL at 216, 219.

[166] Jahrreiss, Legal Argument, 17 IMT, TRIAL at 458, 458–59. The principal French judge, Donnedieu de Vabres, *supra* note 4, at 495, later described Jahrreiss as "a German master of public international law."

was binding,[167] yet he challenged the tribunal as to whether the charter actually made new (i.e., potentially retroactive) law.[168] He then went on to argue strongly that the notion of aggressive war as an individual crime did not exist in international law before World War II and was an ex post facto creation of the charter.[169] This famous and lengthy argument will not be repeated here.

Jahrreiss made a brief argument on conspiracy to commit aggressive war (count one of the indictment), which was picked up by three other counsel. He argued:

> [T]he defendants . . . are strung together into a conspiracy by legal concepts rooted in Anglo-Saxon law and alien to us. . . .
>
> Insofar as the Charter supports all of this by its regulations, it is essentially laying down fundamentally new law if . . . one measures against existing international law.[170]

Stahmer, for Göring, added to this argument. As set out in the charter and the indictment, he said, conspiracy vastly exceeded the scope of joint liability for crime recognized in German law.[171] One could not, therefore, say that any substantive crime for which a defendant might be liable under ex post facto conspiracy law was automatically a crime for which he would be liable under German domestic law. Otto Frieherr Von Lüdinghausen, for defendant Constantin von Neurath, added that conspiracy was particularly inappropriate for international law because it was "foreign to the vast majority of peoples" and was developed solely to deal with common crimes under domestic laws.[172]

Jahrreiss did not specifically address the issues of war crimes and crimes against humanity. Indeed, that was not his brief. He did anticipate one of the claims of the tribunal with regard to them: that acts could be considered criminal in an international tribunal under new law if they were criminal

[167] Jahrreiss, Legal Argument, 17 IMT, Trial at 459–60. See also von Lüdinghausen, 19 IMT, Trial at 219.

[168] Jahrreiss, Legal Argument, 17 IMT, Trial at 459–60.

[169] *Id.* at 461ff.

[170] *Id.* at 480. Accord Stahmer, Argument, 17 IMT, Trial at 508ff.; Steinbauer, Argument, 19 IMT, Trial at 46, 51–52 (conspiracy was not a crime recognized outside the common law world – i.e., not a crime where the defendants acted); von Lüdinghausen, Argument, 19 IMT, Trial at 220. Hans Flächsner, for defendant Albert Speer, 19 IMT, Trial at 177–78, joined Stahmer's arguments on conspiracy, as well as Jahrriess's arguments.

[171] Stahmer, Argument, 17 IMT, Trial at 508 ff.

[172] Von Lüdinghausen, Argument, 19 IMT, Trial at 220.

under national law at the time committed.[173] He applied this argument to the possibility of a hypothetical national law against aggressive war, and he appeared to admit the possibility, at least for common law views, that the *lege* in *nullum crimen sine lege* need not be the written statute in existence at the time of the crime under which the defendant is prosecuted.[174] He then went on to make an extended argument that "the so-called Führer Principle"[175] was so thoroughly incorporated into German governance that no order issued by Hitler could possibly violate the law of Germany: his orders and decrees, and the orders of those under him, were the law.[176] Thus, the portion of the charter abolishing the defense of superior orders,[177] in the context of the Third Reich (and, probably most other governments as well, he said) effectively criminalized acts that were not criminal under national law when committed.[178] This last was necessary not so much to the aggressive war argument as to rebut the argument that the actions of defendants committing or encouraging murders, and so on, were at all times crimes under the German Penal Code.

Many other defense counsel left the arguments on legality of crimes against peace (aggressive war) alone. Because they agreed to let Jahrreiss speak for them on these issues, none of them gave up any legality claim concerning conspiracy and crimes against peace. However, if they wished to maintain legality claims as to war crimes and crimes against humanity, they did need something more than his arguments.

3.B.III.C.III. WAR CRIMES AND CRIMES AGAINST HUMANITY

Remarkably, few counsel attacked the legality of prosecutions for war crimes, or even for crimes against humanity. In fact, a number of counsel made

[173] Jahrreiss, Legal Argument, 17 IMT, Trial at 481. See also Pannenbecker, Argument, 18 IMT, Trial at 167–68 (no defendant could be convicted of the crime of aggressive war, because "one condition for this is lacking, namely, the possibility of establishing that the defendants have offended against a principle of generally valid international custom or a principle of national law which defined the war of aggression at the time it took place and declared it punishable as a crime of which a single individual could be guilty").

[174] Jahrreiss, Legal Argument, 17 IMT, Trial at 481.

[175] *Id.* at 482.

[176] *Id.* at 481ff.

[177] Nuremberg Charter art. 8.

[178] Jahrreiss, Legal Argument, 17 IMT, Trial at 481–94. Cf. Fritz Sauter, Argument for Defendant Walter Funk, 18 IMT, Trial at 247–50 (questioning "whether a state official whose government has been legally recognized by all the governments of the world is liable to legal punishment for putting into effect a law – and I emphasize the word 'law' – passed in accordance with the legislative system of this state").

no independent closing argument on legality.[179] Many appeared to tacitly admit the legality of bringing war-crimes charges, or in some cases even charges of crimes against humanity.[180] In one case, no legality challenge was made even where defense counsel referred to crimes against humanity for acts concerning the Incorporated Territories (i.e., areas such as Austria incorporated into Germany as a result of the Third Reich's actions)[181] – though this is one area in which the definition of crimes against humanity arguably does not overlap with traditional war crimes.[182]

The legality arguments made as to war crimes were various. Only a few directly attacked the legality of prosecutions for traditional war crimes.

Alfred Thoma, for the defendant Alfred Rosenberg, argued in a long section that was not presented orally to the tribunal that there is no agreed-upon morality or criminal law of war that is shared by the international community, and that any creation of such by the tribunal would be unfair and retroactive.[183] In modern terms, he appeared to deny the existence of customary international criminal law, even concerning war crimes. He specifically argued that an emergency threatening the existence of the state can overcome even the treaty-based rules of the Hague regulations that would otherwise bind the state.[184]

[179] Hanns Marx, for defendant Julius Streicher, 18 IMT, Trial at 190; Fritz Sauter, for defendant Walter Funk, 18 IMT, Trial at 220; Rudolf Dix, for defendant Hjalmar Schacht, 18 IMT, Trial at 270; Egon Kubuschok, for defendant Franz von Papen, made essentially no legality argument separate from that of Jahrreiss. Friedrich Bergold, for defendant Martin Bormann in absentia, 19 IMT Trial at 111 did not address legality in the sense of the existence of crimes at the time of the defendant's acts, addressing principally the procedural issue of fairness of defendant's trial in absentia, without possibility of review if the defendant was found alive.

[180] Otto Nelte, Argument for Keitel, 18 IMT, Trial at 3–5, 15–23 (Oradour, Tulle, "Night and Fog" orders), 31–33 (French prisoners of war), 38–40 (war crimes, crimes against humanity); Kurt Kauffmann, Argument for Kaltenbrunner, 18 IMT, Trial at 40, 68 (war crimes, crimes against humanity); Siemers, Argument for Raeder, 18 IMT, Trial at 424 (equating "genuine war crimes, the crimes against humanity"); Sauter, for von Schirach, 18 IMT, Trial at 450–51 (war crimes, crimes against humanity; discussed further at the end of this section); Martin Horn, Argument for von Ribbentrop, 17 IMT, Trial at 555, 588–89 (war crimes).

[181] See Pannenbecker, Argument for Frick, 18 IMT, Trial at 176ff.

[182] This is the view of Taylor, *supra* note 29, at 583, as to the annexation of Austria, before the actual outbreak of war, discussing Nuremberg Judgment, 1 IMT, Trial at 65.

[183] Alfred Thoma, Argument, 18 IMT, Trial at 69, 123–25.

[184] *Id.* at 87–91. Accord, Alfred Seidl, for defendant Hans Frank, Argument 18 IMT, Trial at 129, 154–55 (emphasizing defense of "vital stress," which appears to have included what many common lawyers would call the doctrines of self-defense and duress, as a general principle of criminal law for individuals).

Alfred Seidl, for defendant Hans Frank, argued that the Hague Convention (No. IV) and its Appendix, "The Hague Regulations of Land Warfare," were specifically not meant to bind individuals; and that, in any case, conditions had changed by the time of World War II so that they were no longer law even for nations.[185] Thus:

> It is not possible to adduce the provisions of the Hague Rules for Land Warfare, even indirectly or by way of analogy, to establish individual criminal liability. Seeing that this is the case, it must be looked upon as impossible to give a clear and general definition of the factual characteristics of so-called war crimes.[186]

The last sentence can be read as a claim that there is no sufficiently definite law (*lex certa*) to define war crimes for individuals. However, there is some evidence in the speech that Seidl did not mean this wholly as a legality argument, claiming that there was no law, because he admitted later that "terrible crimes" were committed in the General Government of Poland, the territory managed by his client.[187]

It is possible to see a slightly different argument, based on the means of attributing criminality to the acts of individuals, in the words of Otto Frieherr von Lüdinghausen, for Constantin von Neurath:

> it is because of an entirely new principle of law that my client is facing this Court today. Because for the first time in history the idea is to be carried into practice according to which the statesmen of a nation are to be held personally responsible and are to be punished for the inhuman acts of wars of aggression caused by them.[188]

This endorses the argument of Jahrreiss that aggressive war was being punished ex post facto. It can also be read as arguing that this is the first time that war crimes and crimes against humanity were attributed to the statesmen who caused the wars of aggression in which they occurred. Thus, the establishment of liability for these acts when committed in connection with aggressive war, as is set forth in the charter, establishes a new, ex post facto means of attributing criminal guilt to acts that were previously noncriminal. Presumably, von Lüdinghausen would have admitted that those

[185] Alfred Seidl, Argument 18 IMT, Trial at 143–44, relying on Hague Convention (No. IV) art. 3.
[186] *Id.* at 144.
[187] *Id.* at 160.
[188] Von Lüdinghausen, Argument, 19 IMT, Trial at 217.

who committed the war crimes, and possibly even the military leaders who directly ordered them, were liable for them in international law.

Otto Kranzbühler, for the defendant Grossadmiral Karl Dönitz, asserted that there was no stable customary international law of sea warfare on which criminal law for an admiral could be based, and in fact argued that recent developments in international law had broadened permissible combat operations at sea rather than narrowed them.[189] He also took on the claim that what was an ordinary national crime, such as murder, when committed could later be characterized as an international crime: "the German Supreme Court, during the war crimes trials after the first World War, formulated in this regard . . . : 'The culprit must be conscious of the violation of international law by his actions.'"[190] This is the argument that legality requires that the specific law under which one is convicted must have been in place at the time of the act charged. However, Kranzbühler admitted that a legal basis existed for war crimes in land warfare at least since the time of Hugo Grotius, who traced his own reasoning back to Plutarch.[191]

He made one factual retroactivity argument that is slightly aside from the issue of legality but worth noting because it appears to have been successful. He argued that Dönitz could not have joined the alleged conspiracy to wage aggressive war until his promotion to Commander-in-Chief of the German Navy in 1943, and it would be unjust to hold him retroactively responsible for the earlier acts of the other conspirators. He was convicted of waging aggressive war but not of conspiracy to wage it.[192]

A few other counsel admitted that, in general, war-crimes law existed at the time of their clients' acts but for one reason or another did not apply to their clients. In a paragraph in his written argument, but cut from his oral presentation at the direction of the tribunal to speed up the proceedings, Stahmer argued that legality, especially *nulla poena sine lege praevia*, should be applied "to Germans accused of War Crimes."[193] The point of emphasizing *nulla poena* and adding the word *praevia* is that the punishment for the crime must be laid down in the text applicable before the time of the crime, which was not the case in international law at the time – that is, Stahmer was treating *lege* as positive textual law. He needed to do this

[189] Otto Kranzbühler, Argument, 18 IMT, Trial at 312, 344–46.
[190] *Id.* at 346 (no case citation given).
[191] *Id.* at 312, quoting Grotius, *De jure pacis ac belli*, Bk. II, chap. 24, ¶ 10.
[192] Nuremberg Judgement, 1 IMT, Trial at 310–11, 315.
[193] Stahmer, Argument, 17 IMT, Trial at 496 (request of tribunal to shorten speeches), 505. See also Servatius, Argument, 18 IMT, Trial at 469–70.

because he recognized the argument (from the British chief prosecutor[194]) that a defendant might be convicted if some law made his act criminal at the time, even if not the law under which he is being tried – for example, he might be tried for an act that was a crime under national law when done, or even under international law as a war crime (but without an international law text laying down a punishment), but is now also a crime under the charter and in a new tribunal.[195] Indeed, he recognized that war crimes existed in international law at the time of World War II,[196] and even that Göring considered which acts of Allied aviators might be considered criminal[197]; though elsewhere he argued that breaches of the laws of war did not involve personal liability for Göring.[198]

Martin Horn, for defendant Joachim von Ribbentrop, admitted that "classical international law" allowed that individuals could be held criminally responsible for violation of the usages of war, at least while the war continued, and that the issue of whether war crimes could be prosecuted thereafter was "the subject of many discussions."[199] This was an "exception" to the general rule that international law only binds states.[200] As to war crimes (and, Horn intimated, crimes against humanity), the issue of legality for von Ribbentrop was that conspiracy of the type charged by the prosecution could not implicate him in the crimes committed under either national or international law at the time he acted[201] – that is, the real legality issue concerned conspiracy. Finally, Horn, rebutting the argument of French prosecutor de Menthon that the acts of the defendants violated German law, appears to say that the tribunal cannot convict his client as though it were a German court. He seems to argue that his client could not have been aware of violating international law, and thus the law cannot be applied in a German court. Although interesting on its own terms, this argument appears to be the converse of the actual argument made by de Menthon.[202]

[194] See Shawcross, Opening, 3 IMT, Trial at 106–07.

[195] Stahmer, Argument, 17 IMT, Trial at 506–07.

[196] *Id.* at 515–16, 527ff. At 515–16, he seems to equate crimes against humanity with war crimes (a strategy that made sense to attempt to limit his client's responsibility).

[197] *Id.* at 532 (another paragraph presented to the tribunal in writing but not orally).

[198] *Id.* at 525.

[199] Martin Horn, for Joachim von Ribbentrop, Argument, 17 IMT, Trial at 555, 588–89.

[200] *Id.* at 589.

[201] See *id.* at 592–95. Cf. *id.* at 599 (referring to "norms of actual criminal law laid down in [Charter] Article 6").

[202] Compare Horn, Argument, 17 IMT, Trial at 600–03 with de Menthon, Opening, 3 IMT, Trial at 107–110, 128.

Hans Flächsner, for defendant Albert Speer, was the lawyer who raised most clearly the legality argument that the Hague Convention and Regulations on Land Warfare did not apply on their own terms to at least the war in the East because the Soviet Union was not a party to the Hague Convention.[203] He distinguished between the treaty law and "universally valid international law"[204] (in modern terms, customary international law or *jus cogens* [peremptory norms of international law from which no derogation is permitted]). He then went on to argue that the facts of modern war had made many of the Hague Convention and Regulation rules obsolete.[205] Thus, they were certainly not customary international law.

Robert Servatius, for defendant Fritz Sauckel, argued that the Hague Convention on Land Warfare (to which the Regulations are annexed) distinguished between war crimes that can be committed by individuals, such as murder and ill treatment, and violations that can be committed only by states, such as acts of illegal mobilization of labor during a war.[206] His client only being charged with the latter, there was no law under which he could be convicted.[207] In contrast with Flächsner, Servatius admitted that the Hague Regulations were "an important guide."[208]

Otto Freiherr von Lüdinghausen, for the Reich Protector of Bohemia and Moravia, Constantin von Neurath, made an argument that the tribunal interpreted as a legality argument concerning war crimes. He argued that Bohemia and Moravia were not merely protectorates of Germany but actually had become part of the German Reich.[209] This would have meant that, by the doctrine of subjugation, the rules of land warfare from the Hague Convention (and indeed other laws of war) no longer applied when von Neurath committed his acts there. (This was another argument that the

[203] Hans Flächsner, Argument, 19 IMT, TRIAL at 177, 180–82, relying on Hague Convention (No. IV) on Land Warfare art. 2 ("general participation clause"). Similarly seeking to have the Geneva Prisoner of War Convention arts. 31 & 32 (1929) applied only to the prisoners of war from the western states (because the Soviet Union was not a signatory to the pact), see Hans Flächsner, Argument, 19 IMT, TRIAL at 202–03. Accord, Servatius, Argument, 18 IMT, TRIAL at 470.

[204] Flächsner, Argument, 19 IMT, TRIAL at 182.

[205] *Id.* at 182–84. Accord, Servatius, Argument, 18 IMT, TRIAL at 471–72 (e.g., Hague Regulations on moving workers from occupied territory no longer applied). See also Gustav Steinbauer, Argument for Arthur Seyss-Inquart, 19 IMT, TRIAL at 72–73 (most Hague Regulations outmoded by World War II).

[206] Servatius, Argument, 18 IMT, TRIAL at 478, citing "Article 3 of the introductory agreement to the Hague Convention on Land Warfare."

[207] *Id.*

[208] 18 IMT, TRIAL at 470.

[209] Von Lüdinghausen, Argument, 19 IMT, TRIAL at 291, citing Decree of 16 March 1939 art. 1.

tribunal eventually rejected, holding that Bohemia and Moravia in fact had remained protectorates.)[210]

Walter Siemers, for Grossadmiral Erich Raeder, made much less of an argument on legality than did counsel for his naval codefendant. He did, however, make the point that "a treaty violation cannot *ipso jure* be a crime."[211]

Fritz Sauter, for Hitler Youth leader and later Gauleiter of Vienna Baldur von Schirach, utterly threw in the towel on legality. Indeed, he claimed that not even the Nuremberg Charter limited the tribunal:

> You are, Gentlemen, truly sovereign judges, not bound by any written law, not bound to any paragraph, pledged to serve your conscience only, and called by destiny to give to the world simultaneously a legal order which will preserve for future generations that peace which the past was unable to preserve for them.[212]

Perhaps this was a tactical speech. Yet the charges against von Schirach were largely crimes against humanity committed in Austria after the Anschluss, in which Austria was annexed by Germany, against then nationals of the enlarged Germany or against stateless persons. Thus, he might have had the strongest argument that his crimes against humanity were not, when committed, traditional war crimes.[213]

Sauter also remarked that "the precepts of humanity" would be "an unsteady foundation for a verdict . . . because ideas on what humanity demands or prohibits in individual cases may vary, depending upon the epoch, the people, the party concepts according to which one judges."[214] Although one can imagine a lawyer developing this into a legality-type argument concerning crimes against humanity, Sauter did not do so here.

3.b.iv. The Nuremberg Judgment

Many commentators have discussed whether the Nuremberg Judgment was correct concerning the *nullum crimen nulla poena sine lege* issues. The

[210] Nuremberg Judgment, 1 IMT, TRIAL at 334 (holding that the Decree of 16 March 1939 recognized that the territories were truly protectorates, and that the rules of the Hague Convention applied there as "declaratory of existing international law," even though Czechoslovakia, from which Bohemia and Moravia were taken, was not a party to the Hague Convention.)

[211] Walter Siemers, Argument, 18 IMT, TRIAL at 372, 375.

[212] Sauter, Argument, 18 IMT, TRIAL at 430, 465.

[213] See Taylor, *supra* note 29, at 554, 583.

[214] 18 IMT, TRIAL at 466.

purpose of this discussion is neither to validate nor to condemn the tribunal's reasoning, both of which have been done extensively before,[215] but to examine the tribunal's conception of legality. This will lay the foundation for discussion of later developments. This necessarily covers some of the most famous and familiar language from one of the best-known judicial documents in history; the reader can judge what is new here.

On the principal issues concerning legality and lawmaking, the Nuremberg Tribunal ruled unanimously.[216] Agreement on a text, as we have seen in the case of the charter, does not always require theoretical consistency and may indicate an evasion of difficult issues. Indeed, notes by the American judge Francis Biddle and his alternate judge, John J. Parker, indicate that many of the votes on specific issues (including lawmaking), defendants, charges, and sentences taken before issuance of the judgment were not unanimous among the four voting judges[217]; some of these points will be discussed subsequently. Later discussion of the divided opinions issued by the Tokyo Tribunal will show how fragile the Nuremberg consensus on legality was.[218]

In its majority judgment, the Nuremberg Tribunal viewed authority to establish tribunals and define substantive criminal law in a defeated state first as a national function,[219] not prohibited or limited in any relevant

[215] See, e.g., NINA H.B. JØRGENSEN, THE RESPONSIBILITY OF STATES FOR INTERNATIONAL CRIMES 28 nn.1–2 (2000) (collecting criticisms of Nuremberg trial from English, American and German commentators); SHELDON GLUECK, THE NUREMBERG TRIAL AND AGGRESSIVE WAR 74ff. n.3 (Kraus Reprint Co. 1976) (Alfred A. Knopf 1946), originally appearing in 59 HARV. L. REV. 396, 437 (1946) (collecting early criticisms of the Nuremberg process from American lawyers and then rebutting them).

[216] Judge I. T. Nikitchenko (Soviet Union) dissented as to three not-guilty verdicts as to individuals (Hjalmar Schacht, Franz von Papen, and Hans Fritzsche), one failure to impose a death sentence (Rudolf Hess), and the refusal to declare three organizations to be criminal (the Reich Cabinet, the German General Staff, and the OKW). Dissenting Opinion of the Soviet Member of the International Military Tribunal, 1 October 1946, 1 IMT, TRIAL at 342. He did not dissent on issues of lawmaking authority in the judgment. But see Chap. 3.b.iv.E on differences within the court not expressed in the opinions.

[217] Accounts of the deliberations, including disagreements among the judges, based on the notes of Judges Biddle and Parker and memoranda of their assistants, including Adrian Fisher, Jim Rowe, Robert Stewart, and Herbert Wechsler, have been published in SMITH, *supra* note 26, at 114–299; ROBERT E. CONOT, JUSTICE AT NUREMBERG 481–98 (Chaps. 55–56) (Harper & Row 1983); Taylor, *supra* note 29, at 546–611 (Chaps. 20–21) (Taylor points out specifically, *id.* at 549 n., that his description of the deliberations is based entirely on these notes and memoranda, and that, as a part of the prosecution team, he was not privy to the deliberations in any way). Judge Biddle published his own account, in his autobiography, FRANCIS BIDDLE, IN BRIEF AUTHORITY 465–87 (Doubleday & Co. 1962).

[218] See Chap. 3.d.

[219] See Nuremberg Judgment, 1 IMT, TRIAL at 218.

way by international law. International law itself was an alternate source of substantive criminal law,[220] used to avoid retroactivity issues, and perhaps as an expression of underlying commitment to international criminal law. For example:

> The Charter makes the planning or waging of a war of aggression or a war in violation of international treaties a crime; and it is therefore not strictly necessary to consider whether and to what extent aggressive war was a crime before the execution of the London Agreement. But in view of the great importance of the questions involved, the Tribunal has heard full argument from the Prosecution and the Defense, and will express its view on the matter.[221]

The discussion of *nullum crimen sine lege* excerpted in the introduction to this book immediately follows the preceding extract. The tribunal then enters into its famous construction of the international law crime of aggressive war from the pre–World War II sources.[222]

The judgment has a dual focus that matches the division at the London Conference. The dual focus also matches the reference to the charter and to other substantive law in the indictment.[223] On the one hand, the principle of legality need not be considered by states in creating law for courts such as the IMT. On the other, the tribunal alternatively considered the existence of the crimes within the tribunal's jurisdiction as a matter of international law in general,[224] although not everyone has considered this part of its discussion to be satisfactory. A bit more detailed examination of this discussion may be useful.

The Nuremberg Charter named the crimes within the jurisdiction of the Nuremberg Tribunal as crimes against peace, war crimes, and crimes against humanity, as well as conspiracy. Conspiracy was eventually decided to apply to crimes against peace only (i.e., a conspiracy solely to commit war crimes or crimes against humanity would not be within the jurisdiction of the tribunal).[225]

The Nuremberg Judgment addressed the issue of the creation of the tribunal. It stated that any of the parties to the London Agreement could have set up a military tribunal on its own, given its right as an occupying force

[220] See *id.*
[221] *Id.* at 219.
[222] *Id.* at 219ff.
[223] See Chap. 3.b.iii.A.
[224] Nuremberg Judgment, 1 IMT, Trial at 219.
[225] Nuremberg Charter arts. 6, 9 & 10; on the ambit of conspiracy in the charter, see Nuremberg Judgment, 1 IMT, Trial at 224–26.

"to set up special courts to administer law."[226] By necessary implication, these tribunals could be established retrospectively.

The tribunal itself stated several times that this document was conclusive as to the existence of these crimes and their applicability to the defendants at Nuremberg.[227] That is, the nations adopting the charter were not limited in what they did by the then-current international law of occupation. They defined what classes of acts were crimes and what classes of acts came within the jurisdiction of the court:

> The making of the Charter was the exercise of the sovereign legislative power by the countries to which the German Reich unconditionally surrendered; and the undoubted right of these countries to legislate for the occupied territories has been recognized by the civilized world.[228]

The victors possessed a sovereign right to legislate – both by defining crimes and by creating a tribunal to try them – which overrode all claims that the defendants should not have been brought to trial:

> The Signatory Powers created this Tribunal, defined the law it was to administer, and made regulations for the proper conduct of the Trial. In doing so, they have done together what any one of them might have done singly; for it is not to be doubted that any nation has the right thus to set up special courts to administer law. With regard to the constitution of the Court, all that the defendants are entitled to ask is to receive a fair trial on the facts and law.[229]

It was in this discussion that the Nuremberg Tribunal stated that *nullum crimen sine lege* "is not a limitation of sovereignty, but is in general a principle of justice"[230] that apparently can be overridden by sovereign will. Although the tribunal does not use the word *jurisdiction*, here it is effectively considering the jurisdiction of the Allies to prescribe by stating substantive criminal law and to adjudicate by establishing the tribunal.[231]

Thus far, the Nuremberg Judgment accepts the views of the United States, the Soviet Union, and the United Kingdom as expressed at the London

[226] Nuremberg Judgment, 1 IMT, Trial at 218. For a discussion of the defense challenge to the authority to establish a new jurisdiction, see P. D., *supra* note 42.

[227] See Nuremberg Judgment, 1 IMT, Trial at 173–74, 218, 228, 232, 243, 253.

[228] *Id.* at 218.

[229] *Id.*

[230] *Id.* at 219.

[231] Compare 2 IMT, Trial at 95 (decision 21 November 1945) ("insofar as [the motion] is a plea to the jurisdiction of the Tribunal, it conflicts with Article 3 of the Charter and will not be entertained"), rejecting Motion Adopted by All Defense Counsel, 1 IMT, Trial at 168–70 & n.* (motion 19 November 1945), discussed in Chap. 3.b.iii.A.

Conference. It is in opposition to the French views there, because the judgment places authority to define crimes in the hands of the victors rather than in customary international law. This portion of the discussion does not endorse the Leninist view of prescription, but thus far there is nothing truly inconsistent with it.

Viewing prescription of substantive criminal law as solely or principally a national function (i.e., of the signatory powers) meant, however, that the entire Nuremberg proceeding was subject to a claim that it violated the principle of legality. The Nuremberg Charter had not been established by the victorious nations until after the Nazis had committed their crimes. In response to this, the tribunal argued that the definitions of crimes set out in the charter come from international law existing as of the beginning of World War II. It began by claiming:

> The Charter is not an arbitrary exercise of power on the part of the victorious Nations, but in the view of the Tribunal, as will be shown, it is the expression of international law existing at the time of its creation; and to that extent is itself a contribution to international law.[232]

This, of course, is slightly ambiguous as to whether the charter really restates law existing beforehand or prescribes new law. Nonetheless, the tribunal tries very hard to justify the existence before the war of the various crimes within its jurisdiction, especially aggressive war, the crime against peace.

When the Nuremberg Tribunal considered the German defendants' attack on the definition of the crime against peace and other charter crimes as ex post facto, it acted as though these individuals had the right on their own (without the intervention of Germany) to raise this issue of international authority to define crime, even though no such right had been explicitly granted to these individuals in the charter. This is one beginning of a doctrine of international legal personality of individuals that suggests that individuals have certain rights that other international actors must recognize when the individuals assert them. Challenging the authority of the tribunal to try the defendants for crimes named in the charter goes beyond the procedural protections for defendants specifically set forth in the Nuremberg Charter.[233] Thus, the tribunal goes beyond a doctrine that international agreements may explicitly give individuals rights that they can raise directly against other international actors.

[232] Nuremberg Judgment, 1 IMT, Trial at 218.

[233] See Nuremberg Charter art. 16 (listing "fair trial" rights of defendants; right to challenge existence of law or its meaning not explicit in this section).

3.b.iv.A. The Crime Against Peace (Aggressive War and War in Breach of Treaties) and Conspiracy

For the crime against peace, most of the international law that the tribunal relied on was treaty law, in which states had exercised their sovereign authority to bind themselves. In the indictment, twenty-six treaties and assurances were mentioned,[234] not all of which were important in the tribunal's judgment. The tribunal relied several times on multilateral treaties to which Germany was a party and on documents relevant to their interpretation.[235] For the crime against peace of aggression, these included the Pact of Paris (Kellogg-Briand Pact),[236] the portion of the Treaty of Versailles concerning trying the kaiser "for a supreme Offense against international morality and the sanctity of treaties,"[237] and the never-ratified Protocol for the Pacific Settlement of International Disputes.[238]

At the time the Nazis planned and launched World War II in Europe, such aggressive war was an international delict, at very least under the treaties to which Germany was a party, if not under customary international law. That much can fairly be admitted. However, the Treaty of Versailles is the only one of these that even arguably criminalizes the conduct of planning or waging aggressive war for any individual, and the case against that individual, the kaiser, was never brought.

Thus, it is very difficult to sustain the claim that aggressive war or war in breach of treaties was a customary international law crime for individuals before World War II. It is also difficult to find any other law criminalizing the bare planning and waging of aggressive war by individuals during the period leading up to and beginning World War II. The tribunal overstates the legal purport of, for example, the Kellogg-Briand Pact for the renunciation of war as an instrument of national policy:

> In the opinion of the Tribunal, the solemn renunciation of war as an instrument of national policy necessarily involves the proposition that such a war is illegal in international law; and that those who plan and wage

[234] Indictment, Appendix C, 1 IMT, TRIAL at 84–92.

[235] See Nuremberg Judgment, 1 IMT, TRIAL at 216–18, 219–23, 238–39, 253.

[236] Pact of Paris ("Kellogg-Briand Pact"), 27 August 1928, arts. 1 & 2, 46 Stat. 2343, 2345–46, 94 L.N.T.S. 57, 59–63 (entered into force 24 July 1929), discussed at Nuremberg Judgment, 1 IMT, TRIAL at 219–21.

[237] Treaty of Versailles art. 227, (28 June 1919; entered into force 10 January 1920), discussed at Nuremberg Judgment, 1 IMT, TRIAL at 222.

[238] Protocol for the Pacific Settlement of International Disputes (Geneva Protocol), Preamble, 1924 (never entered into force), discussed at Nuremberg Judgment, 1 IMT, TRIAL at 221.

> such a war, with its inevitable and terrible consequences, are committing a crime in so doing.[239]

The first clause in this sentence was true as a matter of treaty law between states. The clause after the semicolon does not follow from the text of the treaty in the context of international treaty law of the time. Indeed, there are places where the tribunal relies not on the criminality of the defendants' acts in planning and waging an aggressive war but on their wrongfulness:

> To assert that it is unjust to punish those who in defiance of treaties and assurances have attacked neighboring states without warning is obviously untrue, for in such circumstances the actor must know that he is doing wrong, and so far from it being unjust to punish him, it would be unjust if his wrong were allowed to go unpunished.[240]

In other words, beginning World War II was sufficiently wrongful at the time that it was just to transmute that wrong into a crime. Both of these quotations implicitly reject the principle of legality of crimes and punishments as a binding rule of law. It appears that Hans Kelsen's explanation that aggressive war at Nuremberg represented a transformation of an international legal wrong into an individual crime is the most accurate. Accepting the result of the Nuremberg Judgment, he stated, "[a] retroactive law providing for punishment for acts which were illegal though not criminal at the time they were committed, seems . . . to be an exception to the rule against *ex post facto* laws."[241] At very least Kelsen was correct that this was not prohibited by anything then existing in international law. If this explanation is accepted, then implicitly the defense claim of Pannenbecker that *nulla poena sine lege* was a rule of customary international law was rejected.[242]

The tribunal did not much address legality concerning the conspiracy charge. It argued that the counts of conspiracy and aggressive war "are in substance the same."[243] This is because aggressive war by its nature requires

239 Nuremberg Judgment, 1 IMT, Trial at 221.

240 *Id.* at 219.

241 See Hans Kelsen, *Will the Judgment in the Nuremberg Trial Constitute a Precedent in International Law?*, 1 Int'l L.Q. 153, 164–65 (1947), discussed in Bassiouni, *supra* note 26, at 163–65.

242 See Chap. 3.b.iii.C.I, discussing Pannenbecker, Argument, 18 IMT, Trial at 164–65, and the related argument of Steinbauer, 19 IMT, Trial at 52–53 ("this principle *nullum crimen nulla poena sine lege* [is] firmly rooted in almost all law books" – a claim that it is a general principle of law, though the text relies most heavily on the place of the principle in the law of Germany's enemy, and his client's prosecutor, France).

243 Nuremberg Judgment, 1 IMT, Trial at 224.

"[p]lanning and preparation."[244] This, plus the decision to read the charter as allowing conspiracy only for crimes against peace (and not for war crimes or crimes against humanity),[245] represented a partial victory for the French view at London. If the proposition that aggressive war necessarily entails a conspiracy is accepted (and, as a matter of fact, it seems reasonable), then the creation of new criminal liability in the charter is at very least limited. Indeed, it appears that conspiracy was treated as narrower than crimes against peace, because in some cases, defendants were acquitted of the conspiracy but convicted of crimes against peace, but never the opposite.[246]

There was one member of the tribunal, however, who had argued the criminality as well as the illegality of aggressive war before World War II. This was the principal French judge, Professor Henri Donnedieu de Vabres. In 1928, concerning state criminal responsibility, he stated: "*La guerre d'aggression est un crime* (Aggressive war is a crime)."[247] Concerning individual responsibility, he stated that there is no juridical reason to avoid criminal liability even for the head of state who begins "*une guerre injuste* (an unjust war)."[248] Additionally, in 1932, Poland created the crime of public incitement to aggressive war, which carried a penalty of five years' imprisonment. The act of incitement would only be prosecuted if the act is also "recognized as criminal by the laws of the States against which the incitement is directed."[249]

3.b.iv.B. War Crimes

The crime against peace was the focus of the defendants' motion to dismiss on the basis of the principle of legality at the beginning of the trial. Nonetheless, some defendants raised legality claims as to the war crimes as

[244] *Id.*

[245] *Id.* at 224–26.

[246] See verdicts on William Frick, Karl Dönitz, Walter Funk, and Arthur Seyss-Inquart (all convicted of crime against peace but acquitted of conspiracy; no one was convicted of conspiracy but not crime against peace), all in Nuremberg Judgment, 1 IMT, Trial at 298–301 (Frick), 304–07 (Funk), 310–15 (Dönitz), 327–30 (Seyss-Inquart).

[247] Donnedieu de Vabres, *supra* note 6, at 426 (my own translation).

[248] *Id.* at 414–15. Obviously, there is a good deal of "just war" theory that lies behind this passage, which cannot be delved into in detail here. One might wonder if this view had something to do with Donnedieu de Vabres's selection to be the principal French judge at Nuremberg, but I have seen no specific evidence for this.

[249] Polish Criminal Code art. 113 (1932), quoted in translation in 7 UNWCC, Law Rep. at 91. Donnedieu de Vabres, *supra* note 6, at 498 (stating the Penal Code of Roumania had a similar provision).

well.[250] These were rejected on their merits[251] as well as because the charter was binding.[252]

The tribunal recognized customary international law at the time of World War II as a source of substantive criminal prescriptive authority for war crimes. At least two defendants noted that certain provisions of the Hague Convention (No. IV) of 1907[253] and its Regulations were facially inapplicable because not all parties to World War II in Europe were parties to the treaty.[254] The tribunal stated that these provisions may have been new treaty rules in 1907, "but by 1939 these rules laid down in the Convention were recognized by all civilized nations, and were regarded as being declaratory of the laws and customs of war which are referred to in . . . the Charter."[255] The rules adopted by some states through the treaty-making process had later become rules of customary international law, regardless of the applicability of the Hague Convention itself. The prescriptive authority was articulated as "all civilized nations" – the then-recognized international community.

The tribunal also used the Treaty of Versailles provision allowing trial of "persons accused of having committed acts in violation of the laws and customs of war"[256] and the United States' long-term use of the law of nations to define duties of individuals in war.[257] These were evidence that individuals were subject as individuals to criminal liability under the laws and customs of war.

Two other examples show a double reliance on the charter itself and on international law (presumably as existing when the defendants acted) as prescriptive authorities for substantive criminal law of war crimes. In response to the argument that international law binds only states, not individuals, the tribunal stated:

> The very essence of the Charter is that individuals have international duties which transcend the national obligations of obedience imposed by the individual state. He who violates the laws of war cannot obtain immunity

[250] See Chap. 3.b.iii.C.III.

[251] Nuremberg Judgment, 1 IMT, Trial at 253–54.

[252] See *id.* at 218–19.

[253] Hague Convention (No. IV) Respecting the Laws and Customs of War on Land, 19 October 1907, arts. 46, 50, 52 & 56, 32 Stat. 2277, 2306–09, reprinted in 2 A.J.I.L. Supp. 90 (entered into force 26 January 1910).

[254] See Hans Flächsner, Argument, 19 IMT, Trial at 177, 180–82, relying on Hague Convention (No. IV) on Land Warfare, art. 2 ("general participation clause"); Servatius, Argument, 18 IMT, Trial at 470, discussed in Chap. 3.b.iii.C.III.

[255] Nuremberg Judgment, 1 IMT, Trial at 253–54.

[256] Treaty of Versailles art. 228, discussed in Nuremberg Judgment, 1 IMT, Trial at 222–23.

[257] *Ex parte* Quirin, 317 U.S. 1 (1942) (discussing early usage of laws of nations and war in U.S. Supreme Court), quoted and discussed in Nuremberg Judgment, 1 IMT, Trial at 223.

> while acting in pursuance of the authority of the state if the state in authorizing action moves outside its competence under international law.[258]

This assertion about general international law was made immediately after the tribunal relied on the text of its charter as authority for charging individuals with violations of international law.[259]

The judgment immediately followed with a similar pairing of the charter text and an appeal to "the laws of all nations" and "international law" as authority for rejecting the defense of superior orders.[260] "The laws of all nations" here presumably refers to the internal laws of all nations, and thus appears to set out general principles of law deducible from the laws of all nations as a source of international criminal prescription as well.[261]

The defense claims that international law did not cover war crimes in violation of the laws of land warfare as crimes for individuals at the time of World War II were ultimately unconvincing.[262] However, reading the verdict against Grossadmiral Dönitz on war crimes,[263] one has the distinct feeling that the tribunal partly accepted the legality argument that the law of war crimes as to naval warfare was less developed during World War II.[264] It accepted the defense argument that British practice concerning the use of armed merchant ships was relevant to the definition of the rules of submarine warfare that the admiral was accused of violating.[265] The tribunal relied on treaty law concerning neutral merchant shipping for the existence of some individual criminal law applicable during the war that he violated,[266] thus reducing the number of incidents for which he was criminally liable.

3.b.iv.C. Crimes Against Humanity

Perhaps because the defendants paid so little attention to legality concerning crimes against humanity,[267] the tribunal paid little attention to the issue in its judgment. Specifically, counsel for the two persons who in the end were

[258] Nuremberg Judgment, 1 IMT, Trial at 223.
[259] *Id.*
[260] *Id.* at 223–24.
[261] Cf. P.C.I.J. Stat., art. 38. Contra, Dissenting Opinion of Pal at 17, 105 IMTFE Records (opposing the use of general principles of law in international criminal law at Tokyo Tribunal).
[262] Thoma, Argument, 18 IMT, Trial at 87–91. Seidl, Argument, 18 IMT, Trial at 129, 154–55.
[263] Nuremberg Judgment, 1 IMT, Trial at 311–14.
[264] Kranzbühler, Argument, 18 IMT, Trial at 344–46.
[265] Nuremberg Judgment, 1 IMT, Trial at 312.
[266] *Id.* at 312–13, relying on Protocol of 1936 on naval warfare.
[267] See Chap. 3.b.iii.C.III.

convicted solely for crimes against humanity, Julius Streicher and Baldur von Schirach, did not use their closing arguments to argue the ex post facto nature of crimes against humanity.[268]

Indeed, the tribunal never stated that a category of individual crimes called crimes against humanity existed in international law at the time of World War II. The statement that the charter "is the expression of international law existing at the time of its creation" is not fully justified by the discussion of crimes against humanity.[269] The closest that it came to an explanation of crimes against humanity was arguing that

> from the beginning of the war in 1939 War Crimes were committed on a vast scale, which were also Crimes Against Humanity; and insofar as the inhumane acts charged in the Indictment, and committed after the beginning of the war, did not constitute War Crimes, they were committed in execution of, or in connection with, the aggressive war, and therefore constituted Crimes Against Humanity.[270]

In the portion of the judgment convicting Julius Streicher only of crimes against humanity, the tribunal emphasized Streicher's advocacy and incitement of and favorable reporting on the murder of Jews in the occupied Eastern territory, and stated that this constituted "persecution on political and racial grounds in connection with War Crimes, as defined in the Charter, and constitutes a crime against humanity."[271] In French, the judgment is clearer that Streicher encouraged acts that were themselves war crimes:

> *Le fait que Streicher poussait au meurtre et à l'extermination, à l'époque même où, dans l'Est, les Juifs étaient massacrés dans les conditions les plus horribles, réalise «la persecution pour des motifs politiques et raciaux» prevue*

[268] Marx, Argument, 18 IMT, Trial at 190; Sauter, Argument, 18 IMT, Trial at 430, 465.

[269] See Nuremberg Judgment, 1 IMT, Trial at 218, 254–55; see also Leila N. Sadat, The International Criminal Court and the Transformation of International Law: Justice for the New Millenium 30 n.34 (Transnational Publishers 2002), quoting Theodore Meron, *The Role of Custom in the Formation of International Humanitarian Law*, 90 A.J.I.L. 238, 239 (1996) (noting that the Nuremberg Tribunal "paid little attention to the process or rationale by which various provisions of humanitarian conventions were transformed into customary international law").

[270] Nuremberg Judgment, 1 IMT, Trial at 254–55. Bassiouni points out that Control Council Law No. 10, allowing for further trials by occupation authorities, removed the jurisdictional connection between prosecutable crimes against humanity and the 1939–45 war in Europe, M. Cherif Bassiouni, *International Criminal Investigations and Prosecutions: From Versailles to Rwanda*, in 3 International Criminal Law (Enforcement) 31, 52 (M. Cherif Bassiouni, ed., 2d ed., Transnational Publishers 1999), thus undercutting this theory.

[271] Nuremberg Judgment, 1 IMT, Trial at 302–04.

parmi les crimes de guerre défines par le Statut, et constitue également un crime contre l'Humanité.[272]

Those who committed the killings committed the war crime of murder under the charter,[273] for which Streicher was liable as an aider and abettor. He was convicted instead for crimes against humanity of "persecution on political and racial grounds in connection with War Crimes,"[274] because he was only charged with crimes against humanity. Note, however, that the tribunal might have been required to be more explicit about the source of crimes against humanity in the charter had Streicher's counsel raised a retroactivity argument. Some believe there was little or no injustice in convicting persons under the rubric "crimes against humanity" if the acts were also war crimes in the traditional sense. However, some argue that Streicher did not actually aid the murder of Jews in the occupied territory (i.e., that his rantings had no effect on the events of the Holocaust, and thus his execution was in fact unjust).[275] Moreover, it should be noted that the IMT did not have to address the issue whether the laws and customs of war applied to Streicher, who was not a government or military official – though several other courts had no problem finding the laws and customs of war applicable to civilians.[276]

The preceding quotation from the Nuremberg Judgment on crimes against humanity indicates that some of "the inhumane acts charged in the Indictment, and committed after the beginning of the war, did not constitute War Crimes."[277] For these crimes against humanity, the tribunal cited no specific source in law existing during World War II, when the defendants committed their acts. For example, the Gauleiter of Vienna, Baldur von Schirach, was convicted of crimes against humanity, but these were crimes

[272] French version (equally authoritative with English version) of Nuremberg Judgment, quoted and discussed in Donnedieu de Vabres, *supra* note 4, at 526, and in Cassese, *supra* note 124 at 429, 434–35 & n.15.

[273] Nuremberg Charter art. 6(b).

[274] Nuremberg Judgment, 1 IMT, TRIAL at 304.

[275] See Taylor, *supra* note 29, at 264, 562 & 590. Some national systems do not require causation of a crime to convict persons of aiding and abetting, and under these theories, Streicher was an abettor; but this book will not go into the details of aiding and abetting law worldwide.

[276] See *Trial of Bommer*, 9 UNWCC, Law Rep. 62 ([French] Permanent Military Tribunal at Metz, 19 February 1947), and note at 65–66; *Trial of Tesch (The Zyklon B Case)*, 1 UNWCC, Law Rep. 93 (British Military Court, Hamburg, 8 March 1946), and note at 103; *Trial of Klein (Hadamar Trial)*, 1 UNWCC, Law Rep. 46 (U.S. Military Commission, 15 October 1945), and note at 53–54; Notes on *Trial of Weilen*, 11 UNWCC, Law Rep. 31, (Brit. Mil. Ct., Hamburg, Germany, 3 September 1947) and note at 51.

[277] Nuremberg Judgment, 1 IMT, TRIAL at 254–55.

committed against the population of Austria, after the Anschluss made it part of Germany, and principally concerning the deportation of large portions of the population of Austria.[278] Under the traditional view, they could not be war crimes. This is because war crimes could not, at the time, be committed against a nation's own nationals on its own territory. Under the traditional view, he could be guilty only of the crime against humanity of deportation and not the cognate war crime of deportation.[279]

The only source of law given for such crimes is the charter: "they were committed in execution of, or in connection with, the aggressive war, and therefore constituted Crimes Against Humanity"[280] – that is, the acts violated Nuremberg Charter's Article 6(c). The charter, of course, did not exist when von Schirach committed his evil acts. Thus, as to his conviction, the only law that the tribunal appears to claim applied was the ex post facto law of the charter, which could occur only if the charter bound the tribunal, and the rule *nullum crimen, nulla poena sine lege* did not.

There are two possible theories that would make von Schirach's conviction non-retroactive. Because the tribunal saw the annexation of Austria by Germany as illegal under the Treaty of Versailles (and thus a crime against peace under the charter),[281] crimes against the population of Austria should be seen as war crimes against persons in an occupied territory. Telford Taylor, part of the American prosecution team at Nuremberg, believed this was a stretch, however, as the manner in which Austria was annexed did not meet the normal definition of war,[282] and, in fact, the tribunal dated the beginning of World War II from the invasion of Poland, which occurred after the Anschluss.

The second theory was the one advanced by the French prosecutor, François de Menthon, in his opening and by the British prosecutor, Sir Hartley Shawcross, in his closing, that the defendants were charged with acts that were common crimes – violations of general principles of law and of the German Penal Code – at the time committed.[283] The problem is that the Nuremberg Judgment does not directly adopt this theory. The tribunal never explicitly says convicting a person of crimes against humanity would

[278] *Id.* at 318–20.

[279] See *id.*; compare Nuremberg Charter art. 6(c) with *id.* at art. 6(b).

[280] Nuremberg Judgment, 1 IMT, Trial at 254–55.

[281] *Id.* at 217, relying on Treaty of Versailles art. 80.

[282] Taylor, *supra* note 29, at 554, 583. In this he agreed with Steinbauer, counsel for Seyss-Inquart, 19 IMT, Trial at 67–68.

[283] See Chap. 3.b.iii.B, discussing de Menthon, Opening, 3 IMT, Trial at 92, 128, and Shawcross, Closing, 19 IMT, Trial at 433, 448.

be acceptable and non-retroactive because the acts involved were crimes, such as ordinary murders, under national law. However, it never says that it rejects such an argument either. As will be seen subsequently, this argument was applied by tribunals under Control Council Law No. 10 and by other post–World War II courts.[284]

Some of the commentary on Nuremberg attributes the theory of re-characterization of war crimes into crimes against humanity to a number of persons, particularly the French participants. Judge Antonio Cassese, the first President Judge of the International Criminal Tribunal for the Former Yugoslavia, has argued that the French judge Henri Donnedieu de Vabres and the French chief prosecutor François de Menthon believed there were no *nullum crimen* problems concerning crimes against humanity at the main Nuremberg trial, because the crimes against humanity there were also on their facts war crimes.[285] Cassese himself believes that crimes against humanity were newly created at Nuremberg.[286]

To the extent that some or all crimes against humanity from Nuremberg are war crimes by another name, or even crimes under the then-existing German Penal Code, cases have suggested that there is little injustice in convicting defendants for them.[287] This works for one reading of *nullum crimen sine lege*: essentially the view that one may be punished so long as the act for which one is punished was prohibited before it was done (whether the name given to the crime at trial is the same as previously given, or the description of the crime is the same as previously given, or the prescriptive authority is the same), so long as the act charged fits into both the old and the new name and description. This works best for crimes that can be characterized as *malum in se* – evil in themselves. Certainly the atrocities that the Nazis committed fall within that category. To this extent, there was no injustice in holding the defendants accountable for them no matter what the crime's name or what jurisdiction did the accounting. This theory would not convince a firm advocate of the view *nullum crimen sine lege praevia scripta*, that is, that the law under which one has been convicted

[284] See Chap. 3.c.i.

[285] See Cassese, *supra* note 124, at 433–35.

[286] Cassese, *supra* note 124, at 353, 354–55.

[287] See *United States v. Ohlendorff (Einsatzgruppen Case)*, 4 T.W.C., at 485–87. See also *Trial of Rauter*, 14 U.N.W.C.C., Law Rep. 89, 119–20 (Netherlands Special Ct. of Cass. 12 January 1949). Cf. Nuremberg Judgment, 1 IMT, Trial at 254 (discussing inhumane acts in Germany "before the war of 1939" as not "crimes within the meaning of the Charter" because it was not proved that they were done as part of the planning or execution of the conspiracy to commit aggressive war).

must have been written and proclaimed before the act has been committed. It has, however, been adopted, at least as a statement of the law, by modern international criminal tribunals.[288] Arguably, this theory is a step on the intellectual road to universal jurisdiction for these crimes.

Those crimes against humanity that may not be considered war crimes are those acts (e.g., mass killings) against citizens of Germany in Germany, rather than citizens of enemy states or acts committed in occupied territory. Bassiouni finds declaring these to be criminal an acceptable use of the principle of analogy in the interpretation of criminal law, using the principle of ejusdem generis (things of the same kind to be treated similarly).[289] He points out that both the German laws of 1935[290] and the Meiji Constitution of Japan[291] allowed broad applications of analogy. He might have added the Soviet Constitution as well.[292] At the least, Bassiouni is correct that nothing in international law prohibited the use of analogy at the time of Nuremberg. Many critics, of course, deny that crimes can justly be created by analogy after the fact.[293] This view has found expression in the Rome Statute of the International Criminal Court,[294] in other current treaties,[295] and in customary international human rights law.[296]

In terms of both the notice and the arbitrariness goals of the principle of legality, the creation of crimes by analogy is more troubling than taking an act that is already a crime (e.g., deliberate killing as a war crime) and giving it a new criminal name (deliberate killing as a crime against humanity). Creation of crimes by analogy could be seen as raising *ne bis in idem* (here, double punishment) problems for those convicted of both types of crimes (though this is mitigated by the fact that the Nuremberg defendants each received a single sentence for their crimes), and as creating *nulla poena* problems unless it is shown that the re-characterized crime is not given a greater penalty than it could have been given under the law that criminalized the act at the time it was done.

[288] See Chap. 6.a.iv.
[289] Bassiouni, *supra* note 26, at 158–66.
[290] Law of 28 June 1935 Amending the Criminal (Penal) Code § I, published in 1935 Reichgesetzblatt, part I, p. 839 (Germany), translated and reprinted in *Justice Case*, 3 T.W.C. at 176–77, amending German Penal Code, art. 2.
[291] Bassiouni, *supra* note 26, at 160–61, discussing Shigemitsu Dando, Basic Concepts in Temporal and Territorial Limits on the Applicability of the Penal Law of Japan, 9 N.Y. L. Sch. J. Int'l Comp. L. 237 (1988).
[292] USSR Const. (Fundamental Law) (5 December 1936) in Unger at 140.
[293] Cf., e.g., Hall, *supra* note 74, at 172ff.
[294] ICC Statute art. 22(2), discussed in Chap. 6.c.
[295] See Chap. 4.
[296] See Chap. 7.

3.b.iv.D. Summary of the Main Nuremberg Judgment

The Nuremberg Judgment adopted the alternate views that the Charter of the IMT defined substantive crimes and was binding and that the law the charter proclaimed was not ex post facto. Its conclusion that *nullum crimen nulla poena sine lege* was not a limitation of sovereignty, at least in international law, was correct, despite the argument – not wholly without support but with many important exceptions – that it was even at that time a general principle of law.

It held (though many remained unconvinced) that aggressive war was a crime for individuals before World War II. It also stated the view that because the defendants knew that aggressive war was (morally) wrong, there was no injustice in convicting them criminally. It held much more convincingly that traditional war crimes carried individual liability in international law at the time.

As to crimes against humanity, its claim that many of the acts charged were also war crimes was convincing for those acts committed against non-German nationals or committed outside the international boundaries of Germany (at least as recognized before the beginning of the war with Poland in 1939). Whether this is a convincing argument that the law is non-retroactive depends on whether one accepts the proposition that the specific law under which one is convicted must have existed at the time one acted.

As to the crimes against humanity committed against German nationals within Germany, the prosecutors argued that in any case the defendants had committed common crimes. The tribunal did not either expressly accept or reject this proposition.

Even though on these issues the tribunal ruled unanimously, the ambivalence expressed about legality at the London Conference is present in the Nuremberg Judgment. One cannot fairly state that the Nuremberg Judgment as a whole represents the French view at the London Conference. However, those portions of the judgment arguing that the crimes named in the charter were in fact crimes under international law when they were committed are at least consistent with Gros's view that this is a minimum requirement to convict defendants. One might then use common law technique and state that the portions of the judgment that state that the Nuremberg Charter prescribes this same law are obiter dictum. This at least opens up the possibility that the views of Gros are not wholly rejected in the judgment. Of course, the Nuremberg Judgment's version of the history explaining how crimes against peace were not ex post facto rejected the historical views expressed by Gros at the London Conference. Moreover, one can reasonably argue that the crimes against humanity that were not traditional war crimes were criminalized only by the charter: that is, they were applied ex post facto.

3.b.iv.E. Divisions within the Nuremberg Tribunal? Judges Nikitchenko and Donnedieu de Vabres

Notes by the American judge Francis Biddle and his alternate judge John J. Parker indicate that many of the votes on specific issues (including legality), defendants, charges, and sentences that went into the main judgment initially were not unanimous among the four voting judges.[297] This suggests that there was not a true theoretical consensus among the judges participating in the majority judgment, even on the issues concerning which the judgment appears on its face to be unanimous. The opinions, judgments, and criminal sentences of the Nuremberg Tribunal are its juridical acts. International law is based on practice and *opinio juris* – what is actually done and the legal reasons stated for doing it. In fact, one of the arguments of this book is that judgments and opinions of tribunals are practice constitutive of customary international criminal law, even though they are not practice of specific states (the traditional source of practice in international law). In contrast, statements of the judges not in the final text of the judgment may provide insight into the views of the judges on legality, as part of the intellectual history of modern international criminal law. They do not, however, constitute practice of the court, or *opinio juris* of international actors.

The double reliance in the majority judgment on the charter and on customary international law as sources of prescription may well have come from internal disagreements among the judges as to the source of substantive law to be applied. During the deliberations, it appears that Judge I. T. Nikitchenko (Soviet Union) accepted the absolutely binding nature of the charter as to both jurisdiction and the substance of the criminal law, especially against any claim that crimes against peace or conspiracy to wage aggressive war should not be applied to the Nuremberg defendants because they were crimes that had been created ex post facto.[298] This is similar to the views he expressed as the Soviet Union's delegate to the London Conference.[299]

In contrast, it appears that Judge Henri Donnedieu de Vabres (France) argued during the deliberations that the tribunal could, in fact, examine

[297] See note 217.
[298] Taylor, *supra* note 29, at 551, relying on notes of Biddle.
[299] See Chap. 3.b.ii.

whether the crimes listed in the charter were actually crimes under applicable substantive law. It appears that he argued that conspiracy was unknown to continental law (including the German law under which the defendants lived) or international law and therefore would be ex post facto as to these defendants. Therefore, they should not be convicted of such a crime.[300] This is consistent with the lawmaking theory that André Gros advanced on behalf of France at the London Conference, though Gros applied it to the crime of aggressive war rather than to conspiracy.[301] Telford Taylor, a very respected participant in the main Nuremberg Trial, argued that Donnedieu de Vabres opposed the conspiracy count as "incompatible with French criminal procedure."[302] On the evidence that he presents, however, it is fair to conclude that the French judge, whether basing his ex post facto objection on what the defendants would have known about their own law, on international law, or on both, had a genuine substantive law argument that the crime of conspiracy did not exist as to them (or that they would not have had notice concerning conspiracy) and was not merely making a claim about French criminal procedure.[303] In contrast, his endorsement of the substantive crime of aggressive war meant that he accepted that the defendants' acts in fact subjected them to criminal liability at the time done.

After much discussion over the summer of 1945, Donnedieu de Vabres eventually joined the majority judgment that limited the conspiracy charge authorized by the charter to a conspiracy to wage aggressive war (and not a conspiracy to commit war crimes and crimes against humanity). Nikitchenko joined the majority judgment presumably because it contained language that the court was bound by the charter, even though it also discussed grounds for finding crimes against peace, war crimes, and crimes against humanity existed in international law at the time they were committed. The extent to which either or both compromised his principles in joining the Nuremberg Judgment can be left to the reader. The evidence, however, suggests that the final structure of the majority judgment on the issue of ex post facto definitions of crime reflected the fact that the judges held a set of different views rather than that a true consensus had been reached behind a single view of substantive international criminal lawmaking authority.

300 See Taylor, *supra* note 29, at 551, relying on notes of Biddle; Conot, *supra* note 217, at 482 (for view that conspiracy was not part of "international law").

301 See Chap. 3.b.ii.

302 Taylor, *supra* note 29, at 552–53.

303 *Id.* at 551–53. See also Conot, *supra* note 217, at 482.

Donnedieu de Vabres commented on the application of the principle of legality at Nuremberg not long after the trial, using a number of lines of reasoning as to aggressive war. He extended the argument about how the pre–World War II treaties and other documents made aggressive war a crime at the time the Nazi leaders launched World War II. He indicated that the penalty (*sanction pénale*) for the crime of aggressive war might come from the ordinary law of war (i.e., war crimes) at the time.[304]

He admitted that aggressive war belonged to a class of political crimes (*les formes de la déliquance politique*) that is less stable and foreseeable than other crime (*la déliquance de droit commun*).[305] The application of legality of crimes and punishments (*légalité des délits et des peines*) must be applied in this context,[306] but given that context, he argued for the consistency of the judgment with the principle of legality. One of the ways that he did this was to argue that the new order in international law did not begin with the Kellogg-Briand Pact. He took his argument back to the Treaty of Versailles, and particularly the agreement founding the League of Nations.[307] Thus, he gave more importance to the post–World War I prosecutions for war crimes and the failed prosecution of the kaiser than is common today.

In one of his paragraphs on political crimes, Donnedieu de Vabres pointed out that substantive interstate criminal law[308] is "customary law (*un droit coutumier*)," to which the doctrines of legality of crimes and punishments must be applied with "flexibility (*souplesse*)."[309] It is difficult to tell if this was meant to be an independent argument or part of the political crime argument.

However in his discussion of aggressive war as a crime, he also defended the claim of the judgment that *nullum crimen sine lege* does not limit sovereignty.[310] He states that it was unknown to the law of two of the four powers that originally signed the London Agreement, the Soviet Union and Great Britain.[311] The Soviet Union abandoned the principle of legality for many years.[312] Great Britain, however, generally recognized the principle

[304] Donnedieu de Vabres, *supra* note 4, at 497.
[305] *Id.* at 501.
[306] *Id.* at 501–02.
[307] *Id.* at 496.
[308] *Id.* at 484–85 & n.1.
[309] *Id.* at 502.
[310] *Id.* at 503.
[311] *Id.*
[312] See Chap. 2.c.ii.C.

of legality, though in a manner appropriate to a common law jurisdiction that had not yet put all of the major felonies into statutory form.[313] His failure to recognize this is perhaps attributable to the fact that Britain did not have a statutory provision equivalent to the strict civil law version of the principle. This, however, would be odd, considering that he recognized that the principle could be applied with flexibility to customary law. Nonetheless, he recognized the principle of legality of crimes and punishments as a vital principle of justice fundamental to criminal law.[314]

He recognized that war crimes, at least as to the persons who immediately committed the acts, were classical crimes of a much different type than aggressive war. They were neither political crimes nor new crimes, but they had a long history of enforcement. Because a leader who commands the commission of such a crime is its "moral author (*auteur moral*)," Donnedieu de Vabres found no problem with legality of crimes in applying them to the Nazi leaders. This appears to be similar to the notion in common law jurisdictions that persons who incite or command a crime are liable as accomplices or accessories in its commission. Donnedieu de Vabres admitted that penalties were in large measure left to the tribunal but did not find that this violated the principle of legality of punishments, given the flexibility of that doctrine in international law.[315] He could have pointed out that the custom of punishing these crimes with penalties up to death existed in the same way that the crimes existed in customary international law, but he did not. This may be connected to the civil law view that more specificity in limiting the range of available punishments is needed to strictly comply with the doctrine of legality of punishment.

3.c. Legality in Other Postwar Cases (Mostly from Europe)

One famous post–World War II case suggested legality was required in national law by World War II. The *Justice Case* discussed the Nazi laws destroying criminal law legality. They were used as part of the demonstration that the operation of the Nazi justice system during World War II was integral to the crimes against humanity perpetrated by the regime and those participating in it.[316]

[313] See Chap. 2.a.i.

[314] Donnedieu de Vabres, *supra* note 4, at 531.

[315] For the material in this paragraph to this point, see *id.* at 505–512.

[316] Opinion and Judgment of *Justice Case*, 3 T.W.C. at 979, 990–91, 1022, 1082–83 (the anti-legality proclamation "destroyed the feeling of legal security and created an atmosphere of terrorism").

This case is important to the modern recognition that the violation of legality can be a violation of human rights. Nonetheless, it did not repudiate the law of the main Nuremberg Judgment on legality, nor could it have done so. The situation revealed by many of the European postwar cases concerning crimes against humanity, war crimes, and aggressive war is complex and not fully consistent.

3.c.i. *Recognition That an Act Is Criminal under Some Applicable Law When Committed as the Key to Legality of Crimes*

The arguments justifying the legality of crimes against humanity after World War II need some discussion, because they are echoed in some judgments of modern international criminal tribunals. This theory begins with the idea that the doctrine of legality of crimes demands that an act must be criminal under some law applicable to the actor when the act is committed. However, the theory does not necessarily demand the stronger civil law notion that an act be criminal under a particular text of a law that has already been proclaimed at the time of the act (*nullum crimen, nulla poena sine praevia lege scripta*).

Acts that are already crimes under international or national law may, according to this theory, be criminal under a different, retroactively applied name. One might call this theory "retroactive re-characterization" of acts that were criminal under prior law. Retroactive re-characterization has appeared in the rhetoric of international tribunals and Control Council No. 10 courts in two contexts. One is the transformation of some war crimes (already recognized in international law and national military law) into a subset of the new class of international crimes called crimes against humanity, which was seen in the main Nuremberg Judgment. The other is the recognition of acts as customary international crimes that may not have been so when committed but that were criminal either as treaty crimes or crimes under national law at the time committed.

A similar process – re-characterization of international crimes into national crimes – happened in purely national courts as well. French courts allowed conviction of German nationals for violating later-established French law if the acts were violations of the laws of war at the time committed.[317]

[317] *Trial of Wagner*, 3 UNWCC, Law Rep. Case No. 13, p. 23, 43, 45 (French Permanent Military Court, Strasbourg, 3 May 1946, aff'd, Cour de Cassation, 24 July 1946); *id.* at 53–54 (commentary asserting that this was common continental practice with respect

It is very difficult to isolate a category "crimes against humanity" that existed as a juridical concept before the end of World War II. Donnedieu de Vabres, shortly after his service as a Nuremberg judge, pointed out that the main Nuremberg Judgment marked the entry of the concept of crimes against humanity into the judicial arena.[318] Nonetheless, the acts called crimes against humanity committed outside Germany as it existed at the beginning of World War II, and crimes against non-German nationals in Germany (especially those deported to Germany as slaves), were war crimes in international law before World War II.[319] The Nuremberg Judgment itself indicates that the provision in the Nuremberg Charter concerning crimes against humanity largely renamed what were already war crimes under customary international law.[320]

The prosecution at Nuremberg argued that crimes against humanity were also murders and other common crimes as understood in national law.[321] This argument was neither accepted nor rejected explicitly in the Nuremberg Judgment. It was, however, accepted by the U.S. Military Court acting pursuant to Control Council Law No. 10. In the *Einsatzgruppen Case*, the court pointed out: "Murder, torture, enslavement and similar crimes which heretofore were enjoined only by the respective nations now fall within the prescription of the family of nations. Thus murder becomes no less murder because directed against a whole race instead of a single

to war crimes). For further references and later practice, see Jean-Marie Henckaerts & Louise Doswald-Beck, 1 CUSTOMARY INTERNATIONAL HUMANITARIAN LAW (RULES) R. 156 (discussion), p. 572 (Cambridge Univ. Press 2005) (study issued by the International Committee of the Red Cross; also citing similar post–World War II practice of Belgium, similar legislation of France, the Netherlands and Norway, and modern legislation of the Democratic Republic of the Congo); 2(2) *id.* at ¶¶ 521, 523, pp. 3984–85, 3986.

318 Donnedieu de Vabres, *supra* note 4, at 505.

319 Cf. Chap. 3.a. There is controversy as to whether acts committed in Austria and the Sudetenland after annexation by threat of aggression qualify as war crimes under then existing international law. See, e.g., Taylor, *supra* note 29, at 554.

320 See Chap. 3.b.iv.C, discussing Nuremberg Judgment, 1 IMT, TRIAL at 254. See also *Trial of Rauter*, 14 UNWCC, Law Rep., Case No. 88, p. 89, 119–20 (Netherlands Special Ct. of Cass., 12 January 1949). For discussion of this theory, see Chap. 3.b.iii.B, citing A. Cassese, *supra* note 124, at 433–35 (for the proposition that both the French judge Donnedieu de Vabres and original French chief prosecutor François de Menthon at Nuremberg believed that the acts constituting crimes against humanity prosecuted there were war crimes in any event, and therefore there was no *nullum crimen* problem as to them). See also Comment of André Gros, Minutes of Conference Session, 23 July 1945 [Doc. XLIV]; Comment of Gros, Minutes of Conference Session, 24 July 1945 [Doc. XLVII] published in REP. OF JACKSON at 328, 334–35, 360 (during the London Conference that prepared London Agreement and the Nuremberg Charter).

321 See Chap. 3.b.iii.B.

person."[322] The court traced the criminal responsibility of German soldiers for following illegal orders back as far as the Prussian Military Code of 1845.[323] Another of the U.S. Military Court trials indicated that the principle of legality was met where there was a lawful basis for the court to try both a named crime and a crime that existed at the time the defendant acted:

> It is true that this Tribunal can try no defendant merely because of a violation of the German penal code, but it is equally true that the rule against retrospective legislation, as a rule of justice and fair play, should be no defense if the act which he committed in violation of C. C. Law 10 was also known to him to be a punishable crime under his own domestic law.[324]

In the *Einsatzgruppen Case*, the names of the crimes change from murder, torture, or enslavement to the crimes against humanity of murder, torture, and enslavement. Not all murders are crimes against humanity, of course. Additional elements must be met, which have varied through the years in different definitions of crimes against humanity. In the Nuremberg Charter, murder and other crimes must have been committed against a civilian population to qualify as a crime against humanity, and the crime against humanity acts required some connection with another crime within the jurisdiction of the tribunal.[325] Control Council Law No. 10 eliminated the jurisdictional need for a connection between crimes against humanity and aggressive war or another crime under the charter.

That a person be able to recognize the act as criminal under some law applicable to the actor at the time committed is a minimum requirement for the principle of legality. The material elements of the original crime cannot be lessened; thus, the actor is able to recognize the criminality of the act. This is a necessary argument to criminalize, under international law, the barbarities committed by Germans against other Germans in World War II without violating the principle of non-retroactivity of crimes.

[322] *Einsatzgruppen Case*, 4 T.W.C. 411, 497; see also *id.* at 459. This was a case from a U.S. military tribunal whose creation was authorized by an international act (Control Council Law No. 10 of the Allies) of legislation for an occupied state, Germany, applying, as it thought, international criminal law.

[323] *Einsatzgruppen Case*, 4 T.W.C. at 471–72, citing the Prussian Military Code (1845); Saxony Military Penal Code (1857); Bavarian Military Penal Code (1869); Baden Military Penal Code (1870); German Military Penal Code, art. 47 (1872). It also cited the Austro-Hungarian Military Penal Code, art. 158 (1855).

[324] *Justice Case*, 3 T.W.C. 954, 977.

[325] Nuremberg Charter art. 6(c), as amended by October Protocol (changing the semicolon in paragraph c into a comma, at the request of the Soviet Union).

Thus, the non-retroactivity of crimes against humanity committed against Germans in Germany depends on the fact – perhaps a historical accident, perhaps not – that criminal definitions of "murder . . . and similar crimes" were not excised from the German criminal law by the Nazis.[326] The foregoing argument is consistent with the principle that no one may be convicted of a crime for an act that was not criminal when it was committed. This same issue has arisen in more recent years with regard to the question of the applicability of national laws in situations such as the Rwandan genocide and the East German border-guard shootings.[327]

The view that the law against murder and the prohibition of war crimes had not been repealed by the leadership principle (*Führerprinzip*) in German law appears in the *High Command Case.* The German military manuals of the time, including a revision issued during World War II, stated a rule that persons could be criminally liable for implementing orders that were illegal under the law of war, if "'the obeying subordinate knew that the order of the superior concerned an act which aimed at a civil or military crime or offense.'"[328] This quote, was, however, not part of an argument for the re-characterization of national crimes as international crimes, but part of an argument that Control Council Law No. 10 did not itself make law, but punished acts that "then were crimes under international common law."[329]

Even if Control Council Law No. 10 is deemed to be an exercise of German national legislative authority by the occupying powers, and the Control Council Law No. 10 courts are considered domestic courts, the principle of legality would require that crimes against humanity committed by Germans against Germans in Germany under Control Council Law No. 10 must have been crimes under domestic German criminal law when committed. In fact, the occupying powers required this when they promulgated Control

[326] See Paul K. Ryu & Helen Silving, *International Criminal Law: A Search for Meaning*, in 1 A Treatise on International Criminal Law 22, 39 n.23 (M. C. Bassiouni & Ved P. Nanda, eds., 1973).

[327] See Chaps. 4.h (East German border guards), 6.a.i (Rwanda).

[328] United States v. Von Leeb *(High Command Case)*, Opinion and Judgment, 11 T.W.C. 462, 508 (U.S. Military Tribunal V, 27 October 1948) [hereinafter *High Command Case*], quoting from German Military Penal Code (1872), art. 47, and its 1940 revision which changed *civil* to *general* and from an unnamed article of Goebbels, Voelkischer Beobachter, 28 May 1944 (no page given) to the effect that soldiers are not exempt from punishment for acts in violation of international usages of war. Accord, *Einsatzgruppen Case*, 4 T.W.C. at 472.

[329] *High Command Case*, 11 T.W.C. at 508. See also *id.* at 510 (act must be "voluntarily done with knowledge of its inherent criminality under international law").

Council Law No. 11, repealing the Nazi laws destroying the principle of legality, the same day as Law No. 10.[330] Thus, for this part of the legality argument it is irrelevant that Control Council Law No. 10 defines crimes against humanity without regard to their legality in domestic law. It is not, however, irrelevant for the argument of the main Nuremberg Judgment that the laws of the occupying power (e.g., the Nuremberg Charter and hence Control Council Law No. 10) control without any reference to legality and non-retroactivity.

The argument that a crime may be retroactively re-characterized from a national crime to an international crime did not meet with total acceptance. Subsequent British trials of German nationals addressed only war crimes, not crimes against humanity,[331] which indicates some doubt about this doctrine. The royal warrant creating British military courts with jurisdiction over "violations of the laws and customs of war" (but not crimes against humanity) was dated 14 June 1945, before the adoption of the London Charter.[332] Moreover, the text of Control Council Law No. 10 was not based upon this theory. It explicitly allowed prosecutions for crimes against humanity "whether or not in violation of the domestic laws of the country where perpetrated."[333]

Retroactive re-characterization has had some success in the modern period. It has been adopted as doctrine in various modern international criminal tribunals.[334]

3.c.ii. *Against Legality: Retroactive Criminalization of Moral Wrongs and Non-Criminal Legal Violations*

The difference between retroactive re-characterization of a national crime as a crime against humanity and the retroactive change of aggressive war from a state delict or moral wrong to a crime carrying individual responsibility in the main Nuremberg Judgment is apparent today.[335] It was not

[330] Control Council Law No. 11, Official Gazette of the Control Council for Germany, No. 3 (Berlin, 31 January 1946). See also Allied Control Council Law No. 3, and Military Order No. 1 issued in pursuance of it, discussed in Boot at 87.

[331] See Bassiouni, *supra* note 26, at 531–32, 533–34.

[332] [U.K.] Royal Warrant of 14 June 1945, quoted and discussed in British Law Concerning Trials of War Criminals by Military Courts, 1 UNWCC, Law Rep. 105 (Annex I).

[333] Control Council Law No. 10, art. II(1)(c); accord, IMTFE Charter art. 5(c).

[334] See, e.g., *Prosecutor v. Hadzihasanovic*, Judgment ¶ 34 (ICTY App. Ch., 16 July 2003); *Prosecutor v. Norman*, Judgment (SCSL App. Ch., 31 May 2004), discussed in Chap. 6.a.i.

[335] See Nuremberg Judgment, 1 IMT, TRIAL at 216–18, 219–24. Accord, *Justice Case.*

quite as obvious to the British prosecutor Sir Hartley Shawcross at the main Nuremberg trial. He argued on closing that there was "no difference between illegality and criminality" in the breaches of the law beginning World War II.[336] This line of thought continued into some later cases from the British Zone of Occupation.

According to Judge Antonio Cassese's reading, some German Supreme Court cases from the British Zone of Occupation allow retroactive punishment of crimes against humanity, so long as the acts were contrary to "the moral law (*Sittengesetz*)."[337] The German Court saw the retroactive creation of crimes against humanity as "not entail[ing] any violation of legal security (*Rechtssicherheit*) but rather the re-establishment of its basis and presuppositions."[338] It is fascinating that these cases come from the British Zone because the British themselves refused to prosecute charges of crimes against humanity, presumably because of concerns for retrospectivity.[339]

This argument has justly been ignored in most of the more recent national and international tribunals.[340] It is inconsistent with the core of the principle of legality in criminal law: the act must have been criminal at the time committed.

3.c.iii. *Retrospective Expansion of Jurisdiction in the Post–World War II National Courts*

Some post–World War II national laws gave national courts the authority to punish crimes committed in World War II, so long as the acts alleged were crimes under international law at the time committed. This type of

[336] Shawcross, Closing, 19 IMT, TRIAL at 472.

[337] Cassese, *supra* note 124, at 433 n.11, quoting from Judgment of 4 May 1948, *Case against Bl.*, 1 ENTSCHEIDUNGEN DES OBERSTEN GERICHTSHOFES FÜR DIE BRITISCHE ZONE IN STRAFSACHEN 5 (Berlin, 1950) (translated by Cassese). For the point that crimes against humanity could be punished retroactively, Cassese also cites Judgment of 21 March 1950, *Case against M.*, 2 *id.* 378, 380–81.

[338] Cassese, *supra* note 124, at 433 n.11, quoting from Judgment of 4 May 1948, *Case against Bl.*, 1 ENTSCHEIDUNGEN DES OBERSTEN GERICHTSHOFES FÜR DIE BRITISCHE ZONE IN STRAFSACHEN 5 (Berlin, 1950) (translated by Cassese).

[339] Bassiouni, *supra* note 26, at 531–32, 533–34; [U.K.] Royal Warrant of 14 June 1945, quoted and discussed in British Law Concerning Trials of War Criminals by Military Courts, 1 UNWCC, Law Rep. 105 (Annex I).

[340] But see Polyukovich v. Australia (Australia High Court, 14 August 1991), Opinion of Dawson, J., ¶ 18, quoted in Ward N. Ferdinandusse, DIRECT APPLICATION OF INTERNATIONAL CRIMINAL LAW IN NATIONAL COURTS 227 n.1337 (TMC Asser 2006).

law was enacted and applied in Norway[341] and France.[342] Arguably, this also happened in the United States.[343]

Much later, this occurred again in Israel (a jurisdiction that did not exist at the time of the crimes)[344] and France.[345] Under this theory, trials were held in Canada and Australia.[346] The United States extradited a person to Israel on this basis; he was eventually acquitted.[347]

Of course, everything in this argument depends on the correctness of the conclusion that the Nazi war crimes and crimes against humanity were crimes when committed, under either international or national law. This proposition is controversial with respect to the crimes against humanity, unless one accepts the proposition that one can retroactively re-characterize war crimes and crimes under national law as crimes against humanity, as discussed previously.[348]

3.c.iv. *Members of Criminal Organizations in the Nuremberg Charter and Control Council Law No. 10: Retroactivity and Collective Punishment*

There is one part of the postwar proceedings that involves two issues of legality: first, non-retroactivity and, second, the requirement that an individual be somehow involved in a crime before conviction. The Nuremberg Charter allowed the IMT to declare certain organizations to have been

[341] *Trial of Klinge*, 3 UNWCC, Law Rep., Case No. 11, p. 1, 2, 3, 6, 10 & 11 (Supreme Court of Norway, 27 February 1946) (but there were dissents on this issue); see also Annex 1, *id.* at 81 (discussing Norwegian statutes).

[342] *Trial of Wagner*, 3 UNWCC, Law Rep. Case No. 13, p. 23, 43, 45 (French Permanent Military Court, Strasbourg, 3 May 1946, aff'd, Cour de Cassation, 24 July 1946); *id.* at 53–54 (commentary asserting that this was common continental practice with respect to war crimes).

[343] See *Ex parte* Yamashita, 327 U.S. 1 (1946) (military commission formed under different rules from prior military commissions).

[344] Eichmann v. Attorney-General, [1962] 16 Piske Din 2033 (Israel, Sup. Ct., 29 May 1962), reprinted in 36 Int'l L. Rep. 277 (1968), *affirming* 45 Pesakim Mehoziim 3 (Jerusalem Dist. Ct., 11 December 1961), reprinted in 36 Int'l L. Rep. 18, which discussed Judgment of S. Fed. Trib. (Germany), 29 January 1952, 1 St/R 563/51, BGH 562 234, and Law of July 10, 1947, art. 27A (Netherlands) (giving Netherlands courts jurisdiction over war crimes or crimes against humanity as defined at Nuremberg).

[345] See *Matter of Barbie*, 78 ILR 125 (France, Cour de Cassation, 6 October 1983 & 26 January 1984).

[346] Regina v. Finta, 104 ILR 285 (Canada, Sup. Ct., 24 March 1994); *Polyukovich*.

[347] Demanjuk v. Petrovsky, 776 F.2d 571 (6th Cir. 1985), cert. denied, 475 U.S. 1016 (1986) (approving an extradition to Israel on the basis of the Israeli statute applied in *Eichmann*); Demanjuk was acquitted on appeal in the Supreme Court of Israel, on the factual ground that his identity as the concentration camp guard known as "Ivan the Terrible" had not been sufficiently proved.

[348] See Chap. 3.c.i.

illegal.[349] In subsequent proceedings, members of the organizations could not challenge that finding.[350] More important, for our purposes, the charter authorized the criminalization of membership in such an organization,[351] and Control Council Law No. 10 implemented the authorization:

> Each of the following acts is recognized as a crime: . . .
>
> (d) Membership in categories of a criminal group or organization declared criminal by the International Military Tribunal.[352]

The available penalties for this crime included death, imprisonment (with or without hard labor), a fine, forfeiture of property, and restitution.[353]

The concept of group criminality was certainly recognized by the laws of many states, including Germany and the four Allied powers that created the London Agreement and Nuremberg Charter.[354] However, the charter and Control Council Law No. 10 did not require actual participation in, knowledge of, or agreement to support the crimes of the organization before conviction of the crime of membership. It is difficult to see how mere membership in one of the organizations that was part of running Germany was illegal in either German or international law before or during World War II.

This law carried with it the danger both of imposition of retroactive criminal liability and of collective punishment of persons not implicated in specific crimes of the organization. The retroactivity of this portion of postwar law has not been widely commented on. Individual criminal responsibility is another matter.

The Nuremberg Tribunal attempted in its judgment to limit at least the imposition of collective punishment. First, it limited the size and character of the criminal organizations declared guilty. For example, in its decision on the Gestapo (*Die Geheime Staatspolizei*) and the SD (*Der Sicherheitsdienst des Reichsführer SS*) as criminal organizations:

> The Tribunal declares to be criminal within the meaning of the Charter the group composed of those members of the Gestapo and SD holding

[349] Nuremberg Charter art. 9.

[350] *Id.* at art. 10.

[351] *Id.* ("In cases where a group or organization is declared criminal by the Tribunal, the competent national authority of any Signatory shall have the right to bring individuals to trial for membership therein before national, military, or occupation courts.")

[352] Control Council Law No. 10, art. II(1)(d).

[353] *Id.* at art. II(3).

[354] A summary of group criminality in the law of Germany and the four Allies before World War II is contained in [Zivkovic], Notes on the Case [*Trial of Greifelt*], 13 UNWCC, Law Rep., Case No. 73, pp. 1, 36, 42 & 46–47.

> [positions relevant to the commission of War Crimes and Crimes against Humanity by the organizations] who became or remained members of the organization with knowledge that it was being used for the commission of acts declared criminal by Article 6 of the Charter, or who were personally implicated as members of the organization in the commission of such crimes.[355]

The tribunal included similar language limiting the scope of the groups in its rulings declaring the Leadership Corps of the Nazi Party,[356] and the SS (*Die Schutzstaffeln der Nationalsozialistischen Deutschen Arbeiterpartei*)[357] to have been criminal. The tribunal said as to all its declarations of organizational criminality, "Membership alone is not enough to come within the scope of these declarations" and warned that the criminalization of mere group membership "may produce great injustice."[358]

The tribunal also made recommendations concerning how other courts should treat its finding that an organization was criminal. It recommended that Control Council Law No. 10 be amended to limit penalties for membership in these organizations to those authorized under separate denazification laws, that in any case penalties not exceed those under the denazification laws, that individuals not be convicted under both laws, and that the courts of all four zones of occupation in Germany adopt similar sentencing policies.[359]

These recommendations were never enacted into textual law by the Four Powers. The U.S. military tribunals attempted to implement the requirement that persons must have knowledge of criminal acts or have participated in them before conviction.[360] On the basis of current research, the author cannot say that the IMT's limitation on who might be convicted of membership in a criminal organization was fully implemented by all countries that adhered to the London Agreement and Nuremberg Charter.

[355] Nuremberg Judgment, 1 IMT, TRIAL at 267–68.

[356] Nuremberg Judgment, 1 IMT, TRIAL at 261–62.

[357] *Id.* at 273.

[358] *Id.* at 256. Although I was not born until 1951, I understand something of the desire for collective punishment arising from World War II. I remember wondering as a child why all of the Nazis had not been put in jail.

[359] Nuremberg Judgment, 1 IMT, TRIAL at 256–57.

[360] See, e.g., United States v. Brandt *(Medical case)*, Judgment, 2 T.W.C. 171 (U.S.M.T. I, 20 August 1947) (nine persons actually implicated in crimes; one convicted of membership in SS with knowledge of its criminal activity). Five cases in front of U.S. military tribunals and three in front of U.S. general military government courts are discussed in [Zivkovic], Notes on the Case [*Trial of Greifelt*], 13 U.N.W.C.C., Law Rep., Case No. 73, pp. 55–67.

3.d. LEGALITY IN THE IMTFE (TOKYO TRIBUNAL): DISSENSUS REVEALED

The justices of the International Military Tribunal for the Far East (IMTFE or Tokyo Tribunal) did not reach a consensus on their views of legality and non-retroactivity. Their opinions reveal deep splits in the court on legality.

The IMTFE Judgment and the separate opinions have had far less influence on the political imagination and criminal law practice of the world than has the Nuremberg Judgment. Partly this is because it came second and drew some of its most important legal conclusions from Nuremberg. Partly, it is because the IMTFE Judgment and separate opinions simply were not published and circulated as widely as the Nuremberg Judgment.[361] Partly it is because some who have studied the two tribunals assert that the Nuremberg proceedings were, despite problems, essentially fair; but the Tokyo proceedings, despite some virtues, were essentially unfair.[362] Yet only in the IMTFE did one openly see expressed in judicial opinions very deep divisions about the nature of legality in international criminal law, and arguments that most or all of the defendants should be acquitted or should have lesser sentences. These were matters that were present in the discussions of war crimes and war criminals from the European theater but were not expressed in the Nuremberg Judgment or in the one separate opinion in that case.

The majority judgment and separate opinions raise questions about legality that turned out to be of great importance to the development of international criminal law and international criminal tribunals. These opinions did not themselves direct the future course of debate on these issues the way the Nuremberg Judgment did. Yet the dissensus they reveal about legality at the beginning of the modern era of international criminal law had important consequences for the future.

3.d.i. *The IMTFE Charter*

There is one significant difference between the creation of the Nuremberg Tribunal and the IMTFE. The IMTFE was not created by an explicit international agreement, negotiated between states, such as the London Agreement. Instead, the Supreme Allied Commander for the Far East, General Douglas

361 See R. John Pritchard, *The International Military Tribunal for the Far East and the Allied National War Crimes* Trials in Asia, in 3 Bassiouni, ed., *supra* note 270, at 109, 127–28.

362 See, e.g., Bassiouni, *supra* note 26, at 22; RICHARD H. MINEAR, VICTOR'S JUSTICE: THE TOKYO WAR CRIMES TRIAL (Princeton Univ. Press 1971).

MacArthur, created it by special proclamation.[363] The proclamation was based on the authority to implement the terms of surrender, granted to the supreme commander for the Allied powers in the Instrument of Surrender signed by Japan.[364] The surrender document authorized implementation of the Potsdam Declaration, which stated among other things, "stern justice shall be meted out to all war criminals, including those who have visited cruelties upon our prisoners."[365] In the instrument of surrender, the Allied powers were referred to as the three original signatories of the Potsdam Declaration, the United States, China, and Great Britain, as well as the Soviet Union, which later adhered to the declaration. The instrument of surrender was also signed by other Allies: Australia, Canada, France, the Netherlands, and New Zealand.[366] The nine Allied signatories were thus the Nuremberg Four (France, the Soviet Union, the United Kingdom, and the United States), a major victim of Japanese aggression and the fifth of the permanent members of the new United Nations Security Council (China), the

[363] Special Proclamation by the Supreme Commander of the Allied Powers, Establishment of an International Military Tribunal for the Far East (19 January 1946), reprinted as Annex A-4 of the Judgment of 1 November 1948, United States v. Araki, 104 IMTFE Records, with Tokyo Charter (amended 26 April 1946).

[364] Japanese Instrument of Surrender ¶¶ 1 (naming the Allied Powers) & 8 (authorizing "the supreme commander for the Allied Powers... [to] take such steps as he deems proper to effectuate these terms of surrender"), 2 September 1945 [hereinafter Instrument of Surrender], reprinted as Annex A-2 of the Judgment, 104 IMTFE Records at 11.

[365] Instrument of Surrender ¶ 6 (Japan agrees to "carry out the provisions of the Potsdam declaration in good faith, and to issue whatever orders and take whatever action may be required by the supreme commander for the Allied Powers"), referring to Potsdam Declaration of United States, United Kingdom, and China, 26 July 1945 [hereinafter Potsdam Declaration] as Annex A-1 of the Judgment, 104 IMTFE Records at 1. Thus, the Potsdam Declaration was taken into treaty law through the instrument of surrender, and its directions gained legal status, whatever weight it might have been given before. Cf. Weston et al., *supra* note 63, at 172 (describing Potsdam and other major power declarations during and just after World War II as "presumptively non-legal intergovernmental declarations outside the framework of an international organization... [that] settle disputes and chart the course for future relations"), discussing Schachter, *supra* note 63, at 129-30 (describing these declarations as "official State acts" from which "it is appropriate to draw inferences that the States concerned have recognized the principles, rules, status and rights acknowledged"). Compare Chap. 3.b.ii, text at n. 63 on legal status of Moscow Declaration of 1943. See also Madeline Morris, *High Crimes and Misconceptions: The ICC and Non-Party States*, 64 Law & Contemp. Probs. 13, 37–38 (2001). The proclamation also implemented a later agreement among the Soviet Union, the United Kingdom, and the United States. Instrument of Surrender, 104 IMTFE Records at 11; Moscow Conference Agreement §5 (26 December 1945), reprinted as Annex A-3 of the Judgment, 104 IMTFE Records at 15.

[366] Instrument of Surrender. For some reason, Australia was omitted as a signatory in the typed copy in 104 IMTFE Records.

Western colonial power in what became Indonesia (the Netherlands), and three British dominions (Australia, Canada, and New Zealand).

The IMTFE judiciary was a larger body than that of the Nuremberg Tribunal. The IMTFE Charter, as amended, included participation by judges from eleven nations.[367] The justices of the IMTFE came from nine Allied signers of the instrument of surrender and one colonial possession from each of the United Kingdom and the United States, respectively, that had not gained full independence at the time the IMTFE was formed: India and the Philippines. Both India and the Philippines were at the time gaining international legal personality. India had been a member of the League of Nations but was not yet fully independent when the IMTFE Charter was amended. India and the Philippines both became members of the Far Eastern Commission of the Allies, planning for the postwar period, and the committee on war criminality of that commission decided that all members of the commission should be represented on the IMTFE.[368]

The President Justice of the IMTFE was not from one of the Nuremberg Four, but from Australia. Five justices wrote separate opinions. Most of the separate opinions were written by the justices from nations other than the Nuremberg Four, but one, sharply raising the issue of preexisting natural law as the basis for international criminal law, was by the French justice.

For purposes of examining the legality issues, the IMTFE Charter text was nearly identical to the Nuremberg Charter. It contained the same ambiguity about whether the section setting out crimes was merely jurisdictional or contained definitions of crimes that bound the tribunal regardless of whether they were international law crimes at the time the relevant acts were committed.[369] The crimes were defined in similar ways as well.[370]

[367] Amendment to IMTFE Charter, 26 April 1946, 4 Bevans 20.

[368] Amendment to IMTFE Charter; see Arnold C. Brackman, The Other Nuremberg 69 (1987); Elizabeth S. Kopelman, *Ideology and International Law: The Dissent of the Indian Justice at the Tokyo War Crimes Trial*, 23 NYU J. Int'l L. & Politics 373, 383–84 n.34 (1991). By the time of the IMTFE Judgment, both the Philippines and India had become independent.

[369] Compare Nuremberg Charter art. 6 *chapeau* (quoted in Chap. 3.b.ii.A, n.98) with IMTFE Charter art. 5 *chapeau* (quoted in 104 IMTFE Records 19, 21):

> *Jurisdiction Over Persons and Offenses.* The Tribunal shall have the power to try and punish Far Eastern war criminals who as individual or as members of organizations are charged with offenses which include Crimes Against Peace.
>
> The following acts, or any of them, are crimes coming within the jurisdiction of the Tribunal for which there shall be individual criminal responsibility:...

[370] Compare Nuremberg Charter art. 6 (quoted in Chap. 3.b.ii.A, n.98) with IMTFE Charter art. 5 (quoted in 104 IMTFE Records at 21–22).

3.d.ii. *The Majority IMTFE Judgment: Based in Existing International Law?*

Unlike the Nuremberg Tribunal, the IMTFE did not produce a judgment that was unanimous as to any defendant or any crime. On issues of whether IMTFE Charter crimes were ex post facto as to the defendants, there were deep and fundamental divisions among tribunal members. President Justice William Webb of Australia, who also wrote a separate opinion, read the majority judgment in open court from 4 November to 12 November 1948.[371] The judgment covers about 1,200 pages in the typescript record, not including annexes or separate opinions, which were not read in open court.[372]

The majority judgment of the Tokyo Tribunal concurred with the Nuremberg Judgment on the legality issue. It expressly disavowed a wish to revisit issues such as the prior existence of the crime of waging aggressive war, the prior existence of individual criminal liability in international law generally, the application of the *nullum crimen* principle to international criminal proceedings, and the existence of the defense of superior orders.[373] Thus, the majority judgment displays, at least on its surface, the same dual structure as the Nuremberg Judgment, arguing both that the charter of the IMTFE is binding and that, in fact, the law of the charter reflects international law at the time of World War II.

However, the majority judgment rejected the most sweeping view of the claim that "the law of the Charter is decisive and binding on the Tribunal."[374] Its language questioned whether the extreme view that the victors have unlimited criminal lawmaking authority, including the right of retroactive legislation, had ever really been advanced:

> The foregoing expression of opinion [that the Charter is binding] is not to be taken as supporting the view, if such view be held, that the Allied Powers or any victor nations have the right under international law in providing for

[371] R. John Pritchard, *The International Military Tribunal for the Far East and the Allied National War Crimes Trials in Asia*, in 3 Bassiouni, *supra* note 270, at 124–25; Kopelman, *supra* note 368, at 377.

[372] 101 IMTFE Records 48415. In this edition, using the original typescript pagination, the pages are numbered consecutively through the main judgment, but in different ways for the annexes and separate opinions, which were "regarded as part of the proceedings" but not read in open court. See R. John Pritchard, *supra* note 371 at 126. The statement in Kopelman, *supra* note 368, at 378, that the separate opinions were not made part of the record appears to be an overstatement of what was genuine hostility to the dissenting views.

[373] 101 IMTFE Records at 48437–39.

[374] *Id.* at 48435.

> the trial and punishment of war criminals to enact or promulgate laws or vest in their tribunals powers in conflict with recognized international law or rules or principles thereof. In the exercise of their right to create tribunals for such a purpose [i.e., for the trial and punishment of war criminals] and in conferring powers on such tribunals[,] belligerent powers may act only within the limits of international law.[375]

This appears to require that international law be examined to determine the substantive criminal law. However, the arguments contained in the judgment that crimes against peace (conspiracy), aggressive war, and crimes against humanity existed at the time of the Pacific portion of World War II are subject to criticisms similar to those leveled at the Nuremberg Judgment.

Justice Bernard of France found the two views expressed on the binding nature of the charter in the main IMTFE Judgment to be inconsistent. They express an ambiguity of attitude of the majority concerning the ability of the tribunal to examine the facts and the law.[376] This ambiguity did not need to be resolved by the majority judgment, but only because the majority followed the Nuremberg Tribunal decision that the crimes set out in the charter were consistent with international law (a conclusion that was unanimous in the Nuremberg Judgment but that was not unanimous in the IMTFE or the court of scholarly opinion).

3.d.iii. *The Separate IMTFE Opinions*

The separate opinions presented diverse views on the issue of legality. These included views that some of the convictions at Tokyo violated the principle of legality. The opinions disagreed on whether this violation was acceptable.

3.d.iii.A. Justice Jaranilla (Philippines): Retroactivity Permissible in International Criminal Law

Justice Delfin Jaranilla of the Philippines argued that *nullum crimen sine lege, nulla poena sine lege* may be a general principle of criminal law in domestic systems but does not apply to international law. He was less apologetic about this fact than many: "Apart from specific agreements as to fundamental rights of man, which international law sets out to secure, the permanence of the [international] community depends on such variable standards that the

[375] *Id.* at 48436.

[376] Dissenting Opinion of Bernard, 104 IMTFE Records at 8–9, discussed in Chap. 3.d.iii.D.

corresponding acts of violation cannot be predetermined."[377] This, along with a very different argument by Justice Bernard Victor Aloysius Röling,[378] seems to be the closest that any of the Nuremberg or Tokyo judges came to explicit rejection of Jerome Hall's view, "A plausible rationalization of deliberate retroactivity [in criminal law] cannot be made."[379] At the time of World War II, there were no general international treaties protecting individuals from retroactive criminal punishment as a fundamental right.

3.d.iii.B. President Webb (Australia): Retroactivity May Be Permissible

The President of the IMTFE, William Webb, of Australia, questioned the non-retroactivity of one part of the substantive law of the charter, admitting that "aggressive war was not universally regarded as a justiciable crime" at the beginning of the Pacific war.[380] He noted that even after the war, some international lawyers remained unconvinced that the Pact of Paris changed that.[381] It is not clear here whether he was referring only to sufficient acceptance to make aggressive war a customary international crime or whether he was also looking to the fact that most national systems did not make it a crime. In either case, however, he would be correct. Moreover, he suggests that the Nuremberg judges knew this and that this explains why five Nuremberg defendants convicted of conspiracy to make aggressive war were spared the death penalty.[382] Yet he did not dissent from the convictions of the defendants for this crime. He thus admitted that retroactive conviction for aggressive war as an individual crime under international law was acceptable, except that by itself it would not authorize imposition of the death penalty.

3.d.iii.C. Justice Röling (Netherlands): Retroactivity Permissible in International Criminal Law as Alternative to "Political" Disposition; *Nullum Crimen* Not a Principle of Justice

Justice Bernard Victor Aloysius Röling, of the Netherlands, made the remarkable statement set out in the Introduction:

[377] Separate Opinion of Jaranilla at 18–19, 105 IMTFE RECORDS, relying on Jorge Americano, NEW FOUNDATIONS OF INTERNATIONAL LAW 38–39 (Macmillan 1947).
[378] Separate Opinion of Röling, at 47, 109 IMTFE RECORDS.
[379] Hall, *supra* note 74.
[380] Separate Opinion of Webb, President, at 17, 109 IMTFE RECORDS.
[381] *Id.*
[382] *Id.* at 16.

> If the principle of "nullum crimen sine praevia lege" were a principle of *justice*, . . . the Tribunal would be bound to exclude for that very reason every crime created in the Charter ex post facto, it being the first duty of the Tribunal to mete out justice. However, this maxim is not a principle of justice but a rule of policy, valid only if expressly adopted, so as to protect citizens against arbitrariness of courts (nullum crimen, nulla poena sine lege), as well as against arbitrariness of legislators (nulla crimen, nulla poena sine praevia lege).[383]

Here, "a principle of justice" sounds like a command of natural law rather than one of a set of positive rules. Yet one must be very careful. Even when he spoke about the duty of a tribunal to do justice, he appeared to look to positive law to determine what justice is. He stated that the task of the tribunal to "*to do justice*, be it stern justice" came from the duty of the tribunal under the Potsdam Declaration, and hence the IMTFE Proclamation and Charter.[384] The duty of tribunal to do justice was a positive legal direction to the tribunal to examine the international law criminality of acts. Justice Röling indicated that meting out justice in cases before the tribunal means at least "considering the question whether or not the crimes mentioned in the [Nuremberg and IMTFE] Charters were crimes according to international law."[385] Given that *nullum crimen* is not a principle of justice, it is not to be applied unless it appears in positive law.

He also developed a rather unusual argument to show that the international law offense of the crime against peace (i.e., aggressive war) was legally created by the Nuremberg and Tokyo charters, though he admits that they were created ex post facto. One might call his method a judicializing, not to mention a civilizing, of the political practice of dealing with dangerous leaders of defeated forces.

Justice Röling examined essentially the same history as the Nuremberg Judgment and found that international law, as manifested through treaties and state practice, did not make crimes against peace, or the planning or waging of aggressive war, a crime for which there was individual liability as of 1939, or even 1943.[386] Given his insistence that the tribunal could not apply charter crimes where not authorized to do so by international law, he could have ended the matter with a rejection of these crimes. However, he did not.

[383] Separate Opinion of Röling, at 44–45, 109 IMTFE Records (italics substituted for underlining in typewritten original).

[384] *Id.* at 7, 109 IMTFE Records, quoting from Potsdam Declaration.

[385] Separate Opinion of Röling, at 4–5, 109 IMTFE Records.

[386] *Id.* at 11–44.

Justice Röling argued that *crime* has different meanings in international law, and it in fact has different meanings in domestic law as well.[387] One of the key differences he saw is between ordinary crimes and crimes analogous to political crimes under domestic law, "where the decisive element is the danger rather than the guilt."[388] He argued that the crime against peace of aggressive war is a crime of the political type, creating danger to the international community. In contrast, crimes of guilt are "morally and legally condemned in all civilized nations" and include war crimes such as "the torture of prisoners of war."[389]

The Tokyo and Nuremberg trials were "the first at which aggression-as-a-crime is at stake."[390] Long before World War II, however,

> powers victorious in a "bellum justum," and as such responsible for peace and order thereafter, have, according to international law, the right to counteract elements constituting a threat to the newly established order, and are entitled, as a means of preventing the recurrence of gravely offensive conduct, to seek and retain custody of the pertinent persons. Napoleon's elimination [by captivity and exile] offers a precedent.[391]

Justice Röling read the Treaty of Versailles provision concerning the kaiser similarly. He emphasized the facts that the treaty sought to arraign the kaiser not for "crime" but for "a supreme offence against international morality and the sanctity of treaties"; the court to try the kaiser would not be guided by "justice" but "by the highest motives of international policy"; and the Allies' request to the Netherlands for his extradition stated that "their demands . . . contemplate, not a juridical accusation, but an act of high international policy."[392]

According to Justice Röling, "[m]ere political action, based on the responsibilities of power" was an acceptable means under international law for eliminating dangerous defeated war leaders from society. This is why it was just to create the new crimes against peace: "That the judicial way was chosen to select those who were in fact the planners, instigators and wagers of Japanese aggression is a novelty which cannot be regarded as a violation of international law in that it affords the vanquished more guarantees than

[387] *Id.* at 10, 48.
[388] *Id.* at 48.
[389] *Id.* at 10.
[390] *Id.* at 50.
[391] *Id.* at 46. The source of the definition of *bellum justum* in natural or positive law is not clear here.
[392] *Id.* at 13, quoting from Treaty of Versailles art. 227 and Demand of Allied Powers to the Netherlands for Extradition of the Kaiser.

mere political action could do."[393] Here is a justification, by example, for the claim that *nullum crimen* is not a principle of justice in all cases, and another argument against Jerome Hall that perhaps a justification of deliberate retroactivity can be made, at least in very limited circumstances.[394]

Or perhaps Justice Röling was arguing that this result is consistent with the principle of legality. In the rare case when vengeance for a given act (e.g., starting an aggressive war) is lawful, then the principle of legality is not offended by making that act a crime, even after the act is committed. Civilization of a penalty, from vengeance to the sentence of a court of justice, is not a violation of legality, because the penalty has merely been mitigated, or at least regularized.

Like President Webb, Justice Röling questioned issuing a death sentence to one convicted only of these newly created crimes, because "the punishment should only be determined by considerations of security" (i.e., not punishment for guilt). He also pointed out that the Nuremberg defendants who were convicted of crimes against peace without also being convicted of major participation in conventional war crimes were spared the death penalty.[395] He looked at state practice but certainly omitted many examples over the centuries of death being handed out to the leaders of defeated armies and, in modern times, to those accused of what he calls "political" crimes, such as treason and sedition in national courts.

3.d.iii.D. Justice Bernard (France): Natural Law Is Not Retroactive Law

Justice Henri Bernard of France wrote a dissenting opinion.[396] In the course of the opinion, he defended the IMTFE Charter against allegations that the

[393] *Id.* at 47. See also *id.* at 45:

> Positive international law, as existing at this moment, compels us to interpret the "crimes against peace" as mentioned in the Charter, in [this] special way. It may be presupposed that the Allied nations did not intend to create rules in violation of international law.... This indicates that the Charter should be interpreted so that it is in accordance with International Law.

Cf. Glueck, *supra* note 215, at 83 (claiming that the Nazi leaders "knew that they could be executed for their deeds without being granted the privilege of trial at all" and thus they should not be heard to complain that the interpretation of international law which made their act a crime "involve[d] retroactivity"). Glueck's work preceded the IMTFE Judgment and even the Nuremberg Judgment (see Glueck at 101–02), but it is not clear if it was a source for Justice Röling.

[394] Compare Separate Opinion of Jaranilla, at 14, 105 IMTFE Records.

[395] Separate Opinion of Röling, at 47–49, 109 IMTFE Records, citing the cases of Hess, Dönitz, Raeder, Funk, and von Neurath in the main Nuremberg Judgment, 1 IMT, Trial at 365-67 (sentences).

[396] This opinion appears in 105 IMTFE Records and dissents on grounds that the procedure of the trial was essentially unfair. The opinion is printed in English, even though the

law proclaimed therein was ex post facto, using a natural law and internationalist approach unique among the justices. Justice Bernard's view of the substantive criminal law to be applied by the IMTFE was internationalist:

> The crimes committed against the peoples of a particular nation are also crimes committed against members of the universal community. Thus, the de facto authority [here, the Supreme Commander of the Allied Powers] which can organize the trial of crimes against peace and against humanity can, if it finds it opportune, prosecute for crimes against peoples of particular nations along with them. The law to be applied in such cases, however, will not then be of a particular nation, the victor or the defeated, but will be that of all nations.[397]

In other words, there was no problem with the retrospective creation of the IMTFE, so long as it applied international law.

Justice Bernard's opinion was also based in natural law, as shown in this passage on crimes against peace:

> There is no doubt in my mind that such a[n aggressive] war is and always has been a crime in the eyes of reason and universal conscience, – expressions of natural law upon which an international tribunal can and must base itself to judge the conduct of the accused tendered to it.[398]

Natural law existing before World War II, rather than the charter, defined these crimes: "It is because they are inscribed in natural law and not in the constitutive acts of the Tribunal by the writers of the Charter, whose honor it is, however, to have recalled them, that those principles [of individual responsibility] impose themselves upon the respect of the Tribunal."[399]

Natural law provides the basis for "the rejection of the objections of the Defense based upon the principle 'nullum crimen sine lege,' [and] upon the principle of the non-retroactivity of laws."[400] Many Nuremberg and Tokyo judges and commentators have puzzled over how to argue that rules of international law that bind states can be transformed to create individual criminal responsibility. Justice Bernard saw matters the other way. Because the crimes of the charter are "inscribed in natural law," there was individual criminal responsibility for them.[401] The fact that international custom has

defense objected that Justice Bernard did not speak either of the official languages of the IMTFE, English and Japanese. Kopelman, *supra* note 368, at 444.

397 Dissenting Opinion of Bernard at 2, 105 IMTFE Records.

398 *Id.* at 10.

399 *Id.* at 11.

400 *Id.*

401 *Id.* at 10–11.

also created collective (i.e., state) responsibility for them cannot eliminate individual responsibility.[402] The IMTFE could examine whether the persons accused of crimes were actually those who committed them.

Obviously, one can question this reasoning on at least two grounds. First, the human habit of aggressive war suggests that it may not violate natural law. Second, a natural law unformulated in any positive law hardly provides notice to persons that an act is criminal. Reaching either conclusion would suggest a violation of the principle of legality. However, if Justice Bernard's arguments are accepted, then there is no legality violation.

Justice Bernard's views are tied up with the fact that the IMTFE was established to deal with crimes that had already happened. In this way, they resemble the views of Gros at the London Conference.[403] For Justice Bernard, the ordinary case of criminal prescription and adjudication involves "eventual facts which would come within the scope of a penal definition previously established by a qualified legislator"[404] – that is, a promulgated law applied prospectively to acts alleged to be criminal. This was not the case in the IMTFE (or the Nuremberg Tribunal).

Justice Bernard argued that the following was referred to the IMTFE in its charter:

> facts already committed and specified concerning which the Tribunal itself will have to decide whether they were in fact and validly subjected to penal sanctions by a competent authority and to investigate and decide whether the Accused were the authors of them. Under these conditions, the Tribunal has the right to examine the facts submitted to it with due regard to all the qualifications recognized possible by the conscience and universal reason.[405]

In other words, the authority that created the tribunal essentially referred the facts of Japanese aggression and atrocities to the IMTFE.

The IMTFE cannot assume "criminality of the facts or acts in relation to which . . . jurisdiction is assumed."[406] "This is particularly true when the authority which relays the facts to the judges is not the one qualified to legislate on their criminality."[407] The creator of the IMTFE, the supreme

[402] *Id.*
[403] See Chap. 3.b.ii.
[404] Dissenting Opinion of Bernard at 7, 105 IMTFE Records. Justice Röling's views, Separate Opinion of Röling at 6, 109 IMTFE Records, are related to Justice Bernard's views here.
[405] Dissenting Opinion of Bernard at 7, 105 IMTFE Records.
[406] *Id.* at 3. See also Separate Opinion of Röling at 6, 109 IMTFE Records.
[407] Dissenting Opinion of Bernard at 3, 105 IMTFE Records.

commander, acting for the Allied powers, referred the atrocities committed by the Japanese in the Pacific war to this tribunal but was not competent to define the substantive international criminal law.[408] Indeed, if the authors of the charter had intended to make crimes out of specific facts (in the common lawyer's language, to create a conclusive presumption that what the defendants are alleged to have done was criminal), "the Tribunal would be competent to examine ex-officio the legality of those substantive provisions and if it found them beyond the competence of their author, to refuse to apply them."[409] Anything else would "jeopardize the proper administration of justice."[410] This is consistent with Gros's view of the duty of criminal courts. Substantively, Justice Bernard differs from Gros in that Bernard believed that aggressive war was an individual crime in natural and international law,[411] whereas Gros believed that they were not individual crimes in international law at the time the European Axis leaders acted.

In summary, Justice Bernard accepted the notion that *nullum crimen, nulla poena sine lege* applies to international criminal law. He also accepted natural law as a source of international criminal prescription that could provide prior existing law.[412]

3.d.iii.E. Justice Pal (India): Against Retroactive Creation of Crimes; Admitting Retrospective Creation of Tribunals

Justice Radhabinod Pal of India wrote a dissenting opinion of more than 1,200 typescript pages. The material presented here is thus extremely compressed. He agreed that the authority to set up a tribunal retrospectively and authority to define substantive law raise different issues: "Under international law as it now stands, a victor nation or a union of victor nations would have the authority to establish a tribunal for the trial of war criminals, but no

408 Separate Opinion of Röling at 7, 109 IMTFE Records. Cf. material on the 1990s UN ad hoc tribunals, Chap. 6.a, discussing Report of the Secretary-General Pursuant to Paragraph 2 of Security Council Resolution 808 ¶¶ 18-30 (1993), UN Doc. S/25704 (1993) [hereinafter Secretary-General's Rep.]; Prosecutor v. Milutinovic, Decision on Dragojub Ojdanic's Motion Challenging Jurisdiction: Joint Criminal Enterprise ¶ 9, IT-99-37-AR72 (ICTY App. Ch., 21 May 2003).

409 Dissenting Opinion of Bernard at 8–9, 105 IMTFE Records.

410 *Id.* at 9.

411 *Id.* at 10.

412 An extended analysis and critique of Justice Bernard's natural law philosophy must be left for another time.

authority to legislate and promulgate a new law of war crimes."[413] Contrary to the Nuremberg Judgment, he believed the IMTFE must be established "under the authority of international law, and not in the exercise of any sovereign authority. I believe, even in relation to the defeated nationals or to the occupied territory a victor nation is not a sovereign authority."[414]

He argued that the IMTFE Charter respected this limitation. It purported only to provide for "jurisdiction over persons and offenses"[415]:

> The intention, in my opinion is not to enact that these acts [named in IMTFE Charter, art. 5] constitute crimes but that the crimes, if any with respect to these acts, would be triable by the Tribunal. Whether or not these acts constitute any crime is left open for determination by the Tribunal with reference to the appropriate law.[416]

His views on this issue are consistent with those of Justices Röling and Bernard, and probably with President Webb as well. They are generally consistent with the arguments raised by Gros at the London Conference.

The "appropriate law" is "the international law to be found by us."[417] Partly, this wording reflects the judicial tradition that the common law judge finds the law rather than makes it. However, this also reflects a genuine view that the tribunal should enforce only international law that already existed at the time of the acts alleged against the defendants.

Elsewhere, Justice Pal admits the existence of conventional war crimes in international law, and reaffirms the vitality of "*jus-in-bello.*"[418] However, he also suggests that they are individually punishable only if "the act in question is not the act of the enemy state."[419] When he looked, much later in the opinion, at the evidence of conventional war crimes during the Far East phase of World War II, he found that there was a great deal of evidence that war crimes had been committed but insufficient evidence tying the Tokyo defendants to the specific atrocities charged through a common plan

[413] Dissenting Opinion of Pal at 56, 105 IMTFE Records.

[414] Dissenting Opinion of Pal at 56–57, 105 IMTFE Records.

[415] *Id.* at 33–34, interpreting IMTFE Charter art. 5.

[416] *Id.* at 33–34, interpreting IMTFE Charter art. 5. See also Dissenting Opinion of Pal at 55, 105 IMTFE Records ("Extending criminal jurisdiction is one thing, and extending the criminal law itself by defining 'crime' is a different thing"), distinguishing *S.S. Lotus (France v. Turkey)*, 1927 P.C.I.J. (ser. A) No. 10.

[417] Dissenting Opinion of Pal at 66, 105 IMTFE Records.

[418] *Id.* at 16, 1027–49.

[419] *Id.* at 18. See also *id.* at 16 ("War crimes, *stricto sensu*, as alleged here, refer to acts ascribable to individuals concerned in their individual capacity") (underlining in original).

or conspiracy.[420] Justice Pal rejected the theory that the illegality of Japanese aggression in World War II made all killings in furtherance thereof into ordinary murder.[421]

Taken together, this suggests that what he meant when he denied the existence of crimes against peace is that the conception of crime did not apply to the interactions between states that led to decisions concerning war and peace. Those decisions were not yet controllable by law as he defined it.

3.e. IF THE NUREMBERG AND TOKYO JUDGMENTS VIOLATED THE PRINCIPLE OF LEGALITY, CAN THEY NONETHELESS FORM THE BASIS OF LEGITIMATE LAW? JUSTICE PAL ANSWERS

The Nuremberg and Tokyo tribunals were in no sense common law supreme courts of the world. Their judgments did not, of their own force, become the law that all persons coming after must follow. Nonetheless, Nuremberg, and to a lesser extent Tokyo, have been extremely influential and have shaped international criminal law and the standards that individuals must obey. It is difficult to imagine modern international criminal law without them.

This is not the place to address all of the ways in which the charters and judgments have acted prescriptively in national and international courts and other contexts. That could well become its own book. Here, one question will be considered. Can substantive law aspects of the Nuremberg and Tokyo judgments have prescriptive force even if the judgments sanctioned violations of the principle of legality?

Justice Pal, the fiercest dissenter from the majority judgment at Tokyo, set forth two paths to legitimation of the Nuremberg–Tokyo law, even though he found the judgments themselves to contain violations of legality. These were through treaty law and custom. In his dissenting judgment in the Tokyo Tribunal, he attacked the proposition that the IMTFE or the victor states could make international criminal law that would be applicable to the defendants, especially by creating crimes against peace (aggressive war). With the Nuremberg Judgment, the IMTFE majority judgment, and Justice Röling, he agreed that the rule against retroactive creation of criminal law is not absolute. Nonetheless, "if such retroactive operation can be avoided,

[420] *Id.* at 1027–49.
[421] *Id.* at 1029–39.

courts should always do that."[422] Given his reading of the IMTFE Charter as a jurisdictional grant, and not as a set of definitions of crime, he argued that crimes against peace ("aggressive war") could not be applied to the IMTFE defendants, as their acts in planning and waging war were not criminal when done.

Justice Pal raised the issue about the precedential value of the decisions on aggressive war at the main Nuremberg and IMTFE trials. First, he noted that the making of new substantive criminal law in the IMTFE would be illegal, but, consistent with his common law orientation, he continues: "Any law *now* created in this manner *will* perhaps be the law *henceforth*."[423] Note that this is somewhat stronger than the traditional view of international law creation of custom (which requires the action of many states and their *opinio juris*) but is consistent with the modern "instant custom" theory, in which a single act or a small number of acts, if appropriately acquiesced to, can quickly form customary international law.

However, about a hundred pages further on, he returned to an extreme version of the older view of the nature of customary international law, indicating that the IMTFE decision "would not create anything new. It would only create precedent for a victor to bring the vanquished before a tribunal. It can never create precedent for the sovereign states in general, unless such states voluntarily accept such limitations."[424] This, he continued, could be done "by treaties or conventions."[425] These passages can be more or less reconciled if one views the passage that the law made here "*will* perhaps be the law *henceforth*" to mean that it will be the law only if voluntarily accepted by all sovereign states.

Justice Pal's statement about treaties and conventions does not necessarily reject the concept of customary international law. He admits that consent to rules may be expressed "tacitly" as well as "expressly."[426] He remarked early on, "No pact, no convention, has in any way abrogated *jus-in-bello*."[427] That is, the customary law of war still stands. This includes individual responsibility for war crimes, including trial of criminals by the victors, "so long as the belligerent confines himself to punishing breaches of

[422] *Id.* at 33.
[423] *Id.* at 56 (italics substitute for double underlining in original typescript).
[424] *Id.* at 146.
[425] *Id.*
[426] *Id.* at 102.
[427] *Id.* at 15 (italics substituted for single underlining in original typescript).

universally acknowledged laws."[428] Elsewhere, he appears to accept the need for unanimity in formation of rules of international law.[429] This argument has not, however, displaced the view that general acceptance is required for the formation of custom.[430]

In keeping with this rather strict interpretation of the formation of international law, he rejected a third road to legitimacy, which was later endorsed in the International Covenant on Civil and Political Rights (ICCPR)[431]: the use of general principles of law as a basis for international criminal law. Because law is not the basis of international life, "the international community has not authorized transposition of principles of criminality into rules of law in international life."[432]

Justice Pal's construction of convention and custom as ways to legitimacy for the substantive criminal law of Nuremberg and Tokyo proved prescient, even if his rejection of general principles did not. Crimes against humanity have, without much question, passed into customary international law.[433] However, it took more than half a century before crimes against humanity were formulated in a general treaty intended to be worldwide, the Rome Statute of the International Criminal Court.[434] Even that treaty disclaims an intent to formulate international criminal law for purposes other than its own enforcement, and thus does not claim to be a definitive statement or limitation of crimes against humanity in international criminal law.[435]

The vicissitudes of crimes against peace shows that the path to legitimacy is not an easy one. Many believe that the Nuremberg and Tokyo judgments were incorrect when they stated that crimes against peace already existed in international law at the time of World War II. Even as of today (2007), the ICC Statute does not contain any definition of crimes against peace

[428] *Id.* at 17 (italics substituting for double underlining in typewritten original), quoting from an unnamed work of Hall. See also *id.* at 23–25, quoting from opening speech of prosecutor Comyns Carr.

[429] See *id.* at 101.

[430] See, e.g., UN Doc. A/CN.4/16 (3 March 1950) (Manley Hudson, Working Paper).

[431] See ICCPR art. 15(2).

[432] Dissenting Opinion of Pal at 1003–04, 108 IMTFE Records (refusing to apply Statute of the Permanent Court of International Justice art. 38, provision on general principles of law, to substantive international criminal law definition).

[433] See, e.g., Report of the Secretary-General pursuant to Paragraph 2 of Security Council Resolution 808 ¶ 34 (1993), UN Doc. S/25704 (3 May 1993).

[434] Rome Statute of the International Criminal Court art. 7 (17 July 1998; entered into force 1 July 2002).

[435] ICC Statute art. 10.

or aggression, and the International Criminal Court cannot exercise jurisdiction over any such crime.[436] The disappearance of crimes against peace and aggression from practice of states and international organizations after the post–World War II prosecutions and the current difficulty in finding an implementable criminal law definition of aggression at least raises the question of whether such a crime could be prosecuted today under the principles of legality – though, as will be seen, there is a great deal of *opinio juris* from the negotiations for the Universal Declaration of Human Rights and the ICCPR to the effect that the Nuremberg and Tokyo judgments were unquestioned.[437]

3.f. CONCLUSION

The entire Nuremberg process, from the London Conference through the Nuremberg Judgment, was shot through with ambiguities on the issues of legality and retroactivity of criminal law. The fact that the judgment was unanimous did not eliminate the ambiguities – it merely saved them for another day. Whatever consensus existed on legality as a matter of international criminal law at Nuremberg was shattered at Tokyo. Views expressed on legality by some IMTFE justices provided reasoned challenges to the need for legality in international criminal law, at least as to the so-called political crimes against peace. But some justices also provided reasoned challenges to the Nuremberg claim that crimes against peace existed in international law at the time of World War II. When read together, the Nuremberg and IMTFE judgments and opinions reveal deep divisions among the jurists about the nature of legality in criminal law generally. This division set the stage for the modern era in which legality in criminal law was taken up by the international human rights movement.

[436] *Id.* at art. 5.
[437] See Chap. 4(a, b).

4

Modern Development of International Human Rights Law: Practice Involving Multilateral Treaties and the Universal Declaration of Human Rights

The revulsion against the Nazis' rejection of legality, questions about the true application of the principle of legality in the Nuremberg prosecutions, and other factors driving the international human rights movement led to the principle of legality becoming an international human right. The rest of this book is largely concerned with how this happened between World War II and the present and the current status of customary international law concerning legality. This chapter considers the treaty law and other international acts of states concerning legality and non-retroactivity of criminal law. Later chapters will consider the internal and comparative law of legality in modern states,[1] legality in the modern international and internationalized criminal tribunals,[2] and the current status of legality in customary international law.[3]

The emphasis on legality after the war was driven at least in part by a sense of guilt (or perhaps shame) that Nuremberg and Tokyo might have involved violations of legality, specifically concerning the creation of the crime of aggression, and, to a lesser extent, crimes against humanity. Moreover, many hoped to turn the same prosecutions into a onetime set of events that – even if problematic in themselves – would create a solid foundation of law to support later prosecutions for war crimes, crimes against humanity, and crimes against peace.[4]

[1] Chap. 5.
[2] Chap. 6.
[3] Chap. 7.
[4] E.g., Comment of Jackson, Minutes of Conference Session, 25 July 1945 [Doc. LI], Robert H. Jackson, Preface, published in REPORT OF ROBERT H. JACKSON UNITED STATES REPRESENTATIVE TO THE INTERNATIONAL CONFERENCE ON MILITARY TRIALS: LONDON 1945, 384–85, vii–viii (U.S. Gov't Printing Off. 1949 [submitted by Justice Jackson to the Secretary of State 15 December 1947]) [hereinafter REP. OF JACKSON].

Perhaps this was best summed up in a remark by René Cassin, of France, in the negotiations that led to the International Covenant on Civil and Political Rights. As summarized in the United Nations record:

> He pointed out that the rule of non-retroactivity in criminal sentences was not merely humanitarian, but was based on considerations of security. That rule had not yet been established in international law, but its necessity had now been recognized.... [H]e hoped that an international penal law, embodying the principle of non-retroactivity, would shortly be established.[5]

Two theses of this book are encapsulated here. First, Cassin was correct concerning the situation at the end of World War II. Second, his hope that future international penal law would embody the principle of non-retroactivity has largely been fulfilled.

The principle of legality in criminal law has entered the pantheon of international human rights through universal and regional treaties and nonbinding declarations of international organizations. These binding and nonbinding acts have contributed to the growth of this principle into a rule of customary international law, to be addressed in the final chapter of this book. First came the Universal Declaration of Human Rights by the General Assembly of the United Nations. Thereafter, the principle of legality was adopted in varying forms into many binding international conventions. These included general human rights treaties, both worldwide and regional, at least one human rights treaty designed to protect a specific group (the Convention on the Rights of the Child), and international humanitarian law treaties designed to protect civilians, prisoners of war, and others during war and occupation. The principle of legality in the various treaties applies to crimes under international law when prosecuted in the courts of states. The issue of using human rights principles for limiting the acts of international organizations is not overtly discussed in general treaty law.[6]

[5] UN Doc. E/CN.4/SR.112, pp. 2–3 (7 June 1949, reporting session of 3 June 1949). In this chapter are many direct quotes from summary record (/SR.) documents. These may not be exactly the words spoken at the meetings. The summary records are intended to be accurate summaries but do not purport to be complete verbatim quotes from speakers.

[6] But see Chaps. 4.d.v (on European Charter of Human Rights as a control on the European Union) & 6 (on legality in treaties and other organic documents of international and mixed international/national criminal courts).

4.a. THE UNIVERSAL DECLARATION OF HUMAN RIGHTS

4.a.i. *The Text*

Soon after Nuremberg, the Universal Declaration of Human Rights (UDHR)[7] incorporated both *nullum crimen sine lege* and *nulla poena sine lege* into an article on fair criminal process:

> 1. Everyone charged with a penal offence has the right to be presumed innocent until proved guilty according to law in a public trial at which he has had all the guarantees necessary for his defence.
> 2. No one shall be held guilty of any penal offense on account of any act or omission which did not constitute a penal offense, under national or international law, at the time when it was committed. Nor shall a heavier penalty be imposed than the one that was applicable at the time the penal offense was committed.[8]

There must have been applicable law at the time of the criminal act for any criminal penalty to be imposed. This is made clear by the second sentence (*nulla poena*). The provision also recognized that an act could be criminalized by either relevant national or relevant international law. However, the UDHR does not require the existence of a statutory text that had been enacted by a legislature at the time of the criminal act (*praevia lege scripta*). Thus, it respects the common law tradition. However, the fact that some law must exist at the time of the crime means that the common law can no longer develop new crimes out of whole cloth after the fact (though, of course, the provision does not limit how crimes may be proclaimed for the future). It also requires the existence of international criminal law prior to an act charged as an international crime, but it respects the possibility that the law may be customary as well as conventional (treaty based). All of these characteristics of the text were the result of specific choices made during the process of drafting and voting on the text, which is discussed subsequently.[9]

The UDHR is a resolution of the UN General Assembly, adopted without opposition, forty-eight to zero, but with eight abstentions.[10] The legal force of resolutions such as this is one of the great academic controversies of

[7] G.A. Res. 217 (III), art. 11(2) (10 December 1948) [hereinafter UDHR]; UN GAOR, 3d sess., part I, p. 71, rep. in 1948 UNYBHR 466, 467.

[8] UDHR art. 11.

[9] Chap. 4.a.ii.

[10] See 1948 UNYBHR at 465–66, drawing on GAOR, 3d sess., plen. mtgs., pp. 852–934.

modern international law, and it will be discussed a bit further herein.[11] However, the provision of the UDHR on the non-retroactivity of crimes and punishments has been so accepted into later treaty and customary international law that for our purposes the controversy is of little import.[12]

The UDHR set the framework for the treatment of non-retroactivity of criminal law in later treaties. These include the International Covenant on Civil and Political Rights (ICCPR) and the regional human rights treaties. They also include humanitarian treaties such as the Geneva Conventions of 1949 on the law of war (international humanitarian law) and their 1977 Protocols, and one of the specialized human rights treaties, the Convention on the Rights of the Child.

For the most part, as would be expected, the preamble and final articles of the UDHR exhort states to implement the rights set forth in the declaration. Yet the rights in the text are often not limited to being rights against states. Thus, one can read some of the provisions as calling on the United Nations itself, as an international organization, and perhaps other international organizations as well, to recognize and apply these rights where applicable to their missions.[13] For example, the preamble points out that "Member States [of the United Nations] have pledged themselves to achieve, in co-operation with the United Nations, the promotion of universal respect for and observance of human rights and fundamental freedoms."[14] One of the later articles of the UDHR suggests that national law is not the only realm for protection of these rights: "Everyone is entitled to a social and international order in which the rights and freedoms set forth in this Declaration can be fully realized."[15] The final article of the UDHR can be read as suggesting that international organizations should not infringe upon protected rights:

[11] See Chap. 4.k.

[12] Chap. 7 discusses the current status of non-retroactivity in customary international law. For a somewhat partisan view that the UDHR has become customary international law, but discussing opposing views of its limited force, see John P. Humphrey, Human Rights and the United Nations: A great adventure 73–77 (Transnational Publishers 1984). One problem with the approach Humphrey, a vital person in the creation of the UDHR, takes (at least from the point of view of the current study) is that he simply argues that the UDHR as a whole has become customary international law without looking at the customary law status of each of the provisions separately.

[13] See UN Doc. E/CN.4/SR.112, p. 8 (3 June 1949) (René Cassin of France discussing proposal to conform legality provision of draft covenant to that of the UDHR; David Weissbrodt, The Right to a Fair Trial under the Universal Declaration of Human Rights and the International Covenant on Civil and Political Rights 79–80 (Martinus Nijhoff Publishers 2001) [hereafter Weissbrodt].

[14] UDHR, Preamble (6th unnumbered "Whereas" clause).

[15] UDHR art. 28.

"Nothing in this Declaration may be interpreted as implying for any State, *group* or person any right to engage in any activity or to perform any act aimed at the destruction of any of the rights and freedoms set forth herein."[16]

The UDHR is not a piece of binding treaty law itself. Yet because of its broad influence, both on subsequent treaties and on national practice, it is worth looking at the issues that were raised in drafting its legality provisions and how they were resolved.

4.a.ii. *History and* Travaux Préparatoires *of the UDHR Non-retroactivity Provision (and Beginnings of the ICCPR Provision)*

The non-retroactivity provision of the UDHR resulted from a set of deliberate choices.[17] Both *nullum crimen* and *nulla poena* were included, over a claim that only *nullum crimen* should be declared an international human right. Either national or international law may provide a basis for criminal prosecution, but *nullum crimen* and *nulla poena* apply in either case. The UDHR drafters rejected language similar to that which eventually entered the ICCPR on general principles of law. The drafters considered and rejected language that would arguably have required written statutes in effect at the time of the criminal act to provide notice – that is, *praevia lege scripta* was rejected as a requirement of international human rights. Thus, common law and at least customary international law can be sources of criminal proscriptions, as can statutes and treaties. However, where common law is used, the language chosen prohibits the wholly new creation of crimes after the fact. The drafters also included language requiring that any penalty be applicable before it can be imposed. Finally, they chose to limit the right to non-retroactive laws to the criminal sphere.

All of these choices will be discussed herein. Addressing the significance of some of them is the main reason to retell this twice-told tale.[18]

One issue was conspicuously missing from the debates on the UDHR and the ICCPR: what constitutes crime and punishment for the purposes

[16] UDHR art. 30 (emphasis added). Humphrey, *supra* note 12, at 134, claims that at one point in 1950, the Secretariat argued in the UN Administrative Tribunal that the secretary-general is not bound by the provisions of the UDHR; Humphrey denounces this idea.

[17] Technically the term *travaux préparatoires* in the title of this section applies to the preparatory work for treaties, whereas the UDHR is a declaration of the UN General Assembly. However, the usage, by Weissbrodt, seems appropriate here.

[18] The two main secondary sources for this section are Albert Verdoodt, Naissance et signification de la Déclaration Universelle des Droits de L'Homme (E. Warny/Université Catholique de Louvain 1964) [hereafter Verdoot]; and Weissbrodt.

of applying non-retroactivity rules. A few words will be said about this important subject in the chapter on national laws.[19] However, it remains a topic for future study by comparative and criminal law scholars.

The history of the UDHR is closely linked to the early history of the ICCPR.[20] The UN Economic and Social Council (ECOSOC) gave the Commission on Human Rights the tasks of submitting proposals, recommendations and reports to the Council regarding:

> (a) an international bill of rights;
> (b) international declarations or conventions on civil liberties, the status of women, freedom of information and similar matters. . . . [21]

Originally, ECOSOC established a "nuclear Commission on Human Rights," of nine persons serving in their individual capacities to prepare the way for the permanent commission.[22] The nuclear commission chose Mrs. Franklin D. Roosevelt (as the records called Eleanor Roosevelt) (US) as its chair, René Cassin (France) as its vice-chair, and K. C. Neogi (India) as its rapporteur.[23] The majority of the group proposed to ECOSOC that the full Commission on Human Rights be composed of persons serving "as non-governmental representatives."[24] This was, however, opposed by the Soviet Union's representative to the nuclear commission.[25]

Eventually, ECOSOC decided that the Commission on Human Rights would have eighteen members, elected by a complex procedure as representatives of states rather than as individuals.[26] For the purposes of this book, this action had some consequences. Actions and statements of members of the commission in preparing the UDHR and later the ICCPR can be seen as state practice or expression of *opinio juris* of their states. In contrast, this action can be viewed as a defeat for the participation of individuals in their own status within the UN organization early in its history.

There are two other points about the making of international law early in the history of the United Nations here. First, many of the documents submitted during the process of drafting the UDHR and ICCPR were labeled

[19] See Chap. 5.c.viii.
[20] See Weissbrodt at 35–36; Verdoodt at 50–51.
[21] ECOSOC Res. 1/5 (16 February 1946); ESCOR, 1st yr., 1st sess., p. 163, quoted and discussed in 1947 UNYBHR at 422–23, Weissbrodt at 6, and Verdoodt at 50–51.
[22] 1947 UNYBHR at 421–22 n.4, quoting ESCOR, 1st yr., 1st sess., p. 163.
[23] 1947 UNYBHR at 421 nn.2–3.
[24] *Id.* at 421–22 n.4, quoting ESCOR, 1st yr., 1st sess., at 163.
[25] 1947 UNYBHR at 421–22 n.4 (Borisov); Verdoodt at 49.
[26] ECOSOC Res. 2/9 (21 June 1946), discussed in 1947 UNYBHR at 422.

"unrestricted," and important drafts were published in the UN *Yearbook on Human Rights* or elsewhere. Some of the unrestricted documents included important reports of the committees or working groups, the Commission on Human Rights, and ECOSOC,[27] along with proposals and comments of particular states.[28] They can be seen as an effort to implement Woodrow Wilson's ideal of open covenants openly arrived at. Additionally, where these documents are from states, their public nature strengthens their claim to being acts constituting state practice or expressing the *opinio juris* of the issuing state. Where the documents are from an organ of the United Nations acting in its official capacity (e.g., the Secretariat), the public nature of the documents strengthens their claim to being practice of the United Nations or to expressing the *opinio juris* of the United Nations or the issuing organ. By the end of the process, however, some documents were in the less public category of "limited distribution."[29] Some nongovernmental organizations, and even a few individuals in their own capacities, made some proposals for the UDHR and later the ICCPR,[30] and they were present in some of the meetings at which the documents were discussed.[31]

The Commission on Human Rights, meeting 27 January to 10 February 1947, decided, at the prompting of P. C. Chang, representing China, to "work under the assumption that the [international bill of rights] would be adopted as a General Assembly Resolution . . . [and to] draft a declaration rather than a convention, because the declaration could be more promptly adopted by the General Assembly."[32] The commission decided that drafting

[27] E.g., E/CN.4/56 (11 December 1947) (Report of the Working Party on an International Convention on Human Rights); E/CN.4/95 (21 May 1948) (Report of the Drafting Committee to the Commission on Human Rights); E/1681 (Report to the Economic and Social Council on the Work of the sixth session of the Commission [on Human Rights]) (25 May 1950), rep. in ESCOR, 5th yr., 11th sess., Supp. No. 5, especially Annex I at 15, 17 (Draft First International Covenant on Human Rights, art. 11 on non-retroactivity in criminal law).

[28] E.g., E/CN.4/37 (26 November 1947) (U.S. Proposal for a Human Rights Convention); E/CN.4/82/Adds. 7, 8, 11 (4, 6, and 19 May 1948, respectively) (communications of India, France, and Sweden).

[29] See Marc J. Bossuyt, Guide to the "*Travaux Préparatoires*" of the International Covenant on Civil and Political Rights XXIII–XXIV (Martinus Nijhoff Publishers 1987) [hereafter Bossuyt].

[30] See note 43 *infra* and accompanying text.

[31] See, e.g., UN Docs. E/CN.4/21 ¶ 4, p. 2 (two representatives of nongovernmental organizations attended the first session of the Drafting Committee to the Commission on Human Rights as "consultants"); E/CN.4/95 ¶ 4, p. 2 (seventeen people representing fifteen nongovernmental organizations attended the second session of the Drafting Committee as "consultants").

[32] Weissbrodt at 7, citing UN Docs. E/CN.4/SR.7, p. 3 (31 January 1947), and E/259, p. 3 (27 January–10 February 1947).

would be done by a drafting group of the three members of its bureau, "'with the assistance'" of the UN Secretariat.[33] When the Soviet Union and Czechoslovakia objected to this small group a few months later,[34] Chair Eleanor Roosevelt proposed the eight-member Drafting Committee consisting of representatives from Australia, Chile, China, France, Lebanon, the Soviet Union, the United Kingdom, and the United States, which would also be assisted by the Secretariat. ECOSOC, as the parent organ of the Commission on Human Rights, adopted this proposal.[35] The Drafting Committee was also chaired by Roosevelt, and Charles Malik of Lebanon was rapporteur.

The UN Secretariat created the Division of Human Rights, directed by John P. Humphrey of Canada.[36] He and Emile Giraud, of France, produced "a remarkable work of documentation," which was both "a substantial advance draft of a declaration of rights [and] . . . a collection of texts relating to the advance draft."[37] Humphrey asserted that he wrote the draft outline[38] "with some help from Emile Giraud" and that "the Secretariat" (presumably he and his staff) later produced the documentation[39] to support it.[40] The documented outline included extracts from fifty-five national constitutions of UN members then in effect, some declarations and proposals presented by individual countries, and one draft declaration from a nongovernmental organization. The national provisions and the proposals were collated to each article of the outline.[41] This was material that went to the Drafting Committee. Before writing the draft, Humphrey and Giraud also had access to drafts provided by a number of individuals and other nongovernmental organizations, mostly in English and all from "the democratic West."[42] He listed his sources as drafts by the American Law Institute (which he called the best, which had been drafted "by a distinguished group representing many cultures" during World War II and had been introduced by Panama at

[33] 1947 UNYBHR at 432; Weissbrodt at 7, citing UN Docs. E/CN.4/SR.12, p. 5 (3 February 1947); E/259, p. 2.

[34] See Weissbrodt at 7.

[35] ECOSOC Res. No. 46 (IV) (28 March 1947), reproduced in relevant part at 1947 UNYBHR at 468.

[36] See 1947 UNYBHR at 429–30.

[37] Verdoodt at 57 (translation by the current author), discussing UN Docs. E/CN.4/AC.1/3 & Add.1. The text, called "Draft Outline of an International Bill of Rights," also appears in English and French in Report of the Drafting Committee to the Commission on Human Rights, UN Doc. No. E/CN.4/21 (1 July 1947), Annex A.

[38] Draft Outline of International Bill of Rights, UN Doc. E/CN.4/AC.1/3 (4 June 1947).

[39] Documented Outline, UN Doc. E/CN.4/AC.1/3/Add.1 (2 June 1947).

[40] Humphrey, *supra* note 12, at 31–32.

[41] E/CN.4/AC.1/3/Add.1; see Verdoodt at 57.

[42] Humphrey, *supra* note 12, at 31–32.

San Francisco and in the General Assembly); Gustavo Gutiérrez; Irving A. Isaacs; Rev. Wilfred Parsons, SJ; Rollin McNitt; a committee chaired by Viscount Sankey; Hersch Lauterpacht; H. G. Wells; the American Association for the United Nations; the American Jewish Congress; the World Government Association; Institut de Droit International; the editors of *Free World*, and "an enumeration of subjects" from the American Bar Association (which later became an opponent of the UDHR project).[43]

The text set out on non-retroactivity and legality in criminal law in the Secretariat outline was part of an article with more general fair trial guarantees. In English, the whole article read as follows:

> No one shall be convicted of a crime except by judgment of a court of law, in conformity with the law, and after a fair trial at which he has had an opportunity for a full public hearing.
>
> Nor shall anyone be convicted of crime unless he has violated some law in effect at the time of the act charged as an offense, nor be subjected to a penalty greater than that applicable at the time of the commission of the offense.[44]

In French,

> Nul ne peut être condamné pénalement que par jugement d'un tribunal rendu en application de la loi et après un procès régulier et public au cours duquel il aura eu toute faculté de se faire entendre.
>
> Nul ne peut être condamné pénalement à moins qu'il n'ait violé une loi en vigueur au moment où il a commis l'acte qui lui est reproché, ni être condamné à une peine plus grave que celle applicable au dit moment.[45]

Especially in the French-language version, this suggested a requirement that there be a statute in force ("une loi en vigueur") before the charged act is committed (i.e., the French text proposed the requirement of *praevia lege*

[43] *Id.*; for ABA opposition, see *id.* at 46. The documented outline does not refer to all of these sources. It mentions only those nongovernmental drafts that obtained state sponsorship for their introduction, particularly the American Law Institute (Panama) and the Inter-American Juridical Committee (Chile), and one draft from the American Federation of Labor, as an accredited nongovernmental organization. See E/CN.4/AC.1/3/Add.1, p. 219.

[44] Draft Outline of an International Bill of Rights art. 26, UN Doc. E/CN.4/21 ¶¶ 10 & 11 & Annex A, pp. 2–3, 8 & 17–18 (from UN Doc. E/CN.4/AC.1/3), rep. in 1947 UNYBHR at 485. In the documented outline, the text of the provision was a bit mangled. E/CN.4/AC.1/3/Add.1, p. 219. Nonetheless, the documentation provided for Article 26 in the documented outline, *id.*, pp. 219–34, was intended to address the entire article as found in E/CN.4/21, Annex A.

[45] Draft Outline of an International Bill of Rights art. 26 (French version), E/CN.4/21, Annex A, made part of the English document (the original) at p. 18.

scripta). It omitted any direct reference to crimes under international law, though "some law in effect" in the English version could be read to include international law. Note that the grammar at the beginning of the second sentence in the two languages is different. Language and translation issues would continue to be important.

The second paragraph of the article, whether in French or English, is a classic statement of the principle of non-retroactivity as a criminal law doctrine. However, the article preceding it in the Secretariat draft outline showed that in the Secretariat's view, this was not merely about criminal law. It was about how a principle of legality could protect human freedom generally: "Everything that is not prohibited by law is permitted."[46] This notion existed in the French Declaration of the Rights of Man and of the Citizen, and in several contemporary constitutions, mostly from Latin America.[47] Unfortunately for libertarians, this provision did not survive into the final version of either the UDHR or the ICCPR.

Two other versions of the specific provision on non-retroactivity in criminal law were very similar to the Secretariat draft. The version suggested by René Cassin as representative of France on the basis of the draft was exactly the same in its French version except the penalty had to be "légalement *applicable au dit moment*."[48] This suggests a requirement of a statute for punishment as well as criminalization. Even the United States, a common law country, did not have trouble at the beginning with this kind of formulation:

> No one shall be convicted of any crime except . . . for violation of *a law in effect* at the time of the commission of the act charged as an offense, nor be subjected to a penalty greater than that applicable at the time of the commission of the offense.[49]

[46] Draft Outline of an International Bill of Rights art. 25, E/CN.4/21, Annex A, p. 17. In French, *id.*, p. 18, art. 25, reads: "Tout ce qui n'est pas interdit par la loi est permis."
British comic novelist T. H. White, The Once and Future King (G. P. Putnam's Sons 1958), satirized antilibertarian societies with an ant colony slogan, "Everything not forbidden is compulsory."

[47] France Declaration of the Rights of Man and of the Citizen art. 5; various constitutions discussed in Chap. 5.b and collected in Appendix B.

[48] Suggestions Submitted by the Representative of France for Articles of the International Declaration of Human Rights, art. 12, E/CN.4/21 Annex D at 54 (French version made part of the English original of this document).

[49] U.S. Suggestions for Articles to be Incorporated in an International Bill of Human Rights, arts. 9 & 10, UN Doc. E/CN.4/21 Annex C at 42 (third unnumbered paragraph; emphasis added), rep. in 1947 U.N.Y.B.H.R. at 492–93.

Another version was quite different and crystallized two of the important debates surrounding the non-retroactivity article. Charles Dukes, Lord Dukeston, on behalf of Great Britain, submitted a draft that clearly did not require a specific statute at the time of the act charged: "No person shall be held guilty of any offence on account of acts or omissions *which did not constitute such an offence* at the time when they were committed."[50] Here, the source of the definition of the offense is not specified. Thus, there is no prohibition of common law or customary international law as a source of offenses in existence at the time of an act. However, whatever the source of law is, law must have existed at the time of the offense; thus, creation of wholly new common law crimes after the fact would be impermissible. Dukeston's version also omitted the rule that a penalty could not be increased retroactively (i.e., *nulla poena* was not required). This was deliberate, supported by the view that criminals should not have the right to calculate the potential gains of a crime against the penalties to be imposed for it, and concluding that "the question of penalty was not a fundamental human right and should be considered on a different basis."[51]

The text proposed by the Drafting Committee for an International Declaration of Human Rights at the end of its first session retained *nulla poena*. This was a text originally prepared by Cassin. He revised it on the basis of discussions,[52] and then the Drafting Committee revised it further. This version also retained the possibility that it could be read as requiring a written statute in force: "No one can be convicted of crime unless he has violated some law in effect at the time of the act charged as an offence nor be subjected to a penalty greater than that applicable at the time of the commission of the act."[53]

[50] Letter of Lord Dukeston (U.K.) to UN Secretary-General, with Draft International Bill of Human Rights, draft Bill, art. 12, UN Doc. E/CN.4/21 Annex B at 34 (emphasis added), rep. in 1947 U.N.Y.B.H.R. at 490, citing E/CN.4/AC.1/8 referring to Secretariat art. 26. Eagle eyes will note that *offence* and *offense* appear in different portions of E/CN.4/21; but the American spelling disappears later on in the process of drafting the UDHR and the ICCPR.

[51] Geoffrey Wilson (U.K.) (discussing a slightly later Anglo-Indian version of this paragraph) in UN Doc. E/CN.4/SR.54, pp. 13–14 (1 June 1948) (note this is a direct quote from the summary record document, but these documents do not purport to be verbatim transcripts of the proceedings); Weissbrodt, *supra* note 13, at 20. Wilson substituted for Charles Dukes, Lord Dukeston, at meetings of the Drafting Committee to the Commission of Human Rights.

[52] See UN Doc. E/CN.4/21 ¶¶ 14–17 and Appendix F, pp. 4–5, 73, rep. in 1947 UNYBHR at 483, 499. Unfortunately, the French version of the report does not appear in the English original of this document.

[53] Suggestions of the Drafting Committee for Articles of an International Declaration of Human Rights, art. 10 (first unnumbered paragraph), UN Doc. No. E/CN.4/21 Annex F, p. 75, rep. in 1947 UNYBHR at 500.

At the same time, however, the Drafting Committee adopted the U.K. draft on non-retroactivity as a "Draft Article on Human Rights and Fundamental Freedoms to be Considered for Inclusion in a Convention."[54] This was preparatory work for what eventually became the ICCPR. This U.K. text required neither a prior statute nor non-retroactivity of penalties – though it did require preexisting criminal law of some kind. At this early stage, the debate over these issues had been joined.

The full Commission on Human Rights met in its second session, 2–17 December 1947, and quickly established three working groups, one for the International Declaration of Human Rights (also chaired by Eleanor Roosevelt), one for a convention or conventions, and one for issues of implementation.[55] From here on, the histories of the UDHR and the ICCPR begin to diverge.

The Working Group on the Declaration greatly changed the form of the protection against retroactive criminal laws: "No one shall be convicted or punished for crime or other offence [in French, *un crime ou autre infraction pénale*] except... which shall be pursuant to law in effect [in French, *la loi en vigueur*] at the time of the commission of the act charged."[56] The issue of whether non-retroactivity would extend to non-criminal acts arose here. A comment by the Working Group on this article states, "[T]his text covers one of the general principles which are not applicable to minor administrative offences that do not always require legal proceedings."[57] This is clearer in the French text "autre infraction pénale" than in the English text "other offence," as the English could in ordinary usage include non-penal offences.

The Commission on Human Rights, still at its second session, did not like this change in form of the non-retroactivity provision. One reason given by Dukeston for returning the protection against non-retroactivity to a separate sentence was that it corresponded to the ongoing project for a convention on human rights.[58] Another reason might have been that Dukeston's latest proposal did not require statutory criminal law (i.e., it eliminated the requirement of *praevia lege scripta*). At about the same time,

[54] Art. 6, UN Doc. No. E/CN.4/21 Annex G, pp. 82–83, rep. in 1947 UNYBHR at 504.

[55] UN Doc. E/600 ¶¶ 15–16, rep. in 1947 UNYBHR at 536.

[56] Report of the Working Group on the Declaration on Human Rights, UN Doc. E/CN.4/57, Ch. 3, Texts, art. 10, p. 7. The French wording is found in Verdoodt at 133, discussing text of Cassin, from E/CN.4/AC.2/SR.4, p. 8.

[57] UN Doc. E/CN.4/57 at 8. See Weissbrodt at 17–18 (attributing this limitation to Eleanor Roosevelt, "to allow administrative authorities to deal with minor offences without a public trial"); Verdoodt at 132–33.

[58] Verdoodt at 133.

Belgium and the Philippines jointly proposed adding a new sentence in light of the Nuremberg and Tokyo trials.[59] These two nations had both been particularly affected by the aggressive nature of the German and Japanese attacks in World War II, and aggression (the crime against peace) was the most questionable of the crimes in the two international military tribunals. Both of these proposals were adopted, and the non-retroactivity language remained part of the more general article on rights to fair procedure in criminal matters.[60] The article at this point also had a provision against torture, which later became a separate article of the UDHR. The full Commission on Human Rights second session draft of the article containing non-retroactivity became:

1. Any person is presumed to be innocent until proved guilty. No one shall be convicted or punished for crime or other offence except after fair public trial at which he has been given all guarantees necessary for his defence. No person shall be held guilty of any offence on account of any act or omission which did not constitute such an offence at the time when it was committed, nor shall he be liable to any greater punishment than that prescribed for such offence by the law in force at the time when the offence was committed.
2. Nothing in this article shall prejudice the trial and punishment of any person for the commission of any act which, at the time it was committed, was criminal according to the general principles of law recognized by civilized nations.
3. No one shall be subjected to torture, or to cruel or inhuman punishment or indignity.[61]

An article with parallel wording on non-retroactivity was made part of the Draft International Covenant on Human Rights at the same session of the Commission on Human Rights.[62] The draft covenant provision was different only in that it was a separate article on non-retroactivity, divorced from the general procedural issue of fair trial and the substantive issue of

[59] Weissbrodt at 18 n.126 notes that *Nürnburg* is the spelling used in the preparatory documents for the UDHR.

[60] Verdoodt at 133 treats the British and Belgian/Philippines proposals as separate. Weissbrodt at 18–19 treats them as a joint proposal.

[61] Draft International Declaration on Human Rights, art. 7, U.N. Doc. E/600 Annex A (17 December 1947), ESCOR, 3d yr., 6th sess., Supp. No. 1, rep. in 1947 UNYBHR at 541–42.

[62] Draft International Covenant on Human Rights, art. 14, U.N. Doc. E/600 Annex B (17 December 1947), rep. in 1947 UNYBHR at 548.

protection from torture and related practices. Cassin argued that the second paragraph of the draft declaration properly belonged only in the covenant.[63] He lost the point here, though he won eventually.

The full ECOSOC did not vote on the substance of the draft covenant and declaration at its meeting in early 1948, because the matters had been sent to UN member governments for consideration. Ten nations responded to the call for comments, but not all addressed the criminal non-retroactivity provisions of the drafts.[64] The comments that did address criminal non-retroactivity, however, addressed two of the important issues in the discussion.

The Netherlands raised the theoretical issue of what kind of protection the principle of legality provides, though it did not lay out all theoretical views. It merely stated that the provisions on non-retroactivity addressed "a doctrine of a general character."[65] By contrast, the first two sentences of the first paragraph (on fair trial) and the third paragraph (on torture and related practices) dealt with "protection of the individual against unjust treatment."[66] It therefore suggested this be separated into two articles, placing the non-retroactivity provisions in a separate article.[67]

The other comments on non-retroactivity all addressed the "Nuremberg/ Tokyo" provision of paragraph 2 in the draft covenant and/or declaration and were all negative. The United States (on the covenant), Brazil (on both) and Egypt (on the covenant) all believed that including this paragraph "involves an unacceptable derogation of the traditional precept – *nullum crimen sine lege.*"[68] (More than a decade later, the United States changed its view and voted to include this provision in the ICCPR.[69])

Eventually, the Drafting Committee received the declaration again, along with the comments from governments and from other UN bodies.[70] The second session of the Drafting Committee wound up passing the draft of the non-retroactivity provision unchanged from its Commission on Human

[63] Weissbrodt at 19.

[64] Collation of the Comments of Governments on the Draft International Declaration of Human Rights, Draft International Covenant on Human Rights, and the Question of Implementation, UN Doc. E/CN.4/85, pp. 20, 76 (1 May 1948).

[65] UN Doc. E/CN.4/85, p. 20.

[66] *Id.*

[67] See *id.*

[68] *Id.* (Brazil, comment on Draft Declaration, art. 7(2)). Accord, *id.*, p. 76 (United States, Brazil, and Egypt comments on Draft Covenant, art. 14(2)).

[69] UN Doc. A/C.3/SR.1013 ¶ 47; *id.* at ¶ 50.

[70] 1948 UNYBHR at 457.

Rights (2d sess.) form.[71] It did, however, consider and reject (by a two-three vote, with two abstentions) a much different form of the non-retroactivity provision:

> 1. . . . Arrest, detention or imprisonment may be allowed only according to pre-existing law and in accordance with due process.
>
> . . .
>
> 6. Every one accused of an offence must be judged within a reasonable time by courts established beforehand and in accordance with pre-existing laws in a public trial. The foregoing provision shall not prejudice the trial and punishment of any person for the commission of any act which, at the time it was committed, was criminal according to the general principles of law recognized by civilized nations.[72]

This version would have preserved both *nullum crimen* and *nulla poena*, as "pre-existing law" involves both criminal definition and punishment. It does not necessarily require a written statute (*praevia lege scripta*). Indeed, by prohibiting arrest and detention without preexisting law, it appears to prohibit non-criminal detention (e.g., commitment to a mental institution) on the basis of retroactively applicable law.[73] It also contained the "Nuremberg/Tokyo" sentence. Finally, it introduced the idea that not only the substantive law but the court in which crimes are judged must have been established beforehand – which had been an objection made by the United States to retroactive creation of an international criminal court after World War I.[74] This would have prohibited the ex post facto creation of courts such as the Nuremberg and Tokyo tribunals. Although the Drafting Committee defeated this proposal, it "decided to forward it nevertheless to the full Commission [on Human Rights]."[75]

[71] Draft International Declaration of Human Rights, art. 8 (formerly art. 7), in UN Doc. E/CN.4/95 (21 May 1948), p. 6, rep. in relevant part in 1948 UNYBHR at 458.

[72] Note 1, ¶¶ 1 (second unnumbered sentence) & 6, to Draft Declaration, art. 8, in UN Doc. E/CN.4/95, p. 6, rep. in 1948 UNYBHR at 458. The entire rejected revision was a recasting of several provisions of the Draft Declaration.

[73] Cf. ACHR art. 7(2), discussed in Chap. 4.d.ii.

[74] See Robert Lansing & James Brown Scott, *Memorandum of Reservations Presented by the Representatives of the United States to the Report of the Commission on Responsibilities (April 4, 1919), Annex II to Commission on the Responsibility of the Authors of the War and on Enforcement of Penalties, Report Presented to the Preliminary Peace Conference (Versailles, March 29, 1919)*, published at 14 A.J.I.L. 95 (1920), reprinted in 1 The Law of War: A Documentary History 842, 860, 865 (Leon Friedman, ed., Random House 1972).

[75] Note 1 to Draft Declaration, art. 8, in UN Doc. E/CN.4/95, p. 6, rep. in 1948 UNYBHR at 458.

Two other points about the actions of the Drafting Committee are of interest. The first is that it chose not to act on the negative reactions of three states to the asserted derogation of the principle of *nullum crimen* contained in paragraph 2 of the proposal from the second session of the commission. The second is that it did so even though the chair of the Drafting Committee, Eleanor Roosevelt, was from the United States, which was one of the objectors to the paragraph.

The Commission on Human Rights at its third session in May and June 1948, did make substantial changes in the non-retroactivity provisions, and rejected other important proposed changes. Britain, along with the now-independent India, again proposed eliminating non-retroactivity of punishment on the ground that penalties did not go to fundamental human rights.[76] The commission also discussed the issue of the postwar trials and the new paragraph inserted at its second session. The issue was so controversial that Cassin at one point suggested saying that non-retroactivity of laws and sanctions would not apply to the case of war criminals.[77] A subcommittee was appointed to deal with the issue.

Eventually, the third session of the commission dropped *nulla poena.* It also found a new solution was found for the Nuremberg/Tokyo problem – referring to both national and international law as possible sources of penal law:

> 1. Everyone charged with a penal offence [in French, *un délit*] has the right to be presumed innocent until proved guilty according to law in a public trial at which he has had all the guarantees necessary for his defence.
> 2. No one shall be held guilty of any offence on account of any act or omission which did not constitute an offence, under national or international law [in French, *une infraction aux termes du droit national ou international*], at the time when it was committed.[78]

The French version, replacing *un loi* with *aux termes du droit* appears to indicate an acceptance that a preexisting statute would not be required; *loi* being a more limited word than the phrase *termes du droit.* The Belgian representative was concerned that "international law" could be interpreted

[76] Geoffrey Wilson (UK) at UN Doc. E/CN.4/SR.54 at 13–14 (1 June 1948); see Weissbrodt at 20, discussing UN Doc. E/CN.4/99 at 3, art. 8 (24 May 1948) and citing Wilson.

[77] Verdoodt at 134–35.

[78] Draft International Declaration of Human Rights art. 9, published in Report of the Third Session of the Commission on Human Rights, UN Doc. E/800 (28 June 1948), rep. in 1948 UNYBHR at 463. The French version is quoted in Verdoodt at 135.

narrowly, as including only treaty language, and therefore proposed using the phrase "general principles of international law."[79] Geoffrey Wilson of the United Kingdom responded that international law as defined in the Statute of the International Court of Justice (ICJ Statute), included conventions, international custom, recognized principles, judicial decisions, and so on.[80] With Belgium's understanding that "international law" meant the definition in Article 38 of the ICJ Statute (and a similar Soviet admission),[81] this amendment was approved twelve to zero, with three abstentions.[82]

Note also that the first paragraph of this version has a more limited definition of what is covered than does the second paragraph, in both English and French, but that the English and French texts are different. In English, *penal offence* can be construed more narrowly than *offence*, which in ordinary language can include non-criminal wrongs; in French, *délit* is limited to more serious matters than *infraction*, but both of the French words have technical legal meanings. *Penal offence* is different from *délit*; and *offence* is not always used in the same sense as *infraction*.

This version also separated the idea of non-retroactivity from general fair trial guarantees, by placing it in a separate paragraph, if not in a separate article. It also begins with the phrase "No one" rather than "No person." This change had been proposed to ensure that the protection of international human rights laws would apply only to individuals, and not to "juridical persons" such as corporations, which some states recognize.[83]

The Draft Declaration went to ECOSOC. It decided "to transmit to the General Assembly the draft International Declaration of Human Rights submitted to the Council by the Commission on Human Rights in the Report of its third session."[84]

The declaration then proceeded to the Third Committee of the General Assembly, which considered a number of changes. The Panamanian representative objected to the elimination of the rule of *nulla poena* – he felt it was a "universally recognized principle that the penalty for any crime could not be changed *ex post facto*."[85] He proposed an amendment that, with

[79] UN Doc. E/CN.4/SR.56 at 4.

[80] *Id.* at 6; Weissbrodt at 21. Wilson was referring to Statute of the International Court of Justice art. 38 [hereinafter ICJ Statute].

[81] E/CN.4/SR.56 at 6–7.

[82] *Id.* at 7.

[83] Cf. Weissbrodt at 77; Chap. 4.b.ii.A on the change in the draft covenant.

[84] ECOSOC Res. No. 15 (VII) (26 August 1948), in E/1065, p. 15, rep. in 1948 UNYBHR at 464.

[85] GAOR, 3d sess., 1st part, Third Committee, p. 265. See Verdoodt at 135.

some stylistic modification, was accepted as the second paragraph of the article:

> No one shall be held guilty of any offence on account of any act or omission which did not constitute an offence, under national or international law, at the time when it was committed. Nor shall a heavier penalty be imposed than the one that was applicable at the time the offence was committed.[86]

This proposal was not passed without controversy. The vote on the amendment in the Third Committee was nineteen for, six against, and nineteen abstentions.[87]

This change did two things other than restore non-retroactivity of punishments. It restored the idea that a penalty must be *applicable* [the word is the same in French] as well as existing in law before an act may be punished. Also, it did not restore any reading that would require a prior existing statute (*praevia lege scripta*). At least preexisting common law or customary international law would be good enough.

Eleanor Roosevelt, on behalf of the United States, wanted to ensure that the rule of non-retroactivity would apply only to criminal cases, at least as far as the declaration was concerned. She therefore proposed changing "an offence" to "a penal offence" in the non-retroactivity paragraph,[88] matching the usage in the general fair trial paragraph. Again, however, there was dissent. The vote was sixteen in favor, eight against, and fourteen abstentions.[89]

The Greek delegate proposed a change in French that would also make it clear that only criminal law was covered. He proposed the phrase "acte délictueux," to replace both *infraction* in the non-retroactivity paragraph and *délit* in the general fair trial paragraph.[90] He argued that *infraction* was too broad, potentially covering non-criminal matters (i.e., it has meanings beyond its technical meaning in criminal law); but that *délit* was too limited

[86] GAOR, 3d sess., 1st part, Third Committee, p. 269; UN Doc. A/C.3/SR.116; discussed in Weissbrodt at 22. The GAOR indicates that the second sentence here was originally proposed as second independent clause of the first sentence, but by the time the matter went through the Third Committee, it had been made into a second sentence. See UN Doc. A/C.3/400/Rev.1 (4 December 1948), Annex A, art. 9, in English and French at GAOR, 3d sess., 1st part, Third Committee, Annexes to the Summary Records of Meetings, pp. 124–25.

[87] GAOR, 3d sess., 1st part, Third Committee, p. 273; Verdoodt at 136, referring to UN Doc. A/C.3/220.

[88] Weissbrodt at 22, referring to UN Doc. A/C.3/230, p. 10 (6 October 1948) & A/C.3/223.

[89] GAOR, 3d sess., 1st part, Third Committee, p. 273 (29 October 1948), noted in Weissbrodt at 22 n.157.

[90] GAOR, 3d sess., 1st part, Third Committee, p. 270 (29 October 1948), endorsed by France at *id.* p. 271; see Verdoodt at 135; Weissbrodt at 22, referring to UN Docs. A/C.3/SR.111–16.

in juridical terminology.[91] The French agreed "to render the English expression 'penal offense' in French by the words *acte délictueux*."[92] This change passed unanimously.[93]

Another French wording change approved unanimously replaced "aux termes du droit national ou international" with "d'après le droit national ou international."[94] This did not change the sense that law might come from customary or decisional law as well as from a statute.

There was other discussion of how this article interacted with the Nuremberg and Tokyo judgments. In this discussion, only the (prerevolutionary) Cuban delegate explicitly stated that his endorsement of the article was not "a direct or indirect approval of the Nürnberg Judgments."[95] Given the language of the text, this necessarily questions whether some acts for which there were convictions at Nuremberg might not have been crimes when done. Cuba also proposed a right "to be judged by tribunals established prior to the offence . . . charged." This was rejected eighteen to eight, with seventeen abstentions.[96]

The Third Committee passed this article on, with its recommendation for adoption,[97] by a vote of forty-two to zero, with two abstentions.[98] The entire text of the declaration was referred to a subcommittee "solely from the standpoint of arrangement, consistency, uniformity and style."[99] No further substantive changes in the text on non-retroactivity were made.[100] The Third Committee approved the full draft of the UDHR for the General Assembly, twenty-nine to zero, with seven abstentions, the six Communist General Assembly abstainers discussed subsequently plus, perhaps surprisingly, Canada. South Africa and Saudi Arabia, which abstained in the General Assembly, did not vote in the Third Committee.[101]

[91] GAOR, 3d sess., 1st part, Third Committee, p. 270; see Verdoodt at 135 for the point on *délit*; see Weissbrodt at 22 for the point on *infraction*.

[92] GAOR, 3d sess., 1st part, Third Committee, p. 271.

[93] *Id.* at 273–74.

[94] *Id.* at 274.

[95] *Id.* at 267–68; see Weissbrodt at 22.

[96] GAOR, 3d sess., 1st part, Third Committee, p. 274.

[97] Report of the Third Committee ¶¶ 5, 7, UN Doc. A/777, rep. in relevant part in 1948 UNYBHR at 465.

[98] GAOR, 3d sess., 1st part, Third Committee, p. 274; Verdoodt at 137.

[99] GAOR, 3d sess., 1st part, Third Committee, p. 849, referring to UN Doc. A/C.3/400 & Rev. 1.

[100] The two clauses of the original sentence on non-retroactivity were divided into the two sentences of the final UDHR art. 11(2). See note 86 *supra*.

[101] GAOR, 3d sess., 1st part, Third Committee, p. 879–80; see Humphrey, *supra* note 12, at 71–72.

The General Assembly voted on the text by article and adopted this article unanimously.[102] This might suggest that none of the nations that eventually abstained from voting on the UDHR did so because of the non-retroactivity provisions. Perhaps this is so, but perhaps this is reading too much into the preliminary vote. After all, the eight eventual abstainers were six Communist governments (Belorussian SSR, Czechoslovakia, Poland, Ukrainian SSR, USSR, and Yugoslavia), one near-absolute monarchy (Saudi Arabia), and the apartheid Union of South Africa.[103] None of those that abstained from the UDHR vote had a constitutional guarantee of non-retroactivity as of 1946.[104] Today, they (or their successor states) all have constitutional or statutory guarantees of non-retroactivity of both crimes and punishments.[105]

4.b. THE ICCPR

4.b.i. *The Text*

The most prominent of the human rights treaties is the one intended to be universal, the International Covenant on Civil and Political Rights (ICCPR). The ICCPR deals with non-retroactivity of criminal law in an article separate from the general guarantees of fair criminal trials:

> 1. No one shall be held guilty of any criminal offence on account of any act or omission which did not constitute a criminal offence, under national or international law, at the time when it was committed. Nor shall a heavier penalty be imposed than the one that was applicable at the time when the criminal offence was committed. If, subsequent to the commission of the offence, provision is made by law for the imposition of a lighter penalty, the offender shall benefit thereby.
> 2. Nothing in this article shall prejudice the trial and punishment of any person for any act or omission which, at the time when it was committed, was criminal according to the general principles of law recognized by the community of nations.[106]

[102] 1948 UNYBHR at 465, referring to GAOR, 3d sess., plen. mtgs., pp. 852–934.
[103] See 1948 UNYBHR at 465–66, drawing on GAOR, 3d sess., plen. mtgs., pp. 852–934.
[104] See Appendix B.
[105] See Appendix C.
[106] International Covenant on Civil and Political Rights, art. 15, G.A. Res. 2200A (XXI), 21 GAOR Supp. No. 16, p. 52, UN Doc. A/6316, 993 U.N.T.S. 171 (16 December 1966, entered into force 23 March 1976) [hereinafter ICCPR].

The ICCPR, like the UDHR, was adopted by the United Nations General Assembly without dissent. The vote was 106 to 0, with no abstentions.[107] Because the ICCPR is a treaty, the General Assembly's adoption of it was merely the setting of a text. No nation was bound by the ICCPR until it adopted it by signature and ratification, accession, state succession or other legal process for adopting a treaty, and until enough nations adopted it to bring it into force by its own terms. It did not come into force until 23 March 1976, almost nine and a half years after its adoption by the General Assembly. As of today (25 September 2007), 160 states are parties to the ICCPR.[108] The People's Republic of China, the largest nation by population in the world, and by far the largest holdout from ratification, has now signed the ICCPR but has not yet ratified it.[109]

The ICCPR was not the first treaty protecting human rights generally after the passage of the UDHR. The first was the European Convention on Human Rights (ECHR) of 1950, which will be discussed herein, with the other regional human rights conventions.

The first two sentences of the ICCPR provision are nearly identical to the UDHR provision on non-retroactivity, except that *penal* was changed to *criminal* in both sentences, and *when* was added after *time* in the second sentence to make the constructions parallel.[110] The ICCPR added two doctrines to the UDHR provisions on legality. First, if the penalty for a crime changes between commission and conviction, the lighter penalty is to be imposed[111] (*lex mitior*). Second, the so-called Nuremberg/Tokyo paragraph, dropped from the UDHR, was restored in the ICCPR.[112]

General principles of law is one of the canonical sources of international law recognized in the Statutes of the Permanent Court of International Justice and the current International Court of Justice.[113] General principles

[107] See UN Doc. A/PV.1496 ¶ 59, p. 6 (16 December 1966).

[108] See http://www.ohchr.org/english/countries/ratification/4.htm.

[109] See *id.*

[110] Compare ICCPR art. 15(1)(first two unnumbered sentences) with UDHR art. 11(2). No reservations to this portion of the ICCPR provision on legality have been noted at the UN High Commission for Human Rights Web site, http://www.ohchr.org/english/countries/ratification/4_1.htm.

[111] ICCPR art. 15(1). The United States has reserved the right not to apply the mercy principle (*lex mitior*); Italy and Trinidad and Tobago have reserved the right to apply it only to cases still in progress at the time the law is changed; Germany reserves the right not to apply it in extraordinary circumstances. See http://www.ohchr.org/english/countries/ratification/4_1.htm.

[112] ICCPR art. 15(2). Argentina reserves the right to apply this provision on legality only consistently with its own constitution. See http://www.ohchr.org/english/countries/ratification/4_1.htm.

[113] PCIJ Statute art. 38; ICJ Statute, art. 38.

of law were recognized as a subset of international law by the Commission on Human Rights during its debate on the UDHR.[114]

There has been debate about whether the last provision adds anything at all to the principal definition of the rule taken from the UDHR. Some argue that it was simply meant to ratify the post–World War II case law; others that it truly recognizes a different means of crime creation as being consistent with the principle of legality.[115] Although that debate may not have been concluded, it can fairly be said that this provision does not derogate from the clear statement of legality, including a requirement of existing law concerning both the crime and the punishment, in the first portion of the ICCPR section. Moreover, the history of the provision shows that almost all drafters had no intention of creating any ongoing exception to the rule of non-retroactivity. At most, there were fears that the language might be read to create such an exception, and an intention that the language should not be read that way.[116]

On its face, it allows general principles of law to be used as one of the sources of international law that can create international criminal law, if there has been sufficient notice (in the accessibility and foreseeability senses[117]) to persons.[118] The temporal requirement on the face of the ICCPR section – that the act have been criminal according to general principles

[114] Weissbrodt at 21, referring to UN Doc. E/CN.4/SR.56 at 6.

[115] See Public Prosecutor v. Sarmento, Decision on the Defense (Domingos Mendonca) Motion for the Court to Order the Public Prosecutor to Amend the Indictment, Case No. 18a/2001 ¶ 20 (Timor-Leste, Dili District Special Court for Serious Crimes, 24 July 2003) ("general principles of law recognized by the community of nations" treated as a subset of the rules of customary international law, and must have been applicable at time crime committed); Machteld Boot, Genocide, Crimes Against Humanity, War Crimes: Nullum Crimen Sine Lege and the Subject Matter Jurisdiction of the International Criminal Court 137–40, 158–61, 628 (Intersentia 2002) (discussing *travaux préparatoires*, analogous in international law of treaties to legislative history in national law of statutory interpretation of ICCPR art. 15, and the European Convention for the Protection of Human Rights and Fundamental Freedoms art. 7, 213 U.N.T.S. 221 (4 November 1950) [hereinafter ECHR]); Ward N. Ferdinandusse, Direct Application of International Criminal Law in National Courts 233–36 (TMC Asser Press 2006).

[116] See Chap. 4.b.ii.C.

[117] See Chap. 1.b.i & Chap. 7.b.i.

[118] *Sarmento* ¶ 20; Ferdinandusse, at 233–34 (arguing strongly for the significance of "general principles of law" as a permissible source of law under ICCPR, art. 15(2) and ECHR, art. 7.2, seeing them as a type of international law; and admitting reference to them requires consideration of accessibility and foreseeability); Sarah Joseph, Jenny Schultz & Melissa Castan, The International Covenant on Civil and Political Rights: Cases, Materials, and Commentary §15.11 (2d ed., Oxford Univ. Press 2004).

of law "at the time when it was committed"[119] – prohibits the retroactive application of newly developed general principles to create crimes.

Article 4 of the ICCPR permits "[n]o derogation from" the legality and non-retroactivity rules of Article 15.[120] The rights which are non-derogable are the most fundamental in the ICCPR – or at least those deemed most worthy of protection in the times of greatest stress, when the pressure to violate human rights would seem to be the greatest. That Article 15 is included here is yet more evidence of the fundamentality of the non-retroactivity of crimes and punishments in international human rights law and of its broad acceptance by states.

4.b.ii. *History and* Travaux Préparatoires *of the ICCPR Non-Retroactivity Provision*[121]

Almost all of the issues raised by Article 15 of the ICCPR had been discussed during the negotiation of the UDHR. Yet the history of this ICCPR provision is worth following through, as it became a discussion separate from that surrounding the UDHR.

4.b.ii.A. Beginnings, Through Spring 1950 (Sixth Session of the Commission on Human Rights)

As noted previously, at the end of 1947, the second session of the UN Commission on Human Rights passed identical wording on non-retroactivity of criminal law in the Draft Declaration and the Draft Covenant.[122] The only difference was that the Draft Covenant contained a separate article on non-retroactivity, while the Draft Declaration made it part of a more general article on fair trial procedure.

The second session of the Drafting Committee in 1948 considered many changes but in the end changed just one word: "No *person*" at the beginning of the non-retroactivity article became "No *one*,"[123] at Roosevelt's request,

[119] ICCPR art. 15(2).

[120] *Id.* at art. 4(2).

[121] Bossuyt was a very useful source for this section, along with Weissbrodt and, for the early material when the drafting of the UDHR and ICCPR were linked, Verdoodt.

[122] Draft International Declaration on Human Rights art. 7, U.N. Doc. E/600 Annex A (17 December 1947), ESCOR, 3d yr., 6th sess., Supp. No. 1, rep. in 1947 UNYBHR at 541–42. Draft International Covenant on Human Rights art. 14, U.N. Doc. E/600 Annex B (17 December 1947), rep. in 1947 UNYBHR at 548. See Chap. 4.a.i.

[123] Redraft of International Covenant on Human Rights, art. 14, in Report of the Drafting Committee [2d sess.] to the Commission on Human Rights, UN Doc. E/CN.4/95, p. 29 (21 May 1948), rep. in 1948 UNYBHR at 475 (emphasis added). On the change from

apparently to ensure that the provision applied only to natural persons and not to juridical persons such as corporations.[124] (The Drafting Committee did not make even this change to the Draft Declaration, though the change was later made.)

At this session the Drafting Committee at first agreed to delete the "Nuremberg/Tokyo" sentence, which had been criticized by the United States, Brazil, and Egypt as potentially permitting violation of *nullum crimen*.[125] Then, by a vote of five to two, with one abstention, the sentence was restored.[126] Thus, at this point, the text of the Draft Covenant non-retroactivity article was:

> 1. No one shall be held guilty of any offence on account of any act or omission which did not constitute such an offence at the time when it was committed, nor shall he be liable to any greater punishment than that prescribed for such offence by the law in force at the time when the offence was committed.
> 2. Nothing in this article shall prejudice the trial and punishment of any person for the commission of any act which, at the time it was committed, was criminal according to the general principles of law recognized by civilized nations.[127]

This draft was passed on by the Commission on Human Rights, without extensive examination, to ECOSOC.[128] ECOSOC had only "general debate" on the Draft Covenant at its seventh session and passed it on to the General Assembly.[129] The General Assembly's Third Committee considered that the Draft Covenant was "not yet in a state suitable for consideration."[130] The General Assembly therefore asked ECOSOC to "ask the Commission on Human Rights to continue to give priority in its work to the preparation

"No person" to "no one," approved seven to zero, with one abstention, see UN Doc. E/CN.4/AC.1/SR.25, p. 10, discussed at Bossuyt at 322.

[124] See Weissbrodt at 77.

[125] Bossuyt at 322, citing UN Docs. E/CN.4/AC.1/SR.30, p. 11. See Weissbrodt at 77, citing UN Doc. E/CN.4/AC.1/SR.25, p. 9. For the national criticisms, see UN Doc. E/CN.4/85, p. 76 (United States, Brazil, Egypt comments on Draft Covenant, art. 14(2). Accord, *id.*, p. 20 (Brazil, comment on Draft Declaration, art. 7(2)).

[126] See Bossuyt at 322; Weissbrodt at 77, both citing to E/CN.4/AC.1/SR.31, pp. 2–5.

[127] UN Doc. E/800, art. 14, quoted in Bossuyt at 322, rep. in relevant part at UN Doc. E/CN.4/253, p. 3 (24 May 1949).

[128] UN Doc. E/800, art. 14, quoted in Bossuyt at 322 and discussed in 1948 UNYBHR at 478.

[129] 1948 UNYBHR at 478, referring to ECOSOC Res. 151 (VII) (26 August 1948), in UN Doc. E/1065 at 15.

[130] Report of the Third Committee, UN Doc. A/777 ¶ 4, rep. in relevant part in 1948 UNYBHR at 478.

of a draft Covenant on Human Rights."[131] Despite this rather summary treatment of the work of the second session of the Drafting Committee, the debates at that session, discussed in the section on the history of the UDHR, throw light on the choices made in drafting the ICCPR.

Because of a desire to finish what became the UDHR, the Commission on Human Rights did not focus on the covenant for some time. The Commission on Human Rights took up the covenant again at its fifth session, 9 May–20 June 1949, after the General Assembly adopted the UDHR.[132] This session made significant changes to the non-retroactivity provision of the Draft Covenant, in the end conforming it to the parallel UDHR provision. Its debates and decisions are instructive.

For example, one rejected proposal, from the United States, would have changed the focus of the provision:

> No state shall enact any penal laws making punishable an act or omission which did not constitute a penal offence at the time it was committed, or providing a greater punishment for a penal offence than that prescribed by law in force at the time when the offence was committed.[133]

Roosevelt said that this would make non-retroactivity apply only to legislative changes, not to judicial interpretations of statutes.[134]

France objected that non-retroactivity of criminal law should apply no matter how the law was made. Cassin argued that this version was unacceptable, "as it afforded protection from retroactive punishment of crime only on the level of law and was consequently too narrow; a similar protection was necessary against action of judges and administrators."[135] This shows an understanding that non-statutory crime creation can work differently from statutory crime creation in both the civil and the common law systems. Both judges and administrators can abuse their powers no matter what the legal system.

Guatemala and the United Kingdom objected to the U.S. proposal on the ground that this wording focused on the duty of the state not to make a non-retroactive law rather than on the right of individuals to be free from

[131] GAOR, 3d sess., part I, Resolutions, p. 79, rep. in 1948 UNYBHR at 479. This was G.A. Res. 217E (III). See 1949 UNYBHR at 330.

[132] See Weissbrodt at 78.

[133] UN Docs. E/CN.4/170 (6 May 1949) and E/CN.4/253 p. 3 (24 May 1949), discussed in Weissbrodt at 78.

[134] UN Doc. E.CN.4/SR.112, p. 4 (7 June 1949, recording session of 3 June 1949); Weissbrodt at 79.

[135] E.CN.4/SR.112, p. 8.

retroactive punishment. They believed the focus of the covenant should be on individual rights rather than state duties.[136] The U.S. proposal (with a modification from Uruguay) was rejected nine to four, with one abstention.[137]

The United Kingdom reiterated its proposal to drop non-retroactivity of increased punishments (*nulla poena*) from the covenant.[138] This proposal too was not specifically voted on and was not adopted. It was here that Cassin stated most forcefully the French reason for insisting on *nulla poena*: "France, which during the war had seen men executed for crimes which, when committed, had been considered relatively minor, could not accept retroactive increases of penalty."[139] This is the ultimate fear of those who argue for *nulla poena*.

The drafters of the ICCPR recognized that individuals might need protections from abuses by entities other than governments of nation-states. Cassin pointed out that the language of the UDHR, requiring existing "national or international law" at the time an alleged offense is committed, would "protect the individual from arbitrary actions even by international organizations" and urged that the covenant include this language.[140]

Technically, the ICCPR is a treaty among states and was never planned directly to control the acts of international organizations. Yet Cassin was correct that such protection was needed. His point was reaffirmed by the secretary-general in annotations prepared for the General Assembly.[141] The need for these protections against international organizations was discussed decades later, though without direct reference to Cassin, by the secretary-general in his report recommending the establishment of the International Criminal Tribunal for the Former Yugoslavia;[142] and the other international and international/national tribunals have, in one way or another, recognized the need for such protection.[143] Others have continued to note this need for human rights protection, specifically of legality, against the actions

[136] *Id.* at 4–5 (Guatemala) & 7 (United Kingdom); Weissbrodt at 79.
[137] E/CN.4/SR.112, p. 9.
[138] Proposal of U.K., E/CN.4/253, p. 3, referring to UN Doc. E/CN.4/188; E/CN.4/SR.112, p. 4; Weissbrodt at 79.
[139] E/CN.4/SR.112, p. 8.
[140] Quote from Weissbrodt at 79–80, citing to UN Doc. E/CN.4/SR.112, p. 8 (3 June 1949).
[141] UN Doc. A/2929 ¶ 94 (Annotations on the Text of the Draft International Covenant on Human Rights (Prepared by the Secretary-General)) (1 July 1955).
[142] See Report of the Secretary-General pursuant to Paragraph 2 of Security Council Resolution 808, UN Doc. S/25704 ¶ 34 (3 May 1993), available at http://www.un.org/icty/legaldoc-e/basic/statut/s25704.htm [hereinafter Sec-Gen's ICTY Rep.], discussed in Chap. 6.a.
[143] See generally Chap. 6.

of international organizations exercising criminal powers.[144] Finally, the proposed European Union Charter of Fundamental Rights of the European Union,[145] not yet in force, would apply the doctrine of non-retroactivity of crimes and punishments directly to an international and/or supranational organization, the European Union.

At this session, the "Nuremberg/Tokyo" sentence was dropped. Egypt, India, and Uruguay criticized this sentence along lines previously discussed.[146] The elimination of the sentence came as a result of a series of votes that put on the table most of the important issues concerning non-retroactivity of criminal law.

A proposal was made by France to adopt the UDHR language on non-retroactivity into the Draft Covenant, as a replacement for the entire article on non-retroactivity.[147] For purposes of voting, it was divided up into four parts, which essentially required the commission to vote on the most controversial points concerning legality and non-retroactivity in criminal law. The provision was broken up in this manner[148]:

First, the Commission voted on the beginning of the text: "[1] No one shall be held guilty of any penal offence on account of any act or omission which did not constitute a penal offence."[149] This was adopted unanimously.[150] Next was the wording allowing either national or international law to provide the existing law criminalizing acts: "[2] under national or international law."[151] This was adopted by a vote of ten to three, with one abstention.[152] Third, the words, completing the rule of non-retroactivity of criminalization of acts (*nullum crimen*) under either national or international law: "[3] at the time when it was committed."[153] This was adopted twelve to zero, with two abstentions, and this entire sentence was then adopted by twelve to zero, with two abstentions.[154]

[144] Haji N. A. Noor Muhammad, *Due Process of Law for Persons Accused of a Crime*, in THE INTERNATIONAL BILL OF RIGHTS: THE COVENANT ON CIVIL AND POLITICAL RIGHTS 138, 164, 439 n.28 (Louis Henkin ed., Columbia Univ. Press 1981), citing to 10 GAOR Annexes, UN Doc. No. A/2929 ¶ 94 (1955).

[145] Art. 49, 2000/C 364/01 (7 December 2000; pub. date 18 December 2000).

[146] Weissbrodt at 80, citing to UN Docs. E/CN.4/253, p. 3 (proposals of India and Egypt to drop the paragraph), and E/CN.4/SR.112, pp. 3, 4 & 6.

[147] E/CN.4/253, p. 3; Bossuyt at p. 326, citing E/CN.4/228.

[148] UN Doc. E/CN.4/SR.112, pp. 9–10; see Bossuyt at 326; Weissbrodt at 80.

[149] E/CN.4/SR.112, p. 9; see Bossuyt at 326; Weissbrodt at 80.

[150] E/CN.4/SR.112, p. 9; see Bossuyt at 326; Weissbrodt at 80.

[151] E/CN.4/SR.112, p. 9; see Bossuyt at 326; Weissbrodt at 80.

[152] E/CN.4/SR.112, p. 9; see Bossuyt at 326; Weissbrodt at 80.

[153] E/CN.4/SR.112, p. 9; see Bossuyt at 326; Weissbrodt at 80.

[154] E/CN.4/SR.112, p. 9; see Bossuyt at 326; Weissbrodt at 80.

The commission then voted on the provision prohibiting imposition of a heavier penalty that was not applicable at the time of the commission of an act (*nulla poena*), "in order to take into account the United Kingdom amendment to delete [*nulla poena*]"[155]: "[4] Nor shall a heavier penalty be imposed than the one that was applicable at the time the penal offence was committed."[156] The provision retaining *nulla poena* was adopted thirteen to one with no abstentions.[157]

At this point, Cassin explained that this amendment had been "intended as a total substitution for both paragraphs of the original text of [the non-retroactivity] article."[158] This meant that a vote to approve the entire French amendment would eliminate the "Nuremberg/Tokyo sentence, paragraph 2 of the prior version of the Draft Convention legality provision. The Soviet Union (which wanted to replace *civilized* with *democratic* in the description of which nations formed general principles of law)[159] and Chile (which wished the sentence to be limited explicitly to "war criminal[s]"[160]), apparently as a result, decided to withdraw their proposed amendments to that sentence; and the commission proceeded directly to a vote on the entire French proposal.[161] The entire French amendment, as approved in pieces, was then adopted as a whole, by a vote of eleven to zero, with three abstentions.[162]

In the preparation for these votes, Cassin had stated that he could accept the deletion of this sentence if the reference to international law was in the text,[163] as in fact it was. Yet, as will be seen, the fight over the Nuremberg/Tokyo paragraph was not finished.

Acceptance of the *nulla poena* sentence in the French proposal rejected the British proposal excising the doctrine. The vote on the beginning of the first sentence can be seen as a rejection of the U.S. proposal that non-retroactivity of crimes only apply to statutes. It also meant the obverse: a reaffirmation of the decision not to require statutory texts to define crimes (*praevia lege scripta*), thus accepting the existence of common law or customary crimes.

[155] E/CN.4/SR.112, p. 9 (Comment of the Chair, Roosevelt; bracketed material added).
[156] *Id.*; see Bossuyt at 326.
[157] E/CN.4/SR.112, p. 9; see Bossuyt at 326.
[158] E/CN.4/SR.112, p. 10 (bracketed material added).
[159] *Id.* at 7.
[160] *Id.* at 6–7 (bracketed material added).
[161] *Id.* at 10.
[162] *Id.*; see Bossuyt at 326. The assertion that this sentence from the earlier versions of the draft covenant was "not voted upon" by the fifth session of the Commission on Human Rights, Bossuyt at 330, is thus not strictly speaking correct.
[163] E/CN.4/SR.112, p. 3; see Weissbrodt at 80.

Finally, the first vote was a continued insistence that non-retroactivity, as a matter of human rights law applies only to criminal matters.

In the end, the text on non-retroactivity that the fifth session of the Commission on Human Rights "submitted to member governments for consideration and comment"[164] was the same as the text of the UDHR provision on non-retroactivity, except that the covenant version was a separate article.[165] The decisions made in reaching that text resembled, in many ways, the decisions reached when the text was ironed out for the UDHR.

The secretary-general's call for comments from UN member governments on the draft International Covenant on Human Rights produced a few responses on the non-retroactivity article.[166] Only the United Kingdom and the Philippines produced comments in time for the compilation made of the comments.[167] Shortly thereafter, Egypt put forth a proposal.[168]

Each of these was taken up at the sixth session of the Commission on Human Rights, 27 March to 19 May 1950, and had an effect on the final shape of the provision, so they will each be considered here. However, it must be noted that the Soviet Union boycotted this session after the chair ruled out of order a motion to exclude the Nationalist Chinese representative on the commission, and the ruling was upheld by the commission.[169]

The Egyptian proposal, made in the debate by Abdel Meguid Ramadan, essentially reintroduced *lex mitior*, a right to a lower sentence if the legal penalty is reduced after the act.[170] This had been raised by O. Sagues of Chile the year before but had not been part of the provision adopted.[171] In the United States, it was thought that "every accused person" should have the right to benefit from subsequent legislation reducing penalties.[172] Although this has been a widespread sentiment in the United States, it has not been required by United States constitutional law, and in fact, the United States

[164] 1949 UNYBHR at 332.

[165] Draft International Covenant on Human Rights, art. 14, UN Docs. E/1371 and E/CN.4/350, Annex I, p.33, and 1949 UNYBHR at 334.

[166] Secretary-General, note of 29 July 1949, discussed in Compilation of the Comments of Governments on the Draft International Covenant on Human Rights and on the Proposed Additional Articles, UN Doc. E/CN.4/365 ¶ 1, p. 1 (22 March 1950).

[167] E/CN.4/365, p. 42 (comments to art. 14).

[168] UN Doc. E/CN.4/425 (14 April 1950).

[169] UN Doc. E/1681 ¶ (25 May 1950), in ESCOR, 5th yr., 11th sess., Supp. No. 5.

[170] E/CN.4/425 (14 April 1950).

[171] UN Docs. E/CN.4/SR.112, p. 6 (Chile raises issue), 9–10 (for non-adoption), and E/CN.4/SR.159 ¶¶ 61–66, pp. 13–14 (18 April 1950) (discussion of Egyptian proposal); Weissbrodt at 79, 81.

[172] E/CN.4/SR.159 ¶ 48, p. 10; see Weissbrodt at 81–82.

wound up making a reservation to this provision of the ICCPR.[173] This provision further attacks the British view, expressed in the drafting of the UDHR as well as the ICCPR, that *nulla poena* itself is not a fundamental human right.[174] This time, *lex mitior* was adopted, by a vote of seven to three, with five abstentions, in the following language: "If, subsequent to the commission of the offence, provision is made by law for the imposition of a lighter penalty, the offender shall benefit thereby."[175] At the time, the French delegate indicated that this would apply only to mitigations of penalty in effect at the time of sentencing.[176] However, later thought indicated that it might apply to changes in the law after sentencing.[177]

The Philippines proposed some changes in wording, only one of which was accepted. It changed *penal* to *criminal* throughout the article to make the wording consistent with wording in another article related to fairness in criminal proceedings,[178] again ensuring that the human right against non-retroactive laws would not be extended to civil matters.

The Philippines also suggested changing *penalty* to *repression.*[179] It is not clear why this suggestion was made. Thus, it is not clear why it was not accepted, other than that *repression* was not used this way in U.S. law or Anglo-Saxon law generally.[180] However, it is possible those who wanted a clear separation between rights in criminal and civil cases did not want the rule of *nulla poena* to apply to anything other than criminal penalties.

The third Philippine suggestion would have changed *heavier* to *different*– so that the rule would have prohibited giving lighter as well as heavier sentences. As this logic was rejected by the decision to implement *lex mitior*

[173] See http://www.ohchr.org/english/countries/ratification/4_1.htm (documentation of ICCPR ratifications and reservations on the Web site of the UN Office of the High Commissioner for Human Rights).

[174] On British views on Declaration, see Letter of Dukeston (U.K.) to UN Secretary General, with Draft International Bill of Human Rights, draft Bill, art. 12, UN Doc. E/CN.4/21 Annex B at 34 (emphasis added), rep. in 1947 UNYBHR at 490, citing E/CN.4/AC.1/8; E/CN.4/SR.54, p. 13; Weissbrodt at 20 (discussing an Anglo-Indian proposal). On British views on the covenant, see Proposal of U.K., E/CN.4/253, p. 3, referring to UN Doc. E/CN.4/188; E/CN.4/SR.112, p. 3. Weissbrodt at 79.

[175] Draft First International Covenant on Human Rights, art. 11(1) (third unnumbered sentence), in UN Doc. E/1681, Annex I, p. 17 (25 May 1950); on the vote, see E/CN.4/SR.159 ¶ 94, p. 19; Weissbrodt at 81.

[176] E/CN.4/SR.159 ¶ 88, p. 18.

[177] See Noor Muhammad, *supra* note 144, at 164, citing 15 GAOR Annexes, UN Doc. A/4397 ¶ 97 (1960).

[178] Proposal in E/CN.4/365, p.42; adopted at E/CN.4/SR.159 ¶ 92, p. 18; Weissbrodt at 81.

[179] E/CN.4/365, p. 42.

[180] See E/CN.4/SR.159 ¶ 47, p. 10.

on the suggestion of Egypt, this amendment was rejected by a vote of thirteen to one, with one abstention.[181]

Finally, the United Kingdom brought back the so-called Nuremberg/ Tokyo sentence, in the following form: "Nothing in this Article shall prejudice the trial and punishment of any person for the commission at [*sic* – should probably be "of"] any act which, at the time it was committed, was criminal according to the general principles of law recognized by civilized nations."[182] This proposal remained as controversial as ever. It was opposed by Roosevelt for the United States, joined by China, Denmark, and India, because the phrase "under national or international law" already provided for the validity of prosecutions on the basis of international criminal law. Roosevelt "noted that the expression 'the general principles of law recognized by civilized nations' was used in article 38 c of the Statute of the International Court of Justice to designate one of the sources of international law."[183] She later argued, supported by Denmark, that "the words 'under national or international law' . . . had the same meaning as 'according to generally recognized principles of law'; there was no principle of law which did not form part of national or international law."[184] Hansa Mehta of India also believed that the sentence was more suitable for a convention directed specifically at war crimes rather than a general human rights convention.[185] Branko Jevremovic of Yugoslavia agreed with the idea of the sentence but wanted to remove the reference to "civilized nations,"[186] and agreed with an oral suggestion of the United Kingdom to change the wording to "according to generally recognized principles of law."[187] This is part of the larger debate over who it is that makes the general principles of law that are a source of international law. He also argued: "The defendants at Nurnberg and Tokyo had been condemned for having committed acts regarded as criminal not only under international law but also under the common law of all countries."[188]

In the end, Roosevelt as chair put the United Kingdom sentence to a vote. The Commission on Human Rights adopted it by a very close vote of seven to

[181] Proposal in E/CN.4/365, p. 42; rejected at E/CN.4/SR.159 ¶ 93, p. 19.
[182] E/CN.4/365, p. 42.
[183] E/CN.4/SR.159 ¶¶ 49 (U.S., punctuation of quote as in original), 51 (China), 53 (India) & 68 (Denmark), pp. 11, 12 & 15.
[184] E/CN.4/SR.159 ¶ 80, p. 17. "[G]enerally recognized principles of law" had just been suggested as a wording by Bowie of the United Kingdom, *id.* at ¶ 79.
[185] E/CN.4/SR.159 ¶ 53; Weissbrodt at 82.
[186] E/CN.4/SR.159 ¶ 59; cf. *id.* at ¶¶ 79 & 82, p. 17.
[187] *Id.* at ¶ 79, p. 17 (United Kingdom); *id.* at ¶ 82.
[188] *Id.* at ¶ 78, p. 16.

six, with two abstentions.[189] The summary record indicates that the original U.K. sentence was voted on, but the report of the Style Committee left out the reference to "civilized nations," in conformity with the oral amendment proposed by the United Kingdom and supported by Yugoslavia.[190]

The text that came out of the sixth session of the Commission on Human Rights and was submitted to ECOSOC was thus:

> 1. No one shall be held guilty of any criminal offence on account of any act or omission which did not constitute a criminal offence, under national or international law, at the time when it was committed. Nor shall a heavier penalty be imposed than the one that was applicable at the time when the criminal offence was committed. If, subsequent to the commission of the offence, provision is made by law for the imposition of a lighter penalty, the offender shall benefit thereby.
> 2. Nothing in this article shall prejudice the trial and punishment of any person for the commission of any act which, at the time when it was committed, was criminal according to the generally recognized principles of law.[191]

States that were members of the commission had time to submit comments on the Draft Covenant for inclusion in the report to ECOSOC. No comments were addressed to the criminal law non-retroactivity provision, despite the controversy surrounding some of the issues.[192]

This version was particularly significant for two reasons. First, it began to assume the shape of the final ICCPR provision. Second, it was the version that was current when the nations of Europe completed the European Convention on Human Rights on 4 November 1950.[193] The ECHR will be discussed along with the other regional human rights conventions. But it should not be forgotten that the ECHR was the first of the general human rights treaties to be completed, preceding the ICCPR by about sixteen years, and the two treaties' provisions on non-retroactivity of criminal law are nearly identical. The UN Secretariat produced reports comparing

[189] *Id.* at ¶ 96, p. 19.

[190] Compare *id.* at ¶ 96, p. 19 (original summary record) with E/CN.4/L.16, pp. 8–9 (22 May 1950) (Text of Articles 5, 6 and 8–15 of the Draft Covenant on Human Rights as revised by the Style Committee during its meetings held on 16 May 1950).

[191] Draft First International Covenant on Human Rights, art. 11, E/1681, Annex I, p. 17. For the unanimous Resolution transmitting the Draft Covenant to ECOSOC for its eleventh session, see E/1681 ¶ 51, p. 9.

[192] E/1681, Annex II, pp. 23–26.

[193] Cf. Humphrey, *supra* note 12, at 93–94.

the Commission on Human Rights provision with the ECHR draft[194] and comments by the Secretariat, the General Assembly, ECOSOC, and member states on the Draft Covenant.[195] In light of this feedback, the Commission on Human Rights took up the issue of legality in criminal law in 1952.

4.b.ii.B. 1952 and Beyond

The next time that this provision was substantively amended was at the eighth session of the Commission on Human Rights. The discussion focused on two major issues: the requirement of retroactivity of more lenient punishments (*lex mitior*) and the Nuremberg/Tokyo sentence.

Lex mitior is not at the core of this study. For our purposes, it is sufficient to note that there were controversies over the details, but in the end, attempts to change the text or delete the concept passed at the sixth session were rejected.[196] The first paragraph was adopted as a whole by fifteen to zero, with three abstentions.[197]

Two amendments to paragraph 2, the Nuremberg/Tokyo sentence, were passed. The first conformed the language of the second paragraph on what could be a crime. By a vote of thirteen to zero with five abstentions, it changed "the commission of any act" to "any act or omission."[198] This is not simply a matter of style.[199] It indicates that general principles of law may cover types of conduct – both acts and failures to act – as broad as those covered by any other kind of national or international criminal law. One of the most important substantive debates in international criminal law has been the liability of military and civilian superiors for failing or omitting to stop atrocities they knew or had reason to know were occurring.

The second amendment, adopted by a vote of nine to zero, with nine abstentions, changed the phrase "the generally recognized principles of law" to "the general principles of law recognized by the community of nations."[200] Although this statement is technically correct, something deeper was

[194] UN Doc. No. E/CN.4/524 (April 1951).
[195] UN Docs. No. E/CN.4/528 (2 April 1951) and E/CN.4/552 (22 April 1951).
[196] See E/CN.4/SR.324, pp. 16–17; UN. Doc. E/2256 ¶ 226, ESCOR, 14th sess., Supp. 4, pp. 1, 33.
[197] E/CN.4/SR.324, p. 17; E/2256 ¶ 226.
[198] E/2256 ¶ 228, adopting second U.K. amendment from UN Doc. E/1992, Annex III A, art. 11 (17 May 1951), in ESCOR, 13th sess., Supp. 9, p. 31. The summary record, E/CN.4/SR.324, p. 17, mistakenly leaves out the word *general* in the replacement sentence and states that there were only eight abstentions.
[199] *Pace* Weissbrodt at 86.
[200] E/CN.4/SR.324, p. 17; E/2256 ¶ 228.

going on. The ECHR had adopted a similar sentence: "This article shall not prejudice the trial and punishment for any act or omission which, at the time when it was committed, was criminal according to the general principles of law recognized by civilized nations."[201] The language at the end of this sentence parallels one of the sources of international law in the ICJ Statute.[202] The British wished to insert this language into what became the ICCPR, but many Communist and other countries objected to the phrase "civilized nations" as suggesting that some countries, particularly the nations newly freed from colonialism, were not civilized. This resulted in a lively debate over the meaning of the phrase, which is of more import to the political conflicts between East and West, as well as the decolonized states and the colonial powers, than to the principles of legality.[203] The language that was adopted did, in fact, eliminate the reference to "civilized nations," and instead referred to "the community of nations," but nothing in the discussion suggests that these two phrases are meant to refer to different types of law.[204]

The larger issues, which do relate to legality, are whether this sentence should have been included in the covenant at all, and whether the sentence refers to anything broader than a subset of international law. This will be discussed in a later section.[205] Here, it suffices to say that the amended sentence was adopted by a vote of ten to six, with two abstentions. The entire article on legality was adopted by a vote of fourteen to zero, with four abstentions.[206]

It would be fourteen more years before the adoption of the ICCPR by the UN General Assembly in 1966, and another decade before it would come into force. But the article on legality and non-retroactivity in criminal law had assumed the wording in which it would finally be adopted.

In 1955, the Secretariat prepared a set of annotations to the Draft Covenant on Human Rights, which included material on the legality article.[207] However, nothing substantive on legality occurred until the Third Committee of the General Assembly took up the matter in 1960.

[201] European Convention on Human Rights and Fundamental Freedoms art. 7(2).
[202] ICJ Statute art. 38(1)(c).
[203] E/CN.4/SR.324, *passim*.
[204] E/CN.4/SR.324.
[205] See Chap. 4.b.ii.C.
[206] Both votes at E/CN.4/SR.324, p. 17; E/2256 ¶¶ 228–29, and text as adopted at *id.*, Annex I B, art. 13.
[207] Annotations on the text of the Draft International Covenants on Human Rights (Prepared by the Secretary-General), UN Doc. A/2929 ¶ 96 (1 July 1955), in GAOR, 10th sess., Annexes, pp. 1, 45, discussed in Chap. 4.b.ii.C.

The Third Committee devoted several sessions of debate to this article.[208] Many of the prior decisions of the negotiators were reconsidered here. Given the closeness of some of the votes in the Commission on Human Rights, and the fact that all UN member states could participate in the Third Committee, it was not a foregone conclusion that the existing text would be adopted. Although many amendments were proposed, only a few survived to the stage of voting.

Indicating a growing consensus, the United Kingdom did not even request a vote on eliminating *nulla poena*. Yet the Netherlands still considered the inclusion of *nulla poena* in the ICCPR as a progressive development in international human rights law:

> Although *nulla poena sine lege* was a recognized principle of law in many countries, it was regarded as merely a moral principle in others. Hence the inclusion of that last principle in a new international instrument and subsequently in the legislation of many countries could be regarded as real progress.[209]

The first amendment voted on was from Argentina. It proposed to change the phrase "under national or international law" in the first sentence of the first paragraph to "under the applicable law."[210] This would have had the effect of making the covenant agnostic as to whether international criminal law applicable to individuals actually exists but preserving applicability of the rule of non-retroactivity of criminal law to it to the extent it does exist. This was defeated twenty-three votes for, forty-seven against, with ten abstentions.[211]

The second amendment put to the vote, from the United Kingdom, would have limited the rule of *lex mitior* to cases where the law became more lenient before sentence was imposed.[212] It was defeated by a vote of twenty-eight for, thirty-four against, with eighteen abstentions.[213]

Following these amendments, the entirety of paragraph 1, including *nullum crimen* (applying to both national and international law), *nulla*

[208] UN Docs. A/C.3/SR.1007–13 (meetings of 31 October 1960–4 November 1960), in GAOR, 15th sess., Third Committee, pp. 129ff. Some nations discussed their votes recorded in A/C.3/SR.1013 in UN Doc. A/C.3/SR.1014 (meeting of 7 November 1960). All the summary records in this series cited in this section are printed in the GAOR material cited here.

[209] A/C.3/SR.1011 ¶ 28.

[210] UN Doc. A/C.3/L.865 (31 October 1960) (proposal on paragraph 1).

[211] UN Doc. A/C.3/SR.1013 ¶ 44 (meeting of 4 November 1960), in GAOR, 15th sess., Third Committee, pp. 159, 162–63.

[212] A/C.3/SR.1013 ¶ 45.

[213] *Id.*

poena, and *lex mitior* was put to the vote. It passed fifty-six to zero, with twenty-four abstentions.[214]

The Argentine proposal to eliminate paragraph 2, the Nuremberg/Tokyo sentence,[215] was then put to the vote. For all the controversy earlier, the Third Committee vote was not so close. The tally was nineteen votes for deletion, fifty-one against, and ten abstentions.[216] Even the United States came around to favoring the sentence, though Roosevelt had opposed including it in the UDHR (and even after the vote, the United States mentioned that the sentence might better be placed as a footnote[217]). Support for eliminating the paragraph came mostly from the civil law Latin American countries, plus Saudi Arabia, Spain, China, Italy, Japan, and Lebanon. It is interesting to see the support from two of the former Axis nations of World War II (Italy and Japan), an Axis sympathizer (Spain), and one of the nations that suffered most from Japanese aggression (China, still represented by the Nationalists). Two states with large Islamic populations voted to eliminate the paragraph (Lebanon and Saudi Arabia), but several voted against (Morocco, Somalia, Sudan, United Arab Republic, Yemen, Afghanistan, Indonesia, Iran, Iraq, Jordan, and Libya), and Pakistan abstained. No common law country voted to eliminate this paragraph.[218]

Finally, the Third Committee voted on the entire legality/non-retroactivity of criminal law article. It was adopted by a vote of fifty-six to zero, with twenty-three abstentions.[219] This was the text of the article when the entire ICCPR was adopted and opened for signature.[220]

4.b.ii.C. General Principles of Law: No Exception to Legality Intended

The tension over the Nuremberg/Tokyo sentence is clear. The United Kingdom and other states feared that the Nuremberg and Tokyo judgments could be called into question without it.[221] The United States and others

[214] *Id.* at ¶ 46.
[215] UN Doc. A/C.3/L.865 (31 October 1960) (proposal on paragraph 2).
[216] A/C.3/SR.1013 ¶ 47. This was followed, *id.* at ¶ 50, by a vote of fifty-three to four, with twenty-two abstentions, in favor of paragraph 2.
[217] A/C.3/SR.1014 ¶ 3.
[218] A/C.3/SR.1013 records the roll call of votes.
[219] A/C.3/SR.1013 ¶ 51. All these votes are also recorded in the Report of the Third Committee, A/4625 ¶ 20 (8 December 1960).
[220] G.A. Res. 2200 A (XXI).
[221] See E/CN.4/SR.159 ¶ 50, p. 11 (quote from Roosevelt); *id.* at ¶ 57, p. 12 (France, by Ordonneau, not Cassin); *id.*at ¶ 59 (Yugoslavia).

feared that this sentence could itself call into question those judgments, as somehow needing special retroactive justification.[222]

In any case, the sentence does not allow for retroactive crime creation. An act or omission must have been criminal according to general principles of law "at the time when it was committed."[223]

A look at the statements made on this proposal over the history of the ICCPR negotiation is instructive. There are statements in the record, both before and after the sixth session of the Commission on Human Rights in 1950, that indicate a fear that the sentence could be read "to open up a breach in the system of protection against retroactive law which the article was designed to set up," despite there being no intent to allow for violations of legality.[224] Supporters of this sentence argued that this was a needless

[222] See E/CN.4/SR.159 ¶ 60, p. 13 (United States); *id.* at ¶ 68, p. 15 (Denmark); *id.* at ¶ 74, p. 16 (Belgium – U.K. amendment "defeated its own purpose by implying that the defendants at Nurnberg and Tokyo had not been condemned under international law but in virtue of principles of less certain authority"); UN Doc. E/CN.4/85, p. 20 (Brazil, comment on Draft Declaration, art. 7(2)); *id.* at p. 76 (United States, Brazil, Egypt comments on Draft Covenant, art. 14(2)).

[223] ICCPR art. 15(2).

[224] E/CN.4/SR.159 ¶ 51, p. 11 (China); E/CN.4/SR.112, pp. 5–6 (Philippines); *id.* at p. 7 (Soviet Union stated that "the Nürnberg Judgment had become part of international law" and supported principle of non-retroactivity on grounds of humanity and justice; war criminals' claim was that they did not commit crimes under German law); E/CN.4/SR.324, p. 10 (27 June 1952, reporting meeting of 5 June 1952) (Chile, arguing that the sentence was, as the USSR representative had said, a reinforcement of legality, but the sentence might not be read that way); *id.* at p. 12–13 (Belgium); cf. E/CN.4/SR.159 ¶ 70, p. 15 (Chile, fearing that even including "under national or international law" in the first sentence would allow for using international law in national courts "for offences not punishable under the national legislations of these countries, under the pretext they were punishable under international law."). Note that, in 1949 at the fifth session of the Commission on Human Rights, Chile had been willing to retain the sentence on "general principles of law" if it would "refer clearly to war criminals." E/CN.4/SR.112, pp. 6–7.

For later statements, see UN Doc. A/C.3/SR.1007 ¶¶ 3–4 (meeting of 31 October 1960) (Argentina – pointing out danger of this wording to liberty generally, without desiring to pose such a danger), in GAOR, 15th sess., Third Committee, 129; *id.*at ¶ 22 (Saudi Arabia, supporting the deletion of the sentence, proposed by Argentina); *id.* at ¶ 25 (Brazil, finding general principles of law hard to define); UN Doc. A/C.3/SR.1009 ¶¶ 9–10 (meeting of 2 November 1960) (Argentina again); UN Doc. A/C.3/SR.1010 ¶ 20 (second meeting of 2 November 1960), in GAOR, 15th sess., Third Committee, p. 143, 145 (Peru); *id.* at ¶ 25 (Japan); UN Doc. A/C.3/SR.1011 ¶ 3 (Haiti), in GAOR, 15th sess., Third Committee, p. 149 (meeting of 3 November 1960); *id.* at ¶¶ 22–23 (Paraguay); UN Doc. A/C.3/SR. 1012 ¶ 6, in GAOR, 15th sess., Third Committee, p. 155 (meeting of 4 November 1960) (Uruguay); *id.* at ¶ 13 (Cambodia) (supporting the Nuremberg/Tokyo sentence even though it could possibly be misinterpreted, as "general principles" tended to be imprecise); UN Doc. A/C.3/SR.1014 ¶ 7, in GAOR, 15th sess., Third Committee,

fear, because the sentence merely developed what was in the statement of non-retroactivity at the beginning of the article.[225] Some felt that removing the sentence could lead to uncertainty, rather than support for the principle of legality.[226] Other statements in support do not express an intention to allow for retroactive crime creation.[227] Sometimes they look to a possible repetition of the crimes of World War II and seek to preserve the general principles of law used in the Nuremberg Judgment for use again in the future.[228] This would seem to be the opposite of expanding the possibility of retroactive crime creation. The Netherlands' delegate stated the matter a bit more moderately:

> The definition of offences under international law might of course vary at different times and in different places, but if national courts were guided by the principles applied by the Nürnberg and Tokyo tribunals and formulated by the International Law Commission, no infringement of fundamental human rights would result.[229]

Many statements in the UN debate directly or indirectly support the proposition that general principles of law were intended as a subset of international law.[230] The representative of Israel went so far as to indicate

p. 165 (meeting of 7 November 1960) (explaining abstention of Canada on removing the sentence).

[225] E/CN.4/SR.324, p. 14 (Soviet Union).

For a later statement, see A/C.3/SR.1011 ¶ 13 (Kasliwal, India) (purpose of paragraph 2 was "to permit the punishment *a posteriori* of persons responsible for acts deemed to be criminal at the time when they had been committed").

[226] UN Doc. A/C.3/SR. 1012 ¶ 3, in GAOR, 15th sess., Third Committee, p. 155 (4 November 1960) (Belorussian SSR).

[227] E/CN.4/SR.159 ¶ 52, pp. 11–12 (United Kingdom); *id.* at ¶¶ 57–59, pp. 12–13 (France and Yugoslavia).

For later statements, see A/C.3/SR.1007 ¶¶ 19–20 (Afghanistan, suggesting that Argentina might suggest "technically" better language to address its concern about the sentence); UN Doc. A/C.3/SR.1008 ¶ 4 (meeting of 1 November 1960) (India, suggesting that removing this paragraph would be "doubting the existence of international law"), in GAOR, 15th sess., Third Committee, 133; A/C.3/SR.1012 ¶¶ 18–21 (Togo) (supporting view that "criminal laws were not retroactive"; indicating that "States" might be "condemned and severely punished" in the future for discrimination).

[228] UN Doc. E/C.3/SR.1008 ¶¶ 2–3 (meeting of 1 November 1960) (Poland), in GAOR, 15th sess., Third Committee, 133.

[229] A/C.3/SR.1011 ¶ 29.

[230] See E/CN.4/SR.112, pp. 5–6 (Philippines); *id.* at p. 7 (Soviet Union stated that "the Nürnberg Judgment had become part of international law," and supported principle of non-retroactivity on grounds of humanity and justice); E/CN.4/SR.159 ¶ 78, p. 16 (Jesremovic of Yugoslavia, in favor of the paragraph); *id.* at ¶ 80, p. 17 (Roosevelt for the

that the general principles of law expressed in the Nuremberg and Tokyo judgments were by 1960 part of "positive law."[231] The Netherlands and the United Arab Republic argued that these general principles were in fact general principles of international law itself.[232] In 1951, a UN Secretariat memorandum summarized the view as follows:

> there seems to be no clear reason for regarding the provision made in paragraph 2 [the Nuremberg/Tokyo sentence] as being different in content from that made in the first sentence of paragraph 1 of the Articles, [*sic*] particularly in view of the reference made therein to "international law". It seems to be accepted that the generally accepted principles of law are a part, or are a source of, international law. Thus for instance Article 38, paragraph 1 of the Statute of the International Court of Justice includes a provision that "The Court, whose function it is to decide *in accordance with international law* such disputes as are submitted to it, shall apply . . . c. the general principles of law recognized by civilized nations." When, in the proceedings and judgments of war crimes trials and in the literature thereon, reference has been made to "the generally recognized principles of law," these principles have been quoted and relied upon for the sole purpose of demonstrating that certain acts on the part of accused persons could be regarded as punishable under the law of war *as part of international law* (E/L.68, paragraph 72).[233]

United States, opposing this language on the ground that "general principles" are part of international law as defined in the ICJ Statute).

For later statements, see E/C.3/SR.1008 ¶ 4 (meeting of 1 November 1960) (India, suggesting that removing this paragraph would be "doubting the existence of international law"), in GAOR, 15th sess., Third Committee, 133; *id.* at ¶ 14 (Yugoslavia) (in favor of the paragraph as it is consistent with legality; "general principles" are a part of international law); UN Doc. A/C.3/SR.1010 ¶ 1 (second meeting of 2 November 1960), in GAOR, 15th sess., Third Committee, p. 143 (United Arab Republic); *id.* at ¶ 6 (Ceylon); *id.* at ¶ 14 (Iraq); *id.* at ¶ 23 (Czechoslovakia); cf. *id.* at ¶ 29 (Afghanistan); A/C.3/SR.1012 ¶ 15 (Bulgaria); *id.* at ¶ 24 (the Philippines); UN Doc. A/C.3/SR.1013 ¶ 14, in GAOR, 15th sess., Third Committee, p. 159 (second meeting of 4 November 1960) (Yugoslavia again).

[231] A/C.3/SR.1011 ¶¶ 36–37; see also A/C.3/SR.1013 ¶ 19 (Ceylon).

[232] For the statement that "general principles of law" in the covenant should mean "general principles of international law" that arose from events like Nuremberg and Tokyo, and not from the general principles of law recognized in ICJ Statute art. 38 (which arose from rules recognized by most legal systems), see A/C.3/SR.1011 ¶ 31 (Netherlands); see also A/C.3/SR.1012 ¶ 32 (United Arab Republic, "general principles in question were those of international law").

[233] Draft International Covenant on Human Rights and Measures of Implementation, The General Adequacy of the First Eighteen Articles (Parts I and II), Memorandum by the Secretary-General, UN Doc. E/CN.4/528 ¶ 164, at pp. 51–52 (2 April 1951) (bracketed material added).

The 1951 memorandum quotation is an accurate statement of matters as they then stood.

By 1955, the UN Secretariat, in an annotation to the Draft International Covenants on Human Rights, had changed its view. The annotation pointed out the claim in the debates that general principles of law in paragraph 2 were part of international law in paragraph 1. But it then said: "On the other hand, the view was heard that the saving provision set forth in paragraph 2 had no application to past convictions for war crimes, nor was it fully covered by the term 'international law' contained in paragraph 1."[234] The recent scholar Machteld Boot has agreed with the annotation that the phrase "general principles of law" was broader than international law generally.[235] Marc Bossuyt identifies several statements as "relevant" to this assertion of the Secretariat in its 1955 annotation.[236] He does not claim that these statements actually support the Secretariat's assertion.[237]

No one connected with the debate at this point stated any specific idea of what, outside of international law, was to be included here. In the material cited by Bossuyt and Boot,[238] there is no clear reference to what the content of such law might be. Most of the cited references simply do not say that the Nuremberg/Tokyo sentence refers to anything outside of international law as set forth in paragraph 1 of the article. The closest anyone came to such a

[234] See Annotations on the text of the Draft International Covenants on Human Rights (Prepared by the Secretary-General), UN Doc. A/2929 ¶ 96 (1 July 1955), in GAOR, 10th sess., Annexes, pp. 1, 45. Given the format of these annotations, the paragraph did not cite any particular statements, persons, or delegations in support.

[235] Boot, ¶ 125, at pp. 137–38 n.44, citing UN Docs. E/CN.4/SR. 112, 159 & 324 (including views of France, the Soviet Union, the United Kingdom, and Yugoslavia). Boot, ¶ 125 at p. 137 n.43. citing E/CN.4/SR. 112, 159, 199, 324, notes that several states (Australia, Belgium, China, Denmark, Philippines, the United States, Uruguay) believed that general principles of law was a subset of international law in the draft ICCPR.

[236] Bossuyt identifies the following documentation relevant to the claim:

> *[E/CN.4/SR.112, p.3 & p.8 (F), p.7 (RCH) & (SU); E/CN.4/SR.159, §52 & §75 & §79 & § 81 (GB), §57–58 (F), §59 & §78 (YU), § 73 (RCH); E/CN.4/SR.324, p.11 (F), p.14 (SU)]*

Bossuyt at 330, left column, bottom, on A/2929, Ch. 6, ¶ 96. Bossuyt used traffic or related abbreviations for the countries, so RCH is China, F is France, GB is the UK, SU is the USSR, and YU is Yugoslavia.

[237] Bossuyt at xxv, explaining that he cited to "interventions of government representatives relevant to" a given sentence in A/2929 or other report.

[238] See notes referring to their work just previously. See also the extensive documentation to 1955 on the "Prohibition of retroactive application of criminal law" article in UN Doc. A/2929, following ¶ 96, UN GAOR 10th sess., Annexes, p. 45. This is a listing, intended to be complete, of documentation on the article up to that time.

statement was J. M. Bowie, of the United Kingdom, during the 1950 debates. Her view was

> that one of the main arguments of the defence at Nurnberg had been that the acts of which the defendants had been accused had not constituted crimes under international law at the time they had been committed. The words "under international law" were therefore not sufficient to cover acts such as those perpetrated during the war.[239]

In context, though, it is clear that she said the sentence is necessary because of the claims made by the Nuremberg defendants, not because the Nuremberg principles are actually outside of international law. She had just finished pointing out that the United Kingdom thought it wise in this sentence "to reproduce the exact terms of article 38 of the Statute of the International Court"[240] – that is, the definition of general principles of law as part of international law. She had also stated the same day that "[i]t was important to emphasize in the covenant that acts which might not so far be the subject of express provisions of international law, could nevertheless be contrary to the general principles of law recognized implicitly in both national and international legislation."[241] This means that general principles of law in the covenant provision may go beyond the "express provisions" of international legislation (i.e., treaty law). But this is not to say that they are outside of international law as a whole. Bowie's argument, moreover, does not appear to allow retroactive creation of these general principles of law to convict persons of crimes.[242] This probably explains why the 1951 memorandum did not indicate any conflict over whether general principles of law were within international law.

So where did the claim, current as of 1955, arise that general principles of law might include something more than international law? The answer seems to be in the 1952 Report to the Economic and Social Council on the eighth session of the Commission on Human Rights.[243] This report includes the discussion of the commission at its 324th meeting, in 1952. After

[239] E/CN.4/SR.159 ¶ 81.

[240] *Id.* at ¶ 75.

[241] *Id.* at ¶ 52.

[242] See also A/C.3/SR.1008 ¶ 11 (Italy, arguing that with or without the paragraph, nations could apply general principles of law in defining criminal law, so long as they did it non-retroactively).

[243] UN Doc. E/2256 ¶¶ 224–29, in ESCOR, 14th sess., Supp. No. 4, pp. 1, 32–33. This document was approved by the Commission on Human Rights by a vote of eleven to zero, with five abstentions. *Id.* at ¶ 299.

a discussion of the reasons stated against the Nuremberg/Tokyo sentence, the report stated:

> Some representatives, on the other hand, said that the saving provision set forth in paragraph 2 had no application to past convictions for war crimes, nor was it fully covered by the term "international law" in terms of the first paragraph relating to acts or omissions constituting criminal offences under international law.[244]

When one looks at all the statements in favor of the sentence from that meeting in the summary records, there simply is no statement that the "general principles of law" in paragraph 2 was not covered by the phrase "international law."[245] There is indeed only one statement that paragraph 2 has no application to past convictions. This statement was made by P. D. Morosov, of the USSR, and denied that general principles went beyond existing international law:

> With regard to the Belgian representative's statement that the Commission's adoption of paragraph 2 would look like an attempt to justify the Nürnberg judgment *a posteriori*, he thought that the Commission was not concerned with what had been done at Nürnberg. There was no question of giving retroactive force to the Nürnberg procedure, which had been entirely justified by the general principles of international law, which had not been invented at that time to meet that particular case. Paragraph 2 merely developed the general principle already stated in the first sentence of paragraph 1.[246]

There seem to be two possible reasons (other than simple mistake) for the apparent inaccuracy in the 1952 report, which got carried over into the 1955 Secretariat annotations and the later work of scholars. One is that there might have been statements made to the effect of the 1952 report that were not included in the summary records, which, after all, were not verbatim transcripts. It seems unlikely, though, that such an important point to a key debate would have been missed by the rapporteur and staff. Another possibility is that the author of the 1952 report felt that the report was biased toward the reasons against the sentence and inserted the inaccuracy, possibly on the basis of an incorrect memory, to provide balance. Certainly both the

[244] E/2256 ¶ 227.

[245] See UN Doc. E/CN.4/SR.324, pp. 4 (UK), 4–5 (USSR), 6 (France), 7 (UK again), 7–8 (USSR), 8–9 (Poland), 9 (Yugoslavia), 11 (France again), 12 (Australia), 14 (USSR again), 15 (UK again), 16 (Yugoslavia again).

[246] E/CN.4/SR.324, p. 14.

1952 report and 1955 Secretariat annotations would otherwise seem tilted against, if not actively hostile, to the Nuremberg/Tokyo sentence.

From 1960 onward, this claim had disappeared from the official reports. In the Report of the Third Committee to the UN General Assembly, sentiment was discussed as follows: "The draft article [including the Nürnberg/Tokyo sentence] embodied the principle *nullun* [*sic*] *crimen sine lege*, and prohibited the retroactive application of criminal law. It was pointed out that there could be no offences other than those specified by law, either national or international."[247] Even if some might have felt that there was a necessity for a statement to ratify the post–World War II judgments, there was almost no support for an exception to the principle of non-retroactivity going forward. One delegation that feared (rather than hoped) that general principles of law might be other than a subset of international law was that of Brazil. Its delegate, speaking in the Third Committee in 1960, was against using the phrase in the covenant because it had three separate meanings through history. First, general principles of law denoted principles of Roman law that had so influenced the development of the European civil law system. The second was the natural law view that they were the enduring and absolute principles guiding the development of law through history. The third was the positivist view that they emerged from the study of the principles underlying positive law as it has actually developed. Given these differences in meaning, it was not a good idea to use the phrase in a text on non-retroactivity in criminal law.[248]

Also in 1960, Samuel Hoare, for the United Kingdom, came close to suggesting that the reference to general principles of law could be read as retroactively legitimating the Nuremberg proceeding,[249] but he did not suggest that it would legitimate retroactive crime creation in the future. The concern genuinely seems to have been to preserve the value of the Nuremberg/Tokyo proceedings as substantive law precedents for the future, not to approve further retroactive lawmaking.

A Chilean representative made one argument that some crimes of which "the whole community was a victim" should be exempted from the principle of non-retroactivity – "so-called economic offences, including illegal

[247] Draft International Covenants on Human Rights, Report of the Third Committee, UN Doc. A/4625 ¶ 13 (8 December 1960), in GAOR, 15th sess., Annexes at 3, 4.

[248] A/C.3/SR.1011 ¶¶ 19–21.

[249] UN Doc. A/C.3/SR.1009 ¶ 13; cf. *id.*, para. 19 (Ukrainian SSR); A/C.3/SR.1010 ¶¶ 6, 9–10 (Ceylon).

speculation."[250] These, however, are not the sort of crimes dealt with in the post–World War II tribunals. They are not the sort governed by general principles of law, but by very specific statutes in each society. This appears to be Chile's point, given that the representative opposed the U.K. addition of the sentence on "general principles."[251] Thus, the Chilean statement cannot be used to develop a case that this sentence allows a derogation from legality. Moreover, the suggestion that economic crimes should be an exception to non-retroactivity did not make further progress.

There is very little in the record by either supporters or opponents that the Nuremberg/Tokyo sentence is intended to permit retroactive crime creation at any time or for any reason in the future. One remark that could conceivably be read that way is a comment by a Cuban delegate, in 1960, just after the revolution led by Fidel Castro. His argument was that:

> The principle of non-retroactivity, in particular, could not be adopted without due regard to realities; for in seeking to ensure respect for that principle justice might be frustrated.... His delegation therefore ... supported paragraph 2, under which it would be possible to allow for the *de facto* situation in the various countries.[252]

This was consistent with the Communist view of socialist law for some decades after the Russian Revolution.[253] He did not, however, indicate how paragraph 2, and particularly the phrase "general principles of law," could be taken to allow retroactive local crime creation in a particular society based on its peculiar conditions. Moreover, he later expressed support for non-retroactivity in criminal law.[254] There is also a remark by a delegate of Romania, who argued that the Genocide Convention could be used to prosecute persons who committed genocide even before it came into force.[255] This claim, however, is made in the context of a discussion in which he argues that the law proclaimed at Nuremberg and Tokyo had existed previously, even though it had not been codified.[256]

Interestingly, the Soviet Union's representative indicated on the same day that non-retroactivity of crimes and punishments were "at the very basis of

[250] E/CN.4/SR.159 ¶ 71, p. 15.
[251] See *id.* at ¶ 70, p. 15.
[252] A/C.3/SR.1008 ¶ 9.
[253] See Chap. 2.c.ii.C & Chap. 5.c.iv.
[254] A/C.3/SR.1013 ¶ 22.
[255] A/C.3/SR.1010 ¶ 36.
[256] *Id.* at ¶¶ 33–35.

USSR penal law" and that the Nuremberg/Tokyo sentence was consistent with non-retroactivity.[257] The Soviet Union had recently changed its internal law to bring back non-retroactivity in criminal law.[258]

Another fascinating statement was made in 1960 by a representative of Spain, then governed by the authoritarian Francisco Franco regime. He asserted that Spain had observed legality since the seventh century and was against anything in the covenant that might be seen as "prejudicial to the accused."[259] Thus, although Spain does not specifically refer to the Nuremberg/Tokyo sentence, it clearly wanted the sentence eliminated from the treaty. However, Spain did not say that non-retroactivity must utterly disappear from practice. Rather,

> the Covenant on Civil and Political Rights was not designed to be relied upon at the great historical trials of the future; its purpose was to safeguard the dignity of man and to guarantee his everyday freedoms by enabling him to go before courts which interpreted a clearly defined law.[260]

These great historical trials "were rare, and the courts set up on those occasions their own rules of law and their own body of practice in light of the prevailing circumstances."[261] This, from a government of the far right, is as close as any statement to the Cuban view that non-retroactivity should sometimes be acceptable. However, the revolutionary Cuban government wanted non-retroactivity to be permissible within the covenant system, while the Spanish government wanted it available only in extraordinary historical circumstances outside the system. Other delegations did not state support for either of these ideas.

Finally, the view that the Nuremberg/Tokyo sentence could itself call into question the legality of those trials survived late into the discussion of the ICCPR. This was seen as a reason for opposing its inclusion in the text.[262]

As mentioned previously, the final vote keeping the sentence in the covenant was not very close. On an Argentine amendment to delete it, the vote in the Third Committee was nineteen for deletion, fifty-one against, and ten abstentions.[263]

[257] A/C.3/SR.1008 ¶ 22.
[258] See Chap. 5.c.iv.
[259] A/C.3/SR.1011 ¶ 25.
[260] *Id.* at ¶ 26.
[261] *Id.*
[262] A/C.3/SR.1013 ¶ 32 (China).
[263] *Id.* at ¶ 47; *id.* at ¶ 50 was a vote fifty-three to four, with twenty-two abstentions, in favor of the sentence.

4.C. THE CONVENTION ON THE RIGHTS OF THE CHILD: UNIVERSALITY OF *NULLUM CRIMEN* AND PROHIBITING EVEN ACCUSATIONS OF RETROACTIVE CRIME

The UN Convention on the Rights of the Child (CRC) is another treaty, intended to be universal, which requires the internal application of the principle of *nullum crimen* in some cases.[264] Pursuant to this treaty, delinquent acts of juveniles must be defined by national or international law in advance of their commission: "No child shall be alleged as, be accused of, or recognized as having infringed the penal law by reason of acts or omissions that were not prohibited by national or international law at the time they were committed."[265] This convention prohibits accusations of retroactively created crimes and convictions.[266] All UN member states except the United States and Somalia have ratified this convention, and there is no evidence that this provision is what has caused the failure to ratify by those states.[267]

This convention does not contain a *nulla poena* provision. Juvenile delinquency is considered in many places to be a matter of treatment rather than punishment, at least in most cases. Under this logic, new methods of treatment for children should not be prohibited just because they were brought into practice after the young person committed a delinquent act. Although the CRC text does not wholly rule out punishment for juveniles who violate penal law, its text promotes habilitation and rehabilitation over punishment:

> A variety of dispositions, such as care, guidance and supervision orders; counselling; probation; foster care; education and vocation training programmes and other alternatives to institutional care shall be available to ensure that children are dealt with in a manner appropriate to their well-being and proportionate both to their circumstances and the offence.[268]

The broader movement earlier in this century to consider all criminal law sanctions (including for adults) as treatment, and not really as a penalty,

[264] Art. 40(2)(a), G.A. Res. 44/25 (Annex) (20 November 1989), UN Doc. A/RES/44/49 [hereinafter CRC], ratified by all U.N. members except Somalia and the United States. The UN High Commission for Human Rights Web site, http://www.ohchr.org/english/countries/ratification/11.htm (updated 13 July 2007) reveals no specific reservation to this provision by any of the ratifying states.

[265] CRC art. 40(2)(a).

[266] Compare ICCPR art. 15(1).

[267] In the United States, this convention has been opposed by many because of its prohibition of the death penalty for any juvenile. For most of the period since the convention was opened for signature, Somalia has not had a functioning government.

[268] CRC art. 40(4).

has died out,[269] as has the Anglo-Indian suggestion that non-retroactivity of punishment is not a vital human right.[270] At least these ideas no longer threaten to do away with *nulla poena* in criminal law generally.

When the ICCPR and the CRC are taken together, every UN member has accepted, as a matter of international obligation, that the principle of *nullum crimen* applies to its criminal law (whether covering national or international crimes) for both its nationals and nonnationals, at least for children and in most states for everyone.[271] It is hard to see why a state would accept an international law obligation to apply *nullum crimen* for juvenile offenses but object to international law prescribing the principle for adults, given that juvenile justice is generally treated much more flexibly in national systems than adult criminal law. This suggests that the failure of the ICCPR to obtain universal acceptance is not based on an objection to its inclusion of the principle of legality, or at least not on objection to the ICCPR's version of the principle of non-retroactivity of criminal law.

4.d. THE REGIONAL HUMAN RIGHTS TREATIES: EUROPEAN, AMERICAN, AFRICAN, ARAB

Regional treaty regimes requiring legality in criminal law (in both the *nullum crimen* and *nulla poena* senses, and in some cases more broadly) include (in chronological order) the European Convention for the Protection of Human Rights and Fundamental Freedoms (ECHR),[272] the American Convention on Human Rights (ACHR),[273] the African Charter of Human and Peoples' Rights (ACHPR),[274] and the revised Arab Charter on Human Rights (ArCHR).[275] Legality in criminal law also appears in the Charter

[269] See Jerome Hall, *Nulla Poena Sine Lege*, 47 YALE L.J. 165, 182–85 (1938).

[270] See Chap. 4.b.ii.A.

[271] For the ratification status of the Convention on the Rights of the Child (193 parties), see http://www.ohchr.org/english/countries/ratification/11.htm; for the ICCPR (160 parties), see http://www.ohchr.org/english/countries/ratification/4.htm.

[272] Art. 7, 312 U.N.T.S. 221 (4 November 1950) [hereinafter ECHR].

[273] Arts. 7–9, 1114 U.N.T.S. 123 (22 November 1969), reprinted in 9 I.L.M. 673 (1970) [hereinafter ACHR].

[274] Art. 7(2), OAU Doc. CAB/LEG/67/3/Rev. 5, art. 7(2) (27 June 1981), reprinted in 21 I.L.M. 59 (1982) [hereinafter ACHPR].

[275] Art. 15, reprinted in 12 Int'l Hum. Rts. Rep. 893 (2005) (22 May 2004; entered into force 15 March 2008). This document is a revision of ArCHR art. 6, adopted by the Council of the League of Arab States, Resolution 5437, 102d Reg. Sess., 15 September 1994 (text available at http://www.al-bab.com/arab/docs/international/hr1994.htm) (never in force).

of Fundamental Rights of the European Union,[276] whose complicated legal status is bound up with the negotiations over new treaties for the European Union.

The ECHR legality provisions are couched in terms very close to the text of the ICCPR. In contrast, the formulations of some of the other regional treaties differ from those of the UDHR and the ICCPR. They sometimes contain a broader array of rights than these two instruments which are intended to be universal.

4.d.i. *European Convention for the Protection of Human Rights and Fundamental Freedoms*

The 1950 ECHR legality provision is similar to the later final version of the ICCPR, except that "civilised nations" was used in the ECHR instead of "the community of nations":

> 1. No one shall be held guilty of any criminal offence on account of any act or omission which did not constitute a criminal offence under national or international law at the time when it was committed. Nor shall a heavier penalty be imposed than the one that was applicable at the time the criminal offence was committed.
> 2. This article shall not prejudice the trial and punishment of any person for any act or omission which, at the time when it was committed, was criminal according to the general principles of law recognised by civilised nations.[277]

As noted previously, this article is very close to that in the Draft International Covenant at the time the ECHR was finalized.[278] It does not include *lex mitior.*

4.d.ii. *American Convention on Human Rights: Broadening of Procedural Protections*

The ACHR contains three versions of the principle of legality. Article 9 contains a traditional *nullum crimen, nulla poena sine lege* rule but refers to "applicable" law rather than to crimes under national or international

[276] Art. 49, 2000/C 364/01 (7 December 2000; pub. date 18 December 2000).

[277] ECHR art. 7. A heading, "No punishment without law," was added to this section by the 11th Protocol to the ECHR. Persons who truly care about spelling will note the *s* in *recognised* as well, instead of the *z* in the UDHR.

[278] See Chap. 4.b.ii.A.

law in the *nullum crimen* clause. The emphasis is thus on ensuring that the law not only has been previously enacted or made effective (e.g., by the common law process) but also was applicable to the actor at the time of the act:

> No one shall be convicted of any act or omission that did not constitute a criminal offence, under the applicable law, at the time it was committed. A heavier penalty shall not be imposed than the one that was applicable at the time the criminal offense was committed. If subsequent to the commission of the offense the law provides for the imposition of a lighter punishment, the guilty person shall benefit therefrom.[279]

The Inter-American Court of Human Rights has found a violation of this provision where the law existed but was not applicable to a specific actor at the time of the offense.[280] Like the ICCPR and the ECHR, the ACHR contains a rule of mercy applying the lighter penalty if there is a change in penalties between commission and conviction of the crime (*lex mitior*).[281] Unlike those two treaties, the ACHR does not have a special provision concerning crimes under general principles of law. However, there is no evidence of an intent to exclude international criminal law from being a source of applicable law.

Article 7 of the ACHR states a principle of non-retroactivity more procedurally and more broadly: "No one shall be deprived of his physical liberty except for the reasons and under the conditions established beforehand by the Constitution of the State Party concerned or by a law established pursuant thereto."[282] On its face, this extends the principle of legality to non-criminal reasons for depriving a person of liberty, such as institutionalization for mental incompetence. Here "the reasons and . . . the conditions established beforehand" for deprivation of liberty have a role analogous to the previous definition of crime. However, it is limited only to deprivations of physical liberty, not to other negative legal consequences of non-criminal acts. Note that this does prevent holding a person in jail while under charge for a retroactively created crime.

Article 8 of the ACHR adds the rule of prior establishment of courts in both criminal and civil cases: "Every person has the right to a hearing . . . by a competent, independent, and impartial tribunal, previously established

[279] ACHR art. 9.

[280] Castillo Petruzzi v. Peru, Judgement, ¶ 121, Inter-Am. C.H.R., Petition No. 11,319 (30 May 1999).

[281] ACHR art. 9.

[282] *Id.* at art. 7(2).

by law."[283] This is the strongest of the rules against retroactive creation of jurisdictions in the human rights treaties. It reflects the historical experience of many states in the Americas with special, retroactively created courts.

The ACHR also focuses on the guilt of the individual: "Punishment shall not be extended to any person other than the criminal."[284] This effectively outlaws collective punishment, though without using that specific phrase.

4.d.iii. *African Charter of Human and Peoples' Rights: Against Collective Punishment*

The ACHPR contains rules of legality in criminal law as well:

> No one may be condemned for an act or omission which did not constitute a legally punishable offence at the time it was committed. No penalty may be inflicted for an offense for which no provision was made at the time it was committed. Punishment is personal and can be imposed only on the offender.[285]

This is a different way of articulating both *nullum crimen* and *nulla poena* from the other human rights documents. On its face, it is at least as broad as the UDHR/ICCPR version. *Lex mitior* is not included.

The provision allowing imposition of punishment only on the offender disallows collective, communal, or family punishments. In this way, it is similar to the humanitarian law treaties discussed herein.[286] The ACHPR declaration that punishment is personal is more explicit that the ACHR version and is in advance of the other human rights treaties.[287]

4.d.iv. *Revised Arab Charter on Human Rights*

The new revised ArCHR came into force while this book was being prepared for publication. It states a strong version of legality: "No crime and no penalty can be established without a prior provision of the law. In all circumstances, the law most favorable to the defendant shall be applied."[288]

[283] *Id.* at art. 8(1).
[284] *Id.* at art. 5(3).
[285] ACHPR art. 7(2).
[286] Cf. Geneva Convention (No. IV) art. 33; Additional Protocol No. I, art. 75(2)(d); Additional Protocol No. II, art. 4(2)(b).
[287] ACHR art. 5(3).
[288] Revised Arab Charter on Human Rights art. 15, reprinted in 12 Int'l Hum. Rts. Rep. 893 (2005) (22 May 2004; entered into force 15 March 2008).

This appears to include *lex mitior*. The prior version, never brought into force, stated: "There shall be no crime or punishment except as provided by law and there shall be no punishment in respect of an act preceding the promulgation of that provision. The accused shall benefit from subsequent legislation if it is in his favour."[289] In both versions, the prior promulgation of a law appears to be required – that is, *nullum crimen, nulla poena sine praevia lege scripta*. Special mentions guard against retroactive imposition of the death penalty.[290]

4.d.v. *Charter of Fundamental Rights of the European Union: Legality Controlling an International Organization?*

The proposed Charter of Fundamental Rights of the European Union provision includes language similar to the ICCPR. It also contains a new provision that prohibits disproportion between an offense and its punishment.[291] It will apply only to the European Union. This entity has fewer national members than the Council of Europe, to which the ECHR applies. However, the new charter will apply directly to the supranational European Union institutions. This may become an important innovation in the application of human rights to supranational entities.

The question of the legal status of this document is bound up with the question of new treaty documents for the European Union.[292] One cannot therefore draw any firm conclusions yet about whether it will be effective in the long term at the supranational level.

4.e. NON-DEROGABILITY OF LEGALITY IN THE TREATIES

The principle of legality is specifically described as non-derogable even in times of emergency in the ICCPR, the ECHR, the ACHR, and the revised ArCHR.[293] No provision for derogation is made in the Convention on

[289] Arab Charter on Human Rights art. 6, adopted by the Council of the League of Arab States, Resolution 5437, 102d Reg. Sess., 15 September 1994 (text available at unofficial Web site, http://www.al-bab.com/arab/docs/international/hr1994.htm) (never entered into force).

[290] Revised ArCHR arts. 6, 7.

[291] Charter of Fundamental Rights of the European Union art. 49.

[292] See the European Parliament webpage on the European Charter of Human Rights, at http://www.europarl.europa.eu/charter/default_en.htm.

[293] See ICCPR art. 4; ECHR art. 15(2); ACHR art. 27; revised ArCHR art. 4; 1 ICRC CUSTOMARY IHL (RULES) discussion of R. 101, at pp. 371–72; 2 ICRC CUSTOMARY IHL (PRACTICE, PART II) ¶¶ 3677–78, 2681–82, at pp. 2494–95.

the Rights of the Child and the ACHPR, so the issue of derogability does not arise as to them. In the ACHR, both non-retroactivity and the rule against extending punishment beyond the criminal are non-derogable.[294] (The issue of reservation, which is separate from the issue of derogability once a provision is accepted, is discussed subsequently.[295])

4.f. LEGALITY IN THE INTERNATIONAL HUMANITARIAN LAW SYSTEM: APPLICATION TO INTERNATIONAL AND INTERNAL CONFLICTS AND OCCUPATION

4.f.i. *Non-retroactivity*

The principle of legality in both crime creation and sentencing also appears in two of the almost universally accepted humanitarian conventions on the laws of war, the Third and Fourth Geneva Conventions of 1949. The Fourth Geneva Convention forbids retroactive effect of penal provisions against a civilian population by an Occupying Power, which on its face includes sentencing law (*nulla poena*) as well as crime creation (*nullum crimen*): "penal provisions enacted by the Occupying Power shall not come into force before they have been published... [and] [t]he effect of these provisions shall not be retroactive."[296] The Third Geneva Convention provides that a prisoner of war may be punished only for an act "forbidden by the law of the Detaining Power or by international law, in force at the time the said act was committed."[297] In both of these cases, the burden of the text is that the law itself may not have retroactive effects. This indicates that charge, arrest, or other retroactive effects before conviction are also prohibited.

Non-retroactivity of crimes and punishments also appears in Additional Protocols I and II of 1977, in identical language:

> No one shall be accused or convicted of a criminal offence on account of any act or omission which did not constitute a criminal offence under national or international law to which he was subject at the time when it was committed; nor shall a heavier penalty be imposed than that which

[294] ACHR art. 27.

[295] See Chap. 4.g.

[296] Convention Relative to the Protection of Civilian Persons in Time of War (Geneva Convention (No. IV)), art. 65 (1949).

[297] Convention Relative to the Treatment of Prisoners of War (Geneva Convention (No. III)), art. 99 (1949).

> was applicable at the time when the criminal offence was committed; if, after the commission of the offence, provision is made by law for the imposition of a lighter penalty, the offender shall benefit thereby.[298]

As will be seen, the material in this sentence before the second semicolon is perhaps the best summing up of the current principle of legality of crimes and punishments as a matter of international law generally,[299] even though the Additional Protocols themselves have a narrower scope. The Additional Protocols themselves have been widely adopted but not universally so; given that this language was adopted by consensus, there is nothing which suggests that opposition to the first two independent clauses has anything to do with this. There have been a few objections to a similar "lighter penalty" provision in the ICCPR, and thus the last independent clause has not been universally accepted.[300] The Geneva Conventions and their Additional Protocols require that these rules be applied to persons (prisoners of war, civilians, and others) in the power of an enemy state in time of armed conflict or during occupation.

Additional Protocol II applies to non-state actors involved in armed conflict within a state, as well as to state actors involved in non-international conflicts. The Additional Protocols are explicit in forbidding both retroactive increases in penalties and retroactive crime creation. The additional protocols make it clear that the law under which an actor is punished must have been applicable to the actor at the time of the act or omission.

Additional Protocol II is particularly significant because it applies to internal armed conflict. More than 160 states have accepted as an international obligation that *nullum crimen* and *nulla poena* must apply internally even in the desperate strait of civil war. It does not require that states abide by the rule of legality in all prosecutions at all times, as do the ICCPR and the regional human rights treaties. However, it applies specifically to those times when the pressure would be greatest to ignore the rule of law. Therefore, its broad adoption is very strong evidence of the importance of the principle of non-retroactivity of crimes and punishments to the international community.

There is one oddity in the Third Geneva Convention provisions. In certain situations, it seems that the laws of the detaining state may be applied to

[298] Additional Protocol I to the 1949 Geneva Conventions, art. 75(4)(c) (1977); Additional Protocol II to the 1949 Geneva Conventions, art. 6(2)(c) (1977); see 2 ICRC Customary IHL (Practice, part II) ¶¶ 3679-80, at 2492-95 (both of these provisions adopted by consensus).

[299] See Chap. 7.

[300] See Chap. 4.g.

acts of a prisoner of war even before capture.[301] There might be situations when the actor might not have known he was subject to the laws of the detaining state. The better reading, however, is that the law of the detaining power must have been applicable to the prisoner of war at the time of the act. This is made explicit in the Additional Protocols,[302] and is the most sensible reading of the Third Geneva Convention. This would mean that the detaining power could apply its law implementing the international laws and customs of war and prohibiting genocide and crimes against humanity to acts occurring before capture, and to ordinary crimes unconnected with military activities committed in the detaining power's territory (e.g., rape or robbery). In these cases, it is clear that the law involved applied to the person at the time of acting. This reading would be based on consistency with the rest of international humanitarian law and international human rights law, which requires that criminal law have been applicable to an actor at the time that the allegedly criminal acts were committed. In any case, the provision does prevent arbitrary creation of new laws to punish prisoners of war.

There is also a persuasive, if not wholly conclusive, argument that the 1949 Geneva Conventions themselves incorporate the principle of non-retroactivity of criminal law in their regulation of non-international conflict. This is a useful argument because of the near universality of the main conventions as opposed to Additional Protocol II, which is widely, though not universally, accepted. Non-international armed conflict is regulated by Common Article 3 of the Geneva Conventions. In relevant part, these require that:

> 1. Persons taking no active part in the hostilities, including members of armed forces who have laid down their arms and those placed hors de combat by sickness, wounds, detention, or any other cause, shall in all circumstances be treated humanely, without any adverse distinction founded on race, colour, religion or faith, sex, birth or wealth, or any other similar criteria.
>
> To this end the following acts are and shall remain prohibited at any time and in any place whatsoever with respect to the above-mentioned persons:
>
> (a) violence to life and person, in particular murder of all kinds, mutilation, cruel treatment and torture;
>
> (b) taking of hostages;

[301] Geneva Convention (No. III) art. 85.

[302] But cf. Additional Protocol I to the 1949 Geneva Conventions, art. 75(4)(c) (1977); Additional Protocol II to the 1949 Geneva Conventions, art. 6(2)(c) (1977).

(c) outrages upon personal dignity, in particular humiliating and degrading treatment;
(d) the passing of sentences and the carrying out of executions without previous judgment pronounced by a regularly constituted court, affording all the judicial guarantees which are recognized as indispensable by civilized peoples.[303]

It is fair to characterize "all the judicial guarantees which are recognized as indispensable by civilized peoples" as including the non-retroactivity of crimes and punishments. At the time of the 1949 conventions, legality in criminal law had just been declared as a fundamental human right recognized by the UDHR. All of the arguments as to the importance of non-retroactivity of crimes and punishment discussed throughout this book can be used to show that it is a "judicial guarantee recognized as indispensable by civilized peoples."[304] Passing sentences without indispensable judicial guarantees is part of the "grave breaches" regime of the Geneva Convention system:

> Grave breaches to which the preceding Article relates shall be those involving any of the following acts, if committed against persons or property protected by the present Convention: wilful killing, torture or inhuman treatment, including biological experiments, wilfully causing great suffering or serious injury to body or health, unlawful deportation or transfer or unlawful confinement of a protected person, compelling a protected person to serve in the forces of a hostile Power, or *wilfully depriving a protected person of the rights of fair and regular trial prescribed in the present Convention*, taking of hostages and extensive destruction and appropriation of property, not justified by military necessity and carried out unlawfully and wantonly.[305]

The argument that non-retroactivity of crimes and punishments is already in Common Article 3 of the 1949 Geneva Conventions is not conclusive for a simple reason: it is not explicitly listed there. Additionally, the conventions were drafted shortly after the Nuremberg Judgment, at which time, as we have seen, *nullum crimen* was not yet a limitation on sovereignty. Yet these conventions are drafted in a way that suggests that the notion of what is "recognized as indispensable by civilized peoples" was not frozen in time as of 1949, and certainly not as of 1946, the date of the Nuremberg Judgment. Most of the systems which did not have legality in their constitutional or

[303] Geneva Conventions (Nos. I–IV) art. 3(1).
[304] *Id.*
[305] Geneva Convention (No. IV) art. 147 (emphasis added) (the "grave breaches" articles are differently numbered in each of the four conventions).

statutory systems in 1946 do today – for example, the states of the former Soviet Union. Today, non-retroactivity of crimes and punishment are far more likely to be considered "indispensible."[306]

The International Committee of the Red Cross (ICRC), on the basis of the preceding material and abundant further state practice, has found the non-retroactivity of crimes and punishments to have become "a norm of customary international law applicable in both international and non-international armed conflicts"[307]:

> No one may be accused or convicted of a criminal offense on account of any act or omission which did not constitute a criminal offence under national or international law at the time it was committed; nor may a heavier penalty be imposed than that which was applicable at the time the criminal offence was committed.[308]

Note that in situations covered by international humanitarian law, only some of the purposes of legality apply.[309] Notice to actors and prevention of arbitrary government action apply. Purposes such as protecting separation of powers and democratic government may not apply in areas under occupation or to prisoners of war.

4.f.ii. *Against Collective Punishments and Hostage Taking to Ensure Good Behavior*

At the close of World War II, there was some question concerning the lawfulness of reprisals as collective punishment, and some question concerning taking and use of hostages, at least in the context of international war.[310] These questions are no longer open.

The international humanitarian law treaty system has a number of protections against collective punishment for crime or other prohibited behavior. The Fourth Geneva Convention prohibits collective punishments in occupied territory or of civilians caught up in international armed conflict: "No protected person may be punished for an offence he or she has

[306] Cf. Chap. 5(b, c).

[307] Jean-Marie Henckaerts & Louise Doswald-Beck, 1 Customary International Humanitarian Law (Rules), Summary of R. 101, p. 371 (Cambridge Univ. Press 2005) (study issued by the ICRC) [hereinafter ICRC, Customary IHL].

[308] 1 ICRC, Customary IHL (Rules) R. 101, p. 371. Extensive documentation of further state and other practice supporting this rule is collected at 2 ICRC, Customary IHL (Practice) §§3673–3716, pp. 2493–2500.

[309] See Chap. 1.a.

[310] Cf. [Zivkovic], Notes on the Case (*Trial of Rauter*), 14 UNWCC, Law Rep., Case No. 88, pp. 89, 123–38; Wright, *Foreword*, 14 UNWCC, Law Rep., ix, xi–xii (1949).

not personally committed. Collective penalties and likewise all measures of intimidation or of terrorism are prohibited."[311] The Third Geneva Conventions forbids "[c]ollective punishment for individual acts" and "collective disciplinary measures involving food" of prisoners of war.[312] The Third and Fourth Geneva Conventions prohibit "[m]easures of reprisal" against prisoners of war[313] and "[r]eprisals" against civilians or persons in occupied territory.[314] These provisions effectively forbid collective punishment of innocent protected persons as a way of coercing obedience from others.

These latter provisions also forbid individual punishment of individuals who have not committed a prohibited act. This effectively forbids the punishment of prisoners or hostages as a guaranty of good behavior of others.

The 1949 Geneva Conventions directly forbid the taking of hostages, in both international and non-international armed conflicts.[315] Because hostages cannot lawfully be taken, innocent persons cannot lawfully be held as hostages under threat of punishment to ensure the behavior of the population from which they are taken.

The two 1977 Additional Protocols prohibit collective punishments in both international and non-international armed conflicts.[316] Again, the prohibition of collective punishments during civil wars is of most significance for the construction of general human rights law. If governments are willing to give up the right to impose such punishments internally in times of greatest temptation to do so, can it not be considered that they are willing to give up the right to impose collective punishment during normal times?

The ICRC finds that these materials, plus state practice, form two rules of "customary international law applicable in both international and non-international armed conflicts."[317] The first confines criminal responsibility to the actor: "No one may be convicted of an offence except on the basis of individual criminal responsibility."[318] The second says simply: "Collective

[311] Geneva Convention (No. IV) art. 33.

[312] Geneva Convention (No. III) arts. 26(6) (food), 87(3) (collective punishment for individual acts of prisoners of war generally).

[313] Geneva Convention (No. III) art. 13.

[314] Geneva Convention (No. IV) art. 33.

[315] Geneva Convention (No. IV) art. 34 (international conflicts; treatment of civilians); Geneva Conventions (Nos. I–IV) art. 3 (non-international conflicts).

[316] Additional Protocol I, art. 75(d) (international conflicts); Additional Protocol II, art. 4(2)(b) (non-international conflicts).

[317] 1 ICRC, Customary IHL (Rules), Summaries of R. 102 & 103, pp. 372, 374.

[318] 1 ICRC, Customary IHL (Rules), R. 102, p. 372, with additional documentation at 2 ICRC, Customary IHL (Practice) §§3717–3816, pp. 2500–12.

punishments are prohibited."[319] The ICRC states that this last rule covers more than criminal sanctions, and includes "sanctions and harassment of any sort, administrative, by police action or otherwise."[320]

4.g. RESERVATIONS TO PROVISIONS ON LEGALITY BY PARTIES TO THE WORLDWIDE TREATIES

No reservation to the ICCPR by any country explicitly limits or rejects the principles of non-retroactivity of crimes and punishments. A few limit or reject the additional doctrine of *lex mitior*.[321] A reservation by Argentina to the ICCPR provision on "general principles of law"[322] seems aimed to prevent that provision from impairing non-retroactivity.

Similarly, there are no reservations to the Convention on the Rights of the Child explicitly limiting or rejecting the principle of non-retroactivity of crimes.[323] The real issue about reservations comes from those states which purport to reserve or declare against all provisions that conflict with a state's religion or traditions, without specifying which provisions are in conflict.

No reservation to the Third and Fourth Geneva Conventions or Additional Protocols I and II impugns the non-retroactivity of crimes and punishments.[324] Similarly, no reservation to the Third and Fourth Geneva

[319] 1 ICRC, CUSTOMARY IHL (RULES), R. 103, p. 374, with additional documentation at 2 ICRC, CUSTOMARY IHL (PRACTICE) §§3717–3816, pp. 2500–12.

[320] 1 ICRC, CUSTOMARY IHL (RULES), Summary of R. 103, p. 374, quoting from COMMENTARY ON THE ADDITIONAL PROTOCOLS §3055 (Yves Sandoz, Christophe Swinarski, & Bruno Zimmerman, eds., ICRC 1987).

[321] The United States has reserved the right not to apply the mercy principle (*lex mitior*); Italy and Trinidad and Tobago have reserved the right to apply it only to cases still in progress at the time the law is changed; Germany reserves the right not to apply it in extraordinary circumstances. See http://www.ohchr.org/english/countries/ratification/4_1.htm (documentation of ICCPR ratifications and reservations on the Web site of the UN Office of the High Commissioner for Human Rights).

[322] Argentina reserves the right to apply ICCPR art. 15(2) only consistently with its own constitution. See http://www.ohchr.org/english/countries/ratification/4_1.htm.

[323] The UN High Commission for Human Rights Web site, http://www.ohchr.org/english/countries/ratification/11.htm (updated 13 July 2007), reveals no specific reservation to this provision by any of the ratifying states (including all UN members except the United States and Somalia).

[324] See http://www.icrc.org/ihl.nsf/WebSign?ReadForm&id=375&ps=P (Web site of the ICRC) and links therein to reservations to the four Geneva Conventions of 1949; http://www.icrc.org/ihl.nsf/WebSign?ReadForm&id=470&ps=P (Web site of the ICRC) and links therein to reservations to Additional Protocol I of 1977; http://www.icrc.org/ihl.nsf/WebSign?ReadForm&id=475&ps=P and links therein to reservations to Additional Protocol II of 1977.

Conventions or Additional Protocols I and II impugns the prohibition of collective punishment.[325]

4.g.i. *Lack of Reservations in the Treaties for* Ta'azir *Crimes in Islamic Law and Lack of Persistent Objection*

As mentioned previously, *ta'azir* crimes are sometimes seen as an exception to the principle of non-retroactivity of crimes and punishments in Islamic societies (though many disagree).[326] When treaty practice is examined, however, there is very little support for the view that Islamic-law states themselves make the claim that *ta'azir* crimes are exempt from legality. Among the major predominantly Islamic states to have accepted the ICCPR are Afghanistan, Algeria, Azerbaijan, Bangladesh, Egypt, Indonesia, Iran, Iraq, Kazakhstan, Kuwait, Kyrgyzstan, Lebanon, Libya, Syria, Turkey, Turkmenistan, and Uzbekistan.[327] This includes countries that are both majority Sunni and majority Shia, and countries that are both explicitly Islamic-law states as well as secular states. The most prominent majority Islamic states that have not ratified the ICCPR are Pakistan[328] and Saudi Arabia.[329] It is particularly interesting that the revised ArCHR contains no exception to non-retroactivity for *ta'azir* crimes.[330]

All Islamic-law states have accepted the Convention on the Rights of the Child, and none has made specific reservation concerning the convention's

In 1961, while it was still a colonial power and governed by an authoritarian regime, Portugal reserved as to Common Article 3 because of its lack of definition of "a conflict not of an international character." See http://www.icrc.org/ihl.nsf/NORM/663716D11E477ECFC1256402003F977C?OpenDocument.

[325] See http://www.icrc.org/ihl.nsf/WebSign?ReadForm&id=375&ps=P and links therein to reservations to the four Geneva Conventions of 1949; http://www.icrc.org/ihl.nsf/WebSign?ReadForm&id=470&ps=P and links therein to reservations to Additional Protocol I of 1977; http://www.icrc.org/ihl.nsf/WebSign?ReadForm&id=475&ps=P and links therein to reservations to Additional Protocol II of 1977.

[326] See Chap. 2.a.ii.

[327] 2(2) ICRC, Customary IHL, Status of Ratifications Chart, 4153ff.

[328] Pakistan's law embodies Islamic and common law elements. The common law tradition is especially important in criminal law and procedure there. Islamic law is especially important as to family law and related aspects of property law. Portions of Pakistan, especially in the North-West Frontier Province and Baluchistan, remain effectively under the rule of traditional tribal law, much of which is related to, but not identical with, sharia law. See generally *Pushtunwali: Honour among Them*, The Economist, 23 December 2006, at 36.

[329] The Saudi Arabian legal system is based in Islamic sharia.

[330] Revised ArCHR art. 15.

nullum crimen provision.[331] Some Islamic-law states have, however, made declarations or reservations generally concerning the right to exclude application of provisions that are in conflict with the principles of Islam, without stating specifically which principles are involved. These states include Afghanistan,[332] Brunei,[333] Djibouti,[334] Iran,[335] Kuwait,[336] Mauritania,[337] Qatar,[338] Saudi Arabia,[339] and Syria.[340] Pakistan made, and then withdrew,

[331] See http://www.ohchr.org/english/countries/ratification/11.htm (updated 13 July 2007), revealing no specific reservation to this provision by any of the ratifying states (including all UN members except the United States and Somalia). Some militias in Somalia (a non-party to the Convention on the Rights of the Child) wish to make it an Islamic-law state. As of this writing, November 2007, these militias are in retreat, but an effective national government has not yet been formed. Such law as exists in Somalia is local.

[332] Afghanistan Declaration (upon signature): government "reserves the right to express, upon ratifying the Convention, reservations upon all provisions of the Convention that are incompatible with the laws of Islamic Shari'a and the local legislation in effect," noted at http://www.ohchr.org/english/countries/ratification/11.htm. No actual reservations are noted.

[333] Brunei Reservation: government "expresses its reservations on the provisions of the said Convention which may be contrary to the Constitution of Brunei Darussalam and to the beliefs and principles of Islam, the State, religion, and without prejudice to the generality of said reservations, in particular expresses its reservations on [provisions other than the article concerning *nullum crimen*]," noted at http://www.ohchr.org/english/countries/ratification/11.htm.

[334] Djibouti Declaration: government "shall not consider itself bound by any provisions or articles that are incompatible with its religion and its traditional values," noted at http://www.ohchr.org/english/countries/ratification/11.htm.

[335] Iran Reservation: government "reserves the right not to apply any provisions or articles of the Convention that are incompatible with Islamic Laws and the international legislation in effect," noted at http://www.ohchr.org/english/countries/ratification/11.htm.

[336] Kuwait Reservation (upon signature): "[Kuwait expresses] reservations on all provisions of the Convention that are incompatible with the laws of Islamic Shari'a and the local statutes in effect," noted at http://www.ohchr.org/english/countries/ratification/11.htm. Unlike the declaration of Afghanistan upon signature, this reservation does not merely claim the right to make reservations upon ratification. Upon ratification, Kuwait declared that one article not concerning *nullum crimen* is incompatible with Islamic sharia.

[337] Mauritania Reservation (upon signature): "In signing this important Convention, the Islamic Republic of Mauritania is making reservations to articles or provisions which may be contrary to the beliefs and values of Islam, the religion of the Mauritania People and State," noted at http://www.ohchr.org/english/countries/ratification/11.htm.

[338] Qatar Reservation (upon signature, confirmed upon ratification): Qatar makes "a general reservation by the State of Qatar concerning provisions incompatible with Islamic Law," noted at http://www.ohchr.org/english/countries/ratification/11.htm.

[339] Saudi Arabia Reservation: government makes "reservations with respect to all such articles as are in conflict with the provisions of Islamic law," noted at http://www.ohchr.org/english/countries/ratification/11.htm.

[340] Syria Reservation: "The Syrian Arab Republic has reservations on the Convention's provisions which are not in conformity with the Syrian Arab legislations and with the Islamic

a reservation of this type.[341] Of these states, however, Afghanistan, Djibouti, Iran, Kuwait, Mauritania, and Syria are parties to the ICCPR without such reservations or reservations to provisions concerning the principles of legality. Therefore, their general reservations to the Covenant on the Rights of the Child cannot reasonably be read as including the view that Islamic law prohibits application of the doctrine of non-retroactivity of crimes or punishments. Saudi Arabia has a general statutory implementation of non-retroactivity of crimes and punishments.[342] This leaves only Brunei as a state for whom practice concerning these treaties could possibly constitute persistent objection to non-retroactivity as a rule of customary international human rights law, and no evidence has been found that its reservation in fact is designed to detract from legality.

In fact, all of the states mentioned as having general Islamic-law reservations to the Convention on the Rights of the Child, including Brunei, Saudi Arabia, and Pakistan (noted here because it is not a party to the ICCPR), are parties to the 1949 Geneva Conventions. Brunei and Saudi Arabia are parties to the 1977 Additional Protocols I and II to the Geneva Conventions, the latter of which requires the principle of non-retroactivity of crimes and punishments to apply in times of internal armed conflict. As mentioned previously, no states (including Islamic-law states) made reservation to the legality principles embodied in the Third and Fourth Geneva Conventions, and none of those that has accepted the Additional Protocols have made reservations on this ground. No Islamic-law states have made general objections to these humanitarian law treaties, like those that have been made as to the Convention on the Rights of the Child, on the basis of Islamic law.[343]

It is possible, though because of the preceding, quite difficult, to argue that *ta'azir* law is an exception to non-retroactivity of crimes in international human rights law. One might possibly argue that these general Islamic-law reservations do reserve against this principle (though they do not name it). It could then be argued that this is part of the practice of persistent

Shariah's principles, in particular the content of [provisions unconnected to *nullum crimen*]," noted at http://www.ohchr.org/english/countries/ratification/11.htm.

[341] See http://www.ohchr.org/english/countries/ratification/11.htm, at note 20 (Pakistani withdrawal, dated 23 July 1997, of reservation stating that "Provisions of this Convention shall be interpreted in light of the principles of Islamic laws and values").

[342] See Basic System of the Consultative Council [of Saudi Arabia] art. 38.

[343] See http://www.icrc.org/ihl.nsf/WebSign?ReadForm&id=375&ps=P and links therein to reservations to the four Geneva Conventions of 1949. http://www.icrc.org/ihl.nsf/WebSign?ReadForm&id=470&ps=P and links therein to reservations to Additional Protocol I of 1977; http://www.icrc.org/ihl.nsf/WebSign?ReadForm&id=475&ps=P and links therein to reservations to Additional Protocol II of 1977.

objection that these states have been making to a principle of legality that would forbid *ta'azir* crimes. However, it should be noted that not every state believes that general objections such as these are effective in international law. Denmark objected to the general reservations of Brunei and Saudi Arabia as "of unlimited scope and undefined character, and thus "as being incompatible with the object and purposes of the Convention and accordingly inadmissible under international law."[344] Many European states have objected to reliance on internal law (either specific or general) as setting out the scope of reservations to this convention, because of the rule of general international law that domestic law cannot provide a ground for violation of a treaty.[345]

4.h. LIMITS TO RULE OF LEGALITY IN MODERN TREATIES: STATUTORY INTERPRETATION, COMMON LAW CASE DEVELOPMENT, AND CIVIL LAW ANALOGY

There are limits to the strictures of legality in postwar international treaties and national law. International human rights law does not ignore the problem of the indeterminacy of legal language. Courts may interpret criminal law so that conduct on the fringes of the definition of crime is made criminal, so long as the language defining the law, along with published and accessible case law interpretation, makes it foreseeable to the public that the conduct would fall within the prohibition.[346] Case law may clarify statutes even in civil law countries, without offending international law.[347] In many states, there are provisions requiring criminal statutes be strictly construed against the state, but this has not reached the status of customary international law or a general principle of law recognized by the community of nations, as there are many states that do not apply it or that apply it only inconsistently. Some jurisdictions and multilateral human rights systems have allowed for new criminal statutes to be applied, so long as the acts charged were within

[344] Denmark Objection, noted at http://www.ohchr.org/english/countries/ratification/11.htm (updated 19 April 2006).

[345] See http://www.ohchr.org/english/countries/ratification/11.htm (updated 19 April 2006), noting objections of Finland, Germany, Ireland, Italy, Netherlands, Norway, Portugal, Slovakia, and the former Czechoslovakia.

[346] See Kokkinakis v. Greece, Judgment, Eur. Ct. H.R. (25 May 1993), ser. A-260-A, ¶ 40; G. v. France, Judgment, Eur. Ct. H.R. (27 September 1995), ser. A-325-B; Baskaya v. Turkey, Judgment, Eur. Ct. H.R. (8 July 1999), ¶ 39. For a U.S. case limiting unpredictable judicial expansion of criminal liability through statutory interpretation, see Bouie v. City of Columbia, 378 U.S. 347 (1964).

[347] Kokkinakis v. Greece, at ¶ 40; G. v. France.

the old criminal definitions and the penalty given was no greater than that permitted by the law at the time of the criminal act.[348]

Admittedly there are occasional cases that seem to go too far in allowing a so-called predictable change in law. For example, the courts of the United Kingdom abolished the marital defense to rape apparently through the case law process. In *C. R. v. United Kingdom*,[349] a man who was convicted of attempting to rape his wife, from whom he had been separated for some time, alleged that applying this new rule to him violated the legality principle in the ECHR. The European Court of Human Rights (ECtHR) stated that this was not the case, because case law in the United Kingdom eroding the so-called marital defense to rape, coupled with changes in the law elsewhere and changes in societal attitudes, might have led him to conclude that the former law, which made being the husband of the victim a defense to rape, was about to be overruled. Thus he was on notice that what he did was possibly a crime.[350] Interestingly, this court is made up of judges predominantly from the civil law tradition of *nullum crimen sine praevia lege scripta*.[351]

This case discusses the notice and foreseeability rationale for the principle of legality:

> There was no doubt under the law as it stood on 12 November 1989 that a husband who forcibly had sexual intercourse with his wife could, in various circumstances, be found guilty of rape. Moreover, there was an evident evolution, which was consistent with the very essence of the offence, of the criminal law through judicial interpretation towards treating such conduct generally as within the scope of the offence of rape. This evolution had reached a stage where judicial recognition of the absence of immunity had become a reasonably foreseeable development of the law.[352]

[348] Westerman v. Netherlands, Com. 682/1986, UN Doc. A/55/40, Annex IX (UNHRC, 3 November 1999) (Netherlands retrospectively applied new military code provision on "refusal to obey military orders"; acceptable under ICCPR art. 15(1) because the acts charged were punishable under both old and new codes, and the sentence given was permissible under the code in force when the acts were committed), digested in LOUISE DOSWALD-BECK & ROBERT KOLB, JUDICIAL PROCESS AND HUMAN RIGHTS: UNITED NATIONS, EUROPEAN, AMERICAN AND AFRICAN SYSTEMS: TEXTS AND SUMMARIES OF INTERNATIONAL CASE-LAW 279 (Kehl, N.P. Engel, 2004); G. v. France (France retrospectively applied new crime of "indecent assault with violence or coercison by a person in authority"; acceptable under ECHR art. 7 because of *lex mitior* – under law in effect at time of the act, it would have been the more serious crime of rape).

[349] ECHR art. 7.

[350] C. R. v. United Kingdom, Judgment, Case No. 48/1994/495/577, Eur. Ct. H.R. (27 October 1995).

[351] *Id.*

[352] See C.R. v. United Kingdom, at ¶¶ 34, 38 (change foreseeable with "appropriate legal advice"), 41 (quoted excerpt).

The court also claims that the change in law was consistent with the prevention of oppressive criminalization:

> The essentially debasing character of rape is so manifest that the result of the decisions of the Court of Appeal and the House of Lords – that the applicant could be convicted of attempted rape, irrespective of his relationship with the victim – cannot be said to be at variance with the object and purpose of Article 7 of the Convention, namely to ensure that no one should be subjected to arbitrary prosecution, conviction or punishment. . . . What is more, the abandonment of the unacceptable idea of a husband being immune against prosecution for rape of his wife was in conformity not only with a civilised concept of marriage but also, and above all, with the fundamental objectives of the Convention, the very essence of which is respect for human dignity and human freedom.[353]

The ECtHR ignored the opportunity to say that the act in this case could reasonably have been considered a natural expansion of exceptions to the marital-consent doctrine, deeming consent to sexual intercourse withdrawn after certain kinds of separation. Instead, the court stated that this case was a reversal, not a modification of the law.[354] It said that such a complete reversal was foreseeable, and therefore one need not consider whether the law had effectively been previously modified to include the facts raised by the current case.[355]

Certainly the rule that a man cannot be convicted for the rape of his wife should have been abolished. Yet this would not justify convicting a defendant for an act for which he had a valid substantive criminal law defense when he committed it.

The ECtHR does not emphasize one important aspect of the case which might justify its decision. It was only in recent years that rape has been defined by statute in the United Kingdom.[356] That statute, in effect at the time the defendant acted, contains on its face no defense for marital rape, though the defendant argued that the defense was implicit in the fact that to be rape, sexual intercourse must be unlawful. Although there had been cases that partly upheld the marital defense after the passage of the statute, it might have been emphasized that the failure to include the defense in the statute was the legal act which made it foreseeable that the defense would be considered to have been abolished.

[353] *Id.* at ¶ 42.

[354] *Id.* at ¶¶ 9–10 (describing separation of C. R. and his wife at the time of the attempted rape), 22–23 (describing exceptions in the law) & 35.

[355] *Id.* at ¶ 43.

[356] See Sexual Offenses Act 1956 § 1 (1956); Sexual Offenses (Amendment) Act 1976 § 1.1.

Another ECtHR case involving marital rape in the United Kingdom, *S. W. v. United Kingdom*,[357] stands on slightly different ground with respect to non-retroactivity. In this case, there was a separation of only one day (initiated by the husband), not the longer separation there had been in C. R.'s case. However, S. W. did not commit his act until after there had been another important court ruling that had purported to overturn the marital-consent doctrine.[358] The court slightly modified the statement concerning foreseeability from C. R.'s case:

> There was no doubt under the law as it stood on 18 September 1990 that a husband who forcibly had sexual intercourse with his wife could, in various circumstances, be found guilty of rape. Moreover, there was an evident evolution, which was consistent with the very essence of the offence, of the criminal law through judicial interpretation towards treating such conduct generally as within the scope of the offence of rape. This evolution had reached a stage where judicial recognition of the absence of immunity had become a reasonably foreseeable development of the law.[359]

The intervening decision made it more likely that the statute would be read as a complete reversal, even though it was a trial court case that did not bind the judge in S. W.'s case.

One might look here at a recent national case from Singapore. That case pointed out that a reversal of an interpretation that truly creates new criminal liability is prohibited by rules of legality.[360] This correctly warns us that the situations in which a reversal might genuinely be said to be foreseeable will be quite limited.

In another series of cases from the ECtHR, East German border guards who shot people attempting to cross the Berlin Wall had their convictions upheld in the face of claims that criminal law was being retroactively applied to them. They would clearly have been acting criminally at the time they acted, had they not had the claimed defense of following government policy to kill persons attempting to cross the wall illegally. The post-unification

[357] S. W. v. United Kingdom, Judgment, Case No. 47/1994/494/576, Eur. Ct. H.R. (27 October 1995).

[358] *Id.* at ¶¶ 8 (facts), 10 (discussing R.v.R., U.K. Crown Court, Judgment, 30 July 1990, [1991] 1 All E.R. 747, aff'd, Ct. App., Crim. Div., 14 March 1991, [1991] 2 All E.R. 257).

[359] *Id.* at ¶ 43.

[360] Public Prosecutor v. Manogaran, [1997] 2 L.R.C. 288 (Ct. of App. of Singapore), noted in Nihal Jayawickrame, The Judicial Application of Human Rights Law: National, Regional and International Jurisprudence 588 (Cambridge Univ. Press 2002).

German courts found that it would be "unjust and unfair"[361] to allow this defense and convicted a number of persons for the acts.[362] The convictions were upheld by the ECtHR on the ground that the acts were illegal under East German law of the time: the law against deliberate killing had not been abolished or modified by the government's policies.[363]

George Fletcher has recently presented a rationale for these cases, which suggests that they are not mere extensions of the notion of foreseeability. His argument follows the German principle of criminal law which radically separates crime creation from defenses. He argues that under these cases defense destruction can occur retroactively, where the defense is unjust and where, stripped of the defense, the act in question was squarely criminal at the time done. That appears to have been the case both in the marital rape cases and the German border guard cases.[364] This argument, at least has the merit of preventing the retroactive creation of new crimes – it is solely limited to the destruction of unjust defenses. It is, however, inconsistent with the idea that at least some defenses – the justifications – tell us what behavior is legally acceptable, in the same way that crime definitions tell us what behavior is legally unacceptable. If this last idea is correct, then expansion of the set of criminal acts by abolition of justification defenses should be subject to the rule of non-retroactivity.

In contrast, Ward N. Ferdinandusse argues that the border guards cases are overextensions of the doctrine of foreseeability. He argues rather persuasively that the entire East German law at the time suggested that the acts with which they were charged were not criminal; and that the acts were not, at the time done, crimes against humanity. He sees the case as one where a moral wrong was retroactively (and thus illegitimately) transformed into a criminal wrong, because of "anger over an immoral act or regime."[365] Failure to recognize the pressure put on individuals by the East German policy as an important mitigating factor does make the border guard cases seem

[361] Quoted in George P. Fletcher, 1 The Grammar of Criminal Law: American, Comparative, and International (Foundations) 147 (Oxford Univ. Press 2007), attributing this language originally to Gustav Radbruch.

[362] *Id.* at 147, citing to Judgment of the Constitutional Court, 24 October 1996, 95 EBVerfG 96.

[363] Streletz, Kessler and Krenz v. Germany, ¶¶ 54–55, 74–76, 77–106, Case Nos. 34044/96, 35532/97, 44801/98, Eur. Ct. H.R. 2001-II (22 March 2001) (acts were illegal under East German law of the time, and criminal liability was foreseeable); K.-H. W. v. Germany, ¶¶ 49–50, 66–67, 68–91, Case No. 37201/97, Eur. Ct. H.R. 2001-II (22 March 2001) (similar effect).

[364] Fletcher, *supra* note 359, at 145–48.

[365] Ward N. Ferdinandusse, Direct Application of International Criminal Law in National Courts 244–48 (TMC Asser 2006).

harsh; and Ferdinandusse provides a reasonable explanation as to why this mitigating factor was not emphasized. However, these cases do not make it inevitable that moral wrongs will generally be turned retroactively into crimes under the ECHR. One can expect, therefore, that Ferdinandausse's fears for the future of legality will not be realized.

There is one admissibility decision in which a panel of the ECtHR indicates that, where an act was a crime under general principles of law as set out in ECHR, Article 7(2), courts need not examine whether the act was a crime under "international law" in the sense of ECHR, Article 7(1).[366] To the extent that the European Court must have found that the charged act would have been a crime under general principles of law at the time committed, there is no violation of the doctrine of non-retroactivity of crimes. However, the claim that Article 7(1) (or its analogue, ICCPR, Article 15(1)) has no effect at all on this case seems wrong. Article 7(2) does not explicitly contain a *nulla poena* provision, but there seems to be no justification for inserting it with respect to all other forms of international law in Article 7(1) (particularly customary international law or applicable treaties), yet not with regard to crimes which existed under general principles of law. It should be noted that the case in which the aberrational view that Article 7(1) did not apply was not a case involving an allegedly unlawful imposition of punishment by a state, but a case involving pretrial transfer from Croatia to the International Criminal Tribunal for the Former Yugoslavia (ICTY). Certainly legality arguments, including any *nulla poena* argument insufficiently addressed by the ECtHR and the courts of Croatia, could be addressed to the ICTY.[367] Further, the case did not deal so much with the availability of punishments under international law at the time of the act but with whether the ICTY was authorized to give a greater punishment than the courts of Croatia.[368] That by itself would not make a stiffer international punishment illegally retroactive, unless the punishment was not available under international law at the time of the crime.

These examples do not show that the ECtHR does not apply the principle of legality. They merely demonstrate that application of the principle will not always be without controversy. This has its necessary roots in the indeterminacy of language, which affects any statement of the principle of legality as much as it affects any other articulation of a rule of law. In fact, I believe that the ECHR cases on marital rape contain language that undercuts

[366] Naletilic v. Croatia, Admissibility Decision, Eur. Ct. H.R. (4 May 2000).
[367] See Chap. 6.a.
[368] See *Naletilic.*

the principle of legality of non-retroactivity of crimes by broadening the concept of foreseeability too much. When such a controversy arises in international criminal law, as with the issue of rape as a violation of the laws and customs of war,[369] one cannot expect an easier solution than is found in regional human rights law or domestic constitutional law. This no more voids the project of international criminal law than it voids the legitimacy of domestic law. Nor does it void the project of articulating a rule of legality in international law.

The multilateral human rights treaties herein do not specifically mention crime creation by analogy on the civil law model. However, one can infer that they all prohibit retroactive analogical creation of crime by their language, at least to the extent that the technique is used specifically to criminalize an act that is not within the meaning of a statute.[370] If this is done retroactively, then the act was not a crime at the time it was performed, and criminalization is prohibited by each of the treaties. Note that these treaties do not prohibit prospective statements expanding the definition of crimes, whether using common law or civil law techniques. Whether to allow the judiciary to participate in crime definition this way is part of the internal constitutional law of each state and does not in itself impugn the principle of legality as applied in international human rights law and international criminal law.

One generally civilian form of *nulla poena* is not generally followed in common law jurisdictions or required by international human rights law or in international criminal law. That version prescribes specific penalties for specific crimes, with little or no discretion in the courts to vary the penalties.[371] The common law, by contrast, focuses on whether a maximum possible penalty has been set before the crime is committed. Any retroactive increase above that maximum would violate *nulla poena*. International criminal law simply has not developed any generally accepted schedule of penalties. Penalties have been established in international criminal law through customary international law. As mentioned, many states also simply set maximum penalties for many crimes, without having a tariff, or a narrow range of tariffs, for each crime. Thus, it cannot be said that a textual specification of a penalty for each crime is a necessity under the treaty law.

[369] See Prosecutor v. Furundzija, Judgement ¶¶ 165–69, Case No. IT-95-17/1-T (ICTY Tr. Ch., 10 December 1998), aff'd (ICTY App. Ch., 21 July 2000).

[370] See C. R. v. United Kingdom, at ¶ 33.

[371] See M. Cherif Bassiouni, Crimes against Humanity in International Criminal Law 176 (2d ed., Transnational Publishers 1999).

Specification, whether by statute or custom, of the maximum penalty for which the offender is eligible before the commission of the crime is all that is required.

4.i. PATTERNS OF TREATY NONPARTICIPATION

There are a few patterns of nonparticipation in the worldwide (ICCPR) and regional (ACHR, ACHPR, ArCHR, ECHR) human rights treaties that have general provisions prohibiting retroactive crimes and punishments. The patterns do not suggest a special hostility to legality, though it is conceivable that there are one or two states that might be excepted. The discussion here is focused on legality in criminal law, but it must be remembered that these treaties contain many more provisions, and usually it is the freedom of expression and religion that receive the most attention.

The first pattern is that small island nations often do not participate in the human rights treaty regime. In the Atlantic, those island nations outside the treaty system include Antigua and Barbuda, the Bahamas, St. Kitts and Nevis, St. Lucia, and Cuba. All of these have constitutional provisions endorsing non-retroactivity of crimes and punishments. In the Pacific, the island states that do not participate include Brunei, Fiji, Kiribati, the Marshall Islands, Micronesia, Palau, Papua New Guinea, Samoa, Tonga, Tuvalu, and Vanuatu. All of these except Brunei have constitutional provisions endorsing non-retroactivity of crimes and punishments. Brunei is party to the Convention on the Rights of the Child. Many of these states have common law traditions, having gained independence from either the United Kingdom or the United States. Two other island entities with disputed international status might fall into this category. One is the Republic of China (Taiwan), which signed the ICCPR but had not ratified it before the People's Republic of China was recognized as the holder of the seat of China at the United Nations. Its constitution does not refer to the principle of legality in criminal law. Another island entity with a constitution endorsing non-retroactivity that has not gained general recognition as a state is the Turkish Republic of Northern Cyprus.

Some other states that do not participate are also small, either in geography or in population, or both. These include Bhutan, Oman, Singapore, the United Arab Emirates (UAE), and Vatican City. Oman, Singapore, and the UAE all have constitutions endorsing non-retroactivity in criminal law. The constitution of Singapore, however, has an exception concerning subversion,[372] which is important enough that one might conclude that its failure to participate in the ICCPR might be based in part on the non-derogability of criminal law legality in that treaty. Bhutan participates in the Convention on the Rights of the Child and Vatican City does as well, along with the 1977 Additional Protocol II to the 1949 Geneva Conventions.

That leaves only a few larger mainland states outside the general human rights treaty system. Malaysia, Myanmar, and Pakistan have constitutional provisions endorsing non-retroactivity of crimes and punishments. Pakistan's constitution has an exception for subversion of its various constitutions, which is narrower than Singapore's exception, but given that exception, its refusal to join the ICCPR could be seen as partly based in objections to the non-derogability of legality. Two other important countries that have stood outside the human rights treaty system, the People's Republic of China and Saudi Arabia, now have statutory embodiments of the non-retroactivity of crimes and punishments. In addition, the People's Republic of China has signed the ICCPR, and Saudi Arabia has signed the revised ArCHR.[373]

The existence of internal rules of non-retroactivity in most countries outside the international human rights treaty system suggests that non-retroactivity is not the reason that they stayed out. Similarly, the most pervasive patterns of nonparticipation, size and geography as islands, seems to be completely fortuitous, at least in terms of commitment to principles of legality in criminal law.

4.j. INDIVIDUAL, STATE, AND INTERNATIONAL ORGANIZATION ABILITY TO RAISE LEGALITY IN CRIMINAL PROCEEDINGS AS AN INTERNATIONAL LAW CLAIM UNDER THE TREATIES

States may complain to other states about violations of all international human rights of the complaining state's citizens. States often complain about the international human rights of other persons being violated, including the rights of persons who are citizens of the state being addressed. This is a major reason for the development of the United Nations Human Rights Council,[374] and the United Nations Commission on Human Rights, which it replaced. Thus, internationally protected human rights of all persons – not just rights

[372] See Chap. 5.c.vi, discussing Singapore Const. arts. 11 & 149(1).
[373] All the states mentioned in this section are discussed in Chap. 5.
[374] G.A. Res. 60/251, UN Doc. A/RES/60/251 (3 April 2006).

of nationals of complaining states – have entered the arena of international law. This suggests that earlier case law, to the effect that only the state of one's nationality may offer international protection,[375] is being modified at least where international human rights are concerned. Both states and appropriate international organizations may make claims concerning violations of human rights – including the principle of legality in criminal law.

There is a general trend through treaty systems setting up international organizations to make it possible for the individual to raise a claim that a prosecution or sentence violates the principle of legality. Indeed these treaty systems are general and allow individuals to make claims that many different types of government action violate a large number of rights specified in international human rights treaties. Legality issues may be raised before the ECtHR, whose judgments have binding force for the states adhering to the ECHR and its protocols.[376] The same rule applies to the Inter-American Court of Human Rights (IACtHR) concerning violations by parties to the ACHR that have accepted the jurisdiction of the IACtHR.[377] The African human rights system now includes a court with binding authority over those states that have accepted it.[378]

The individual here has the legal personality to make complaints against states for treaty violations in these regional international organizations. If accepted (and the procedural and substantive obstacles to consideration are considerable), the judicial arms of the organizations can issue binding judgments against member states. Individuals, groups, and nongovernmental organizations have the right to bring complaints about violations of human rights under the ECHR to the ECtHR, though the procedural requirements for this are substantial.[379] Thus, in the European human rights system, the individual has international legal personality to make a complaint that may result in a binding judgment against a state.

However, the procedural and substantive obstacles to consideration in regional human rights systems may limit the international legal personality

[375] See Nottebaum Case (Leichtenstein v. Guatemala), [1955] I.C.J. 4; Flegenheimer Claim, 25 I.L.R. 91 (Italian-U.S. Conciliation Comm'n, 1963); both discussed in Myres S. McDougal, Harold D. Lasswell & Lung-chu Chen, *Nationality and Human Rights: The Protection of the Individual in External Arenas*, 83 YALE L.J. 900 (1974) (collecting materials on the rule that only the state of nationality may make a claim to protect the individual).

[376] ECHR art. 46.

[377] ACHR arts. 62 & 68.

[378] Protocol to the African Charter on the Establishment of the African Court on Human and Peoples' Rights, adopted by the Organization of African Unity Assembly of Heads of State and Government (34th Ordinary Session, 1998), entered into force 25 January 2004.

[379] ECHR arts. 32 & 34–39.

of the individual. For example, the ACHR allows individuals to lodge a petition with the Inter-American Commission on Human Rights about human rights violations by a State Party to the ACHR.[380] The commission has conciliation, investigation, and recommendatory authority.[381] However, individuals dissatisfied with the results of the commission's process do not have an individual right to bring the matter to the IACtHR. Only the commission and states parties have the authority to present matters to the IACtHR.[382] Thus the individual does not have full international legal personality with regard to complaints about human rights under the ACHR.

In contrast, the Human Rights Committee, working under the First Optional Protocol to the ICCPR,[383] can only issue "'views', [which] are, in effect, recommendations to the States concerned."[384] The African Commission on Human and Peoples' Rights, which remains active for those states which have not become party to the protocol to the ACHPR, has recommendatory powers.[385] In both of these systems, individuals have power to make complaints and may receive statements of law vindicating their positions, but the statements have no binding power.

The African commission has stated a rule that would appear to allow legality challenges by individuals more broadly than is customary in other systems. It condemned criminal laws that have a purportedly retroactive effect even before a prosecution is undertaken. The African Charter provisions:

> must be read to prohibit not only condemnation and infliction of punishment for acts which did not constitute crimes at the time they were committed, but retroactivity itself. . . . If laws change with retroactive effect, the rule of law is undermined since individuals cannot know at any moment if their actions are legal. For a law abiding citizen, this is a terrible uncertainty, regardless of the likelihood of eventual punishment.[386]

This apparent ability to raise the issue of legality before one is prosecuted may represent the beginning of a further expansion of the international

[380] ACHR art. 44.
[381] *Id.* at arts. 48–51.
[382] *Id.* at arts. 57, 61 & 62.
[383] First Optional Protocol to the ICCPR, 999 U.N.T.S. 171 (1967).
[384] Doswald-Beck & Kolb, *supra* note 346, at 5.
[385] See ACHPR art. 45(1)(a).
[386] Communications 105/93, 128/94, 130/94 & 152/96, Media Rights Agenda & Constitutional Rights Project v. Nigeria (ACommHPR, Twelfth Activity Report 1998–99), quoted and discussed in Christof Heyns, Civil and Political Rights in the African Charter, in The African Charter on Human and Peoples' Rights: The System in Practice, 1986–2000 137, 160–1 (Malcolm Evans and Rachel Murray, eds., Cambridge Univ. Press 2002).

legal personality of the individual. It recognizes that laws may impinge on rights of individuals through deterrence and fear even when they are not enforced. Indeed, in the case of the non-retroactivity provision, this fear may be a fear not of what laws exist but of what law may at some future time be brought into force retroactively. Thus, lawful activity may be deterred – in American legal jargon, "chilled."

There is no means for individuals to complain directly to an international forum under the ICCPR concerning those states that have not adopted its First Optional Protocol. The international legal personality of individuals under the ICCPR thus remains strictly limited to matters concerning those states that have specifically agreed to accept such personality. Those that complain under the regional human rights treaties similarly do so within a treaty system to which the relevant state belongs. Again, the international legal personality of the individual in these systems is defined by the treaty instrument.

Most states do not participate in a regional human rights organization with the authority to make binding rulings on the basis of individual complaints. Many states, including China, India, the United States, and Indonesia, four of the five most populous countries in the world, do not even participate in the recommendatory system of the First Optional Protocol to the ICCPR,[387] which is based on the right of individuals to complain. This means that the individual has not obtained full international legal personality, even with regard to human rights.[388]

States do not complain to one another over every violation of legality or other individual human rights. Indeed, this is a significant weakness of international human rights treaties without clear and mandatory enforcement mechanisms.[389] Thus, some violations of the principle of legality by states may go unremedied for the foreseeable future.

4.k. STATUS OF ACTIONS DISCUSSED IN THIS CHAPTER UNDER INTERNATIONAL LAW

A word here needs to be said about the international law status of the materials described in this chapter, because these materials are important

[387] The fifth, Brazil, has ratified the ACHR but not the First Optional Protocol to the ICCPR.

[388] But cf. Chap. 6.a (on personality in the ICTY, ICTR, SCSL) & 6.c (on personality in ICC).

[389] See MARK SACHLEBEN, HUMAN RIGHTS TREATIES: CONSIDERING PATTERNS OF PARTICIPATION, 1948–2000 159 (Routledge 2006), relying on Louis Henkin, *International Law: Politics, Values, and Functions*, 216 RECUEIL DE COURS 27 (1989).

to the construction of the rules of customary international law concerning the principle of legality in Chapter 7. Treaty adoptions are acts of the states involved, which is why they are discussed here. The treaties are also relevant to the *opinio juris* of states.

No claim is made here that widespread adoption of a multilateral treaty, such as the ICCPR, by itself transforms the content of the treaty into customary international law. It is, however, one of those factors that goes into determining the content of modern customary international law. Universal or near-universal acceptance of a treaty provision, along with other state practice and expressions of *opinio juris*, can lead to a conclusion that a treaty rule has become a rule of customary international law. One of the expressions of the importance of criminal law legality in the ICCPR is its status as a non-derogable right. Thus, the treaty provisions discussed in this chapter will be brought back in Chapter 7.

Some acts discussed here are the practice or expression of the *opinio juris* of international organizations. These include the UDHR (an act of the UN General Assembly) and the decisions of human rights bodies (such as the ECtHR) interpreting and applying treaties.

The UDHR also represents the *opinio juris* of the states voting for it, and of the General Assembly as a principal organ of the United Nations. The votes of those states can also be seen as part of state practice. After the decision was made that members of the Commission on Human Rights would represent their states,[390] actions and statements of Human Rights Council members can also be seen as state practice that may express an *opinio juris*. Further, the fact that those nations which did not vote for the UDHR or for the final version of the non-retroactivity provisions in the Third Committee at least abstained on them reflects an acquiescence in the practice that it represents, almost two decades before similar votes on the ICCPR. The lack of opposition (even if there were abstentions) to the non-retroactivity of crimes and punishments in particular, indicates the general acquiescence of states to this as a norm of international law.[391]

The UDHR is not a treaty document. It is ambiguous as to whether it represents a statement of the law as the General Assembly (and the approving states) believed that it was at the time it was adopted or a statement of the law that was in the process of development. The document was "[p]roclaim[ed] . . . as a common standard of achievement for all peoples

[390] See 1947 UNYBHR at 421–22 n.4.

[391] Cf. Manley O. Hudson, Working Paper, UN Doc. A/CN.4/16 (3 March 1950) (general acquiescence one element in creation of customary international law).

and all nations."[392] Its tremendous influence in the field of human rights generally, and on the issue of legality in criminal law in particular, justifies the close scrutiny of its text and *travaux* given here, and its place in the creation of the customary international law rule of non-retroactivity of crimes and punishments.

The decisions of the human rights bodies are acts of international organizations but are so closely related to the treaties that they are more sensibly (if not more logically) discussed here rather than later. To the extent that they find the challenged national activities acceptable, they also report on a state practice that has been found acceptable.

National and international courts and publicists have been relying on international tribunals and international monitoring agencies as sources of international law, especially international human rights law and criminal law.[393] A bit more on the legal status of the practice and the *opinio juris* of international organizations will be found at the end of Chapter 6.

In summary, the international materials examined in this chapter testify to the tremendous change in attitude toward legality in criminal law. As pointed out, it is accepted by treaty law at least as to some important classes of crimes and/or actors by every UN member state. The study of national materials in the next chapter will show that all but two UN member states have accepted the non-retroactivity of crimes and punishments more generally.

[392] UDHR, preamble.

[393] L. Zegfeld, *The Bouterse Case*, 32 Netherlands Y.B.I.L. 97, 99–100 (2001), relying on Prosecutor v. Tadic, Decision on Defence Motion for Interlocutory Appeal on Jurisdiction Case IT-94-1-AR71 ¶ 99 (ICTY App. Ch., 2 October 1995), along with the work of Prof. C. J. R. Dugard in the *Bouterse* case (referring to human rights monitoring bodies created by international and regional conventions) and Wijngaarde v. Bouterse, Court of Appeal of Amsterdam, 20 November 2000, rev'd in the interest of law, Hoge Raad der Nederlanden (Supreme Court of the Netherlands), 18 September 2001, translated into English at 32 Netherlands Y.B.I.L. 282 (2001).

5

Modern Comparative Law Development: National Provisions Concerning Legality

This chapter examines how states have accepted various aspects of the principle of legality as a matter of law. These aspects include non-retroactivity of crimes (*nullum crimen sine lege*), non-retroactivity of punishments (*nulla poena sine lege*), requirement of a preexisting statutory text (*praevia lege scripta*), limitation or prohibition of special courts for crimes or retroactively created courts, and prohibition of collective punishments. It also looks at which states require retroactivity of more lenient punishment (*lex mitior*). It considers these materials in the context of the different legal systems in which they arise. It concludes with a section on the meaning of these national materials for international law.

5.a. CONTENT AND LIMITATIONS OF THE MATERIAL IN THIS CHAPTER AND THE APPENDICES ON NATIONAL LAW

The material used in this study of criminal law legality in national systems is collected in three appendices to this book. Appendix A lists in chart form the states that accept *nullum crimen* and *nulla poena*, and those that implement *lex mitior*. Appendix B lists the constitutional provisions, and in a few cases, other provisions, existing in 1946–47, after the end of World War II.[1] Appendix C sets out the texts of the provisions as they exist today (or the most recent available texts).[2] Appendix C also includes statutory and other

[1] Unless otherwise stated, the provisions effective in 1946–47 are taken from one of two UN sources, Documented Outline of an International Bill of Rights, UN Doc. E/CN.4/AC.1/3/Add.1 (2 June 1947), or [UNITED NATIONS] YEARBOOK ON HUMAN RIGHTS 1946, UN Sales No. 1948.XIV.1 (rep. William S. Hein & Co. 1996) [hereinafter 1946 UNYBHR].

[2] Unless otherwise stated, the current constitutional texts and translations are taken from the exhaustive set, CONSTITUTIONS OF THE COUNTRIES OF THE WORLD (Rüdiger H.

material that has been found on these subjects in states where there are no constitutional materials. In addition to matters concerning retroactivity of crimes and punishments, Appendix C includes constitutional material that has been found concerning personality of punishment, collective punishment, retroactivity of establishment of courts, and establishment of special courts.

This chapter first covers legality in the constitutions of countries around the world in 1946–47. This portion of the chapter discusses the documentation produced by the UN Secretariat in its Documented Outline of 1947 and the material in the 1946 *Year Book on Human Rights.* Because a number of states were not UN members during its early period, the *Year Book,* which included practice of non-UN member states, is particularly useful as a supplement to the Documented Outline. This portion of the study provides a baseline against which subsequent changes in national laws can be measured.

The chapter then considers the modern status of legality in criminal law around the world. It examines the constitutions of all nation-states around the world (along with some entities whose claim to the status of state is contested or not generally recognized) to look for these provisions. United Nations membership is taken as a marker of statehood at present, even though not every member of the UN has bilateral relations with every other member. The current constitutional materials on which this study is based were last verified September–October 2007. A few subsequent developments have been taken into consideration, particularly the Pakistan constitutional crisis of November–December 2007 and the declaration of independence of Kosovo (recognized by many, but not all, states; not a UN member) and the presentation of its proposed constitution to its president, which occurred while this book was going to press.[3]

Because constitutional provisions generally control all other domestic law, the constitution of a state is the preferred document for purposes of this study. The texts of these constitutional provisions (in English translation where necessary) are collected in Appendix C. The listing of constitutional

Wolfrum, Rainer Grote & Gisbert H. Flanz eds., Oxford Univ. Press [formerly published by Oceana], various dates, including both paper version and online subscription version at http://www.oceanalaw.com) [hereinafter CCW]. Every effort has been made to be current through November 2007, but constitutional law changes quickly in many states, particularly those emerging from conflict situations.

[3] Proposed Kosovo Const. art. 33, presented to the President of Kosovo, 7 April 2008, from Kosovo Constitutional Commission website, www.kosovoconstitution.info.

provisions in Appendices A and C is intended to be complete for all of the entities included.

In some states, however, there is no written constitution (e.g., the United Kingdom). In others there may be no constitutional provision on legality in criminal law (e.g., People's Republic of China). In these cases, an effort was made to find other domestic law that would indicate the state's acceptance of non-retroactivity of crimes and punishments as an obligation. The preferred sources here are available statutes and binding court decisions. These also are collected in Appendix C. Although it cannot be guaranteed that every state with solely statutory or caselaw provisions as to non-retroactivity of crimes and punishments has been listed here, the listing in Appendix A should be reasonably complete.

This chapter also discusses various forms in which states have implemented the requirement that crimes be defined by statute or other promulgated texts (*nullum crimen sine praevia lege scripta*). A number of different rhetorical and structural devices are used by various states. For reasons discussed subsequently, however, a definitive listing of states following this rule could not be made.[4]

As to *lex mitior*, special or retroactively created courts, and personal punishment, the statutory research in states where there is no constitutional provision on these issues is less complete than it is for whether the state has rules on non-retroactivity of crimes and punishment. The nations in which these have been found should, however, be reasonably representative of the group in which these provisions exist.

The multilateral treaty law imposing obligations concerning legality in domestic law, described in more detail in Chapter 4, has also been consulted here. These treaties include the regional treaties with court-based enforcement mechanisms binding states to apply principles of legality internally, the European Convention on Human Rights (ECHR)[5] and the American Convention on Human Rights (ACHR).[6] The African regional treaty system (African Charter of Human and Peoples' Rights) has a commission system for issuing determinations,[7] and some members of the system have recently

[4] See Chap. 5.c.ii.

[5] Arts. 7, 46, 312 U.N.T.S. 221 (4 November 1950), *as amended* [hereinafter ECHR].

[6] Arts. 7–9, 69, 1114 U.N.T.S. 123 (22 November 1969), reprinted in 9 ILM 673 (1970) [hereinafter ACHR].

[7] Arts. 7(2), 45, OAU Doc. CAB/LEG/67/3/Rev. 5 (27 June 1981), reprinted in 21 I.L.M. 59 (1982) [hereinafter ACHPR].

brought into force a protocol to establish an African court of human rights.[8] The ICCPR[9] has an optional protocol[10] for obtaining recommendatory views. The revised Arab Charter on Human Rights (ArCHR)[11] entered into force 15 March 2008 as this book was going to press. Because these treaties impose international obligations on states to act in accordance with the principle of legality in criminal law in their internal acts, they are relevant to determining the internal legal situation of states, and are noted in Appendices A and C, whether or not there are constitutional, statutory, or case law provisions on legality.

This treaty research is intended to be complete, except that information on the current status of the revised ArCHR in the various countries of the Arab League has been difficult to come by. States that have ratified such a treaty and do not have constitutional or statutory provisions implementing non-retroactivity of crimes and punishments and/or *lex mitior* are listed as having accepted these doctrines by treaty.

There are other treaties that require the application of the principle of legality in some situations, such as the Convention on the Rights of the Child, the Third and Fourth Geneva Conventions of 1949, and the First and Second Additional Protocols of 1977 to the Geneva Conventions.[12] Among these, the most important provisions for consideration in this comparative law chapter are those that bind states to apply the principle of legality to their own nationals in the relevant situations. These are the Convention on the Rights of the Child, which prohibits retroactive crime creation as to all children,[13] and the Second Additional Protocol to the Geneva Conventions, which prohibits both retroactive crime creation and increases in punishment during non-international conflicts (i.e., in civil wars).[14] These two treaties are noted in Appendices A and C only if the state has

[8] Protocol to the African Charter on Human and Peoples' Rights on the Establishment of an African Court on Human and Peoples' Rights (Ouagadougou, Burkina Faso, 9 June 1998; entered into force 25 January 2004), available at http://www.achpr.org/english/_info/court_en.html (official Web site of African Commission on Human and Peoples' Rights).

[9] ICCPR art. 15.

[10] First Optional Protocol to the ICCPR.

[11] Revised ArCHR art. 15, reprinted in 12 Int'l Hum. Rts. Rep. 893 (2005) (22 May 2004; entered into force 15 March 2008); see UAE ratifies Arab charter on human rights at http://www.uaeinteract.com/docs/UAE_ratifies_Arab_charter_on_human_rights/28218.htm (UAE Interact, Web site of National Media Council, posted 16 January 2008).

[12] See Chapter 4.c & f.

[13] Convention on the Rights of the Child art. 40 (*nullum crimen* only).

[14] Additional Protocol (No. II) to the 1949 Geneva Conventions art. 6(2)(c).

no constitutional or statutory provisions on non-retroactivity of criminal law and is not a party to the ICCPR or to a relevant regional human rights treaty embodying the requirement of non-retroactivity of crimes and punishments.

The collection of this material began to determine which states have rules of law prohibiting retroactive criminalization of acts and retroactive increases of penalties. If provisions to this effect were not found in the constitutions of countries, they were searched for in statutes. This study makes no claim to being exhaustive as to statutes and cases, especially where there is a constitutional provision on legality. It is quite possible that there are statutes or cases that have been missed providing protections beyond what is explicitly stated in national constitutions. This is most likely true for that great majority of the world in which English is not the language of the legislature and the courts.

This project was expanded to a few other areas concerning or related to legality and rule of law, at least as far as the constitutions of the countries. It examines whether the constitution prohibits special or retroactively created criminal courts. Finally, it looks at whether specific constitutional provisions state that penalties are personal or otherwise prohibit collective punishments. Unfortunately, it has proved much more difficult to do a thorough statutory search for these provisions and such has not been done.

This kind of overview of provisions on legality in criminal law has not been done in recent times. The material has changed and grown substantially since the constitutional provisions on legality were collected by John P. Humphrey and his UN Secretariat colleagues as part of the Documented Outline of all constitutional human rights provisions in UN member states in 1947.[15]

Studying national material is useful in its own right as a matter of comparative law. National legal acts may also be useful in determining the international law of human rights, because human rights law deals mostly, though not exclusively, with governments' treatment of their own nationals and other persons on their territories.

As it turns out, the law is not always clear from the facial statements of the constitutions involved. This is why Appendix C includes the constitutional or other statutory texts relied upon: the reader can use them to determine

[15] Documented Outline arts. 25–26, pp. 215–34, UN Doc. E/CN.4/AC.1/3/Add.1.

whether the author's interpretation is reasonable and for beginning more in-depth research as to any given country. In a few cases, there is unclarity in a constitutional text as to whether both retroactive crime creation and retroactive increase of penalties are prohibited. Where this is so, and the state involved is party to one of the general international human rights documents prohibiting both retroactive crime creation and increase of penalties in all cases (ACHR, ACHPR, ECHR, revised ArCHR, ICCPR), the constitutional text is read with that meaning.

Another limitation to this study concerns the issue of translation. Translation of legal terms and concepts, as with translation of any other words and ideas, is inherently imperfect. Thus, one cannot do too much analysis of a foreign legal text in a foreign language. This study of legality, for example, must deal with the fact that words translated into English as *law* or *laws* might mean "statutes," "statutes, regulations and other binding legal texts," "binding rules of conduct however made," or something slightly different. Often other sources of law, such as cases, which might clarify the usage, are not readily available in translation. Indeed, in English, *laws* is used in these different senses and others, often ambiguously.

For example, it may be difficult to tell whether a requirement that an act be "prohibited by *a law* at the time the act was committed" truly means that a state follows the rule of *praevia lege scripta*, or whether there merely be some binding legal obligation in effect, which might occur through common law or customary law as well as through statute or regulation. This has prevented development of a definitive list of countries following *praevia lege scripta.* Complete accuracy would require knowing every text in its original language and legal context.

Realistically, an in-depth study of every nation's constitutional, statutory, treaty, and case law jurisprudence on legality is not possible here. Most interpretations of constitutional provisions are not noted. Given the exigencies of worldwide statutory legal research, it is possible, if not likely, that a number of existing statutes have been missed. Violations of legality provisions that governments may have committed may not have come to light through the author's research. Because of these issues, plus the issue of translation, a lawyer with a case involving any of these countries can use the material here only as a starting point for a detailed consideration of national law relating to criminal law legality. A truly detailed comparative study of the principle of legality in criminal law as applied in states around the world remains to be done.

5.b. LEGALITY IN CONSTITUTIONS OF THE WORLD IN 1946–47

Early in its history, officials at the United Nations studied the law of human rights of UN member states and other states. This produced two major results. One was the documented outline that was used in preparing the UDHR and the early drafts of the ICCPR.[16] It examined and categorized human rights provisions in the constitutions of UN member states as of 1946–47. The other was a comprehensive compilation of human rights provisions in national constitutions (including those of non-UN members), along with some country studies by national experts, which was printed in the first UN *Year Book on Human Rights*, dated 1946 and published in 1948 (1946 UNYBHR).[17] At this time, UN staff did not do an exhaustive study of the statutory or other law of human rights of states, though some information was included in the country studies. The 1946 UNYBHR included information on non–UN member states, including the former enemy states of World War II. The provisions on the principle of legality in criminal law are collected from both the documented outline and the 1946 UNYBHR in Appendix B.

At the close of World War II, many nations had constitutional provisions requiring a rather weak form of legality in criminal law – specifically, that crimes and punishments may only be determined by law – but did not have constitutional provisions that on their face required non-retroactivity of crimes and punishments. These were spread though many parts of the world and were principally, though not exclusively, from civil law systems. In Western Europe, these countries included Belgium, Eire (Ireland), Liechtenstein, Luxembourg, and Monaco.[18] In Eastern Europe, these countries included Albania (which allowed administrative organs to award jail for misdemeanors), Czechoslovakia, Poland, Romania, and Yugoslavia.[19] In Asia, these countries were Afghanistan, Iran, Iraq, Lebanon and Syria,[20]

[16] UN Doc. E/CN.4/AC.1/3/Add.1 (2 June 1947), discussed in Chap. 4.a.ii above.

[17] 1946 UNYBHR.

[18] All constitutions as of 1946–47 from Appendix B: Belgium Const. art. 9; Eire (Ireland) Const. art. 40(4)(1); Liechtenstein Const, art. 33; Luxembourg Const. arts. 12–14; Monaco Const. art. 7.

[19] All constitutions as of 1946–47 from Appendix B: Albania Const. art. 19; Czechoslovakia Const. art.111(2); Poland Const. art. 98 (1921; declared in force in its "basic provisions" by Polish Committee on National Liberation, 22 July 1944); Romania Const. art. 14; Yugoslavia Const. art. 28.

[20] All constitutions as of 1946–47 from Appendix B: Afghanistan Fundamental Principles of the Government art. 11; Iran Supplementary Fundamental Laws art. 12 (8 October 1907); Iraq Organic Law art. 7 (21 March 1925); Lebanon Const. art. 8; Syria Const. art. 9.

which were all either majority Islamic or (in the case of Lebanon) containing large populations of both Christians and Muslims. In Africa, Ethiopia and Liberia had this type of constitution.[21] In the Americas, the Dominican Republic, Haiti (specifically allowing for retroactivity concerning events of a transitional period), and Uruguay had this kind of constitution.[22]

This does not generally mean that these nations did not observe non-retroactivity of crimes and punishments. The material discussed in the UN study was, in most cases, limited to constitutional law. Many countries, especially from the civil law code-based tradition, may have observed non-retroactivity of criminal law through statute (e.g., Lebanon and Italy[23]). Some may even have inferred it from the idea that crimes and punishments can only be defined by law – to punish retroactively would allow for targeting of punishment at certain individuals who are known to have done certain things, not criminal when done. This would be contrary to the rule of law.

In contrast, a significant number of countries did have explicit constitutional guarantees of non-retroactivity as to both crimes and punishments. These were mostly New World states, principally civil law, plus the United States. France, an originator of the modern movement to place legality in governing texts,[24] and a few other Old World states also had such provisions. The civil law states in the Americas included Argentina, Bolivia, Brazil, Chile, Colombia (which also observed *lex mitior* in its constitution), Costa Rica, Cuba (also with *lex mitior* except for public corruption crimes and offenses against constitutional rights), Ecuador, El Salvador (also with *lex mitior*), Guatemala (also with *lex mitior*), Honduras (also with *lex mitior*), Mexico, Nicaragua, Panama, Paraguay, Peru, and Venezuela.[25] The United States was a common law representative here, and unlike the other countries,

[21] All constitutions as of 1946–47 from Appendix B: Ethiopia Const. arts. 23–24; Liberia Const. art. 8.

[22] All constitutions as of 1946–47 from Appendix B: Dominican Rep. Const. art. 88; Haiti Const. arts. 15 and "D"; Uruguay Const. art. 10.

[23] Lebanon Code Pénal arts. 1–14 (1943); see also Italy Penal Code arts. 1, 2 (1931) (with no constitutional provision on legality in criminal law).

[24] See France Declaration of the Rights of Man and of the Citizen art. 8 (1789).

[25] All constitutions as of 1946–47 from Appendix B: Argentina Const. art. 18; Bolivia Const. arts. 29, 31; Brazil Const. arts. 14(29), 141(27); Chile Const. arts. 26, 28; Costa Rica Const. arts. 26, 43; Cuba Const. arts. 21, 22; Ecuador Const. art. 169; El Salvador Const. arts. 24, 25; Guatamala Const. art. 49; Honduras Const. art. 54; Mexico Const. art. 14; Nicaragua Const. art. 43; Paraguay Const. art. 26; Peru Const. art. 26; Venezuela Const. art. 17(II).

phrased its prohibition in terms of forbidding any "ex post facto Law."[26] Other countries with such constitutional provisions were mostly European civil law systems, France, Greece, Norway, and Portugal (with constitutional *nullum crimen* provision only).[27] Egypt and the Philippines (with an American-style ex post facto provision) also had constitutional provisions.[28]

Some constitutions couched legality in libertarian terms that inspired the article in the Draft Outline of an International Bill of Rights: "Everything that is not prohibited by law is permitted."[29] This happened mostly but not exclusively where there were also specific criminal non-retroactivity provisions in the constitutions. This sort of general protection of freedom to do what is not prohibited by law appeared in Argentina, Bolivia, Brazil, Costa Rica, Dominican Republic, France, Guatemala, Nicaragua, Paraguay, Peru, and Uruguay.[30] As with the more specific provisions on non-retroactivity in criminal law, this type of provision came from the 1789 French Declaration of the Rights of Man and of the Citizen.[31]

There were also many states that had no constitutional provisions on legality in criminal law.[32] Some of these were common law jurisdictions, specifically Australia, Canada, India (still in the midst of its independence struggle in 1946, though a UN member), New Zealand, South Africa (with a mixed Anglo-Dutch legal heritage), and the United Kingdom. Others included the Soviet Union and two of its constituent republics, the Belorussian and Ukrainian SSRs (also UN members), and the Mongol People's

[26] U.S. Const. art. I, §§9, 10, first interpreted and applied in *Calder v. Bull*, 3 Dallas (3 U.S.) 386 (1798).

[27] All constitutions as of 1946–47 from Appendix B: France Const., preamble (27 October 1946) ("reaffirms the rights and freedoms of man and the citizen consecrated by the Declaration of Rights of 1789"); Greece Const. art. 7; Norway Const. art. 97; Portugal Const. art. 8(9).

[28] All constitutions as of 1946-47 from Appendix B: Royal Rescript No. 42 Establishing the Constitutional Regime of the Egyptian State art. 6 (19 April 1923); Philippines Const. art. III(11).

[29] Draft Outline of an International Bill of Rights, art. 25, E/CN.4/21, Annex A, p. 17, reprinted from E/CN.4/AC.1/3.

[30] All constitutions as of 1946–47 from Appendix B: Argentina Const. art. 19; Bolivia Const. art. 29; Brazil Const. art. 140(2); Costa Rica Const. art. 36; Dominican Rep. Const. art. 88; France Declaration of the Rights of Man and of the Citizen art. 8; Guatemala Const. art. 23; Nicaragua Const. art. 41; Paraguay Const. art. 30; Peru Const. art. 24; Uruguay Const. art. 10.

[31] France Declaration of the Rights of Man and of the Citizen art. 5 (1789).

[32] For all the material in this paragraph, see Appendix B, with material from Documented Outline, UN Doc. E/CN.4/AC.1/3/Add.1, pp. 219–34, and 1946 UNYBHR.

Republic (as it was called),[33] all Communist countries with the Marxist-Leninist hostility to legality. Hungary is an interesting case; it had no constitutional provision on legality in criminal law in 1946, but from 1949 throughout the Communist era it did have such a provision.[34] Some civil law nations without legality in constitutional provisions at the time included Denmark, Finland, Iceland, Italy, the Netherlands, Spain, Sweden, and Switzerland. Other states without such a constitutional guarantee included China, Saudi Arabia, Siam (now Thailand), and Turkey.

Again, the fact that there is no non-retroactivity provision in a constitution does not necessarily mean that there was no non-retroactivity in the law. The material discussed in the UN studies was, in most cases, limited to constitutional law. A good example is Italy, which never gave up its statutory non-retroactivity provisions even under Fascism.[35] However, some common law countries mentioned here had not completely given up the right of courts to make up new common law crimes retroactively.[36] The Soviet Union remained actively hostile to legality in criminal law.[37] Finland had a provision which might have retroactively authorized detention for a person who may have "contributed to an aggravation of" Finland's relationships with another country.[38] This may have been designed to protect its relationship with the Soviet Union.

The 1946 UN *Year Book* noted a few states had not yet established post-War legal orders. These included Austria, Bulgaria, and Germany.[39] The study noted, however, that the German laws abrogating non-retroactivity of criminal law by allowing for definition of "any crime 'by analogy' or by so-called 'sound popular instinct'" had themselves been repealed by Control Council Law No. 3 of the Allies.[40]

Examining this material as a whole, as of 1946, one certainly could not say that non-retroactivity in criminal law was a worldwide standard. The

[33] See excerpts from Mongol People's Republic Constitution (Fundamental Law) (30 June 1940; as amended 28 September 1944), 1947 UNYBHR at 247–49.
[34] See Hungary Const. art. 57(4) (1949) (*nullum crimen*), discussed in Chap. 5.c.iv.
[35] See Italy Crim. Code of 1931 art. 1, discussed in M. Cherif Bassiouni, Crimes Against Humanity in International Criminal Law 130–31 (2d rev. ed., Kluwer Law Int'l, 1999); Chap. 2.c.ii.C.
[36] See discussion in Chap. 2.a.i.
[37] See discussion in Chap. 2.c.ii.C.
[38] See Finland Decree Regarding Restrictions of Personal Freedom, No. 899 (30 December 1946), 1946 UNYBHR at 104.
[39] 1946 UNYBHR at 35, 51, 116.
[40] See Control Council Proclamation No. 3 (20 October 1945), in 1946 UNYBHR at 117–18. See also Control Council Law No. 11, Official Gazette of the Control Council for Germany, No. 3 (Berlin, 31 January 1946).

conclusion of the Nuremberg Judgment that *nullum crimen sine lege* was not a limitation of sovereignty but might be a principle of justice did not cite to national provisions.[41] The fact that only a minority of nations had constitutional provisions embodying this principle certainly supported this conclusion.[42]

5.C. NON-RETROACTIVITY OF CRIMES AND PUNISHMENTS IN NATIONAL LEGAL SYSTEMS TODAY: AT LEAST A GENERAL PRINCIPLE OF LAW

By now, virtually all states have accepted the rule of non-retroactivity of crimes and punishments. Most have done so through adoption of constitutional provisions. Some do not have constitutional provisions but have adopted it through statutory or other provisions of domestic law. Most have also adopted treaties with provisions requiring non-retroactivity of criminal law. Those states that have adopted constitutional or statutory provisions include almost all of those remaining outside the international human rights treaty system. Non-retroactivity is a worldwide standard.

All but two UN members accept general non-retroactivity of crimes and punishments by constitution, statute, treaty (the ICCPR and/or the regional human rights treaties), or some combination of these three forms of law. The other two UN member states (Bhutan and Brunei), plus the Vatican (Holy See), at least accept non-retroactivity of crime creation for juveniles, through the Convention on the Rights of the Child.[43] Brunei and the Vatican (Holy See) accept non-retroactivity of both crimes and punishments during non-international armed conflict by accepting the 1977 Additional Protocol II[44] to the Geneva Conventions of 1949.

The treaties are important, even for national law, because they represent a commitment not to use internal law to criminalize or punish acts

[41] *United States v. Göring*, Judgment of 30 September 1946, 1 Trial of the Major War Criminals Before the International Military Tribunal: Nuremberg 14 November 1945-1 October 1946 171, 219 (International Military Tribunal 1947) [hereinafter IMT, Trial].

[42] Sharp eyes will notice an anachronism here, as the Nuremberg Judgment was written in 1946 but the Draft Outline was not completed until 1947, and the 1946 UNYBHR was not published until 1948. Nonetheless, the fact that the United Kingdom and the Soviet Union had no constitutional guarantee of non-retroactivity in criminal law was no secret at Nuremberg.

[43] Convention on the Rights of the Child art. 40(2)(a).

[44] Additional Protocol II art. 6(2)(c).

retroactively. Consideration of the treaties allows completion of the circle of states accepting this core of the principle of legality. By now, every UN member state has accepted that non-retroactivity of crimes is applicable to at least some crimes in its internal law. Every UN member state except Bhutan either has accepted non-retroactivity of crimes and punishments generally or has at least accepted it (through Additional Protocol II) in the situation of non-international armed conflict (i.e., civil war) – the case in which there is likely to be the most pressure to violate legality.

One cannot infer directly from the adoption of the ICCPR or a regional human rights treaty that the terms of the treaty automatically apply in domestic courts. Australia, for example, accepts a moderate version of the dualist theory of international law. That is, international law and national law exist in their own spheres, and international law applies only in national courts where a national legal act has incorporated it. Australia has neither a constitutional provision compelling non-retroactivity of crimes and punishments nor such a provision in its criminal code. It has a history allowing retroactive expansion of jurisdiction, at least where the acts involved are crimes everywhere. However, the Australian government has warned against the use of devices such as the expansion of jurisdiction to provide an excuse for retroactive criminalization of innocent acts.[45] Australia, by adopting the ICCPR and its First Optional Protocol (allowing consideration of individual complaints by the Human Rights Committee), has undertaken a legal obligation not to apply definitions of crimes and punishments retroactively to persons within its jurisdiction.

This near unanimity demonstrates that non-retroactivity of crimes and punishments is a general principle of law accepted by the community of nations, or in the words of the ICJ Statute, "by civilized nations."[46] It is accepted by almost all nations from all of the major legal systems in the world. Later in this book, a synthesis of national and international law and practice will show that the non-retroactivity of crimes and punishments is a rule of customary international law as well.[47]

[45] Charles Sampford, Retrospectivity and the Rule of Law 134 (Oxford Univ. Press 2006), quoting from Criminal Code Amendment (Offenses Against Australians) Bill 2002, Explanatory Memorandum, p. 3.

[46] ICJ Statute art. 38(1)("civilized nations"); accord ECHR art. 7. Compare ICCPR art. 15(2) ("community of nations").

[47] Chap. 7, synthesizing the materials in Chaps. 4, 5 & 6.

5.c.i. *Sources of the Requirement of Non-retroactivity of Crimes and Punishments in National Law*

More than four-fifths of United Nations members (162 of 192, or about 84 percent) recognize non-retroactivity of criminal definitions (*nullum crimen*) in their constitutions.[48] More than three-quarters (147 of 192, or

[48]This material is summarized in Appendix A, with documentation in Appendix C: Afghanistan Const. art. 24 (alternatively numbered ch. 2, art. 7); Albania Const. art. 29(1); Algeria Const. arts. 46, 140; Andorra Const. arts. 3(2), 9(4); Angola Const. Law, art. 9(3, 4); Antigua & Barbuda Const. art. 15(4); Argentina Const. art. 18; Armenia Const. art. 22; Azerbaijan Const. art. 71(VIII); Bahamas Const. art. 20(4); Bahrain Const. art. 20(a); Bangladesh Const. art. 35(1); Barbados Const. art. 18(4); Belarus Const. art. 104; Belize Const. art. 6(4); Benin Const. arts. 7, 17; Bolivia Const. arts. 16(II), 33; Bosnia & Herzegovina Const. art. II(2); Botswana Const. art. 10(4); Brazil Const. art. 5(XXXIX, XL); Bulgaria Const. art. 5(3); Burkina Faso Const. art. 5; Burundi Const. arts. 19, 39, 41; Cambodia Const. art. 31 (incorporation of UDHR and human rights covenants); Cameroon Const., preamble; Canada Const. Act, art. 11(g); Cape Verde Const. arts. 16(5), 30(2); Central African Rep. Const. art. 3; Chad Const. art. 23; Chile Const. art. 19(3); Colombia Const. arts. 28, 29; Comoros Const. art. 48; Dem. Rep. of Congo Const. art. 17; Costa Rica Const. arts. 34, 39; Côte d'Ivoire Const. art. 21; Croatia Const. art. 31; Cuba Const. art. 59; Cyprus Const. art. 12(1); Czech Rep., Const. art. 3 and Czech Rep. Charter of Fundamental Rights and Basic Freedoms art. 40(6); Djibouti Const. art. 10; Dominica Const. art. 8(4); Dominican Rep. Const. art. 47; East Timor Const. art. 31(2, 5); Ecuador Const. art. 24(1); Egypt Const. arts. 66, 187; El Salvador Const. art. 15; Equatorial Guinea Fundamental Law art. 13(s); Eritrea Const. art. 17(2); Estonia Const. art. 23; Ethiopia Const. art. 22(1); Fiji Const. art. 28(1)(j); Finland Const., ch. 2(8); France Const. preamble and France Declaration of the Rights of Man and the Citizen art. 8; Gabon Const. art. 79 (as to high government officials only; Gabon is bound to *nullum crimen* and *nulla poena* for crime generally through the ACHPR and ICCPR); Gambia Const. art. 24(5); Georgia Const. art. 42(5); Germany Basic Law art. 103(2); Ghana Const. arts. 19(5, 6, 11), 107; Greece Const. art. 7(1); Grenada Const. art. 8(4); Guatamala Const. arts. 15, 17; Guinea Fundamental Law art. 59; Guinea-Bissau Const. art. 33(2); Guyana Const. art. 144(4); Haiti Const. art. 51; Honduras Const. arts. 95, 96; Hungary Const. art. 57(4); Iceland Const. art. 69; India Const. art. 20(1); Indonesia Const. art. 28I(1); Iran Const. art. 169; Iraq Const. art. 19(2, 10); Ireland Const. art. 15(5)(1); Italy Const. art. 25; Jamaica Const. art. 20(7); Japan Const. art. 39; Kazakhstan Const. art. 77(3, 5, 10); Kenya Const. art. 77(4, 8); Kiribati Const. art. 10(4); Rep. of Korea, art. 13(1); Kuwait Const. art. 32; Kyrgyzstan Const. art. 85(10); Latvia Const. art. 89 (constitutional requirement of protecting fundamental human rights in accordance with international agreements binding on Latvia, which appears to require implementation of ECHR and ICCPR); Lesotho Const. art. 12(4); Liberia Const. art. 21(a); Macedonia Const. arts. 14, 52; Madagascar Const. art. 13; Malawi Const. art. 42(2)(f)(vi); Malaysia Const. art. 7(1); Maldives Const. art. 17(1); Mali Const. art. 9; Malta Const. art. 39(8); Marshall Is. Const. art. II(8)(1); Mauritius Const., ch. II, art. 10(4); Mexico Const. art. 14; Micronesia Const. art. IV(11); Moldova Const. art. 22; Monaco Const. art. 20; Montenegro Const. arts. 33, 34; Morocco Const. art. 4; Mozambique Const. art. 99; Myanmar Const. art. 23; Namibia Const. art. 12(3); Nauru Const. art. 10(4); Nepal Interim Const. [2007] art. 24(4); Netherlands Const. art. 16; Nicaragua Const. arts. 34(11), 38, 100; Niger Const. arts. 15, 16, 17;

about 76 percent) apply non-retroactivity of increased punishments (*nulla poena*) through their constitutions as well.[49] This means that a significant

Nigeria Const. art. 36 (8, 12); Norway Const. arts. 96, 97; Oman Basic Statute of the State art. 75; Pakistan Const. art. 12(1); Palau Const. art. IV(6); Panama Const. arts. 31, 46; Papua New Guinea Const. art. 37(2, 7, 21, 22) (though in village courts, *nullum crimen* and *nulla peona* appear to be statutory); Paraguay Const. arts. 14, 17(1); Peru Const. art. 2(24)(d); Philippines Const. art. III(22); Poland Const. art. 42(1); Portugal Const. art. 29(1); Qatar Const. art. 40; Romania Const. art. 15(2); Russia Const. art. 54; Rwanda Const. preamble ¶ 9, arts. 18, 20; St. Kitts & Nevis Const. art. 10(4); St. Lucia Const. art. 8(4); St. Vincent & the Grenadines Const. art. 8(4); Samoa Const. art. 10(2); São Tomé and Príncipe Const. arts. 7, 36; Senegal Const. art. 9; Serbia Const. arts. 34, 197; Seychelles Const. art. 19(4); Sierra Leone Const, art. 23(7); Singapore Const. art. 11(1); Slovakia Const. art. 50(6); Slovenia Const. arts. 28, 153, 155; Solomon Is. Const. art. 10(4); Somalia Const. art. 34; South Africa Const. art. 35(3)(l); Spain Const. art. 9(3), 25(1); Sri Lanka Const. art. 13(6); Sudan Interim Nat'l Const. art. 34(4); Suriname Const. art. 131(2); Swaziland Const. Act. §21(5); Sweden Instrument of Gov't, ch. 2, art. 10; Syria Const. art. 30; Tajikistan Const. art. 20; Tanzania Const. art. 13(6)(c); Thailand Const. §39; Togo Const. art. 19; Tonga Const. art. 20; Tunisia Const. art. 13; Turkey Const. art. 38; Turkmenistan Const. art. 43; Tuvalu Const. §22(6); Uganda Const. art. 28(7); Ukraine Const. art. 58; United Arab Emirates Const. art. 27; U.S. Const. art. I(9, 10); Vanuatu Const. art. 5(2)(f); Venezuela Const. arts. 24, 49(6); Yemen Const. arts. 46, 103; Zambia Const. art. 18(4, 8); Zimbabwe Const. art. 18(5). Exceptions to these provisions are discussed in Chap. 5.c.vi and are noted in Appendix A and documented in Appendix C. Numbers in text do not include one state which applies *nullum crimen* constitutionally only to high government officials and have other sources of law applying it to crime in general.

[49] This material is summarized in Appendix A, with documentation in Appendix C: Afghanistan Const. art. 24 (alternatively numbered ch. 2, art. 7); Albania Const. art. 29(2); Algeria Const. arts. 140, 142; Andorra Const. arts. 3(2), 9(4); Angola Const. Law, art. 9(4); Antigua & Barbuda Const. art. 15(4); Argentina Const. art. 18; Armenia Const. art. 22; Bahamas Const. art. 20(4); Bahrain Const. art. 20(a); Bangladesh Const. art. 35(1); Barbados Const. art. 18(4); Belarus Const. art. 104; Belize Const. art. 6(4); Benin Const. arts. 7, 17; Bolivia Const. art. 33; Bosnia & Herzegovina Const. art. II(2); Botswana Const. art. 10(4); Brazil Const. art. 5(XXXIX, XL); Burkina Faso Const. art. 5; Burundi Const. arts. 19, 39, 41; Cambodia Const. art. 31 (incorporation of UDHR and human rights covenants); Cameroon Const. preamble; Canada Const. Act art. 11(i); Cape Verde Const. arts. 16(5), 30(2); Central African Rep. Const. art. 3; Chile Const. art. 19(3); Colombia Const. arts. 28, 29; Comoros Const. art. 48; Dem. Rep. of Congo Const. art. 17; Costa Rica Const. art. 34; Côte d'Ivoire Const. art. 112 (as to high government officials only – as to crime in general *nulla poena* is statutory); Croatia Const. art. 31; Cuba Const. art. 59; Cyprus Const. art. 12(1); Czech Rep., Const. art. 3 and Czech Rep. Charter of Fundamental Rights and Basic Freedoms art. 40(6); Djibouti Const. art. 10; Dominica Const. art. 8(4); Dominican Rep. Const. art. 47; East Timor Const. art. 31(3, 5); Ecuador Const. art. 24(1); Egypt Const. arts. 66, 187; El Salvador Const. art. 15; Equatorial Guinea Fundamental Law, art. 13(s); Estonia Const. art. 23; Ethiopia Const. art. 22(1); Fiji Const. art. 28(1)(j); Finland Const., ch. 2(8); France Const. preamble and France Declaration of the Rights of Man and the Citizen art. 8; Gabon Const. art. 79 (as to high government officials only; Gabon is bound to *nullum crimen* and *nulla poena* for crime generally through the ACHPR and ICCPR); Gambia Const. art. 24(5); Georgia Const. art. 42(5); Ghana Const.

majority has accepted both doctrines as part of the supreme document of national law. In addition, the Palestinian Authority (claiming a right to achieve statehood) and the Turkish Republic of Northern Cyprus (recognized as a state only by Turkey, and the UN Security Council has called on all states not to recognize it[50]) have constitutions implementing these

arts. 19(5, 6, 11), 107; Greece Const. art. 7(1); Grenada Const. art. 8(4); Guatamala Const. arts. 15, 17; Guinea Fundamental Law, art. 59; Guinea-Bissau Const. art. 33(2); Guyana Const. art. 144(4); Haiti Const. art. 51; Honduras Const. arts. 95, 96; Hungary Const. art. 57(4); Iceland Const. art. 69; India Const. art. 20(1); Indonesia Const. art. 28I(1); Iraq Const. art. 19(2, 10); Italy Const. art. 25; Jamaica Const. art. 20(7); Kazakhstan Const. art. 77(3, 5); Kenya Const. art. 77(4, 8); Kiribati Const. art. 10(4); Kuwait Const. art. 32; Kyrgyzstan Const. art. 85(10); Latvia Const. art. 89 (constitutional requirement of protecting fundamental human rights in accordance with international agreements binding on Latvia, which appears to require implementation of ECHR and ICCPR); Lesotho Const. art. 12(4); Liberia Const. art. 21(a); Macedonia Const. arts. 14, 52; Madagascar Const. art. 13; Malawi Const. art. 42(2)(f)(vi); Malaysia Const. art. 7(1); Maldives Const. art. 17(2); Mali Const. art. 95 (as to high government officials only – as to crime in general *nulla poena* is required by ACHPR and ICCPR); Malta Const. art. 39(8); Marshall Is. Const. art. II(8)(1); Mauritius Const., ch. II, art. 10(4); Mexico Const. art. 14; Micronesia Const. art. IV(11); Moldova Const. art. 22; Monaco Const. art. 20; Montenegro Const. arts. 33, 34; Morocco Const. art. 4; Mozambique Const. art. 99(2); Myanmar Const. art. 23; Namibia Const. art. 12(3); Nauru Const. art. 10(4); Nepal Interim Const. [2007] art. 24(4); Nicaragua Const. arts. 34(11), 38, 100; Niger Const. arts. 16, 17; Nigeria Const. art. 36 (8, 12); Norway Const. arts. 96, 97; Oman Basic Statute of the State arts. 21, 75; Pakistan Const. art. 12(1); Palau Const. art. IV(6); Panama Const. art. 46; Papua New Guinea Const. art. 37(2, 7, 21, 22) (though in village courts, *nullum crimen* and *nulla peona* appear to be statutory); Paraguay Const. arts. 14, 17(1); Peru Const. art. 2(24)(d); Philippines Const. art. III(22); Poland Const. art. 42(1); Portugal Const. art. 29(4); Qatar Const. art. 40; Romania Const. art. 15(2); Russia Const. art. 54; Rwanda Const. preamble ¶ 9, art. 20; St. Kitts & Nevis Const. art. 10(4); St. Lucia Const. art. 8(4); St. Vincent & the Grenadines Const. art. 8(4); Samoa Const. art. 10(2); São Tomé and Príncipe Const. arts. 7, 36; Senegal Const. art. 9; Serbia Const. arts. 34, 197; Seychelles Const. art. 19(4); Sierra Leone Const. art. 23(8); Singapore Const. art. 11(1); Slovakia Const. art. 50(6); Slovenia Const. arts. 28, 153, 155; Solomon Is. Const. art. 10(4); Somalia Const. art. 34; South Africa Const. art. 35(3)(n); Spain Const. art. 9(3); Sri Lanka Const. art. 13(6); Suriname Const. art. 131(2); Swaziland Const. Act §21(6); Sweden Instrument of Gov't, ch. 2, art. 10; Syria Const. art. 30; Tajikistan Const. art. 20; Tanzania Const. art. 13(6)(c); Thailand Const., sec. 39; Togo Const. art. 129 (as to high government officials only; Togo is bound to *nulla poena* for crime generally through the ACHPR and ICCPR); Tonga Const. art. 20; Tunisia Const. art. 13; Turkey Const. art. 38; Turkmenistan const. art. 43; Tuvalu Const. §22(7); Uganda Const. art. 28(8); Ukraine Const. art. 58; UAE Const. art. 27; U.S. Const. art. I(9, 10); Vanuatu Const. art. 5(2)(g); Venezuela Const. art. 24; Yemen Const. arts. 46, 103; Zambia Const. art. 18(4, 8); Zimbabwe Const. art. 18(5). Exceptions to these provisions are discussed in Chap. 5.c.vi and are noted in Appendix A and documented in Appendix C. Numbers in text do not include those states which apply *nulla poena* constitutionally only to high government officials and have other sources of law applying it to crime in general.

[50] UN Security Council Res. 541, UN Doc. S/RES 541 (18 November 1983).

principles.[51] Kosovo's proposed constitution would implement them as well.[52]

A significant minority of countries still recognizes non-retroactivity of crimes and, especially, punishments in other ways. There do not seem to be clear patterns in which nations recognize non-retroactivity of crimes and punishments only nonconstitutionally. Many nations in each of the common law, civil law, and Islamic law traditions recognize these doctrines in their constitutions. A few in each system do not. Where there is a statutory recognition of these principles, the vast majority includes these rules in the general part of their criminal codes. A few common law countries recognize the rules in their human rights statutes.

Somewhat more than fifteen countries implement both doctrines through statutes without constitutional provisions. These represent a variety of groups. About half are civil law countries that have traditionally implemented these doctrines in their penal codes: Austria, Belgium, Denmark, Liechtenstein, Luxembourg, Switzerland, and Uruguay.[53] Most of these are in Europe, and most have a large proportion of Germanic language speakers. Israel, Lebanon, and Mauritania, each with a European legal connection as well as a religious tradition, also have these sorts of statutes,[54] though Israel's codification of the doctrines was recent. Two countries with this scheme are former republics of the Soviet Union, Lithuania and Uzbekistan.[55]

The People's Republic of China, with the largest population in the world, recently introduced non-retroactivity of crimes and punishment by statute. It has placed these rules in both its criminal law and its law on legislation.[56]

Two common law countries have recently adopted criminal non-retroactivity statutes outside their general criminal laws. They have institutionalized the doctrines through new human rights statutes. These statutes are the means that these states are using to implement their international human rights treaty obligations. The placing of these criminal law protections in general human rights law also demonstrates the resistance of some

[51] Turkish Rep. of Northern Cyprus Const. art. 18(1); Palestine Amended Basic Law art. 15.

[52] Proposed Kosovo Const. art. 33, presented to the President of Kosovo, 7 April 2008, from Kosovo Constitutional Commission website, www.kosovoconstitution.info.

[53] Austria StGB § 1; Belgium Crim. Code art. 2; Denmark Crim. Code §§ 3, 4; Liechtenstein StGB § 1; Luxembourg Code Pénal art. 2; Switzerland Code Pénal arts. 1, 2; Uruguay Código Penal art. 15.

[54] Israel Penal Law §§ 1–6; Lebanon Code Pénal arts. 1–3, 6–8, 12–14; Mauritania Code Pénal art. 4.

[55] Lithuania Penal Code art. 3; Uzbekistan Crim. Code art. 13.

[56] People's Republic of China Criminal Law art. 12; People's Republic of China Legislation Law art. 84.

common law jurisdictions to the codification of basic principles of criminal law – what civil lawyers call the "general part" of criminal law.[57]

Great Britain and New Zealand have no written constitution. In Great Britain, as discussed in Chapter 2, retroactivity in criminal law was traditionally treated as "odious," and common law crimes were generally fairly stable.[58] Yet criminal law legality was not definitively part of binding law until recently. In 1973, the House of Lords by judicial decision prohibited retroactive crime creation by common law.[59] In 1998, Parliament passed the Human Rights Act, enshrining many internationally recognized human rights in domestic legislation. This act states non-retroactivity of criminal law in the language of the ECHR.[60]

New Zealand enacted legality through the 1990 Bill of Rights Act. The provision, which enacts *nullum crimen*,[61] is modeled on the ICCPR, to which New Zealand is a party. Interestingly, this article is headed "Retroactive penalties," demonstrating that legislators do not always make distinctions between *nullum crimen* and *nulla poena*. The Act has a combined *nulla poena/lex mitior* section, stating that if the penalty has varied between the time of the act and the sentencing, the person has "[t]he right . . . to . . . the lesser penalty."[62]

Saudi Arabia has criminal law non-retroactivity provisions in a decree called the Basic System of the Consultative Council.[63] This example illustrates a difficulty of characterization for this type of study. The Basic System of the Consultative Council serves many of the structural purposes of a constitution in the Saudi system. However, by this decree of the king, the Quran and Sunna of the Prophet are the constitution of Saudi Arabia.[64] Thus, officially, the basic system serves the function of a set of important statutes, which is how it is interpreted here, rather than a constitution. It is also subject to change at the will of the monarch.[65]

The People's Republic of China, New Zealand, Saudi Arabia, and the United Kingdom all come from outside the civil law system. Because they

[57] See GEORGE P. FLETCHER, 1 THE GRAMMAR OF CRIMINAL LAW: AMERICAN, COMPARATIVE, AND INTERNATIONAL (FOUNDATIONS) 18 (Oxford Univ. Press 2007).

[58] See Chap. 2.a.i.

[59] Knuller (Publishing, Printing and Promotions), Ltd. v. DPP, [1973] AC 435 (H.L.).

[60] U.K. Human Rights Act 1998, sched. 1, pt. 1, art. 7.

[61] New Zealand Bill of Rights Act art. 26(1).

[62] *Id.* at art. 25(g).

[63] See Saudi Arabia Basic System of the Consultative Council art. 38, Decree A-90 (1 March 1992).

[64] *Id.* at art. 1.

[65] Cf. *id.* at art. 83.

have less of a tradition of comprehensive but single subject legislative codes, it is not surprising to see non-retroactivity of crimes and punishments in various places in their laws.

Another group of thirteen countries has a *nullum crimen* provision on the face of their constitutions but not *nulla poena*. The continuing existence of such a group might give some force to a U.K. claim in the early negotiations for the UDHR and ICCPR. It argued that *nulla poena* should not be made part of either document because non-retroactivity of crime creation was universally recognized as a human right, but non-retroactivity of punishments was not.[66] Such an argument would be hard to sustain today because every one of these states has now accepted the obligation not to apply new punishments retroactively.[67] Five of these countries have done so by statute. These include the two strongest former Axis powers, Germany and Japan, along with Axis power Bulgaria.[68] One is a former French colony, Côte d'Ivoire.[69] One is the Netherlands.[70]

All these thirteen countries have adopted one or more of the human rights treaties containing these doctrines discussed in Chapter 4.[71] The eight states that have constitutional provisions for non-retroactivity of crimes and have a treaty obligation to recognize non-retroactivity of punishments (without a statute to that effect found) do not fall into any neat pattern, though most of them have substantial Islamic populations. They include old and new states; European, African, and Asian states; and at least one civil law, common law, post-socialist law, and Islamic law state among them: Azerbaijan, Chad, Eritrea, Iran, Ireland, South Korea, Mali, and Sudan.[72]

There is also a group of states that have accepted treaty obligations to apply both *nullum crimen* and *nulla poena*, but for which neither constitutional nor statutory provisions to this effect have been found. One, Australia, is a

[66] See Chap. 4.a.ii.

[67] The material in this and the follow sentences of this paragraph is collected from Appendix A, with documentation in Appendix C.

[68] Bulgaria Const. art. 5(3) and Penal Code art. 2; Germany Basic Law art. 103(2), and §§ 1, 2, StGB; Japan Const. art. 39, and Crim. Code art. 6.

[69] Côte d'Ivoire Const. art. 21, and Code Pénal arts. 19–21.

[70] Netherlands Const. art. 16, and Penal Code art. 1.

[71] Algeria, ICCPR; Bulgaria, ECHR and ICCPR; Côte d'Ivoire, ACHPR and ICCPR; Germany, ECHR and ICCPR; Japan, ICCPR; Netherlands, ECHR and ICCPR; other states discussed subsequently.

[72] Azerbaijan Const. art. 71(VIII), with ECHR, ICCPR; Chad Const. art. 23, with ACHPR, ICCPR; Eritrea Const. art. 17(2), with ACHPR, ICCPR; Iran Const. art. 169, with ICCPR; Ireland Const. art. 15(5)(1) with ECHR, ICCPR; Rep. of [South] Korea Const. art. 13(1), with ICCPR; Mali Const. art. 9, with ACHPR, ICCPR; Sudan Interim National Const. art. 34(4), with ACHPR, ICCPR.

common law country without a general criminal code or human rights code but that is a party to the ICCPR. Three are Asian Communist countries, Laos, Vietnam, and North Korea, all parties to the ICCPR. Others include Republic of the Congo, Gabon, Jordan, Libya, Mongolia, San Marino, and Trinidad and Tobago.[73] Additionally, the Sahrawi Arab Democratic Republic (Western Sahara), an entity that has earned recognition from a substantial minority of states, has accepted the ACHPR. The Republic of China also signed (but did not ratify) the ICCPR before it was replaced at the United Nations by the People's Republic of China.

A number of nations have specific constitutional references to crimes or punishments being defined only by law, or some other constitutional commitment to rule of law in substantive criminal law, but do not include specific reference to the non-retroactivity of crimes and punishments in those definitions. These include Belgium, Gabon, Lebanon, Libya, Liechtenstein, Lithuania, Luxembourg, Mauritania, and Uruguay.[74] Cambodia may also be in this group.[75] The constitution of the Netherlands specifically prohibits retroactive crime creation but merely says that punishments must be defined by law; it endorses non-retroactivity of punishments by statute.[76] All of these states are parties to the ICCPR, ACHR, ACHPR, and/or ECHR. Statutes providing for non-retroactivity of crimes and punishments were found in most of these states, except for Gabon and Libya. Two entities struggling for recognition as states have provisions committing to the rule of law in criminal law without specifically referring to non-retroactivity: Somaliland[77] and the Sahrawi Arab Democratic Republic.[78] As discussed

[73] Rep. of Congo, Gabon, and Libya are parties to ACHPR and ICCPR; Jordan, ICCPR, and has signed the Revised ArCHR(information on ratification not currently available); Mongolia, ICCPR; San Marino, ECHR and ICCPR; Trinidad and Tobago, ACHR and ICCPR.

[74] Belgium Coord. Const. arts. 12, 14; Gabon Const. art. 47; Lebanon Const. art. 8; Constitutional Proclamation of the Revolutionary Command Council of Libya art. 31(a) (1969) (there is some question about whether this remains in force); Liechtenstein Const. art. 33(2) Lithuania Const. art. 31; Luxembourg Const. art. 14; Mauritania Const. art. 13 (additionally, the preamble mentions the ACHPR and UDHR without specifically incorporating all of their provisions); Uruguay Const. art. 10.

[75] See Cambodia Const. arts. 31, 38. ICCPR.

[76] Netherlands Const. arts. 16 (*nullum crimen*), 89(2) (crimes and punishments only by law, but without specification of non-retroactivity) and Penal Code art. 1. ECHR, ICCPR.

[77] Revised Const. of Somaliland art. 26, translated text at http://www.somalilandforum.com/somaliland/constitution/revised_constitution.htm. Translation by Ibrahim Hashi Jama. Somaliland is not generally recognized as a state by the international community.

[78] Const. of Sahrawi Arab Democratic Republic [Western Sahara] art. 26, in French at http://www.arso.org/03-const.99.htm. Sahrawi (sometimes spelled Saharawi) ADR is recognized by a substantial minority of states and is a party to the ACHPR.

previously, the existence of general legality provisions in constitutional law may have been considered in some countries as protecting against retroactivity in criminal law.[79] This can be added to the fact that every UN member state with these provisions has today adopted non-retroactivity through one device or another.

Of particular importance, especially as to the construction of customary international law, is the fact that almost all UN member states that are outside the ICCPR and regional human rights treaty systems have accepted non-retroactivity of crimes and punishments. The vast majority of these have placed non-retroactivity of crimes and punishments in their constitutions: Antigua and Barbuda, the Bahamas, Cuba, Fiji, Kiribati, Malaysia, the Marshall Islands, Micronesia, Myanmar, Nauru, Oman, Pakistan (with exceptions for subversion of constitution), Palau, Papua New Guinea, Qatar, St. Kitts and Nevis, St. Lucia, Samoa, Singapore (with exceptions for political crimes), Solomon Islands, Tonga, Tuvalu, the United Arab Emirates, and Vanuatu.[80] Two states that are considering entering the international human rights treaty system, the People's Republic of China and Saudi Arabia, have statutes endorsing non-retroactivity of crimes and punishments.[81]

As mentioned previously, the two UN members without provisions on non-retroactivity of crimes and punishments in their constitutions or statutes that have not joined the ICCPR or other treaty systems are Bhutan and Brunei. They do, however, have general provisions that crimes or penalties can be created only by law, without express mention of non-retroactivity.[82] As also mentioned, they have accepted the juvenile *nullum crimen* obligation of the Convention on the Rights of the Child (CRC), and

[79] See Chap. 5.b (on similar provisions in 1946–47).

[80] Antigua & Barbuda Const. art. 15(4); Bahamas Const. art. 20(4); Cuba Const. arts. 59, 61; Fiji Const. art. 28(1)(j); Kiribati Const. art. 10(4); Malaysia Const. art. 7(1); Marshall Islands Const. art. II(8); Micronesia Const. art. IV(11); Myanmar Const. art. 23; Nauru Const. art. 10(4) (has signed ICCPR); Oman Basic Statute of the State arts. 21, 75, Sultani Decree No. 101/96 (1996); Pakistan Const. art. 12; Palau Const. art. IV(6); Papua New Guinea Const. art. 37(2, 7, 21 & 22); Qatar Const. art. 40; St. Kitts & Nevis Const. art. 10(4); St. Lucia Const. art. 8(4); Samoa Const. art. 10(1 & 2); Singapore Const. arts. 11(1), 149(1); Solomon Is. Const. art. 10(4); Tonga Const. art. 20; Tuvalu Const., sec. 22(6, 7); UAE Const. art. 27; Vanuatu Const. art. 5(2)(f & g).

[81] People's Republic of China Criminal Law arts. 3, 12; People's Republic of China Legislation Law arts. 9, 84; Saudi Arabia Basic System of the Consultative Council art. 36. The People's Republic of China has signed the ICCPR. Saudi Arabia has signed the Revised ArCHR, and has taken internal steps needed to ratify it. See *Shura Council ratifies Arab Charter on Human Rights*, at http://www.saudiembassy.net/2008News/News/RigDetail.asp?cIndex=7698 (Web site of the Royal Embassy of Saudi Arabia in the U.S., 24 February 2008).

[82] Bhutan Penal Code art. 6; Brunei Penal Code § 2 and Brunei Laws, Ch. 4 (Interpretation and General Clauses) § 39(a).

Bhutan has accepted the non-retroactivity provisions of Additional Protocol II (APII) (concerning non-international conflicts) to the 1949 Geneva Conventions. Vatican City is a party to the CRC and APII. Two entities not generally recognized as states without constitutional, statutory, or treaty provisions endorsing general non-retroactivity of crimes and punishments are Chechnya and Somaliland.

The existence of these legal protections in so many countries does not mean that non-retroactivity is never violated. The research here cannot prove that.[83] It does show, however, that nearly every country asserts to its population and to the world that non-retroactivity of crimes and punishments is a vital part of criminal law and human rights. In this regard, the constitutions are of great importance, because they are the documents in which states – both as peoples and governments – present themselves to the world. For purposes of generating international standards, the treaties are vital as well.

5.c.ii. *Non-retroactivity in the Constitutional Texts: Act Focus and Law Focus*

As was pointed out in the ICCPR debates, one can write non-retroactivity protections differently, on the basis of the differences that one perceives in the evil to be protected against. For example, Eleanor Roosevelt for the United States at one point suggested that legality should protect only against the retroactive passage of statutes, not new judicial interpretations of statutes.[84] This encountered two theoretical objections. Cassin for France argued that legality must protect against retroactivity in criminal law coming from "judges and administrators as well as legislators."[85] Representatives of Guatemala and the United Kingdom argued that the covenant ought to provide protections for individuals (e.g., to prohibit prosecution of individuals for an act not criminal when done) rather than limitations on state power (to forbid a legislature to pass a retroactive law).[86] The ICCPR

[83] See especially Chap. 5.c.vi on exceptions. Additionally, the research here has not canvassed the cases in every state for counterexamples.

[84] UN Doc. E/CN.4/SR.112, p. 4 (7 June 1949, recording session of 3 June 1949); David Weissbrodt, The Right to a Fair Trial under the Universal Declaration of Human Rights and the International Covenant on Civil and Political Rights 79 (Martinus Nijhoff Publishers 2001) [hereafter Weissbrodt], discussed in Chap. 4.b.ii.A.

[85] E/CN.4/SR.112, p. 8, discussed in Chap. 4.b.ii.A.

[86] E/CN.4/SR.112, pp. 4-5 (Guatemala), 7 (United Kingdom); Weissbrodt at 78–79. For an example of a constitutional provision aimed at authority of the national and sub-national legislatures, see U.S. Const. art. I(9, 10).

text represents a victory for both the French and the Guatemalan/British views.

The ICCPR text, however, does not purport to be a required text for implementation of the principle of legality in the law of states that adopt the treaty. Any implementation that in fact protects individuals from retroactivity in crime creation or increase of punishments implements the provision adequately. Indeed, a state that does not criminalize acts or increase punishments retroactively appears to satisfy the non-retroactivity provision of the ICCPR,[87] whether or not it has a text specifically forbidding these practices.[88]

One major pattern of the prohibition against retroactivity of crimes and punishments in national constitutions is to follow the path of the UDHR and the ICCPR. The UDHR prohibits conviction for "any penal offense on account of any act or omission which did not constitute a penal offense, under national or international law, at the time when it was committed" and imposing "a heavier penalty . . . than the one that was applicable at the time the penal offense was committed."[89] On its face, a provision like this prohibits retroactive crime or punishment creation whether by statute, the common law process or otherwise. Grammatically, this type of provision protects individuals by focusing on whether a given act was criminal when done, rather than on the particular form of the prohibition might have taken at that time. As noted before, this idea dates back at least to 1780 in the United States and 1789 in France.[90]

A large number of national constitutional provisions are set up in this way, though this does not mean they adopt the exact wording of either the UDHR or the ICCPR. Most countries with this type of provision are parties to the ICCPR and/or one of the regional human rights conventions.[91]

[87] ICCPR art. 15(1) (first two sentences).

[88] But cf. ICCPR art. 2(2) (on the requirement of implementation of the ICCPR in domestic law by "legislative or other measures").

[89] UDHR art. 11(2); to the same effect, see ICCPR art. 15(1) (first two sentences); ECHR art. 7(1).

[90] Massachusetts [U.S.] Bill of Rights, art. XXIV (1780), reprinted in DOCUMENTS OF AMERICAN HISTORY No. 70 at 107, 109 (Henry Steele Commager, ed., 4th ed. 1948).

[91] Azerbaijan Const. art. 71(VIII); Barbados Const. art. 18(4); Belize Const. art. 6(4); Benin Const. art. 17; Croatia Const. art. 31; Rep. of Cyprus Const. art. 12(1); Eritrea Const. art. 17(2); Ethiopia Const. art. 22; Fiji Const. art. 28(1)(j); Gambia Const. art. 24(5); Georgia Const. art. 42(5); Grenada Const. art. 8(4); Guyana Const. art. 144(4); Jamaica Const. art. 20(7); Japan Const. art. 39 (*nullum crimen*); Lesotho Const. art. 12(4); Malawi Const. art. 42(2)(f)(vi); Malta Const. art. 39(8); Mauritius Const. art. 10(4); Namibia Const. art. 12(3); Nepal Interim Const. art. 24(4); St. Vincent & the Grenadines Const. art. 8(4); Seychelles Const. art. 19(4); Sierra Leone Const. art. 23(7, 8); Somalia Const. art. 34 (but Somalia

Several, however, are not, including the Bahamas, Kiribati, Malaysia, Nauru, Palau, St. Kitts and Nevis, St. Lucia, the Solomon Islands, and Tuvalu.[92] Additionally, Singapore has a constitutional provision of this type (though with important exceptions for political crimes).[93] An entity not generally recognized as a state, the Turkish Republic of Northern Cyprus, has a similar provision.[94]

The presence of a fair number of constitutions of this form among non-parties to the ICCPR and regional human rights treaties may have two meanings. First, it can fairly be called a testament to the influence of the UDHR on the question of legality: all of these states have gained independence since the adoption of the UDHR. Second, it may be taken as evidence that some states consider the statement of non-retroactivity of crimes and punishments in the ICCPR to be required by customary international law.

Many but not all of the countries with legality provisions of this type have a common law tradition or a former colonial or other relationship with the United Kingdom. This is not surprising, as the UDHR formulation was adapted to deal with non-retroactivity in the common law states, where not all criminal definitions have been put into statute, as well as civil law states. Two important common law states, the United Kingdom and New Zealand, have followed this approach in human rights statutes in implementing their human rights treaty obligations.[95] However, some of the states with this type of constitution are from different traditions, for example, two former Communist states (Croatia and Georgia), a few other states with civil law traditions (e.g., Benin, Republic of Cyprus, Suriname, Sweden, Togo), and two other states with large populations (Japan and Turkey).

Thus, a constitutional provision of this type does not necessarily mean that a state recognizes non-statutory means of crime creation. Other sources of law or legal tradition and practice may limit crime creation to statutes

has been without an effective government under the constitution for many years); South Africa Const. art. 35(3)(l) (*nullum crimen*); Sri Lanka Const. art. 13(6); Suriname Const. art. 131(2); Sweden Instrument of Government, ch. 2, art. 10; Tanzania Const. art 13(6)(k); Togo Const. art. 19; Turkey Const. art. 38; Uganda Const. art. 28(7, 8); Zimbabwe Const. art. 18(5).

[92] Bahamas Const. art. 20(4); Kiribati Const. arts. 10(4); Malaysia Const. art. 7(1); Moldova Const. art. 22; Nauru Const. art. 10(4); Palau Const. art. IV(6); St. Kitts & Nevis Const. art. 10(4); St. Lucia Const. art. 8(4); Solomon Is. Const. art. 10(4); Tuvalu Const. art. 22(6, 7).

[93] Singapore Const. art. 11(1) (but see art. 149(1) for important exceptions).

[94] Turkish Rep. of Northern Cyprus Const. art. 18(1) (recognized as a state only by Turkey).

[95] New Zealand Bill of Rights Act 1990 arts. 25(g), 26(1); U.K. Human Rights Act, sched. 1, pt. 1, art. 7.

only. As these have not been fully researched worldwide, the author cannot conclude how common such other sources might be.[96]

Another major pattern of the prohibition against retroactivity of crimes and punishments comes from the tradition requiring a public legal text (generally a statute, but sometimes a regulation,[97] or in dictatorships a decree) effective at the time of the act (*nullum crimen sine praevia lege scripta*). This was the form of the 1789 French Declaration of the Rights of Man and of the Citizen: "nobody may be punished except by virtue of a Law which was adopted and published prior to the offense."[98] Similar provisions exist in the constitutions of Algeria, Burkina Faso, Burundi, Chad, Chile, Colombia, Côte d'Ivoire, Djibouti, Egypt, El Salvador, Kyrgyzstan, Madagascar, Mali, Mexico, Nigeria, Serbia, Spain, Syria, the United Arab Emirates, and the Palestinian Authority (which claims the right to become a state); the requirement of a public legal text may appear in various wordings.[99] A few

[96] See this section, notes 124–26, below for a few examples of constitutions recognizing other sources of law.

[97] See Macedonia Const. art. 14 ("law, or other regulation"); Israel Penal Law art. 2 (allowing authorized regulatory bodies to "designate offences and to set penalties for their commission" of up to six months imprisonment, if approved by a Knesset committee); Nigeria Const. art. 36(12) ("written law" includes "subsidiary legislation or instrument under the provisions of law").

Many jurisdictions allow the sharing of power concerning regulatory offenses between the legislature and a regulatory body, as where the legislature makes it an offense to exceed a posted speed limit, but a regulatory agency such as a highway department determines the actual speed limit in each place; or where the legislature makes it an offense to sell an unapproved drug or medicine but an administrative agency decides which medicines are approved for sale.

[98] France Declaration of the Rights of Man and of the Citizen art. 8 (1789).

[99] Algeria Const. art. 46 ("duly promulgated"); Burkina Faso Const. art. 5 ("promulgated and published"); Burundi Const. art. 39 ("promulgated"); Chad Const. art. 23 ("promulgated"); Chile Const. art. 19(3) ("enacted"); Colombia Const. art. 29 ("written"); Côte d'Ivoire Const. art. 21 ("promulgated"); Djibouti Const. art. 10 ("promulgated"); Egypt Const. art. 66 ("promulgation"); El Salvador Const. art. 15 ("promulgated"); Kyrgyzstan Const. art. 41 ("publication"); Madagascar Const. art. 13 ("promulgated and published"); Mali Const. art. 9 ("promulgated"); Mexico Const. art. 14 ("enacted"); Nigeria Const. art. 36(12) ("written law... [which] refers to an Act of the National Assembly or a law of a State, any subsidiary legislation or instrument under the provisions of law"); Serbia Const. art. 196 ("published"); Spain Const. art. 25(1) ("legislation" required; "publication of norms" required); Syria Const. art. 30 ("Laws are binding only following the date of their enactment"); UAE Const. art. 27 ("issue[ance]"); see Amended Basic Law of Palestine art. 15 ("promulgation") (Palestine claims the right to become a state). Note that this list does not include a complete study of those constitutions that, in their provisions on the legislature, lay out requirements for the enactment, promulgation, or effectiveness of statutes.

states that allow direct application of treaty law to individuals do so only after publication in the state.[100]

This type of provision serves three important policies. The requirement of legislative action and publication ensures notice and accessibility of the law. Indeed, notice is still a primary purpose of this requirement. A second policy is ensuring that there actually is a law (i.e., that the requirements for making a legal rule binding the populace have actually been met). These two policies apply both in democratic and in authoritarian regimes. Finally, this type of provision now protects democratic governance in many places. Where the legislature is democratically chosen, this type of provision ensures that criminal law is created by the institution of representative democracy.

The protection that the *praevia lege scripta* version of legality extends in authoritarian (as well as democratic) regimes is notable. In nondemocratic regimes, this requirement may be met by decrees, proclamations, orders, or statutes by a leader rather than by a parliamentary body. Interestingly, non-retroactivity of criminal law has occasionally been proclaimed by such leaders.[101] Legality has also been proclaimed by outside leaders establishing transitional regimes designed to lead to democracy. At the end of World War II, it may be remembered, the four Allied powers restored the general application of legality to German law by proclamation.[102] Chapter 6 will discuss legality imposed by decree of UN officials in Kosovo and East Timor.

The French Declaration of the Rights of Man and of the Citizen quoted previously shows another important development. Like constitutions that follow the UDHR/ICCPR, it protects individuals by focusing on whether a given act was punishable when done, but it also requires *scripta*. Other constitutions that follow this pattern include Afghanistan, Algeria, Argentina, Bahrain, Bangladesh, Botswana, Burkina Faso, Burundi, Cameroon, Central African Republic, Chad, Chile, Cuba, Czech Republic, Djibouti, Egypt,

[100] Ward N. Ferdinandusse, Direct Application of International Criminal Law in National Courts 236 (TMC Asser 2006) [hereinafter Ferdinandusse], citing Netherlands Constitution art. 93; and *Publication of Treaties Case* (Belgium Ct. of Cassation, 25 November 1993). He also cites a case from interwar Germany, *Publication of Treaties Case* (Reichsgericht in Strafsachen, 25 September 1920), partial translation into English in Annual Digest 1919–1922, No. 234, p. 323, but it is not clear whether this would continue to be true in the current German constitutional order.

[101] E.g., Oman Basic Statute of the State of Oman arts. 21, 75; Saudi Arabia Basic System of the Consultative Council art. 38 (1 March 1992).

[102] Control Council Law No. 11, Official Gazette of the Control Council for Germany, No. 3 (31 January 1946). See also Allied Control Council Law No. 3 (25 October 1945), and Military Order No. 1 issued in pursuance of it.

El Salvador, Estonia, Finland, Germany, India, Iran, Kenya, Kuwait, Madagascar, Oman, Slovakia, Slovenia, Spain, and the United Arab Emirates.[103] Most of these have some tie to the civil law tradition. A few have some tie to the common law (Bangladesh, Botswana, and India) and several have majority Islamic populations (Afghanistan, Algeria, Bahrain, Bangladesh, Djibouti, Egypt, Iran, Kuwait, Oman, and United Arab Emirates).

As discussed earlier, ambiguities of usage and translation make it very difficult to produce a definitive listing of those countries following any of the above versions of *nullum crimen, nulla poena sine praevia lege scripta.*[104] The author does not wish to conclude simply that because a state comes from the civil law tradition that it necessarily implements a strict requirement for the existence of a statute. The discussion should therefore be treated as providing indicative, rather than exhaustive, lists of which states follow which theories.

The United States follows a different path. It has constitutional provisions prohibiting "ex post facto law[s]."[105] On their faces, these prohibit retroactive statutes. These were interpreted early on to prohibit retroactive crime creation or increase of punishment by statute but not to apply to noncriminal statutes.[106] They are not *praevia lege scripta* provisions, because they have not been interpreted to require criminal statutes as opposed to common law crimes. Indeed, they do not, on their face, prohibit retroactive common law crime creation. As a nonconstitutional matter, it was determined early on that there would be no common law crime creation in the federal (i.e., national) courts.[107] It was only much later that a provision of

[103] Afghanistan Const. art. 27 [alternately numbered ch. 2, art. 6]; Algeria Const. art 46 (*nullum crimen* only); Argentina Const. art. 18; Bahrain Const. art. 20(a); Bangladesh Const. art. 35(1) (except for international law crimes specified in *id.* art. 47(3)); Botswana Const. art. 10(4, 8); Burkina Faso Const. art. 5; Burundi Const. art. 41; Cameroon Const., Preamble; Central African Rep. Const. art. 3; Chad Const. art. 23 (*nullum crimen* only); Chile, art. 19(3); Cuba Const. art. 59; Czech Republic Charter of Fundamental Rights and Freedoms [of former Czechoslovakia] arts. 39, 40(6), available at http://www.nssoud.cz/en/docs/charter.pdf (official Web site of Supreme Administrative Court of Czech Republic); Djibouti Const. art. 10; Egypt Const. art. 66; El Salvador Const. art. 15; Estonia Const. art. 23; Finland Const., ch. 2(8); Germany Const. art. 103(2) (*nullum crimen* only); India Const. art. 20(1); Iran Const. art. 169; Kenya Const. art. 77(4, 8); Kuwait Const. art. 32; Madagascar Const. art. 13 (*nulla poena*); Oman Basic Statute, arts. 21, 75; Slovakia Const. art. 50(6); Slovenia Const. art. 153; Spain Const. art. 25(1); UAE Const. art. 27.

[104] See Chap. 5.a.

[105] U.S. Const. art. I(9, 10) (prohibiting such laws by both the national and state governments).

[106] Calder v. Bull, 3 U.S. (3 Dallas) 386, 391, 396 (1798).

[107] See United States v. Wiltburger, 5 Wheat. (18 U.S.) 76 (1820).

the constitution prohibiting deprivation of "life, liberty or property without due process of law" was interpreted to prohibit unforeseeable retroactive judicial expansion of criminal liability by the courts of U.S. states.[108] Thus, the limitation of the ex post facto clauses of the Constitution to statutory criminal law no longer limits the principle of legality in the United States.

A few countries with historic ties to the United States have constitutional provisions modeled on the U.S. ex post facto clauses. These include the Philippines, the Marshall Islands, and Micronesia.[109] The Marshall Islands' provision prohibits "ex post facto punishment,"[110] whether by statute or otherwise.

In civil law countries, phrasing legality in terms of non-retroactivity of all means of creating punishment may be less important than in common law countries such as the United States. If a legal tradition requires a statute to define crimes and punishments, then a prohibition of retroactive criminal statutes essential prohibits retroactivity of crimes and punishments.

Some other states do not use the phrase "ex post facto." Yet they also have constitutions focusing on non-retroactivity of law rather than using some formulation concerning time of the particular act charged. For example, the Cape Verde Islands Constitution says, "Retroactive application of criminal law shall be prohibited unless the subsequent law is more favorable to the accused."[111] The Indonesian Constitution states that "the right not to be tried under a law with retrospective effect [is a] human right that cannot be limited under any circumstances."[112] Some other countries with similar constitutional provisions include Belarus, Bolivia, Guinea, Honduras, Monaco, Syria, and Yemen.[113] Most of these have some sort of civil law background.

A few constitutions essentially prohibit retroactivity twice. One provision requires that crimes and punishments be in existence at the time of the act charged, as in the UDHR and ICCPR. The other provision prohibits the

[108] U.S. Const., amend. XIV(1), was held to prohibit unforeseeable judicial expansion of criminal liability in Bouie v. City of Columbia, 378 U.S. 347 (1964), and Rogers v. Tennessee, 532 U.S. 451 (2001).

[109] Marshall Is. Const. art. II(8); Micronesia Const. art. IV(11); Philippines Const. art. III(22).

[110] Marshall Is. Const. art. II(8).

[111] Cape Verde Const. art., 30(2). See also Costa Rica Const. art. 34; Dominican Rep. Const. art. 47; Guinea-Bissau Const. art. 33(2).

[112] Indonesia Const. art. 28I(1).

[113] Belarus Const. art. 104; Bolivia Const. art. 33; Guinea Fundamental Law art. 59; Honduras Const. art. 96; Monaco Const. art. 20; Syria Const. art. 30; Yemen Const. arts. 46, 103 (Yemen accepts sharia as well as statutes as a source of criminal law).

retroactivity of law, similarly to the just quoted Cape Verde Islands provisions. Such constitutions include those of Armenia, Costa Rica, Croatia, Egypt, Guatemala, Macedonia, Nicaragua, Niger, Paraguay, Peru, Rwanda, Serbia, Slovenia, and East Timor.[114] These are generally but not exclusively countries from the civil law tradition. Of these, Oman is not a party to the ICCPR.

Liberia has a single constitutional article protecting individuals from retroactive criminal law and prohibiting the legislature to pass such laws: "No person shall be made subject to any law or punishment which was not in effect at the time of commission of an offense, nor shall the Legislature enact any bill of attainder or ex post facto law."[115] Botswana, Brazil, Iraq, Nigeria, Papua New Guinea, Russia, and Zambia have a similar structure but divide the provisions into different subarticles.[116] Papua New Guinea is not a party to the ICCPR or the regional human rights conventions.

A few countries have constitutions that, on their faces, incorporate international human rights documents into national law, without mentioning each incorporated right separately.[117] It has not been possible in this study to determine how well legality in criminal law is enforced through this device. Some countries both define a right to non-retroactivity and have general provisions incorporating international human rights law.[118] Most of these latter countries are parts of the African human rights regime. The two that are not are Portugal and Slovenia. The former emerged from the Salazar dictatorship in the 1970s and the latter more recently emerged from the authoritarian Titoist Yugoslavia.

These different constitutional formulations of the principle of legality may have different significances. Some, but not all, of the reasons for choosing a formulation may have legal significance for the content and scope of

[114] Armenia Const. arts. 22, 42; Costa Rica Const. arts. 34, 39; Croatia Const. arts. 31, 89; East Timor Const. arts. 24, 31; Egypt Const. arts. 66, 187; Guatemala Const. arts. 15, 17; Macedonia Const. art. 14, 52; Nicaragua Const. arts. 34(11), 38; Niger Const. arts. 15, 16, 17 (three versions); Oman Const. arts. 21, 75; Paraguay Const. arts. 14, 17; Peru Const. arts. 2(24)(d), 103; Rwanda Const. arts. 18, 20; Serbia Const. arts. 34, 197; Slovenia Const. arts. 28, 155.

[115] Liberia Const. art. 21(a).

[116] See Botswana Const. art. 10(4, 8); Brazil Const. art. 5(XXXIX, XL); Iraq Const. art. 19(2, 10); Nigeria Const. art. 36 (8, 12); Papua New Guinea Const. art. 37(2, 7); Russia, art. 54(1, 2); Zambia Const. arts. 18(4, 8).

[117] Bosnia & Herzegovina Const. art. II(2); Cambodia Const. art. 31; Latvia Const. art. 89.

[118] Benin Const. arts. 7, 17; Burundi Const. arts. 19, 41; Cameroon Const. preamble; Portugal Const. arts. 8(4), 29; Rwanda Const. preamble & arts. 18, 20; Seychelles Const. arts. 19(4), 48; Slovenia Const. arts. 28, 153, 155.

the provision. For example, the original French provision in the Declaration of the Rights of Man and of the Citizen embodies the non-retroactivity of crimes and punishments and the requirement that crime definition be done by a legislature and published to the citizenry.[119] It embodies a revolutionary spirit of liberty[120] and a direct limitation on the power of government to make arbitrary laws. It also retains the power to define crime in the legislative arm of the state. It is thus the model for those states implementing the principle *nullum crimen, nulla poena sine praevia lege scripta.*

On the other hand, adoption of a provision modeled after that of another state or of an international treaty can be principally a matter of political convenience. If a right has already been formulated, then accepting the existing formulation can avoid political controversies that might arise with an independent consideration of how such a provision should be drafted. Moreover, where a provision has proved effective for a nation's purpose, even during a colonial period, it may be repeated in the nation's independence constitution. Again, this may avoid the political controversy that might come from a redrafting. An example of this is the Philippines' provision, "No *Ex Post Facto* Law . . . shall be enacted."[121] This echoes the similar provision of the Philippines most recent colonial ruler, the United States.[122] The Marshall Islands, in contrast, adopted the phrase "ex post facto" but reconstructed the provision to prohibit all "ex post facto punishment"[123] whatever the source of law.

Finally, adoption of a provision like this may be an indication that a state believes that adoption is required by international law. This law may be either the law of a human rights treaty system to which the state belongs or the customary international law of treaty rights. This would be especially true of new states (or states with new constitutions) that adopt provisions with wording like the UDHR or a human rights treaty system to which they belong or which they intend to join.

A few constitutions recognize sources of law other than statutes and common law case development. These other sources include sharia[124] and

[119] France Declaration of the Rights of Man and of the Citizen art. 8.

[120] *Id.* at arts. 5, 8.

[121] Philippines Const. art. III(22). See also Micronesia Const. art. IV(11).

[122] U.S. Const. art. I(9).

[123] Marshall Is. Const. art. II(8).

[124] Yemen Const. art. 46. Saudi Arabia has proclaimed the Quran and Sunna of the Prophet to be its constitution, and the Basic System of the Consultative Council, art. 38, recognizes crimes according to sharia.

custom (here meaning traditional local law rather than customary international law).[125] Constitutions including references to customary international law and general principles of law are discussed subsequently.[126]

As has been seen, the UDHR/ICCPR general formulation of non-retroactivity has been particularly influential. This is not surprising, given the adoption of the UDHR in the period just before the great wave of decolonization and the adoption of the ICCPR text by a unanimous UN vote during the height of the decolonization period. Many of the countries with this sort of language that have been decolonized or otherwise become independent since World War II in fact have a common law heritage.[127] Other such states adopting this kind of provision do not. Some are former members of the Soviet Union.[128] Some are states with majority Islamic populations.[129] Others may not fit neatly into an easy characterization of their legal history as civil, common, or Islamic law.[130]

A good example of why focus on the act in national constitutions is so important comes from Uruguay, which passed a statute criminalizing membership in banned political parties. After passage of the statute, certain parties were banned. Persons were prosecuted for membership in those parties after passage of the statute but before the decree banning them. The Human Rights Committee under the ICCPR Optional Protocol declared that this was impermissible retroactive criminalization of an act that was not criminal when done.[131] The prior passage of the statute here is irrelevant. The act of belonging to the specific organization was not criminal when done and therefore cannot be criminalized retroactively. This case also indicates the limitations of the principle of legality: by itself, legality does not prevent the possibility of banning political parties, no matter how legitimate.

[125] Vanuatu Const. art. 5(2)(f) ("written or custom law"). Cf. Papua New Guinea Const. arts. 37(21, 22), 172(2) (preserving village courts' authority to refer to custom or customary procedures or both).

[126] Chap. 5.c.iii.

[127] See, e.g., Bahamas Const. art. 20(4); Barbados Const. art. 18(4); Sri Lanka Const. art. 13; Tanzania Const. art. 13(6).

[128] See, e.g., Azerbaijan Const. art. 71(8); Georgia Const. art. 42(5); Moldova Const. art. 22.

[129] See, e.g., Turkey Const. art. 38; Sudan Interim Nat'l Const. art. 34(4).

[130] See, e.g., Ethiopia Const. art. 22; Malaysia Const. art. 7(1); Nepal Interim Const. art. 24(4). Cf. Cyprus Const. art. 12(1) (generally recognized as a state; UN, Council of Europe, and European Union member) and Turkish Republic of Northern Cyprus Const. art. 18(1) (recognized as a state only by Turkey; UN Security Council has called on states not to recognize it as a state).

[131] Weinberger Weisz v. Uruguay, Human Rights Committee Communication No. 28/78.

The common law countries that have not completely codified their criminal law and other countries allowing non-statutory sources of law to be taken into account make up a substantial number of states. The requirement of a previous statute or other regulatory text, *praevia lege scripta*, is not a worldwide legal standard, though it is adhered to by many and perhaps a majority of countries. Especially in the states without *praevia lege scripta*, focus on whether the act was criminal when done is one of the chief benefits of legality.[132]

5.c.iii. *Crimes According to International Law and General Principles of Law in the Constitutional Non-retroactivity Provisions and in National Judicial Practice*

For all the passion with which the Nuremberg/Tokyo general principles of law sentence[133] was argued in the ICCPR debates, it has not had a great deal of influence in the drafting of national constitutional provisions. Similarly, only a few national constitutions specifically refer to international law as a source of criminal law acceptable under the principle of legality.

All states with constitutional provisions allowing for conviction on the basis of a crime defined by general principles of law require the general principle of law which criminalizes the act to have existed before the act was done. There are four: Canada, Cape Verde, Poland, and Sri Lanka.[134] The courts of Sri Lanka have held (without a great deal of discussion) that this provision allows conviction where the general principle of law had formed before the act in question was committed. In this case, the general principle of law appears to have come from various international conventions against hijacking.[135] This is possibly the only example of a claim that general principles of law have described any substantive crime other than the international crimes of aggressive war (crimes against peace),

[132] Cf. Stefan Glaser, *La méthode d'interpretation en droit international pénal*, 9 Rivista Italiana di Diritto e Procedura Penale 757, 762–66 (1966).

[133] ICCPR art. 15(2).

[134] Canada Const. Act art. 11(g); Cape Verde Const. art. 30; Poland Const. art. 42(1); Sri Lanka Const. art. 13(6).

[135] Ekanayake v. The Attorney-General, C.A. 132/84 (Sri Lanka Ct. of App., 28 May 1986), app. dis., S.C. App. No. 68/86 (Sri Lanka S.Ct., 9 December 1987) [both available through official Sri Lanka government Web site, http://www.lawnet.lk], discussed without citation in Richard Clayton, Hugh Tomlinson, et al., The Law of Human Rights ¶ 11.512, at p. 769 (Oxford Univ. Press 2000).

crimes against humanity, genocide or war crimes,[136] and contempt of court.[137]

Only a few other states have even adopted the UDHR/ICCPR formulation that national or international law may provide a source of criminalization. Three are Croatia, Rwanda, and South Africa,[138] all of which have recent historical reasons to ensure that protections of international humanitarian law are fully applicable to their peoples. The Canadian Constitution Act also allows for conviction under "international law" as well as "general principles of law."[139] Provisions to similar effect as the two formulations, but with different specific wording, have been adopted by Albania, Bangladesh (for military personnel and prisoners of war only), Germany, Poland, and Seychelles.[140]

A few of these provisions are worth looking at separately. The Bangladesh Constitution states that statutes punishing these crimes when committed by members of the Bangladesh armed forces or prisoners of war of Bangladesh may not be declared unconstitutional.[141] The Bangladesh Constitution generally endorses the rules of non-retroactivity of crimes and punishments, and in fact appears to require a prior written criminal law (*praevia lege scripta*).[142] The savings provision essentially means that *praevia lege scripta* does not apply to the core international crimes. If an act was criminal under international law when done, the fact that the Bangladeshi statute bringing the prohibition into national law was subsequent to the act does not invalidate a prosecution for the act. This provision may also be meant to deal with the common belief (which this book argues is incorrect) that the principles of *nullum crimen* and *nulla poena* do not apply to the core international crimes. Essentially, this provision would work the same way that some of the post–World War II retroactive characterization cases worked.[143]

[136] The crimes against humanity (including genocide) described in the post-World War II cases have by now become crimes under customary international law and/or treaty law, and it is fair to say that the war crimes in those cases were crimes under customary international law even at the time of World War II.

[137] See Chap. 6.a.i, on contempt in the International Criminal Tribunal for the Former Yugoslavia.

[138] Croatia Const. art. 31; Rwanda Const. art. 20; South Africa Const. art. 35(3)(l).

[139] Canada Const. Act art. 11(g).

[140] Albania Const. art. 29(1); Bangladesh Const. art. 47(3); Germany Basic Law [*Grundgesetz*] art. 96(5) (precise application of this provision depends on the specific federal characteristics of the current German state); Poland Const. art. 42(1); Seychelles Const. art. 19(4).

[141] Bangladesh Const. arts. 47(3), 47A.

[142] *Id.* at art. 35(1).

[143] See Chap. 3.c.i.

The Seychelles Constitution has a provision that appears to exempt genocide and crimes against humanity from the rules of *nulla crimen* and *nulla poena*, but the constitution goes on to require compliance with international human rights. This includes human rights treaties.[144] This would appear to have a similar effect to the provisions discussed just previously – allowing application of customary international law definitions of those crimes existing at the time of the act, regardless of the state of Seychelles criminal law at that moment.

By statute, Lithuania appears to permit exceptions to the *praevia lege scripta* principle for some or all of the modern core international crimes (genocide, crimes against humanity, war crimes). That is, it requires pre-existing statutes for criminal law generally but appears to accept that these international crimes may be defined by customary international law rather than by statute at the time punishable acts were committed.[145]

Note that a failure to adopt such a provision does not always mean that a state will necessarily be opposed to prosecuting crimes under international law in its own courts. A state that does not require a previously promulgated statute for criminalization could, conceivably, accept international law as a source of criminal law in its courts, so long as the act involved was criminal under international law when done.[146] Even France, which generally requires prior written statutes, has allowed prosecution of a Nazi war criminal because his acts were criminal according to general principles of law when committed.[147] Slovenia has decided similarly.[148] The Hungarian Constitutional Court has determined that the international law version of non-retroactivity of crimes and punishments applies to crimes against humanity and war crimes, not the text-based national law of such crimes.[149] Germany has allowed prosecutions in its own courts for murder under German law where the acts involved were the war crime of murder committed in the former Yugoslavia.[150]

[144] Seychelles Const. arts. 19(4), 48.

[145] Lithuania Penal Code art. 3(3).

[146] See generally Ferdinandusse.

[147] Barbie Case No. 2, Bull. Crim. No. 34, 78 ILR 132 (France Cour de Cassation, 26 January 1984), quoted in Ferdinandusse at 226 n.1327.

[148] *Case U-1-248/96*, para. 14 (Slovenia Const. Ct., 30 September 1998), quoted in Ferdinandusse at 226 n.1330.

[149] Ferdinandusse at 213–14, 227, quoting from, discussing and analyzing *On War Crimes and Crimes Against Humanity*, Decision No. 53/1993 (Hungary Const. Ct., 13 October 1993).

[150] See cases discussed in Jean-Marie Henckaerts & Louise Doswald-Beck, 1 Customary International Humanitarian Law (Rules) R. 156 (discussion), p. 572 (Cambridge Univ. Press 2005) (study issued by the International Committee of the Red Cross)

The United States has a different way of accepting international criminal law into its courts. In its federal court system, it requires statutory crime creation. However, a statute may refer to the law of nations for its definition of crime, as it does for the law of piracy.[151]

Not every state that requires a previously promulgated statute for criminalization will give up that requirement simply because the crime is of an international nature. Some may not allow prosecution for international crimes that were not implemented by statute in domestic law, even if the crimes existed in customary international law that existed at the time of the act charged. For example, the Supreme Court of the Netherlands held that the Netherlands had no jurisdiction to try an alleged torturer who was accused of committing crimes outside the Netherlands in 1982, before the Netherlands passed its statute implementing the Torture Convention.[152] It held this even though it believed that the acts charged would have been crimes under Netherlands law at the time, had jurisdiction over them existed.[153] The Supreme Court noted a claim by a Netherlands parliamentary committee that the "general principles of law" provisions of the ICCPR and ECHR[154] are "exceptions" to the general rule of non-retroactivity in those treaties.[155] It did not endorse this view, and the result of the case does not depend upon it. It does, however, state that a specific treaty provision requiring retroactive expansion of jurisdiction (not contained in the Torture Convention) could have required the Netherlands to accept jurisdiction, even retroactively.[156] It suggests that a valid treaty might even require retroactive criminalization of acts,[157] though again the result of the case does not depend upon this statement.[158]

[hereinafter ICRC, CUSTOMARY IHL] (also citing similar post-World War II practice of Belgium, similar legislation of France, the Netherlands and Norway, and modern legislation of the Democratic Republic of the Congo); 2(2) *id.*, ¶¶ 521, 523, pp. 3984–85, 3986.

[151] See United States v. Smith, 18 U.S. (5 Wheat.) 153 (1820).

[152] [Wijngaarde v. Bouterse] Appeal in cassation in the interests of the law (Hoge Raad der Nederlanden [Supreme Court of the Netherlands], 18 September 2001), translated into English at 32 Netherlands Y.B.I.L. 282 (2001).

[153] Appeal in cassation in the interests of the law, ¶ 4.6, 32 Netherlands Y.B.I.L. at 291.

[154] ICCPR art. 15(2); ECHR art. 7(2).

[155] Appeal in cassation in the interests of the law, ¶ 4.3.2, 32 Netherlands Y.B.I.L. at 287–88.

[156] Appeal in cassation in the interests of the law, ¶¶ 4.4.1, 4.5, 32 Netherlands Y.B.I.L. at 289, 291.

[157] Cf. Appeal in cassation in the interests of the law, ¶ 4.5, 32 Netherlands Y.B.I.L. at 291.

[158] In the common law tradition, a statement of law by a court that has no effect on the decision would be called "dictum," whereas a statement of law on which the decision depends would be called "holding."

5.c.iv. *Modern Adoption or Readoption of Legality by Major States That Had Rejected It*

Almost all states that rejected the principle of legality at some point in the twentieth century have by now adopted non-retroactivity of crimes and punishments in their constitutions or other law. It is worth looking at some of these instances. They are important to the argument that non-retroactivity of crimes and punishments has become a matter of customary international human rights law in the decades since Nuremberg.

The Federal Republic of Germany (now including the former Democratic Republic of [East] Germany) reintegrated it into its law shortly after World War II and definitively repudiated the 1935 acceptance of analogy. This was done first under occupation, through the laws of the allied Control Council.[159] The occupation forces were also responsible for the government of the *Länder* (states), the subnational units of Germany. The state constitutions developed in the American zone had prohibitions of retroactive crime creation and, in some cases, prohibitions of retroactive punishments.[160] The state constitutions in the French zone prohibited both retroactive crimes and punishments.[161] Three constitutions from the Soviet zone had legality generally, with no mention of criminal law non-retroactivity.[162] Two other Soviet zone constitutions contained non-retroactivity of crimes and punishments (though one of them excepted war crimes and crimes against

[159] See Control Council Proclamation No. 3 (20 October 1945), in 1946 UNYBHR at 117–18. See also Control Council Law No. 11.

[160] Bavaria (Germany, American Zone) Const. art. 104(1) (1 December 1946), 1946 UNYBHR at 119-20 (*nullum crimen* only); Bremen (Germany, American Zone) Const. art. 7 (12 October 1947), 1947 UNYBHR at 126, 127 (*nullum crimen* only, but also contains *lex mitior*); Hesse (Germany, American Zone) Const. art. 22 (1 December 1946), 1946 UNYBHR at 124-25 (*nullum crimen, nulla poena*, and personality of punishment); Wuerttemberg-Baden (Germany, American Zone) Const. art. 4 (24 November 1946) (*nullum crimen, nulla poena*), 1946 UNYBHR at 128.

[161] Baden (Germany, French Zone) Const. art. 116 (18 May 1947), 1947 UNYBHR at 100, 105 (*nullum crimen, nulla poena*, and personality of punishment); Rhineland-Palatinate (Germany, French Zone) Const. art. 6 (18 May 1947) (*nullum crimen, nulla poena*) 1947 UNYBHR at 106, 107; Württemberg-Hohenzollern (Germany, French Zone) Const. art. 17(1) (18 May 1947) (*nullum crimen, nulla poena*), 1947 UNYBHR at 113, 114.

[162] Saxony (Germany, Soviet Zone) Const. art. 9 (28 February 1947), 1947 UNYBHR at 117–18 ("restriction or deprivation of personal freedom is admissible only in accordance with the law"); Saxony-Anhalt (Germany, Soviet Zone) Const. art. 9(1) (10 January 1947), 1948 UNYBHR at 80 (similar to Saxony); Thuringia (Germany, Soviet Zone) Const. art. 3(3) (20 December 1946), 1947 UNYBHR at 122 ("freedoms may be restricted only within the framework of general legislation").

humanity committed during the war).[163] By the end of 1947, no state constitutions had been written for the British zone.[164] Interestingly, the texts of the constitutions varied, even within a single zone, for constitutions written at about the same time.

In 1949, the Federal Republic of (West) Germany and the Democratic Republic of (East) Germany were created, though not yet as entities wholly independent of occupation. The Basic Law [*Grundgesetz*] of the Federal Republic of Germany (created out of the French, United States, and British zones) contained a prohibition of retroactive crime creation, in the Administration of Justice section rather than the Basic Rights section.[165] The Constitution of the Democratic Republic of Germany, created out of the Soviet zone, prohibited retroactive creation of crimes and punishments but had an apparent exception for war crimes and crimes against humanity committed before the capitulation of Germany in May 1945.[166] Presumably, the Soviet Union was willing to have such a provision in East Germany's Constitution when it did not have one in its own as part of the program to denazify the German legal system.

Today the text of the German constitutional provision only contains the rule of *nullum crimen*, though the title of the section refers to "prohibition of retroactive criminal laws" generally.[167] Retroactive creation or increase of penalty is prohibited by statute.[168] Germany now participates in the human rights treaty regimes of the ECHR and ICCPR, both of which implement *nulla poena*.[169]

Japan's post–World War II constitution also was written under the influence of occupation. It contains the rule of *nullum crimen*, and its criminal code contains *nulla poena*.[170]

The new Soviet Union rejected legality shortly after the Russian Revolution.[171] This position lasted through the end of Joseph Stalin's life. In 1958, the Soviet Union adopted new Fundamental Principles of Criminal

[163] Brandenburg (Germany, Soviet Zone) Const. art. 41(2) (6 February 1947), 1948 UNYBHR at 74, 75; Mecklenburg (Germany, Soviet Zone) Const. art. 66 (15 January 1946), 1948 UNYBHR at 76, 78 (allowing retroactive penal laws only for war crimes or crimes against humanity committed before 8 May 1945).

[164] Germany, Note on the State Constitutions, 1947 UNYBHR at 100.

[165] Federal Republic of Germany Basic Law art. 103(2) (23 May 1949), 1949 UNYBHR at 79, 82.

[166] Dem. Rep. of Germany Const. art. 135 (30 May 1949, effective 7 October 1949), 1949 UNYBHR at 73, 78.

[167] Federal Republic of Germany Basic Law art. 103(2); see also § 1, Strafgesetzbuch [StGB] [Germany Crim. Code].

[168] Germany § 2, StGB.

[169] ECHR art. 7(1); ICCPR art. 15(1).

[170] Kenpō, [Japan Const.] art. 39; Japan Crim. Code art. 6.

[171] See Chap. 2.c.ii.C.

Legislation of the USSR and the Union Republics, which embodied a number of aspects of the principle of legality.[172] These were implemented in new criminal codes for the Soviet republics. A crime was to be "a socially dangerous act provided for by law"; one could be guilty of a crime only by doing such an act "intentionally or negligently," and criminal punishment may be "applied only by judgment of a court."[173] Non-retroactivity of crimes and punishments was set out clearly but in language somewhat different from the treaty language discussed in the prior chapter:

> Article 6. *Operation of a criminal law in time.* The criminality and punishability of an act shall be determined by the law prevailing at the time of commission of that act.
>
> A law eliminating the punishability of an act or reducing the punishment for it shall have retroactive force, that is, it shall extend also to acts committed before its promulgation.
>
> A law establishing the punishability of an act or increasing the punishment for it shall not have retroactive force.[174]

However, legality was not fully put in place for minor offenses treated as non-criminal by nonprofessional Comrades' Courts.[175] Legality in criminal law was also undermined by the existence of the so-called noncrime of parasitism, "introduced [by edict] in the various republics between 1957 and 1961."[176] Parasitism could be punished by internal exile.[177] Parasitism was made a crime by enactments between 1970 and 1975, and the punishment limited to deprivation of freedom for one year, but the legal definition of the crime remained vague.[178]

[172] *Osnovy ugolovnogozakonodatel'stva Soiuza SSR I soiuznykh respublik* (Fundamental Principles of Criminal Legislation of the USSR and the Union Republics), arts. 3, 6 & 7, 25 December 1958, *Vedomosti SSSR* (1959), no. 1, item 6 [hereinafter 1958 USSR Fundamental Principles].

[173] 1960 RSFSR Crim. Code art. 3 ("*Basis of criminal responsibility*") (27 October 1960), implementing (and identical to) 1958 USSR Fundamental Principles art. 3, trans. in HAROLD J. BERMAN, SOVIET CRIMINAL LAW AND PROCEDURE: THE RSFSR CODES 145 (Harvard Univ. Press 1966) (translations from this book are by Berman and James W. Spindler); *id.* at 47 (for identity of texts). To similar effect is article 7 ("*The concept of crime*") of the same documents. *Id.* at 47, 147.

[174] 1960 RSFSR Crim. Code art. 6, implementing (and identical to) 1958 USSR Fundamental Principles art. 6, trans. in Berman at 146-47; *id.* at 47 (for identity of provisions).

[175] See Berman at 8, 47, discussing 1961 RSFSR Statute on Comrades' Courts, *Vedomosti RSFSR* (1961), no. 4, item 83.

[176] ARYEH L. UNGER, CONSTITUTIONAL DEVELOPMENT IN THE USSR 131 (Pica Press 1981) [hereinafter Unger].

[177] Unger at 131.

[178] *Id.*

After the dissolution of the Soviet Union, all of the states formed from it accepted the non-retroactivity of crimes and punishments. Most of them (including Russia) placed this rule in their constitutions.[179] Latvia placed in its constitution the obligation to "protect fundamental human rights in accordance with . . . international agreements binding upon Latvia"[180]; it is a party to the ICCPR and the ECHR. Two of the former Soviet states placed non-retroactivity of crimes and punishments in their criminal codes.[181]

Not all of the European Communist countries joined the Soviet Union in rejecting legality. For example, *nullum crimen* was part of the Constitution of Hungary from 1949 onward,[182] and as noted previously both *nullum crimen* and *nulla poena* were part of the East German Constitution from 1949.[183] Today, non-retroactivity of crimes and punishment has been accepted by Albania,[184] Bosnia and Herzegovina,[185] Bulgaria,[186] Croatia,[187] Czech Republic,[188] Macedonia,[189] Montenegro,[190] Poland,[191] Romania,[192] Serbia,[193] Slovakia,[194] and Slovenia.[195]

In 1960, revolutionary Cuba expressed doubts about a strict rule against non-retroactivity of crimes and punishments during the ICCPR negotiations.[196] However, it is now part of the nation's constitution.[197]

Imperial China, as noted previously, had recognized the principle of analogy in penal law in the Qing Code,[198] even though it did not really

[179] Armenia Const. art. 22; Azerbaijan Const. art. 71(VIII); Belarus Const. art. 104; Estonia Const. art. 23; Georgia Const. art. 42(5); Kazakhstan Const. art. 77(3, 5, 10); Kyrgyzstan Const. art. 85(10); Moldova Const. art. 22; Russia Const. art. 54 (1993); Tajikistan Const. art. 20; Turkmenistan Const. art. 43; Ukraine Const. art. 58.

[180] Latvia Const. art. 89.

[181] Lithuania Penal Code art. 3; Uzbekistan Crim. Code art. 13.

[182] Hungary Const. (1949) art. 57(4). For *nulla poena*, see Hungary Crim. Code §2.

[183] Dem. Rep. of Germany Const. art. 135 (1949).

[184] Albania Const. art. 29.

[185] Bosnia & Herzegovina Const. art. II(2) (by incorporating ECHR provisions).

[186] Bulgaria Const. art. 5(3); Bulgaria Penal Code art. 2.

[187] Croatia Const. art. 31.

[188] Czech Rep. Const. art. 3 (incorporating Czechoslovak Charter of Fundamental Rights and Freedoms).

[189] Macedonia Const. arts. 14, 52.

[190] Montenegro Const. art. 34.

[191] Poland Const. art. 42(1).

[192] Romania Const. art. 15(2).

[193] Serbia Const. art. 197.

[194] Slovakia Const. art. 50(6).

[195] Slovenia Const. art. 28.

[196] UN Doc. A/C.3/SR.1008, ¶ 9, discussed in Chap. 4.b.ii.C.

[197] Cuba Const. arts. 59, 61.

[198] See Chap. 2.a.iii, citing Qing Code art. 44.

distinguish between criminal and non-criminal law in the same way as Western countries. Until 1979, the People's Republic of China effectively had no overall criminal code, and from 1979 until 1997, the criminal code allowed for crime creation by analogy, though this is said to have been used sparingly.[199]

The People's Republic of China now has a statutory provision on non-retroactivity of crimes and punishments in its criminal law:

> If an act committed after the founding of the People's Republic of China and before the entry into force of this Law was not deemed a crime under the laws at the time, those laws shall apply. If the act was deemed a crime under the laws in force at the time and is subject to prosecution under the provisions of Section 8, Chapter IV of the General Provisions of this Law, criminal responsibility shall be investigated in accordance with those laws. However, if according to this Law the act is not deemed a crime or is subject to a lighter punishment, this Law shall apply.
>
> Before the entry into force of this Law, any judgment that has been made and has become effective according to the laws at the time shall remain valid.[200]

This provision can possibly be read as applying non-retroactivity only to the change from earlier law to this particular new law rather than being a general rule of non-retroactivity.[201] However, it is not the only legality provision in Chinese law. The criminal law also contains a general legality provision without specific reference to non-retroactivity. A person can be convicted and punished only for acts "explicitly defined as criminal acts in law."[202] The legislation law provides for non-retroactivity more generally,

[199] See Gu Minkang, *Criminal Law*, in CHINESE LAW 591, 594–95 & n.10 (Wang Guiguo & John Mo, eds., Kluwer Law Int'l 1999) (indicating that no more than ninety-two prosecutions were carried out under this law). *Id.* at 594 n.9, quotes Criminal Law of the People's Republic of China 1979 art. 79: "Crimes that are not expressly defined in the Specific Provisions of this Law may be determined and punished in accordance with whichever Article in the Specific Provisions of this Law that covers the most closely analogous crime, but the judgment shall be submitted to the Supreme People's Court for approval." The decision to allow for analogy and to reject a strict *nullum crimen* provision was a subject of extended debate from 1957 through 1979. THE CRIMINAL CODE OF THE PEOPLE'S REPUBLIC OF CHINA 13–15, 46 (Chin Kim trans., Fred B. Rothman & Co. 1982) (providing a slightly different translation of art. 79).

[200] Criminal Law of the People's Republic of China art. 12 (as revised at the Fifth Session of the Eighth National People's Congress on 14 March 1997), translated at U.S. gov't website http://www.cecc.gov/pages/newLaws/criminalLawENG.php.

[201] This was pointed out to me by my research assistant Samuel P. Trenchi.

[202] Criminal Law of the People's Republic of China art. 3, translated at U.S. gov't Web site http://www.cecc.gov/pages/newLaws/criminalLawENG.php.

though it provides for exceptions that are not wholly clear: "National law, administrative regulations, local decrees, autonomous decrees and special decrees, and administrative or local rules do not have retroactive force, except where a special provision is made in order to better protect the rights and interests of citizens, legal persons and other organizations."[203]

The People's Republic of China has also joined the regime of the CRC, the Geneva Conventions and Additional Protocols I and II,[204] and has signed, but not yet ratified, the ICCPR.

These acts demonstrate that the People's Republic of China has joined the ranks of the overwhelming majority of countries that accept non-retroactivity of crimes and punishments as part of its domestic legal order. It has also accepted non-retroactivity of crimes and punishments as part of the international legal order of human rights. However, events must be watched carefully to ensure that this remains the reality in the future.

The immediate successor of the Qing dynasty was the Republic of China, now limited to governing Taiwan. Like the People's Republic, the Republic of China has no legality provision in its constitution. It, too, signed the ICCPR and, unlike the People's Republic, signed the First Optional Protocol. Before it ratified, however, the UN seat for China was given to the representative of the People's Republic of China, and no further action was taken.

Asian Communist countries have accepted non-retroactivity of crimes and punishments, usually but not only through the ICCPR. Cambodia is a party to the ICCPR, and its constitution states that it shall respect human rights as stipulated in the UDHR and human rights covenants.[205] Laos and Vietnam are parties to the ICCPR. Myanmar (Burma), with a very repressive government, has a constitutional provision, "No penal law shall have retrospective effect,"[206] but has not adopted the ICCPR. In north Asia, North Korea has accepted the ICCPR, as has former Communist state Mongolia.

As Haider Ala Hamoudi has pointed out, in classical Islamic law "for the wide variety of 'discretionary' crimes known as the *ta'azir*, there was no concept of *nulla poena/nullum crimen*."[207] Yet, by now, nearly all Islamic nations have accepted *nulla poena/nullum crimen*, "even those purported

[203] Legislation Law of the People's Republic of China art. 84.

[204] 2(2) ICRC, Customary IHL, Status of Ratifications Chart 4153ff.

[205] Cambodia Const. art. 31.

[206] Myanmar Const. art. 23.

[207] Haidar Ala Hamoudi, *The Muezzin's Call and the Dow Jones Bell: On the Necessity of Realism in the Study of Islamic Law*, 56:2 Am. J. Comp. L. (forthcoming) (sec. II.A) [hereinafter Hamoudi].

to be governed by *shari'a*."[208] Among majority-Islamic countries, the principle of non-retroactivity of crimes and punishments only recently entered the Constitution of Indonesia.[209] In 2006, Indonesia became a party to the ICCPR. Like many of the other countries discussed here, Indonesia has recently emerged from a period of authoritarian rule, the Suharto regime.

Following a coup in 2006, Thailand suspended its constitution, which had provided for non-retroactivity of crimes and punishments.[210] It has now approved a new constitution restoring this protection.[211]

5.c.v. *Other Legality Issues in the Constitutional Texts*

5.c.v.A. *Lex mitior*, and the Issue of Mixing *Nullum crimen*, *Nulla poena*, and *Lex mitior*

The mercy doctrine, *lex mitior*, appears in fewer constitutions than does non-retroactivity of crimes and punishments. Nonetheless, it appears in a substantial number of constitutions and appears in the statutory regime of several other countries.

Some version of the doctrine appears in almost fifty constitutions: Albania, Angola, Armenia, Azerbaijan, Belarus, Bolivia, Brazil, Burundi, Cambodia, Canada, Cape Verde, Chile, Colombia, Croatia, Cuba, Czech Republic, Democratic Republic of the Congo, Dominican Republic, East Timor, Ecuador, Ethiopia, Georgia, Guatemala, Guinea-Bissau, Haiti, Honduras, Iraq, Kazakhstan, Kyrgyzstan, Latvia, Macedonia, Montenegro, Mozambique, Nicaragua, Panama, Paraguay, Peru, Portugal, Romania, Russia, São Tomé and Príncipe, Serbia, Slovakia, Slovenia, South Africa, Spain, Tajikistan, and Ukraine.[212] This amounts to more than one-quarter of UN

[208] Hamoudi, sec. II.A; accord, Chaps. 4.g.i, 5.c (introductory section) and Appendices A & C.

[209] Compare Const. of Indonesia as existing through 1998 in CCW (print edition) with Const. of Indonesia art. 28I, at CCW online at www.oceanalaw.com. Many other basic human rights have also recently been added to the Indonesian Constitution, joining freedom of assembly, association, speech, press, and worship, which were in the constitutional text since 1945. Const. of Indonesia (1945)arts. 28, 29.

[210] Thailand Interim Const. art. 18 (2006), (after suspension of Thailand Const. art. 32 (1997)).

[211] Thailand Const. art. 39 (2007) (English translation at http://www.parliament.go.th/parcy/sapa_db/sapa25-upload/25-20070217151204_2007.pdf), approved in referendum 19 August 2007, formally approved by king of Thailand 24 August 2007, http://jurist.law.pitt.edu/paperchase/2007/08/new-thailand-constitution-formally.php (academic Web site).

[212] Albania Const. art. 29(3); Angola Const. Law, art. 36(4); Armenia Const. art. 22; Azerbaijan Const. art. 71(VIII); Belarus Const. art. 104; Bolivia Const. art. 16(II); Brazil Const. art.

member states. This is substantial but significantly below the support for the core doctrines of *nullum crimen* and *nulla poena*.

It appears by statute in at least nineteen more: Algeria, Austria, Belgium, Bulgaria, People's Republic of China, Côte d'Ivoire, Denmark, Germany, Hungary, Iceland, Israel, Japan, Lebanon, Lithuania, Luxembourg, Netherlands, New Zealand, Papua New Guinea, Switzerland, Uruguay, and Uzbekistan.[213] This brings the total applying the doctrine through positively stated internal law to more than one-third of UN members. Because of the way in which this research was conducted, there may be some statutes that have been missed. However, this should be a representative sample of those countries adopting a rule of *lex mitior* by statute.

The bulk of these states are from the civil law tradition in one way or another, and several of them are current or former Communist states. The only common law states are Canada and New Zealand. Two others with common law connections are Israel and South Africa (a mixed Anglo-Dutch legal heritage). Although a number of these states have majority Islamic populations, they tend to have more secular rather than strictly Islamic legal orders. The People's Republic of China has its own legal tradition as well as its tie to Socialist law.

5(40); Burundi Const. art. 19 (incorporating International Covenants on Human Rights into constitution); Cambodia Const. art. 31 (incorporating covenants and conventions on human rights; Cambodia has ratified the ICCPR); Canada Const. Act art. 11(i); Cape Verde Const. art. 30(2); Chile Const. art. 19(3); Colombia Const. art. 29; Democratic Rep. of the Congo Const. art. 17; Croatia Const. art. 31; Cuba Const. art. 61; Czech Rep. Charter of Fundamental Rights and Freedoms [former Czechoslovakia] art. 40(6); Dominican Rep. Const. art. 47; East Timor Const. art. 31(5); Ecuador Const. art. 24(2); Ethiopia Const. art. 22(2); Georgia Const. art. 42(5); Guatemala Const. art. 15; Guinea-Bissau Const. art. 33(2); Haiti Const. art. 51; Honduras Const. art. 96; Iraq Const. art. 19(10); Kazakhstan Const. art. 77(3,5); Kyrgyzstan Const. art. 85(10); Latvia Const. art. 89 (incorporating provisions of human rights agreements; ICCPR has been adopted); Macedonia Const. art. 52; Montenegro Const. art. 34; Mozambique Const. art. 99(2); Nicaragua Const. art. 38; Panama Const. art. 46; Paraguay Const. art. 14; Peru Const. art. 103; Portugal Const. art. 19(6)(4); Romania Const. art. 15(2); Russia Const. art. 54(1, 2); São Tomé and Príncipe Const. art. 36(2); Serbia Const. art. 197; Slovakia Const. art. 50(6); Slovenia Const. art. 28; South Africa Const. art. 35(3)(n); Spain Const. art. 9(3); Tajikistan Const. art. 20; Ukraine Const. art. 58.

[213] Algeria Penal Code art. 2; Austria § 1, StGB; Belgium Crim. Code art. 2; Bulgaria Penal Code art. 2; Crim. Law of the People's Rep. of China art. 12; Côte d'Ivoire Penal Code arts. 19-20; Denmark Crim. Code §§ 3-4; Germany §§ 2(3, 4), StGB; Hungary Crim. Code § 2; Iceland Gen. Penal Code art. 2; Israel Penal Law §§ 4-6; Japan Crim. Code art. 6; Lebanon Code Pénal arts. 2, 3, 8; Lithuania Penal Code art. 3; Luxembourg Penal Code art. 2; Netherlands Penal Code art. 1(2); New Zealand Bill of Rights Act art. 25(g); Papua New Guinea Criminal Code Act art. 11(2); Switzerland Code Pénal art. 2(2); Uruguay Código Penal art. 15; Uzbekistan Crim. Code art. 13.

Statutes of Belgium, Luxembourg, New Zealand, and Papua New Guinea limit the effect of reductions in legal punishment to those occurring between the act and the judgment.[214] The People's Republic of China's statute appears to limits the effect of *lex mitior* to changes between the old law and the 1997 Criminal Law of the People's Republic and limits its effects to changes in the law between crime commission and sentencing.[215] Switzerland's wording appears to be similar.[216] Lebanon limits reductions in legal punishments to those occurring between the act and the judgment,[217] except where the entire act is decriminalized, in which case "the criminal condemnations cease to have effect."[218]

A few of these provisions deal with the issue of temporary crimes, which was discussed in the ICCPR negotiations.[219] They allow for continued punishment even after the expiration of the law making the acts criminal, in cases where the acts were committed while they were criminal.[220]

A number of constitutions combine the non-retroactivity of criminal law (*nullum crimen sine lege* and *nulla poena sine lege*) with the doctrine that an offender is entitled to a subsequent reduction in penalties or removal of criminal liabilities (*lex mitior*). To legal academics, these provisions seem to confuse legality in criminal law with the doctrine of mercy. In fact, some argued that *lex mitior* should not be part of the ICCPR.[221] However, these provisions often make sense in ordinary language terms. The Brazilian Constitution is one of several that say, "the criminal law shall not be retroactive, except to benefit the defendant."[222] Cuba's provision, though worded differently, is similar.[223] The Constitution of the Democratic Republic of the Congo is to similar effect, except that the mercy rule is limited to the time of sentencing.[224] Some constitutions keep non-retroactivity of crime creation (*nullum crimen*) separate but combine *nulla poena* and *lex mitior*. Canada, for example, has a *nullum crimen* provision paralleling

[214] Belgium Crim. Code art. 2; Luxembourg Penal Code art. 2; New Zealand Bill of Rights Act art. 25(g) (sentencing); Papua New Guinea Crim. Code Act art. 11(2) (conviction).

[215] Crim. Law of the People's Rep. of China art. 12.

[216] Switzerland Penal Code art. 2(2).

[217] Lebanon Code Pénal arts. 3, 8.

[218] Quote from Lebanon Code Pénal art. 2 (translation from French by the current author).

[219] See Chap. 4.b.ii.

[220] Germany § 2(4) StGB; Israel Penal Law art. 6; Lebanon Code Pénal art. 2; cf. Denmark Crim. Code § 3(1).

[221] See Chap. 4.a.ii & 4.b.ii.

[222] Brazil Const art. 5(XL). See also Guatemala Const. art. 15.

[223] Cuba Const. art. 61.

[224] Dem. Rep. of the Congo Const. art. 17.

the ICCPR. It then states that a person charged with crime has the right "if found guilty of [an] offence and if the punishment for the offence has varied between the time of the commission and the time of sentencing, to the benefit of the lesser punishment."[225] Chile has a similar constitutional provision,[226] and the Netherlands has a similar provision in its penal code.[227]

5.c.v.B. Legality and Freedom in the Modern Constitutions

The view that legality protects freedom – that everything not forbidden by law is permitted – has continued since 1946.[228] It persists in Argentina, Bolivia, Brazil, Costa Rica, Dominican Republic, France, Guatemala, Nicaragua, Paraguay, Peru, and Uruguay.[229] However, this type of provision has not expanded its reach much since then. Only a few states, such as Afghanistan,[230] Burkina Faso,[231] Czech Republic,[232] and El Salvador[233] have added provisions that were not found in the United Nations' 1946-47 review of constitutions.

Plain, bare statements of legal and moral theory in constitutional documents do not always represent practice in the states. A good number of the states that had these provisions in 1946 continue to have them today. However, during this time, many of them have suffered through substantial periods of authoritarian or otherwise antilibertarian government, often of more than one type.

5.c.v.C. *Lex certa* in the Constitutions

Few constitutions specifically address the requirement of certainty in criminal law (*lex certa*). Chile, for example, states, "No law may establish penalties without the conduct that it punishes being expressly described therein."[234]

225 Canada Const. Act art. 11(i).
226 Chile Const. art. 19(3).
227 Netherlands Penal Code art. 1(2).
228 See Chap. 5.b, citing Draft Outline of an International Bill of Rights art. 25, E/CN.4/21, Annex A, p. 17, reprinted from E/CN.4/AC.1/3 and the several national constitutions that inspired it.
229 Argentina Const. art. 19, Bolivia Const. art. 32; Brazil Const. art. 5(II); Costa Rica Const. art. 28; Dominican Rep. Const. art. 8(5); France Declaration of the Rights of Man and of the Citizen art. 5; Guatemala Const. art. 5; Nicaragua Const. art. 32; Paraguay Const. art. 9; Peru Const. art. 2(24)(a); Uruguay Const. art. 10.
230 Afghanistan Const. art. 24 [alternately numbered ch. 2, art. 3].
231 Burkina Faso Const. art. 5.
232 Czech Republic Charter of Fundamental Rights and Basic Freedoms art. 2(3).
233 El Salvador Const. art. 8.
234 Chile Const. art. 19(3). See also Ghana Const. art. 19(11); Greece Const. art. 7(1).

On the other hand, the protection against retroactivity in criminal law in the UDHR and the ICCPR implies an important provision requiring certainty. The requirement that an act have been an offense at the time it was committed implies that it must have been knowable or foreseeable as an offense at that time. Whether the crime was defined by statute or common or customary law, the application of the crime to the act cannot have been unpredictable.[235] This approach is generally implicit in all constitutions that focus on the act, whether or not they follow the specific language of the ICCPR or UDHR.

The entire principle of legality in criminal law contains within itself this much requirement of certainty in definitions of crime. That is, non-retroactivity and legality itself make little sense if an utterly vague law can be read expansively in an unpredictable manner to condemn new acts. The author has found no evidence that any state reads its constitutional provisions on non-retroactivity to permit this.

Eleanor Roosevelt for the United States raised the possibility, in the negotiations for the ICCPR, that the non-retroactivity provision should apply only to the later passage of statutes and not to any judicial interpretations of statutes.[236] Her theory would have had the unintended consequence of allowing both utter vagueness in crime definition and utter unpredictability in judicial interpretation of statutes. In this instance, her views were strongly opposed and were rejected.[237]

More recently, the ICC Statute did not explicitly address *lex certa*, but provided a set of rules that should enforce the requirement. The statutes require that definitions of crimes be "strictly construed," and "[i]n case of ambiguity" should be interpreted in favor of the person under investigation, charge, or conviction.[238] This essentially requires that any criminal liability to be imposed under the statute have been foreseeable to the actor at the time of the act.

5.c.v.D. Narrow Interpretation and Analogy in the Constitutions

As with *lex certa*, the principle of narrow interpretation has specifically been incorporated in only a few constitutions. For example, the Ecuador

[235] See, e.g., Shum Kwok Sher v. HKSAR, [2002] HKCEA 17 (Hong Kong), noted in RICHARD CLAYTON & HUGH TOMLINSON, THE LAW OF HUMAN RIGHTS, 2D ANNUAL SUPP. ¶ 11.475A, p. 185 (Oxford Univ. Press 2003) [hereinafter Clayton & Tomlinson Supp.].

[236] UN Doc. E.CN.4/SR.112, p. 4 (7 June 1949, recording session of 3 June 1949); Weissbrodt at 79; discussed in Chap. 4.b.ii.A.

[237] E.CN.4/SR.112, p. 8 (France); *id.* pp. 4–5 (Guatemala); *id.* p. 7 (United Kingdom); *id.* p. 9 (vote); Weissbrodt at 79; discussed in Chap. 4.b.ii.A.

[238] ICC Statute art. 22(2).

Constitution states, "In case of a conflict between two laws that contain punishments, the less rigorous shall be applied, even if its promulgation was after the infraction; and[,] in case of doubt, the norm that contains punishments shall be applied in the manner most favorable to the accused."[239]

Additionally, only a few constitutions mention analogy. Only the Kazakh Constitution explicitly prohibits it.[240] Iceland[241] and Mexico[242] severely limit its use to ways that prohibit retroactive crime creation.

The ICC Statute embodies this principle, essentially in the same provision implying *lex certa*. In addition to requiring strict construction and resolution of ambiguities in favor of the defense, the ICC Statute forbids the use of analogy to create crime.[243] It may well be that some states will adopt similar provisions in the future.

5.c.v.E. Retroactive Expansion of National Jurisdiction: Domestic Incorporation of Crimes under the Law of Another State or Crimes under International Law – A Current Version of Retroactive Re-characterization?

Occasionally, national legislation has expanded the criminal jurisdiction of national courts to include offenses that have already been committed, but were not within the jurisdiction of the courts at the time committed. For example, after the Bali, Indonesia, bombings that killed many Australians, Australia passed an act giving its courts jurisdiction over certain offenses committed in foreign countries against Australians[244] (an exercise of so-called passive personality jurisdiction). The official explanatory memorandum of the law pointed out that the "'conduct which is being criminalized – causing death or serious bodily injury – is conduct which is universally known to be conduct which is criminal in nature.'"[245] It warned against expanding jurisdiction to criminalize acts not criminal in all other systems.[246] The retrospective expansion of jurisdiction here can be seen as

[239] Ecuador Const. art. 24(2). See also Equatorial Guinea Const. art.13(s).
[240] Kazakhstan Const. art. 77(3, 10).
[241] Iceland Const. art. 69.
[242] Mexico Const. art. 14.
[243] ICC Statute art. 22(2).
[244] Criminal Code Amendment (Offenses Against Australians) Act 2002 (Cth).
[245] Sampford, RETROSPECTIVITY at 134, quoting from Criminal Code Amendment (Offenses Against Australians) Bill 2002, Explanatory Memorandum, p. 3.
[246] Sampford, RETROSPECTIVITY at 134, quoting from Criminal Code Amendment (Offenses Against Australians) Bill 2002, Explanatory Memorandum, p. 3.

similar to the reasoning of the *Einsatzgruppen Case*,[247] in which the court indicated that national crime was being re-characterized as also a crime against humanity. In Australia, certain crimes under Indonesian law were simply being re-characterized as crimes under Australian law if their victims were Australian.

Some nations have allowed expansions of jurisdiction covering genocide, crimes against humanity, and war crimes in international law to be applied retrospectively in their national courts, so long as the crimes existed in international law at the time of the acts.[248] This is accepted in the French and Norwegian World War II cases.[249] Slovenia has also allowed such expansion of jurisdiction.[250] As mentioned previously, some constitutions allow for subsequent substantive national statutes to be applied in the case of some or all international crimes where the acts involved were criminal under international law when committed.[251] That a power to bring international crimes into domestic law is stated in a constitution does not necessarily mean that it has ever been exercised retrospectively.

Some nations do not permit this sort of retroactive expansion of their own jurisdiction, even for torture, equating it with impermissible retroactive

[247] United States v. Ohlendorff (Einsatzgruppen Case), 4 Trials of War Criminals before the Nuremberg Military Tribunals under Control Council Law No. 10, 411, 485–87, 497 (U.S. Military Tribunal, 10 April 1948).

[248] Regina v. Finta, 104 I.L.R. 285 (Canada Sup. Ct. 24 March 1994) (requires that act must have been crime both under international law and Canadian law, but jurisdiction may have expanded retrospectively to include extraterritorial acts); *On War Crimes and Crimes against Humanity*, Decision No. 53/1993 (Hungary, Const. Ct., 13 October 1993), discussed in Ferdinandusse at 213-14, 227, 231; War Crimes Act (U.K., 1991); but cf. Polyukovich v. Commonwealth, 172 CLR 501 (Australia High Ct., 14 August 1991) (did not appear to require inquiry into status of crimes under international law, as Australia did not have constitutional protection against retroactive criminal statutes). See generally Theodore Meron, War Crimes Law Comes of Age 246 (Oxford Univ. Press 1998), quoting from United Nations War Crimes Commission, History of the United Nations War Crimes Commission and the Development of the Laws of War 232 (1948).

[249] See *Trial of Wagner*, 3 UNWCC, Law Reports of Trials of War Criminals, Case No. 13, p. 23, 43, 45 (French Permanent Military Court, Strasbourg, 3 May 1946, aff'd, Cour de Cassation, 24 July 1946); *id.* at 53–54 (commentary asserting that this was common Continental practice with respect to war crimes); *Trial of Klinge*, 3 UNWCC, Law Reports, Case No. 11, p. 1, 2, 3, 6, 10, 11 (Supreme Court of Norway 27, February 1946) (but there were dissents on this issue); see also Annex 1, *id.* at 81 (discussing Norwegian statutes). For a more recent example from France, see Barbie Case No. 2, Bull. Crim. No. 34, 78 ILR 132 (France Cour de Cassation, 26 January 1984), quoted in Ferdinandusse at 226 n.1327.

[250] Case U-1-248/96 ¶ 14 (Slovenia Const. Ct., 30 September 1998), quoted in Ferdinandusse at 226 n.1330.

[251] See Chap. 5.c.iii, discussing about ten constitutions of countries such as Canada, Croatia, Bangladesh, Germany, and Rwanda.

crime creation. The Netherlands[252] and the United Kingdom[253] appear to be in this group.

Even where retroactive expansion of jurisdiction to adjudicate is permissible, there are important issues of legality unconnected to retroactivity that continue to have vitality. Criminal courts must be independent, impartial, and created by law. This is recognized in treaty law.[254] Nothing in the practice of states creating new courts or expanding jurisdiction retrospectively permits these aspects of legality to be undermined, nor do any of the cases permit such undermining. Recently, the U.S. Supreme Court has held that the military commissions created to try Taliban and al-Qaeda members at Guantánamo Bay had not been created by law,[255] indicating that this doctrine retains importance.

5.c.vi. *Exceptions and Possible Exceptions to Non-retroactivity of Crimes and Punishments*

No UN state has a constitutional provision specifically rejecting non-retroactivity of criminal law in general. Some states have narrow limitations on the non-retroactivity of crimes and punishments in their constitutions. In some cases, apparent exceptions to the rule turn out not to be so.

Some of these provisions deal with contempt of court.[256] Botswana, Kenya, and Zambia, for example, prohibit creating crimes and punishments except by "written law" and have an exception in nearly identical language: "Provided that nothing in this subsection shall prevent a court of record from punishing any person for contempt of itself notwithstanding that the act or omission constituting the contempt is not defined in a written law and

[252] See [Wijngaarde v. Bouterse] Appeal in cassation in the interests of the law (Hoge Raad der Nederlanden [Supreme Court of the Netherlands], 18 September 2001), translated into English at 32 Netherlands Y.B.I.L. 282 (2001) (refusing to apply Netherlands Act [1988] Implementing the Torture Convention to murders committed in Suriname in 1982, allegedly at the direction of Suriname leader Bouterse, on grounds of legality and on other grounds.

[253] See Regina v. Bartle (Pinochet), U.K. House of Lords, 24 March 1999, 38 I.L.M 581 (1999).

[254] ICCPR art. 14(1); ECHR art. 6(1); ACHR art. 8(1); ACHPR art. 7(1) (not including "created by law" language); Revised ArCHR art. 13.

[255] Hamdan v. Rumsfeld, 548 U.S. 557 (2006).

[256] Crim. Code art. 4, citing Denmark, Crim. Code arts. 56–61 & 62–70; § 2(6) StGB (Germany), Lithuania, Penal Code art. 3(4).

the penalty therefor is not so prescribed."[257] Papua New Guinea has a similar provision.[258] This essentially allows contempt to be a common law offense as to both crime and punishment. It is an exception to the requirement of *praevia lege scripta.*

Zambia and Zimbabwe allow the disciplinary law of disciplined forces (i.e., military forces) of their nations to apply regardless of many constitutional rights, including the provisions on legality.[259] Zimbabwe also excepts from protection of its own constitution the disciplined forces of other nations or of international organizations present in Zimbabwe by permission.[260] These, however, ought to be protected by human rights guarantees from their own jurisdictions. It also exempts members of disciplined forces of a country at war or in hostilities with Zimbabwe from these protections.[261] As to this last group, however, the rules of non-retroactivity would apply to crimes through the Third Geneva Convention and its First Additional Protocol.[262]

Statutory exceptions related to retroactive non-punishment are discussed subsequently.[263] These exist at least in Canada, Denmark, Germany, Lithuania, and the United States.

Venezuela permits retroactive change of "a minor penalty."[264] Israel does not consider "updating the amount of a fine" to be "setting a more severe penalty."[265]

The Papua New Guinea Constitution appears to allow waiver of the non-retroactivity of crimes and punishments for village courts applying traditional law and/or procedure. However, implementing statutes and regulations define crimes and punishments within the jurisdiction of these courts in a way that complies with the rule of non-retroactivity.[266]

[257] Botswana Const. art. 10(8). Kenya Const. art. 77(8) is the same except for omission of the words *of record* and the words *of itself.* Zambia Const. art. 18(8) is also nearly identical to Botswana's provision.

[258] Papua New Guinea Const. art. 37(2).

[259] Zambia Const. Act art. 32(2); Zimbabwe Const. art. 26.

[260] Zimbabwe Const. art. 26(6).

[261] *Id.* art. 26(7).

[262] See Geneva Convention (No. III) art. 99; Additional Protocol I to the 1949 Geneva Conventions art. 75(4)(c) (1977).

[263] Chap. 5.c.viii.

[264] Venezuela Const. art. 24.

[265] Israel Penal Law sec. 3.

[266] Papua New Guinea Criminal Code Act 1974 art. 11; Papua New Guinea Village Courts Act 1989 arts. 41, 42; Village Court Regulation 1974 (as amended through 25 November 2006) art. 3; cf. Papua New Guinea Const. art. 37.

Two modern constitutions have limited but more significant anti-legality provisions. Both countries involved, Pakistan and Singapore, have general constitutional provisions prohibiting retroactive creation of crimes or increase of punishments, but both also have exceptions for certain subversive acts. Neither country is party to the ICCPR or other general human rights treaty regime, though both are parties to the CRC.

The Pakistan Constitution has a general constitutional provision prohibiting retroactivity of crimes and punishments.[267] There is a specific exception, however, for "any law making acts of abrogation or subversion of a Constitution in force in Pakistan at any time since the twenty-third day of March, one thousand nine hundred and fifty-six, an offence."[268] This provision rather narrowly defines the sort of acts that may be criminalized retroactively. Moreover, it is presumably for a court to determine whether the retroactively criminalized act was an act of abrogation or subversion of a constitution of Pakistan. Pakistan has had a number of military coups during its history of independence and is, as this book goes to press, governed by a president who came to power in such a coup, sharing power with an elected government.

Singapore has a general prohibition of retroactivity of crimes and punishments, which is enforced.[269] However, it has an exception for activity perceived as subversive. This exception allows for a criminal law to apply retroactively (or to violate other constitutional rights) if it recites certain facts:

> If an Act recites that action has been taken or threatened by any substantial body of persons, whether inside or outside Singapore –
>
> (a) to cause, or to cause a substantial number of citizens to fear, organised violence against persons or property;
> (b) to excite disaffection against the President or the Government;
> (c) to promote feelings of ill-will and hostility between different races or other classes of the population likely to cause violence;
> (d) to procure the alteration, otherwise than by lawful means, of anything by law established; or

[267] Pakistan Const. art. 12(1).
[268] Pakistan Const. art. 12(2).
[269] Singapore Const. art. 11(1); see Public Prosecutor v. Manogaran, [1997] 2 L.R.C. 288 (Ct. of App. of Singapore), noted in Nihal Jayawickrame, The Judicial Application of Human Rights Law: National, Regional and International Jurisprudence 588 (Cambridge Univ. Press 2002) [hereinafter Jayawickrame].

(e) which is prejudicial to the security of Singapore, any provision of that law designed to stop or prevent that action or any amendment to that law or any provision in any law enacted under clause (3) is valid notwithstanding that it is inconsistent with Article . . . 11 . . . or would, apart from this Article, be outside the legislative power of Parliament.[270]

The classes of acts for which retroactive criminalization is acceptable is much broader in this Singapore provision than in the Pakistan Constitution. It covers not only acts of subverting the constitution but also exciting disaffection against the president or government and promoting ill will between groups within society. It also claims the right to do so extraterritorially. Perhaps as important, the decision as to whether retroactive crime creation is justified is entirely for the political authority. Such a statute is justified under the Singapore Constitution by the political recital of certain circumstances alone.

Because of the asserted extraterritorial reach of the Singapore constitutional provision, it is easy to see how it might become a matter of controversy between states. If a national of another state were to be charged by Singapore on the basis of a retroactive statute, the state of nationality could assert that the law violated the customary international law protection against retroactivity of definition of crimes and punishments. Of course, the Singapore provision allows punishment for some political activities that could be considered protected in international human rights law. Thus, a claim and resolution might not turn solely, or even principally, on the issue of non-retroactivity.

The Vatican has a provision that, if broadly interpreted, would allow for the retroactive creation of crimes and punishments in any criminal case. Its new Fundamental Law provides that in any civil or criminal case, the supreme pontiff may "transfer the examination and decision to a special body with the right to make a decision according to equity to the exclusion of any further appeal."[271] On its face, this does not prohibit the special body from making criminal an act which was not a crime when done, or increasing penalties retroactively. The Vatican's adherence to the CRC and the Second Additional Protocol to the Geneva Conventions suggests, however, that the state does not insist on the unlimited right to make criminal law retroactively.

[270] Singapore Const. art. 149(1).
[271] Vatican City Fundamental Law art. 16.

5.c.vii. Representation (or Vicarious) Jurisdiction: A Challenge for Legality

Often lost, at least among common lawyers, in the discussion of types of criminal jurisdiction recognized by international criminal law is representation jurisdiction. In this type of jurisdiction, national courts take jurisdiction over cases where a person allegedly commits a crime in one country and is found in another, of which he is not a national. The state where the alleged criminal is found (called the *judex deprehensionis*) for some reason (unrelated to the nature of the crime) cannot extradite or is not requested to extradite. If the defendant is a national of the state of refuge,[272] the case would fit comfortably into nationality jurisdiction (i.e., the claim that a state may exercise criminal jurisdiction over its nationals even when they act outside its territory) so long as the state of refuge exercises nationality jurisdiction under its internal law. The names given to this type of jurisdiction are *representation jurisdiction* (because the state trying the case represents the interests of the state where the crime allegedly occurred or that has some other interest in the matter)[273]; *vicarious jurisdiction* (because the state with the principal interest in the matter sees its interests vindicated vicariously by another state)[274]; *subsidiary universal jurisdiction* (because it is universal in the sense that there may be no connection between the crime and the site of the trial other than the presence of the accused, and subsidiary in the sense that there must be a state where it would, in the abstract, be more appropriate to try the case); and the *co-operative general universality principle.*[275]

[272] "State of refuge" is used here simply as a description of the place that the accused criminal has gone. As Henri Felix August Donnedieu de Vabres, Les principes modernes de droit pénal international 137 (Librairie du Recueil Sirey 1928), noted, this type of jurisdiction is a denial of the existence of the right of asylum or refuge from criminal prosecution. It is not, however, a denial of the right to be treated fairly and humanely in the criminal process; and fear of unfair process, torture, or inhumane punishment can be one of the reasons for denying extradition.

[273] See Iain Cameron, *Jurisdiction and Admissibility Issues under the ICC Statute*, in The Permanent International Criminal Court: Legal and Policy Issues 65, 77 (Dominic McGoldrick, Peter Rowe & Eric Donnelly eds., Hart Publishing 2004); Marc Henzelin, Le principe de l'universalité en droit pénal inernational: Droit et obigation pour les États de poursuivre et juger selon le principe de l'universalité ¶¶ 75–79, pp. 30–32 (Helbing & Lichtenhahn 2000).

[274] Jürgen Meyer, *The Vicarious Administration of Justice: An Overlooked Basis of Jurisdiction*, 31 Harv. Int'l L.J. 108 (1990) [hereinafter Meyer].

[275] Luc Reydams, Universal Jurisdiction: International and Municipal Legal Perspectives 29–35 (Oxford Univ. Press 2003) [hereinafter Reydams].

This section will briefly introduce representation jurisdiction and explain why, in a few cases, it can pose a challenge to legality. It will then look at means that have been used to reconcile the exercise of jurisdiction with legality. However, this is not an exhaustive worldwide study of this practice. The conclusion reached is at best tentative.

Representation jurisdiction is far more accepted in the civil law world, particularly in the Germanic and Nordic traditions, than in the common law world.[276] Henri Donnedieu de Vabres traced it back to its modern popularization by Grotius of Holland.[277] More recently, Luc Reydams traced it further, to the sixteenth-century Spanish author Covarruvias, and to his source in the practice of medieval Italian city-states.[278] Where it is generally accepted, it applies to serious common crimes.[279] The reason for its acceptance in the civil law world may be connected to the fact that many civil law countries refuse to extradite their nationals and are familiar with the notion of prosecuting a crime committed elsewhere in their own courts as a substitute for extradition.

One motivation of this type of jurisdiction has colorfully been called "le scandale, ou le prejudice social resultant de l'impunité [the scandal, or social prejudice resulting from impunity]."[280] Social disutility occurs in the state of refuge of the malefactor and the state where the crime was committed and in the case of some crimes within the international community as a whole.[281]

[276] Cameron, *supra* note 273, at 76–7; Meyer at 115-16; Reydams at 30. For national statutes, see, e.g., Austria, Strafgesetzbuch [StGB] §65 (requiring that the sentence not exceed that of the place of the crime); Denmark Straffeloven [Strfl.] §8(6) (requiring a rejected request for extradition for a crime carrying more than a one year sentence in Denmark); Germany StGB §7(2)(2).

[277] Donnedieu de Vabres, *supra* note 272, at 136. Interestingly, current Netherlands law does not adopt this doctrine.

[278] Reydams at 29, discussing D. Covarruvias, PRACTICORUM QUAESTIONUM, Ch. 11, no. 7 (no date given) and relying on G. GUILLAUME, *La competence universelle, formes anciennes et nouvelles*, in MELANGES OFFERTS À GEORGES LEVASSEUR: DROIT PÉNAL, DROIT EUROPÉEN 23, 24 (Paris 1992) (for Covarruvias), along with J. KOHLER, INTERNATIONAL STRAFRECHT 37 (1917) and G. SOLNA, DAS WELTRECHTSPRINZIP IM INTERNATIONALEN STRAFRECHT 13 (1925) (for practice of Italian city-states). See also Donnedieu de Vabres, *supra* note 272, at 136, discussing the Italian practice, specifically in the Lombard cities.

[279] Germany, StGB § 7(2)(2).

[280] Donnedieu de Vabres, *supra* note 272, at 161 (discussing universal jurisdiction generally but focusing on the problem of impunity of the criminal who could not be brought to prosecution in the territorial state). Accord, MAURICE TRAVERS, 1 LE DROIT PÉNAL INTERNATIONAL ET SA MISE EN OEUVRE EN TEMPS DE PAIX ET EN TEMPS DE GUERRE 106 (1920–22) [hereinafter Travers].

[281] Donnedieu de Vabres, *supra* note 272, at 161–62. See *id.* at 135 ("un intérêt humain [a human interest]" is what is protected).

To the extent that it is the social order of the state where the offender is found that is protected from the criminal, this type of jurisdiction can be seen as having some territorial basis.[282] A second motivation is generally seen as its promotion of the solidarity of states in fighting serious crime.[283] A third is the promotion of effective cooperation in criminal justice between the specific states involved, even where extradition is not possible.[284]

Representation jurisdiction presents an interesting challenge for legality, especially for *nulla poena*. The question is how to reconcile the principles of notice and foreseeability to a case where the offense was committed in one jurisdiction, where one law applies, and is tried in another jurisdiction, using another criminal law. In representation jurisdiction cases, the forum state usually purports to apply its own substantive criminal law (*lex fori*).[285] This has been the general rule at least since the French Revolution, though in earlier ages, this was not always true.[286]

However, most states that use the doctrine of representative jurisdiction also apply rules of law indicating that the law of the place of the crime (*lex loci delicti*) is included in the prescription of law for the case. Most states applying the doctrine require double criminality – that is, that the act charged be a crime under both the law of the place of the crime and the law of the forum state, unless the place where the crime was committed has no criminal law.[287] Some states also allow defenses that would be available in

[282] This idea is attributed to Brusa by Reydams at 30–31, relying on A. Mercier, *Le conflit des lois pénales en matière de competence*, [1931] ANNUAIRE L'INSTITUTE DE DROIT INTERNATIONAL, I, 87, 134 [hereinafter Mercier]; Travers at 75–76.

[283] Reydams at 30, using Mercier at 134, attributes this idea to Ludwig von Bar. *Id.* at 32–33, quotes from Travers at 11, 75–76, rejecting this reason, but accepting the threat to the social order of the state of refuge.

[284] See Meyer at 116.

[285] Meyer at 115–16, discussing Germany Strafgesetzbuch (StGB) § 7(2)(2) (the statute allowing the courts of Germany, formerly West Germany, to exercise representative jurisdiction over persons who for one reason or another cannot be extradited); Donnedieu de Vabres, *supra* note 272, at 161-62 (stating it as the generally accepted rule, and accepting this doctrine if avoiding social harm to the state of refuge of the criminal is the principal purpose of the doctrine, but criticizing a strict application of it). See also Austria StGB §65(1&3). For a proposal to allow the forum state to apply the law of the state where the crime allegedly occurred in some cases, reversing the rule that one state will not apply the criminal law of another sovereign, see M. CHERIF BASSIOUNI, INTERNATIONAL EXTRADITION AND WORLD PUBLIC ORDER 428 (A.W. Sijthoff 1974).

[286] Christine van den Wyngaert, *Double Criminality as a Requirement to Jurisdiction* [hereinafter van den Wyngaert], in DOUBLE CRIMINALITY: STUDIES IN INTERNATIONAL CRIMINAL LAW 43, 44–45 (Nils Jareborg, ed., Iustis Förlag AB 1989) [hereinafter Jareborg].

[287] See Meyer at 115; van den Wyngaert at 49–50. The issue of crime occurring in a place with no functioning law is peculiar. Cf. Cvjetkovic Case, Austria, Supreme Court, 1994, discussed in Arrest Warrant Case, Judgment, Joint Separate Opinion of Judges Higgins, Kooijmann & Buergenthal ¶ 22.

the state where the crime was committed to be raised in the forum state, whether or not they would be defenses under forum law – this has been described as "apply[ing] the principle of double criminality in concreto."[288] These defenses may be either substantive (e.g., justification defenses)[289] or procedural (e.g., statute-of-limitations defenses).[290]

Many states will also impose a penalty no greater than that allowed where the crime was committed.[291] This rule was included in the Institute of International Law's Munich Resolutions of 1883. That document proposed that a state "which has custody over an offender may try and punish him" when extradition cannot be granted to the state where the crime occurred or the offender's home state: "In this case, the court will apply the most favourable law to the accused, taking into account the probable place of the crime, the nationality of the accused, and the law of the forum state."[292] This followed the 1852 Austrian Penal Code. Under that code, a person prosecuted in Austria because the state of the offense would not receive him would "generally" be treated under the Austrian code, but: "If, however, more lenient treatment is prescribed by the criminal law of the place where he committed the act, he shall be treated according to this more lenient law."[293] This appears to be the general practice when representative jurisdiction is exercised. Besides Austria, the states with statutes taking into account some version of the law more favorable to the accused include Israel[294] and Switzerland.[295] German doctrine requires that punishment in Germany

[288] Cameron, *supra* note 273, at 77.

[289] Van den Wyngaert at 51–52.

[290] See commentary on Germany, StGB § 7(2)(2) in Reydams at 143–44 & n.20; van den Wyngaert at 52.

[291] See Cameron, *supra* note 273, at 77–78; Meyer at 116 (Germany).

[292] L'Institute de droit international, Session de Munich, Résolution 10 (23 September 1883), 7 *Annuaire de l'Institut de droit international* 157 (1885), quoted with approval in Donnedieu de Vabres, *supra* note 272, at 466 and in Reydams at 30 (where the above translation appears). This report was based upon earlier work of von Bar and Brusa on criminal conflict of laws.

[293] Austria Penal Code art. 40 (1852), trans. in Harvard Research in International Law, Jurisdiction with Respect to Crime, 29 A.J.I.L. Supp. 435, 574–75 (1935).

[294] See Israel Penal Law § 17(b) (on "vicarious applicability" of Israeli penal law), translation ed. by Aryeh Greenfield, PENAL LAW 5737–1977 PART ONE 9-10 (5th ed., Aryeh Greenfield-A.G. Publications 2005) (through Amendment 63). Similar situations treated using the less onerous penalty in Israel Penal Law §§14(c) (offenses against Israel citizen or resident – i.e., passive personality jurisdiction), 15(b) (offenses committed by Israel citizen or resident - i.e., nationality or active personality jurisdiction), & 16(b) (offenses against international law). The suggestion in Reydams at 159 that Israel does not apply more lenient foreign law looks at Israel Penal Law, §9 only, and not the succeeding sections, which make clear that a foreign law, if more lenient as to penalty, would limit the ability of the court to punish.

[295] Switzerland Code Pénal art. 6bis(1) (1982), quoted in English translation in Reydams at 194; see also *id.* at 201.

"should not exceed that which would be imposed by the law where the criminal conduct occurred. This qualification reflects both the idea of the vicarious administration of justice and the fact that the perpetrator could not have known of the applicability of foreign law."[296] German doctrine and statutory interpretation principles also require that justification and excuse defenses of the place of commission of the crime be allowed.[297]

These rules together amount to implementation of *nullum crimen, nulla poena sine lege*.[298] Indeed, this book argues that international human rights law requires implementation of *nullum crimen* and *nulla poena*.[299] To those who accept the substantive view of international criminal law, these limitations are more clearly required by *nullum crimen, nulla poena*. To them, international human rights law comfortably serves to require the importation of these limitations as part of the substantive limits on jurisdiction to prescribe imposed on states by international law.

This logic of how representation jurisdiction should work is persuasive. Nonetheless, it cannot be said that it works this way all the time in all countries using representation jurisdiction. Jürgen Meyer indicates that German courts do not always apply the penalty of the country where the crime occurs if that penalty is more lenient than the German penalty.[300]

Instances of true representation jurisdiction are not common.[301] To truly require representation jurisdiction, the crime must have no connection with the state where the fugitive is found (or territorial, protective or passive

[296] Meyer at 116, relying on D. Oehler, Internationales Strafrecht ¶¶ 892–94 (2d ed., 1983).

[297] Meyer at 111, relying in part on Germany StGB § 7(2)(1); Van den Wyngaert at 53–54. But cf. Per Ole Träskman, *Should We Take the Condition of Double Criminality Seriously?*, in Jareborg 148–52, esp. 149 (considers the existence of the law as sufficient to meet *nulla poena* but that rules of jurisdiction can prevent persons from being tried for crimes where there was no applicable law).

[298] Cf. Henzelin, *supra* note 273, ¶¶ 645–47, at pp. 208–09.

[299] Chap. 7; cf. Michael Akehurst, *Jurisdiction in International Law*, 46 Brit. Y.B. Int'l L. 145, 188 (1972-73) (international law may impose some limitations on state prescription); Susan Lamb, *Nullum crimen, nulla poena sine lege* in International Criminal Law, in 1 The Rome Statute of the International Criminal Court: A Commentary 733, 735 (Antonio Cassese, Paola Gaeta & John R. W. D. Jones, eds. 2002)(principle of legality has become "clearly and firmly entrenched in customary international law" since World War II); M. Cherif Bassiouni, Crimes against Humanity in International Criminal Law 144, 162 (2d ed., Transnational Publishers, 1999).

[300] Meyer at 116.

[301] Fiction is replete with criminals who flee with huge amounts of money into an exile where they have no connections but from which they cannot be extradited. Although such cases are not unheard of in life, they are not as common as fantasy would have it.

personality jurisdiction could apply). The fugitive cannot be a national of that state (or nationality jurisdiction could apply). Yet the state of refuge must be unwilling or unable to extradite for reasons unconnected to the nature of the crime. In the future, if a German court were to apply a penalty beyond the maximum that could have been applied in the state where the crime occurred or the state of nationality of the fugitive, the fugitive might seek review from the ECtHR. The fugitive could argue that such a penalty violates the ECHR legality provision[302] because a penalty is being imposed that was not available in the law that applied to the fugitive at the time of the act. The fugitive might have a valid claim to reduction of sentence, and it would be interesting to see if the ECtHR would agree. Obviously, the same situation might arise within the other human rights treaty systems.

5.c.viii. *What Is Punishment for Purposes of Invoking the Non-retroactivity Rules of Criminal Law? A Brief Note*

One of the issues where penology intersects with criminal law is: What measures constitute punishment for purposes of legality in criminal law, and what measures are merely preventative or therapeutic, and may be imposed regardless of retroactivity? It is unfortunate that this book is unable to deal with this issue in the theoretical and practical depths that it deserves. As will be seen from the few examples of state practice below, it is a very live issue in a wide variety of legal systems.

The issue of what is a punishment for purposes of criminal law legality needs to be considered as an autonomous legal issue. That is, a state cannot simply say that certain things are or are not criminal penalties – though a decision by a state that a legal consequence is a criminal penalty would be conclusive as to that state. One needs to make an independent legal determination. So, for example, the action of an administrative agency is not automatically a non-punishment just because it is not labeled a criminal court or what it does is not labeled a criminal sanction.[303] However, the range of matters that have not been considered penalties for purposes of the non-retroactivity of punishments in national courts or under national statutes is quite broad.

For example, the U.S. Supreme Court has decided it is constitutional to hold dangerous sexual predators for mental health treatment even when

[302] ECHR art. 7(1).

[303] Cf. Jayawickrame at 530, citing MacIsaac v. Canada, Human Rights Committee Communication No. 53/79 (1983).

the state (i.e., subnational) statute involved was not enacted until after their predatory acts. The court determined that the treatment was not punishment for purposes of the rules prohibiting ex post facto increases of punishment.[304]

A number of countries provide for some sort of therapeutic treatment in their general criminal codes, without regard to the date of the crime. German law states: "Unless the law provides otherwise, decisions as to measures of reform and prevention shall be according to the law which is in force at the time of judgment,"[305] but other "collateral consequences" of conviction are according to the law in force at the time of the act.[306] Lithuania has a similar provision.[307] Denmark allows for conditions of probation and community service, as well as means for dealing with persons who have been acquitted by reason of mental illness or defect to be determined as of the time of the criminal proceeding rather than the time of the act.[308]

Lebanon prohibits the retroactive introduction of "security and education measures" as well as punishment where an act was not a crime when committed.[309] However, where an act was a crime when committed, new education and security measures can be applied until the judgment of the last court with appropriate jurisdiction.[310] Superseded measures of security and education can be eliminated or replaced by newly imposed measures even after final judgment.[311]

Canada increased the mandatory supervision of parolees and applied the new supervision to those then on parole. The Human Rights Committee under the ICCPR determined that this was not a retroactive penalty but acceptable as "a measure of social assistance intended to provide for the rehabilitation of the convicted person, in his own interest."[312]

This brief survey almost certainly understates the prevalence of retrospective application of nonpunitive measures. No constitution authorizes retroactive application of nonpunitive therapeutic measures to offenders. All of these examples come from statutory authorization. The focus of this

[304] See Kansas v. Hendricks, 521 U.S. 346, 361 (1997).
[305] Germany § 2(6), StGB.
[306] Germany § 2(1-5), StGB.
[307] Lithuania Penal Code art. 3(4).
[308] Denmark Crim. Code art. 4, citing Denmark Crim. Code arts. 56–61 & 62–70.
[309] Lebanon Code Pénal art. 1.
[310] Lebanon Code Pénal art. 13.
[311] Lebanon Code Pénal art. 14.
[312] A. R. S. v. Canada, HRC Comm. No. 91/81, para. 5(3), quoted in SARAH JOSEPH, JENNY SCHULTZ & MELISSA CATAN, THE INTERNATIONAL COVENANT ON CIVIL AND POLITICAL RIGHTS: CASES, MATERIALS AND COMMENTARY 463–64 (Oxford Univ. Press 2004).

book, however, is on punishment for crime. Thus, it is very likely that legal consequences of crime that societies do not see as criminal punishment may be treated in some nations as exempt from their constitutional or statutory bans on retroactively increasing punishments.

Some nations make distinctions between punishment and non-punishment for purposes other than retroactivity of criminal law. Although these cannot necessarily be treated as applying directly to the non-retroactivity problem, they may be illuminating. Some Sunni Islamic schools of jurisprudence draw a line between restitution (to the victims and their families) and retribution (the punishment inflicted on the offender) for many killings and batteries. They do this for the purpose of determining what legal consequences of the offense may be imposed on the family of the offender.[313] Many states draw a distinction between restitution and recompense provided to a victim or a victim's family and a penalty awarded to the state in determining what is "penal" for purposes of the conflict of laws/private international law principle that states will generally not enforce another's penal laws.[314] Daniel Warnotte has warned against the dangers of the Belgian practice of using harsh administrative remedies as a substitute for the perceived inadequacy of criminal punishments.[315] All these examples would suggest that when the state seeks to impose its will on an individual because of criminal acts, such imposition should be considered penal. However, current practice in some states allows a broader definition of non-punishment in analyzing legality issues.

Expanding the principle of retroactive non-punishment can lead to the sort of abuses perpetrated by the system of "mental health treatment" for dissidents that prevailed in the former Soviet Union.[316] There is, however, a counterargument. In many, if not most, countries, strict non-retroactivity is limited to crimes and punishments.[317] In these nations, the rule does not

[313] See discussion in Chap. 5.e.

[314] E.g., Loucks v. Standard Oil Co. of New York, 224 N.Y. 99, 120 N.E. 198 (1918).

[315] Daniel Warnotte, Commentary on Belgium, 1946 UNYBHR at 38.

[316] See, e.g., 1926 RSFSR Crim. Code art. 7 (trans. Harold J. Berman & James W. Spindler), quoted in HAROLD J. BERMAN, SOVIET CRIMINAL LAW AND PROCEDURE: THE RSFSR CODES 25 (Harvard Univ. Press 1966) [hereinafter Berman]. JOHN N. HAZARD & ISAAC SHAPIRO, THE SOVIET LEGAL SYSTEM: POST-STALIN DOCUMENTATION AND HISTORICAL COMMENTARY 4 n.3 (Parker School of Foreign & Comparative Law, Columbia University/Oceana 1962) [hereinafter Hazard & Shapiro] document the 1926 RSFSR Crim. Code as Decree of 22 November 1926, [1926] I Sov. Uzak. RSFSR, No. 80, Item 600 (effective 1 January 1927).

[317] But see Chap. 1.a for a list of countries that appear to require non-retroactivity of all laws to the detriment of individuals.

apply to non-criminal causes of action and remedies. Arguably, if a remedy may apply retroactively in a non-criminal case, it should similarly apply in a case where the law has previously defined a wrong in very strong terms (i.e., by calling it a crime). It is thus very interesting that what constitutes crime and what constitutes punishment were not major topics of discussion in the negotiations for the UDHR and ICCPR.

The dangers of retroactive non-punishment for criminal acts far exceed the potential benefits of the practice, at least where the nonpunitive measures include deprivations of liberty such as institutionalization that could not be supported by other law.[318] However, as a matter of customary international human rights law, the practice is not currently prohibited. The current extent and appropriate limitations of this practice are matters that need further study by scholars of comparative and criminal law.

5.d. NON-RETROACTIVITY OF COURT CREATION AND PROHIBITIONS OF SPECIAL COURTS

Some have regarded non-retroactivity of court creation as a part of the principle of legality in criminal law.[319] Some have also seen the creation of special criminal courts as a threat to the fairness and legality of criminal proceedings. As a result, many national constitutions and at least one regional human rights system have prohibitions against these practices.

The states whose constitutions prohibit retroactive creation of criminal tribunals include Argentina, Bolivia, Chile, El Salvador, Italy, Peru, and Sweden.[320] All states that are parties to the ACHR have agreed to this prohibition by treaty.[321]

[318] The discussion here is limited to the retroactivity of non-punishment. It does not deal with other issues, such as double punishment when the so-called non-punishment is added only at the completion of the criminal's sentence, as in the U.S. case of *Hendricks*.

[319] See Chap. 2.c.i.

[320] Argentina Const. art. 18; Bolivia Const. art. 14; Chile Const. art 19(3); El Salvador Const. art. 15; Italy Const. art. 25 (judge to be "pre-established by law"); Peru Const. art. 139(3) (person may not "be turned away from a jurisdiction predetermined by the law, or be subjected to a procedure different from those previously established, or adjudicated by the [state of] exception judicial organs or by special commissions created for that purpose no matter how denominated"); Sweden Instrument of Government, ch. 2, art. 11 ("No court of law shall be established on account of an act already committed, or for a particular dispute or otherwise for a particular case").

[321] ACHR art. 8.

Some states phrase the protection in terms of a prohibition of removing a person from the jurisdiction of that person's "lawful judge" or similar formulation. These states include Burundi, Democratic Republic of the Congo, Germany, Italy, Kazakhstan, Liechtenstein, Luxembourg, Nigeria, Peru, Portugal, São Tomé and Príncipe, Slovakia, Suriname, and Venezuela.[322] One entity not generally recognized as a state with a similar provision is the Turkish Republic of Northern Cyprus.[323] This sort of provision has some of the same effects as provisions on the non-retroactivity of court creation because it prevents removal of a case to any other jurisdiction, whether or not the jurisdiction is new.

States that prohibit the creation of special tribunals for the trial of particular cases include Costa Rica, Nepal, Portugal, and Sweden.[324] Again, this has the effect of protection from the retroactive creation of special courts.

Many states prohibit the creation of special tribunals either in criminal cases or more generally. The prohibitions take a variety of forms in constitutions. The states with constitutional prohibitions include Albania, Andorra, Angola, Armenia, Azerbaijan, Belarus, Bolivia, Brazil, Bulgaria, Chile, Comoros, Denmark, East Timor (except for the national/international UNTAET courts transferred to East Timor sovereignty on independence), Ethiopia, Finland, Germany, Haiti, Iraq, Italy, Japan, Lithuania, Luxembourg, Macedonia, Montenegro, Mexico, Mozambique, Papua New Guinea,

[322] Burundi Const. art. 39; Dem. Rep. of Congo, art. 19 ("judge who has been assigned to hear his/her case"); Germany Basic Law art. 101(1); Italy Const. art. 25; Kazakhstan Const. art. 77(3); Liechtenstein Const. art. 33(1); Luxembourg Const. art. 13; Nigeria Const. art. 4(8) (law may not oust jurisdiction of courts); Peru Const. art. 139(3) (person may not "be turned away from a jurisdiction predetermined by the law, or be subjected to a procedure different from those previously established, or adjudicated by the [state of] exception judicial organs or by special commissions created for that purpose no matter how denominated"); São Tomé and Príncipe Const. art. 39(7) ("No case may be removed from the court whose competence has been established in prior law"); Slovakia Const. art. 48(1); Suriname Const. art. 11; Venezuela Const. art. 49(4) ("Any person has the right to be judged by his legitimate [*naturales*] judges in the ordinary, or special, jurisdictions with the guarantees established in this Constitution and the law. No person can be sentenced to judgment without cognizance of the identity of those who judge him, nor can [a person] be processed by tribunals of exception or by commissions created to this effect").

[323] Turkish Rep. of Northern Cyprus Const. art. 17(1).

[324] Costa Rica Const. art. 35; Nepal Interim Const. art. 101(2); Portugal Const. art. 209(4) (except military courts "courts with exclusive jurisdiction to try specific categories of offense" prohibited); Sweden Instrument of Government art. 11 ("No court of law shall be established on account of an act already committed, or for a particular dispute or otherwise for a particular case").

Paraguay, Romania, Russia, Rwanda (though the constitution has retrospectively established special quasi-traditional *gacaca* courts to deal with many persons accused in the 1994 genocide), Switzerland, Ukraine, Uruguay, and Venezuela.[325] Israel establishes this prohibition by statute.[326] Qatar prohibits

[325] Albania Const. art. 135(2) ("extraordinary court" prohibited); Andorra Const. art. 85(2) ("special jurisdiction" prohibited); Angola Const. Law arts. 125, 126 ("the constitution of courts with sole powers to try determined offenses shall be prohibited," but military courts may be established); Armenia Const. art. 92 ("emergency tribunals" forbidden); Azerbaijan Const. art. 125(VI) ("The use of legal means not specified by law in order to change the competence of judges and create extraordinary courts is prohibited"); Belarus Const. art. 109 ("exceptional courts"); Bolivia Const. arts. 14 ("special commissions"), 116(II) ("exceptional tribunals or courts"); Brazil Const. art. 5(XXXVII); Bulgaria Const. art. 119(3); Chile Const. art. 19(3)("special commissions"); Comoros Const. art. 48 ("penal jurisdiction of exception"); Denmark Const. Act, art. 61 ("Extraordinary courts of justice with judicial power"); East Timor Const. arts. 123(2) ("courts of exception" prohibited), 163 (saving the national/international tribunals); Ethiopia Const. art. 78(4) ("Special or ad hoc courts which take judicial powers away from the regular courts or institutions legally empowered to exercise judicial functions and which do not follow legally prescribed procedures shall not be established"); Finland Const., ch. 9, § 98 ("provisional courts"); Germany Const. art. 101 ("extraordinary courts" prohibited; but courts for particular fields of law may be established); Haiti Const. art. 173–2 ("special court"); Iraq Const. arts. 92, 130 ("Special or exceptional courts" other than the Iraqi High Criminal Court); Italy Const. art. 102 ("Extraordinary or special judges"); Japan Const. art. 76 ("extraordinary tribunals" and giving "final judicial power" to the executive); Liechtenstein Const. art. 33(1) ("special tribunals"); Lithuania Const. art. 111 ("Courts with special powers may not be established in the Republic of Lithuania in times of peace"); Luxembourg Const. art. 86 ("extraordinary commission or courts"); Macedonia Const., amend. XXV(1) ("Emergency courts"); Montenegro Const. art. 118; Mexico Const. art. 13 ("special tribunals"); Mozambique Const. art. 167(2) (courts for "specific categories of crimes"); Papua New Guinea Const. art. 159 (National Judicial System has exclusive authority to impose penalties for criminal offence, but disciplined forces may give penalties other than death, and in various non-criminal situations special or private courts may be established); Paraguay Const. art. 17(3) (in criminal cases, no "special tribunals"); Philippines Const. art. VII(18)(4) (martial law does not authorize military jurisdiction over civilians); Poland Const. art. 175(2) ("extraordinary courts or summary procedures" only allowed in time of war); Romania Const. art. 126(5) ("courts with special jurisdiction" prohibited, but specialized courts may be established by organic law); Russia Const. art. 118(3) ("extraordinary courts"); Rwanda Const. arts. 143 (no "exceptional courts"), 152 (establishing *gacaca* courts for genocide and crimes against humanity from 1990 through 1994); Switzerland Const. art. 30(1); Ukraine Const. art. 125 ("extraordinary and special courts"); Uruguay Const. art. 19 ("trials by commission"); Venezuela Const. art. 49(4) ("Any person has the right to be judged by his legitimate [*naturales*] judges in the ordinary, or special, jurisdictions with the guarantees established in this Constitution and the law. No person can be sentenced to judgment without cognizance of the identity of those who judge him, nor can [a person] be processed by tribunals of exception or by commissions created to this effect"); Zimbabwe Const. art. 81(4) (complex provision apparently preventing new jurisdictions from being established after day appointed for hearing a case; see text in Appendix C).

[326] Israel Basic Law: The Judiciary art. 1(c).

civilians and civilian crimes to be tried in military courts except under martial law.[327]

A few states do the opposite. States that specifically allow special tribunals (beyond military tribunals to try military offenses) include Ireland, Jordan, Nepal, and Poland (during wartime).[328]

The constitutional protections against special tribunals or retroactively created tribunals are geographically widespread. They are overwhelmingly in countries with civil law traditions.

This is one area of criminal law and procedure where national and international practices are diverging rather sharply. Since Nuremberg, special and retroactively established criminal tribunals have become the norm in international criminal practice. The establishment of the ICC may reverse this trend but has not stopped it completely.[329]

This is another area in which further research by scholars is necessary. The collection of constitutional provisions concerning establishment of special or retroactive criminal jurisdictions has been possible. This section does not collect the jurisprudence on the way these provisions are implemented. This is obviously important, as what an "extraordinary" court is, is not self-evident. Many of the provisions deserve further study.

5.e. PERSONAL PUNISHMENT AND REJECTION OF COLLECTIVE PUNISHMENT: ALSO GENERAL PRINCIPLES OF LAW

The ideas that punishment is personal to the offender and that collective punishments should be prohibited is one idea that has grown in modern constitutions. It also appears in the African human rights system,[330] the American human rights system,[331] and the Geneva Convention system of international humanitarian law. Essentially, criminal punishment may not be imposed on one who is not a criminal offender, whether the punishment is imposed individually or collectively.

The states that recognize the doctrine of personality of punishment explicitly in their constitutions include Afghanistan, Algeria, Bahrain, Brazil,

[327] Qatar Const. art. 132.

[328] Ireland Const. art. 38(3)(1); Jordan Const. art. 110; Nepal Interim Const. art. 101(2) (except to try particular case); Poland Const. art. 175(2) ("extraordinary courts or summary procedures" allowed, but only in time of war).

[329] See Chap. 6, discussing special tribunals established since the 1998 adoption of the text of the ICC Statute.

[330] ACHPR art. 7(2).

[331] ACHR art. 5(3).

Burkina Faso, Chad, Democratic Republic of the Congo, Egypt, Iraq, Mali, Qatar, Togo, and Tunisia.[332] Yemen states, "Crime shall be the sole responsibility of the culprit."[333] Saudi Arabia declares punishment to be personal in its Basic System of the Consultative Council.[334] Libya has such a provision in one of its revolutionary documents.[335] The Palestinian Authority prohibits collective punishment.[336] Somaliland, a breakaway portion of Somalia seeking recognition as a state, states that "the punishment for crime shall be confined to the offender only."[337] These are all African or Islamic-majority states or entities seeking recognition as states. Outside Africa and the Arab world, Slovakia limits punishment to "the offender."[338] Switzerland makes this the first principle of its penal code.[339]

The prevalence of this provision in constitutions of Islamic-majority states may be related to an issue in the history of Islamic criminal law. As Bassiouni points out, "the principle of individual criminal responsibility is fundamental in Islam."[340] However, the Sunni schools of jurisprudence disagree on whether compensation (*diyya*) for certain crimes of homicide or battery (*quesas*) may be imposed only on the individual perpetrator or may be imposed on the perpetrator's family as well.[341] The victim or victim's family must seek physical punishment (as execution in a case of murder) only against the perpetrator, not against uninvolved members of the perpetrator's family.[342] The inclusion of a provision that punishment is personal in these constitutions may be aimed to limit the applicability

[332] Afghanistan Const. art. 26 [alternately numbered ch. 2, art. 5]; Algeria Const. art. 142; Bahrain Const. art. 20(b); Brazil Const. art. 5(XLV); Burkina Faso Const. art. 5; Chad Const. art. 26; Dem. Rep. of Congo Const. art. 17; Egypt Const. art. 66; Iraq Const. art. 19(8); Mali Const. art. 9; Qatar Const. art. 40; Togo Const. art. 19; Tunisia Const. art. 13.

[333] Yemen Const. art. 46.

[334] Saudi Arabia Basic System of the Consultative Council art. 38.

[335] Constitutional Proclamation of the Revolutionary Command Council of Libya art. 31(b) (1969).

[336] Amended Basic Law of Palestine art. 15.

[337] Somaliland Const. art. 26.

[338] Slovakia Const. art. 49.

[339] Switzerland Code Pénal art. 1.

[340] M. Cherif Bassiouni, *Quesas Crimes* [hereinafter Bassiouni, *Quesas Crimes*], in The Islamic Criminal Justice System 203, 207–09 (M. Cherif Bassiouni, ed., Oceana Publications 1982) [hereinafter Bassiouni, Islamic Criminal Justice]; accord, Ahmad Fathi Bahnassi, Criminal Responsibility in Islamic Law, in Bassiouni, Islamic Criminal Justice 171, 175.

[341] Bassiouni, *Quesas Crimes* at 207–09. See also Ahmad Abd al-Aziz al-Alfi, *Punishment in Islamic Criminal Law*, in Bassiouni, Islamic Criminal Justice 227, 230.

[342] Bassiouni, *Quesas Crimes, passim.*

of family responsibility strictly to what can be characterized as restitution rather than expand it to include punishment or retribution.[343]

The issue of restitution versus retribution seen in the case of *quesas* crimes raises again the importance and autonomy of the question of what is punishment for the purposes of legality in criminal law. Those Islamic schools that permit the compensation (*diyya*) to be imposed on the family of the criminal determine that compensation is not punishment in this sense. Note that the question of legality here (requirement of individual criminal responsibility) is somewhat different than the question where the autonomy of punishment was previously addressed (non-retroactivity of punishment).[344]

The personality of punishment and rejection of collective punishment is deeply connected to the notion of the individuation of desert. If one becomes deserving of punishment only through fault, then punishment should not extend to those not at fault. That excludes punishment of families, clans, villages or cities, and other groups. As the mental element in criminal law developed, the idea that there should be punishment for anyone utterly without fault – connected to the crime only by blood, geographical, or other relationship to the offender – receded.[345]

Togo felt it necessary to specifically state that persons other than the direct actor may become criminally liable under the law.[346] This is to validate the doctrines of accomplice, conspiracy, command, or other types of criminal liability under national or international law that may attach to persons who are morally at fault for crimes, and who may have aided, encouraged, agreed to, or failed in a duty to suppress their perpetration but who did not commit the primary criminal acts themselves.

The prohibition of collective punishments does not directly limit what acts may be criminalized. It does not impinge upon the authority of states to reasonably define group criminality or to impose duties to report or

[343] Cf. Chap. 5.c.viii (on what is not punishment for purposes of invoking the rule of non-retroactivity).

[344] See Chap. 5.c.viii.

[345] The example of strict liability crimes in the Western traditions is related to the concept of individuation of punishment, though not directly to the issue of collective punishment. These crimes require a voluntary act as a minimum condition of culpability. For example, the traditional strict liability crime of statutory rape (sexual intercourse with an underage person) presumes that the actor commits a voluntary act of sexual intercourse, taking the risk that the person will turn out to be underage.

[346] See Togo Const. art. 19 ("Besides the cases provided by the law, no one may be prosecuted or sentenced for acts reproached to others.")

(in the case of command responsibility for core international crimes) to suppress crime. The protection against collective punishment alone would not, for example, prevent a state from criminalizing membership in a collective, such as a terrorist group or even a political party. The prohibited act, which would allow for individual punishment, would be joining or remaining a member of the group. Protection against criminalization of legitimate groups (as the political group in this hypothesis) in this manner must come from the substantive protections of constitutional and human rights law, such as protection of freedom of association, which are beyond the scope of this book.

Although only a minority of constitutions specifically prohibit collective punishment, one can infer this prohibition from the structure of most others. Many constitutions are of the form of the ICCPR, and are to the effect that, "No one shall be held guilty of any criminal offence on account of any act or omission which did not constitute a criminal offence . . . at the time when it was committed."[347] One most naturally reads this as limiting the "one" who can be held criminally liable to a person who committed a relevant act or omission. More than one hundred states have constitutional or statutory provisions to this effect.[348]

[347] ICCPR art. 15(1).

[348] National constitutions most naturally read to this effect include at least Albania Const. art. 29; Algeria Const. art. 46; Andorra Const. art. 9(4); Argentina Const. art. 18; Armenia Const. art. 22; Bahamas Const. art. 20(4); Bangladesh Const. art. 35(1); Barbados Const. art. 18(4); Belize Const. art. 6(4); Benin Const. art. 17; Botswana Const. art. 10(4); Bulgaria Const. art. 5(3); Burundi Const. arts. 39, 40; Cameroon Const. preamble; Canada Const. Act art. 11(g); Central African Rep. Const. art. 3; Chad Const. art. 23; Chile Const. art. 19(3); Comoros Const. art. 48; Dem. Rep. of Congo Const. art. 17; Costa Rica Const. art. 39; Côte d'Ivoire Const. art. 21; Croatia Const. art. 31; Cuba Const. art. 59; Rep. of Cyprus Const. art. 12(1); Djibouti Const. art. 10; Dominica Const. art. 8(4); East Timor Const. art. 31(2); Ecuador Const. art. 24(1); El Salvador Const. art. 15; Equatorial Guinea Fundamental Law, art. 13(s); Eritrea Const. art. 17(2); Estonia Const. art. 23; Ethiopia Const. art. 22(1); Fiji Const. art. 28(1)(j); Finland Const., ch. 2, sec. 8; France Declaration of the Rights of Man and of the Citizen art. 8; Gambia Const. art. 24(5); Georgia Const. art. 42(5); Germany Basic Law art. 103(2) (*nullum crimen*); Ghana Const. art. 19(5); Greece Const. art. 7(1); Grenada Const. Order, art. 8(4); Guyana Const. art. 144(4); Hungary Const. art. 57(4); Iceland Const. art. 69; India Const. art. 20; Iran Const. art. 169; Jamaica Const. art. 20(7); Japan Const. art. 39; Kenya Const. art. 77(4, 8); Kiribati Const. art. 10(4); Rep. of (South) Korea Const. art. 13(1); Kyrgyzstan Const. art. 85(10); Lesotho Const. art. 12(4); Macedonia Const. art. 14; Madagascar Const. art. 13; Malawi Const. art. 42(2)(f)(vi); Malaysia Const. art. 7(1); Maldives Const. art. 17; Malta Const. art. 39(8); Marshall Is. Const. art. II(8); Mauritius Const. art.10(4); Mexico Const. art. 14; Moldova Const. art. 22; Mozambique Const. art. 99; Namibia Const. art. 12(3); Nauru Const. art. 10(4); Nepal Interim Const. art. 24(4); Nicaragua Const. art. 34(11); Niger Const. art. 17; Nigeria Const. art. 36(8); Pakistan Const. art. 12(1); Palau Const. art. IV(6); Papua New Guinea Const. art. 37; Paraguay Const.

Similarly, many states prohibit conviction or punishment of a person except upon judgment of a regularly constituted court and/or according to law, fair procedures, or due process. These constitutions are naturally read to allow punishment to be visited only upon the persons so convicted, not on others. Several of these states have not already been listed as prohibiting collective or individual punishments of non-criminals either directly or by inference.[349]

Finally, all states that have adhered to the ACHPR and ACHR have agreed to implement this rule domestically. All states that have adhered to Additional Protocol II to the Geneva Conventions have agreed to implement it domestically in the case of civil wars.

Failure explicitly to prohibit collective punishment in its constitution does not mean that a state uses or endorses the practice. No constitution that the author has found recognizes a right to punish groups for crimes for which the individuals punished bear no individual responsibility.

When all of this is taken together, it is fair to conclude that the requirement that criminal punishment be limited to those who act criminally and the prohibition of collective punishment are (like non-retroactivity) general principles of law recognized by the community of nations. The evidence

art. 17(3); Peru Const. art. 2(24)(d); Poland, Const. art. 42(1); Portugal Const. art. 29(1); Russia Const. art. 52(1); Rwanda Const. arts. 18, 20; St. Kitts & Nevis Const. ¶ 10(4); St. Vincent & the Grenadines Const. art. 8(4); Samoa Const. art. 10(2); São Tomé and Príncipe Const. art. 36; Senegal Const. art. 9; Serbia [former Serbia and Montenegro] Charter of Human and Minority Rights and Civil Liberties art. 20; Seychelles Const. art. 19(4); Sierra Leone Const. art. 23(7); Singapore Const. art. 11(1); Slovakia Const. arts. 49, 50(6); Slovenia Const. art. 28; Solomon Is. Const. art. 10(4); Somalia Const. art. 34; South Africa Const. art. 35(3)(l); Spain Const. art. 25(1); Sri Lanka Const. art. 13(6); Sudan Interim National Const. art. 34(4); Tajikistan Const. art. 20; Tanzania Const. art. 13(6)(c); Thailand Const., 2007 §39; Turkey Const. art. 38; Turkmenistan Const. art. 43; Tuvalu Const. §22(6); Ukraine Const. art. 58; Vanuatu Const. art. 5(2)(f); Venezuela Const. art. 49(6); Zambia Const. art. 18(4); Zimbabwe Const. art. 18(5); cf. Guatemala Const. art. 17. For statutory law to similar effect see People's Republic of China Crim. Law arts. 3, 12; Denmark Crim. Code §3; New Zealand Bill of Rights Act art. 26(1); U.K. Human Rights Act art. 7. For an entity not generally recognized as a state, see Const. of Turkish Rep. of Northern Cyprus art. 18(1). Accord, Proposed Kosovo Const., art. 33.

[349] See Belgium Coord. Const. arts. 12, 13; Czech Rep. Charter of Fundamental Rights and Freedoms [of the Former Czechoslovakia] art. 40; Lebanon Const. art. 8; Mauritania Const. art. 13; Norway Const. art. 96; Romania Const. art. 23(12); Trinidad & Tobago Const. art. 5; U.S. Const. amends. V, XIV(1); Uruguay Const. art. 12; Uzbekistan Crim. Code art. 4. For similar statutory law indicating that only actors can be punished, see Bhutan Penal Code art. 6; Brunei Penal Code § 2. The Bhutan and Brunei provisions are of particular interest because they are the only two UN member states that have not clearly rejected retroactive creation of crimes and punishments. For an entity not universally recognized as a state, see Sahrawi Arab Democratic Rep. Const. art. 26.

supports the inference that they are accepted by most nations from all of the major legal systems in the world. Even if the legal texts are not quite as universal, and in some cases not quite so clear, as in the case of non-retroactivity, it is almost impossible to find support in them for criminal punishment of those not involved in criminal acts. Later in this book, a synthesis of national and international law and practice will show that these are rules of customary international law as well.[350]

Collective punishment, when performed by states today, is usually an adjunct of war, other outbreaks of mass violence, or occupation. In these cases, it is almost always done outside the judicial system. Enforcement of its prohibition thus falls more to the field of humanitarian law than to criminal law and procedure.[351] This has been the point of objections to Israeli policies of destruction of the family homes of apparent terrorists.

Where state authority is weak, collective punishment has existed as a social or even a legal reality in the modern period. As late as the 1950s, a "collective penalty of special contribution" existed by decree in the UN Trust Territory of Somaliland.[352] There have been recent examples of punishment of a non-wrongdoer, as in a 2002 case in a Pakistani tribal area in which members of an offended family raped the sister of an offender; complaints from an Islamic leader, the rape victim, and her family eventually resulted in state action against the perpetrators of the revenge.[353]

Of course, this does not mean that no one but the convict may suffer from a criminal conviction and punishment. Incarceration obviously affects families of those incarcerated very deeply. In those countries where criminal liability of business corporations exists, fining or dissolving those corporations will affect the assets of investors. These effects are generally not prohibited by law. Wrongdoing is not immunized from punishment because others might also feel the effects of punishing a wrongdoer.[354]

[350] Chap. 7.f.

[351] See Geneva Convention (No. III) art. 13; Geneva Convention (No. IV) art. 33; Additional Protocol No. I, art. 75(d); Additional Protocol No. II, art. 4(2)(b); see Geneva Conventions (Nos. I-IV) arts. 3 (prohibiting hostage taking in non-international conflicts; all discussed in Chap. 4.f.ii).

[352] Judicial Regs. of Somaliland arts. 23, 24, suspended for two years by Somaliland Ord. No. 14 (2 August 1954), Bulletino Officiale No. 8 (16 August 1954), all noted in 1954 UNYBHR at 321.

[353] See BBC News, Mukhtar Mai – history of a rape case, http://news.bbc.co.uk/2/hi/south_asia/4620065.stm (28 June 2005).

[354] This fact should not deter efforts to lessen the economic and other effects on the families of incarcerated persons and to support the family as the incarcerated person is reintegrated into society.

5.f. THE STATUS OF NATIONAL CONSTITUTIONS AND OTHER INTERNAL LEGAL ACTS OF STATES AS STATE PRACTICE FOR CONSTITUTING CUSTOMARY INTERNATIONAL HUMAN RIGHTS LAW

The adoption of internal law, constitutional or otherwise, is state practice, at least in terms of the creation of international human rights law. Some older definitions of *state practice* in international law would not include internal constitutional or statutory provisions as instances of state practice but would include only acts between or among states.[355] By now, however, consistent internal practice of states can be among the acts that constitute international law, especially international human rights law.

Consistent internal practice among many states is traditionally seen as creating a "general principle of law recognized by the community of nations."[356] Certainly this includes "basic principles of criminal law," such as legality.[357] By World War II, some believed, "if a practice is generally regarded by states in their conduct of internal affairs as representing a principle of justice, it is also enforceable as a rule of customary international law."[358] Whether or not this statement is by itself true, it indicates that practice concerning internal affairs could be considered as part of the practice relevant to determining a rule of customary international law.

Human rights law primarily deals with interactions between states and individuals. Although sometimes these individuals are foreigners, most of us are present in the state of our nationality most of the time. Thus, international human rights treaties generally protect individual human rights without regard to whether the person involved is a national of the concerned state party or of another state. Human rights treaty obligations generally protect political rights of nationals and allow greater limitations of political rights of nonnationals.[359] These international human rights are

[355] [George Brand], *The Sources of International Criminal Law*, 15 UNWCC, LAW REP. at 5, 6–10 (authorship attributed by Foreword by [Lord] Wright [of Durley], *id.* at x) [hereinafter Brand].

[356] See ICJ Statute art. 38(1)(c).

[357] Henzelin, *supra* note 273, ¶ 641.

[358] Brand at 6–7, relying on United States v. List (Hostages Case), as excerpted in 8 *id.* 34, 49–50 (19 February 1948), and citing to analysis of Schonfeld Case, 11 *id.* 64, 72–73 (British Military Ct., Essen, 19 June 1946).

[359] See generally ICCPR arts. 2 (distinctions of nationality not generally made), 25 (political participation rights are for "citizen[s]" of a state); ECHR arts. 14 (distinctions of nationality not generally made), 16 (political participation rights of "aliens" may be restricted); ACHR arts. 1 (distinction of nationality not generally made), 23 (right to participate in government

protected for nationals against their own states. The notion of customary international human rights law makes little sense without it protecting such persons. Thus, it is most reasonable to include state practice, including constitutional provisions and statutes, which affects a state's own nationals as part of the state practice that makes up international human rights law.

Recently, in *Case Concerning the Arrest Warrant of 11 April 2000 (Democratic Republic of Congo v. Belgium)*, the International Court of Justice "carefully examined state practice, including legislation and those few decisions of national higher courts" in determining whether customary international law permits prosecution of a sitting foreign minister in the courts of another nation for crimes against humanity, against a claim of immunity by the state of which he was foreign minister.[360] Thus, it appears that internal state practice, including legislation, is now accepted as practice constituting evidence of customary international law. Indeed, court decisions are being treated as such practice where relevant, though traditionally they have only been considered "subsidiary means for the determination of rules of law."[361] This case is particularly important for the purposes of this work because it dealt with criminal law, albeit in the area of immunity from jurisdiction to adjudicate rather than directly concerning legality. This focus on internal practice did not require states to justify their internal practice by reference to international law to use it for the construction of customary international law. It thus appeared to give less importance than in the past to a need for statements of *opinio juris*,[362] at least where practice is widespread. One can hardly doubt the widespread nature of non-retroactivity of crimes and punishments as a human right in national constitutions and law.

The practice of states both within and without the international human rights treaty system is important. The practice of almost all states standing outside the treaty system having non-retroactivity of crimes and punishments in their constitutions and codes is of particular importance to the creation of customary international law. So too is the fact that the states that had particularly rejected legality during the twentieth century have now

may be limited to "citizen[s]"); ACHPR arts. 2 (distinction of nationality not generally made), 13 (right to participate in government may be limited to "citizen[s]"); Revised ArCHR arts. 3 (distinction of nationality not generally made), 24 (political rights may be limited to "citizen[s]").

360 Case Concerning the Arrest Warrant of 11 April 2000 (Democratic Republic of Congo v. Belgium), Judgment, ¶ 58 (ICJ, 14 February 2002).

361 ICJ Statute art. 38(1)(d).

362 Compare North Sea Continental Shelf Cases (Fed. Rep. of Germany v. Denmark, Fed. Rep. of Germany v. Netherlands), 1969 I.C.J. 3.

accepted it. A pattern of respect for legality in criminal law is reflected in the constitutions of restored Germany and Japan – these came into being before the current international human rights treaty system. It is finally reflected in more recent UN administration of territories such as East Timor and Kosovo. These indicate international practice that legality in criminal law is one of the international human rights to be promoted by the UN Charter.

International humanitarian law similarly protects the rights of nationals during non-international armed conflicts. This is true both of treaty law[363] and customary international humanitarian law.[364] This makes sense because it is most often nationals of the state in question who are affected by civil wars. Internal practice of states is a vital source for determining customary international humanitarian law for non-international conflicts.[365] In this sense, international humanitarian law resembles international human rights law, and in the case of non-retroactivity of crimes and punishments, they embody some of the same rules. By now, both international humanitarian law and international human rights law provide some limits on the criminal law of states.

Where state practice follows international humanitarian law in human rights areas – as where states accept and apply non-retroactivity of crimes and punishments in civil wars – this will generally constitute state practice following international human rights law as well. However, international humanitarian law is limited to situations of armed conflict and occupation. Therefore, more is needed to show that states consistently accept and apply any given rule as a matter of human rights law – that is, as a protection of persons in peacetime as well as wartime.

5.g. THE TRANSFORMATION OF LEGALITY IN NATIONAL LAW SINCE WORLD WAR II

Since the end of World War II, non-retroactivity of crimes and punishments has changed from a rule recognized by fewer than one-third of national constitutions to a rule contained in over three-fourths. Almost all other states

[363] Geneva Conventions (Nos. I-IV) common art. 3; Additional Protocol II, *passim*.

[364] 1 ICRC, CUSTOMARY IHL (RULES), *passim*, points out extensive customary international law rights for nationals which are protected during non-international armed conflicts. Indication that a customary rule applies in non-international armed conflicts generally immediately follow the statement of that rule.

[365] 2 (pts. 1 & 2) ICRC, CUSTOMARY IHL (PRACTICE), *passim*, provides extensive documentation from both internal and international state practice for the rules of international humanitarian law applicable in non-international conflicts set forth in 1 *id.*

recognize the rule by statute or as the result of undertaking international human rights treaty obligations.

The transformation has been particularly sharp in common law nations. As has been noted, few such states recognized the principle in their constitutions in the 1946–47 period. Admittedly, the constitutional material from that time probably underestimates the applicability of non-retroactivity as a principle of interpretation in common law countries. However, the theory of parliamentary supremacy in most of them meant that this principle of interpretation was subject to derogation by the legislature.[366] Today, all common law countries recognize the rule, most by constitutional law, but some by statute or adoption of an international human rights treaty.

The near-universal acceptance has also been striking among the decolonized states and other states that have attained independence since World War II. This has been a pattern from the independence constitution of the Philippines shortly after the war and the Constitution of India, adopted in 1950, a few years after independence and about a year after the adoption of the UDHR. Today, almost every generally recognized state created since World War II (except Brunei) accepts the general non-retroactivity of crimes and punishments by constitution, statute, or treaty. Thus the claim which is sometimes made that Western-inspired individual rights are not appropriate for all societies seems inapplicable to the non-retroactivity of crimes and punishments.

Similarly, the treatment of non-retroactivity of crimes and punishments by those states which had rejected it in the twentieth century is remarkable. Many states that rejected it for ideological reasons, particularly Fascism and Communism, have by now rejected those ideologies and accepted non-retroactivity. Yet even those states that continue to endorse Communism, such as the People's Republic of China and Cuba, have adopted non-retroactivity of crimes and punishments.

One can hardly doubt that today the non-retroactivity of crimes and punishments is a worldwide human rights rule recognized by the laws of the community of nations. As noted earlier, the evidence for personality of punishment and the prohibition of collective punishment is, perhaps, a bit less overwhelming than for non-retroactivity. Yet these too appear to be at least general principles recognized by the laws of the community of nations.

[366] See R. A. Melikan, *Pains and Penalties Procedure: How the House of Lords "Tried" Queen Caroline*, in DOMESTIC AND INTERNATIONAL TRIALS, 1700-2000: THE TRIAL IN HISTORY, VOLUME II 54, 57 (R. A. Melikan, ed., Manchester Univ. Press 2003).

6

Legality in the Modern International and Internationalized Criminal Courts and in the UN Trust Territories

Those designing and implementing the statutes of the various modern international and internationalized criminal courts and tribunals have adopted the principle of legality as a core principle. The way in which this has been done has, however, varied among the courts.

All of the international and internationalized criminal courts have accepted the rule of *nullum crimen sine lege* (nothing is a crime without [preexisting] law) in one way or another. The ad hoc UN Tribunals for the Former Yugoslavia and for Rwanda (ICTY and ICTR, respectively) and the Special Court for Sierra Leone (SCSL) have done so without a formal provision in their statutes. The Rome Statute of the International Criminal Court (ICC) has several provisions implementing the principle. Three of the internationalized courts (Kosovo, East Timor, and now Cambodia) adopted the principle by reference to major international documents on human rights, and the East Timor court incorporated it explicitly into the law. The Iraqi Special Tribunal incorporated the principle by reference to applicable Iraqi domestic law.

The principle of *nulla poena sine lege* (no penalty may be imposed without [preexisting] law) has been slightly more problematic. Some theorists have stated that *nulla poena* does not truly apply to international criminal law. However, the author has not found a single case in which the rule as stated in the International Covenant on Civil and Political Rights (ICCPR) and similar international documents has been violated, at least so far as permitting a penalty that was not available under a relevant law at the time the alleged crime was committed.

The statutes of the international and internationalized criminal courts and tribunals are in fact documents with very different statuses in international and national law. These include a multilateral treaty between states

(ICC), treaties between a state and the United Nations (e.g., the SCSL), acts of the UN Security Council (ICTY, ICTR), acts of UN administrators of local territories (East Timor and Kosovo), and an act of a national legislature still under international occupation (Iraq). Some of these statutes have now in fact been readopted through statutes and constitutional provisions under national law (East Timor [Timor-Leste] and Iraq).

The section on the internationalized courts includes a note on practice concerning legality in UN Trust Territories and the states that emerged from them.[1] This, like much of the material on the internationalized courts, reflects international organization and national practice concerning legality in territories under some degree of international supervision. It represents a different solution to some of the issues of criminal justice existing where there has been international and multinational control of territory in places such as East Timor, Kosovo, Iraq, and even Germany after World War II. This material is thus appropriate for inclusion in this chapter.

6.a. LEGALITY IN THE ICTY, ICTR, AND SCSL (AND THE NASCENT LEBANON TRIBUNAL)

The statutes of the International Criminal Tribunals for the Former Yugoslavia (ICTY) and for Rwanda (ICTR), as well as the Special Court for Sierra Leone (SCSL), do not contain explicit statements of the principle of legality. Nonetheless, *nullum crimen sine lege* was an important principle applied in drafting them and has been adopted as a rule of law in applying them.

These three courts are considered first because the ICTY and ICTR were the first of the modern international tribunals. The SCSL is considered with them because all three have international organization status. The ICTY and ICTR are subsidiary organs created by a primary organ of an international organization, the UN Security Council. The SCSL is an international organization in its own right, created by agreement between the United Nations and the state of Sierra Leone. This section will conclude with a note on the Special Tribunal for Lebanon (STL), whose formation was recently approved by the Security Council.[2]

[1] Chap. 6.b.ii.

[2] SC Res. 1757, UN Doc. S/RES/1757 (30 May 2007), with appended agreement between the United Nations and Lebanon and Statute of the STL.

6.a.i. *Non-retroactivity (*Nullum crimen, nulla poena sine lege*) in These Courts Generally*

In 1993, as the Balkan Wars were in progress, the UN Secretary-General, at the request of the Security Council, issued a report with a draft statute for an International Criminal Tribunal for the Former Yugoslavia.[3] This report framed the legality issue for international criminal tribunals, as it did with many other issues in international criminal law.

As to substantive crimes in the ICTY Statute, the Report of the UN Secretary-General stated that the statute included only crimes "undoubtedly" customary under international law. This was done "so that the problem of adherence of some but not all States to specific conventions does not arise,"[4] thus avoiding problems of *nullum crimen sine lege.* This assumes that, at the time of the atrocities in the former Yugoslavia, customary international criminal law in fact existed. The report does not, however, state that customary international law crimes are the only crimes that could be tried by an international court consistent with the principle of legality. Many of those participating in the Security Council debate and discussions concerning the creation of the ICTY agreed with the view that the ICTY should only prosecute crimes under existing international law, though some of the statements were ambiguous about whether this would encompass all of existing international criminal law or would be limited to existing customary (as opposed to treaty based) international criminal law.[5]

[3] Report of the Secretary-General pursuant to Paragraph 2 of Security Council Resolution 808, UN Doc. S/25704 (3 May 1993), available at http://www.un.org/icty/legaldoc-e/basic/statut/s25704.htm [hereinafter Sec-Gen's ICTY Rep.].

[4] Sec-Gen's ICTY Rep. ¶ 34.

[5] See Prosecutor v. Tadic, Decision on the Defence Motion on Interlocutory Appeal on Jurisdiction ¶ 143, Case No IT-94-1 (ICTY App. Ch., 2 October 1995), available at http://www.un.org/icty/tadic/appeal/decision-e/51002.htm (discussing statements of the United States, the United Kingdom, and France from Provisional Verbatim Record, SCOR, 3217th mtg., at 11, 15, 19, UN Doc. S/PV.3217 (25 May 1993)); Machteld Boot, GENOCIDE, CRIMES AGAINST HUMANITY, WAR CRIMES: NULLUM CRIMEN SINE LEGE AND THE SUBJECT MATTER JURISDICTION OF THE INTERNATIONAL CRIMINAL COURT ¶¶ 218–19, at pp. 235 & n.55, 236 & n.57, 237 & n.60 (Intersentia 2002) [hereinafter Boot] (quoting and citing statements of Russia, the Organization of the Islamic Conference, Canada, Venezuela, Brazil, Spain, and Mexico, though the quotations from Venezuela, Brazil, and Spain do not include direct references to current international criminal law; Canada referred specifically to crimes against humanity under "customary or conventional law").

The Secretary-General's ICTY Report expresses the *opinio juris* of the Secretariat as an organ of the United Nations, an international organization, that *nullum crimen sine lege* must be observed by a UN criminal tribunal, and perhaps international criminal tribunals generally. The Security Council resolution establishing the ICTY is practice of an international organization.[6] The resolution also expresses the *opinio juris* of the Security Council as a UN organ, because it accepts the secretary-general's report. One argument of this book is that international organizations now participate, along with states, in the process of creating and maintaining customary rules of law. Their acts may be used to show development of practice and of *opinio juris* (the opinion or belief that the acts are permissible or required by law, as the case may be).[7]

The ICTY Appeals Chamber has held that treaties ratified by the parties to a conflict may also be considered in deciding on the content of international criminal law applicable to persons involved in the conflict[8]; that is, treaty law may be part of the law that defines crimes. Where treaty law defining crimes might have been involved, the Appeals Chamber took care to note that the law had been embodied in the relevant domestic law at the relevant time.[9] The Appeals Chamber appears to have adopted the view that *nullum crimen* is a principle that it applies in determining whether the tribunal has jurisdiction, though the procedural posture of the case in which this first arose did not allow for square determination of this issue.[10]

The ICTR Statute included treaty-based crimes that might or might not have been customary, but applied to Rwanda through its ratification of the instruments involved and the adoption of the substance of the instruments into national law of Rwanda.[11] The SCSL has held that the recruitment of

[6] SC Res. 827, UN Doc. S/RES/827, with appended Statute of the International Tribunal.

[7] See discussion in Chap. 4(h, k) & Chap. 6.d.

[8] *Tadic*, Decision on Appeal on Juris. ¶¶ 143–45.

[9] *Id.* at ¶ 135.

[10] *Id.* at ¶¶ 143–45. See also Prosecutor v. Aleksovski, Appeals Judgement ¶¶ 126–27, Case No. IT-95-14/1 (ICTY App. Ch., 24 March 2000), available at http://www.un.org/icty/aleksovski/appeal/judgement/ale-asj000324e.pdf; Prosecutor v. Delalic, Appeals Judgement ¶¶ 178–80, Case No. IT-96-21 (ICTY App. Ch. 20 February 2001).

[11] Statute of the International Criminal Tribunal for Rwanda art. 4 [hereinafter ICTR Statute] (applying law under 1949 Geneva Conventions, common art. 3, and 1977 Protocol II), discussed in Prosecutor v. Akayesu, Judgement ¶ 617, Case No. ICTR-96-4-T (ICTR Trial Ch., 2 September 1998), available through ICTR Web site http://69.94.11.53/default.htm (relying on ratification of Additional Protocol II by Rwanda on 19 November 1984, and the adoption of its provisions into domestic criminal law, as well as the status of those provisions as customary international law).

child soldiers was a crime under customary international law during the Sierra Leone civil war,[12] although this proposition might be controversial to some.

Non-retroactivity of crimes includes non-retroactivity of complicitous acts that will incur criminal liability. A person may not be convicted for the criminal acts of others through the use of a newly stated type of liability (e.g., joint criminal enterprise) unless his or her own complicitous acts would have incurred criminal liability under the law existing at the time of the accused person's alleged complicity.

> [T]here is no reference in the Report of the Secretary-General limiting the jurisdiction *ratione personae* [personal jurisdiction] of the International Tribunal to forms of liability as provided by customary law. However, the principle of legality demands that the Tribunal shall apply the law which was binding upon individuals at the time of the acts charged. And, just as is the case in respect of the Tribunal's jurisdiction *ratione materiae*, that body of law must be reflected in customary international law.[13]

The emphasis is on whether the person's act was criminal under some binding law at the time done, no matter what legal theory is used to connect it to the acts of the principals to the crime.

There have certainly been controversies about what is covered by the statutes: the issue of when a crime has been previously defined remains a live and difficult issue.[14] This reflects difficulties in applying the principle of legality, not a rejection of the principle. William A. Schabas has written that the interpretation of legality of substantive criminal law in these tribunals reflects a "relatively relaxed,"[15] Nuremberg-style version of legality. This is

[12] Prosecutor v. Norman, Decision on Preliminary Motion Based on Lack of Jurisdiction, Case No. SCSL 04-14-AR72(E) (SCSL App. Ch., 31 May 2004), available at http://www.sc-sl.org/documents/scsl-04-14-AR72(E)-131-7383.pdf. The accused in this case died in custody before judgment.

[13] Prosecutor v. Milutinovic, Decision on Dragoljub Ojdanic's Motion Challenging Jurisdiction: Joint Criminal Enterprise ¶ 10 (bracketed material added; footnote omitted), Case No. IT-99-37-AR72 (ICTY App. Ch., 21 May 2003), available at http://www.un.org/icty/milutinovic/appeal/decision-e/030521.pdf.

[14] See Prosecutor v. Furundzija, Judgement ¶ 165-69, Case No. IT-95-17/1 (ICTY Tr. Ch., 10 December 1998), available at http://www.un.org/icty/furundzija/trialc2/judgement/fur-tj981210e.pdf (on rape); *Delalic*, Appeals Judgement ¶¶ 175–80 (on whether serious violations of common article 3 of the 1949 Geneva Conventions have been taken into customary international criminal law); *Norman* (crimes involving child soldiers).

[15] William A. Schabas, The UN International Criminal Tribunals: The Former Yugoslavia, Rwanda and Sierra Leone 63 (Cambridge Univ. Press 2006) [hereinafter Schabas, UN ICT].

correct to the extent that the statutes of the ad hoc tribunals do not contain *nullum crimen, nulla poena sine praevia lege scripta* (no act is a crime and no act may be punished without a previous written enactment; i.e., a statute). It is an overstatement if it is taken to suggest that the modern tribunals have permitted true retroactive crime creation, similar to the creation of the crime of aggressive war by the Nuremberg Tribunal.

As to sentencing, the statutes of all three tribunals allow terms of imprisonment. In the ICTY and ICTR, this is not specifically limited, and the ICTR has handed down a number of life sentences. The SCSL "shall impose upon a convicted person, other than a juvenile offender, imprisonment for a specified number of years."[16] This appears to prevent sentences denominated "life imprisonment" but not long, determinate sentences that would have the effect of imprisoning someone for life.

The SCSL has jurisdiction over certain crimes under Sierra Leone law as well as international humanitarian law.[17] Its sentencing provisions do not specifically require adherence to Sierra Leone sentencing law.[18] However, its provision on individual criminal responsibility states: "Individual criminal responsibility for the crimes referred to in article 5 [crimes under Sierra Leone law] shall be determined in accordance with the respective laws of Sierra Leone."[19] If this is interpreted to include the extent of criminal responsibility, as is most natural, then it would limit the sentences available for these crimes to those available under Sierra Leone law. It is difficult to imagine that the SCSL would impose sentences greater than those authorized under Sierra Leone law solely for crimes under that law. As will be seen, the same issue exists concerning the proposed Special Tribunal for Lebanon.[20]

[16] Special Court for Sierra Leone [SCSL] Statute art. 19(1), available at http://www.sc-sl.org/scsl-statute.html.

[17] SCSL Statute art. 5.

[18] SCSL Statute art. 19 (Penalties):

1. The Trial Chamber shall impose upon a convicted person, other than a juvenile offender, imprisonment for a specified number of years. In determining the terms of imprisonment, the Trial Chamber shall, as appropriate, have recourse to the practice regarding prison sentences in the International Criminal Tribunal for Rwanda and the national courts of Sierra Leone.
2. In imposing the sentences, the Trial Chamber should take into account such factors as the gravity of the offence and the individual circumstances of the convicted person.
3. In addition to imprisonment, the Trial Chamber may order the forfeiture of the property, proceeds and any assets acquired unlawfully or by criminal conduct, and their return to their rightful owner or to the State of Sierra Leone.

[19] SCSL Statute art. 6(5).

[20] See Chap. 6.a.v.

6.a.i.A. The Special Case of Contempt in the ICTY

The ICTY has convicted persons for contempt of the tribunal, which is not specifically provided for in its statute but is set forth in the ICTY Rules of Procedure and Evidence.[21] The ICTY Appeals Chamber has held that *nullum crimen sine lege* applies to contempt of the tribunal.[22]

The ICTY Appeals Chamber did not depend on the definitions of contempt that it has given at various times in the Rules of Procedure and Evidence for the *lege* on which it based the existence of the crime of contempt. These, it said, were procedural and could not be used to create new crimes.[23] Instead, it held that it had the inherent judicial power to punish persons for contempt since its creation.[24]

In deciding that it had the inherent power to punish for contempt, the Appeals Chamber considered "the usual sources of international law."[25] It first held that there was no relevant customary international law.[26] It rather deduced the power, and the definition of contempt, from "the general principles of law common to the major legal systems of the world, as developed and refined (where applicable) in international jurisprudence."[27] It found a very broad and deep history of contempt as an inherent power of common law courts.[28] It also found a trend in civil law countries toward creating statutory crimes similar to contempt and cited examples from Germany, France, Russia, and (interestingly, as a country that could be said to have a legal system different from either civil or common law) China.[29] It did not survey all civil law countries, and in particular, did not address the situation concerning contemptlike acts in the former Yugoslavia or its successor states or in the Netherlands, where the ICTY sits.

It also made reference to the practice of international courts and tribunals. It referred to the power of the International Military Tribunal at Nuremberg to punish "any Defendant or his Counsel" for "any contumacy."[30] It noted

[21] ICTY Rules of Procedure and Evidence [hereinafter ICTY RPE], R. 77 (existing in different forms from the first version of the RPE).

[22] Prosecutor v. Aleksovski (Appeal of Nobilo), Judgment on Appeal by Anto Nobilo against Finding of Contempt, Case No. IT-95-14/1-AR77 ¶ 38 (ICTY App. Ch., 30 May 2001).

[23] Prosecutor v. Tadic (Appeal of Vujin), Judgement on Allegations of Contempt against Prior Counsel, Milan Vujin, Case No. IT-94-1-A-R77 ¶¶ 19–24 (ICTY App. Ch., 27 February 2001).

[24] *Vujin* ¶¶ 13, 27–28.

[25] *Id.* at ¶ 13.

[26] *Id.* at ¶ 14.

[27] *Id.* at ¶ 15.

[28] *Id.* at ¶ 15–17.

[29] *Id.* at ¶¶ 15, 17 n.20.

[30] *Id.* at ¶ 14, citing Nuremberg Charter art. 18(c).

that three of the later Control Council Law No. 10 military tribunals, all of the United States, punished persons for contempt.[31] It also referred to the practice of the International Court of Justice and the ICTY's own prior practice, which authorized actions to ensure that "the exercise of the jurisdiction [which it possesses as an international judicial organ] . . . is not frustrated and that its basic judicial functions are safeguarded."[32] The Appeals Chamber did not specifically say that it was using the practice of other tribunals as part of the demonstration of the existence of a general principle of law. The Appeals Chamber noted that the IMT Charter mention of contumacy was "an international analogue available, by way of conventional international law."[33] However, the London Agreement and the IMT Charter are not applicable as treaty law in the ICTY. Using the international tribunal practice as instances that go to the building of a general principle of law is the most natural way to find that these matters were relevant to persons accused of contempt in an international criminal tribunal.

Together, this is evidence that there is a general principle of law that contempt can be a crime punishable by a criminal court. They are perhaps less convincing that the entire definition of contempt of court existed as a general principle of law of which the accused had notice at the time. Therefore, it might have been safer, from the point of view of legality, for the Appeals Chamber to have held that the specific implementation of

[31] *Vujin* ¶ 14 & n.14, citing as authority:

> "Trials of War Criminals Before the Nuernberg Military Tribunals under Control Council Law No 10": *US v Karl Brandt*, 27 June 1947, at 968-970 (where a prosecution witness assaulted one of the accused in court); *US v Joseph Altstoetter*, 17 July 1947, at 974–975, 978, 992 (where defence counsel and a private individual attempted improperly to influence an expert medical witness by making false representations, and mutilated an expert report in an attempt to influence the signatories of the report to join in altering it); and *US v Alfried Krupp von Bohlen und Halbach*, 21 Jan 1948, at 1003, 1005-1006, 1088, 1011 (where defence counsel staged a walk out, and then failed to appear, in protest of a ruling against their clients, but which conduct was ultimately dealt with on a disciplinary basis).

[32] *Vujin* ¶ 13 & n.11, citing as authority:

> *Nuclear Tests Case*, ICJ Reports 1974, pp 259-260, par 23, followed by the Appeals Chamber in *Prosecutor v Blaskic*, Case IT-95-14-AR108*bis*, Judgment on the Request of the Republic of Croatia for Review of the Decision of Trial Chamber II of 18 July 1997, 29 Oct 1997 ("*Blaskic Subpoena Decision*"), footnote 27 at par 25. See also *Northern Cameroons Case*, ICJ Reports 1963, p. 29.

[33] *Vujin*, para. 14.

contempt in the Rules of Procedure and Evidence at the time the accused acted provided accessible notice that his acts would be considered criminal. When the opinion is read as a whole, this conclusion would have been quite reasonable.[34]

There is also another issue which has arisen with regard to contempt in the ICTY. In an important decision that has not received sufficient notice, the ICTY Appeals Chamber punished for contempt journalists who revealed confidential information concerning a proceeding.[35] In this type of case, to comply with the principle of legality, it must be established that the ICTY has jurisdiction to prescribe (i.e., to define crimes) for persons who otherwise have no connection with the tribunal. That is, it is one thing to say that the ICTY has jurisdiction to prescribe contempt law for persons such as defendants, lawyers, and witnesses who are connected with the court. It is another to say that the ICTY has jurisdiction to define contempt law for all persons in the world, which is essentially what the tribunal does when it convicts journalists for revealing information. The issue of the extent of jurisdiction to prescribe is a matter of authority of international organizations that would require an inappropriately extended discussion here. What can be said here is that the decision of the ICTY to impose contempt on journalists is correct if but only if the ICTY had legitimate authority to impose its law on persons unconnected with the tribunal, and that notice requirements concerning the journalists were met.

From the beginning, the ICTY rule has set a maximum limit on the penalty for contempt available in the tribunal.[36] Thus, whenever it has been clear that the crime of contempt has been in existence, the penalty has been defined.

6.a.ii. *Legality as a Jurisdictional and Substantive Issue, Right of the Individual to Complain, and the International Legal Personality of the Individual*

The ICTY, ICTR, and SCSL all treat legality as an issue that the individual can raise as a matter of right in these international fora.[37] The cases deal

[34] *Id.*, esp. at ¶ 19 (noting that witness tampering and intimidation had specifically been added to ICTY RPE, R. 77 in January 1995; the acts complained of in this case began in 1997).

[35] *Prosecutor v. Marijacic*, Case No. IT-95-14-R77.2 (ICTY App. Ch., 10 March 2006).

[36] ICTY RPE, R. 77.

[37] See *Tadic*, Decision on Appeal on Juris.; Proscutor v. Hadzihasanovic, Decision on Interlocutory Appeal Challenging Jurisdiction in Relation to Command Responsibility

specifically with the legality issues of *nullum crimen* and the right to be tried in a tribunal that has been established by law. The international legal personality of the individual is developing here, even if it has not fully developed in the international system generally.[38]

The issue of legality has been treated as both jurisdictional and as a matter of substantive law. At least once, this has happened in the same case, where the issue of retroactivity of a criminal definition was treated as a matter of the subject matter jurisdiction of the court, whereas the issue of retroactivity of a type of criminal liability (joint criminal enterprise) was treated as a matter of substantive criminal law.[39]

6.a.ii.A. Claim of Violation of Non-retroactivity as Issue Individuals May Raise and Court Must Consider

Both the ICTY and the SCSL consider issues of legality as raising a challenge to the jurisdiction of the court over the acts charged.[40] The ICTY treats this as an issue of subject-matter jurisdiction:

¶¶ 10–36, Case No. IT-01-47-AR72 (ICTY App. Ch., 16 July 2003), available at http://www.un.org/icty/hadzihas/appeal/decision-e/030716.htm; *Akayesu*, Trial Judgement ¶¶ 611–17; Prosecutor v. Kanyabashi, Decision on Defence Motion on Jurisdiction, Case No. ICTR-96-15-T (ICTR Tr. Ch., 18 June 1997), available at http://69.94.11.53/default.htm [this case is still sub judice as of 2007]; *Norman*.

[38] See also Chap. 4(h, j) (on individual ability to raise legality issues in international human rights courts and commissions); Chap. 6.c.iii (on individual ability to raise legality issues in the ICC).

[39] *Milutinovic*, Decision on Dragoljub Ojdanic's Motion Challenging Jurisdiction: Joint Criminal Enterprise ¶ 10.

[40] *Hadzihasanovic*, Decision on Interlocutory Appeal Challenging Jurisdiction in Relation to Command Responsibility ¶¶ 10–36 (question whether command responsibility in non-international conflict was a crime under customary international law at time accused acted treated as jurisdictional), and *id.* Decision Pursuant to Rule 72(E) as to Validity of Appeal (ICTY App. Ch. Bench, 21 February 2003), available at http://www.un.org/icty/hadzihas/appeal/decision-e/030221.htm (holding that the appeal was jurisdictional); *Milutinovic*, Decision on Dragoljub Ojdanic's Motion Challenging Jurisdiction: Joint Criminal Enterprise ¶ 9 & n.28, citing Prosecutor v. Vasiljevic, Trial Judgment ¶¶ 193ff., Case No. IT-98-32-T (ICTY Trial Chamber, 29 November 2002), available at http://www.un.org/icty/vasiljevic/trialc/judgement/vas021129.pdf (the *Milutinovic* Appeals Chamber noted this matter had not been appealed); Prosecutor v. Blaskic, Appeals Judgement ¶¶ 140–41, Case No. IT-95-14-A (ICTY App. Ch, 29 July 2004), available at http://www.un.org/icty/blaskic/appeal/judgement/bla-aj040729e.pdf; *Norman* (both majority and dissent treated the question of whether recruitment of child soldiers was a crime under customary international law at the time Norman allegedly acted as a question of jurisdiction).

> The scope of the Tribunal's jurisdiction *ratione materiae* [subject matter jurisdiction] may therefore be said to be determined both by the Statute... and by customary international law, insofar as the Tribunal's power to convict an accused of any crime listed in the Statute depends upon its existence *qua* custom at the time this crime was allegedly committed.[41]

The next paragraph indicated that this issue was not a matter of personal jurisdiction, but "the principle of legality demands that the Tribunal shall apply the law which was binding upon individuals at the time of the acts charged."[42] This includes whether, at the time of the acts charged, those acts could subject one to criminal liability for the acts of others. In other words, legality is also a principle of substantive criminal law on which individuals can rely.

The SCSL has allowed a defendant to challenge, as a matter of jurisdiction, the existence of the crime of recruitment of child soldiers under customary international law at the time of the acts alleged. This *nullum crimen* claim has been rejected on its merits, on the ground that the crime existed in customary international law at the time.[43]

The ICTR has discussed the fact that its statute authorizes prosecutions for violations of Additional Protocol II of 1977 to the Geneva Conventions, which may contain provisions that are not customary international law. The court allowed an accused to raise this issue as a matter of jurisdiction and rejected the claim on its merits, because Rwanda had adopted the relevant protocol and had criminalized the relevant acts in domestic law, and because the crime in question was in fact a crime under customary international law.[44]

These courts have allowed defendants to argue that they (the courts) were not established by law. These claims have been rejected on their merits, as matters of the jurisdiction of the tribunals.[45] The courts have heard challenges claiming that they were not "impartial," again rejecting the claims on their merits.[46]

[41] *Milutinovic*, Decision on Dragoljub Ojdanic's Motion Challenging Jurisdiction: Joint Criminal Enterprise ¶ 9 (bracketed material added).

[42] *Milutinovic*, Decision on Dragoljub Ojdanic's Motion Challenging Jurisdiction: Joint Criminal Enterprise ¶ 10.

[43] *Norman, passim.*

[44] *Akayesu*, Trial Judgement ¶¶ 611–17.

[45] *Tadic* ¶¶ 26–63; *Kanyabashi, passim*; *Norman.*

[46] E.g., *Furundzija*, Trial Judgement ¶¶ 164–216.

6.a.ii.B. Argument That Court Created by an International Organization Should Not Examine Whether a Prosecution Is Prohibited by Rule of *Nullum crimen*, so Long as the Crime Is Named in the Organic Documents of the Court

William A. Schabas argues that the better view is that international courts may not question whether crimes named in their organic documents were crimes applying to those within their jurisdiction at the relevant times.[47] When a crime is set forth in the organic documents of such a court, the court has no authority to question whether the crime can be applied to any person – specifically to determine whether the act involved was a crime under law applicable to a given person at the time of the act. This essentially encapsulates the American and Soviet view at the beginning of the negotiations that led to the Nuremberg Charter.

Schabas argues that international organizations may define crimes that have not yet passed into customary international law. International organizations, he suggests, need not follow any rules of international law in defining crimes except those which are peremptory norms of international law – i.e., *jus cogens*.[48]

There are several responses to this view. First, and perhaps most important, international organizations are not generally free to act in violation of applicable customary international law, especially customary international human rights law.[49] They are international legal persons – different from states in significant ways, and some of the rules controlling their behavior are different – but nothing in their creation suggests they are generally exempt from the rule of customary human rights law. This is consistently recognized in the practice of the Security Council and the modern international criminal tribunals. Specifically, all of the courts have applied the principles of non-retroactivity in their rulings.[50] One might say that what states cannot separately do to individuals they cannot do together through the guise of an international organization. Practice concerning legality in these courts

[47] Schabas, UN ICT at 63, 66.

[48] See Schabas, UN ICT at 67.

[49] Cf. Prosecutor v. Tadic (Appeal of Vujin), Appeal Judgement, Case No. IT-94-1-A-AR77 (ICTY App. Ch., 27 February 2001) (fourth introductory "Considering" clause), available at http://www.un.org/icty/tadic/appeal/vujin-e/vuj-aj010227e.pdf, discussed in Salvatore Zappalà, Human Rights in International Criminal Proceedings 154 & n.8 (Oxford Univ. Press 2003), on the requirement that international criminal tribunals follow "imperative" norms of international human rights law, in this case the right to appeal that appears in the International Covenant on Civil and Political Rights art. 14 (hereinafter ICCPR).

[50] See cases discussed in other parts of Chap. 6.a.

has reflected more closely the views of the French, particularly André Gros, than those of the Americans and Soviets at the London Conference.[51]

Second, under the current statements of law by international criminal courts and tribunals, matters that were not customary international law crimes at the time may in fact be punished if they were crimes under other law applicable to the actor at the time of the action.[52] One does not need to destroy the doctrine of non-retroactivity of crime creation to broaden the definition of crimes that a court can try beyond customary international law crimes.

Third, so long as the body creating the court also has the authority to define crimes in a given situation, there is no problem with defining crimes that will be enforced in the future. Thus, as will be seen below, the Security Council allowed the UN administrations in Kosovo and East Timor to define crimes that would be enforced in the future.[53] The courts, however, were bound to apply all criminal law only in accordance with international human rights, including the rules of non-retroactivity.[54]

Fourth, nothing in what the Security Council has passed suggests that it intended to prohibit the courts that it has created or that have been created pursuant to its authority from applying the defenses of *nullum crimen* and *nulla poena*. Challenging the retroactive application (and only the retroactive application) of criminal definitions is not challenging the "constitutionality" of the criminal definitions.[55]

Fifth, the Security Council has not claimed the authority to act in violation of customary international human rights law. Perhaps at some time it will encounter a situation in which acts of great evil, not prohibited by any criminal law when done, prevent the maintenance or restoration of international peace and security because they have not been addressed. If this situation is reached, the Security Council may need specifically to address its authority to evade customary international human rights law.

Sixth, there are those like Judge Theodore Meron who argue forcefully that non-retroactivity of criminal enactments has already become *jus cogens*, a peremptory, non-derogable norm of international law.[56] This book con-

[51] See generally Chap. 3.b.ii.

[52] *Akayesu*, Trial Judgement ¶¶ 611–17; Prosecutor v. Galic, Judgement ¶¶ 16–25, 28–32, Case No. IT-98-29 (ICTY Tr. Ch., 5 December 2003), available at http://www.un.org/icty/galic/trialc/judgement/gal-tj031205e.pdf.

[53] See Chap. 6.b.

[54] See *id.*

[55] Schabas, UN ICT at 64–65.

[56] Theodore Meron, War Crimes Law Comes of Age 244 (Oxford Univ. Press 1998) [hereinafter Meron].

cludes that, at very least, the principle of non-retroactivity of crimes and punishments is beginning to emerge as a *jus cogens* norm.[57]

Finally, there is one way of reading Schabas's objection that would bring his position closer to the position advanced here. He points out that some of the rhetoric of these tribunals does allow them to go beyond customary international criminal law.[58] One might say he accepts the principle of non-retroactivity as being something like *nullum crimen, nulla poena sine praevia iure* (in Bassiouni's formulation). Schabas would state that more than customary international law may make up *praevia iure.* This much would be acceptable. Non-retroactivity as currently practiced allows for prosecution under non-customary rules of criminal law (e.g., rules created by treaty law), so long as those rules were applicable to the actor at the time of the act alleged.

6.a.iii. *Legality of Courts*

6.a.iii.A. Claims That These Courts Are Not Established by Law: Powers of International Organizations, the International Legal Personality of Individuals, and the Issue of Special Courts

As mentioned, these courts have treated the question of whether they have been established by law as matters of jurisdiction, and they have accepted their creation as valid.[59] This has consequence for the view of international organizations as legal entities with authority over individuals, and hence for the international legal personality of both international organizations and individuals. In the cases of the ICTY and ICTR, the Security Council asserted the authority, as a matter of legal right, to establish international criminal courts to try and to punish individuals as part of its authority to restore and maintain international peace and security.[60] This direct authority over individuals may or may not have been in the mental contemplation of those who framed the UN Charter in San Francisco or who participated in its ratification by its various state members thereafter. It was not explicitly included in the charter. Neither, however, do the adopted texts explicitly exclude this authority. In addition to earning judicial acceptance, this view of the lawfulness of criminal court creation by the United Nations has become part of the generally accepted repertoire of UN practice.[61] As will be

[57] Chap. 7.i.

[58] Schabas, UN ICT at 65–66.

[59] *Tadic*, Decision on Appeal on Juris., ¶¶ 26–63; *Kanyabashi, passim*; *Norman.*

[60] See *Tadic*, Decision on Appeal on Juris., ¶¶ 26–48; *Kanyabashi*, ¶¶ 17–29. This issue has been discussed at greater length in Sec-Gen's ICTY Rep.

[61] See Chap. 6.b.i (on creation of internationalized courts).

seen, this has been extended into the sphere of participating in the creation of national (East Timor, Kosovo) criminal courts.[62]

Indeed, in other contexts the Security Council has asserted authority to impose non-criminal sanctions (e.g., freezing of assets) on individuals without giving the individuals the right to defend themselves as they can in the criminal tribunals.[63] Even though they do not involve criminal liability, these resolutions raise their own questions for human rights, which cannot be discussed in full here.[64]

The ICTY and ICTR have considered challenges to their creation as special courts or courts created after the crimes in question and rejected them on their merits.[65] The ICTY, ICTR, and SCSL have considered challenges to their creation as beyond the authority of the United Nations and rejected them on their merits as well.[66]

Schabas's concern about "constitutional" challenges to Security Council acts is better placed here,[67] though ultimately unconvincing. He is right that acceptance of a claim that a court was not created by law is a challenge to the actions of the international organization establishing it as being ultra vires its own organic documents. The ICTY Trial Chamber in fact refused to consider the right of the Security Council to bring it into existence, though the ICTY Appeals Chamber overruled it on this point.[68] Although Schabas is correct about what occurs when a court considers a challenge to its own existence, the decision of international criminal tribunals to undertake such investigations is by now well accepted and reflects a willingness of these tribunals to consider legal questions important to human rights.

Even the Nuremberg Tribunal felt the need to justify its own existence. It discussed the right of the Allies to do together what any of them could do separately (i.e., create a military tribunal).[69] Modern international courts have followed this precedent by allowing accused persons to challenge their establishment. Thus, as already pointed out, the ICTY Appeals Chamber specifically adopted the view that an international criminal tribunal could

[62] See *id.*

[63] See, e.g., Security Council Resolutions 1267, 1373, 1390 (sanctions on persons accused of terrorist involvement).

[64] The issue of when individual sanctions ought to be considered criminal punishment is addressed briefly in Chap. 5.c.viii.

[65] *Tadic*, Decision on Appeal of Juris., ¶¶ 45–48, 61–64; *Kanyabashi*, ¶¶ 33–36.

[66] *Tadic*, Decision on Appeal on Juris.; *Kanyabashi*; *Norman*.

[67] Cf. Schabas, UN ICT at 66.

[68] *Tadic*, Decision on Appeal on Juris., ¶¶ 4–48 (ICTY App. Ch., 2 October 1995), revising on this ground Decision on the Defence Motion on Jurisdiction, ¶¶ 1–40 (ICTY Trial Ch., 10 August 1995), available at http://www.un.org/icty/tadic/trialc2/decision-e/100895.htm.

[69] Nuremberg Judgment, 1 IMT, TRIAL at 218.

indeed examine its own establishment to determine whether it was established according to law.[70]

The real innovation in accepting challenges to the lawfulness of courts is the growth of the international legal personality of individuals. The real issue is the right of individuals to test whether they are being imprisoned by an entity, whether the United Nations or a state, that is acting beyond its legitimate authority. The challenge to the lawfulness of the establishment of a court is one device to test the legality of a person's detention. It thus serves a purpose analogous to the writ of habeas corpus in common law systems, and other procedural devices in other systems, ensuring that detentions in criminal matters are lawful.

The right to have the legality of one's detention determined is recognized in treaty law.[71] It is also recognized by the Secretary-General of the United Nations, in his ICTY Report,[72] and by the Security Council in its adoption of the report.[73]

There is no real alternative to judicial self-examination if individuals are entitled to challenge the legality of their detention by international criminal law bodies. There is no moral or legal value in allowing an illegitimately established tribunal to convict and imprison persons. It is also difficult to see the moral or legal value of restricting the legal personality of those individuals whom the international legal system seeks to imprison to the extent that they cannot ensure the legality of the process against them.

6.a.iii.B. Creating New Jurisdictions Retrospectively

The above material presents issues of court creation and grants of jurisdiction that continue to have vitality, that is, that criminal courts must be independent, impartial, and created by law. In its strongest form, this requires that a jurisdiction be "previously" established by law – that is, established before the commission of the allegedly criminal act.[74] This last

[70] *Tadic*, Decision on Appeal on Juris., ¶¶ 4–48, revising on this ground Decision on the Defence Motion on Jurisdiction, ¶¶ 1–40 (ICTY Trial Ch.).

[71] ICCPR art. 9; European Convention on Human Rights and Fundamental Freedoms art. 5 [hereinafter ECHR]; American Convention on Human Rights art. 7 [hereinafter ACHR]; Revised Arab Charter on Human Rights art. 14 (2004); cf. African Charter of Human and Peoples Rights arts. 6, 7(1)(a) (creates right against unlawful detention but does not specifically require existence of remedy for illegal detention) [hereinafter ACHPR].

[72] Sec.-Gen's ICTY Rep. ¶¶ 16, 18–30.

[73] SC Res. 827.

[74] See ACHR art. 8(1). Accord, Christoph J. N. Safferling, Towards an International Criminal Procedure 88 (2001) [hereinafter Safferling] ("it can be said that international

rule, however, is not a requirement for the establishment of international criminal courts and tribunals.

The creation of new jurisdictions to try previously defined crimes has become accepted in international criminal law. The requirement of a preexisting jurisdiction continues to exist in some national laws and in one regional human rights system.[75] However, this particular jurisdictional interpretation of legality has been rejected as a requirement of international criminal law in both national and international tribunals.[76]

The Nuremberg[77] and Tokyo[78] tribunals were created exclusively to deal with crimes that had already happened. The United States, a leader in the effort to create the Nuremberg Tribunal, reversed its post–World War I position on the legality of new jurisdictions.[79] The ICTY,[80] ICTR,[81] and

human rights law considers it necessary for a criminal tribunal and its competence to have been established by a legislative act before a criminal offence occurs"). Safferling objectively points out that the American Convention on Human Rights, art. 8, requires a preexisting tribunal, whereas the International Covenant on Civil and Political Rights, art. 15, does not have such a requirement, especially in light of the fact that a Chilean proposal to include this requirement in the ICCPR was rejected. *Id.*, 87-88, citing UN Doc. E/CN.4/SR.110, 4.

[75] See ACHR, art. 8; discussion of national constitutions in Chap. 5.d; Safferling at 87–88.

[76] See national constitutions cited in Chap. 5.d; charters and statutes of international tribunals cited in notes below; *Tadic*, Decision on Appeal on Juris.; Sharon A. Williams, Article 11, *Jurisdiction ratione temporis*, in COMMENTARY ON THE ROME STATUTE OF THE INTERNATIONAL CRIMINAL COURT: OBSERVERS' NOTES, ARTICLE BY ARTICLE ¶ 2, pp. 323–24 (Otto Triffterer ed., Nomos Verlagsgesellschaft 1999) [hereinafter OBSERVERS' NOTES]. Contra, Safferling at 88.

[77] London Agreement of 8 August 1945, preamble, 59 Stat. 1544 [hereinafter London Agreement], with annexed Charter of the International Military Tribunal arts. 1, 6 [hereinafter Nuremberg Charter].

[78] Special Proclamation by the Supreme Commander of the Allied Powers, Establishment of an International Military Tribunal for the Far East, 19 January 1946 [hereinafter MacArthur Proclamation] with annexed Charter of the International Military Tribunal for the Far East arts. 1, 5 [hereinafter IMTFE Charter].

[79] Compare Lansing and Scott, Memorandum of Reservations Presented by the Representatives of the United States to the Report of the Commission on Responsibilities, reprinted in LEON FRIEDMAN, 1 THE LAW OF WAR 860, 860–67 (opposing creation of new jurisdiction after World War I on ex post facto grounds) with REPORT OF ROBERT H. JACKSON UNITED STATES REPRESENTATIVE TO THE INTERNATIONAL CONFERENCE ON MILITARY TRIALS: LONDON, 1945, *passim* (Washington: U.S. Gov't Printing Off. 1949) [submitted by Justice Jackson to the Secretary of State 15 December 1947] (setting out U.S. efforts to create the Nuremberg Tribunal). See ARIEH J. KOCHAVI, PRELUDE TO NUREMBERG: ALLIED WAR CRIMES POLICY AND THE QUESTION OF PUNISHMENT (Chapel Hill: Univ. of N.C. Press 1998).

[80] ICTY Statute art. 8.

[81] ICTR Statute art. 1.

SCSL[82] were all created principally[83] or exclusively to deal with crimes that had already happened. The Special Tribunal for Lebanon is being created to deal with a specific assassination, that of former prime minister Rafiq Hariri on 14 February 2005, and related crimes.[84] The internationalized chambers or panels in Kosovo and East Timor were created at least in part to deal with offenses that had already occurred when they were formed; the Iraqi Special Tribunal was created to deal with crimes committed during the former Saddam Hussein regime[85]; and the Extraordinary Chambers in Cambodia are being created to deal with crimes committed during the former Khmer Rouge regime.

In contrast, the International Criminal Court is without jurisdiction over cases arising before its creation.[86] Yet it may (through Security Council referral or retroactive state acceptance of jurisdiction[87]) obtain jurisdiction over some persons who were outside its jurisdiction to prescribe or to adjudicate when they acted and jurisdiction over some criminal acts that were outside its jurisdiction at the time they were committed.

Retroactive court creation has an important danger, the potential for targeting specific individuals or groups for prosecution and punishment. Ad hoc international tribunals are generally brought into existence only after official reports have identified crimes and/or possible suspects.[88] This is yet another reason why non-retroactivity of crime creation is a vital safeguard in international criminal justice, both as a protection for potential accused persons and as a guarantee to the public that prosecutions will have a legal, rather than merely a political, basis.

6.a.iv. *Retroactive Re-characterization of Crime in These Tribunals?*

Language from cases in the ICTY and SCSL might be seen to reopen the argument about retroactive re-characterization in the post–World War II

[82] SCSL Statute art. 1(1).

[83] The cases arising out of ethnic cleansing in Kosovo arose after the creation of the ICTY. See, e.g., Prosecutor v. Milosevic, Indictment, IT-02-54 (24 May 1999) available at http://www.un.org/icty/indictment/english/mil-ii990524e.htm.

[84] Report of the Secretary-General on the establishment of a special tribunal for Lebanon ¶¶ 11–26, UN Doc. S/2006/893 (15 November 2006).

[85] Statute of the Iraqi Special Tribunal arts. 1 & 10 (created by the then-existing Coalition Provisional Authority, 10 December 2003, available at http://www.cpa-iraq.org/human_rights/Statute.htm (Web site of the former Coalition Provisional Authority).

[86] Rome Statute of the International Criminal Court art. 11 [hereinafter ICC Statute].

[87] ICC Statute arts. 12, 13.

[88] E.g., Report of the Secretary-General on the establishment of a special tribunal for Lebanon ¶ 10, UN Doc. S/2006/893 (15 November 2006).

prosecutions.[89] This argument posits that it is acceptable to change the name of a crime within the international legal system[90] or to take criminal acts from one legal system (applicable to the actor at the time of the crime) into another legal system.[91] The arguments of the ICTY and SCSL appear to accept the possibility of retroactive re-characterization of behavior (as criminal under international as well as national law) as consistent with the principle of legality.[92] However, the acts re-characterized must actually be crimes carrying individual criminal responsibility in the appropriate legal system; the cases in the modern tribunals do not permit the retroactive criminalization of international wrongs bearing only state responsibility or retroactive criminalization of moral wrongs.

International criminal courts have not applied the strictest definition of legality, the rule that there must be a prior written criminal statute specifically encompassing the act charged (*nullum crimen, nulla poena sine praevia lege scripta*), to international criminal law. Both the ICTY and the SCSL merely ask whether the act of the accused was a crime as generally understood at the time of the offense charged:

> [a]s to foreseeability, the conduct in question is the concrete conduct of the accused; he must be able to appreciate that the conduct is criminal in the sense generally understood, without reference to any specific provision. As to accessibility, in the case of an international tribunal such as this, accessibility does not exclude reliance being placed on a law which is based on custom.[93]

This clearly rejects the requirement that there be a specific text naming a crime before the principle of legality can be met. Thus, crimes may be defined by customary international law.

[89] See Chap. 3.c.i.

[90] Nuremberg Judgment, 1 IMT, TRIAL at 254 (acts being both "War Crimes" and newly named "Crimes against Humanity"). See also *Rauter Case*, 14 UNWCC, Law Reports of Trials of War Criminals 89, 119–20 (Netherlands Special Ct. of Cass. 12 January 1949); Comment of André Gros, Minutes of Conference Session, 23 July 1945 [Doc. XLIV]; Comment of Gros, Minutes of Conference Session, 24 July 1945 [Doc. XLVII] published in REP. OF JACKSON at 328, 334–35, 360 (during the London Conference that prepared London Agreement and the Nuremberg Charter).

[91] See Chap. 3.c.i, citing United States v. Ohlendorff (Einsatzgruppen Case), in 4 TRIALS OF WAR CRIMINALS BEFORE THE NUERNBERG MILITARY TRIBUNALS UNDER CONTROL COUNCIL LAW No. 10 [hereinafter T.W.C.] 411, 497 (U.S. Military Tribunal, 10 April 1948) ("[m]urder, torture, enslavement and similar crimes which heretofore were enjoined only by the respective nations now fall within the prescription of the family of nations").

[92] See *Furundzija*, Trial Judgement ¶¶ 165–69 (on rape); *Delalic*, Appeals Judgement ¶¶ 178–80; *Norman*.

[93] *Hadzihasanovic*, Decision on Interlocutory Appeal Challenging Jurisdiction in Relation to Command Responsibility ¶ 34; accord, *Norman* ¶ 25.

This argument goes further, however. Mere appreciation of conduct as "criminal in the sense generally understood," is a weak requirement that might allow for reclassification of crimes, both within the international system of criminal law and between national and international crimes.

Retroactive re-characterization has not often been explicitly treated in discussion of legality. One author who did so in some detail and accepted it as consistent with legality is Judge Theodore Meron,[94] though he did not explicitly name this as a separate way of dealing with issues of legality. In considering the criminalization of Common Article 3 of the Geneva Conventions and Additional Protocol II, he pointed out that the provisions "are treaty obligations binding on Rwanda, that they clearly proscribe certain acts, and that those acts are also prohibited by the criminal law of Rwanda, albeit in different terms."[95] He accepted the proposition that the acts prohibited by these treaty provisions were criminal in both national and international law when committed.

Without referring to penalties existing under international law,[96] he argued that they are not being subject to retroactive penal sanctions "if the penalties do not exceed those previously established by their national states,"[97] which in the case of Rwanda was death. Therefore nothing in the ICTR Statute could violate the requirements in ICCPR Article 15(1) of previous prohibition of acts and no retroactive increase in penalties.[98] Note that Judge Meron would not require that acts that were clearly customary international law crimes at the time committed be punished at the level prescribed by national law.

M. Cherif Bassiouni, in contrast, appears to treat re-characterization as an example of analogy.[99] The core element of the re-characterization process as practiced, however, is that the act involved was criminal under some law before it was committed. This is stricter than the true civil law analogical process, which allows some acts that are outside a statutory criminal definition to be treated as crimes. To preserve legality in international criminal law, loose references to analogy cannot permit application of international criminal law to acts that were outside the scope of any applicable criminal law when committed.

[94] Meron at 244–48.
[95] *Id.* at 245.
[96] See *id.* at 246: "The Geneva Conventions define offenses but leave it to the contracting states to determine penal sanctions."
[97] *Id.*
[98] *Id.*
[99] Cf. M. Cherif Bassiouni, Crimes Against Humanity in International Criminal Law 158-59 (2d rev. ed., Kluwer Law Int'l 1999).

If retroactive re-characterization occurs, care must be taken in assignment of penalties, as Judge Meron pointed out. A penalty greater than that available under the law that forbade the act at the time it was committed would violate the principle of *nulla poena sine lege.*[100] The cases in which the retroactive re-characterization rhetoric has been used in the modern tribunals, however, do not concern acts that were clearly crimes only under national law at the time committed; or at least the courts have also held that the acts involved were crimes under customary international law when they were performed.[101] Therefore this issue has not arisen squarely.

The possibility of re-characterization from a national to an international crime affects the debate over superior orders, duress and similar defenses, and sentencing policies. Essentially, the process allows reliance on an existing national crime to ensure that the principle of legality is observed.

Sometimes these cases arise in the context of a government policy that encourages atrocity. These policies have included the Nazi German *Führerprinzip*, the Rwandan extremist Hutu policy of attacking Tutsis, and the East German Communist policy of shooting persons attempting to cross the Berlin Wall.[102] Such a policy does not override the existence of national criminal law against crimes such as murder, at least so long as that law is not specifically repealed or made inapplicable to these situations. It emphatically does not override existing international criminal law.

In form, this accurately describes the state of the law. In practice, however, it may not reflect the actual pressures brought to bear on a person who commits a criminal act. For example, in Rwanda, many of those killed in the bloodletting of 1994 were moderate Hutus who did not approve of or wish to participate in the genocide against the Tutsis. One can imagine a Rwandan Hutu reasonably believing that death would be the consequence of nonparticipation in the slaughter: this is one of the most terrible aspects of the events. This example illustrates why duress can be a defense under the

[100] See Meron at 246; Chap. 7.c.iii.

[101] See, e.g., *Akayesu* ¶¶ 611–17; *Furundzija*, Trial Judgement ¶¶ 165–69.

[102] See K.-H.W. v. Germany, Eur. Ct. H.R. App. No. 37201/97, ¶¶ 10-33, 71 (22 March 2001) (on the policy of shooting persons attempting to cross the Berlin wall), discussed in Ward N. Fedinandusse, Direct Application of International Criminal Law in National Courts 244–49 (TMC Asser 2006). Note that this case came out of the national courts of the reunified Germany, not from an international criminal tribunal. Cf. United States v. Von Leeb ("The High Command Case"), Opinion and Judgment, 11 T.W.C. 462, 508 (USMT V, 27 October 1948), quoting from German Military Penal Code (1872) art. 47, and its 1940 revision, which changed *civil* to *general*, and from an unnamed article of Goebbels, Voelkischer Beobachter, 28 May 1944 (no page given) to the effect that soldiers are not exempt from punishment for acts in violation of international usages of war; *Einsatzgruppen Case*, 4 T.W.C. at 463; both discussed at Chap. 3.c.i above.

Statute of the International Criminal Court (ICC) and why superior orders can serve as a reason in the ICC for mitigating sentences.[103]

The facts of many of the ICTY, ICTR, and SCSL cases, however, have not required actual retroactive re-characterization, at least in the opinion of the tribunals deciding the cases.[104] One example, however, does require the use of this technique. This is the situation where criminal liability has been alleged on the basis of "joint criminal enterprise,"[105] which is a new name for complicity in criminal law, but includes many acts which have long constituted criminal complicity in international and national criminal systems.

6.a.v. *Note on Legality in the Special Tribunal for Lebanon*

In mid-2007, the UN Security Council moved to establish a Special Tribunal for Lebanon (STL) to try persons suspected in the assassination of former Lebanese Prime Minister Rafiq Hariri and related crimes.[106] The Security Council intends that this tribunal will be operated by the United Nations in consultation with the government of Lebanon. The substantive criminal law of the tribunal will be Lebanese.[107] The STL therefore represents a slightly different international model for court creation than the previous tribunals.

The STL will have jurisdiction only over crimes defined under Lebanese law.[108] Because Lebanese law includes the non-retroactivity of crimes and punishments,[109] that rule should be read into the law of the statute. Unfortunately, that rule is not explicit in the STL Statute. In particular, the sentencing provision of the STL Statute merely states that Lebanese sentencing "practice" will be taken into account.[110] However, with the combination of substantive Lebanese criminal law being applicable in the tribunal, the recognition of human rights generally and non-retroactivity in particular in the other modern international criminal tribunals, and the recognition of non-retroactivity of crimes and punishments in the ICCPR, to which Lebanon is a party, the maximum sentence that the STL may issue for a vio-

[103] ICC Statute arts. 31(1)(d).
[104] See, e.g., *Akayesu* ¶¶ 611–17; *Furundzija*, Trial Judgement ¶¶ 165–69; *Norman*.
[105] See *Milutinovic*, Decision on Dragoljub Ojdanic's Motion Challenging Jurisdiction: Joint Criminal Enterprise ¶ 10.
[106] SC Res. 1757, UN Doc. S/RES/1757 (30 May 2007), with appended agreement between the United Nations and Lebanon and Statute of the STL.
[107] STL Statute art. 6.
[108] *Id.*
[109] Lebanon Code Pénal arts. 1–3.
[110] STL Statute art. 24.

lation of Lebanese law should not exceed the maximum sentence allowable under Lebanese law.

6.b. LEGALITY IN THE INTERNATIONALIZED TRIBUNALS AND A NOTE ON LEGALITY IN INTERNATIONALLY SUPERVISED TRUST TERRITORIES

6.b.i. *The Internationalized Tribunals*

The organic documents of the "internationalized" criminal tribunals (Kosovo, East Timor, Cambodia, and Iraq) go beyond the statutes of the ad hoc tribunals in protecting against retroactive criminalization. The first three tribunals at least incorporated by reference human rights documents requiring implementation of both parts of the legality principle of *nullum crimen* and *nulla poena*. The organic document of the Iraqi Special Tribunal used the law applicable at the time of the crime as its substantive law.

The UN Interim Administration in Kosovo (UNMIK) proclaimed:

> 1.3 In exercising their functions, all persons undertaking public duties or holding public office in Kosovo shall observe internationally recognized human rights standards, as reflected in particular in:
>
> *The Universal Declaration on Human Rights* of 10 December 1948;
>
> *The European Convention for the Protection of Human Rights and Fundamental Freedoms* of 4 November 1950 and the Protocols thereto;
>
> *The International Covenant on Civil and Political Rights* of 16 December 1966 and the *Protocols* thereto;
>
> ...
>
> *The International Convention on the Rights of the Child* of 20 December 1989.
>
> 1.4 No person undertaking public duties or holding public office in Kosovo shall discriminate against any person on any ground such as sex, race, colour, language, religion, political or other opinion, natural, ethnic or social origin, association with a national community, property, birth or other status. In criminal proceedings, the defendant shall have the benefit of the most favourable provision in the criminal laws which were in force in Kosovo between 22 March 1989 and the date of the present regulation.[111]

[111] UN Interim Administration Mission in Kosovo UNMIK Regulation No. 2000/59, UN Doc. UNMIK/REG/2000/59, Amending UNMIK Regulation No. 1999/24 [10 June 1999] On the

Here we have adoption (or incorporation by reference) of multiple human rights instruments into the law that courts will use to govern a local population, proclaimed by the Special Representative of the Secretary-General of the United Nations, claiming authority pursuant to a Security Council resolution.[112]

Interestingly, the documents incorporated include a General Assembly declaration as well as three treaties, one regional and two universal. Once the legitimacy of the UN administration to proclaim this law is admitted, there can be no objection to the legislative adoption of human rights standards from other texts. However, the substance of these treaties is not applied here as treaty law, but as law incorporated into the "domestic" law of Kosovo – that is, the law for Kosovo as prescribed by the UN administration.

The UN Transitional Administrator for East Timor (UNTAET) originally placed a similar provision in the UNTAET Regulations. This regulation relied on the same international human rights instruments as the Kosovo documents, except that the ECHR was not relied on and the "mercy principle" in the paragraph quoted previously was not included.[113] Explicit recognition of the principle of legality was added shortly thereafter, in terms similar to those found in the ICC Statute,[114] and the mercy principle was also added.[115] Penalties for crimes under East Timor law within the jurisdiction of the special panels for serious criminal offenses are the penalties that exist under East Timor law.[116]

The Dili Special Court for Serious Crimes, in a case beginning under the UNTAET regime but ending under the independent Constitution of Timor-Leste, stated that it was allowing UNTAET regulations concerning crimes against humanity and genocide to be applied retrospectively. It held the acts involved were criminal under customary international law and under general principles of law before they were committed,[117] and thus they could

Law Applicable In Kosovo (27 October 2000) §§ 1.3, 1.4 (italics substitute for underlining in original), available at http://www.unmikonline.org/regulations/2000/re2000_59.htm.

112 UNMIK Reg. No. 1999/24, relying on S.C. Res. 1244, UN Doc. S/RES/1244 (10 June 1999).

113 UNTAET Regulation No. 1999/1, UN Doc. UNTAET/REG/1999/1, On the Authority of the Transitional Administration in East Timor § 2 (27 November 1999), relying on Security Council Resolution 1272, UN Doc. No. S/RES/1272 (25 October 1999).

114 Compare UNTAET Regulation No. 2000/15, UN Doc. UNTAET/REG/2000/15, On the Establishment of Panels with Exclusive Jurisdiction over Serious Criminal Offenses §§ 12, 13 (6 June 2000) with ICC Statute arts. 23, 24.

115 UNTAET Reg. No. 2000/15 § 3.2.

116 UNTAET Reg. No. 2000/15 § 10.1(a).

117 Public Prosecutor v. Sarmento, Decision on the defense (Domingos Mendonca) motion for the Court to order the Public Prosecutor to amend the indictment, Case No. 18a/2001

be prosecuted in the East Timor courts. Although some language appears to reject legality here, what is actually being rejected is the stricter civil law version of legality that the statute implementing international criminal law must have been in place before the act (i.e., *nullum crimen sine praevia lege scripta* is rejected). The ICCPR version of legality is accepted: the act must have been criminal under some applicable law when done.[118]

In the creation of the new Extraordinary Chambers for Cambodia, the UN General Assembly and the government of Cambodia have approved an agreement that incorporates human rights protections "as set out in" the ICCPR, in particular Articles 14 and 15.[119] Thus, the legality principle again should apply to the chambers. Interestingly, though, the crimes over which the Extraordinary Chambers will have jurisdiction are defined by reference to international documents, not all of which were in existence at the time of the Khmer Rouge atrocities.

The adoption of definitions of crime from international documents is different from the issue of adoption of human rights standards. This is because the definitions of crime are subject to the principle of legality,

¶¶ 19–30 (Timor-Leste, Dili District Special Court for Serious Crimes, 24 July 2003), available at http://www.jsmp.minihub.org/Court%20Monitoring/SPSC/Documents/2001/18-2001%20Benjamin%20Sarmento%20et%20al/18-2001%20Domingos%20Mendonca%20Int%20Decision%20on%20defense%20motion%20for%20court%20to%20order%20amendment%20of%20indictment%20Eng.doc (Web site of the [East Timor] Judicial System Monitoring Programme, a nongovernmental organization). In ¶ 20, the court says "under customary international law crimes against humanity are criminal under general principles of law recognized by the community of nations," thus treating "general principles of law recognized by the community of nations" as a subset of the rules of customary international law.

118 *Sarmento* at ¶¶ 6–10, 19–30, rejecting the reasoning of Prosecutor v. dos Santos, Applicable Subsidiary Law Decision, Case No. 16/2001 (Timor-Leste, Court of Appeal, 15 July 2003), available at http://www.jsmp.minihub.org/Judgements/courtofappeal/Ct_of_App-dos_Santos_English22703.pdf (slightly earlier court of appeal case applying *nullum crimin sine praevia lege scripta*, voiding a conviction under the UNTAET Regulations because they had not been in force when the crime was committed, and applying a Portuguese prohibition of genocide that the court held had been lawfully in force). See WARD N. FERDINANDUSSE, DIRECT APPLICATION OF INTERNATIONAL CRIMINAL LAW IN NATIONAL COURTS 225–26 (TMC Asser 2006).

119 Draft Agreement between the United Nations and the Royal Government of Cambodia concerning the Prosecution under Cambodian Law of Crimes Committed during the Period of Democratic Kampuchea art. 12(2), approved in and annexed to Khmer Rouge Trials, G.A. Res. 57/228 B, UN Doc. A/RES/57/228 B (22 May 2003), incorporates ICCPR arts. 14 & 15. The *Agreement Between the United Nations and the Royal Government of Cambodia Concerning the Prosecution under Cambodian Law of Crimes Committed During the Period of Democratic Kampuchea* was signed at Phnom Penh on 6 June 2003. In accordance with its Article 32, it entered into force on 29 April 2005.

As of the current writing, the Extraordinary Chambers have just begun to deal with cases.

as set forth in the Cambodia–UN agreement. This structure requires the Extraordinary Chambers to determine whether a given act was in fact a crime under some applicable law at the time of the act. It thus explicitly adopts the view of André Gros at the London Conference that a court must determine whether there was a criminal law applicable to a defendant at the time of the act charged.[120] This type of issue has been regularly presented to and considered by international criminal courts and tribunals.[121]

The Iraqi Special Tribunal was allowed to have international judges, but it is now a national tribunal. It was directed to have international staff members and was originally established by the Coalition Interim Authority, representing the United States and the United Kingdom, the occupying powers in Iraq. They were acting pursuant to Security Council authorization in administering Iraq after the 2003 removal of the Baathist regime of Saddam Hussein.[122] Those who characterized it as partially international point to the fact that it was created by a multinational occupying authority authorized to act by a Security Council resolution and to the fact of international staffing. Those who saw it as primarily a national tribunal emphasize that the Coalition Provisional Authority exercised the sovereignty of Iraq as an occupying force.

It has now been renamed the Iraqi High Criminal Tribunal and is operated by the once-again sovereign government of Iraq. Thus, it is similar to the Dili Special Court for Serious Crimes, which began its existence under UNTAET but is now a court of the state of East Timor. The jurisdiction of the Iraqi High Tribunal is retrospective, covering crimes committed between 17 July 1968 and 1 May 2003. Its statute contains provisions which require that general principles of criminal law be applied as existing at the time of the crime,[123]

[120] Cf. Chap. 3.b.ii.

[121] See Chap. 6.a.ii.

[122] See Statute of the Iraqi Special Tribunal arts. 4, 6, 8 (10 December 2003); Security Council Res. 1483, UN Doc. S/RES.1483 (22 May 2003).

[123] Statute of the Iraqi Special Tribunal art. 17(a–c):

(a) Subject to the provisions of this Statute and the rules made thereunder, the general principles of criminal law applicable in connection with the prosecution and trial of any accused person shall be those contained:
  (i) in Iraqi criminal law as at July 17, 1968 (as embodied in The Baghdadi Criminal Code of 1919) for those offenses committed between July 17, 1968 and December 14, 1969;
  (ii) in Law Number 111 of 1969 (the Iraqi Criminal Code), as it was as of December 15, 1969, without regard to any amendments made thereafter, for those offenses committed between December 15, 1969 and May 1, 2003; and
  (iii) and in Law Number 23 of 1971 (the Iraqi Criminal Procedure Law).

provisions that are much more specific than those of other tribunals. The new Constitution of Iraq specifically recognizes the continuing existence of the Iraqi High Criminal Tribunal but prohibits the creation of any new "special or exceptional" courts.[124]

The Iraqi High Criminal Tribunal adopts sentencing provisions for domestic law violations from the relevant provision of the Iraqi penal code.[125] As to sentencing for any international law crimes not in the Iraqi penal law at the relevant time, it permits reference to international sentencing practice, as well as the facts of the case.[126] The Iraq Interim Constitution in force from 1970 (i.e., for most of the period within the temporal jurisdiction of the tribunal) contained a fairly standard implementation of the principle of legality.[127] The new Iraqi Constitution has similar material, though in a slightly different format.[128]

> (b) In interpreting Articles 11 to 13, the Trial Chambers and the Appellate Chamber may resort to the relevant decisions of international courts or tribunals as persuasive authority for their decisions.
> (c) Grounds for exclusion of criminal responsibility under the said Iraqi Criminal Code shall be interpreted in a manner consistent with the Statute and with international legal obligations concerning the crimes within the jurisdiction of the Tribunal.

[124] See Const. of Iraq arts. 92 (prohibiting "special or exceptional" courts), 130 (transitional provision recognizing continuation of Iraqi High Criminal Tribunal).

[125] Statute of the Iraqi Special Tribunal art. 24(a-b).

[126] Statute of the Iraqi Special Tribunal art. 24(e):

> (e) The penalty for any crimes under Articles 11 to 13 which do not have a counterpart under Iraqi law shall be determined by the Trial Chambers taking into account such factors as the gravity of the crime, the individual circumstances of the convicted person and relevant international precedents.

[127] Iraq Interim Constitution art. 21(b) (1970):

> (b) There can be no crime, nor punishment, except in conformity with the law. No penalty shall be imposed, except for acts punishable by the law, while they are committed. A severer penalty than that prescribed by the law, when the act was committed, cannot be inflicted.

[128] Iraq Const. art. 19(2, 9–10):

> (2) There is no crime or punishment except by stipulation. The punishment shall only be for an act that the law considers a crime when perpetrated. A harsher sentence than the applicable sentence at the time of the offense may not be imposed.
> (9) A law does not have a retroactive effect unless the law stipulates otherwise. This prohibition shall not include laws relating to taxes and fees.
> (10) Criminal law does not have a retroactive effect, unless it is to the benefit of the accused.

The Iraqi High Tribunal has issued its first judgments, death sentences against Saddam Hussein and two others, and they have been carried out.[129] It has recently had three more death sentences for crimes against humanity in poison-gas attacks upheld on appeal.[130] Because Iraqi sovereignty has now been restored, these are most properly seen as issuing from a national tribunal.

6.b.ii. A Note on Legality in UN Trust Territories as Another Example of International Organization and National Practice

In the 1950s and early 1960s, after the UDHR but before the adoption of the ICCPR, practice concerning legality existed in UN Trust Territories, as reported in the UN *Year Books on Human Rights.* This information is collected here, because, like information on some of the internationalized criminal tribunals, it reflects international organization and national practice concerning legality in territories under some degree of international supervision.

Trustee nations imposed non-retroactivity of crimes and punishments in at least the Trust Territory of the Pacific Islands (now–UN members the Marshall Islands, Micronesia, and Palau, and the not-fully-independent Northern Marianas), Cameroun, and Togoland.[131] The *Year Books* do not report such internal practice in other trust territories (though it may have existed in some of them), but many had non-retroactivity of crimes and punishments in their immediate or near-immediate postindependence constitutions.[132] Two nations formed from former trust territories after the

[129] *Saddam Hussein*, Lawsuit No.1/Criminal/2005 (Iraqi High Tribunal), judgment delivered orally 5 November 2006, aff'd 26 December 2006 (Iraqi High Tribunal Appeals Commission). On the night of 29-30 December 2006, Saddam Hussein was executed by hanging. The other two defendants were hanged soon thereafter.

[130] Bushra Juhi, *Death Sentences Upheld in Iraq For 'Chemical Ali,' Two Others, Washington Post*, 5 September 2007, p. A-11; for trial judgment, see *Al Anfal*, Special Verdict Pertaining to Case No 1/ CSecond/2006 (24 June 2007), unofficial English translation available at http://www.law.case.edu/grotian-moment-blog/anfal/opinion.asp.

[131] Trust Territory of the Pacific Islands Code art. 5 (22 December 1952), 1952 UNYBHR at 344 (United States acting as Trustee); Decree No. 57-501, setting forth the Statute of the Cameroons art. 15 (16 April 1957), 1957 UNYBHR at 273, 274 (France Trustee; incorporating the 1789 French Declaration of the Rights of Man and of the Citizen by reference to France Const., preamble); Decree No. 58-187, setting forth the Statute of Togoland art. 32 (22 February 1958) (similar; France Trustee), 1958 UNYBHR at 277, 278.

[132] Libya Const. art. 17 (7 October 1951), 1951 UNYBHR at 225, 226; Rwanda Const. art. 13 (24 November 1962) (by incorporating UDHR), 1962 UNYBHR at 256; Western Samoa [now Samoa] Const. art. 10(1, 2) (1 January 1962), 1962 UNYBHR at 336, 337; Somalia Const. art. 42, 1963 UNYBHR at 259, 262 (approved by referendum 20 June 1961; provisionally

drafting of the ICCPR, but before its entry into force had non-retroactivity of crimes and punishments in their constitutions.[133]

One fairly clear counterexample is Tanganyika, a former British Trust Territory now part of Tanzania, which did not have non-retroactivity of crimes and punishments in its postindependence constitution.[134] Similarly, when the British mandate was laid down in Palestine, neither Jordan nor Israel appears to have had non-retroactivity of crimes and punishments explicitly in its law (at least as available through the *Year Books*).

By now, all of the UN member states formed from the trust territories have adopted non-retroactivity of crimes and punishments by constitution or statute or through adoption of one or more of the international human rights treaties. The breakaway territory of Somaliland, not generally recognized as a state, does not appear to have such a provision, though its constitution does recognize legality in criminal law without specific mention of non-retroactivity.[135]

6.c. THE ICC AND THE PRINCIPLE OF LEGALITY

The principle of legality in the ICC Statute is generally broad. The statute does not conform its language to that of the UDHR, the ICCPR and related documents, or to other standard formulations of legality doctrines, except in two article titles.[136] Thus, close textual analysis is necessary to elucidate the law of legality in the statute.

In the end, however, the essential principles of legality from the UDHR and ICCPR exist both in the particular legality provisions of the ICC Statute,[137] and in its commitment to international human rights law. Indeed, the ICC Statute's requirement that the interpretation and application of law

in force 1 July 1960) (part of Somalia was the former Trust Territory of Somaliland), also printed in 1960 UNYBHR at 301, 304; cf. Burundi Const. art. 9 (1 July 1962), 1962 UNYBHR at 23 ("No penalty may be established or applied save in pursuance of a law").

[133] Nauru Const. (31 January 1968) art. 10(4), 1968 UNYBHR at 294, 296; Papua New Guinea Const. (16 September 1975) § 37(2) (*nullum crimen, nulla poena sine praevia lege scripta* except for contempt of court), 1975 UNYBHR at 218, 221.

[134] See 1961 UNYBHR at 325, printing excerpts of Tanganyika Const. (9 December 1961).

[135] Somaliland Revised Const. art. 26(1) ("Crimes and [their] punishment shall be laid down by the law, and no punishment shall be administered in a manner which is contrary to the law").

[136] ICC Statute arts. 22 (titled "*Nullum crimen sine lege*"), 23 (titled "*Nulla poena sine lege*").

[137] ICC Statute arts. 11, 22-24. These provisions read (bracketed materials added):

Part II. Jurisdiction, Admissibility and Applicable Law

...

"must be consistent with internationally recognized human rights"[138] immediately incorporates the principles of legality that have become customary international law, as described subsequently.[139] Nonetheless, it is worth considering the specific legality provisions of the ICC, to show how they in fact provide protections at least the equivalent of legality as understood in customary international human rights law today: no act may be criminally punished unless it was a criminal act under law applicable to the actor at the time done, and no greater punishment may be imposed than the maximum penalty applicable at the time of the act.

> *Article 11 Jurisdiction ratione temporis*
>
> 1. The Court shall have jurisdiction only with respect to crimes committed after the entry into force of this Statute.
> 2. If a State becomes Party to this Statute after its entry into force, the Court may exercise its jurisdiction only with respect to crimes committed after the entry into force of this Statute for that State, unless that State has made a declaration under article 12, paragraph 3 [concerning retroactive acceptance of jurisdiction by that State].
>
> . . .
>
> Part 3. General Principles of Criminal Law
>
> *Article 22 Nullum crimen sine lege*
>
> 1. A person shall not be criminally responsible under this Statute unless the conduct in question constitutes, at the time it takes place, a crime within the jurisdiction of the Court.
> 2. The definition of a crime shall be strictly construed and shall not be extended by analogy. In case of ambiguity, the definition shall be interpreted in favour of the person being investigated, prosecuted, or convicted.
> 3. This article shall not affect the characterization of any conduct as criminal under international law independently of this Statute.
>
> *Article 23 Nulla poena sine lege*
>
> A person convicted by the Court may be punished only in accordance with this Statute.
>
> *Article 24 Non-retroactivity ratione personae*
>
> 1. No person shall be criminally responsible under this Statute for conduct prior to the entry into force of this Statute.
> 2. In the event of a change in the law applicable to a given case prior to a final judgement, the law more favourable to the person being investigated, prosecuted or convicted shall apply.

Compare UDHR art. 11(2); ICCPR art. 15(1).

[138] ICC Statute art. 21(3).
[139] See generally Chap. 7.

The Pre-Trial Chamber recently issued the first decision on legality in the ICC. It has treated legality as an issue that the individual accused has a right to raise,[140] similar to the right of the individual in the ICTY, ICTR, and SCSL.[141] As will be seen subsequently,[142] many issues of legality are called jurisdictional in the ICC Statute, and individuals can challenge jurisdiction under the statute.[143] Other issues are treated as matters of substantive criminal law, which are customarily litigable in criminal proceedings.

The legality provisions of the ICC Statute, like many other provisions, operate differently depending on whether only states party to the ICC Statute at all relevant times are involved. The easier case, where all are states party at all relevant times, will be considered first.

A preliminary point on how matters reach the ICC: First, a situation may be referred to the prosecutor by a state party to the ICC Statute.[144] Second, a situation may be referred by the UN Security Council.[145] Third, a situation may be investigated by the prosecutor proprio motu (on his or her own motion).[146]

Another preliminary point: the discussion of the ICC is placed before the discussion of legality as a matter of customary international law today, which is Chapter 7. Yet one must remember that the ICC Statute incorporates customary international human rights law as a vital part of its own law.[147] Additionally, the ICC Statute is not meant to inhibit the growth of customary international law outside the context of the statute, including international criminal law and procedure and international human rights law.[148] Thus, the material here and in Chapter 7 needs to be considered together.

6.c.i. *Situations Involving Only States Parties to the ICC Statute at All Relevant Times*

In all cases, the ICC has "jurisdiction only with respect to crimes committed after the entry into force of [the] Statute."[149] Thus, the plain language of

[140] Procureur c. Dyilo, No. ICC-01/04-01/06, Décision sur la confirmation des charges (Version publique) (La Chamber Préliminaire I), ¶¶ 294–316, 29 January 2007 (available in French only as of 7 February 2007).
[141] See Chap. 6.a.ii.
[142] Chap. 6.c.iii.
[143] See ICC Statute arts. 17–19.
[144] ICC Statute art. 13(a).
[145] ICC Statute art. 13(b).
[146] ICC Statute art. 13(c).
[147] ICC Statute art. 21(3).
[148] See ICC Statute arts. 10, 22(3).
[149] ICC Statute art. 11(1).

the statute does not allow for prosecutions of acts arising before its effective date.[150]

As to states that accede to the statute after it has come into force generally, the court has jurisdiction only with respect to crimes that are committed after it comes into force for that state, unless the state has authorized the exercise of jurisdiction over prior cases. This applies whenever the basis of jurisdiction of the court is referral by a state party or initiation of an investigation by the prosecutor proprio motu.[151] It does not apply where there is a Security Council referral of a situation involving events happening before the state accepted jurisdiction. These instances will be covered in the next section.

Amendments to the criminal definitions of the ICC Statute do not apply retroactively to nationals of or persons committing crimes in states parties. Again, this applies to referrals by states parties or prosecutions initiated proprio motu.[152]

Penalties may only be imposed "in accordance with this Statute."[153] Thus, for cases where only states party to the ICC Statute are involved, there will not be retroactive increases in the maximum penalties involved.

These provisions obviously protect against many retroactivity problems. For state referrals of situations in states parties to the ICC Statute and for investigations of situations in states parties begun by the prosecutor proprio

[150] ICC Statute arts. 11(1), 24(1). This date was 1 July 2002. A contrary argument that the Security Council could make a referral concerning crimes committed before that date, Luigi Condorelli & Santiago Villalpando, *Referral and Deferral by the Security Council*, in 1 The Rome Statute of the International Criminal Court: A Commentary 627, 630–31 (Antonio Cassese, Paola Gaeta & John R. W. D. Jones, eds., Oxford Univ. Press 2002), is not persuasive. It would improperly allow one international organization (the United Nations, acting through the Security Council) to require another international organization (the ICC) to violate the explicit terms of its organic document. See Kenneth S. Gallant, *The International Criminal Court in the System of States and International Organizations*, 16 Leiden J.I.L. 553 (2003) [hereinafter Gallant, ICC IO]. Security Council Resolution No. 748 ¶ 7, UN Doc. S/RES/748 (31 March 1992), "*Calls upon* all States, including States not members of the United Nations, and international organizations, to act strictly in accordance with the provisions of the present resolution, notwithstanding the existence of any rights or obligations conferred or imposed by any international agreement or any contract entered into or any license or agreement granted prior to 15 April 1992)." Given that this resolution does not "*Decide*" that international organizations "shall" comply with it, it cannot be read as requiring other international organizations to violate their charters, though it might be asking them to do so if necessary. Cf. José Alvarez, International Organizations as Law Makers 71–72 n.25 (Oxford Univ. Press 2005), and sources cited therein, including UN Charter art. 103.

[151] ICC Statute arts. 11(2), 12(2-3).

[152] ICC Statute arts. 121(4-6), 123. The text is not explicit as to the effective date of amendments when there is a Security Council referral. Compare *id.*, arts. 121, 123, with *id.*, art. 13(b).

[153] ICC Statute art. 23.

motu they conform to the UDHR/ICCPR formulations of legality. In these cases, no person may be convicted of a crime "on account of any act or omission which did not constitute a penal offense, under [law applicable to the actor], at the time when it was committed. Nor [may] a heavier penalty be imposed than the one that was applicable at the time the penal offense was committed."[154]

In fact, as to these cases, the ICC Statute meets the stronger version of legality in crime definition: *nullum crimen sine praevia lege scripta.* There is a treaty, the ICC Statute, defining the crimes prohibited. The explicit use of a treaty to define criminal law for individuals, without any requirement of adoption into national law, is an important development for international law. It does not, however, prevent satisfaction of the legality requirement of notice.

The first ICC decision on legality involved a case concerning a person acting in a state party, the Democratic Republic of the Congo. The Pre-Trial Chamber held that the statutory crime of recruitment of child soldiers met the requirements of prior law "(lex *praevia* [*sic*])," sufficient definition of crime and punishment "(*lex certa*)," crime creation in the ICC Statute and not by analogy "(*lex stricta*)," and crime defined in a promulgated writing "(*lex scripta*)."[155] One point that might be noted here is that the Pre-Trial Chamber treated the ICC Statute, a treaty, as legislative, at least for those persons acting in states that had ratified the statute. It refused to accept the argument that there had been no actual communication of the terms of the statute to persons like the accused, relying on the provisions limiting the error-of-law defence.[156] This raises the issue of ensuring that international humanitarian law, including its criminal aspects, is communicated to forces fighting in inaccessible locations.

The ICC Statute meets the notion of *nulla poena sine praevia lege scripta* because it allows sentences of thirty years' imprisonment for most offenses and life imprisonment for the most serious offenses, along with fines and forfeitures for all crimes, as the maximum penalties permitted.[157] It does not meet the strongest requirements, present in the laws of some nations, that there be a specific penalty or reasonable range of penalties attached to each offense. This, however, has not always been the tradition in international criminal law.

[154] UDHR art. 11(2) [bracketed material not in original].

[155] *Dyilo* ¶ 303, relying on K. Ambos, *Nulla Poena Sine Lege in International Criminal Law*, in SENTENCING AND SANCTIONING IN INTERNATIONAL CRIMINAL LAW 17 (R. Haveman & O. Olusanya, eds.).

[156] *Dyilo*, ¶¶ 296–97.

[157] ICC Statute arts. 75, 77.

One potential legality issue does exist in the ICC Statute, even where all relevant states are states parties at all relevant times. Problems of legality in crime definition should arise only if crimes are not sufficiently clearly defined (do not meet *lex certa*) or if the court interprets them in a broad and unforeseeable manner, in violation of its statute.[158] The most obvious place for this possibility to arise is in the catchall provision of the definition of crimes against humanity, which defines as a crime "other inhumane acts of a similar character [to those specifically listed] intentionally causing great suffering, or serious injury to body or to mental or physical health."[159] The ICC Statute itself provides for strict construction of crime definitions, and in case of ambiguity "shall be interpreted in favour of the person being investigated, prosecuted, or convicted."[160] As long as the court applies the ICC Statute in this way, there should not be a problem. However, if the court uses expansive methods of interpretation, foreseeability of whether a given act is a crime when committed could become a problem.

The UN Security Council may refer a situation to the ICC whether or not any state involved in the situation is a party to the ICC Statute and whether or not any state involved gives its consent. In these situations, the date of invoking the exercise of the jurisdiction of the ICC appears to be either the date the statute entered into force, 1 July 2002, or such later date specified by Security Council as the beginning of the "situation" referred to the court.[161] Where all states involved have been states party to the ICC Statute at all relevant times, the legality provisions of the statute work in the same way to prevent retroactive application of either crimes or penalties as they do in the other means of invoking an exercise of the court's jurisdiction. In all of these cases, all of the relevant persons are covered by the prescription of criminal law in the ICC Statute at all relevant times. The case where some states are not parties to the statute (or were not parties at some relevant time) will be discussed subsequently.[162]

Some of the ICC Statute provisions on legality express a state-centric view of temporal jurisdiction, in that the effective date of the substantive law of

[158] See ICC Statute art. 22(2).

[159] ICC Statute art. 7.

[160] ICC Statute art. 22(2) (*nullum crimen sine lege*).

[161] See ICC Statute art. 13 (on "exercise of jurisdiction"). Cf. ICTY Statute art. 8; ICTR Statute art. 1 (both of which have beginning dates for crimes within the jurisdiction of the court, and the latter of which has an ending date; suggesting that the Security Council can limit the jurisdiction of an international criminal tribunal with respect to the time of commission of crimes).

[162] Chap. 6.c.ii.

the statute is controlled by state acceptance of the statute. One scholar has pointed out that many states insisted on this temporal restriction to crimes occurring after the effective date of the statute as a condition of their acceptance of the statute.[163] One would expect this demand from those states that require the previous establishment of a court system within their own national definitions of legality.

Another ICC Statute provision on effective dates is based in individual rights and substantive criminal law. The rule excluding crimes committed before the entry into force of the ICC Statute from the jurisdiction of the court is repeated in Part 3 as a rule of the court's substantive law, preventing an individual from being "criminally responsible under this Statute for conduct prior to the entry into force of the Statute."[164]

Finally, the principle of complementarity plays into the notion that one should not be removed from one's natural judge.[165] Complementarity means, in this context, that the ICC may not prosecute a case unless national courts are unwilling or unable to genuinely investigate and prosecute the matter. This creates a policy of *jus de non evocando* (against removal of trial to special criminal courts).[166] By allowing the accused to challenge admissibility of a case, the ICC Statute allows the accused to raise this issue.[167] This is not an absolute right of accused persons, however. The rules of complementarity require the ICC determine the willingness and ability of the state concerned to prosecute. The accused has no right to prevent the ICC from handling a case in that situation or to force a willing and able state to end its prosecution and refer the matter to the ICC for investigation and prosecution.[168]

6.c.ii. *Security Council Referrals of Situations Involving Nonparty States and Retroactive Acceptances of Jurisdiction by States*

There are at least two ways in which the ICC may gain jurisdiction of a case over which it did not have the authority to exercise jurisdiction at the time of the crime. The first occurs when a state that is not a party to the ICC

[163] Williams, *supra* note 76, at ¶ 4, pp. 324–25.
[164] ICC Statute art. 24(1) (article headed "Non-retroactivity *ratione personae*").
[165] Cf. Chap. 5.d (on national constitutions which protect against creation of special courts or removal from one's "natural judge").
[166] See generally *Kanyabashi*, ¶¶ 30–32; *Tadic*, Decision on Appeal on Juris., ¶¶ 45–48, 61–64.
[167] See ICC Statute arts. 17, 19(2)(a).
[168] See ICC Statute art. 17.

Statute issues a retroactive acceptance of "the exercise of jurisdiction by the Court with respect to the crime in question."[169] The second occurs when the UN Security Council refers a situation involving a state not party to the ICC Statute to the prosecutor because of crimes that have allegedly been committed in that situation.[170] ICC Prosecutor Luis Moreno Ocampo has recently suggested that there might be a third way the ICC could exercise such retrospective jurisdiction.[171] This would occur when a state has exempted itself from jurisdiction over war crimes for seven years as permitted by the ICC Statute, and then withdraws that exemption, which is also permitted, with retrospective effect.[172]

Each of these cases will typically involve persons, places, acts, and/or crimes over which the court had no prescriptive jurisdiction (authority to proclaim criminal law) or adjudicative jurisdiction (authority to try allegations of crime) at the time of the act. In these situations, at the time the alleged crime was committed, the state involved was not a party to the ICC Statute. A person who is a national of a nonparty state and who commits an act in a nonparty state is not bound by the force of any of the ICC Statute provisions at the time of the act.[173] The ICC Statute's substantive criminal provisions do not prohibit any acts of that person, at least until the time of referral or acceptance of jurisdiction by the relevant state. That is, third-party states and individuals subject to their criminal jurisdiction are not generally bound by treaties purporting to make international criminal

[169] ICC Statute art. 12(3) (allowing states to accept the jurisdiction of the ICC over events that have already occurred).

[170] See ICC Statute art. 13(b). *Id.*, art. 11(2), is not intended to prohibit Security Council referrals from being heard by the court for crimes in a state or by a state's nationals committed between the entry into force of the ICC Statute and the accession of that state to the ICC Statute. Cf. Stéphane Bourgon, *Jurisdiction Ratione Temporis*, in 1 ANTONIO CASSESE *et al.*, ROME STATUTE COMMENTARY 543, 553. Otherwise, a state that is not a party to the ICC Statute could avoid a Security Council referral by becoming a party but refusing to make a declaration of retroactivity. The first Security Council referral was recently made, with respect to the situation in Darfur, the Sudan, which is not a party to the ICC Statute. S.C. Res. No. 1593, UN Doc. S/RES/1593 (31 March 2005).

[171] Andrés Garibello y Jhon Torres Martínez, *Corte Penal Internacional sigue pista a la parapolítica, asegura su fiscal jefe, Luis Moreno Ocampo*, ElTiempo.com, 21 October 2007, available at http://www.eltiempo.com/justicia/2007-10-22/ARTICULO-WEB-NOTA_INTERIOR-3776563.html.

[172] ICC Statute art. 124. The ability of the state to make the withdrawal retrospective is not explicit in the statute. The comments in this section are about whether a retroactive withdrawal would be consistent with legality as required by other provisions of the ICC Statute and customary international law.

[173] Cf. ICC Stat. art. 12(2). In Ocampo's hypothesized case, the war crimes definitions of ICC Statute, art. 8, did not apply to the actor at the time of the action.

law simply because the treaties have come into effect for some other states. Note that this assumes that, where the relevant states have become party to a treaty (e.g., the ICC Statute), such a treaty can bind individuals as well as states – a key element of the system of the ICC.

The prosecution of persons for acts committed before the referral or acceptance of jurisdiction requires some other source of substantive law, applicable to the person at the time of the acts, prohibiting the acts. The most likely source of this law would be customary international law existing at the time of the acts. Where this is the case, there will be no *nullum crimen* problem. If, as seems reasonable, it is the case that all penalties up to life imprisonment are still available under customary international law for all customary international humanitarian law crimes, there is no *nulla poena* problem either.

However, it is not enough to say that genocide, crimes against humanity, and war crimes are core crimes under international criminal law and therefore customary international law crimes. Each specific crime named within these classes must be examined to determine whether it is a customary international law crime. For example, it is not clear that long-term and severe environmental damage as a war crime existed in customary international law at the time the ICC Statute came into effect or exists in customary international law today.[174] This provision may become one of the most important progressive developments of the ICC Statute, but it may not yet be customary international criminal law, principally because of the lack of many actual prosecutions.[175] Thus, a further search for applicable law may need to be undertaken if the act alleged occurred before a referral by the Security Council or a relevant state's retroactively effective acceptance of jurisdiction.

Technically, one could also look to see whether the act was a crime according to general principles of law recognized by the community of nations at the time it was committed. This is also a potential source of international law criminalizing acts. Whether any of the crimes listed in the ICC

[174] See ICC Statute art. 8(2)(b)(iv).

[175] But see Jean-Marie Henckaerts & Louise Doswald-Beck, 1 Customary International Humanitarian Law (Rules) R. 156 (discussion), pp. 568, 580, 582–83 (Cambridge Univ. Press 2005) (study issued by the International Committee of the Red Cross) [hereinafter ICRC, Customary IHL] (asserting that environmental damage as criminalized in the ICC Statute is also a war crime in international armed conflict under customary international law). However, no prosecutions or other state practice is cited, and the only evidence given beyond the provision of the ICC Statute is the fact that this provision was not controversial when adopted and the claim that it is encompassed in the concept of attacks on civilian objects.

Statute are criminal according to these general principles but not according to customary international law is doubtful. For example, many states have begun to criminalize environmental damage, but the criminalization of such damage has probably not yet become a general principle of law around the world.

Another source of applicable law would be treaty law applicable to persons at the time of the acts, paralleling the prohibition in the ICC Statute, particularly where that treaty prohibition has been adopted into the criminal law of the relevant state.[176] As shown in the discussion of this matter in the ad hoc tribunals, this would not present a legality problem.[177]

A final possibility – though a controversial one – would be that an ICC statutory crime could be prosecuted in the ICC even if, at the time of the act, it was prohibited for the person involved solely by the law of the relevant state at the time committed. This would be similar to the notion of retrospective re-characterization from national to international law discussed previously.[178] Here, the act that is criminal under national law would be retrospectively re-characterized as a violation of the ICC Statute. It would appear that this would not be prohibited by customary international human rights law.[179] It is not clear, however, that the court would allow for re-characterization under its statute, because of the requirement that it exercise jurisdiction under the provisions "of this Statute."[180] If it does (considering the statements of the ICTY and ICTR discussed earlier), it is to be hoped that the period in which this process is necessary will be brief.

If there is no source of law criminalizing the act in question at the time committed there can be no prosecution, because of the principle stated as "Non-retroactivity ratione personae" in the ICC Statute.[181] The Security Council referral or the retroactive acceptance of jurisdiction has changed the law applicable to the case to the detriment of the person being prosecuted – by applying the law of substantive crimes of the ICC Statute. The person is entitled to be judged by the "more favorable" law from the time of the act[182] – the ICC Statute cannot retroactively make a person's act criminal if the act was non-criminal under all applicable law when done. This is one point at which the doctrine of applicability rather clearly applies in the ICC Statute.

[176] Cf. *Tadic*, Decision on Appeal on Juris., ¶¶ 135, 143–45; *Akayesu*, Judgement ¶¶ 611–17.
[177] See Chap. 6.a.iv.
[178] See Chaps. 3.c.i, 6.a.iv.
[179] See Chap. 7.b.ii.
[180] ICC Statute art. 1.
[181] See ICC Statute art. 24 (caption).
[182] ICC Statute art. 24(2).

The same result is reached under the provision of the ICC Statute labeled "*Nullum crimen sine lege.*"[183] Without a source of law criminalizing an act, there is no crime, and therefore no "crime within the jurisdiction of the Court"[184] at the time and place of the act. There is a conceivable argument that this section is only meant to apply to the question of whether a crime is within the subject-matter jurisdiction of the court – that is, is the act named covered by any of the substantive provisions of the statute at the time of the act? This would, however, seem a cramped reading of this section. Even if this argument were accepted, the prosecution would be unacceptable under the other two theories discussed here.

A third means of applying *nullum crimen* also exists and reaches the same result. As discussed earlier, the ICC Statute must be applied and interpreted consistently with international human rights law.[185] An act may not be punished if it "did not constitute a penal offense, under national or international law, at the time when it was committed."[186] Without a source of law applicable to the actor that criminalizes the act, punishment would constitute a violation of the customary international human rights law version of *nullum crimen* as well.

Even if there was relevant law criminalizing the charged act at the time, the legality of sentence (*nulla poena*) remains an issue. If the relevant source of law criminalizing the act at the time committed prescribed a maximum sentence less than that authorized by the ICC Statute, that earlier sentencing maximum must be respected. This is required by the non-retroactivity *ratione personae* provision, as described earlier. The court must apply the "more favorable" sentencing provision from the time of the criminal act[187] – there can be no retroactive increase in maximum available sentence any more than there can be a retroactive criminalization of a non-criminal act. Similarly, under the general human rights provision of the statute, an increased penalty for a crime may not be imposed retroactively.[188]

The statute's provision labeled "*Nulla poena sine lege*" is by itself weak. It states: "A person convicted by the Court may be punished only in accordance

[183] ICC Statute art. 22 (caption).
[184] ICC Statute art. 22(1).
[185] ICC Statute art. 21(3).
[186] ICCPR art. 15(1). This provision embodies customary international human rights law. See Chap. 7(a, c), also quoting UDHR, art. 11(2).
[187] ICC Statute art. 24(2).
[188] ICC Statute art. 21(3). The version of the principle *nulla poena sine lege* existing in customary international human rights law is that of the ICCPR art. 15(1). See Chap. 7(a, c), also quoting UDHR, art. 11(2).

with this Statute."[189] It does not specifically deal with the question of what happens when a punishment is authorized by the statute but was not applicable to the actor at the time of the alleged act. Nonetheless, it is quite clear from the analysis herein that the ICC Statute prohibits retroactive increases in all sentences through its non-retroactivity *ratione personae* provision,[190] as well as its general human rights provision.[191]

The possible retroactive application of non-customary international criminal law, especially after a Security Council referral, is not an imaginary problem. Many of the framers of the ICC Statute sought a progressive development of international criminal law and procedure.[192] Therefore, they did not necessarily limit their drafting of the criminal law of the statute to that which was customary international law.[193] It is not self-evident that all of the crimes listed in the statute are customary international law crimes.

Some respected commentators have suggested that all of the crimes set forth in the ICC Statute automatically apply when the Security Council has referred a situation to the ICC.[194] This would be inconsistent with the legality analysis both of the statute and of international human rights law and with fundamental rules of treaty law.

Schabas, for example, claims that such an application would be permissible because it is "foreseeable" that the court would attempt to apply the statute to such people.[195] The problem with this argument is that the states adopting the ICC Statute have no authority to prescribe new criminal law either for non-ICC states or for persons with no relevant connection to any ICC state. The ICC Statute can apply to a national of a non-ICC state who commits a criminal act in, or with effect in, an ICC state, as an instance of territorial jurisdiction.[196] The states adopting the ICC Statute could not make law to apply to someone who is wholly unconnected with any ICC state party, and whose allegedly criminal acts are unconnected with such a state party, unless the crime were a customary international law crime over which there is universal jurisdiction (which, by hypothesis, the crime here

[189] ICC Statute art. 23.
[190] ICC Statute art. 24(2).
[191] ICC Statute art. 21(3).
[192] Leila Nadya Sadat, The International Criminal Court and the Transformation of International Law 12 (Transnational Publishers 2002) [hereinafter Sadat].
[193] Sadat at 12–13.
[194] See Sadat at 12, 138–39; William A. Schabas, An Introduction to the International Criminal Court 71–72 (2d ed., Cambridge Univ. Press 2004) [hereinafter Schabas, Introduction].
[195] Schabas, Introduction at 71–72.
[196] Cf. ICC Statute art. 12(2).

is not). *Foreseeability* in the sense of legality can include a development in the law of a jurisdiction with legitimate authority over a person. It cannot mean foreseeability that an international organization will later attempt to impose its prescriptive jurisdiction on a person over whom it has no legitimate authority.

Schabas argues that the application of new, non-customary crimes in the ICC Statute to such persons is acceptable by pointing out that aggressive war was effectively a new crime at Nuremberg.[197] The problem with this argument is that international human rights law has changed since that time. The claim by the Nuremberg Tribunal that *nullum crimen sine lege* was, in international law, merely a principle of justice was true then but is not so now. Now it is a rule of customary international law and perhaps a *jus cogens* rule at that.[198] It is less clear whether Schabas argues that conventional war crimes were applied retroactively at Nuremberg.[199] This argument, to the extent that it is made, is not correct, because conventional war crimes were seen as crimes under customary international law at the time of World War II, even if the Hague and Geneva conventions of the time did not explicitly criminalize them.[200]

6.c.iii. *Legality as a Jurisdictional Issue in the ICC*

The ICC Statute articulates aspects of the principle of legality as both jurisdictional and substantive rules.[201]

The provision prohibiting application of the statute to crimes before its entry into force, or before its entry into force for a relevant state, are in a section headed "Jurisdiction *ratione temporis*" (jurisdiction with regard to time) in Part 2, covering "Jurisdiction, Admissibility and Applicable Law."[202] This provision, therefore, can fairly be considered jurisdictional without much debate.

In contrast, the other specific legality provisions are in Part 3, headed "General Principles of Criminal Law."[203] This would indicate that they may be treated as matters of substantive criminal law rather than of jurisdiction. However, to the extent that the issue of what law can apply to a matter is

[197] See Schabas, INTRODUCTION at 70–71.
[198] Chap. 7 below will discuss this on the basis of the materials in Chaps. 4, 5 & 6.
[199] Cf. Schabas, INTRODUCTION at 70–71.
[200] See Chap. 3.a.
[201] Cf. Williams, *supra* note 76, ¶¶ 2, 4, pp. 323–25.
[202] ICC Statute, art. 11.
[203] ICC Statute arts. 22–24.

affected by issues of legality, the ICTY case discussed earlier has a point in holding that this issue is a matter of "jurisdiction *ratione materiae*"[204] (subject-matter jurisdiction). And the description of key provisions of the ICC legality rules as "Non-retroactivity *ratione personae*" (with regard to the person)[205] suggests that these rules might be considered to cover personal jurisdiction issues: what law of crime and punishment covers this particular actor at the time of the action?

There is procedural significance to considering a matter as jurisdictional. A decision on jurisdiction is appealable without waiting for trial and judgment.[206] The reason that jurisdictional issues are immediately appealable is that the court system has no authority (i.e., no legitimate power) to bring and continue the proceedings where it has no jurisdiction. Such proceedings themselves are a violation of the accused person's rights.

6.d. STATUS OF ACTIONS OF THE SECURITY COUNCIL, OTHER UN BODIES, AND THE RECENT INTERNATIONAL CRIMINAL COURTS AND TRIBUNALS UNDER INTERNATIONAL LAW

As the material in the preceding sections is used in the development of the rules of customary international law of legality, it is important to mention the international legal status of the material discussed in this section. The acts of the UN Security Council establishing the ICTY and ICTR are acts of an international organization – in this case, pursuant to Chapter VII of the UN Charter, with binding legal force worldwide, or at least as to all UN members. The acts of the ICTY and ICTR themselves, including their decisions, are also acts of an international organization, in this case, judicial organs acting as authorized by the UN Security Council. Note that the Security Council acts by the votes of its members; its resolutions are thus individual state practice as well as practice of an international organization. The acts of the tribunal in prosecuting, rendering judgment, and punishing, however, are independent of the wills of the individual states.

An international organization (the United Nations) and the state of Sierra Leone made an international agreement (treaty) to create the SCSL. The

[204] *Milutinovic*, Decision on Dragoljub Ojdanic's Motion Challenging Jurisdiction: Joint Criminal Enterprise ¶ 9, citing *Vasiljevic*, Trial Judgment ¶¶ 193–97, discussed in Chap. 6.a.ii.

[205] ICC Statute art. 24.

[206] See ICC Statute art. 82(1).

SCSL, however, is an independent international organization, and its decisions are its acts.[207]

Individuals may challenge actions of all three of these courts, including the exercise of jurisdiction over them, and may litigate the meaning of criminal definitions and whether they have committed the acts charged. They may do this without approval of the state of their nationality and sometimes in opposition to the views of that state. This is seen most easily in the presentation of defenses in the ICTR, where the state of Rwanda is generally seen as favoring the position of the prosecution over that of the Hutu Rwandan nationals who are the accused. These are direct acts of individuals under international law and the law of the appropriate international organization.

A very interesting pattern appears to be developing concerning individuals who have been turned over to the ad hoc international courts. Once in the custody of these courts, it appears that the individual is the sole "person" who can raise a challenge to the legality of the proceedings against him or her. Except for the ICC, there does not appear to be a political/legal mechanism for a state, even the state of the person's nationality, to make such a complaint. Perhaps such a complaint could be made through the UN Security Council, but even this is unclear. No mechanism has been contemplated. Yet states have in effect "objected" to acts of the ICTY and ICTR by withdrawing (or threatening to withdraw) lawfully required cooperation from the tribunals.[208] In the ICC, states may make challenges to the jurisdiction of the court.[209] Presumably, this would include challenges to legality in a prosecution, as we have seen that the ad hoc tribunals have treated this as a jurisdictional matter.[210]

The UNTAET and UNMIK Regulations are acts of the United Nations as an international organization made in the interests of peace and security. The regulations act as domestic law of the administered territory. The decisions made by courts operating pursuant to them during the period of UN administration are also acts of an international organization. In the case of the UNTAET regulations, however, East Timor has now gained

[207] See Agreement between the United Nations and the Government of Sierra Leone on the Establishment of a Special Court for Sierra Leone (16 January 2002).

[208] Consider the long-time failure of Serbia to cooperate with the arrest of General Ratko Mladic and Radovan Karadzic. Karadzic was arrested as this book went to press in mid-2008.

[209] ICC Statute art. 17.

[210] See Chap. 6.a.ii.

independence as Timor-Leste and is continuing cases begun under UNTAET law through its own tribunals, as its own acts.[211]

Late in the process of the preparation of this book for publication, Kosovo declared its independence. Its Constitutional Commission recently presented a draft Constitution containing non-retroactivity of crimes and punishments.[212] The international-law status of matters in the Kosovo courts after the declaration of independence is not as clear as the status of matters from East Timor, because not all other states recognize Kosovo.

In form, acts of individuals defending themselves in these courts while under UN administration are similar to acts defending themselves in the ICTY and ICTR. The UNTAET and UNMIK, however, have effectively been local administrations operated by an international organization. Thus, the acts of individuals and the courts there have not had the same impact on international law as the acts in and of the ICTY and ICTR. Nonetheless, the administrators made international human rights law, including the principle of legality, a core part of the law of the administered territories and allowed individuals to make claims in UNTAET and UNMIK courts against them. This is another important step in the growth of the international legal personality of individuals.

The Extraordinary Chambers in the Courts of Cambodia were formed by an international agreement between the United Nations and Cambodia. They will be staffed by both national and international personnel. Unlike the SCSL, the chambers themselves are part of the state institutions of Cambodia.[213] Thus, it appears that their acts will be acts of Cambodia, not of an international organization. However, it remains to be seen how the international agreement will be treated, specifically whether claims about legality made under it will be treated as claims directly under international law.

The Iraqi Special Tribunal was established by the Iraqi Governing Council[214] during the occupation of Iraq by U.S. and British forces (acting as the

[211] See *dos Santos*; *Sarmento*.

[212] Proposed Kosovo Constitution Draft, art. 33, presented 8 April 2008, at Constitutional Commission Web site, www.kosovoconstitution.info. Kosovo declared its independence 17 February 2008.

[213] See Cambodia Law on the Establishment of the Extraordinary Chambers (as amended through 27 October 2004), NS/RKM/1004/006; G.A. Res. 57/228 Khmer Rouge Trials, UN Doc. No. A/RES/57/228 B (22 May 2003).

[214] Statute of the Iraqi Special Tribunal, Statute No. 1, Iraqi Governing Council, 10 December 2003.

Coalition Provisional Authority, which was approved by the Security Council). Iraq has now regained sovereignty, and the decisions of that tribunal are acts of Iraq.

The ICC is an international organization in its own right, with its own international legal personality.[215] Its decisions are its acts. The ICC has a "relationship agreement" with the United Nations,[216] but it is not an organ or part of the United Nations. However, the UN Security Council and states parties to the ICC Statute can perform legal acts relating to the ICC, as by referring situations to the prosecutor.[217]

As with the ICTR, ICTY and SCSL, individuals may challenge actions of the ICC, including the exercise of jurisdiction over them,[218] and may litigate the meaning of criminal definitions and whether they have committed the acts charged. They may do this without approval of the state of their nationality. These will be direct acts of individuals under international law and the law of the ICC as an international organization.

6.d.i. *Practice and* Opinio juris *of International Organizations, Including International Tribunals, as Contributing to Customary International Law and General Principles of Law*

Acts of international organizations within their charters have begun to affect the development of customary international law. For example, the Security Council resolutions creating UNMIK and UNTAET are actions that constitute "practice" of the Security Council as a UN organ allowing for an international organization to administer a territory emerging from conflict and as an expression of *opinio juris* that this is lawful. It is also an act (to the same effect) of each state voting for the resolutions.

The decision of the Security Council need not be unanimous. Thus, the acts of the Security Council are not merely the joint acts of all of its members. They are also acts of an organ of an international organization.

The acts of the UNTAET and UNMIK administrators implementing laws that require observance of internationally recognized human rights in

[215] ICC Statute, preamble; art. 4(1).

[216] Relationship Agreement between the United Nations and the International Criminal Court; see ICC Statute art. 2. This provision is broad enough to allow the ICC to become a specialized agency within the UN system. See Kenneth S. Gallant, *The International Criminal Court in the System of States and International Organizations*, 16 LEIDEN J.I.L. 553 (2003). This, however, has not been done.

[217] See ICC Statute art. 13(b).

[218] See ICC Statute art. 19.

these territories, including the principle of legality, are the practice of an authorized body of an international organization. They can fairly be seen as expressing the *opinio juris* that observance of legality and other internationally recognized human rights by international organizations exercising power over individuals is necessary under international law.

This can also be seen in the Security Council resolutions creating the ad hoc tribunals for the Former Yugoslavia and for Rwanda. The *opinio juris* that the principle of legality must be observed in these tribunals is expressed most clearly in the Secretary-General's Report proposing the ICTY.[219] The act of adoption of this report by the Security Council is also practice to this effect.

Cases in international criminal courts have been treated as practice defining customary international criminal law. This was seen early on in the UN General Assembly's recognition of the principles of law developed in the main Nuremberg Judgment and the International Law Commission's statement of those principles.[220] In the process of establishing the ICTY, the UN Secretary-General and then the UN Security Council used the practice of the Nuremberg Tribunal in determining what crimes were "beyond doubt part of customary law."[221]

The ICTY and ICTR have continued the practice of treating case law as an element of the practice that goes into the formation and statement of customary international criminal law.[222] Note, however, that the courts

[219] Sec-Gen's ICTY Rep. ¶ 34.

[220] Affirmation of the Principles of International Law Recognized by the Charter of the Nürnberg Tribunal, G.A. Res. 95 (I), 1st sess., UN Doc. A/236 (11 December 1946) (General Assembly "*Affirms* the principles of international law recognized by the Charter of the Nürnberg Tribunal and the Judgment of the Tribunal"); International Law Commission, Principles of International Law Recognized in the Charter of the Nürnberg Tribunal and in the Judgment of the Tribunal, UN Doc. A/1316, 2 YBILC 374 ¶¶ 97–127 (2 August 1950). In its introductory material, Formulation of the Nürnberg Principles, *id.* ¶ 96, the ILC indicates that it is not expressing an opinion on the status of the Principles in international law, because "the Nürnberg Principles had been affirmed by the General Assembly," which had asked the ILC to "formulate" the principles in G.A. Res. 177(II) (21 November 1947).

[221] Sec.-Gen's ICTY Rep. ¶¶ 34, 42–44 (on violations of the laws and customs of war), 47–49 (on crimes against humanity), approved in S.C. Res. 827 (establishing the ICTY on the basis of the statute presented in the report).

[222] See, e.g., Prosecutor v. Kayishema, Judgement (Reasons), Case No. 95-1-A, ¶ 161 & n.241 (ICTR App. Ch., 1 June 2001), available through http://69.94.11.53/default.htm, relying on Prosecutor v. Tadic, Appeals Judgment ¶ 269, Case No. IT-94-1-A (ICTY App. Ch. 15 July 1999), available at http://www.un.org/icty/tadic/appeal/judgement/tad-aj990715e.pdf; *Aleksovski*, Appeals Judgment ¶¶ 107–09 (stating general rule of following its own prior practice absent "cogent reasons in the interests of justice"). See also L. Zegfeld, *The Bouterse*

must be careful that in doing so they do not treat cases that were decided after the act as though they had been decided before the act. For purposes of legality, only cases decided before an act can conceivably count as providing notice of what acts are criminal.

The conjunction of practice and *opinio juris* concerning legality is apparent in the judgments and other decisions of the ICTY and ICTR. These are the purposes of a judicial order and opinion: to order or perform a legal act and to explain its legal basis. The opinions of all of these tribunals discuss legality,[223] demonstrating both the practice of considering legality and the legal opinion that such consideration is required.

In the Statute of the International Court of Justice[224] and most books of doctrine, judicial opinions are a subsidiary source of international law.[225] In international criminal law and procedure, however, judgments and decisions of international criminal courts and tribunals from Nuremberg onward have been a primary, if not the primary, source of law. This is not surprising, because there has not been a general legislative authority for international criminal law. Thus, decisions of such courts have been the primary way in which both core international crimes and the human rights of persons brought before such courts have been defined. In fact the ICTY and ICTR have been very influential in the development of the law of the international crimes within their jurisdiction. Perhaps more important, their decisions directly control the liability of individuals for violations of criminal law.

The international criminal tribunals apply customary international law definitions of crimes. These must be formed by the concordance of practice and *opinio juris* as with other customary international law. However, Theodore Meron has pointed out that the ICTY has not always required the same degree of actual enforcement practice that might be required in general international law to create a custom. He argues that the ICTY uses methods of international humanitarian law and international human rights law, which depend more on *opinio juris* and less on practice than other

Case, 32 NETHERLANDS Y.B.I.L. 97, 99-100 (2001), relying on *Tadic*, Decision on Defence Motion for Interlocutory Appeal on Jurisdiction ¶ 99.

223 Chap. 6.a.

224 ICJ Statute art. 38(d).

225 For one source stating that the decisions of international criminal courts and tribunals remain "secondary" sources of international criminal law, see L. J. VAN DEN HERIK, THE CONTRIBUTION OF THE RWANDA TRIBUNAL TO THE DEVELOPMENT OF INTERNATIONAL LAW 275 (Martinus Nijhoff 2005).

international law. He indicates that this draws on the method of deducing general principles of law for law creation.[226]

This does create a danger that must be recognized. Unless this method is strictly limited, it can result in courts saying that customary international law crimes exist on the basis of very thin evidence. At worst, it can result in convictions where a defendant could have no reason to foresee that an act would be considered a crime. That is, this method can result in violations of the rules of non-retroactivity applicable in these courts and tribunals.[227]

It cannot be denied that the core international crimes are under-enforced. Many persons in many countries have committed such crimes without being prosecuted, even since World War II. Yet, as with domestic crimes, the fact that some individuals commit such crimes and escape detection or punishment does not mean that law forbidding the crimes does not exist. This emphasizes the difference between the international legal personality of international organizations and that of individuals. It makes clear that the role of practice of international organizations is growing in importance in determining the customary international law of crime. In contrast, the acts of individuals in committing crimes (whether or not they are punished) are not in the current system constitutive for the definition of crime.

The ICTY has held that the crime of contempt exists through general principles of law rather than through customary international law. Although the tribunal is not completely clear on the issue, its judgment is most naturally read to include both national and international judicial practice as instances from which general principles are deduced.[228]

In contrast, the states parties to the ICC Statute have brought it into force and created the ICC. The inclusion of both specific human rights (including legality) and the general requirement of consistency with international human rights[229] in the ICC Statute are the act of those states. However, the application and development of the law under the statute will principally be carried out by the court as a judicial organ. The court as a judicial organ may use its prior case law in making its decisions.[230] For the most part, its substantive criminal law decisions will probably amount to interpretation of a treaty text (i.e., the ICC Statute). However, as discussed earlier, some substantive law decisions following Security Council referrals or retroactive

[226] Meron at 263–64.
[227] Cf. Meron at 265.
[228] See Chap. 6.a.i.A.
[229] ICC Statute art. 21(3).
[230] ICC Statute art. 21(2).

acceptances of jurisdiction will need to be decisions based in customary international criminal law.[231]

Certain decisions, such as how to implement the statute in the Rules of Procedure and Evidence and the Elements of Crimes, devolve to the Assembly of States Parties (ASP) of the International Criminal Court. One can see the acts of states in the assembly as state practice but, because unanimity is not required, one can also see these acts as the acts of the ASP as an organ of the international organization called the International Criminal Court.[232]

As international organizations gain increasing authority, especially but not exclusively over individuals, this pattern may become more familiar. The acts of international organizations may gain in lawmaking force over both member states and (in the case of international criminal law and possibly other appropriate subjects) individuals over whom they have jurisdiction to prescribe. Their acts may also become acts relevant to the formation of other appropriate aspects of customary international law, as the judgments of international criminal courts and tribunals contribute to customary international criminal law today.

[231] See Chap. 6.c.ii.

[232] Cf. Gallant, ICC IO at 559–61 (considering the extent to which the ASP is the plenary quasi-political organ of the ICC as an international organization, even though it is not named as an organ of the court in the ICC Statute).

7

Legality in Customary International Law Today

7.a. THE CORE RULES OF LEGALITY IN CUSTOMARY INTERNATIONAL LAW

The history since World War II, set out in previous chapters, shows that the law has changed since Nuremberg. The central aspects of the principle of legality in criminal law, especially the non-retroactivity of crimes and punishments, are now rules of customary international law.

The statement of the principle of non-retroactivity of crimes and punishments from the Universal Declaration of Human Rights (UDHR) has become customary international law:

> No one shall be held guilty of any penal offense on account of any act or omission which did not constitute a penal offense, under national or international law, at the time when it was committed. Nor shall a heavier penalty be imposed than the one that was applicable at the time the penal offense was committed.[1]

The prohibition of the act and the maximum penalty must not only have been in existence at the time of the act. They must also have been applicable to the actor and the action at the time. An act cannot constitute an offense carrying a penalty except pursuant to some national or international law applicable to the actor and the act at the time committed.

This summary of the customary international human rights rules of legality is based on the practice and *opinio juris* of states, the organic documents, other documents, practice and *opinio juris* of international organizations

[1] Universal Declaration of Human Rights art. 11(2), G.A. Res. 217 (III), 10 December 1948 [hereinafter UDHR], GAOR, 3d sess., pt. I, p. 71.

(especially but not only international criminal courts and tribunals), writings of publicists, and other evidence.[2] Evidence that this is customary international law comes not only from the UDHR but also from the International Covenant on Civil and Political Rights (ICCPR),[3] the European Convention on Human Rights (ECHR),[4] the American Convention on Civil and Political Rights (ACHR),[5] the African Charter of Human and People's Rights (ACHPR),[6] the national constitutions and statutes in which the prohibition of retroactive crimes and punishments appears in similar formats to the treaties,[7] and the constitutions and statutes in which it appears in different formats.[8] All but two UN member states have adopted non-retroactivity of crimes and punishments by constitution or statute, or as a matter of treaty obligation.[9] Importantly for the creation of customary international law, almost all of the states that have not joined in the international human rights treaty system have accepted the rules of *nullum crimen* and *nulla poena*, most by constitution, but some by statute.[10]

This rule also appears in the organic documents or the jurisprudence, or both, of the modern international and internationalized criminal courts, as a matter required by law.[11] The rule appears throughout modern international

[2] Material collected in Chaps. 4 (state treaty practice and *opinio juris* and international human rights court practice), 5 (internal state practice), & 6 (international and hybrid national-international criminal tribunal practice).

[3] International Covenant on Civil and Political Rights art. 15, G.A. Res. 2200A (XXI), 21 GAOR Supp. No. 16, p. 52, UN Doc. A/6316, 993 U.N.T.S. 171 (16 December 1966, entered into force 23 March 1976) [hereinafter ICCPR].

[4] Also known as the European Convention on Human Rights and Fundamental Freedoms art. 7, 312 U.N.T.S. 221 (4 November 1950) [hereinafter ECHR].

[5] American Convention on Human Rights art. 9, 1114 U.N.T.S. 123 (22 November 1969), reprinted in 9 I.L.M. 673 (1970) [hereinafter ACHR].

[6] African Charter of Human and Peoples' Rights art. 7(2), OAU Doc. CAB/LEG/67/3/Rev. 5, art. 7(2) (27 June 1981) reprinted in 21 I.L.M. 59 (1982) [hereinafter ACHPR].

[7] See the list of more than one hundred national constitutions in Chap. 5.e note 348 (collected there because they support the proposition that individual criminal responsibility is required, but they also support the non-retroactivity of crimes and punishments in a format similar to that of the UDHR).

[8] See discussion in Chap. 5.c and 5.c.i, including the listing of all constitutions implementing non-retroactivity of crimes, note 48, and non-retroactivity of punishments, note 49.

[9] See discussion in Chap. 5.c.

[10] See Chap. 5.c.i notes 80–1, citing constitutions of Antigua and Barbuda, the Bahamas, Cuba, Fiji, Kiribati, Malaysia, Marshall Islands, Micronesia, Myanmar, Nauru, Oman, Pakistan (with exceptions for subversion of constitution), Palau, Papua New Guinea, Qatar, St. Kitts and Nevis, St. Lucia, Samoa, Singapore (with exceptions for political crimes), Solomon Islands, Tonga, Tuvalu, the United Arab Emirates, and Vanuatu, and citing statutes of the People's Republic of China and Saudi Arabia.

[11] See generally Chap. 6.

humanitarian law, including the law applicable to internal armed conflicts: states have bound themselves to the rules of legality in times of greatest stress.[12] Leading publicists declare it to be customary international law (both international human rights law and international humanitarian law) and even a peremptory norm.[13]

These rules do not prohibit statutory interpretation or development of the criminal law through common law or (in the case of international crimes) customary international law processes. However, to count as "a criminal offence under national or international law at the time [an act] was committed," the statute, common law, treaty law, or customary international law rules applicable to the actor at the time must have made it foreseeable that the act would be held to be criminal.[14]

This statement of the law is supported by the consistent application and restatement of these principles in multiple treaties and other state practice, both external and internal, including adoption of constitutional and other legal provisions and decisions of national courts,[15] and by practice of international organizations, including decisions of international criminal tribunals

[12] Geneva Convention (No. IV) art. 65 (forbidding retroactivity of crimes and punishments as to protected civilians); Geneva Convention (No. III) art. 99 (same as to prisoners of war); Additional Protocol I to the 1949 Geneva Conventions art. 75(4)(c) (1977); Additional Protocol II to the 1949 Geneva Conventions art. 6(2)(c) (1977) (both Additional Protocol provisions adopted by consensus; Additional Protocol II provision applies to internal armed conflicts); JEAN-MARIE HENCKAERTS & LOUISE DOSWALD-BECK, 1 CUSTOMARY INTERNATIONAL HUMANITARIAN LAW (RULES) R. 101 (Cambridge Univ. Press 2005) (study issued by the ICRC) [hereinafter ICRC, CUSTOMARY IHL] (rule of customary international law applying to internal as well as international armed conflict), supported by extensive documentation in 2 (pt. 2) ICRC, CUSTOMARY IHL (PRACTICE) §§3673–3716, pp. 2493–2500.

[13] THEODORE MERON, WAR CRIMES LAW COMES OF AGE 244 (Oxford: Oxford Univ. Press 1998) [hereinafter Meron] ("customary, even peremptory, norm"); Susan Lamb, *Nullum crimen, nulla poena sine lege* in 1 THE ROME STATUTE OF THE INTERNATIONAL CRIMINAL COURT: A COMMENTARY 735 (Antonio Cassese, Paola Gaeta & John R. W. D. Jones, eds., Oxford Univ. Press 2002) [hereinafter CASSESE, ET AL., COMMENTARY] (principle of legality has become "clearly and firmly entrenched in customary international law" since World War II, i.e., in customary international human rights law); 1 ICRC, CUSTOMARY IHL, R. 101, p. 371 (non-retroactivity of crimes and punishments is part of international humanitarian law). For a discussion of views that legality does not fully apply to the core international crimes, see Chaps. 7.b.iv, 7.c.ii.

[14] See Chap. 7.b.i. For general principles of law as a part of international law, see Chap. 7.b.iii.

[15] See generally Chap. 5. Note that the adoption of the ICC Statute, on which the discussion of Chap. 6.c is based, was an act of the states becoming parties to the statute. We do not yet have a great deal of practice on the issues of legality emerging from the court as an international organization.

and international human rights bodies and organs.[16] It encapsulates the customary international human rights law principle of legality in national and international courts.

There has even been international imposition of these principles into national and local administration outside of the context of treaties where legality is directly required. This occurred in occupied Germany, Japan, and Iraq, and UN-administered areas.[17] As mentioned earlier, the UN Charter does not explicitly list non-retroactivity of crimes and punishments as an international human right. Thus, this practice, when done under the charter in recent times (i.e., through direct UN Administration in Kosovo and East Timor, and through the Security Council-approved Coalition Provisional Authority in Iraq) is particularly indicative that this right has become customary international law.[18]

To echo Jerome Hall, deliberate retroactive creation of new crimes and increased punishments is not plausible now, even in international criminal law, if it ever was.[19] Any failure to enforce the core principles of legality at Nuremberg, Tokyo, and the other post–World War II tribunals (as by the retroactive creation of the crime against peace and the arguably retroactive creation of crimes against humanity) has been decisively rejected by state and international organization practice and *opinio juris* since then. However, the substantive criminal law made in those tribunals, particularly the law of crimes against humanity, has been accepted as legitimate for use in the process of creating international criminal law.[20]

This version of legality applies as a matter of international human rights law in both national and international tribunals, whether national or international crimes are charged. Stronger versions of the principle of legality exist in many national systems and even in one regional human rights system.[21] However, these stronger versions have not become customary international law binding states and/or international organizations outside the treaty context.

[16] Chap. 6, and the material from Chap. 4(h, j, k) above on decisions of the ECtHR, IACtHR, African Commission on Human and Peoples' Rights, and the Human Rights Committee.

[17] See Chap. 5.c.iv & 5.f.i. For the UN Trust Territories, see Chap. 6.b.ii.

[18] See Chaps. 5.f.i & 6.b.

[19] Cf. Jerome Hall, *Nulla Poena Sine Lege*, 47 YALE L.J. 165, 172 (1937) [hereinafter Hall].

[20] See, e.g., Report of the Secretary-General pursuant to Paragraph 2 of Security Council Resolution 808, UN Doc. S/25704 ¶ 47 (3 May 1993), available at http://www.un.org/icty/legaldoc-e/basic/statut/s25704.htm [hereinafter Sec-Gen's ICTY Rep.].

[21] See ACHR arts. 7–9.

For example, the rule *nullum crimen sine praevia lege scripta* is followed by many civil law and other countries, and is the rule followed in the ICC (except in cases of retroactive acceptance of jurisdiction or Security Council referral of a situation involving a non-state party to the ICC Statute). However, this rule has not yet become customary international law.[22] It is not yet a universal requirement of the common law tradition. As another example, the prohibition against retroactive creation of criminal jurisdictions is part of the ACHR and the laws of a number of states. Yet, many non-ACHR states have not adopted this as part of their law. It is not in the ICCPR and has been rejected by the creation of courts such as the ICTY, ICTR, SCSL, the Iraqi Special Tribunal, and the currently developing Extraordinary Chambers for Cambodia.[23] A third example is that there is no "detailed catalogue of crimes and penalties" in international criminal law, as required by the version of *nulla poena* applied in some states.[24] Even a commentator steeped in the civil law tradition, Stefan Glaser, points out that the key aspect of legality is the refusal to criminalize an act that was innocent when done.[25] Finally, the rule of *lex mitior* (applying any less onerous criminal law enacted after the criminal act) has not yet passed into customary international law, though it is widely adopted by treaty law.[26]

One can characterize the development of non-retroactivity of crimes and punishments as a rule of customary international law in several ways. One can view it as a change in the substantive law of international human rights,[27] as a limitation on jurisdiction to define crime,[28] as a limitation on sovereignty,[29] or as all three. Certainly the legitimate authority to define

[22] In addition to the evidence in Chap. 5.c.ii, see WARD N. FERDINANDUSSE, DIRECT APPLICATION OF INTERNATIONAL CRIMINAL LAW IN NATIONAL COURTS 233 (TMC Asser 2006) [hereinafter Ferdinandusse].

[23] See Chap. 6.

[24] See SALVATORE ZAPPALÀ, HUMAN RIGHTS IN INTERNATIONAL CRIMINAL PROCEEDINGS 195 (Oxford Univ. Press 2003).

[25] Stefan Glaser, *La méthode d'interpretation en droit international pénal*, 9 RIVISTA ITALIANA DI DIRITTO E PROCEDURA PENALE 757, 762–64 (1966) [hereinafter Glaser, *La méthode*].

[26] ICCPR art. 15(1), except for such states that have reserved against this rule, discussed in Chap. 4.g.

[27] See, e.g., *Milutinovic*, Decision on Dragoljub Ojdanic's Motion Challenging Jurisdiction: Joint Criminal Enterprise ¶ 10 (to effect that principle of legality is substantive rule of criminal law protecting the accused, not a matter of personal jurisdiction).

[28] Cf., e.g., *id.* at ¶¶ 9, 10 (to effect that retroactive creation of crime would exceed ICTY's subject matter jurisdiction).

[29] Compare Nuremberg Judgment, 1 IMT TRIAL at 219.

crime is a traditional attribute of sovereignty. The principle of legality is a limitation upon it, as are many of the human rights protections of modern international law. Judge Theodore Meron has pointed out that, in some cases, customary international human rights law has been found to exist largely on the basis of *opinio juris*, with little practice required.[30] To the extent that this is true, much of the material in this book – surveying state and international organization practice through treaties, constitutions, statutes, other binding legal texts, and case law – might not be necessary to a conclusion that the non-retroactivity of crimes and punishments is a matter of customary international human rights law. However, this conclusion is far safer and more secure if it is grounded in study of practice as well as *opinio juris.*

This book discusses some aspects of legality other than the non-retroactivity of the definition of crimes and punishments. The doctrine that punishment is personal and may not be imposed collectively, or on persons unconnected with the commission of a crime, is also customary international law, although the evidence for it may not be quite as "thick" as the evidence for non-retroactivity of crimes and punishments.[31] As a matter of customary international law, both national and international criminal courts must be independent, impartial, and created by law.[32]

7.b. ELABORATION OF THE CORE RULES: *NULLUM CRIMEN*

The retroactive creation of new crimes by national or international law (including treaty law, customary international law and general principles of law recognized by the community of nations) is prohibited – that is, acts not prohibited by some law applicable to an act at the time of the act may not be criminalized retroactively. As a corollary, retroactive creation of new crimes by analogy is prohibited, to the extent that acts that are not criminal under the statute in force at the time of commission of an act may not be criminalized retroactively just because there is an analogy between the prohibited act and the non-prohibited act that suggests that the non-prohibited act should be criminalized.

A person may be convicted for the criminal acts of others (e.g., on the basis of joint criminal enterprise liability) only if, at the time of the accused person's alleged complicity, the law allowed for the imputation of liability from

[30] Meron at 264.
[31] See Chap. 7.f.
[32] See, e.g., *Tadic* (created by law); *Furundzija*, Trial Judgement (impartiality).

the acts that the accused committed.[33] For example, a plurality opinion of the U.S. Supreme Court recently emphasized that conspiracy to commit a violation of the law of war does not exist as a crime in international criminal law.[34] Without some act or omission by an accused person that was illegal under applicable law at the time, the "legality of the charge" against that person is called into question. Unless the accused can be charged under some theory of criminal involvement that applied to his or her acts at the time committed, the accused would not have committed any act that was criminal under law applicable to him or her when done.[35]

This version of *nullum crimen sine lege* (or, as some would say, *nullum crimen sine iure*[36]) has become part of customary international law. It is irrelevant whether the crime in question is created through national or international law (including the subset of international law called "general principles of law recognized by the community of nations"). This is demonstrated by the preceding history as well as the opinions of publicists.[37] As will be seen, though, some publicists disagree on the applicability of *nulla poena* to crimes under international law.[38]

The applicable law (*lege* or *iure*) may include crimes previously defined by the judiciary (through common law processes) and by international law (including customary international law, applicable treaty law, and general principles of law recognized by the community of nations). The applicable law may include national law defining ordinary crimes, so far as it demonstrates what acts persons might have notice would be considered criminal.[39] How the system deals with the uncertainty inherent in language (either statutory or case law) defining crimes will be discussed next.

[33] See *Milutinovic, supra* note 27, at ¶ 10 (treating this as matter of substantive criminal law rather than jurisdiction).

[34] Hamdan v. Rumsfeld, 548 U.S. 557 (2006) (plurality opinion as to this issue).

[35] See *Hamden* (pt. V of plurality opinion).

[36] See Chap. 1 (introductory section), discussing Glaser, *La méthode*, at 766; M. Cherif Bassiouni, Crimes against Humanity in International Criminal Law 144, 162 (2d ed., Transnational Publishers 1999) [hereinafter Bassiouni, CAH-ICL]; Ferdinandusse at 232–36; Geert-Jan Knoops, Defenses in Contemporary International Criminal Law 156–57 (Transnational Publishers 2001).

[37] Gerhard Werle et al., Principles of International Criminal Law ¶ 93 at 33 (TMC Asser Press 2005); Susan Lamb, *Nullum crimen, nulla poena sine lege* in 1 Cassese, et al., Commentary at 735 (principle of legality has become "clearly and firmly entrenched in customary international law" since World War II); Bassiouni, CAH-ICL at 144, 162; as well as material discussed in Chapter 1.b.v.

[38] See material discussed in Chap. 7.c.ii.

[39] See the material on retroactive re-characterization in Chaps. 3.c.i & 6.a.iv.

7.b.i. *Foreseeability*

Within limits, interpretation and clarification of statutes and development of criminal law (either national or international) through judicial decision is not prohibited by customary international law. When this is done, any arguable expansion of criminal liability from prior decisions by this means must have been foreseeable to the person being charged and the relevant public at the time that the crime was committed.[40] In other words, an act or omission may constitute a criminal offense only if it was foreseeable that national or international criminal law to which the actor was subject at the time would be applied to the act.

7.b.i.A. Indeterminacy of Language and the Necessity of a Foreseeability Doctrine

Foreseeability is a critical element of any theory of legality meant to apply to most or all current legal systems. Most criminal acts were clearly criminal at the time committed. However, to paraphrase Jerome Hall, we can say that "not all acts found criminal at trial"[41] were within the hard core of criminal acts defined by a statute, code, or common law rule. In many systems, there is no binding requirement that the absolutely narrowest definition of crimes set forth in statutes, codes, or case law be adopted. The current system of international human rights law does not require this.

What the current system of international law does require is that the act have at least been foreseeably criminal – reasonably likely to be held criminal – under existing law applicable to the actor when the act is done. This makes sense of the fact that the strictest modes of interpretation are not universal under either national or international law. It also imposes a real legal limitation on the creativity of prosecutors and the discretion of courts in applying criminal law. It maintains the prohibition on retroactive criminal legislation (except for mitigating legislation).

In a perfect world, a doctrine of foreseeability would not be necessary. Criminal law would be perfectly clear, and no one would act at an unclear boundary of the law. In this world, legality could be enforced on the basis of

[40] Cf. William A. Schabas, The UN International Criminal Tribunals: The Former Yugoslavia, Rwanda and Sierra Leone 63 (Cambridge Univ. Press 2006) [hereinafter Schabas, UN ICT].

[41] Hall at 171. See also Charles Sampford, Retrospectivity and the Rule of Law 16–17, *passim* (Oxford Univ. Press 2006).

clear meanings. In a slightly less perfect world, courts would always apply the doctrine of *lex stricta* (always applying the narrower of two reasonable meanings for the definition of a crime). Unfortunately, neither of these reflects the current practice in the international sphere, or in many national spheres. They may not even reflect possible states of this world of imperfect language.[42]

Many national jurisdictions do enforce fairly strict, narrow limits on the interpretation of criminal law. In these systems, something greater than mere foreseeability may properly be required. Yet perfect congruence with the narrowest possible reading of statutes or decisions is not a rule that has ever been enforced by international law. It is also possible that such a world could not reasonably exist, because with every narrowing of criminal definition, new areas of ambiguity might open up, leading to constant erosion of definitions of crime.

This transforms the principle of legality and the particular rules of non-retroactivity that are enforced into pragmatic rules rather than absolutely clear-cut ones. That is the price that we pay for operating in the current world, with our limited human understanding of rules and our ambiguous languages.

7.b.i.B. Foreseeability and the Development of Criminal Law by Judicial Decision, Statutory Interpretation, and Analogy

Hall's conception of the extent to which the criminal law may expand in a common law case can be generalized.[43] It can apply to both common and civil law countries and to both statutory and case law definition of crime, and will provide appropriate boundaries for statutory interpretation, use of analogy, and development of case law.

If an act can reasonably be construed as within the ambit of definition of crime existing at the time of the act (whether statutory, common law, or international law), the actor is sufficiently warned so that a conviction will not violate the customary international law version of *nullum crimen sine lege.* This is true even if no case decided before the act was committed had held the specific act to be criminal. This articulation provides an operational

[42] An argument that such a world would be possible on the basis of consistent application of the rule of lenity (*lex stricta*) is found at Matthew H. Kramer, Objectivity and the Rule of Law 120 (Cambridge Univ. Press 2007). To the extent that Kramer suggests that existing liberal democracies apply this rule with sufficient consistency to state that this world actually exists, he is unfortunately incorrect.

[43] See Hall at 171–72.

definition for the meaning of a foreseeable development in criminal law that does not violate the principle of legality.

This formulation rationalizes the limitations on statutory interpretation (in both the civil and the common law systems), common law criminal law development, and civil law use of the techniques of analogy. It harmonizes the principle of legality with the understanding that all definitions of crimes and defenses will have some degree of indeterminacy.

This formulation does not require any given national system to adopt a strict or liberal construction of penal statutes, nor does it prevent common law development of the law of crimes. Civil law systems may continue to use the language of analogy.[44] Instead, this formulation limits the use of these techniques of crime definition to applications where the criminalization was foreseeable at the time of the act.

Foreseeability in this sense can also be used to rationalize the issue of alleged new modes of committing crimes, such as joint criminal responsibility. The question remains the same. At the time the person acted, was that person's act foreseeably within the then-current definition of criminal acts (i.e., could it reasonably have been construed as being within the ambit of the definition of crime existing when it was done?). If so, then the naming of the method of commission as "joint criminal responsibility,"[45] for example, is permissible. On the other hand, if the act was not foreseeable as falling within the definition of criminal acts at the time, then saying that a doctrine such as joint criminal responsibility exists would not justify the prosecution.

The fact that a case arguably imposed criminal liability in excess of that permitted by the principle of legality does not prohibit that case from being used in the definition of crime in the future.[46] This is clearly true for case law, such as the main Nuremberg Judgment, which arose before the principle of legality crystallized into a rule of customary international law. It continues to be true today. Even cases that arguably violate legality state the views of the court concerning the law to be applied in the future. Thus, for example, even if one disagrees with the courts of the United Kingdom and the European Court of Human Rights about the proper application of the principle of legality to the abolition of the marital defense to rape,[47]

[44] Cf. Iceland Const. art. 69; Mexico Const. art. 14; Chap. 5.c.v.D.
[45] See *Milutinovic, supra* note 27, at ¶ 10.
[46] See IMTFE Judgment, Dissenting Opinion of Pal at 56, 105 IMTFE Records.
[47] See *C. R. v. United Kingdom.*

that doctrine has now been abolished for acts committed after those cases were decided, and there can be no more claims based on violations of legality.

The rule requiring narrow interpretation of criminal statutes and lenity in their application is a theoretical desideratum. It is present in the ICC Statute and is set forth in the internal law of many states. However, it has not become a requirement of current customary international law. Even in states generally requiring narrow interpretation of criminal statutes, the narrowest possible reading of a statute is not always followed. Broad interpretation applied to acts that have already occurred is permitted by the international law version of legality, so long as the particular interpretation chosen would have been foreseeable to the person in question from the law available at the time of the act.

7.b.i.C. Foreseeability, *Lex certa*, and the Void-for-Vagueness Doctrine

The standard of clarity in criminal law was recently well stated by Ward N. Ferdinandusse: "The essence of the principle of legality, that an individual may not be prosecuted for conduct she could not know was punishable, requires the law to be so clear as to make its consequences foreseeable."[48] This articulation of foreseeability addresses one of the philosophical problems of the principle of legality. The rule of non-retroactivity of crimes is itself subject to the bane of all legal rules: the indeterminacy of language.[49] It will never be perfectly clear that a set of possible actions are within a definition of crime; and that the complement of the set will be outside the definition of the crime – that is, that there are no close or difficult cases. The rules of non-retroactivity as they exist today admit this. This is why reasonable foreseeability is the standard: the understanding that certain acts may likely be held culpable provides all the protection that can be guaranteed. Even that issue will sometimes be arguable on either side. Yet, this may well be the best that can be achieved.

The principles of notice and avoidance of oppressive government behavior underlie modern rules of non-retroactivity of crimes.[50] They are hardly coherent without some notion of reasonable certainty of the law. This

[48] Ferdinandusse at 238, relying on *G. v. France*, Judgment, Eur. Ct. H.R. ¶¶ 24–25 (27 September 1995), and *Sunday Times v. United Kingdom*, Judgment, Eur. Ct. H.R. ¶¶ 48–49 (26 April 1979). For a clear explication of foreseeability in the context of the core international crimes, see generally Ferdinandusse at 238–48.

[49] See Chap. 1.c.i.

[50] See Chap. 1.a.

certainly was one point of the substantive portion of the PCIJ *Advisory Opinion on the Consistency of Certain Danzig Legislative Decrees with the Constitution of the Free City.*[51] The U.S. Supreme Court has dealt with this issue by holding that statutes that are not reasonably certain may be considered "void for vagueness."[52]

Internationally, there have not been many decisions concerning *lex certa* since the Danzig case that would clarify exactly how much play there can be in the meaning of a criminal enactment before it violates the rule that there can be no crime unless a wrongful act has been previously defined. The Human Rights Committee of the ICCPR, in a General Comment on states of emergency, stated that criminal law must be "limited to clear and precise provisions in the law that was in place and applicable at the time the act or omission took place."[53] The European Commission on Human Rights has pointed out that methods of statutory interpretation must produce results compatible with the requirement that the meaning of the statute have been reasonably certain at the time a defendant acted.[54]

The doctrine that an unclear law is void for vagueness is not currently required by customary international law. There are other actions that a court can take with respect to a law with an impermissible degree of unclarity, such as judicial clarification or determination of whether a given case is within the clear core of meaning of the statute. The international obligation is that the law give a reasonable understanding of what is prohibited. How this is enforced is largely left to the legal systems concerned.

7.b.i.D. Foreseeability and Accessibility

Part of the requirement of notice and foreseeability is accessibility of the law to those who are required to obey it. This is the point of promulgation and publication rules that appear in some of the constitutions that require statutes for criminalization.[55] As has been pointed out, common law systems

[51] 4 December 1935 PCIJ (ser. A/B) No. 65.

[52] See, e.g., Papachristou v. City of Jacksonville, 405 U.S. 156 (1972).

[53] Raija Hanski & Martin Scheinin, Leading Cases of the Human Rights Committee (Turku, Finland: Institute for Human Rights, Åbo Akademi University 2003) 157, citing General Comment No. 29 (72), UN Doc. CCPR/C/21/Rev.1/Add.11 ¶ 7.

[54] See *X, Ltd. v. UK* ¶ 9, 28 DR 77, Eur. Comm. H.R. (1982), noted in Richard Clayton & Hugh Tomlinson, The Law of Human Rights ¶ 11.260, p. 672 (Oxford Univ. Press 2000) [hereinafter Clayton & Tomlinson].

[55] See Chap. 5.c(ii, iii).

have created definitions of crime that are known by the general populace about as well as those produced by civil law systems, even when there were no statutory texts involved.[56] Similarly, the heart of the core international crimes of genocide, crimes against humanity, and war crimes (i.e., the forbidding of killing, maiming, torturing, and other inhumane mistreatment) is well known to be criminal everywhere,[57] whether or not all individuals understand the substance, or even the existence, of international criminal law.

There are different views of whether accessibility is a separate element of legality from foreseeability or it is merely one fact that makes criminal liability for an act foreseeable.[58] To some extent, these are academic distinctions. Two things can be said. The law by which persons are convicted of crimes cannot be kept secret. However, ignorance of the law – the fact that a given person does not know a given law – is not an excuse, so long as that law is accessible.

7.b.i.E. Dangers of the Foreseeability Doctrine and Limitations on the Doctrine

The doctrine of foreseeability must be carefully applied and circumscribed. Otherwise, it may swallow the principle of legality whole.

Foreseeability assumes a law applicable to the actor in some existing legal system. A political force with its own vision of criminal law may not take over a state and retroactively apply its own new criminal definitions. It could not argue that its preannounced intentions made the new law foreseeable to the citizenry.[59] What is still permissible is that existing law applicable to an actor may be re-characterized as law existing in a new or different legal system (e.g., where acts that are war crimes under existing customary

[56] See Chap. 2.a.i.

[57] See, e.g., United States v. Ohlendorff (Einsatzgruppen Case), 4 Trials of War Criminals before the Nuernberg Military Tribunals under Control Council Law No. 10, 411, 459, 497 (US Military Tribunal II-A, 10 April 1948) [hereinafter *Einsatzgruppen Case*, 4 T.W.C.]. Ferdinandusse, at 237, agrees and points out that this reasoning is applicable "[w]hether one believes that the core crimes constitute a modern form of natural law or not."

[58] See Ferdinandusse at 236–38.

[59] William A. Schabas, An Introduction to the International Criminal Court 71–72 (2d ed., Cambridge Univ. Press 2004), appears to indicate it is permissible for the ICC to apply non-customary international law to persons with no connection to an ICC party state after a Security Council referral. This is an overstatement of the doctrine of foreseeability. See Chap. 6.c.ii.

international law are punished by a new international tribunal or a state which had not previously exercised jurisdiction over them).

Thus, foreseeability does not allow an international organization created by treaty to apply its own substantive criminal law in derogation of the public international law rules specifying to whom treaties may apply. Specifically, the International Criminal Court (ICC) may not retroactively apply non-customary international criminal law to persons with no relevant connection with an ICC state party, unless there is some source of law applicable to the person which made the act alleged against the person criminal when committed.[60] The principle of legality requires that there must have been a law applicable to the actor which criminalized the acts. In these cases, by hypothesis, the law of the ICC did not apply to the actor under the customary international law rules of treaty law.

Perhaps the greatest danger of explicitly recognizing a doctrine of foreseeability is this: courts may, without thought or analysis, simply declare that an arguable expansion of criminal liability was "foreseeable."[61] Certainly this is the danger most commonly faced in applying rules of legality. It is particularly a danger because there is no internationally required set of rules of interpretation (whether of statutes or of common law cases), and in fact interpretation in criminal law varies from jurisdiction to jurisdiction. Each jurisdiction must develop a means for ensuring foreseeability in its own interpretive system. Consider, for example, Meron's point that the ICTY sometimes states that a crime exists in customary international law even though the evidence of actual practice of prosecution of the crime is quite thin.[62] There is a great danger that this method of interpretation can open persons to prosecution when there was no reason to foresee that act would be held criminal at the time it was done. The danger is greatest if a court changes the method of interpretation (e.g., by adopting a different and looser definition of how customary international law criminalizes acts), especially where that change is not acknowledged. Obviously, the closer a jurisdiction comes to the ideal of narrow interpretation of criminal law, the smaller danger is posed here.

Indeed, some of this risk inheres in any system of law based on foreseeability or reasonable expectations. That is, foreseeability and expectations are based on both the existing articulations of rules of law and the methods

[60] See Chap. 6.c.ii.

[61] This criticism has been leveled at the Eur. Ct. H.R. judgments on legality discussed in Chap. 4.h.

[62] Meron at 263–64.

used to interpret and develop them. When the latter change without explicit examination and acknowledgement, developments in the law might be called "foreseeable" when, under the conditions existing at the time of the act, they were not. This danger can never be wholly avoided where there is a need to interpret and apply statutory or other enacted texts (as in virtually all legal systems existing today) or to apply rules developed through cases (as in the common law system and sometimes other systems). This difficulty may well inhere in the inability of any linguistic expression of a general rule (in any language) to precisely cover a specific set of situations that have not occurred yet and to precisely exclude all other situations.

Another danger is that acts that are clearly not criminal under the law as currently stated will be retroactively proscribed on the ground that it was "foreseeable" that the law was going to change.[63] To avoid retroactive law-making, and to preserve freedom of non-criminal action, this cannot be the meaning given to foreseeability.[64] Rather, the question must be whether the conduct could have been expected to fall within a reasonable interpretation of the criminal law as it existed at the time of the act. This is a danger to which the common law is particularly vulnerable. In all modern legal systems observing principles of legality, statutes expanding criminal liability simply do not apply to crimes committed before their effective date. To avoid this danger, it is useful to avoid language suggesting that "illegality" or even "manifest illegality"[65] of an act is enough to make it foreseeably criminal. A phrase such as "manifest criminality" is less subject to misinterpretation or abuse.

Note, however, that the person involved need not actually have foreseen the applicability of the law to his or her actions. It is a question of what might be called "publicly available meaning" of the law in effect at the time of the actions: could the law as then existing have been reasonably understood to proscribe the conduct involved?

Language and modes of interpreting language work to provide reasonably certain meanings in most areas of life. It is not too much to insist that they do so in setting forth the criminal law that all must obey. When the concept of foreseeability is properly applied, it can provide such reasonable certainty.

[63] This criticism too has been made concerning the retroactive marital rape cases from the United Kingdom and the Eur. Ct. H.R. See *C. R. v. United Kingdom*; *S. W. v. United Kingdom*, discussed in Chap. 4.h.

[64] Cf. Peter Westen, *Two Rules of Legality in Criminal Law*, 26 LAW & PHILOSOPHY 229, 239 (2006).

[65] This is the formulation of Ferdinandusse at 242–48.

7.b.ii. *Re-characterization in International and National Courts*

The doctrine of legality of crimes demands that an act must be criminal under some law applicable to the actor when the act is committed. Issues of characterization affecting legality may arise, in either national or international law, and in either national or international courts.

7.b.ii.A. Retroactive Re-characterization of a Crime as International, or as a Different Type of International Crime, in National or International Courts

If an act was not a crime in customary international law and was not a crime under general principles of law when committed,[66] international human rights law permits its prosecution in a national or international criminal tribunal as an international crime only if it was a crime under applicable national law or applicable conventional international law at the time of its commission.[67] The change in designation of an international crime, for example, from being a war crime to being a crime against humanity, after the commission of the crime is not prohibited by international human rights law either.[68] In both cases, the core rule of legality, that the act must have been a crime when committed, is met.

Retroactive re-characterization is an exceptional technique that is not frequently used in any system. For the most part, in all systems, the courts, lawyers, and people at large consider whether an act is a crime under the laws of their given system. Retroactive re-characterization thus seems anomalous, and in fact is anomalous. Nonetheless, it appears to exist and not to be prohibited by customary international human rights law.

Courts must strictly comply with three requirements to avoid the great potential for abuse in retroactive re-characterization. First, the act must be a crime under applicable international law at the time it is prosecuted in court. Courts need to avoid short-circuiting the discussion of this issue.

[66] See ICCPR art. 15(2), discussed in Chap. 4.b.ii.C.

[67] See Prosecutor v. Hadzihasanovic ¶ 34 (ICTY App. Ch., 16 July 2003). Accord, *Norman* (SCSL App. Ch. 31 May 2004); Prosecutor v. Furundzija, Trial Judgement ¶¶ 168–69, Case No. IT-95-17/1 (ICTY Tr. Ch. 1998) (on rape); Prosecutor v. Delalic, Appeals Judgement ¶¶ 178-80, Case No. IT-96-21 (ICTY App. Ch. 20 February 1991); Prosecutor v. Akayesu, Judgement ¶ 617, Case No. ICTR-96-4-T (2 September 1998); Chap. 6.a.iv; cf. cases discussed in Chap. 3.c.i (no injustice in convicting under Control Council Law No. 10, where the act charged was a crime under German law).

[68] Nuremberg Judgment, 1 IMT, Trial at 254. See also *Trial of Rauter*, 14 UNWCC, Law Rep., Case No. 88, p. 89, 119–20 (Netherlands Special Ct. of Cass., 12 January 1949).

They must examine practice and *opinio juris* closely in deciding whether any given acts are crimes under customary international law.[69] Otherwise courts run the risk of exceeding their own subject-matter jurisdiction.[70]

Second, the act must have been a crime under some law binding the actor at the time that the act was committed. As has been shown, this law may be national criminal law, international conventional (treaty) law applying criminal law to the actor, or international customary law under another name (as where what were formerly solely war crimes are also called crimes against humanity). Again, courts need to examine closely the specific law alleged to support the claim that the accused had notice that the act performed was criminal rather than simply claim that the act was so.[71] Courts must be sure that the specific law was in fact applicable to the actor at the time he or she acted. Here it is even clearer that an error would cause the court to exceed its subject-matter jurisdiction and subject an accused to a wrongful conviction.

Third, as discussed subsequently, sentencing procedures are needed to ensure that sentences do not exceed the maximum that could have been given for the crime as to which the accused has notice (*nulla poena sine lege*).[72] Where the crime is related to the military under national law, this frequently is not a problem, because military offenses often carry harsh penalties. Indeed, after the World War II trials, one could reasonably conclude that international crimes all carried the death penalty as their maximum punishment.[73] But where the act was simply a crime under national law when committed, there is a danger of a harsher sentence being meted out under international law.

This re-characterization process is strictly limited to crimes that were arguably new under international humanitarian law but that cover acts

[69] Cf. Meron at 265 (criticizing ICTY Appeals Chamber in *Tadic* Interlocutory Appeal on Jurisdiction for not doing more "to identify actual state practice, whether evincing respect for, or violation of, [relevant] rules"), citing Military and Paramilitary Activities in and against Nicaragua (Nicaragua v. United States), Merits, 1986 I.C.J. Rep. 14, 98 ¶ 96 (27 June 1986).

[70] Cf. *Milutinovic* at ¶ 9.

[71] Compare *Akayesu*, Judgement ¶ 617 (relying on adoption of provisions of Additional Protocol II by Rwanda into domestic criminal law as basis for notice to accused) with *Einsatzgruppen Case*, 4 T.W.C. at 497 (conclusory statement, quoted in Chap. 3.c.i, that murder, etc., that were domestic crimes are now international crimes as well).

[72] See Chap. 7.c.iii.

[73] See Nuremberg Charter art. 27; Nuremberg Judgment; Tokyo Judgment. [Brand,] Punishment of Criminals, 15 U.N.W.C.C., Law Rep. 200–01, cites post–World War II cases from Norwegian and Australian courts. The Australian cases involved death sentences imposed for rape; William A. Schabas, *Nulla poena sine lege*, in OBSERVERS' NOTES 463.

that were previously crimes only under national law applying to the actor or were previously crimes under a different name in international law applying to the actor. It cannot be used, for example, as an excuse for an occupying power to broaden its general criminal law authority over persons in occupied territory.

The era of re-characterization of crimes that were solely national into crimes that are international may be drawing to a close, as substantive international criminal law stabilizes. Most of the war crimes in the ICC Statute are clearly crimes under customary international law already, including those crimes which may be committed in non-international armed conflicts. The same can be said of genocide and crimes against humanity. There will be fewer and fewer situations in which one needs to determine whether a crime under the ICC Statute is also a crime under customary international law or a crime under national law, unless the states parties to the ICC Statute amend the statute to add new crimes that arguably depart from then-existing customary international criminal law.[74]

At some point in the not-too-distant future, one may see a principle of legality emerge that will not permit re-characterization of crimes. This will not quite be *nullum crimen sine lege praevia scripta* (requiring prior written legislation) because common law systems may retain judicially developed, rather than legislative, crime definition. However, crimes will need to be previously proclaimed by the system in which prosecution is occurring.

As a scholar, I cannot avoid reporting on the existence of re-characterization as a method of applying international criminal law and its permissibility in the current scheme of customary international human rights law. As a supporter of human rights at the national and international levels, I believe that this doctrine is too easily subject to abuse, and hope that this practice will soon wither away.

7.b.ii.B. Legality and the Debate over Direct Application of International Criminal Law in National Courts

In national courts, prosecutions for violations of international criminal law (genocide, crimes against humanity, war crimes) are generally conducted pursuant to national statutes that, in one way or another, incorporate the

[74] But cf. H. Donnedieu de Vabres, *Le procès de Nuremberg devant les principes modernes du droit pénal international,* 70(I) Recueil des Cours 477, 574–5 (1947) (expressing pessimism about legality ever having a stronger meaning in the changing world of international affairs than it did at Nuremberg).

substance of international criminal law. There is a current debate over whether and to what extent this is application of international law directly in national courts, and whether and to what extent this is an extraterritorial application of national law.[75] To the extent that national law is used, one can treat these cases as cases of re-characterization of an international law crime as a national law crime. Such prosecutions may be conducted on the basis of universal jurisdiction (i.e., where there is no connection between the forum state and the offense, the victim or the alleged perpetrator).

The non-retroactivity principle of international human rights law applies in the same way no matter how the debate over the source of law is resolved. An actor may be prosecuted if the act alleged was a crime under international criminal law applicable to him or her at the time of the act. Such a prosecution does not violate international human rights law, even if the national statute granting national jurisdiction or defining the crime for national law purposes was passed after the alleged act.[76]

Some states are a bit more strict. The House of Lords, in the *Pinochet* case, required that the national law implementing the Torture Convention have been in effect before the act alleged, or extradition for torture could not be allowed.[77] This stronger version of legality is not required by customary international human rights law. Legality in customary international human rights law as it exists today focuses on the law applicable to the actor at the time of the action rather than the law of some other forum that eventually deals with the actor. This does not mean that the House of Lords' action was prohibited by the customary international law of legality – merely that it was not compelled by such law.

7.b.ii.C. Universal Jurisdiction over International Law Crimes

The principle of non-retroactivity as described here would logically have consequences for the exercise of universal jurisdiction in national courts over international crimes. States may or may not claim to be re-characterizing such a crime from international to national law; but this point is so closely related to the one just addressed that it should be considered here.

[75] See generally Ferdinandusse, *passim*.

[76] See *Eichmann*; *Polyukovich*; and other late prosecutions arising from World War II.

[77] See Regina v. Bartle (Pinochet), U.K. House of Lords, 24 March 1999, reprinted in 38 I.L.M. 581 (1999); see also [Wijngaarde v. Bouterse,] Appeal in cassation in the interests of the law (Hoge Raad der Nederlanden [Supreme Court of the Netherlands], 18 September 2001), translated into English at 32 Netherlands Y.B.I.L. 282 (2001).

Customary international law applies everywhere,[78] so that no one can object, on international-law legality grounds, of being prosecuted for acts committed anywhere if they were criminal when committed. The point is that there must be some criminal law that binds the person at the time of the act. If the act violates customary international criminal law when committed, there is no issue of legality, because the actor has violated binding criminal law. The forum state may characterize its criminal proceedings as an application of its own substantive criminal law on the basis of universal jurisdiction. In fact, the forum state may even apply new municipal statutes.[79]

There have been debates about whether international law or national law defines the crime when a state prosecutes on the basis of universal jurisdiction. These debates reached the point of theoretical abstraction where it was stated that whether international criminal law defines substantive crimes or merely defines the crimes over which states may exercise universal jurisdiction "may not make an important difference."[80] In either case, some sense must exist in international law of what acts give rise to the ability of states to exercise universal jurisdiction to punish, either pursuant to municipal law enforcing criminal law defined by "the law of nations" or to municipal law in the strict sense. Universal jurisdiction of core international crimes requires that persons have notice that certain acts are criminal everywhere. This type of notice must come from international law.

Note that logically, re-characterization can sometimes occur where a state is not required to invoke universal jurisdiction. For example, a state may treat an international law war crime as a crime against national law but might claim to apply territorial, nationality, protective, or passive personality jurisdiction, as the facts of the case might allow.

7.b.ii.D. Representation (Vicarious) Jurisdiction and Legality

In representation or vicarious jurisdiction, a state prosecutes an allegation of an ordinary national crime committed elsewhere because it cannot extradite the accused person.[81] In this case, the accused is generally prosecuted under

[78] This disregards the possibility of persistent objection, cf. Chap. 4.g.i (on treaty reservations as persistent objection).

[79] See statutes cited in Chap. 3.c.iii.

[80] American Law Institute, Restatement (Third), Foreign Relations Law §404, Rptr's n.1 (1987).

[81] See Chap. 5.c.vii.

the law of the forum, but in fact is prosecuted for breaking the law where the crime was committed. Thus, as with the cases just discussed, there is re-characterization of the crime from a crime defined by the state where it was committed to a crime defined by the forum state. This type of re-characterization is unlikely to disappear so long as many states have severe limitations on extradition, yet are willing to prosecute persons whom they are unwilling to extradite.[82]

To be convicted, the person must have committed an act that was criminal under a law applicable to the actor. Thus, there must be "double criminality" at least: there must be a crime under the law of the state where the crime was committed. Of course, this is part of the raison d'être of representative jurisdiction. As discussed earlier,[83] most states apply the most lenient law. This, however, is required by the international law rule of non-retroactivity of crime creation only to the extent that an act that would be justified (i.e., would not be a crime) under the law of the state where committed must not result in a conviction under representative jurisdiction. In sentencing, however, the requirement ought to be stricter. The maximum sentence under the law of the state where the act was committed should be the maximum sentence available, even if a harsher sentence would be available under the law of the forum state. That is the sentence that applied when the actor committed the act and should not be increased retroactively.

This is supported by doctrine and state practice,[84] though, as we have seen, there is some contrary authority.[85] It is possible that the regional international human rights courts or the advisory human rights bodies will at some point be presented with cases or communications raising this issue under the appropriate treaty.

7.b.ii.E. Purely National Re-Characterization

Sometimes a person is prosecuted under a new national law which may change the name of a crime. If the act was criminal under the old law, and the penalty under the old law for that act was equal to or greater than the penalty under the new law, applying the new law does not violate the customary international law version of the rule of non-retroactivity of crimes and

[82] See generally Chap. 5.c.vii.
[83] See *id.*
[84] See *id.*
[85] See *id.*

punishments.[86] This rule effectively allows *lex mitior* to be implemented by applying new, more lenient statutes directly.

7.b.iii. *General Principles of Law as a Source of Applicable Criminal Law*

Whether general principles of law can be a source of applicable criminal law independent of and different from customary international law is still a matter of debate. Note that this is a different issue from that raised in Chapter 5, where it was shown that the non-retroactivity of crimes and punishments is itself a general principle of law recognized by "civilized nations"[87] (or, as stated in more recent documents, "the community of nations"[88]).

A person can be convicted for an act that is a criminal violation of a general principle of law only if the act was criminal under a general principle of law existing at the time of the act. This rule is clear from the text of the treaty provisions on general principles of law as a source of criminalization[89] and from the national constitutions implementing general principles of law as a source of criminalization.[90] It is also clear from the ICTY Appeals Chamber Judgment treating contempt of court as a crime under general principles of law.[91]

[86] See G. v. France, Judgment, Eur. Ct. H.R., Case No. 29/1994/476/557, Application No. 15312/89 (27 September 1995) (France retrospectively applied new crime of "indecent assault with violence or coercison by a person in authority"; acceptable under ECHR art. 7 because of *lex mitior* – under law in effect at time of the act, it would have been the more serious crime of rape); Westerman v. Netherlands, Com. 682/1986, UN Doc. A/55/40, Annex IX (UNHRC, 3 November 1999) (Netherlands retrospectively applied new military code provision on "refusal to obey military orders"; acceptable under ICCPR art. 15(1) because the acts charged were punishable under both old and new codes, and the sentence given was permissible under the code in force when the acts were committed), digested in LOUISE DOSWALD-BECK & ROBERT KOLB, JUDICIAL PROCESS AND HUMAN RIGHTS: UNITED NATIONS, EUROPEAN, AMERICAN AND AFRICAN SYSTEMS: TEXTS AND SUMMARIES OF INTERNATIONAL CASE-LAW 279 (Kehl, N.P. Engel, 2004).

[87] See Chap. 5.c; ICJ Statute art. 38(1)(c).

[88] ICCPR art. 15(2).

[89] ICCPR art. 15(2); ECHR art. 7(2).

[90] See Chap. 5.c.iii, discussing Canada Const. Act art. 11(g); Cape Verde Const. art. 30; Sri Lanka Const. art. 13(6), all of which require that a general principle of law used to criminalize an act be in existence at the time of the act. See Ekanayake v. The Attorney-General, C.A. 132/84 (Sri Lanka Ct. of App., 28 May 1986), app. dis., S.C. App. No. 68/86 (Sri Lanka S.Ct., 9 December 1987) [both available through official Sri Lanka government Web site, http://www.lawnet.lk].

[91] Prosecutor v. Tadic (Appeal of Vujin), Judgement on Allegations of Contempt against Prior Counsel, Milan Vujin, Case No. IT-94-1-A-R77 ¶¶ 13–28 (ICTY App. Ch., 27 February 2001).

This rule makes sense of the odd structure of the *nullum crimen, nulla poena* articles of the ICCPR and ECHR. "General principles of law" is a subset of international law, as is seen from the Statute of the International Court of Justice.[92] Arguments that general principles went beyond the definition of international law were rare and not generally accepted in the ICCPR debates.[93] In the ICCPR and ECHR, *nullum crimen* provisions apply to crimes defined by international law and by national law.[94] Thus, general principles of law can be a source of applicable criminal law, so long as they are applied to facts occurring after the general principle in question formed.

7.b.iv. *Criticism of International Criminal Law as Generally Violating Principles of Legality*

Some positivists criticize the possibility of an international criminal law in the current environment – in which there is no general international legislative body – as inconsistent with the principle *nullum crimen, nulla poena sine praevia lege scripta.*[95] This may well cause them to oppose the entire project of a substantive international criminal law.[96] Once it is understood, however, that common or customary law creation can meet the goals of the principle of legality as well as statutory enactments (or nearly as well), then there is no a priori problem with the notion of an international criminal law binding individuals in the current world situation. This is why some have suggested the slogans might be changed to "*nullum crimen, nulla poena sine iure.*"[97]

Allied to this point is the claim that international criminal law is not in fact developed enough to give notice to individuals and to protect them against arbitrary law creation and enforcement.[98] International criminal law is subject to the same pressures toward arbitrary expansion as criminal law in many countries with strong rule-of-law traditions. The claim that unpredictable expansion of criminal law has been greater in this system than in national systems because there is no general international legislative body is becoming less sustainable.

[92] ICJ Statute art. 38. Cf. Ferdinandusse at 236.
[93] Chap. 4.b.ii.C.
[94] ICCPR art. 15(2); ECHR art. 7(2).
[95] See, e.g., Alfred P. Rubin, The Law of Piracy 343 (Naval War College Press 1988); Alfred P. Rubin, *An International Criminal Tribunal for the Former Yugoslavia?*, 6 Pace Int'l L.J. 7 (1994) [hereinafter Rubin, An ICTY?].
[96] This is certainly Professor Rubin's view.
[97] See Chaps. 1 (introductory section) & 7.b.
[98] See Rubin, Piracy.

Nonetheless, the possibility of such unpredictable expansion is real. Ensuring that it does not occur requires vigilance in enforcing the principle, and particularly, where necessary, in examining whether a particular act truly is criminal in customary international law or other applicable law.

Within the ICC system, as to cases involving states parties to the ICC Statute, claims that there is no compliance with the principle of legality have even less force. In those cases, the states parties to the ICC Statute act as the legislative body, and the statute itself serves as the positive law text.[99]

7.b.v. *Defenses*

Without question, the rule of non-retroactivity of crime creation has reached customary international law status. What is perhaps arguable is whether retroactivity of the elimination of defenses concerning what acts are non-criminal[100] is also prohibited by customary international law.

Logic and the language of the treaties and many national constitutions and laws suggest that the rule of non-retroactivity should apply to this sort of change of law.[101] After all, it takes an act that, in the circumstances in which it was performed, would not incur criminal liability (because of the defense) and makes it into an act that does incur criminal liability (after the defense is removed). The treaties state that if an act was not "criminal" when done, it cannot be made so by any retroactive change of law.[102] This would seem to include acts that were innocent, or even encouraged, because of the existence of substantive law defenses. Many of the national constitutions are similar to the treaties in this regard.[103] Retroactive destruction of defenses has been rejected by some jurisprudence for a long time.[104] Moreover, allowing retroactive removal of defenses would allow the targeting of specific persons retroactively.

[99] See ICC Statute art. 22.

[100] This wording is used to avoid the theoretical issue of whether a defense is a "justification" or an "excuse." The question here is not whether it falls into a particular category but whether it concerns a way in which a person can choose to do or omit something that would avoid criminality. Compare, e.g., the claim that East German government policy authorized shooting persons crossing the Berlin wall (i.e., made the acts non-criminal) with the claim that John Hinckley was insane when he shot U.S. President Ronald Reagan (i.e., a criminal act which was excused by insanity).

[101] See Paul H. Robinson, *Fair Notice and Fair Adjudication: Two Kinds of Legality*, 154 U. Pa. L. Rev. 335 (2005) [hereinafter Robinson, *Fair Notice*].

[102] ICCPR art. 15(1); ECHR art. 7(1); ACHR art. 9; ACHPR art. 7(2).

[103] See Chap. 5.e, which lists more than one hundred constitutions that take this form.

[104] See Kring v. Missouri, 107 U.S. 221 (1883).

There are, however, a few examples of recent international organization and national practice that can be read to suggest non-retroactivity of defense destruction has not passed into customary international law. These are the German border guard cases and common law cases of the marital defense to rape in the ECtHR and in German and British courts.[105] This argument would state that, unlike crime creation, defense destruction can occur retroactively, where the defense is unjust and where, stripped of the defense, the act in question was squarely criminal at the time done. There are reasonable arguments that in both the border guards and the marital rape cases, it was foreseeable from the law existing at the time of the act that the act would be held criminal.[106] Thus, the cases provide at best ambiguous support for the proposition that there is a practice of allowing retroactive destruction of defenses that decriminalize acts.

The abolition of defenses that decriminalize acts is functionally equivalent to the creation of crimes when it comes to taking currently non-criminal acts and criminalizing them. Thus, in any given legal system, retroactive abolition of a defense that decriminalizes an act is a violation of the rule of non-retroactivity in criminal law. Nonetheless, this section would not be honest without pointing out the doubt on the part of some that retroactive destruction of defenses is prohibited by customary international law, at least when current thought considers the defenses in question to be immoral.

7.b.vi. *The Right Not to Be Prosecuted*

Most of the research in this book has focused on the issue of what might be called "substantive criminal law legality" – that is, the right not to have substantive criminal law applied retroactively by conviction and punishment. Substantial evidence also supports the slightly broader proposition that arrest and prosecution for acts that were not crimes at the time committed is also banned. In other words, governments may not use retroactively

[105] See discussion in Chap. 4.h; George P. Fletcher, 1 The Grammar of Criminal Law: American, Comparative, and International (Foundations) (Oxford Univ. Press 2007) 145–48 (hereinafter Fletcher, Grammar) (quoting Gustav Radbruch); Streletz, Kessler and Krenz v. Germany, Judgment, Eur. Ct. H.R., Applications Nos. 34044/96, 35532/97 & 44801/98 (22 March 2001); K.-H. W. v. Germany, Judgment of 22 March 2001, Eur. Ct. H.R., 2001-II, Applications Nos. 37201/97 (22 March 2001); C. R. v. United Kingdom, Judgment, Eur. Ct. H.R., Case No. 48/1994/495/577, Application No. 20190/92 (27 October 1995); S. W. v. United Kingdom, Judgment, Eur. Ct. H.R., Case No. 47/1994/494/576 (27 October 1995).

[106] See Chap. 4.h.

created crimes as a device for holding individuals until courts get around to declaring their rights.

The International Committee of the Red Cross (ICRC) has stated this as a rule of customary international humanitarian law applicable in both international and non-international armed conflicts:

> No one may be accused or convicted of a criminal offense on account of any act or omission which did not constitute a criminal offence under national or international law at the time it was committed; nor may a heavier penalty be imposed than that which was applicable at the time the criminal offence was committed.[107]

The key phrase here is, "No one may be accused," demonstrating that the prosecution itself is prohibited. This is very similar to the formulation of two international humanitarian law treaties, Additional Protocols Nos. I and II to the Geneva Conventions of 1949.[108] As previously pointed out in other contexts, Protocol II is particularly important because it applies to non-international conflicts – that is, civil wars in which the pressure to violate rights, such as legality, is greatest within states. Even though the field of international humanitarian law is limited to protections in times of armed conflict or occupation, the customary and treaty obligations applying the legality rules in such times of stress are relevant to showing that they are customary rules to protect human rights at all times.

In more general international human rights law, support for this proposition comes from the provisions prohibiting arbitrary arrest and detention without law. In other words, arrests and detentions on the basis of retroactive (or wholly nonexistent) criminal law are a subset of the sorts of arbitrary arrests and detentions banned in international human rights law.[109]

In the ICTY and the SCSL, this principle appears in the rule that a violation of legality is a matter that goes to the jurisdiction of the courts, as well as a matter of the substantive criminal law applicable to the person.[110]

[107] 1 ICRC, CUSTOMARY IHL at R. 101, p. 371, supported by extensive documentation in 2 (pt. 2) ICRC, CUSTOMARY IHL (PRACTICE) §§3673–3716, pp. 2493–2500.

[108] Additional Protocol I to the 1949 Geneva Conventions art. 75(4)(c) (1977); Additional Protocol II to the 1949 Geneva Conventions art. 6(2)(c) (1977); see 2 ICRC CUSTOMARY IHL (PRACTICE, PART II) ¶¶ 3679–80, at 2492–95 (both of these provisions adopted by consensus).

[109] ICCPR art. 9; ACHPR art. 6; ACHR art. 7; see ECHR art. 5.

[110] See Prosecutor v. Hadzihasanovic, Case No. IT-01-47-AR72 ¶¶ 10–36 (ICTY App. Ch., 16 July 2003) (question whether command responsibility in non-international conflict was a crime under customary international law at time accused acted treated as jurisdictional), and *id.* (ICTY App. Ch. Bench, 21 February 2003) (holding that the appeal was

In the processes of these tribunals, the fact that an issue is jurisdictional means that it is immediately appealable – that is, that the trial itself would violate the rights of the accused.

Arbitrary detention without law is already prohibited by national and international law. So, today the prohibition of being held for trial on a charge that involves retroactively created crime may fairly be considered a violation of the rules of legality as an international human right. Given the inherent problems of language, there may be times when it is not wholly clear whether a given act has been previously defined by law as a crime.[111] The prosecuting authorities are not prohibited from seeking a determination in good faith as to the criminality of the act when committed. More research is necessary to determine whether a holding, sought by the prosecution in good faith, that a charge violates the principle of legality should have legal effects under international human rights law other than dismissal of the charge.

7.C. ELABORATION AND DISCUSSION OF THE CORE RULES: *NULLA POENA*

National and international tribunals may not impose increased penalties that were not available for a crime at the time the acts constituting the crime were done. So long as the penalty given is within the maximum allowable under applicable law at the time of the crime, there is no violation of the international human rights law version of *nulla poena*. The ICCPR and regional human rights treaties all contain this principle as a rule of law, as do constitutions of the vast majority of states.

As with *nullum crimen*, this principle applies to all crimes, regardless of whether the crime has been defined by national or international law. As with *nullum crimen* as well, many states choose to apply a stricter definition of *nulla poena*, requiring specification of penalties in statutory law. This stricter

jurisdictional); *Milutinovic* at ¶¶ 9, 10 & n.28, citing Prosecutor v. Vasiljevic, Trial Judgment ¶¶ 193 *et seq.*, IT-98-32-T (ICTY Trial Chamber, 29 November 2002); Prosecutor v. Blaskic, Appeals Judgment ¶¶ 140–41, IT-95-14-A (ICTY App. Ch, 29 July 2004); Prosecutor v. Norman, Case Number SCSL-2003-14-AR72(E) (SCSL App. Ch., 31 May 2004) (both majority and dissent treated the question of whether recruitment of child soldiers was a crime under customary international law at the time Norman allegedly acted as a question of jurisdiction). Cf. Chap. 6.c.iii on whether issues of legality are immediately appealable under the ICC Statute.

[111] See discussion in Chaps. 1.c.i, 4.h.

version, however, is not required as a matter of customary international human rights law.

Most states have accepted the internal application of this rule as an international obligation through the ICCPR and the regional human rights agreements. The vast majority of states also have integrated *nulla poena* into domestic law through constitutional and other provisions. The principle applies nearly universally through constitution, statute, or treaty, with only Bhutan and Brunei excepted among UN member states. It is also nearly universally accepted through the Geneva Conventions when states come into control of nonnationals through international armed conflict.[112] More than 160 states have accepted the more detailed obligations of legality in the additional protocols to the Geneva Conventions, including the obligation to apply *nulla poena* in non-international (internal) armed conflicts.[113]

Thus, the evidence that this version of *nulla poena sine lege* is a matter of customary international law is nearly as strong as the evidence for *nullum crimen.* Nonetheless some publicists have questioned the applicability of *nulla poena* to crimes under customary international criminal law.[114]

7.c.i. Nulla poena *as Applicable to Crimes under International Law*

Relevant worldwide treaties (ICCPR and Additional Protocols I & II to the Geneva Conventions) and one regional treaty (ECHR) make it clear that the rule prohibiting heavier penalties than available at the time of the crime applies to crimes under international law and to crimes under national law.[115] They follow the form of the UDHR in requiring the existence of a crime (or "penal offense") at the time of an offense (including a crime under international law), and that no heavier punishment may be imposed for that crime than was available at the time of the offense. Two other regional treaties do not distinguish among sources of law (national or international) for crime creation, and their prohibitions of retroactive increase in penalties apply, on their face, to international as well as national

[112] Geneva Convention (No. IV) art. 65; Geneva Convention (No. III) art. 99.

[113] Additional Protocol No. I art. 75; Additional Protocol No. II art. 6 (non-international conflicts).

[114] See Bassiouni, CAH-IHL at 143–44.

[115] ICCPR art. 15(1) (made non-derogable by art. 4); Additional Protocol No. I to Geneva Conventions of 1949 art. 75(4)(c) (1977) (adopted by consensus); Additional Protocol No. II to Geneva Conventions of 1949 art. 6(2)(c) (1977) (adopted by consensus); ECHR art. 7(1) (made non-derogable by art. 15(2)).

crimes.[116] The Fourth Geneva Convention, protecting civilians and others in time of armed conflict, prohibits retroactive application of penal provisions. It does not distinguish between crime creation and punishment provisions, or between the national or international source of the law.[117] Given the ordinary meaning of "penal provisions" as including punishment, the face of the Fourth Geneva Convention includes retroactive increases in penalties. The new ICC Statute states: "In the event of a change in the law applicable to a given case prior to a final judgment, the law more favourable to the person being investigated, prosecuted or convicted shall apply."[118]

Thus, in the ICC, no greater penalty may apply than would have applied at the time of the act.[119] Three internationalized tribunals (Kosovo, East Timor, and Cambodia), as described earlier, all import the human rights rules from treaty law.[120] They have adopted *nulla poena* in its internationally accepted form, forbidding penalties greater than those authorized at the time of the crime.

Support for this rule can be found in the 2005 report, *Customary International Humanitarian Law*, from the International Committee of the Red Cross. This report states unambiguously that law increasing sentences for a crime may not be applied retroactively.[121] This is the law covering international conflicts, non-international conflicts,[122] and occupation,[123] including international criminal law violations. As well as the treaty law discussed earlier, the ICRC includes extensive documentation from national civil and military law and practice supporting its view, including common law, civil law, and Islamic law countries.[124] The ICRC in its statement of doctrine did

[116] ACHR art. 9 (made non-suspendable by art. 27); ACHPR art. 7.

[117] Geneva Convention (No. IV) arts. 65, 67.

[118] ICC Statute art. 24(2).

[119] Accord, on the meaning of this provision, Raul C. Pangalangan, *Article 24, Non-retroactivity ratione personae*, in COMMENTARY ON THE ROME STATUTE OF THE INTERNATIONAL CRIMINAL COURT: OBSERVERS' NOTES, ARTICLE BY ARTICLE ¶¶ 14–15, pp. 467, 472–73 (Otto Triffterer, ed., Nomos-Verlagsgesellschaft 1999) .

[120] Chap. 6.b.

[121] 1 ICRC, CUSTOMARY IHL (RULES), R. 101, p. 371.

[122] *Id.*

[123] *Id.* at 371–72.

[124] In addition to the treaty law discussed above, see 2 (pt. 2) ICRC, CUSTOMARY IHL (PRACTICE) ¶¶ 3687 (Yugoslavia and Croatia (27 November 1991) agreed that civilians be treated in accordance with Additional Protocol I art. 75), 3688 (representatives of Republic of Bosnia-Herzegovina, ethnic Serbs in Bosnia, and ethnic Croats in Bosnia agreed to same, 27 May 1992), 3691–92 (Argentina, Law of War Manual §§3.30, 5.025, 5.026 (1969), "legal provisions" to be applied only if existing at time of offense), 3693 (Canada LOAC Manual §49(a), pp. 12–16 (1999), "penal provisions enacted by the occupant must not be retroactive"), 3696 (New Zealand Military Manual §§1327(1)(a), 1815(2)(c) (1993) "penal

not distinguish between trials in national and international tribunals. The evidence presented by the ICRC specifically applies only to international law limitations on punishment in national courts, whether the source of law is national or international. The ICRC report can be treated as something more than an opinion of publicists, partly because of the massive amount of state practice that it compiles, and partly because the ICRC itself has more status in international law than individual publicists and nongovernmental organizations generally. The focus of the ICRC, and this report in particular, is on international humanitarian law rather than international human rights law. The report focuses on rights and duties of persons in times of armed conflict rather than on rights of individuals at all times. Its value for human rights law exists largely in the fact that it deals with rights of persons in internal armed conflict, in which the pressures to violate human rights is generally very great. Its value for legality in international criminal law comes from the fact that the core crimes of customary international criminal law – genocide, crimes against humanity, and war crimes – are the crimes defined by international humanitarian law.

In the modern international criminal courts, one cannot find examples where sentences have been outside the range of permissible international sentences for crimes that were international crimes at the time they were committed. To the extent that there have been cases re-characterized from

provisions" language concerning occupation similar to Canada's; in non-international armed conflicts, no punishment may "be more severe than was applicable at [the time of the offence]," with the mercy principle applied), 3698 (Sweden, International Humanitarian Law Manual §2.2.3, p. 19 (1991) considers all of Additional Protocol I to be part of customary international law), 3699-700 (U.K. Military Manual §233 (1958) "no prisoner of war may be tried or sentenced for an act which is not forbidden by the law of the Detaining Power or by international law in force at the time the act was committed"; U.K. LOAC Manual (1981) to similar effect), 3701 (U.S. Field Manual, applies Geneva Convention (No. 4) art. 65 to situations of occupation); 3703 (Bangladesh, International Crimes (Tribunal) Act §3(2)(e) (1973), "violation of any humanitarian rules applicable in armed conflicts laid down in Geneva Conventions of 1949" is a crime), 3705 (Ireland Geneva Conventions Act as amended §4(1&4) (1962) provides that "minor breach" of Geneva Conventions or Additional Protocol I, or "contravention" of Additional Protocol II (including the provisions on legality of all the conventions) are punishable offences), 3706 (Norway Military Penal Code, making "anyone who contravenes or is accessory to the contravention of provisions related to the protection of persons or property [of the Geneva Conventions of 1949 and the Additional Protocols] . . . liable to imprisonment"); 3708 (Jordanian practice (1997) holds that Additional Protocol I, art. 75 embodies customary law), 3709 (same for Syria), 3710 (U.S. practice (1997) accepts Additional Protocol II art. 6, and military necessity will not derogate from those rights), pp. 2495–99. Of all the citations in support of the principle of legality in the ICRC material, the only ones listed here are those that go to including the principle of legality in sentencing in documents that deal with the possibility of international law violations.

national law to international law crimes after commission, one cannot find claims that the sentence exceeded what would have been available under national law at the time the crimes were committed.[125] What can be found are cases where persons convicted of international crimes received greater sentences than the sentences they might have received under the law of the state where the acts were committed. The courts in these cases decided that there was no retroactivity in the application of an international crime to the defendant,[126] and thus there was no retroactive re-characterization of national to international crimes. National law cannot of its own force reduce the penalty available for a violation under international law, at least in international criminal courts and tribunals, and such sentencing does not violate the international law version of *nulla poena.*

Of course, there is a reason that it is relatively easy to state that modern penalties for core international crimes have not exceeded those available in customary international law at the time committed. During the period of development of war crimes, military offenses, including war crimes, were generally punishable by death or any term of imprisonment. It is fair to say that this was the penalty available for them in customary international law. During the post–World War II period, when crimes against humanity became a separate core international crime, the same rule was followed: these crimes earned death or any term of imprisonment. Genocide, which began as a subset of crimes against humanity, thus in general has followed the same rule. To say that there is a customary international law penalty for these crimes is little harder than to say that death was the penalty prescribed for common law felonies in early modern England. In each case, there may have been no preexisting statute to this effect, but there was a preexisting law defining the maximum available penalty, thus meeting the requirement of

[125] See Prosecutor v. Furundzija, Trial Judgment ¶¶ 168–69, Case No. IT-95-17/1 (ICTY Tr. Ch., 1998) (on rape); Prosecutor v. Delalic, Appeals Judgement ¶¶ 178–80, Case No. IT-96-21 (ICTY App. Ch. 20 February 1991). *Hadzihasanovic*, ¶ 34 (ICTY App. Ch., 16 July 2003). Accord, *Norman*, ¶ 25 (SCSL App. Ch. 31 May 2004); Prosecutor v. Akayesu, Judgement ¶ 617, Case No. ICTR-96-4-T (2 September 1998) (relying on ratification of Additional Protocol II by Rwanda on 19 November 1984, and the adoption of its provisions into domestic criminal law, as well as the status of those provisions as customary international law).

[126] See Prosecutor v. Delalic, Appeal Judgement ¶ 813, 817 (ICTY App. Ch. 20 February 2001) (allowing heavier sentence of imprisonment under international law than might be available under Yugoslav law); Prosecutor v. Erdemovic, Sentencing Judgment ¶ 38 (ICTY Tr. Ch. 29 November 1996); Prosecutor v. Serushago, Case No. ICTR 98-39-A ¶ 30 (ICTR App. Ch., 6 April 2000).

nulla poena. More will be said about this in response to criticisms discussed in the next section.

7.c.ii. *Criticism of* Nulla poena *as Inapplicable to International Criminal Law*

Despite the strong evidence that *nulla poena sine lege* is a rule of customary international human rights law, it has had a checkered career in the modern academic writing about criminal violations of international humanitarian law. Some publicists remain skeptical of the full application of *nulla poena* to criminal responsibility for violations of international humanitarian law – that is, genocide, crimes against humanity, and war crimes – whether tried in national or international tribunals. These include persons who support the project of international criminal law,[127] as well as those who oppose it.[128] For example, M. Cherif Bassiouni suggests that *nulla poena sine lege* applies in international criminal law only "by analogy."[129] Salvatore Zappalà argues that in international criminal proceedings, this rule is a principle of "equity" but "cannot really be considered as giving rise to a right of the individual."[130]

This issue is being treated separately here because the literature on it is confusing. However, practice is less confusing than the literature might suggest.

The reason for this confusion is that *nulla poena sine lege* has different meanings in different legal systems. Interestingly, much of this focuses on the same problem of the meaning of *lege* that no longer poses such great problems when considering the meaning of *nullum crimen sine lege.* What is needed, then, is an understanding that the international law application of the principle of legality in sentencing to the so-called core international crimes requires no more than it does in crime definition. *Lege* (or, in Bassiouni's usage defining legality in crime definition, *iure*[131]) can come from customary international law of punishment as well as from specific statutory enactments.

[127] See Bassiouni, CAH-ICL at 158–59, 162, 176; Zappalà at 196; GUÉNAËL METTRAUX, INTERNATIONAL CRIMES AND THE *AD HOC* TRIBUNALS 356–57 (Oxford Univ. Press 2005) [hereinafter Mettraux]; Rottleuthner & Mahlmann.

[128] See Rubin, *An ICTY?*

[129] Bassiouni, CAH-ICL at 158–59, 162.

[130] Zappalà at 196.

[131] Bassiouni, CAH-IHL at 144.

The most important source of confusion was pointed out by Dr. Zivkovic, a UN War Crimes Commission commentator, writing about the *Trial of Rauter*, a 1948–49 Netherlands case arising out of World War II: "In continental law . . . penalties for criminal offenses are provided for in express terms and with the designation of the specific penalty or penalties attached to each offence, as a rule in terms of the maxima and/or minima punishments."[132] Such a tariff of penalties was not provided for war crimes in Netherlands law before Rauter committed his war crimes, including murder, enslavement, pillage and illegal confiscation of property, illegal arrests and detentions, collective penalties imposed on innocents, illegal reprisals, and persecution on religious grounds. Much later, the statutes of the ICTY and ICTR also omitted such a tariff of penalties, as has the ICC Statute.

The lack of a specific sentencing scheme in the law of the criminalizing authority is the source of many of the claims that *nulla poena* does not apply to international crimes.[133] Bassiouni asserts that the failure of the statutes of the ICTY and ICTR to set forth authorized penalties for each crime amounted to a failure to comply with the principle *nulla poena sine lege.*[134] Zappalà would allow the use of the sentencing law of the place where the crimes were committed, and he argues that the failure of the ICTY and ICTR to follow Yugoslav and Rwandan sentencing practices is what violates *nulla poena.*[135]

Bassiouni's claim reflects the practice in many states, especially civil law jurisdictions with extensive tariffs of penalties for specific crimes. This strong version of *nulla poena*, however, does not reflect universal practice among states for either national or international law. It also goes far beyond the requirements of legality in sentencing in the international human rights law and international humanitarian law treaties discussed earlier.

All that is required by the international human rights law principle of legality in sentencing is that a heavier penalty not be imposed than that available at the time the crime was committed. Actors must be able to foresee only the maximum penalty for a crime. International human rights law shows that this can be provided by custom, including custom developed through cases, in the same way that customary international law crimes

[132] [Zivkovic,] Notes on *Trial of Rauter*, 14 UNWCC, Law Rep. at 111, 120 (attribution, without given name, from Foreword by [Lord] Wright [of Durley], *id.* at xii).

[133] See Ferdinandusse at 248–49; cf. Bassiouni, CAH-IHL at 133–34; Zappalà at 199–201, 208.

[134] Bassiouni, CAH-ICL at 176.

[135] See Zappalà at 196.

themselves develop. The existence of a continental-style schedule of penalties is not required by this weaker version of the principle of legality in sentencing that exists in international human rights law and is applicable to international as well as national crimes.

For war crimes and crimes against humanity in customary international law, the maximum penalties of death or life imprisonment existed at the time of World War II,[136] and have not been changed, at least for prosecutions in national courts.[137] Life imprisonment continues to be available in international courts.[138] Forfeiture of property and fines were also available,[139] and continue to be so.[140] For crimes against humanity (including what later was broken off into genocide) in customary international law, one can argue about the existence of international law penalties before World War II. Since the World War II charters and prosecutions,[141] however, it has

[136] U.S. Army, Rules of Land Warfare, Field Manual 27–10 ¶ 357 (1 October 1940) ("all war crimes are subject to the death penalty, although a lesser penalty may be imposed"), quoted in Lamb, in CASSESE ET AL., 1 COMMENTARY at 757 n.95; [George Brand,] Punishment of Criminals, 15 U.N.W.C.C, Law Rep. at 200, citing cases of death sentences passed for non-homicidal war crimes such as torture and rape in Norwegian and Australian courts; William A. Schabas, *Article 23, Nulla poena sine lege*, in OBSERVERS' NOTES, ¶ 1, at 463.

[137] Death sentences for genocide (a subset of crimes against humanity in the post–World War II cases) were imposed in Rwandan courts and have recently been imposed by the Iraqi Special Tribunal for war crimes and crimes against humanity. Rwanda: see *Ministère Public v. Karamira*, 1 RECUEIL DE JURISPRUDENCE CONTENTIEUX DU GENOCIDE ET DES MASSACRES AU RWANDA 75 (1st inst., Kigali, 14 February 1997), cited and discussed in Schabas, UN ICT at 124–25 & n.7; Mark A. Drumbl, *Punishment, Postgenocide: From Guilt to Shame to* Civis *in Rwanda*, 75 NYU L. REV. 1221, 1287 n.314 [hereinafter Drumbl] (suggesting some three hundred death sentences arose from the Rwandan genocide). Iraq: *Saddam Hussein*, Iraqi High Tribunal, Lawsuit No. 1/Criminal/2005 (verdict delivered orally, 5 November 2006) (3 persons, including former head of state Saddam Hussein sentenced to death for war crimes; the executions have been carried out).

I generally oppose the death penalty. Yet I remember being opposed to the death penalty as a ten-year-old, and still thinking that I would willingly have executed Adolf Eichmann.

[138] See Chap. 6(a, c).

[139] Control Council Law No. 10 art. II(3)(c-e) (allowing for "fine," "forfeiture of property" or "restitution of property wrongfully acquired"); *Trial of Krupp*, 10 U.N.W.C.C., Law Rep. Case No. 58, pp. 69, 158 (USMT, 30 June 1948) (forfeiture of all property of defendant Krupp); Brand, 15 U.N.W.C.C., Law Rep. at 200, citing *Trial of Goeth*, 7 U.N.W.C.C., Law Rep. 1, 4 (Sup. Nat. Trib. of Poland, 5 September 1946), *Trial of Hoess*, 7 U.N.W.C.C., Law Rep. 11, 17 (Sup. Nat. Trib. of Poland, 29 March 1947) (both imposing "forfeiture of all property"); *Trial of Greiser*, 13 U.N.W.C.C., Law Rep., Case No. 74, pp. 70, 104 (Sup. Nat. Trib. of Poland, 7 July 1946) (forfeiture of all property; court linked case to Free City of Danzig as well as Polish interests).

[140] ICC Statute arts. 75–77.

[141] See Nuremberg Charter art. 27; IMTFE Charter art. 16.

surely become customary international law that these crimes carry the same potential penalties as war crimes.[142] Thus, the principle of legality applicable in international human rights law has been met for these customary international law crimes.[143]

It seems incorrect to conclude that there are no penalties stated in the statutes of the modern international criminal tribunals. One can justify the high maximums because all of the crimes within the jurisdiction of these courts are extremely serious. If one accepts the notion that there are customary international law penalties for these crimes, then there is no violation of *nulla poena*, insofar as that principle requires the statement of a maximum lawful penalty for any given criminal act.

Note that the statement of a penalty in the ICTY and ICTR Statutes would not, by itself, be sufficient to comply with *nulla poena*.[144] These tribunals were established primarily to deal with crimes committed before their establishment, so the penalties must have been available at the time of commission of the crime (i.e., in international law or the law of the state where the crime was committed). If life imprisonment is to be a sentence in, for example, the ICTR, only the availability of at least life imprisonment in some law applicable to the accused at the time those crimes were committed can truly satisfy the non-retroactivity aspect of the principle of *nulla poena*.

Therefore the argument described herein remains intact. The international community has clearly come to accept crimes against humanity and war crimes as set forth at Nuremberg and under Control Council Law No. 10 as crimes defined under international law.[145] The international community has considered the imposition of penalties, including death or life imprisonment, for these crimes by the IMT and other courts after World War II

[142] Consider the death sentences in Rwandan national courts for genocide and the life sentences for genocide in the ICTR. See Drumbl at 1287 n.314.

[143] See Brand, 15 U.N.W.C.C., Law Rep. at 200; see Ferdinandusse at 253–54, relying on *Trial of Klinge*, 3 U.N.W.C.C., Law Rep., Case No. 11, p. 1; Prosecutor v. Delalic, Appeals Judgement ¶ 817 (App. Ch., 20 February 2001); Prosecutor v. Erdemovic, Sentencing Judgment ¶ 40 (ICTY Tr. Ch., 29 November 1996); Prosecutor v. Akayesu, Sentencing Judgment (ICTR Tr. Ch., 2 October 1998) (noting that Rwanda allowed the severest punishments, including death, for genocide).

[144] But cf. Per Ole Träskman, *Should We Take the Condition of Double Criminality Seriously?*, in DOUBLE CRIMINALITY: STUDIES IN INTERNATIONAL CRIMINAL LAW 151 (Nils Jareborg ed., Iustis Förlag AB, 1989) (appearing to make an argument that law of the forum is good enough for purposes of legality).

[145] Later international practice has not been as consistent concerning crimes against peace (aggression).

as being authoritative as well.[146] Since World War II, many states have rejected the death penalty domestically. In recent years, however, Rwanda and Iraq have issued and carried out sentences of death for genocide and war crimes.[147] The United Nations (through the ICTY, ICTR, and joint national/international tribunals) refused to authorize the death penalty in international criminal courts.[148] The states establishing the ICC have refused to apply the death penalty through that court or to give sentences of more than thirty years' imprisonment except for the worst crimes.[149] But this does not mean that there is no penalty in customary international law for these crimes. One penalty – death – available in customary international law has simply been eliminated by the positive textual law of the ICC Statute and the organic documents of the other international criminal tribunals.

The current author's argument is different from an analysis of *nulla poena* by Zappalà. He argues that the ICTY and ICTR do not comply with *nulla poena* because they are not bound by Yugoslav and Rwandan sentencing law and practice.[150] In Zappalà's view, there is no real international law of sentencing yet. In terms of an overall coherent policy that can accurately guide courts in giving specific sentences in specific cases, he is correct. However, the customary international law rule of *nulla poena* does not require so specific a sentencing scheme.

There is a general international law of sentencing for crimes under international humanitarian law – genocide, crimes against humanity, and war crimes – a sentence of up to life imprisonment or death. Fines and confiscation of property are also permissible. The only crimes for which this law does not apply are those crimes re-characterized from national law crimes to international humanitarian law crimes between the time they were committed and the time of trial. For such crimes, the only sentence that existed when the act was committed was the national law sentence. The maximum sentence available under international law should, in those cases, be no more than the maximum sentence available under the national law

[146] See, e.g., Eichmann v. Attorney-General, [1962] 16 PISKE DIN 2033 (Israel, Sup. Ct., 29 May 1962), reprinted in 36 INT'L L. REP. 277 (1968), aff'g 45 PESAKIM MEHOZIIM 3 (Jerusalem Dist. Ct., 11 December 1961), reprinted in 36 INT'L L. REP. 18 (Eichmann was executed); [George Brand], Punishment of Criminals, 15 UNWCC, Law Rep. 200 (1949).

[147] Rwanda: *Karamira*, cited in Schabas, UN ICT at 124–25 (reporting Karamira's execution); Drumbl at 1287 n.314. Iraq: *Saddam Hussein*; Bushra Juhi, *Death Sentences Upheld in Iraq for 'Chemical Ali,' Two Others, Washington Post*, 5 September 2007, p. A-11 (sentences not carried out as of 9 November 2007).

[148] ICTY Statute art. 24; ICTR Statute art. 23; SCSL Statute art. 19.

[149] ICC Statute art. 77.

[150] See Zappalà at 196.

that applied when the crime was committed. This will be discussed further subsequently.[151]

The ad hoc tribunals have rejected the claim that, in applying international criminal law, they are bound to the sentencing tariffs of the states where the crimes occurred.[152] The Netherlands courts after World War II, as well as the ad hoc tribunals, make it clear that persons who do these acts could have foreseen that international law condemned their actions in the harshest terms, whether through the law of war existing during World War II or the newer discipline of international humanitarian law. Rauter, for example, committed crimes which were war crimes in customary international law before World War II. The statutes of the ICTY, ICTR (and the ICC, for especially serious crimes) allow any sentence up to life imprisonment for any of the crimes within its jurisdiction, with no mandatory minimums for any of them. This is sufficient to meet the principle of legality of punishments in international criminal law.

Zappalà goes too far when he asserts that *nulla poena sine lege* does not grant individuals any rights in international criminal law. The rule of non-retroactivity of punishments is somewhat more limited as a matter of international human rights law and international criminal law than it is in some national systems. It is, however, real, and may be invoked by individuals in international criminal proceedings.

This discussion of the arguments of Bassiouni and Zappalà illustrates one of the general points of this book. Claims that *nullum crimen* and *nulla poena* do not apply in international criminal law often arise from the fact that the proponent of the claim is using a very strong definition of non-retroactivity. This very strong definition does not apply to international human rights law and international criminal law. Yet international criminal law applies a true rule of non-retroactivity of crimes and punishments, in slightly weaker forms, to international criminal law, and as a matter of international human rights law generally.

If the penalty for the core international crimes is anything up to and including death (except that torture and other cruel and degrading punishments are always unacceptable and illegal), why does the argument

[151] See Chap. 7.c.iii.

[152] Prosecutor v. Delalic, Appeal Judgement ¶¶ 813, 817 (ICTY App. Ch., 20 February 2001) (allowing heavier sentence of imprisonment under international law than might be available under Yugoslav law); Prosecutor v. Erdemovic, Sentencing Judgment ¶ 38 (ICTY Tr. Ch., 29 November 1996); Prosecutor v. Serushago, Case No. ICTR 98-39-A ¶ 30 (ICTR App. Ch., 6 April 2000).

about whether *nulla poena* applies matter at all?[153] First, political and other support for the project of international criminal law depends in large part, as it should, on observance of human rights norms. Therefore, demonstrating that this norm is in fact met in international criminal law is more useful to generating support for this law than merely claiming that the norm does not apply. Second, as international criminal law matures, stricter limits may emerge, to which the application of *nulla poena* may be easier to understand. Third, to the extent that there are acts retroactively re-characterized from national to international law, those acts are punishable only to the extent of the law applicable to them at the time the accused acted.[154]

In summary, modern international criminal law has generally satisfied the internationally recognized principle of legality in sentencing. This does not mean that the issue of sentencing policy has been dealt with adequately in international criminal law. It has not been.[155] Even less does it mean that the theory of criminology and the purposes of international criminal law, including deterrence, restorative justice, and reconciliation, have been adequately addressed by current law. These subjects need extensive development,[156] and they are beyond the scope of this book.

7.c.iii. Nulla poena *and Re-Characterization*

7.c.iii.A. *Nulla poena* Where There Has Been a Retroactive Re-Characterization of a National Crime into an International Crime

Assume for the moment that someone is charged with an act that was a crime under national law when committed and is now prosecuted internationally through the process of re-characterization described previously. In this situation, the role of the principle of legality in sentencing may become important.

For example, if intentional extensive and long-lasting environmental damage is now treated as a war crime, when it might not have been so treated at the time of the offense, the general rule that war crimes may

[153] Cf. Lamb, in 1 Cassese, et al., Commentary at 757–58.

[154] See Chap. 7.c.iii.A.

[155] See, e.g., Mark A. Drumbl, *Collective Violence and Individual Punishment: The Criminality of Mass Atrocity*, 99 Northwestern L. Rev. 539 (2005) [hereinafter Drumbl, *Collective Violence*]; Mettraux at 357.

[156] See, e.g., Drumbl, *Collective Violence.*

incur any legal punishment will not apply. The most that could be imposed without violating the principle of *nulla poena sine lege* would be the maximum that the offender might have received for the crime that he could have known he was committing at the time he was committing it. This would require an examination of national law to determine whether the act was criminal under national law when committed (to satisfy *nullum crimen*). Then, the maximum penalty available at the time the crime was committed should be consulted (to satisfy *nulla poena*). In fact, this examination does not appear to be done in the few cases in which courts have stated that they are re-characterizing national crimes as international crimes.[157] However, the author has not found any cases where the only basis for the criminality of the act at the time it was done was national law but where the sentences given have been longer than those available under national law.

The articulation of the appropriate rule here reflects the manner in which the general rule of *nulla poena* in international human rights law applies to these cases. However, practice has not developed in these cases. Thus, this statement is not opposed (or supported) by the statements of law in the arguable cases of re-characterization from national to international law in the ICTY or ICTR. Additionally, statements by those tribunals that national law generally does not bind international courts in sentencing do not necessarily imply that national law might not limit international sentencing practice in this one very limited instance. In this case, however, it would be international human rights law that imposed the national law limits on sentencing – the national law would not control international criminal law of its own force.

7.c.iii.B. *Nulla poena* and Re-Characterization of Crimes in National Courts: Universal Jurisdiction over International Law Crimes

Similar logic applies to sentencing for international crime when prosecuted in national courts. Any sentence available under international law at the time of the act is acceptable under the international human rights law implementation of *nulla poena*. However, as a matter of national law, a state may choose to apply a lesser penalty than the maximum available under international law.

[157] See *Einsatzgruppen Case*, 4 T.W.C. at 497.

7.c.iv. Nulla poena *and Representation (Vicarious) Jurisdiction*

Nulla poena should have greater significance as a limit on sentencing in representation (vicarious) jurisdiction cases. Where representation or vicarious jurisdiction is the only basis for jurisdiction over an accused person, the law applicable to that actor at the time of the act was the law of the place where the crime was committed. If that law would apply a lesser penalty than available under the law of the forum, only the penalty to which the offender was subject when the act was committed should be available.

As was seen previously, states generally apply this rule, and doctrine supports it.[158] This rule implements the logic of the requirement of fair warning of potential penalties that underlines the principle of legality. However, some states that apply the doctrine of representation jurisdiction do not have this rule in their applicable statutes.[159] Little or no practice appears to exist on the issue of whether states do or do not accept claims from other states on this basis. As mentioned earlier,[160] it is possible that regional international human rights courts (the ECtHR, ACtHR, and the new ACtHPR) or advisory human rights bodies (e.g., the ICCPR's HRC) will at some point be presented with cases or communications raising this issue.

7.c.v. Nulla poena *and General Principles of Law*

To the extent that general principles of law operate as a subset of international law that can define international criminal law, *nulla poena* simply requires that crimes created in this way be treated as any other crime under international criminal law. One must consider, along with whether the crime existed at the time of the act, what the maximum available punishment for the act was. This is probably the most difficult aspect of fitting crimes under general principles of law into the general system of legality in criminal law.

There was some discussion in the post–World War II cases of crimes against humanity as violations of general principles of law.[161] Even if they are still crimes pursuant to general principles of law (rather than having become crimes under customary international law), these crimes remain punishable by penalties up to death or life imprisonment. To the extent that

158 See Chap. 5.c.vii.

159 See, e.g., Germany § 7(2) StGB; Chap. 5.c.vii.

160 See Chap. 7.b.ii.D.

161 *United States v. Göring*, Count Four – Crimes Against Humanity §X, 1 IMT, Trial at 65; *cf.Einsatzgruppen Case*, 4 T.W.C. at 459, 497.

they are war crimes or national crimes by another name, it is fair to say that the penalties available under the law when committed were severe.

The ICTY used general principles of law as the basis for the crime of contempt. However, the ICTY Rules of Procedure and Evidence contained, from the beginning, a maximum penalty for contempt.[162] Thus, to the extent that contempt always existed as a crime in the tribunal, there has not been a question of *nulla poena* being inapplicable.

There is one case in which a national court did not apply any sort of *nulla poena* analysis. The Court of Appeal of Sri Lanka allowed retrospective acceptance of jurisdiction over hijacking committed on an Italian-flagged flight from India to Thailand, apparently on the theory that hijacking had become criminal under general principles of law before the act was committed.[163] The High Court had sentenced the hijacker to life imprisonment. The Court of Appeal reduced the sentence to five years rigorous imprisonment, on the basis of the individual circumstances of the case, and the Supreme Court affirmed the reduction.[164] Neither appellate court discussed the *nulla poena* issue, and it is not clear that it had been raised. Nonetheless, it would be difficult to imagine that the defendant would not have been subject to conviction and a sentence of at least five years under Indian, Italian, or Thai law for the acts committed, and thus it is likely that there was no actual violation in this case.

There is very little reported practice on this issue. Except for the preceding comments, all that can be said is that the articulation given here – that there must, at the time of the act, be some law applicable to the defendant that authorized the penalty imposed – implements the general rule of non-retroactivity of punishments in international human rights law.

7.c.vi. Nulla poena *as Applying to Punishments Only, and Not to Other Sanctions*

The international human rights movement has limited non-retroactivity as a human right to the criminal sphere only. Non-retroactivity of non-criminal law does not appear as a general human right in the major human rights

[162] ICTY Rules of Procedure and Evidence, R. 77, in its various versions; see discussion in Chap. 6.a.i.A.

[163] Ekanayake v. The Attorney-General, C.A. 132/84 (Sri Lanka Ct. of App., 28 May 1986), aff'd, S.C. App. No. 68/86 (Sri Lanka S.Ct., 9 December 1987) [both available through official Sri Lanka government Web site, http://www.lawnet.lk], discussed without citation in Clayton & Tomlinson ¶ 11.512, p. 769.

[164] *Ekanayake.*

treaties.[165] There is one provision of the ACHR that appears to prohibit retroactive non-punishment consequences involving deprivations of liberty,[166] but the other human rights treaties do not have such a provision. Several states have non-retroactivity provisions in their constitutions that are not limited to criminal law,[167] but most do not.

Some state practice indicates that "non-punishment" consequences of crime are not subject to the rule of non-retroactivity.[168] For example, the U.S. Supreme Court has approved indefinite post-imprisonment commitment of violent sexual predators in mental institutions, even as to persons who committed their sex crimes before the law was passed.[169] At some point, this issue may arise in the international organization law context, given that the UN Security Council has begun imposing "non-criminal" sanctions, such as requiring states to freeze assets and deny entry, upon individuals and other non-state entities.[170]

A worldwide survey of practice concerning what legal consequences of criminal acts may be considered non-punishment for purposes of the prohibition of retroactive punishment has not been possible here. Such a survey would be very useful. What can be said now, is simply that what is punishment for purposes of criminal law is an "autonomous" (i.e., independent) legal question from the question of what constitutes a crime. As an international human rights law matter, it is also separate from what any given state considers not to be punishment (though a given state's practice is part of the practice that defines customary international law).[171]

7.d. *NULLUM CRIMEN, NULLA POENA* AS BINDING INTERNATIONAL ORGANIZATIONS AND INTERNATIONAL COURTS

International organizations, including international criminal courts and internationalized criminal courts operated in whole or part by international organizations, are bound by the customary international law versions of the principles of *nullum crimen, nulla poena sine lege.* The modern international criminal courts and tribunals have consistently applied these doctrines,

[165] See generally Chap.4.
[166] ACHR art. 7, discussed in Chap. 4.d.ii.
[167] See Chap. 1.a.
[168] See Chap. 5.c.viii.
[169] See Chap. 5.c.viii, discussing Kansas v. Hendricks, 521 U.S. 346, 361 (1997).
[170] See UN S.C. Res. 1267, 1373, 1390, UN Docs. S/RES/1267 (15 October 1999), S/RES/1373 (28 September 2001), S/RES/1390 (16 January 2002).
[171] See Chap. 5.c.viii.

even in the absence of express statement of these principles in their organic documents.[172]

7.e. LEGALITY AND JURISDICTION OF COURTS

7.e.i. *Creation of New Courts or Expansion of Jurisdiction of Existing Courts*

The retrospective creation of jurisdictions to hear cases is not prohibited by customary international law. Customary international law does not prohibit the establishment of new courts, either national, international, or mixed, to hear cases concerning crimes that have already been committed so long as the acts were prohibited by some applicable criminal law at the time committed. It also does not prohibit expansion of jurisdiction of existing courts to hear cases concerning crimes that have already been committed, again so long as the acts were prohibited by some applicable criminal law at the time committed.

Courts have been created to try specific groups of persons, more or less identifiable in advance, after the fact of some or all of the crimes involved. These would include the Nuremberg and Tokyo Tribunals, the Sierra Leone Special Court, the Iraqi Special Tribunal, and the Cambodian Extraordinary Chambers. At the time of this writing, a special court to deal with certain political murders in Lebanon is being established.

Some national provisions and the ACHR prohibit such retrospective court creation.[173] Nothing in customary international law prevents these stricter rules from being applied nationally and regionally.

One point of general interest: where there is no requirement of a preexisting jurisdiction, the traditional view of a single prescribing authority may be divided in two – the substantive lawmaker may not be the authority that establishes the court to try the crime in question. However, the creators of such a court must use a body of substantive criminal law applicable to the alleged criminals and their crimes at the time of their commission, to avoid violation of the principle of legality.[174] Even where there is a preexisting jurisdiction, the legislating authority for that court may implement substantive criminal law created by another authority, such as the international community.[175]

[172] See generally Chap. 6.

[173] See Chap. 5.d (national provisions); ACHR art. 8.

[174] Cf. Sec-Gen's ICTY Rep. ¶¶ 33–35 (on finding an existing body of substantive criminal law to be applied in the ICTY).

[175] Cf. Ferdinandusse, *passim*.

7.e.ii. *Requirement that Court Be Established by Law*

The court given jurisdiction to adjudicate criminal law must be independent, impartial, and created by law.[176] This is an issue of legality that goes beyond retroactivity but is intellectually and practically connected to the issue of retroactive court creation.

The practice of states and international organizations suggests that states can lawfully combine to create a military court (Nuremberg) and delegate to a military authority the authority to create a military court (Tokyo). They can also combine to create a tribunal intended to be permanent (the ICC). International organizations acting within their mandate can create criminal tribunals to deal with specific situations (ICTY, ICTR). They can also work with states to create a court either as an independent international organization (SCSL) or as a state judicial organ (Extraordinary Chambers for Cambodia). Finally, an international organization may create courts as part of the administration of a territory emerging from conflict (UNMIK, UNTAET). A recent U.S. court decision on the creation of military commissions demonstrates that the doctrine requiring tribunals to be established by law has continuing vitality at the national level.[177]

7.f. PERSONALITY OF PUNISHMENT AND PROHIBITION OF COLLECTIVE PUNISHMENTS

Criminal punishment of non-offenders, whether individual or collective, is prohibited. A natural person punished for crime must have some individual criminal responsibility.

It would be difficult to argue that collective criminal punishments – or individual punishments of non-criminals – are permissible under customary international law today. There is a political and moral consensus against it that has been building in such documents as the African Charter of Human and Peoples Rights, the American Convention on Human Rights, international humanitarian law treaties, national constitutions and elsewhere. Many of those constitutions that do not explicitly contain this rule are fairly read as including it.[178]

Nonetheless, care is warranted here. Specific national provisions concerning personality of punishment and prohibiting collective punishments

[176] ICCPR art. 14(1); ECHR art. 6(1); ACHR art. 8(1); ACHPR art. 7(1) (not including "created by law" language); Revised ArCHR art. 13.

[177] *Hamdan.*

[178] See Chap. 5.e.

are not as widespread as those enacting *nullum crimen* and *nulla poena*. Reasonably, however, some would argue that this is because personality of punishment is so fundamental to criminal systems that it goes unstated in most systems.

One might also argue that today the real issue of collective punishment occurs outside the criminal law systems of almost all countries. It occurs in situations of war, armed conflict, and occupation. It also occurs when political decisions are made to punish groups within a population. This may be why many of the strongest statements against it come from the field of international humanitarian law, where it is part of both customary international law and treaty law.[179] As has been pointed out in other contexts, the existence of the rule in international humanitarian law does not prove its existence in the more general field of human rights law. However, its existence as a rule of international humanitarian law applicable to internal armed conflicts is one piece of evidence that it is a rule of human rights law. If states have agreed that they cannot impose collective punishment when under the immense pressures of civil war, they are unlikely to condone collective punishment during other times.

Moreover, modern hostage taking is often carried out by terrorists and is aimed to compel a specific outcome, whether a political result, the release of prisoners, or the payment of ransom. The holding of hostages for the purpose of insuring "good" behavior by a population (because "bad" behavior by any members of the population would result in the hostages' deaths) is less prevalent today, at least in international situations.

Despite all these caveats, the inclusion of this norm as a rule of international human rights law concerning legality in criminal law has value. Whether a sanction is punishment for purposes of criminal law legality is, as discussed, an autonomous legal question, not simply controlled by whether a state claims that an act is punishment.[180] This can be seen especially in issues where an occupier takes action, such as destruction or deprivation of property because of a wrong done by a family member, that would squarely be considered punishment if done in the context of a case directly against the criminal. One can see the possibility of collective punishments like this outside the context of occupation; for example, a dictator could punish families or villages of "criminals" with destruction or confiscation of property. This is illegal under customary international human rights law.

[179] See Chap. 4.f.ii and material discussed therein.
[180] See discussion in Chap. 5.c.viii.

7.g. RIGHT OF THE INDIVIDUAL TO RAISE CLAIM OF VIOLATION OF LEGALITY AS A MATTER OF INTERNATIONAL LAW, AND THE INTERNATIONAL LEGAL PERSONALITY OF INDIVIDUALS

As a matter of customary international law, international or internationalized criminal courts and tribunals operated by international organizations or as independent international organizations must allow individuals to raise questions of legality on their own behalf. This includes issues of non-retroactivity of crimes and punishments and the establishment of the tribunal according to law.

All of the international criminal courts and tribunals have thus far allowed individuals to raise claims of legality in their own right. This includes the internationalized criminal tribunals operated by the United Nations as part of its territorial administrations of Kosovo (UNMIK) and East Timor (UNTAET). Even the Nuremberg and Tokyo Tribunals allowed these issues to be raised in circumstances in which some wished to deny that right. It is difficult to imagine that any international criminal tribunal would deny the ability of the individual to raise such a claim.

The matter is different where prosecutions in the internal courts of states are concerned. Many states belong to treaty regimes that allow legality to be raised in regional international courts of human rights, specifically the European Court of Human Rights, the Inter-American Court of Human Rights, and the African Court of Human and Peoples' Rights. Many other states allow persons prosecuted to address claims to the UN Human Rights Committee through the First Optional Protocol to the ICCPR. Persons may address claims to the African Commission on Human and Peoples Rights as to those ACHPR parties who have not ratified the Protocol creating the new African Court of Human and Peoples Rights.[181] These UN Human Rights Committee and the African Commission only have the authority to express "views" and do not make judgments enforceable at the international level. In any event, these individual rights to raise issues are based in treaty law that has not nearly been universally adopted.

At this time, then, customary international law does not require states to permit individuals being prosecuted in their courts to raise legality in their own right as a matter of international law. Where no treaty mechanisms for the individual to raise the issue exist, the issue must be raised through the

[181] Protocol to the African Charter the Establishment of the African Court on Human and Peoples' Rights, adopted by the Organization of African Unity Assembly of Heads of State and Government (34th Ordinary Session, 1998), entered into force 25 January 2004.

normal state-centric mechanisms of international law. Nothing in customary international law or relevant treaty law suggests that states have given up their right to complain to other states about violations of the customary international law principles of legality.

7.h. INTERNATIONAL LAW LEGALITY, NATIONAL LAW LEGALITY, AND THE PROSECUTION OF CORE INTERNATIONAL LAW CRIMES IN NATIONAL COURTS

A problem arises where a national doctrine of legality requires internal adoption of a criminal law before a crime can be prosecuted, even if the crime already exists in treaty or customary international law. This is a very common state of affairs in national systems.[182]

Many states have versions of the principle of legality stricter than the international criminal law version. Many follow the rule *nullum crimen, nulla poena sine praevia lege scripta* requiring a specific criminal statute, including sentencing provisions, to have been in place before an act may be prosecuted. This would, on its face, prohibit using new statutory implementations of international criminal law retroactively in such courts, even where the act involved was a crime under customary international criminal law when committed. Some states also prohibit the creation of new or special courts to prosecute crime retrospectively, a rule not required by customary international law.

In general international law, there is no problem with a state limiting its authority to prosecute crime. There is no general obligation to exercise jurisdiction in every conceivable case.

However, there has been a movement since World War II to remove procedural objections to prosecution for criminal violations of international humanitarian law (genocide, crimes against humanity, and war crimes). For example, there is a great deal of authority for the proposition that customary international law prohibits application of statutes of limitations to these crimes. Arguments are sometimes made that states have a customary international law obligation to prosecute these crimes when they can and to exercise universal jurisdiction for that purpose.

At the current time, neither practice nor *opinio juris* prohibits states from applying constitutional or statutory implementations of principles of legality stronger than those applying in international law. However, such a national rule does not prohibit a court of another state with jurisdiction,

[182] See Chap. 5.c.v.E.

or an international court with jurisdiction, from prosecuting the case. The ICC Statute allows it to prosecute cases pursuant to the principle of complementarity with national systems only if a state claiming jurisdiction shows an "inability or unwillingness" genuinely to investigate or prosecute.[183]

Whether refusal to prosecute because national law has a principle of legality stronger than that required by international law (including the ICC Statute) will be construed as an inability or unwillingness to prosecute remains to be seen. This situation should arise very rarely where the concerned states are parties to the ICC Statute. Such states, it is hoped, will have incorporated crimes in the ICC Statute into their own domestic law as part of the ICC Statute implementation process. The situation may, however, arise in cases of Security Council referral of situations in states that are not party to the ICC Statute. The rejection of impunity in the ICC Statute would suggest, at least as a matter of legality, that the ICC be allowed to prosecute acts that were criminal under customary international law when committed.

7.i. *JUS COGENS* STATUS FOR NON-RETROACTIVITY OF CRIMES AND PUNISHMENTS?

The introduction to this book quoted Meron's assertion, "The prohibition of retroactive penal measures is a fundamental principle of criminal justice, and a customary, even peremptory, norm of international law that must in all circumstances be observed in all circumstances by national and international tribunals."[184] The universal acceptance of criminal law legality as an international law obligation through one or another of the international human rights treaties or international humanitarian law treaties certainly points in this direction.

On the basis of the earlier discussion and sources, there may be an exception to legality as a rule of international law, on the basis of "persistent objection" to the creation of customary international law. As noted previously, there is an argument that *ta'azir* offences in Islamic law do not comply with the principle of legality (though some Islamic scholars disagree).[185] Even if *ta'azir* law as traditionally applied in some Islamic societies conflicts

[183] ICC Statute arts. 17–19.

[184] Meron at 244. Some still question whether and how customary international human rights law comes to bind the United Nations and other international organizations. See José E. Alvarez, International Organizations as Law-makers 179–81 (Oxford Univ. Press 2005).

[185] See Kamel, at 159–68, discussed in Chap. 2.a.ii.

with legality – and the material discussed herein suggests that it does not[186] – the customary rule is not destroyed. An Islamic state might not subscribe to the ICCPR or a regional human rights treaty making *nullum crimen* binding in national law for all persons. If such a state has persistently insisted on maintaining *ta'azir* offenses within its system during the time that the customary international law rule requiring domestic application of *nullum crimen* has been evolving and in a manner inconsistent with that customary international law rule, it may continue to apply *ta'azir* practice consistently with international human rights law. A persistent objector may act inconsistently with customary international law, but such objection does not destroy the obligation of the custom for other states.

However, all states using the Islamic law system have adopted the International Convention on the Rights of the Child,[187] which contains the principle of *nullum crimen*, if not the principle of *nulla poena*. Thus, even these states appear to have admitted that legality is a principle of international human rights law that will bind them in their internal affairs. None of these states have specifically reserved the principle of legality in the convention. A few have general reservations to any provision that might conflict with Islam, but the behavior of these states with regard to other treaties and/or their own internal law suggests they do not believe legality conflicts with Islam.[188] Moreover, as we have seen, most Islamic law states have directly adopted non-retroactivity of crimes and punishments in their internal legal systems.[189] This suggests that these states have committed to an application of *ta'azir* law that does not conflict with non-retroactivity of crimes and punishments. Thus, it cannot be said that any of these states truly remain persistent objectors to this custom.

Suppose, however, evidence were to show that *ta'azir* law is still being applied in some states through the use of preexisting religious and community norms but in a way that allowed new crimes to be retrospectively created.[190] The possible existence of an exception by persistent objection suggests that the *nullum crimen* principle has not yet reached the status of *jus cogens*, a peremptory norm of international law from which no

[186] See Chaps. 4.g.i & 5.c.

[187] At the time of writing, Somalia (a non-signatory to the convention) has not adopted Islamic law as national law, though some militias are seeking to apply it.

[188] See Chaps. 4.g.i, 5.c(i, ii, iv).

[189] See Chap. 5.c.

[190] See Chap. 2.a.ii, discussing source material indicating that this is how *ta'azir* worked early in the Islamic period.

derogation is ever permitted – in this case, by the states and other actors making criminal law.

As discussed earlier, Russia (the major successor state to the former Soviet Union) and the People's Republic of China have now put the principle of legality into their domestic law.[191] All the successor states to the Soviet Union and the other Communist and former Communist states have implemented non-retroactivity of crimes and punishments through constitutional or statutory law or have accepted it through treaty law.[192] All have accepted the International Covenant on the Rights of the Child without reservations as to the *nullum crimen* principle. To the extent that these states were objectors to such a custom, it would seem that they are no longer.

A statement, not necessary to the decision, in a Netherlands Supreme Court case suggests that treaty law could require retroactive creation of crimes.[193] It is hard to imagine a new treaty retroactively making criminal something that was not already criminal under customary international law, general principles of law, or some source of municipal law – though international instruments have several times retroactively created new jurisdictions to try already existing crimes.[194] The existence of such a treaty would challenge the *jus cogens* status of non-retroactivity of crimes, because it would be an attempt to derogate from the rule. There will be time enough to consider this exception if such a treaty comes into existence and there is a retroactive prosecution under its provisions. For now, the lack of such things counts in favor of the universality of the rule of non-retroactivity.

Any view that *nullum crimen* and *nulla poena* have not reached the status of peremptory norms of international law has an interesting consequence for analysis of the ICCPR and some of the regional human rights treaties. It suggests that the non-derogability provisions of these treaties are progressive. They may have included as non-derogable rights certain rights that are not yet *jus cogens* rights, which there is an obligation *erga omnes* to observe.

Yet it seems more reasonable to suggest that there are no longer objectors to the principle of legality, in the version stated here, as a rule of international human rights law. This does not automatically make it a *jus cogens* standard. Nonetheless, its repeated recognition in near-universal treaty law, its adoption as a matter of domestic law by so many states, and the lack of

[191] See Chap. 5.c.iv.
[192] See Chap. 5.c.iv.
[193] See [*Bouterse*] Appeal in cassation in the interests of the law ¶ 4.5, 32 Netherlands Y.B.I.L. at 291, discussed in Chap. 5.c.iii.
[194] See generally Chap. 6.

opposition to it in modern times suggest that Meron is correct. At very least, the principle of non-retroactivity of crimes and punishments is beginning to emerge as a *jus cogens* norm.

7.j. INTERNATIONAL ORGANIZATIONS AS PARTICIPANTS IN THE PROCESS OF CREATING CUSTOMARY AND OTHER BINDING INTERNATIONAL LAW

International organizations – especially international courts and tribunals – have by now become accepted participants in the process of making customary international law and other forms of international law applicable to individuals and states. This is demonstrated by the materials discussed throughout the latter chapters of this book.[195] A few more comments can be added here.

The international criminal tribunals refer to their own judgments and one another' s judgments in determining the customary international law defining crimes. A fighter or commander in the Sudan who ignores the cases declaring that rape can, in certain circumstances, be a war crime or a crime against humanity may be sent to prison. He may be sent to prison either by an international tribunal or by a national authority that allows for incorporation of international criminal law into the law that it will enforce. That is lawmaking, in the sense of proclaiming rules that human beings must follow at the risk of adverse legal consequences.

Since Nuremberg, the international tribunals and international organizations have been among the most important actors in making customary international criminal law. One can argue whether the Nuremberg Tribunal was a true international organization. What seems clear is that the Nuremberg Judgment – that is, the Tribunal acting through its judges as a single entity – was the most important act in the creation of modern customary international criminal law, as far as states, officials and the general public have been concerned. It captured the public imagination and affected state practice even more than the Four Powers acting as individual states in creating the London Agreement and International Military Tribunal Charter. The United Nations and the tribunals that it created or participated in creating (ICTY, ICTR, SCSL, East Timor courts, Kosovo courts) have been the principle entities defining and refining customary international criminal law since 1993. Indeed, it is difficult to imagine a customary international criminal law, in the sense that it has developed, without these institutions.

[195] See Chaps. 4(h, j, k), 6.

Similarly, both the international criminal tribunals and the regional human rights courts participate in making rules of law concerning human rights in criminal proceedings. Within each of the regional human rights systems, this is done through the authority of treaty law. A state which is party to the European Convention on Human Rights may find that the validity of some of its criminal convictions are at risk if it chooses to ignore the decisions of the European Court of Human Rights on legality in criminal law. Along with state practice (in deciding what rights to place in the human rights treaties and how to word them, and how to implement them in domestic law), the human rights courts participate in interpreting these treaties and defining further the rights specified in them. Similarly, the Human Rights Committee (under the ICCPR) and similar regional bodies participate in this process. These courts and other bodies do not of themselves make customary international human rights law. They do not yet appear to be as central to the formation of customary international human rights law as the international criminal tribunals are to the formation of customary international criminal law, at least partly because they each apply treaty texts. One can fairly say this: to the extent that the treaty texts are substantively similar, these decisions are at least becoming part of the practice defining customary international human rights law.

CONCLUSION

The Endurance of Legality in National and International Criminal Law

By now, the principle of legality has come to play a central role in international practice of criminal justice that it did not play before World War II. Even in international criminal law, the rule *nullum crimen, nulla poena sine lege* has obtained customary international law status. Whether or not the entire rule of *nullum crimen, nulla poena sine lege* has become *jus cogens*, the principle of legality is a principle of justice whose enforcement is vital to the rule of law. No national, international, or comparative criminal jurisprudence can ignore it.

The exercise of criminal jurisdiction in violation of the rule of non-retroactivity of crimes and punishments is a violation of an international human right of the accused. The principle of legality implicates jurisdiction, as it concerns the unfairness of both retroactive definition of crimes and penalties (jurisdiction to prescribe) and retroactive application of these rules (jurisdiction to adjudicate and enforce). This is the real answer to those who argue (with some force) that issues of retroactivity have traditionally been considered separately from issues labeled "jurisdictional." The principle also implicates the more traditionally jurisdictional issue of whether a court has been created by law.

There are those who argue that the Nazi mass murders, of the Roma as well as the Jews, made retroactive crime creation at Nuremberg acceptable. This is the force of the statement that it would have been "unjust" to let the Nazi leaders escape.[1] The horror of the events led many positivists to decide that a natural law of humanity prohibits these acts.

[1] *United States v. Göring*, Judgment of 30 September 1946, 1 Trial of the Major War Criminals Before the International Military Tribunal: Nuremberg 14 November 1945–1 October 1946, 171, 219 (Nuremberg: International Military Tribunal 1947).

Retroactive crime creation may have been acceptable at the time of Nuremberg. This is certainly a view that I held before I became a lawyer. At an emotional, though not an intellectual or scholarly level, I am still tempted to believe it. This emotional belief that legality might sometimes be dispensed with is one reason legality is so necessary today to the prevention of tyranny. The view that this emotional force can justify retroactive crime creation is no longer part of international human rights law.

The reason for its unacceptability has a great deal to do with the success of international criminal law as an enterprise. Any criminal law system with the strength to deter, prevent, and punish crime has the strength, if misused, to commit abuses. Abandonment of legality has inevitably led to such abuses. As the international criminal law system becomes more effective, the need for strict enforcement of legality increases rather than decreases.[2] Reliance on the Nuremberg precedent to suggest that retroactive crime creation and increases in available punishment are acceptable is dangerous and, fortunately, incompatible with international law as it now stands.[3] The international legal system has grown to the point where it both can define crimes under international law and create courts (both permanent and ad hoc) to adjudicate allegations of criminality. These courts and tribunals themselves participate in the prescriptive process. Individuals have both substantive and procedural rights in these courts and tribunals, among them the right not to be tried and convicted for acts that were not crimes when committed and the right not to be sentenced to a punishment not available when the acts were committed.

The transformation of the principle of legality from a principle of justice to a binding rule of customary international law, applicable to international organizations such as international tribunals, as well as to states, means that Nuremberg and Tokyo and the rest of the post–World War II prosecutions retroactively creating crimes against peace (aggressive war and conspiracy to wage it) should be a one-time event. Similarly, to the extent that crimes against humanity in the Nuremberg Charter were not already war crimes or crimes under relevant domestic law,[4] the post–World War II creation of

[2] My colleague Josh Silverstein, arguing for the Nuremberg Judgment position, helped me understand why this needed to be said.

[3] William A. Schabas, An Introduction to the International Criminal Court 70–72 (2d ed., Cambridge Univ. Press 2004).

[4] Nuremberg Charter art. 6(c), as amended by Protocol, 6 October 1945, to London Agreement. The issue of applying "whether or not in violation of the domestic law of the country where perpetrated" to crimes against humanity such as murder, as well as persecution became known as the "Great Semicolon Controversy." See Chap. 3.b.ii.A.

these crimes must be a one-time event. *Nullum crimen sine lege* was not, at the time, an international law limitation on the authority of states or the international community. The current state of international law prohibits the retrospective application of a newly created customary international crime where the acts involved were not criminal under law applying to the actor at the time of the act.

Indeed, the era of re-characterization of crimes that were solely national into crimes that are international should be drawing to a close as well. Most of the war crimes in the ICC Statute are clearly crimes under customary international law already, including those crimes that may be committed in non-international armed conflicts. The same can be said of genocide and crimes against humanity. There will be fewer and fewer situations in which one needs to determine whether a crime under the ICC Statute is also a crime under customary international law or a crime under national law, unless the states that are parties to the ICC Statute amend the statute to add new crimes that arguably depart from then-existing customary international criminal law.

At some point in the not-too-distant future, one may see a principle of legality emerge that will not permit re-characterization of crimes. This will not quite be *nullum crimen sine lege praevia scripta* (requiring prior written legislation) because common law systems may retain a common law, rather than a legislative, crime definition. However, crimes will need to be previously proclaimed by the system in which prosecution is occurring. This outcome is not, however, a given. The ICC Statute may be updated with progressive criminal provisions, pursuant to its amendment provisions. If this happens, then under the current structure, these new provisions could raise the same sort of legality problems as the current list of crimes.

Avoiding legality problems is one reason that the ICC Statute provisions on aggression are correct, so far as they go. The failure to hold prosecutions for the crime of aggression outside the World War II context raises the question whether it is currently a customary international law crime, and, if so, what the crime is. Thus, before the ICC can exercise its jurisdiction over aggression, the states party to the statute must adopt a statutory definition of aggression.[5] Although the provisions regarding the coming into force of amendments to the statute are not perfectly clear,[6] the most sensible reading of the statute as a whole is that new, expanded definitions of crimes

[5] ICC Statute art. 5.
[6] See *id.* at arts. 121, 123.

or punishments may not be applied retroactively to acts before the coming into force of those provisions. This would be consistent with the spirit of the statute, which prohibits the current definitions from applying to acts committed before they came into force[7] – that is, when the statute itself came into force.

This does, however, leave the problem of application of a new ICC definition of aggression as an individual crime to a situation involving a non–ICC state referred to the court by the UN Security Council. The issue would be whether aggression is a crime under customary international law at the time that the accused committed the act alleged. There has been an extended debate on this issue, which need not be repeated here. All that needs to be said here is that the addition of aggression to the ICC Statute would not automatically make it a customary international law crime for individuals.[8]

In any case, it is extremely difficult to see how a definition of aggression that included acts other than the planning, ordering, or leading of attacks by one sovereign state on territory within the jurisdiction of another sovereign state for the purpose of conquest – essentially the World War II-type of situation – could be considered a current customary international criminal law definition of aggression as an individual crime. Therefore, it is very difficult to see how a broader definition could be applied to such situations, consistent with *nullum crimen* and the principle that treaty law does not bind third states or persons connected only to them. In other words, the states parties to the ICC Statute are not yet a general criminal law legislature for the entire world.[9]

The principle of legality, despite its limitations, is exceptionally useful for analyzing problems of jurisdiction in international criminal law. Attempts to exercise criminal adjudicative jurisdiction where there has not been prescription of criminal law applicable at the time and place of the act in question violates the principle of legality, and at the very least calls into question the legitimacy of the exercise of jurisdiction.

One challenge of this type may come from outside the area of substantive international criminal law. A view is taking shape that globalization of the economy and communication is making strict rules of jurisdiction

[7] *Id.* at art. 11.

[8] Cf. *id.* at art. 10.

[9] But cf. the views of Leila Nadya Sadat, The International Criminal Court and the Transformation of International Law (Transnational Publishers 2002) (to the effect that the ICC Statute represents a constitutional moment in international law).

obsolete.[10] However, this view plays out in non-criminal private international law, its flexibility poses a danger to individual human rights if it is implemented to its fullest extent in criminal law. If not limited strictly, this type of theory poses a grave threat to the principle of legality. One cannot, under this type of theory, say with any certainty in advance whether a person performing a certain act in a certain place will be subjected to the laws of another given place. Yet the essence of legality is that a person should reasonably be able to tell what laws will be applied to her or him, and the rest of society should be able to determine if such laws are being applied arbitrarily to her or him. The principle of legality will be called upon as a vital reason for limiting unrestrained growth both of jurisdiction to prescribe and jurisdiction to adjudicate.

Flexible-jurisdiction theories grow naturally out of one of the dominant schools of jurisprudence in modern international law, the so-called New Haven school championed by Professors Myres McDougal and W. Michael Reismann. In their view, international law is a constitutive process of authoritative decision making rather than a set of rules. It goes beyond the theory that language is indeterminate at its edges. For all of the success of this view in explaining the sociology of international law, human rights jurisprudence challenges the infinite malleability of international law in the hands of governments and international institutions. A vigorous human rights regime needs rules of some (albeit incomplete) determinacy to protect the individual against both old and new Leviathans.

As Jerome Hall and Lon Fuller pointed out,[11] enforcement of the principle of legality is inherently imperfect. Issues of interpretation of statutes and the evolution of criminal law by judicial decision will always remain, given the imperfections of human language. The epigraph of this book, "To the rule of law as a just and certain guide to human conduct," states an unachieved and possibly unachievable goal, at least if absolute certainty is demanded. Yet it is a goal that it is worth striving to reach, or at least striving to approximate as well as possible.

Non-retroactivity of crimes and punishments is the most important rule implementing the principle of legality today. It challenges dogmatic views of jurisprudence that require rules to be applied to their fullest logical extent,

[10] See generally Paul Schiff Berman, *The Globalization of Jurisdiction*, 151 U. PA. L. REV. 311 (2002).

[11] Lon L. Fuller, THE MORALITY OF LAW 45 (rev. ed., Yale Univ. Press 1969) (1964) ("the utopia of legality cannot be viewed as a situation in which each desideratum of the law's special morality is realized to perfection"); Jerome Hall, *Nulla Poena Sine Lege*, 47 YALE L.J. 165, 171–2 (1938); see also Chap. 1.c.i.

at the risk of not being considered rules at all. Non-retroactivity is a non-derogable rule[12] that will be implemented as well as reasonably possible. This makes it a rule that only pragmatists can love.

[12] See ICCPR art. 4; ECHR art. 15(2); ACHR art. 27; revised ArCHR art. 4; all discussed in Chap. 4.e. See also JEAN-MARIE HENCKAERTS & LOUISE DOSWALD-BECK, 1 CUSTOMARY INTERNATIONAL HUMANITARIAN LAW (RULES) R. 101, discussion at pp. 371–2 (Cambridge Univ. Press 2005) (study issued by the International Committee of the Red Cross); 2 (pt. 2) *id.* (PRACTICE) ¶¶ 3677–78, at p. 2494.

APPENDIX A

Chart of Non-retroactivity Provisions in Criminal Law by Nations

The following chart indicates provisions concerning non-retroactivity in criminal law adopted by the various nations of the world. It also covers the related doctrine of mercy (*lex mitior*) where a later law mitigates a penalty. All UN member states are included in this chart, plus Chechnya, the Republic of China (Taiwan), Kosovo, Turkish Republic of Northern Cyprus, the Palestinian Authority, Sahrawi Arab Democratic Republic (Western Sahara), Somaliland, and the State of Vatican City (the Holy See). These entities each make claims to be a state (Chechnya, Kosovo, N. Cyprus, W. Sahara, Somaliland, Vatican), to be the legitimate government of a state (Rep. of China), or to have the right to become a state (Palestine).[1] Non–UN members are indicated with "x" on the chart.

C = Constitutional provision (including constitutional provisions incorporating human rights treaties with legality provisions, and constitutional provisions that may not be clear on their face but have been authoritatively interpreted by the court of highest jurisdiction in the nation) (Cols. 2-4).

S = Statutory provision (with no clear constitutional provision). Also included here would be case law not tied to a constitutional provision (Cols. 2-4). Note that in a few countries, it is difficult to distinguish between constitutional and statutory provisions.

T = Treaty provision (with no clear constitutional provision, and no statutory provision found) (Cols. 2-4, relevant treaties listed in Col. 5 whether or not there are constitutional provisions).

[1] The Tibetan government-in-exile is not included because the Dalai Lama does not make a claim for independence of Tibet, and because this government has never exerted actual governing power in the territory of Tibet.

Treaties in Column 5 (listed whether or not there are relevant constitutional or statutory provisions for the country):

ACHR = American Convention on Human Rights
ACHPR = African Covenant on Human and Peoples' Rights
ACHPR(P) = ACHPR with Protocol to establish African Court of Human and Peoples' Rights
ArCHR = Revised Arab Charter on Human Rights (information on signatures and ratifications may be incomplete[2])
ECHR = European Convention on Human Rights
ICCPR = International Covenant on Civil and Political Rights
ICCPR(P) = ICCPR with Optional Protocol I allowing reference of complaints to Human Rights Committee

Where there are no constitutional or statutory provisions found, and none of the preceding treaties are applicable, the Convention on the Rights of the Child (CRC) and the 1977 Additional Protocol II to the Geneva Conventions of 1949 (APII) are noted in Column 5. These require application of non-retroactivity in criminal law in limited circumstances, described in Chapter 4.

Treaties or protocols signed, but not ratified, acceded to or succeeded to are so indicated.

The text of constitutional and statutory provisions by country are set forth in Appendix C, so that the reader may check his or her interpretations against the author's.

The material relied on herein was generally verified for the last time in September–October 2007. A few more recent developments have been taken into account, particularly the imposition and subsequent lifting of emergency rule in Pakistan in November-December 2007, the coming into force of the Revised Arab Charter of Human Rights on 15 March 2008, and the presentation of the proposed Kosovo Constitution on 7 April 2008. AFP reported that the new Kosovo Constitution entered into force 15 June 2008, but the President of Serbia said Serbia does not accept the proclamation of the new Kosovo Constitution "as a legal fact."

[2]Entered into force 15 March 2008; for recent news reports on ratification, see *UAE ratifies Arab charter on human rights* from Emirates News Agency at http://www.uaeinteract.com/docs/UAE_ratifies_Arab_charter_on_human_rights/28218.htm (UAE Interact, Web site of National Media Council, posted 16 January 2008) and *Shura Council ratifies Arab Charter on Human Rights*, at the Web site of the Royal Embassy of Saudi Arabia in the U.S., http://www.saudiembassy.net/2008News/News/RigDetail.asp?cIndex=7698 (24 February 2008), which are the sources for current ratification information here.

(1) Country	(2) Retroactive criminalization of acts prohibited (*nullum crimen*)	(3) Retroactive increase of penalties prohibited (*nulla poena*)	(4) Provision on mitigation of punishment (*lex mitior*)	(5) Treaties
Afghanistan	C	C	T	ICCPR
Albania	C	C	C	ECHR, ICCPR
Algeria	C	C	S	ArCHR, ICCPR(P)
Andorra	C	C	T	ECHR, ICCPR(P)
Angola	C	C	C	ACHPR, ICCPR(P)
Antigua & Barbuda	C	C		
Argentina	C	C	T	ACHR, ICCPR(P)
Armenia	C	C	C	ECHR, ICCPR(P)
Australia	T	T	T	ICCPR(P)
Austria	S	S	T	ECHR, ICCPR(P)
Azerbaijan	C	T	C	ECHR, ICCPR(P)
Bahamas	C	C		
Bahrain	C	C	T	ArCHR, ICCPR
Bangladesh[3]	C	C	T	ICCPR
Barbados	C	C	T	ACHR, ICCPR(P)
Belarus	C	C	C	ICCPR(P)
Belgium	S	S	S	ECHR, ICCPR(P)
Belize	C	C	T	ICCPR
Benin	C	C	T	ACHPR(P-signed), ICCPR(P)
Bhutan				CRC only
Bolivia	C	C	C	ACHR, ICCPR(P)
Bosnia & Herzegovina[4]	C	C	C	ECHR, ICCPR(P)
Botswana	C[5]	C	T	ACHPR(P-signed) ICCPR
Brazil	C	C	C	ACHR, ICCPR
Brunei				CRC, APII only
Bulgaria	C	S	S	ECHR, ICCPR(P)
Burkina Faso	C	C	T	ACHPR(P), ICCPR(P)
Burundi[6]	C	C	C	ACHPR(P), ICCPR

(*continued*)

[3] Apparent constitutional exception to constitutional provisions for soldiers and prisoners of war accused of genocide, crimes against humanity and war crimes.
[4] Constitutional provision is specific constitutional incorporation of ECHR.
[5] Excluding contempt of court.
[6] In addition to *nullum crimen* and *nulla poena* requirements being directly in Constitution, *nullum crimen*, *nulla poena* and *lex mitior* are all in the Constitution by incorporation of ICCPR and ACHPR.

(1) Country	(2) Retroactive criminalization of acts prohibited (*nullum crimen*)	(3) Retroactive increase of penalties prohibited (*nulla poena*)	(4) Provision on mitigation of punishment (*lex mitior*)	(5) Treaties
Cambodia[7]	C	C	C	ICCPR(P-signed)
Cameroon[8]	C	C	C	ACHPR(P-signed), ICCPR(P)
Canada	C[9]	C	C	ICCPR(P)
Cape Verde	C[10]	C	C	ACHPR, ICCPR(P)
Central African Rep.	C	C	T	ACHPR(P-signed), ICCPR(P)
Chad	C	T	T	ACHPR(P-signed), ICCPR(P)
x Chechnya[11]				
Chile	C	C	C	ACHR, ICCPR(P)
China,[12] People's Rep. of	S	S	S	ICCPR-signed
x China,[13] Rep. of (Taiwan)	T(signed)	T(signed)	T(signed)	ICCPR&P-signed[14]

[7] General legality provision without regard to retroactivity in constitution. Non-retroactivity in constitution by reference to UDHR and non-retroactivity and *lex mitior* by "covenants and conventions related to human rights," which the author takes as reference to ICCPR.

[8] In addition to *nullum crimen* and *nulla poena* requirements being in constitution, preamble, *nullum crimen, nulla poena* and *lex mitior* are all in the constitution by preamble's incorporation of UDHR and ACHPR.

[9] Allows criminalization of act that at the time done was "criminal according to the general principles of law recognized by the community of nations."

[10] Allows criminalization for acts or omissions that at time committed "were considered criminal according to the principles and norms of International Law."

[11] Claims independence from Russia. Not generally recognized as a state by the international community. By the time of completion of this manuscript, the power of those claiming independence appeared to have weakened substantially.

[12] People's Republic of China claims that there is a single state of China, and it is the sole legitimate government of China. The United Nations and most states recognize the People's Republic as the legitimate government of China.

[13] Constitution of Republic of China maintains that there is one state of China, and government of Republic of China has not formally declared independence from People's Republic of China. Some in the Republic of China seek full independence as a nation under the name of Taiwan. The People's Republic strongly opposes this.

[14] A number of UN members from the socialist group objected to the signing of the ICCPR by the Republic of China in 1967 on the grounds that the government of the People's

(1) Country	(2) Retroactive criminalization of acts prohibited (*nullum crimen*)	(3) Retroactive increase of penalties prohibited (*nulla poena*)	(4) Provision on mitigation of punishment (*lex mitior*)	(5) Treaties
Colombia	C	C	C	ACHR, ICCPR(P)
Comoros	C	C		ACHPR(P)
Congo, Dem. Rep. of	C	C	C	ACHPR(P-signed), ICCPR(P)
Congo, Rep. of	T	T	T	ACHPR(P-signed), ICCPR(P)
Costa Rica	C	C	T	ACHR, ICCPR(P)
Côte d'Ivoire	C	S[15]	S	ACHPR(P), ICCPR(P)
Croatia	C	C	C	ECHR, ICCPR(P)
Cuba	C	C	C	
Cyprus	C	C	T	ECHR, ICCPR(P)
x Cyprus,[16] Turkish Rep. of Northern	C	C		
Czech Rep.[17]	C	C	C	ECHR, ICCPR(P)
Denmark	S	S[18]	S	ECHR, ICCPR(P)
Djibouti	C	C	T	ACHPR(P-signed), ICCPR(P)

(*continued*)

Republic was the only legitimate government of China that could sign such a document. See http://www.ohchr.org/english/countries/ratification/4.html, http://www.ohchr.org/english/countries/ratification/5.html & note 5.

[15] A constitutional provision prevents retroactive increase of penalties for high government officials charged in the High Court of Justice, which in some countries might be called a combined court of impeachment and criminal court for these officials.

[16] Recognized as a state only by Turkey. The UN Security Council "[*c*]*alls upon*" states not to recognize it as a state. UN Security Council Res. 541, S/RES/541 (18 November 1983).

[17] Constitutional provision is specific constitutional incorporation of the Charter of Fundamental Rights and Freedoms (Czechoslovakia, 1991).

[18] Also applies to "legal consequences other than punishment" except for certain issues concerning probation, community service, and mental illness treatment, or debarment from businesses requiring permission for participtation.

(1) Country	(2) Retroactive criminalization of acts prohibited (*nullum crimen*)	(3) Retroactive increase of penalties prohibited (*nulla poena*)	(4) Provision on mitigation of punishment (*lex mitior*)	(5) Treaties
Dominica	C	C	T	ACHR,[19] ICCPR
Dominican Rep.	C	C	C	ACHR, ICCPR(P)
East Timor	C	C	C	ICCPR
Ecuador	C	C	C	ACHR, ICCPR(P)
Egypt	C	C	T	ACHPR (P-signed), ArCHR (signed), ICCPR
El Salvador	C	C	T	ACHR, ICCPR(P)
Equatorial Guinea	C	C	T	ACHPR(P-signed), ICCPR(P)
Eritrea	C	T	T	ACHPR, ICCPR
Estonia	C	C	T	ECHR, ICCPR(P)
Ethiopia	C	C	C	ACHPR(P-signed), ICCPR
Fiji	C	C		
Finland	C	C	T	ECHR, ICCPR
France[20]	C	C	T	ECHR, ICCPR(P)
Gabon[21]	T	T	T	ACHPR(P), ICCPR
Gambia	C	C	T	ACHPR(P), ICCPR(P)
Georgia	C	C	C	ECHR, ICCPR(P)
Germany	C	S[22]	S	ECHR, ICCPR(P)

19 Has not accepted the jurisdiction of the Inter-American Court of Human Rights.

20 From Declaration of the Rights of Man and the Citizen (France, 1789), given current constitutional status through reference in Const. of France (1958), preamble, and Decision of the Constitutional Council of 16 July 1971 (Liberty of Association).

21 A constitutional provision prevents retroactive creation of crimes or increase of penalties for high government officials charged in the High Court of Justice, which in some countries might be called a combined court of impeachment and criminal court for these officials.

22 Punishment may not be retroactive, but certain measures of "reform and prevention" may be imposed as of time of judgment. See Germany § 2 StGB.

(1) Country	(2) Retroactive criminalization of acts prohibited (*nullum crimen*)	(3) Retroactive increase of penalties prohibited (*nulla poena*)	(4) Provision on mitigation of punishment (*lex mitior*)	(5) Treaties
Ghana	C	C	T	ACHPR(P), ICCPR(P)
Greece	C	C	T	ECHR, ICCPR(P)
Grenada	C	C	T	ACHR,[23] ICCPR
Guatemala	C	C	C	ACHR, ICCPR(P)
Guinea	C	C	T	ACHPR(P-signed), ICCPR(P)
Guinea-Bissau	C	C	C	ACHPR(P-signed), ICCPR&P-signed
Guyana	C	C	T	ICCPR(P[24])
Haiti	C	C	C	ACHR, ICCPR
Honduras	C	C	C	ACHR, ICCPR(P)
Hungary	C	C	S	ECHR, ICCPR(P)
Iceland	C[25]	C	S	ECHR, ICCPR(P)
India	C	C	T	ICCPR
Indonesia	C	C	T	ICCPR
Iran	C	T	T	ICCPR
Iraq	C	C	C	ICCPR
Ireland	C	T	T	ECHR, ICCPR(P)
Israel	S	S[26]	S	ICCPR
Italy	C	C	S	ECHR, ICCPR(P)

(*continued*)

[23] Has not accepted the jurisdiction of the Inter-American Court of Human Rights.

[24] Guyana reserved against the ability the Human Rights Committee to receive and consider communications from persons under sentence of death for murder or treason. It did not reserve against any of its substantive obligations under the ICCPR, including legality in criminal matters. A number of states objected to this reservation. See http://www.ohchr.org/english/countries/ratification/5.html, including list of reservations and declarations & n.2.

[25] But some use of strict analogy allowed.

[26] But "updating the amount of a fine shall not be deemed the setting of a more severe penalty." Israel Penal Code § 3.

(1) Country	(2) Retroactive criminalization of acts prohibited (*nullum crimen*)	(3) Retroactive increase of penalties prohibited (*nulla poena*)	(4) Provision on mitigation of punishment (*lex mitior*)	(5) Treaties
Jamaica	C	C	T	ACHR,[27] ICCPR[28]
Japan	C	S	S	ICCPR
Jordan	T	T	T	ArCHR, ICCPR
Kazakhstan	C	C	C	ICCPR
Kenya	C	C	T	ACHPR(P), ICCPR
Kiribati	C	C		
Korea, Dem. People's Rep. of (North)	T	T	T	ICCPR
Korea, Rep. of (South)	C	T	T	ICCPR(P)
x Kosovo[29]	C	C	C	
Kuwait	C	C	T	ICCPR
Kyrgyzstan	C	C	C	ICCPR(P)
Laos	T	T	T	ICCPR
Latvia[30]	C	C	C	ECHR, ICCPR(P)
Lebanon	S	S	S	ICCPR
Lesotho	C	C	T	ACHPR(P), ICCPR(P)
Liberia	C	C	T	ACHPR(P-signed), ICCPR (P-signed)
Libya	T	T	T	ACHPR(P), ArCHR, ICCPR(P)
Liechtenstein	S	S	T	ECHR, ICCPR(P)
Lithuania	S	S[31]	S	ECHR, ICCPR(P)

[27] Has accepted the jurisdiction of the IACtHR to consider communications from other states parties to ACHR.

[28] Has denounced its prior acceptance of ICCPR Optional Protocol I, http://www.ohchr.org/english/countries/ratification/5.html n.5.

[29] Declared Independence in 2008. Recognized by some but not all states. Entry based upon proposed Kosovo Constitution presented 7 April 2008 by the Kosovo Constitutional Commission, entered into force 15 June 2008. See AFP report 15 June 2008 (also noting Serbian objection to Kosovo Constitution.

[30] Latvia Const. art. 89 requires state to "recognize and protect fundamental human rights in accordance with this Constitution, laws and international agreements binding upon Latvia." Thus, implementation of ECHR, ICCPR appears constitutionally required.

[31] Certain measures of education or medical treatment may be imposed as of time of judgment. See Lithuania Penal Code art. 3(3).

(1) Country	(2) Retroactive criminalization of acts prohibited (*nullum crimen*)	(3) Retroactive increase of penalties prohibited (*nulla poena*)	(4) Provision on mitigation of punishment (*lex mitior*)	(5) Treaties
Luxembourg	S	S	S	ECHR, ICCPR(P)
Macedonia	C	C	C	ECHR, ICCPR(P)
Madagascar	C	C	T	ACHPR(P-signed), ICCPR(P)
Malawi	C	C	T	ACHPR(P-signed), ICCPR(P)
Malaysia	C	C		
Maldives	C	C	T	ICCPR(P)
Mali	C	T[32]	T	ACHPR(P), ICCPR(P)
Malta	C	C	T	ECHR, ICCPR(P)
Marshall Islands	C	C		
Mauritania[33]	S	S	T	ACHPR(P), ICCPR
Mauritius	C	C	T	ACHPR(P), ICCPR(P)
Mexico	C	C	T	ACHR, ICCPR(P)
Micronesia[34]	C	C		
Moldova	C	C	T	ECHR, ICCPR(P-signed)
Monaco	C	C	T	ECHR, ICCPR
Mongolia	T	T	T	ICCPR(P)
Montenegro	C	C	C	ECHR, ICCPR(P)[35]
Morocco	C	C	T	ArCHR(signed), ICCPR
Mozambique	C	C	C	ACHPR(P), ICCPR

(continued)

[32] A constitutional provision prevents retroactive increase of penalties for high government officials charged in the High Court of Justice, which in some countries might be called a combined court of impeachment and criminal court for these officials.

[33] Mauritania Const., preamble, contains references to ACHPR and UDHR without specifically incorporating their obligations.

[34] Micronesia Const art. IV(11), with prohibition of ex post facto law.

[35] The UN OHCHR considers that Montenegro succeeded to the ICCPR and Optional Protocol I, see n.33, http://www.ohchr.org/english/countries/ratification/4.htm, http://www.ohchr.org/english/countries/ratification/5.html.

(1) Country	(2) Retroactive criminalization of acts prohibited (*nullum crimen*)	(3) Retroactive increase of penalties prohibited (*nulla poena*)	(4) Provision on mitigation of punishment (*lex mitior*)	(5) Treaties
Myanmar	C	C		
Namibia	C	C	T	ACHPR(P-signed), ICCPR(P)
Nauru	C	C	T[36]	ICCPR&P-signed
Nepal[37]	C	C	T	ICCPR(P)
Netherlands	C	S	S	ECHR, ICCPR(P)
New Zealand	S	S	S	ICCPR(P)
Nicaragua	C	C	C	ACHR, ICCPR(P)
Niger	C	C	T	ACHPR(P), ICCPR(P)
Nigeria	C	C	T	ACHPR(P), ICCPR
Norway	C	C	T	ECHR, ICCPR(P)
Oman[38]	C	C		
Pakistan[39]	C	C		
Palau	C	C		
x Palestinian Authority[40]	C	C		ArCHR
Panama	C	C	C	ACHR, ICCPR(P)
Papua New Guinea[41]	C/S	C/S	S	
Paraguay	C	C	C	ACHR, ICCPR(P)
Peru	C	C	C	ACHR, ICCPR(P)
Philippines[42]	C	C	T	ICCPR(P)
Poland	C	C	T	ECHR, ICCPR(P)

[36] Nauru Const. art. 81(6), appears inconsistent with the *lex mitior* provision of ICCPR art. 15. See Appendix C.

[37] Status prior to meeting of 2008 Constituent Assembly to write a new constitution.

[38] The Basic Statute of the State of Oman, proclaimed by the sultan, is treated here as serving the function of a constitution.

[39] *Nullum crimen* and *nulla poena* provisions do not apply "to any law making acts of abrogation or subversion of a Constitution in force in Pakistan at any time since the twenty-third day of March, one thousand nine hundred and fifty-six, an offence." Pakistan Const. art. 12(2).

[40] As of early 2008, not yet a state, but gaining international legal personality. Observer at United Nations. West Bank remains under occupation by Israel. Amended Basic Law of Palestine serves purpose of a Constitution.

[41] Constitutional *nullum crimen, nulla poena praevia lege scripta* provision does not apply to contempt of court, and may not apply in Village Courts applying traditional law. However, statutory provisions appear to have rejected any right of Village Courts to create retroactive crimes and punishments.

[42] Philippines Const. art. III, § 22, with prohibition of "*Ex Post Facto* Law."

(1) Country	(2) Retroactive criminalization of acts prohibited (*nullum crimen*)	(3) Retroactive increase of penalties prohibited (*nulla poena*)	(4) Provision on mitigation of punishment (*lex mitior*)	(5) Treaties
Portugal	C	C		ECHR, ICCPR(P)
Qatar	C	C		
Romania	C	C	C	ECHR, ICCPR(P)
Russia	C	C	C	ECHR, ICCPR(P)
Rwanda	C	C	T	ACHPR(P), ICCPR
x Sahrawi Arab Dem. Rep. (W. Sahara)[43]	T	T		ACHPR
St. Kitts & Nevis	C	C		
St. Lucia	C	C		
St. Vincent & the Grenadines	C	C	T	ICCPR(P)
Samoa	C	C		
San Marino	T	T	T	ECHR, ICCPR(P)
São Tomé & Príncipe	C	C	C	ACHPR, ICCPR&P-signed
Saudi Arabia[44]	S	S	T-signed	ArCHR-signed[45]
Senegal	C	C	T	ACHPR(P), ICCPR(P)
Serbia	C	C	C	ECHR, ICCPR(P)
Seychelles[46]	C	C	T	ACHPR(P-signed), ICCPR(P)

(*continued*)

[43] Recognized by a substantial minority of states. Territory claimed by Morocco.

[44] By decree of the king, the Quran and Sunna of the Prophet are the constitution of Saudi Arabia. The king has promulgated the Basic System of the Consultative Council, from which the text in Appendix C is taken. It is treated here as a statute.

[45] Internal steps have been taken to allow for ratification. See *Shura Council ratifies Arab Charter on Human Rights*, at http://www.saudiembassy.net/2008News/News/RigDetail.asp?cIndex=7698 (Web site of the Royal Embassy of Saudi Arabia in the U.S., 24 February 2008).

[46] Constitutional text excepts genocide and crimes against humanity from operation of *nullum crimen* and *nulla poena*. However, text shall be interpreted in accordance with treaty obligations relating to human rights and freedoms.

(1) Country	(2) Retroactive criminalization of acts prohibited (*nullum crimen*)	(3) Retroactive increase of penalties prohibited (*nulla poena*)	(4) Provision on mitigation of punishment (*lex mitior*)	(5) Treaties
Sierra Leone	C	C	T	ACHPR(P-signed), ICCPR(P)
Singapore[47]	C	C		
Slovakia	C	C	C	ECHR, ICCPR(P)
Slovenia	C	C	C	ECHR, ICCPR(P)
Solomon Islands	C	C		
Somalia[48]	C	C		ACHPR, ICCPR(P)
x Somaliland[49]				
South Africa	C	C	C	ACHPR(P), ICCPR(P)
Spain	C	C	C	ECHR, ICCPR(P)
Sri Lanka	C[50]	C	T	ICCPR(P)
Sudan	C	T	T	ACHPR(P-signed), ICCPR
Suriname	C	C	T	ACHR, ICCPR(P)
Swaziland	C	C	T	ACHPR(P-signed), ICCPR
Sweden	C	C	T	ECHR, ICCPR(P)
Switzerland[51]	S	S	S	ECHR, ICCPR
Syria	C	C	T	ArCHR, ICCPR
Tajikistan	C	C	C	ICCPR(P)
Tanzania	C	C	T	ACHPR(P), ICCPR

[47] Constitutional text excepts several security and other measures from operation of *nullum crimen* and *nulla poena*, including acts by a "substantial body of persons, whether inside or outside Singapore . . . tending to excite disaffection against the President or the Government."

[48] Somalia has had no effective national government for many years. The constitutional text in Appendix C is the last effective constitution.

[49] From 1960–91, a portion of Somalia. Has claimed independence since 1991. Not generally recognized as a state but has had a more effective government than Somalia since 1991.

[50] Allows criminalization of act that was at the time "criminal according to the general principles of law recognized by the community of nations."

[51] Statutes for Swiss Federation. The laws of all the Swiss cantons have not been searched.

(1) Country	(2) Retroactive criminalization of acts prohibited (*nullum crimen*)	(3) Retroactive increase of penalties prohibited (*nulla poena*)	(4) Provision on mitigation of punishment (*lex mitior*)	(5) Treaties
Thailand[52]	C	C	T	ICCPR
Togo	C	T[53]	T	ACHPR(P), ICCPR(P)
Tonga	C	C		
Trinidad & Tobago	T	T	T	ICCPR[54]
Tunisia	C	C	T	ACHPR(P-signed), ICCPR
Turkey	C	C	T	ECHR, ICCPR(P)
Turkmenistan	C	C	T	ICCPR(P)
Tuvalu	C	C		
Uganda	C	C	T	ACHPR(P), ICCPR(P)
Ukraine	C	C	C	ECHR, ICCPR(P)
United Arab Emirates	C	C		ArCHR
United Kingdom of Great Britain & N. Ireland	S[55]	S	T	ECHR, ICCPR
United States of America[56]	C	C		ICCPR
Uruguay	S	S	S	ACHR, ICCPR(P)
Uzbekistan	S	S	S	ICCPR(P)
Vanuatu	C	C		

(*continued*)

[52] Constitution of 2007 restoring *nullum crimen* and *nulla poena* replaced interim constitution (containing legality provisions without specific mention of non-retroactivity), which was enacted after 2006 coup.

[53] A constitutional provision prevents retroactive increase of penalties for high government officials charged in the High Court of Justice, which in some countries might be called a combined court of impeachment and criminal court for these officials.

[54] Has twice ratified and then denounced Optional Protocol I, which is currently not in effect for Trinidad and Tobago. Acceded to, then denounced, ACHR.

[55] Allows criminalization of act that was at the time "criminal according to the general principles of law recognized by civilized nations."

[56] Constitutional provisions prohibiting ex post facto laws and due process of law as authoritatively interpreted and applied by Supreme Court of the United States. Has reserved against *lex mitior* provision of ICCPR.

(1) Country	(2) Retroactive criminalization of acts prohibited (*nullum crimen*)	(3) Retroactive increase of penalties prohibited (*nulla poena*)	(4) Provision on mitigation of punishment (*lex mitior*)	(5) Treaties
x Vatican City (Holy See)[57]				CRC, APII only
Venezuela	C	C[58]	T	ACHR, ICCPR(P)
Vietnam	T	T	T	ICCPR
Yemen	C	C		ICCPR
Zambia	C	C	T	ACHPR(P-signed), ICCPR(P)
Zimbabwe[59]	C	C	T	ACHPR(P-signed), ICCPR

[57] Recognized by many states. Holy See recognized as non-member observer at UN General Assembly. However, Vatican City does not have a permanent population in the same way as most states.
[58] Retroactive creations of minor penalty acceptable.
[59] *Nullum crimen* and *nulla poena* may not apply in Village Courts applying traditional law.

APPENDIX B

Legality and Non-retroactivity Provisions as of 1946–47

The following materials on the status of legality and non-retroactivity provisions come from the Documented Outline prepared by the Secretariat for the Commission on Human Rights Drafting Committee for the International Bill of Rights, UN Doc. E/CN.4/AC.1/3/Add.1, pp. 215–34 (2 June 1947) (sources for Articles 25 and 26) and the first [UN] YEAR BOOK ON HUMAN RIGHTS 1946 [hereinafter 1946 UNYBHR], which was designed to "'include all declarations and bills on human rights now in force in the various countries.'"[1] The Documented Outline included constitutional provisions of UN member states. The 1946 UNYBHR included constitutional provisions of UN member states; where no human rights provisions existed in the relevant constitutions, it sometimes included statutory provisions and in some cases materials from experts describing the law of the jurisdiction; there were also provisions from non–member states.

This material represents a good snapshot of the constitutional law of legality as of 1946, and a very incomplete view of statutory and other law. The UN member constitutions represent material that was available to the drafters of the UDHR as well as those involved in the early stages of drafting the ICCPR. The other material in the 1946 UNYBHR would have been available by 1948, though it is less easy to say how much of it was actually used by the delegates who participated in drafting the UDHR and the later ICCPR.

The material excerpted here only concerns issues of legality in criminal law. The Article 26 material in the Documented Outline included other constitutional rights related to criminal law and procedure, because Article 26 of the outline, like the eventual UDHR Article 11, covered other criminal law and procedure rights as well. The material in the 1946 UNYBHR includes

[1] 1946 UNYBHR at ix.

material on all human rights provisions in the constitutions, as well as some other material on human rights in the various states.

For those of us looking back at this material from the standpoint of the early twenty-first century, it should be noted that there was a great deal of statutory material on non-retroactivity in criminal law, especially in the criminal or penal codes of civil law countries, which is not noted here. Many of those participating in the process, especially lawyers from civil law countries, would have known of the existence of this material, even if they did not know the exact texts of the codes of countries other than their own. Thus, many of the states where the constitution discusses the rule of law, without reference to retroactivity, may well have had criminal codes enforcing non-retroactivity of crimes and punishments.

Afghanistan

Fundamental Principles of the Government of Afghanistan art. 11:

> . . . No one is imprisoned or punished without an order in accordance with the Shariat or the appropriate laws.

Albania (non-UN member; from 1946 UNYBHR only)

Albania Const. art. 19:

> . . .
>
> No punishment shall be perpetrated or inflicted except as prescribed by law.
>
> . . .
>
> The administrative organs of the state may give jail for misdemeanours as prescribed by law.

Argentina

Argentina Const. art. 18 as in Appendix C.

Argentina Const. art. 19:

> No inhabitant of the nation shall be obliged to do what the law does not command nor deprived of what it does not forbid.
>
> . . .

Australia

No provision on legality in criminal law noted in Documented Outline or in commentary by Geoffrey Sawer, 1946 UNYBHR at 31.

Austria (non-UN member; from UNYBHR only)

Postwar constitution not yet approved.

Belgium

Belgium Const. art. 9 in 1946/47 documents similar to current Belgium Coord. Const. art. 14 (minor translation differences) as in Appendix C.

Commentary by Daniel Warnotte, 1946 UNYBHR at 38, noted a "dangerous" practice of imposing administrative penalties in some cases, as a substitute for inadequate criminal penalties imposed by courts.

Bolivia

Bolivia Const. art. 13:

> No person shall be tried by special commissions or submitted to judges other than those previously designated for such suits.

Bolivia Const. art. 29 in 1946/47 documents similar to current Bolivia Const. art. 32 except for minor translation differences. See Appendix C.

Bolivia Const. art. 31:

> The law provides only for future circumstances and does not have retroactive effect.

Brazil

Brazil Const. art. 14(29):

> Penal law shall be retroactive only when it benefits the accused.

Brazil Const. art. 140(2) in 1946/47 documents same as current Brazil Const. art. 5(2) in Appendix C

Brazil Const. art. 141(27):

> No one shall be prosecuted or sentenced except by a competent authority and in the form of a previous law.

Bulgaria (non–UN member; from 1946 UNYBHR only)

Postwar constitution not yet approved

Belorussian SSR [then a UN member, now a UN member as independent Belarus]

No constitutional provision on legality in criminal law noted in Documented Outline or 1946 UNYBHR

Canada

No provision on legality in criminal law noted in Documented Outline or in commentary by F. R. Scott, 1946 UNYBHR at 56-57.

Chile

Chile Const. art. 11:

> No one may be sentenced unless he is legally tried and by virtue of a law promulgated prior to the act upon which the sentence rests.

China, Rep. of

No provision on legality in criminal law noted in Documented Outline or in commentary of Chung-fu Chang, 1946 UNYBHR at 61-67.

Colombia

Colombia Const. art. 26:

> No one shall be tried except in conformity with laws antedating the offence with which he is charged....
>
> In criminal matters, the law favourable to the defendant, even if enacted after the commission of the alleged offence, shall be applied in preference to the restrictive or unfavourable law.

Colombia Const. art. 28:

> No person shall, even in time of war, be punished ex post facto except in accordance with a law, order, or decree in which the act has been previously prohibited and corresponding punishment determined.
>
> If there are serious reasons to fear a disturbance of the public order, this provision shall not prevent, even in time of peace, the arrest and detention, by order of the Government upon previous advice of Ministers, of any person suspected with good reason of attempting to disturb the public peace.

Costa Rica

Costa Rica Const. arts. 26, 36, 38, 43:

> 26. The law has no retroactive effect.
>
> 36. No one can be disturbed or prosecuted for any act that does not infringe the law, or for the declaration of his political opinions.
>
> 38. Jurisdiction in civil and criminal trials is exclusive in the authorities established by law. No commission, tribunal or judgeship may be created

> for specified trials, nor shall anyone be subjected to military jurisdiction except individuals of the army....
>
> 43. Punishment can be imposed upon no one except by a pre-existent law that names the crime or offence committed.

Cuba

Cuba Const. arts. 21, 22:

> 21. Penal laws shall have retroactive effect when favorable to the offender. This advantage is denied in cases of perpetration of fraud by public officials or employees who may be delinquent in the exercise of their office, and of persons responsible for electoral crimes and crimes against the individual rights guaranteed by this constitution. The penalties and qualifications of the law in force at the moment of the offence shall be applied to those found guilty of these crimes.
>
> 22. No other laws shall have retroactive effect unless the law itself so provides for reasons of public order, social utility, or national necessity, as may be expressly stipulated in that law by a vote of two-thirds of the total number of members of each co-legislative body. If the basis of the retroactivity should be challenged as unconstitutional, it shall be within the jurisdiction of the tribunal of constitutional and social guarantees to decide upon the same, without the power of refusing to render decision because of form or for any other reason.
>
> In every case the same law shall concurrently establish the degree, manner and form of indemnification for injuries, if any, and of retroactivity affecting rights legitimately acquired under the protection of prior legislation.

Czechoslovakia

Const. Charter of the Czechoslovak Rep. of 1920 art. 94(2):

> No one shall be tried other than before his legal judge.

Const. Charter of the Czechoslovak Rep. of 1920 art. 111(2):

> [O]nly by law may fines and punishments be prescribed and imposed.

Zdenek Peska, 1946 UNYBHR at 86 points out that at this time a new constitution was being considered; Const. Charter art. 111(2) noted only in UNYBHR.

Denmark

No provision on legality in criminal law noted in Documented Outline or in 1946 UNYBHR.

Dominican Republic

Dominican Rep. Const. art. 88:

> No one can be obliged to do that which the law does not command, or be impeded from doing that which the law does not prohibit.

Ecuador

Ecuador Political Const. art. 169:

> ... No one may be removed from the jurisdiction of his proper judges; nor ... punished without previous trial, in accordance with a law passed prior to the act committed; ....

Egypt

Royal Rescript No. 42 of 19 April 1923 Establishing the Constitutional Regime of the Egyptian State art. 6:

> No offense and no penalty may be established, save in pursuance of the law. Penalties may be inflicted only in respect of offenses committed after the law providing for them has been promulgated.

Eire (Ireland) (non–UN member; material from 1946 UNYBHR only)

Eire Const. art. 40(4)(1):

> No citizen shall be deprived of his personal liberty save in accordance with law.

El Salvador

El Salvador Const. art. 24:

> The laws cannot have retroactive effect, except in penal matters when the new law may be more favorable to the offender.

El Salvador Const. art. 25:

> No one may be tried except by laws enacted prior to the offence and by a tribunal that the law had previously established.

Ethiopia

Ethiopia Const. art. 23:

> No Ethiopian subject may be arrested, sentenced or imprisoned, except as prescribed by law.

Ethiopia Const. art. 24:

> No Ethiopian subject may, against his will, be deprived of the right to trial by the legally established tribunal.

Only Ethiopia Const. art. 24 listed in Documented Outlined under art. 26.

Finland (non–UN member; material from 1946 UNYBHR only)

Finland Const. art. 13 (1919):

> No Finnish citizen shall be tried by any other court than that which has jurisdiction over him in accordance with the law.

Material noted includes Decree Regarding Restrictions of Personal Freedom, No. 899, 30 December 1946, allowing non-appealable measures including "detention" for an "activity which has contributed to an aggravation of the relations of the State with other States."

France

France Const. (27 October 1946), preamble, "solemnly reaffirms the rights and freedoms of man and the citizen consecrated by the Declaration of Rights of 1789" (quoted in Appendix C).

Germany (non–UN member; still under Four Powers' occupation; material from 1946 UNYBHR only)

Repeal of the Nazi laws allowing for use of "analogy" or "sound popular instinct" by Control Council Law No. 3 of 20 October 1945 noted.

Greece

Greece Const. art. 7:

> No punishment may be inflicted unless previously fixed by law.

Guatemala

Guatemala Const. art. 23(2):

> No person may be hindered in that which the law does not prohibit.

Guatemala Const., art. 49:

> Acts of omission or commission that are not qualified as crimes or offences and subject to a penalty by a law prior to their perpetration are not punishable. Penal laws shall have retroactive effect when they may be favourable to the offender.

Haiti

Haiti Const. (22 November 1946) arts. 15 (similar to current art. 51) and "D":

> 15. No law shall have retroactive effect except in penal cases where it favors the delinquent.
>
> "D". The principle of non-retroactivity of laws does not preclude all such measures of reconstruction and punishment as dictated by the national interest being taken within legal limits and in respect of the period of five years immediately preceding the present constitution.

Honduras

Honduras Const. art. 43:

> No person shall be tried by special commissions . . . .

Honduras Const. art. 54 (similar to current art. 96 in Appendix C):

> No law shall have retroactive effect, except in criminal matters when the new law favours the offender or indicted person.

Hungary

No reference to legality in criminal law noted in Act I on the State Form of Hungary of 31 January 1946.

Iceland

No reference to legality in criminal law noted in Documented Outline or in 1946 UNYBHR.

India

UN member even though not fully independent of British rule. No reference to legality in criminal law noted in Documented Outline or in 1946 UNYBHR.

Iran

Iran Supplementary Fundamental Laws of 8 October 1907 art. 12:

> No punishment can be decreed or executed save in conformity with the law.

Not mentioned in Documented Outline art. 26.

Iraq

Iraq Organic Law of 21 March 1925 art. 7:

> ... None of them [Iraqis] shall be arrested, detained, punished or obliged to change their place of residence, or be placed in bonds, or compelled to serve in the armed forces, except in conformity with law. [Bracketed material added.]

Not mentioned in Documented Outline art. 26.

Italy (non–UN member)

No reference to non-retroactivity of criminal law noted in 1946 UNYBHR (but see discussion of non-retroactivity in Italy Penal Code arts. 1, 2, in Chap. 2.c.ii.C).

Japan (non–UN member; not yet fully restored to sovereignty after World War II; information from 1946 UNYBHR only)

Japan Const. art. 39, same as relevant part of current provision in Appendix C.

Lebanon

Lebanon Const. art. 8 same as relevant part of current provision in Appendix C.

Choucri Cardahi, Lebanon, in 1946 UNYBHR 177-78 translated portions of Lebanese [Penal] Code of 1943 arts. 1 ("no infringement of the law may be punished by a penalty or a security measure, unless such infringement was provided for by law at the time of its commission") & 6 ("no penalty may be inflicted unless it was prescribed by law at the time the infringement was committed").

Liberia

Liberia Const. art. 8:

> No person shall be deprived of life, liberty, property or privilege, but by the judgment of his peers or the law of the land.

Liechtenstein (non–UN member; information from 1946 UNYBHR only)

Liechtenstein Const. art. 33:

> ... Penalties may not be inflicted except within the limits of the law. ...

Luxembourg

Luxembourg Const. arts. 12, 13, 14 same as relevant part of current provisions in Appendix C, except for translation differences.

Mexico

Mexico Const. art. 14 same as relevant part of current provision in Appendix C except for minor differences in translation; *id.*, art. 13 also similar.

Monaco (non–UN member; information from 1946 UNYBHR only)

Monaco Const. art. 7:

> No penalty may be introduced or inflicted except in pursuance of the law.

Mongol Peoples' Republic (non–UN member; information from 1946–47 UNYBHR only)

> No translation of constitution available for 1946 UNYBHR; no provisions on legality in criminal law noted in 1947 UNYBHR.

Netherlands

Netherlands Const. art. 162:

> All judgments shall state the grounds on which they are based, and in penal cases they shall indicate the legal provisions upon which condemnation is based.

New Zealand

No provision on legality in criminal law noted in Documented Outline or 1946 UNYBHR.

Nicaragua

Nicaragua Const. arts. 23, 43 in 1946/47 documents same as current arts. 32, 38 except for minor differences in translation. See Appendix C.

Nicaragua Const art. 44:

> Only acts and transgressions declared punishable by laws prior to their commission may be punished.

Norway

Norway Const. arts. 96, 97, same as current provisions in Appendix C.

Panama

Panama Const. arts. 31, 33, 44 same as current arts. 31, 33, 43 in Appendix C except for minor differences in translation.

Paraguay

Paraguay Const. art. 26:

> No law may have retroactive effect. No inhabitant may be punished except by a prior judgment founded upon some law prior to the violation under prosecution, nor may be judged by special tribunals. . . . Guilt or dishonor that persons may incur does not affect their relatives.

Paraguay Const. art. 30:

> No inhabitant shall be obliged to do anything that the law does not command him to do, nor shall he be deprived of what the law does not prohibit.

Peru

Peru Const. art. 26:

> No law has retroactive force or effect.

Peru Const. art. 30 in 1946/47 documents similar to current Peru Const. art. 2(24)(a) except for minor translation differences. See Appendix C.

Peru Const. art. 57:

> No one may be condemned for an act or an omission which at the time of being committed was not qualified in the law in an express and unequivocal manner as a punishable violation, or be judged except by tribunals established by the laws. . . .

Peru Const. art. 64:

> The ordinary tribunals shall have jurisdiction over crimes of the press.

Philippines

Philippines Const. art. III(11) same as current art. III(22) in Appendix C except for capitalization.

Poland

Poland Const. (17 March 1921; declared by Polish Committee on National Liberation to be in force in its "basic provisions" on 22 July 1944, pending adoption of new constitution), art. 98:

> No one may be deprived of the court to which he is subject by law. Exceptional courts are admissible only in cases determined by statutes, which statutes must have been issued before the offense was committed. A citizen may be prosecuted and punishment inflicted only by virtue of a statute actually in force. . . .

Portugal (non–UN member; information from 1946 UNYBHR only)

Portugal Const. art. 8(9):

> No one shall receive a penal conviction except by virtue of a law of earlier date which declares the act or omission to be punishable.

Romania (non–UN member; information from 1946 UNYBHR only)

Romania Const. art. 14:

> No penalty may be created or applied except in pursuance of a law.

Saudi Arabia

No provision on legality in criminal law noted in Documented Outline or 1946 UNYBHR

Siam (now Thailand)

No provision on legality in criminal law noted in Documented Outline or 1946 UNYBHR

Spain (non–UN member; information from 1946 UNYBHR only)

No provision on legality in criminal law noted

Sweden

Sweden Const. art. 16:

> The King shall cause everyone to be tried by court to the jurisdiction of which he is properly subject.

Switzerland (non–UN member; information from 1946 UNYBHR only)

No provision on legality in criminal law noted.

Syria

Syria Const. art. 9:

> No offense shall be punished and no conviction may be pronounced, except in conformity with the law.

Transjordan (non–UN member; information from 1946 UNYBHR only)

Not independent of Britain in 1946–7. No reference to non-retroactivity of criminal law in Organic Law.

Turkey

No provision on legality in criminal law noted in Documented Outline or 1946 UNYBHR.

Ukranian SSR (then a UN member, now a UN member as independent Ukraine)

No provision on legality in criminal law noted in Documented Outline or in 1946 UNYBHR.

Union of South Africa (now Republic of South Africa)

No bill of rights in force, as noted in UNYBHR.

Union of Soviet Socialist Republics

No provision on legality in criminal law noted in Documented Outline or in 1946 UNYBHR.

United States of America

U.S. Const. art. I(9-10) same as set forth in Appendix C

Uruguay

Uruguay Const. art. 10:

> ... No inhabitant of the Republic shall be obliged to do what the law does not command, nor be prevented from doing what it does not prohibit.

Venezuela

Venezuela Const. art. 17(II):

> No citizen may be judged by specially created tribunals or commissions, but by the usual judges and by virtue of pre-existing laws.

Yugoslavia

Yugoslavia Const. art. 28:

> ... No person may be punished for a criminal act except by sentence of a court on the basis of the law establishing the competence of the court and defining the offence.
> Punishments may be determined and pronounced only on the basis of the law.

APPENDIX C

Constitutional and Other National Provisions Implementing the Principle of Legality Today

Constitutional provisions and translations are taken from CONSTITUTIONS OF THE COUNTRIES OF THE WORLD (Rüdiger H. Wolfrum, Rainer Grote & Gisbert H. Flanz eds., Oxford Univ. Press, various dates, including both paper version and online subscription version at http://www.oceanalaw.com) [hereinafter CCW], unless otherwise indicated. Texts quoted herein are constitutional texts unless noted as statutes or other texts. Non-derogability provisions may be noted but not quoted. Headings or article titles are generally omitted unless they are particularly useful to understanding the provision in question or its place in the law.

The material herein was generally verified for the last time in September–October 2007. A few more recent developments have been taken into account, particularly the imposition and subsequent lifting of emergency rule in Pakistan in November–December 2007, the coming into force of the Revised Arab Charter of Human Rights on 15 March 2008, and the presentation of the proposed Kosovo Constitution on 7 April 2008.

The texts are formatted as uniformly as reasonably possible. Thus, in some cases the typesetting here might not exactly match the source material.

Notations at the beginning of each country's entry summarize the material from Appendix A and some other information collected and discussed in Chapter 5:

NC = *Nullum crimen* – Retroactive criminalization of acts prohibited by constitution, statute, or treaty (Appendix A, Column 2)

NP = *Nulla poena* – Retroactive increase of penalties prohibited by constitution, statute, or treaty (Appendix A, Column 3)

LM = *Lex mitior* – Provision on mitigation of punishment in constitution (Appendix A, Column 4)

SJ = Special jurisdiction – Provision (usually but not always prohibitory) on special or extraordinary tribunals or courts in constitution, or on removal of persons from their lawful or natural judges. Not noted if the only special tribunal mentioned is the permission to have military courts for those in the armed services.
PP = Punishment is personal or prohibition of collective punishments (only noted here where the provision is explicit – substance inferred in other constitutions as discussed in Chap. 5.e)
X = Not a UN member state

Where no constitutional provisions are available, statutes are referenced. The principal statutes researched have been criminal and penal codes or their equivalent, though occasionally other provisions, such as human rights acts, have been found. It is believed and hoped that references to prohibition of retroactive criminalization of acts (*nullum crimen*), and prohibition of retroactive increase of penalties (*nulla poena*) are reasonably complete. Statutory references to application of more lenient penalties (*lex mitior*), personality of punishment (including prohibitions of collective punishment), and provisions concerning special jurisdiction are not necessarily complete, though it is hoped that the constitutional references are reasonably complete. Failure to note such statutes cannot be taken to demonstrate their nonexistence, unless specifically indicated.

These treaties are listed whether or not there are relevant constitutional or statutory provisions for the country:

ACHR = American Convention on Human Rights
ACHPR = African Covenant on Human and Peoples' Rights
ACHPR(P) = ACHPR with Protocol to establish African Court of Human and Peoples' Rights
ArCHR = Revised Arab Charter on Human Rights (material on signatures and ratifications may be incomplete[1])
ECHR = European Convention on Human Rights
ICCPR = International Covenant on Civil and Political Rights

[1]Entered into force 15 March 2008; for recent reports on ratification, see *UAE ratifies Arab charter on human rights* from Emirates News Agency at http://www.uaeinteract.com/docs/UAE_ratifies_Arab_charter_on_human_rights/28218.htm (UAE Interact, Web site of National Media Council, posted 16 January 2008) and *Shura Council ratifies Arab Charter on Human Rights*, at the Web site of the Royal Embassy of Saudi Arabia in the U.S., http://www.saudiembassy.net/2008News/News/RigDetail.asp?cIndex=7698 (24 February 2008), which are the sources for current ratification information here.

ICCPR(P) = ICCPR with Optional Protocol I allowing reference of complaints to Human Rights Committee

The treaties above are those with non-retroactivity provisions applying to internal criminal cases generally. The protocols above are those allowing some sort of enforcement or supervision of treaty implementation. See Chapter 4. References to parties to these treaties are complete, except for difficulties in determining the current status of the Revised Arab Charter on Human Rights for all members of the Arab League.

The following treaties are listed only if a country has no relevant constitutional or statutory provision found (or such are substantially limited or ambiguous) and is a party to none of the above treaties:

CRC = Convention on the Rights of the Child
APII = 1977 Additional Protocol II to the 1949 Geneva Conventions

These treaties are chosen because they have non-retroactivity provisions applying to a limited category of internal criminal cases. See Chapter 4.

Treaties or protocols signed, but not ratified, acceded to or succeeded to are so indicated.

Because the primary foci of this book are *nullum crimen* and *nulla poena*, these are the only provisions for which a statutory search has been done, and only where constitutional provisions are missing or incomplete. In a few cases non-English documents have been left in their original languages.

Afghanistan – NC, NP, LM, PP

Afghanistan Const. art. 24 [alternately numbered ch. 2, art. 3]:

> Liberty is the natural right of human beings. This right has no limits unless affecting the rights of others or public interests, which are regulated by law. . . .

Afghanistan Const. art. 26 [alternately numbered ch. 2, art. 5]:

> Crime is a personal action.
>
> The prosecution, arrest, and detention of an accused and the execution of penalty cannot affect another person.

Afghanistan Const. art. 27 [alternately numbered ch. 2, art. 6]:

> No act is considered a crime, unless determined by a law adopted prior to the date the offense is committed.
>
> No person can be pursued, arrested or detained but in accordance with provisions of law.

No person can be punished but in accordance with the decision of a competent court and in conformity with the law adopted before the date of the act.

Unofficial translation found at http://www.afghan-web.com/politics/current_constitution.html (private Web site)

TREATY: ICCPR

Albania – NC, NP, LM, SJ

Albania Const. art. 29 (made non-derogable by art. 175(1)):

1. No one may be accused or declared guilty of a criminal act that was not considered as such by law at the time of its commission, with the exception of cases, which at the time of their commission, according to international law, constitute war crimes or crimes against humanity.
2. No punishment may be given that is more severe than that which was contemplated by law at the time of commission of the criminal act.
3. A favorable criminal law has retroactive effect.

Albania Const. art. 135(2):

The Assembly may establish by law courts for particular fields, but in no case an extraordinary court.

TREATIES: ECHR, ICCPR

Algeria – NC, NP, LM, PP

Algeria Const. art. 46:

No one may be considered guilty except by virtue of a law, duly promulgated before the incriminating act.

Algeria Const. art. 140:

Justice is founded on the principles of legality and equality.

. . .

Algeria Const. art. 142:

The criminal sanctions conform [*obeisant*] to the principles of legality and personality.

STATUTE:

Algeria Penal Code art. 2:

La loi pénale n'est pas rétroactive, sauf si elle est moins rigoureuse.

Statute is latest version available from private Web site http://www.lexalgeria.net.

TREATIES: ArCHR, ICCPR(P)

Andorra – NC, NP, LM, SJ

Andorra Const. art. 3(2):

> The Constitution recognizes the principles of equality, hierarchy, publicity of the judicial rules, non-retroactivity of the rules restricting individual rights or those that are unfavourable in their effect or sanction, juridical security, accountability of public institutions and prohibition of any kind of arbitrariness.

Andorra Const. art. 9(4):

> No one shall be held criminally or administratively liable on account of any acts or omissions which were lawful at the time when they were committed.

Andorra Const. art. 85(2):

> The whole judicial power is vested in a uniform organization of Justice. Its structure, functioning and the legal status of its members shall be regulated by a *Llei Qualificada*. No special jurisdiction shall be established.

TREATIES: ECHR, ICCPR(P)

Angola – NC, NP, LM, SJ

Angola Const. Law art. 36 (made non-derogable by art. 52(2)):

> (1) No citizen may be arrested or put on trial except in accordance with the law, and all accused shall be guaranteed the right to defense and the right to legal aid and counsel.
> ...
> (3) No one shall be sentenced for an act not considered a crime at the time when it was committed.
> (4) The penal law shall apply retroactively only when beneficial to the accused.
> ...

Angola Const. Law art. 126:

> Without prejudice to the provisions of the foregoing article, the constitution of courts with sole powers to try determined offenses shall be prohibited.

Referring to: Angola Const. Law art. 125:

> (1) Apart from the Constitutional Court, courts shall be structured, in accordance with the law, as follows:
> (a) Municipal courts;
> (b) Provincial courts; and
> (c) The Supreme Court.
> (2) The organization and functioning of military justice shall be set out in an appropriate law.
> (3) Military, administrative, auditing, fiscal. maritime and arbitration courts may be constituted in accordance with the law.

Angola Constitutional Law at http://www.oefre.unibe.ch/law/icl/a000000_.html.

TREATIES: ACHPR, ICCPR(P)

Antigua and Barbuda – NC, NP

Antigua & Barbuda Const. art. 15(4):

> No person shall be held to be guilty of a criminal offence on account of any act or omission that did not, at the time it took place, constitute such an offence, and no penalty shall be imposed for any criminal offence that is more severe in degree or description than the maximum penalty that might have been imposed for that offence at the time when it was committed.

Argentina – NC, NP, LM, SJs

Argentina Const. art. 18:

> No inhabitant of the Nation may be punished without prior trial based on a law in force prior to the offense, or tried by special commissions, or removed from the jurisdiction of the judges designated by the law in force prior to the offense.

Argentina Const. art. 19:

> The private actions of men that in no way offend public order or morality, nor injure a third party, are reserved only to God, and are exempt from the authority of the magistrates. No inhabitant of the Nation shall be compelled to do what the law does not order, or be deprived of what it does not forbid.

TREATIES: ACHR, ICCPR(P)

Armenia – NC, NP, LM

Armenia Const. art. 22 (made non-derogable by art. 44):

> . . .
>
> The imposition of a heavier punishment than the one in effect at the time when the crime was committed shall be prohibited.
>
> No one shall be held guilty for a crime on account of any act which did not constitute a crime under the law at the time when it was committed.
>
> The law eliminating or mitigating the penalty for the offense shall be retroactive.
>
> The law prescribing or increasing liability shall not be retroactive.
>
> . . .

Armenia Const. art. 42 (made non-derogable by art. 44):

> . . .
>
> Everyone shall have the right to act in a way not prohibited by law and not violating others' rights and freedoms. No one shall bear obligations not stipulated by law.
>
> The laws and other legal acts exacerbating the legal status of an individual shall not be retroactive.
>
> The legal acts improving the legal status of an individual or eliminating or mitigating his/her liability shall be retroactive if prescribed by the acts in question.

Armenia Const. art. 92:

> In the Republic of Armenia, function [as] the court of general jurisdiction of the first instance, the Courts of Appeals and the Court of Cassation and, in cases prescribed by law, the specialized courts as well.
>
> Establishing emergency tribunals shall be forbidden.

TREATIES: ECHR, ICCPR(P)

Australia – NC, NP, LM

TREATY: ICCPR(P)

Austria – NC, NP, LM

STATUTES:

Austria, StGB §1 Keine Strafe ohne Gesetz:

> (1) Eine Strafe oder eine vorbeugende Maßnahme darf nur wegen einer Tat verhängt werden, die unter eine ausdrückliche gesetzliche

Strafdrohung fällt und schon zur Zeit ihrer Begehung mit Strafe bedroht war.

(2) Eine schwerere als die zur Zeit der Begehung angedrohte Strafe darf nicht verhängt werden. Eine vorbeugende Maßnahme darf nur angeordnet werden, wenn zur Zeit der Begehung diese vorbeugende Maßnahme oder eine der Art nach vergleichbare Strafe oder vorbeugende Maßnahme vorgesehen war. Durch die Anordnung einer bloß der Art nach vergleichbaren vorbeugenden Maßnahme darf der Täter keiner ungünstigeren Behandlung unterworfen werden, als sie nach dem zur Zeit der Tat geltenden Gesetz zulässig war.

Text from University of Salzburg Web site http://www.sbg.ac.at/ssk/docs/stgb/stgb1_16.htm.

TREATIES: ECHR, ICCPR(P)

Azerbaijan – NC, NP, LM, SJ

Azerbaijan Const. art. 71(VIII):

> No one can be responsible for a deed which at the time of being committed was not considered a violation of law. If after violating the law a new law removed or mitigated the responsibility for such actions the new law is applied in that case.

Azerbaijan Const. art. 125(VI):

> The use of legal means not specified by law in order to change the competence of judges and create extraordinary courts is prohibited.

TREATIES: ECHR, ICCPR(P)

Bahamas – NC, NP

Bahamas Const. art. 20(4) (made non-derogable by art. 29(4)):

> No person shall be held to be guilty of a criminal offence on account of any act or omission that did not, at the time it took place, constitute such an offence that is severer in degree or description than the maximum penalty that might have been imposed for that offence at the time when it was committed.

[Although the text appears to inadvertently leave out a few words at the beginning of the non-retroactivity of punishments portion, the sources are consistent that this is correct. —*KSG*]

Bahrain – NC, NP, LM, PP
Bahrain Const. art. 20(a-b):

a. There shall be no crime and no punishment except under a law, and punishment only for acts committed subsequent to the effective date of the law providing for the same.
b. Punishment is personal.

TREATIES: ArCHR, ICCPR

Bangladesh – NC, NP, LM
Bangladesh Const. art. 35(1):

(1) No person shall be convicted to any offence except for violation of a law in force at the time of the commission of the act charged as an offence, nor be subjected to a penalty greater than, or different from, that which might have been inflicted under the law in force at the time of the commission of the offence.

Bangladesh Const. art. 47(3):

(3) Notwithstanding anything contained in this Constitution, no law nor any provision thereof providing for detention, prosecution or punishment of any person, who is a member of any armed or defence or auxiliary forces or who is a prisoner of war, for genocide, crimes against humanity or war crimes and other crimes under international law shall be deemed void or unlawful, or ever to have become void or unlawful, on the ground that such law or provision of any such law is inconsistent with, or repugnant to, any of the provisions of this Constitution.

Bangladesh Const. art. 47A:

(1) The rights guaranteed under article 31, clauses (1) and (3) of article 35 and article 44 shall not apply to any person to whom a law specified in clause (3) of article 47 applies.
(2) Notwithstanding anything contained in this Constitution, no person to whom a law specified in Clause (3) of Article 47 applies shall have the right to move the Supreme Court for any of the remedies under this Constitution.

TREATY: ICCPR

Barbados – NC, NP, LM
Barbados Const. art. 18(4):

No person shall be held to be guilty of a criminal offence on account of any act or omission that did not, at the time it took place, constitute such an offence, and no penalty shall be imposed for any criminal offence that is more severe in degree or nature than the most severe penalty that might have been imposed for that offence at the time when it was committed.

TREATIES: ACHR, ICCPR(P)

Belarus – NC, NP, LM, SJ

Belarus Const. art. 104:

> . . .
>
> The law has no retroactive force except when it extenuates or revokes the responsibility of citizens.

Belarus Const. art. 109:

> The judicial power in the Republic of Belarus is exercised by the courts.
> The court system is based on the principles of territoriality and specialization.
> The judicial system in the Republic of Belarus is determined by the law.
> The formation of exceptional courts is prohibited.

TREATY: ICCPR(P)

Belgium – NC, NP, LM, SJ

Belgium Coord. Const. art. 12:

> . . . No person may be prosecuted except in cases established by the law and in the form it prescribes. . . .

Belgium Coord. Const. art. 13:

> No person may be deprived of his/her lawfully-assigned judge without his/her consent.

Belgium Coord. Const. art. 14:

> No punishment may be decreed nor applied except in accordance with the law.

Belgium Coord. Const. art. 146:

> No court or contentious jurisdiction may be established other than by law.
> No extraordinary commissions or courts may be created under any name.

STATUTE:

Belgium, Criminal Code art. 2:

> Nulle infraction ne peut être punie de peines qui n'étaient pas portées par la loi avant que l'infraction fût commise.

> Si la peine établie au temps du jugement diffère de celle qui était portée au temps de l'infraction, la peine la moins forte sera appliquée.

TREATIES: ECHR, ICCPR(P)

Belize – NC, NP, LM

Belize Const. art. 6(4):

> A person shall not be held to be guilty of a criminal offence on account of any act or omission that did not, at the time it took place, constitute such an offence, and no penalty shall be imposed for any criminal offence that is severer in degree or description than the maximum penalty that might have been imposed for that offence at the time when it was committed.

TREATY: ICCPR

Benin – NC, NP

Benin Const. art. 7:

> The rights and duties proclaimed and guaranteed by the African Charter on Human and Peoples' Rights adopted in 1981 by the Organization of African Unity and ratified by Bénin on January 20, 1986 shall be an integral part of the present Constitution and of Béninese law.

Benin Const. art. 17:

> . . .
>
> No one shall be condemned for actions or omissions which, at the moment when they were committed, did not constitute an infraction according to the national law. Likewise, he may not have a more severe penalty inflicted than that which was applicable at the time when the offense was committed.

TREATIES: ACHPR(P-signed), ICCPR

Bhutan

STATUTE:

Bhutan Penal Code art. 6:

> A defendant convicted of a criminal offense shall not be sentenced otherwise than in accordance with this penal code.

Translated text from Bhutan government judiciary Web site http://www.judiciary.gov.bt/html/act/PENAL%20CODE.pdf.

TREATY: CRC only

Bolivia – NC, NP, LM, SJ

Bolivia Const. art. 16(II):

> II. . . . A criminal conviction shall be founded on a law that was in effect prior to the trial, and subsequent laws shall only apply if they are more favorable to the accused.

Bolivia Const. art. 32:

> No one shall be compelled to do what the Constitution or the laws do not order, or to deprive himself of things which they do not prohibit.

Bolivia Const. art. 33:

> The law shall provide only for the future and has no retroactive effect, except in social matters when expressly so stated and in criminal matters when it benefits the offender.

Bolivia Const. art. 14:

> No one may be tried by special commissions nor turned over to judges other than those designated before the offense was committed. . . .

Bolivia Const. art. 116(II):

> No exceptional tribunals or courts may be established.

TREATIES: ACHR, ICCPR(P)

Bosnia and Herzegovina – NC, NP, LM

Const. of Bosnia & Herzegovina art. II(2):

> 2. International Standards. The rights and freedoms set forth in the European Convention for the Protection of Human Rights and Fundamental Freedoms and its Protocols shall apply directly in Bosnia and Herzegovina. These shall have priority over all other law.

Const. of Rep. of Srpska [i.e., the constitution of the subnational entity the Republic of Srpska, which together with the subnational entity the Federation of Bosnia and Herzebovina, makes up the state of Bosnia and Herzegovina] art. 20:

> No one may be sentenced for any act which did not constitute a criminal offence under law at the time it was committed, nor may a penalty be imposed which was not prescribed by law for such an act at the time of its commission.
>
> . . .

> Const. of the Federation of Bosnia & Herzegovina [i.e., the constitution of the subnational entity the Federation of Bosnia and Herzegovina, which together with the subnational Republic of Srpska makes up the state of Bosnia and Herzegovina], pt. II(A), art. 2 and Annex incorporates the UDHR, ECHR, and ICCPR(P).

TREATIES: ECHR, ICCPR(succeeded)(P-ratified)

Botswana – NC, NP, LM

Botswana Const. art. 10(4):

> No person shall be held to be guilty of a criminal offence on account of any act or omission that did not, at the time it took place, constitute such an offence, and no penalty shall be imposed for any criminal offence that is severer in degree or description than the maximum penalty that might have been imposed for that offence at the time when it was committed.

Botswana Const. art. 10(8):

> No person shall be convicted of a criminal offence unless that offence is defined and the penalty therefor is prescribed in a written law.
>
> Provided that nothing in this subsection shall prevent a court of record from punishing any person for contempt of itself notwithstanding that the act or omission constituting the contempt is not defined in a written law and the penalty therefor is not so prescribed.

TREATIES: ACHPR(P-signed), ICCPR

Brazil – NC, NP, SJ, PP

Brazil Const. art.5(II, XXXVII, XXXIX, XL):

> Everyone is equal before the law, with no distinction whatsoever, guaranteeing to Brazilians and foreigners residing in the Country the inviolability of the rights to life, liberty, equality, security and property, on the following terms:
>
> ...
>
> II – no one shall be compelled to do or refrain from doing something except by force of law;
>
> ...
>
> XXXVII – there shall be no exceptional courts or tribunals;
>
> ...
>
> XXXIX – there are no crimes unless defined in prior law, nor are there any penalties unless previously imposed by law;

XL – the criminal law shall not be retroactive, except to benefit the defendant;

. . .

XLV – no punishment shall extend beyond the person convicted, but liability for damages and a decree of loss of assets may, as provided by law, extend to successors and be enforced against them up to the limit of the value of the assets transferred;

. . . .

TREATIES: ACHR, ICCPR

Brunei

STATUTE:

Brunei Penal Code §2:

> Every person shall be liable to punishment under this Code, and not otherwise, for every act or omission contrary to the provisions thereof of which he shall be guilty within Brunei Darussalam.

Text in English at Brunei Government Web site, http://www.agc.gov.bn/pdf/Cap22.pdf.

Brunei Laws of Brunei, Ch. 4 (Interpretation and General Clauses) §39:

> Whenever, in or by virtue of any written law, a penalty, whether of imprisonment or fine, is prescribed for an offence the same shall imply –
>
> (a) that such offence shall be punishable upon conviction by a penalty not exceeding the penalty prescribed; and
> (b) if the amount of the fine is unspecified, that such offence shall, without prejudice to any provision of law against excessive and unreasonable fines and assessments, be punishable by a fine of any amount.

Text in English at Brunei government's Web site http://www.agc.gov.bn/pdf/Cap4.pdf.

TREATIES: CRC, APII only.

Bulgaria – NC, NP, LM, SJ

Bulgaria Const. art. 5(3):

> No one may be convicted for action or inaction that did not constitute a crime according to law at the time when it was done.

Bulgaria Const. art. 119(3):

> Extraordinary courts are not permitted.

STATUTE:

Bulgaria Penal Code art. 2:

(1) To each crime applied shall be that law, which was in force at the time of its perpetration.
(2) If by the entry of the sentence into force different laws are issued, that law shall be applied which is most favourable for the perpetrator.

Penal Code translation from Republic of Bulgaria Ministry of Justice. Originally promulgated in State Gazette No. 26/02.04, 1968, with no amendments to this article noted.

TREATIES: ECHR, ICCPR(P)

Burkina Faso – NC, NP, PP

Burkina Faso Const. art. 5:

> Anything which is not forbidden by the law cannot be enjoined and no one can be constrained to do that which it does not order.
>
> The penal law does not have retroactive effect. No one can be judged and punished except in virtue of a law promulgated and published before the punishable act.
>
> Punishment is personal and individual.

Burkina Faso Const. art. 140:

> The High Court of Justice is bound by the definition of crimes and misdemeanors and by the determination of punishments resulting from the penal laws in force at the time when the acts had been committed.

TREATIES: ACHPR(P), ICCPR(P)

Burundi – NC, NP, LM, SJ

Burundi Const. art. 19:

> The rights and duties proclaimed and guaranteed, among others, by the *Universal Declaration of Human Rights*, the *International Covenants on Human Rights*, the *African Charter on Human People's Rights*, the *Convention on the Elimination of all Forms of Discrimination against Women* and the *Convention on the Rights of the Child* are an integral part of the Constitution of the Republic of Burundi.
>
> . . .

Burundi Const. art. 39:

> . . .

> No one may be indicted, arrested, detained or judged except in the cases determined by a law which has been promulgated prior to the commission of the acts with which they are charged.
>
> . . .
>
> No one may be removed, against their will, from the jurisdiction of their lawful judge.

Burundi Const. art. 41:

> No one may be convicted for acts or omissions which, at the time they were committed, did not constitute an infraction.
>
> In the same way, no punishment more severe than that which was applicable at the time the infraction was committed may be inflicted.

TREATIES: ACHPR(P), ICCPR

Cambodia – NC, NP

Cambodia Const. art. 31:

> The Kingdom of Cambodia shall recognize and respect human rights as stipulated in the United Nations Charter, the Universal Declaration of Human rights [*sic*], the covenants and conventions related to human rights, women's and children's rights. . . .

Cambodia Const. art. 38:

> . . .
>
> The prosecution, arrest, or detention of any person shall not be done except in accordance with the law.
>
> . . .

TREATIES: ICCPR(P-signed)

Cameroun – NC, NP, LM

Cameroun Const. preamble:

> *We, the people of Cameroon,*
>
> Declare that the human person, without distinction as to race, religion, sex or belief, possesses inalienable and sacred rights;
>
> Affirm our attachment to the fundamental freedoms enshrined in the Universal Declaration of Human Rights, the Charter of United Nations and The African Charter on Human and Peoples' Rights, and all duly ratified international conventions relating thereto, in particular, to the following principles:

. . .

the law may not have retrospective effect. No person may be judged and punished, except by virtue of a law enacted and published before the offence committed;

. . . .

TREATIES: ACHPR(P-signed), ICCPR(P)

Canada – NC, NP, LM

Canada Const. Act art. 11(g, i):

Whereas Canada is founded upon principles that recognize the supremacy of God and the rule of law:

. . .

11. Any person charged with an offence has the right

. . .

(g) not to be found guilty on account of any act or omission unless, at the time of the act or omission, it constituted an offence under Canadian or international law or was criminal according to the general principles of law recognized by the community of nations;

. . .

(i) if found guilty of the offence and if the punishment for the offence has been varied between the time of commission and the time of sentencing, to the benefit of the lesser punishment.

TREATIES: ICCPR(P)

Cape Verde – NC, NP, LM, SJ

Cape Verde Const. art. 16(5):

Laws restricting rights, liberties, and guarantees must be general and abstract, may not be retroactive, may not reduce the extent and essential content of constitutional norms, and must be limited to what is necessary for the safeguard of other constitutionally protected rights.

Cape Verde Const. art. 30(2, 4 & 7):

. . .

(2) Retroactive application of criminal law shall be prohibited unless the subsequent law is more favorable to the accused.

. . .

(4) Penalties and security measures may not be applied unless they are expressly stated by law.

(7) The provisions of paragraph 2 shall not prevent punishment, within the limits of internal law, for actions or omissions which, at the time they were committed, were considered criminal according to the principles and norms of International Law.

Cape Verde Const. art. 222(2):

Courts of exception shall be prohibited.

TREATIES: ACHPR, ICCPR(P)

Central African Republic – NC, NP, LM

Central African Rep. Const. art. 3.

Everyone has the right to life and to corporal integrity. These rights may only be affected by application of a law.

. . .

No one may be condemned except by virtue of a law which had been in force before the act in question was committed.

TREATIES: ACHPR(P-signed), ICCPR(P)

Chad – NC, NP, LM

Chad Const. art. 23:

No one may be arrested nor charged except by virtue of a law promulgated prior to the acts *[faits]* for which he is blamed.

Chad Const. art. 26:

Customary and traditional rules concerning collective penal responsibility are forbidden.

TREATIES: ACHPR(P-signed), ICCPR(P)

Chechnya[2] – X

No relevant provisions noted.

Chile – NC, NP, LM, SJ

Chile Const. art. 19(3):

The Constitution guarantees to all persons:

[2] Claims independence from Russia. Not generally recognized as a state by the international community. By the time this book went to press, the power of the independence movement had weakened substantially.

3. . . .

No one may be judged by special commissions, but only by the court which is determined by law and which has been established by it prior to the perpetration of the act in question.

. . .

The law may not presume penal liability.

No crime may be subject to penalties other than those prescribed by a law enacted prior to the perpetration of the crime, unless a new law is more favorable to the person concerned.

No law may establish penalties without the conduct that it punishes being expressly described therein;

. . . .

TREATIES: ACHR, ICCPR(P)

China, People's Republic of[3] – NC, NP

STATUTES:

People's Republic of China Criminal Law art. 3 states that a person can be convicted and punished only for acts "explicitly defined as criminal acts in law."

People's Republic of China Criminal Law art. 12:

If an act committed after the founding of the People's Republic of China and before the entry into force of this Law was not deemed a crime under the laws at the time, those laws shall apply. If the act was deemed a crime under the laws in force at the time and is subject to prosecution under the provisions of Section 8, Chapter IV of the General Provisions of this Law, criminal responsibility shall be investigated in accordance with those laws. However, if according to this Law the act is not deemed a crime or is subject to a lighter punishment, this Law shall apply.

Before the entry into force of this Law, any judgment that has been made and has become effective according to the laws at the time shall remain valid.

Criminal Law of the People's Republic of China (as revised at the Fifth Session of the Eighth National People's Congress on 14 March 1997), translated at U.S. government Web site http://www.cecc.gov/pages/newLaws/criminalLawENG.php.

[3] The People's Republic of China claims that there is a single state of China, and it is the sole legitimate government of China. The United Nations and most states recognize the People's Republic as the legitimate government of China.

People's Republic of China Legislation Law, Ch. 2 National Law, §1 Scope of Lawmaking Authority, art. 9:

> In the event that no national law has been enacted in respect of a matter enumerated in Article 8 hereof, the National People's Congress and the Standing Committee thereof have the power to make a decision to enable the State Council to enact administrative regulations in respect of part of the matters concerned for the time being, except where the matter relates to crime and criminal sanctions, the deprivation of a citizen's political rights, compulsory measure and penalty restricting the personal freedom of a citizen, and the judicial system.

People's Republic of China Legislation Law, Ch. 5 Scope of Application and Filing, art. 84:

> National law, administrative regulations, local decrees, autonomous decrees and special decrees, and administrative or local rules do not have retroactive force, except where a special provision is made in order to better protect the rights and interests of citizens, legal persons and other organizations.

Legislation Law of the People's Republic of China (promulgated 15 March 2000), translated in CCW (headings included for clarification.).

TREATY: ICCPR-signed

China, Republic of (Taiwan)[4] – X

TREATIES: ICCPR&P – Signed before People's Republic of China took the seat of China at the United Nations. A number of UN members from the Socialist group objected to this signature on the grounds that the government of the People's Republic of China was the only legitimate government of China with authority to sign such a document.

Colombia – NC, NP, LM

Colombia Const. art. 28:

> Every individual is free. No one may be importuned in his/her person or family, sent to jail or arrested, nor may his/her home be searched except on the basis of a written order from a competent judicial authority, subject to the legal procedures and for reasons previously defined by law. . . .

[4] Constitution of Republic of China maintains that there is one state of China, and government of Republic of China has not formally declared independence from People's Republic of China. Some in the Republic of China seek full independence as a nation under the name of Taiwan. The People's Republic of China strongly opposes this.

Colombia Const. art. 29:

> Due process will be applied in all cases of legal and administrative measures.
>
> No one may be judged except in accordance with previously written laws, which will provide the basis of each decision before a competent judge or tribunal following all appropriate forms.
>
> In criminal law, permissive or favorable law, even when *ex post facto*, will be applied in preference to restrictive or unfavorable alternatives.
>
> . . .

TREATIES: ACHR, ICCPR(P)

Comoros – NC, NP, LM, SJ

Comoros Const. art. 48:

> The organization, the competences and the functioning of the jurisdictions are established by an organic law which puts into effect, among other things, the following principles:
>
> – the singular nature *[unicité]* of justice;
>
> – the sitting magistrates are irremovable;
>
> . . .
>
> – no one may be prosecuted, searched, arrested , detained or judged according to a law retroactive *[posterieur]* to the act committed;
>
> – any penal jurisdiction of exception is prohibited
>
> . . . .
>
> The judicial power, guardian of the individual freedom assures the respect of these principles.

TREATIES: ACHPR(P)

Congo, Democratic Republic of – NC, NP, LM, SJ, PP

Dem. Rep. of the Congo Const. art. 17:

> Individual liberty is guaranteed. It is the rule, detention the exception.
>
> No one may be prosecuted, arrested, detained or sentenced except by virtue of a law and in the manner which the latter prescribes.
>
> No one may be prosecuted for an act or omission which does not constitute a violation of the law at the time it was committed and at the time of the prosecution.

No one may be sentenced for an action or omission which does not constitute a violation of the law both at the time it was committed and at the time of the sentencing.

No harsher punishment than that which was applicable at the time the violation was committed may be imposed.

The execution of the punishment is stopped if, by virtue of a law issued after judgment is rendered:

– the punishment is cancelled;
– the act for which it has been imposed no longer constitutes a violation of the law.

In the case of the reduction of the punishment by virtue of a law issued after judgment is rendered, the punishment is executed in accordance with the new law.

Criminal responsibility is individual. No one may be prosecuted, arrested, detained or sentenced for acts committed by others.

. . .

Dem. Rep. of the Congo Const. art. 19:

No person may be removed or transferred against his will from the judge who has been assigned to hear his/her case.

. . .

Dem. Rep. of the Congo Const. art. 149:

The judicial power is independent from the Legislative Power and the Executive Power.

It is entrusted to the following courts and tribunals: the Constitutional Court *(Cour Constitutionnelle)*, the Court of Cassation *(Cour de Cassation)*, the Council of State *(Conseil d'Etat)*, the Military High Court *(Haute Cour Militaire)*, the civil and military courts and tribunals as well as the prosecutor offices attached to these jurisdictions.

. . .

No extraordinary or special tribunals may be created, no matter what the name is.

The law may establish specialized jurisdictions.

. . .

TREATIES: ACHPR(P-signed), ICCPR(P)

Congo, Republic of the – NC, NP, LM
TREATIES: ACHPR(P-signed), ICCPR(P)

Costa Rica – NC, NP, LM, SJ

Costa Rica Const. art. 28:

> No one may be disturbed or persecuted for the expression of his opinions or for any act which does not infringe the law.
>
> Private actions which do not harm the morals or public order, or which do not cause any damages to third parties are outside the scope of the law.
>
> However, clergymen or secular individuals cannot make political propaganda in any way invoking religious motives or making use of religious beliefs.

Costa Rica Const. art. 34:

> No law shall have retroactive effect to the detriment of any person whatsoever or his acquired property rights, or to the detriment of any consolidated legal situations.

Costa Rica Const. art. 39:

> No one shall be made to suffer a penalty except for crime, unintentional tort or misdemeanor punishable by previous law, and in virtue of final judgment entered by competent authority, after opportunity has been given to the defendant to plead his defense, and upon the necessary proof of guilt.
>
> Judicial compulsion in civil or labor matters or detentions ordered in cases of insolvency, bankruptcy or bankruptcy involuntary proceedings are not violations of this article or of the two preceding articles.

Costa Rica Const. art. 35:

> No one may be tried by a commission, court, or judge specially appointed for the case, but exclusively by the courts established in accordance with this Constitution.

TREATIES: ACHR, ICCPR(P)

Côte d'Ivoire – NC, NP

Côte d'Ivoire Const. art. 21:

> No one can be prosecuted, arrested, detained [*gardé a vue*] or charged, except by virtue of a law previously promulgated to the acts of which he is accused.

Côte d'Ivoire Const. art. 112[5] :

> The High Court of Justice is bound by the definition of the crimes and misdemeanors and by the determination of the resultant penalties of the penal laws in force at the time of the acts accounted for in the prosecution.

STATUTE:

Côte d'Ivoire Code Pénal arts. 19–21:

Section 3: Application dans le temps

Article 19

> Nul ne peut être poursuivi ou jugé en raison d'un fait qui aux termes d'une disposition nouvelle ne constitue plus une infraction.
>
> Si antérieurement à cette disposition, des peines et mesures de sûreté ont été prononcées pour ce fait, il est mis fin à leur exécution, à l'exception de l'internement dans une maison de santé et de la confiscation mesure de police.
>
> Toutefois, en cas d'infraction à une disposition pénale sanctionnant une prohibition ou une obligation limitée à une période déterminée, les poursuites sont valablement engagées ou continuées et les peines et mesures de sûreté exécutées, nonobstant la fin de cette période.

Article 20

> Toute disposition pénale nouvelle s'applique aux infractions qui n'ont pas fait l'objet d'une condamnation devenue définitive au jour de son entrée en vigueur, si elle est moins sévère que l'ancienne.
>
> Dans le cas contraire, les infractions commises avant l'entrée en vigueur de la disposition pénale nouvelle, continuent, à être jugées conformément à la loi ancienne.
>
> Toute loi prévoyant une mesure de sûreté est immédiatement applicable aux infractions qui n'ont pas fait l'objet d'une condamnation devenue définitive même dans le cas où la législation ancienne prévoyait l'application d'une peine aux lieu et place de la mesure de sûreté.

Article 21

> Est définitive, toute condamnation résultant d'une décision autre que par contumace qui n'est pas ou n'est plus susceptible de la part du Ministère public ou du condamné d'une voie de recours ordinaire ou extraordinaire.

[5] The High Court of Justice tries high government officials, and in some countries might be called a combined court of impeachment and criminal court for these officials.

Statutory text from a specialized website of the Organisation Internationale de la Francophonie, droit.francophonie.org/df-web/publication.do?publicationId = 198#H_05.

TREATIES: ACHPR(P), ICCPR(P)

Croatia – NC, NP, LM

Croatia [Republike Hrvatske] Const. art. 31:

> No one can be punished for an act which, at the time when it was committed, did not constitute a penal offence, under domestic or international law, nor shall be sentenced to a penalty which was not applicable at the time the offence was committed. If a less severe penalty is determined by law after the commission of an offence, such a penalty shall be imposed.
>
> . . .

Croatia [Republike Hrvatske] Const. art. 87:

> The Croatian Sabor may empower the Government of the Republic of Croatia, for a maximum period of one year to regulate by decrees certain issues from its competence, except those relating to the elaboration of constitutionally guaranteed human rights and fundamental freedoms, national rights, the electoral system, the organization, competences and operation of governmental bodies and local self-government.
>
> Decrees based on statutory authority cannot have a retroactive effect. Decrees passed on the basis of legal authority shall cease to be valid after the expiry of the period of one year from the date the House of Representatives granted such authority, unless the Croatian Sabor decides otherwise.

Croatia [Republike Hrvatske] Const. art. 89:

> . . .
>
> The laws and other regulations of state bodies, and which have public relevance, cannot have retroactive effect.
>
> Only individual provisions of a law can have retroactive effect.

TREATIES: ECHR, ICCPR-succeeded(P-ratified)

Cuba – NC, NP, LM

Cuba Const. art. 59:

> Nobody can be tried or sentenced except by the competent tribunal by virtue of laws which existed prior to the crime and with the formalities and guarantees that the laws establish.
>
> . . .

Cuba Const. art. 61:

> Penal laws are retroactive when they benefit the accused or person who has been sentenced. Other laws are not retroactive unless the contrary is decided for reasons of social interest or because it is useful for public purposes.

Cyprus, Republic of – NC, NP

Const. of the Rep. of Cyprus, art. 12(1):

> No person shall be held guilty of any offense on account of any act or omission which did not constitute an offense under the law at the time when it was committed; and no person shall have a heavier punishment imposed on him for an offense other than that expressly provided for it by law at the time when it was committed.

TREATIES: ECHR, ICCPR(P)

Cyprus, Turkish Republic of Northern[6] – X, NC, NP, SJ

Turkish Rep. of Northern Cyprus Const. art. 18(1):

> No person shall be considered guilty on account of any act or omission which did not constitute an offence under the law at the time when it was committed; and no person shall have a heavier punishment imposed on him/her for an offence other than that expressly provided for it by law at the time when it was committed.

Turkish Rep. of Northern Cyprus Const. art. 17(1):

> No person shall be denied access to the court assigned to him/her by or under this Constitution. The establishment of judicial committees or special courts under any name whatsoever is prohibited. . . .

Text from Constitutions of Dependencies and Territories (Philip Raworth, ed., Oxford Univ. Press, various dates).

[6] Recognized as a state only by Turkey. The UN Security Council "[*c*]*alls upon*" states not to recognize it as a state. UN Security Council Res. 541, S/RES/541 (18 November 1983).

Czech Republic – NC, NP, LM

Czech Rep. Const. art. 3:

> The Charter of Fundamental Rights and Freedoms is part of the constitutional order of the Czech Republic.

Source: CCW

Czech Republic Charter of Fundamental Rights and Basic Freedoms art. 2(3):

> Everyone may do that which is not prohibited by law; and nobody may be compelled to do that which is not imposed upon him by law.

Czech Republic Charter of Fundamental Rights and Basic Freedoms art. 39:

> Only a law may designate the acts which constitute a crime and the penalties or other detriments to rights or property that may be imposed for committing them.

Czech Republic Charter of Fundamental Rights and Basic Freedoms art. 40(6):

> The question whether an act is punishable or not shall be considered, and penalties shall be imposed, in accordance with the law in effect at the time the act was committed. A subsequent law shall be applied if it is more favourable to the offender.

Source for Czech Republic Charter of Fundamental Rights and Basic Freedoms: http://www.nssoud.cz/en/docs/charter.pdf (official Web site of Supreme Administrative Court of Czech Republic, taken from the 1991 document of the same name of Czechoslovakia).

TREATIES: ECHR, ICCPR(P)-succeeded

Denmark – NC, NP,[7] SJ

Denmark Const. Act art. 61:

> The exercise of judicial authority shall be governed only by Statute. Extraordinary courts of justice with judicial authority shall not be established.

STATUTE:

Denmark Crim. Code §3:

[7] Except for matters discussed in Denmark Crim. Code § 4.

(1) Where the penal legislation in force at the time of the criminal proceedings in respect of any act differs from that in force at the time of the commission of the act, any questions concerning the punishable nature of the act and the punishment to be imposed shall be decided according to the more recent Statute, provided that the sentence may not be more severe than under the earlier Statute. If the repeal of the Statute is due to extraneous circumstances irrelevant to guilt, the act shall be dealt with under the earlier statute.

(2) If, in circumstances other than those provided in the last sentence of Subsection 1 above, an act cease to be lawfully punishable, any punishment imposed for such an act, but not yet served, shall be remitted....

Denmark Crim. Code §4:

(1) The question whether the punishable act shall have legal consequences of the nature referred to in Sections 56–61 [on suspension of sentences and probation], 62–70 [on community service, mental illness or defect, and safe custody in lieu of imprisonment, 73 [on after-acquired mental illness or defect] and 79 [on persons debarred by criminal conviction from engaging in businesses requiring public authorization or permission] of this Act shall be decided under the law in force at the time of the criminal proceedings.

(2) Unless otherwise provided, other legal consequences shall take effect only if also provided for by the law in force at the time the act was committed.

(3) The provision contained in Section 3(2) of this Act shall similarly apply to legal consequences other than punishment, provided such consequences arise as a direct result of the punishable nature of the act.

Statute trans. by Malene Frese Jensen, Vagn Greve, Gitte Høyer & Marten Spencer, THE DANISH CRIMINAL CODE & THE DANISH CORRECTIONS ACT 3 (2d ed., CJØF Publishing, 2003) (material in brackets added).

TREATIES: ECHR, ICCPR(P)

Djibouti – NC, NP, LM

Djibouti Const. art. 10:

...

No one may be prosecuted, arrested, accused or convicted other than by virtue of a law promulgated prior to the actions of which he is accused.

...

TREATIES: ACHPR(P-signed), ICCPR(P)

Dominica – NC, NP, LM

Dominica Const. art. 8(4):

> No person shall be held to be guilty of a criminal offence on account of any act or omission that did not, at the time it took place, constitute such an offence, and no penalty shall be imposed for any criminal offence that is severer in degree or description than the maximum penalty that might have been imposed for that offence at the time when it was committed.

Dominica Const. art. 49(4):

> No law made by Parliament shall come into operation until it has been published in the *Official Gazette* but Parliament may postpone the coming into operation of any such law and may make laws with retrospective effect.

TREATIES: ACHR(but has not accepted the jurisdiction of the IACtHR), ICCPR

Dominican Republic – NC, NP, LM

Dominican Rep. Const. art. 8(5):

> No one shall be obligated to do what the law does not demand nor be prevented from doing what the law does not prohibit; the law is equal for all; it may not order more than what is just and useful for the community nor may it prohibit more than would be prejudicial to it.

Dominican Rep. Const. art. 47:

> A law only provides for and is applicable to the future. It has no retroactive effect except when it is favorable to persons subject to it or serving a sentence. In no case may a law or any public power affect or alter the juridical security deriving from situations established in conformity with previous legislation.

TREATIES: ACHR, ICCPR(P)

East Timor [Timor-Leste] – NC, NP, LM, SJ

East Timor [Timor-Leste] Const. art. 24(2):

> Laws restricting rights, freedoms and guarantees have necessarily a general and abstract nature and may not reduce the extent and scope of the essential contents of constitutional provisions and shall not have a retroactive effect.

East Timor [Timor-Leste] Const. art. 31(2, 3 & 5):

...

(2) No one can be tried and convicted for an act that does not qualify in the law as a criminal offence at the moment it was committed, nor endure security measures the provisions of which are not expressly established in previous law.
(3) Penalties or security measures not expressly provided for by law at the moment the criminal offence was committed cannot be enforced.

...

(5) Criminal law cannot be enforced retroactively, except when the new law is in favor of the accused.

East Timor [Timor-Leste] Const. art. 123(2):

Courts of exception shall be prohibited and there shall be no special courts to judge certain categories of criminal offence.

East Timor [Timor-Leste] Const. art. 163 (Transitional Judicial Organization):

(1) The collective judicial instance existing in East Timor, integrated by national and international judges with competences to judge serious crimes committed between the 1st of January and the 25th of October 1999, shall remain in effect for the time deemed strictly necessary to conclude the cases under investigation.
(2) The judicial Organization existing in East Timor on the day the present Constitution enters into force shall remain in effect until such a time as the new judicial system is established and starts its functions.

TREATY: ICCPR

Ecuador – NC, NP, LM

Ecuador Const. art. 24(1-2):

The following basic guarantees, without impairing others established in the Constitution, international instruments and laws or jurisprudence, must be observed to ensure due process:

(1) No one may be punished for an act or omission that[,] at the time of perpetration[,] was not classified as a penal or administrative infraction or infraction of some other nature, nor can a punishment be applied if it is not foreseen in the Constitution or in the law. Also[,] one may not punish a person in manner that is not in

conformance with the preexisting law, [or that does not] observe the proper transactional steps [*tramite*] of each procedure.

(2) In case of a conflict between two laws that contain punishments, the less rigorous shall be applied, even if its promulgation was after the infraction; and[,] in case of doubt, the norm that contains punishments shall be applied in the manner most favorable to the accused.

TREATIES: ACHR, ICCPR(P)

Egypt – NC, NP, LM, PP

Egypt Const. art. 66:

Penalty shall be personal.

There shall be no crime or penalty except by virtue of the law. No penalty shall be inflicted except by judicial sentence. Penalty shall be inflicted only for acts committed subsequent to the promulgation of the law prescribing them.

Egypt Const. art. 187:

Legal provisions apply only from the date of their entry into force, and shall have no retroactive effect. However, provisions to the contrary may be adopted, in other than criminal matters, with the approval of the majority of the members of the People's Assembly.

TREATIES: ACHPR(P-signed), ArCHR-signed, ICCPR

El Salvador – NC, NP, LM, SJ

El Salvador Const. art. 8:

No one is obligated to do what the law does not order nor deny themselves of what it does not prohibit.

El Salvador Const. art. 15:

No one shall be tried except in conformity with laws promulgated prior to the action in question, and by courts previously established by the law.

TREATIES: ACHR, ICCPR(P)

Equatorial Guinea – NC, NP, LM

Equatorial Guinea Fundamental Law art. 13(s):

All Citizens shall enjoy the following rights and liberties:

. . .

(s) The right not to be punished for any act or omission which at the time it was committed was not punishable as a crime; no penalty may be imposed which is not provided for by law. In case of doubt, the law shall be applied in favor of the defendant.

TREATIES: ACHPR(P-signed), ICCPR(P)

Eritrea – NC, NP, LM

Eritrea Const. art. 17(2) (made non-derogable by art. 27(3)):

No person shall be tried or convicted for any act or omission which did not constitute a criminal offense at the time when it was committed.

TREATIES: ACHPR, ICCPR

Estonia – NC, NP, LM

Estonia Const. art. 23:

No one shall be convicted of an act, which did not constitute a criminal offence under the law in force at the time the act was committed.

No one shall have a more severe sentence imposed on him or her than the one that was applicable at the time the offence was committed. If, subsequent to the commission of an offence, the law provides for a lesser punishment, the lesser punishment shall apply.

. . .

TREATIES: ECHR, ICCPR(P)

Ethiopia – NC, NP, LM, SJ

Ethiopia Const. art. 22(1& 2):

1. No one shall be held guilty of any criminal offence on account of any act or omission which did not constitute a criminal offence at the time when it was committed. Nor shall a heavier penalty be imposed on any person than the one that was applicable at the time when the criminal offence was committed.
2. Notwithstanding the provisions of sub-Article 1 of this Article, a law promulgated subsequent to the commission of the offence shall apply if it is advantageous to the accused or convicted person.

Ethiopia Const. art. 78(4):

Special or ad hoc courts which take judicial powers away from the regular courts or institutions legally empowered to exercise judicial functions and which do not follow legally prescribed procedures shall not be established.

TREATIES: ACHPR(P-signed), ICCPR

Fiji – NC, NP

Fiji Const. art. 28(1)(j):

> Every person charged with an offence has the right:
>
> . . .
>
> (j) not to be found guilty in respect of an act or omission unless the act or omission constituted an offence at the time it occurred, and not to be sentenced to a more severe punishment than was applicable when the offence was committed;
>
> . . . .

Finland – NC, NP, LM, SJ

Finland Const. [Valtiosääntö], ch. 2 §8:

> The principle of legality in criminal cases
>
> No one shall be found guilty of a criminal offence or be sentenced to a punishment on the basis of a deed, which has not been determined punishable by an Act at the time of its commission. The penalty imposed for an offence shall not be more severe than that provided by an Act at the time of commission of the offence.

Finland Const. [Valtiosääntö], ch. 9 §98:

> The Supreme Court, the Courts of Appeal and the District Courts are the general courts of law.
>
> The Supreme Administrative Court and the regional Administrative Courts are the general courts of administrative law.
>
> Provisions on special courts of law, administering justice in specifically defined fields, are laid down by an Act.
>
> Provisional courts shall not be established.

TREATIES: ECHR, ICCPR(P)

France – NC, NP, LM

France Declaration of the Rights of Man and the Citizen (1789) (given current constitutional status through France Const., preamble, and Decision of the Constitutional Council of 16 July 1971 (Liberty of Association)), art. 5:

> The law may prohibit only those actions which are harmful to society. Nothing which is not expressly forbidden by the Law may be prohibited, and nobody may be forced to do anything which it does not ordain.

France Declaration of the Rights of Man and the Citizen art. 8:

> The Law may not establish punishments other than those which are strictly and evidently necessary, and nobody may be punished except by virtue of a Law which was adopted and published prior to the offense, and is legally applied.

TREATIES: ECHR, ICCPR(P)

Gabon – NC, NP, LM

Gabon Const. art. 47:

> Outside of the cases expressly provided for by the Constitution, the law establishes the rules concerning:
>
> . . .
>
> – the determination of crimes and misdemeanors as well as the penalties which are applicable to them, the penal procedure, the penitentiary and amnesty system;
>
> . . .

Gabon Const. art. 79 (concerning court that only tries high government officials):

> The High Court of Justice is constrained, with the exception of judgement of the President of the Republic, by the definition of crimes and misdemeanors as well as by the determination of penalties such as they result from the penal laws in force at the moment when the acts were committed.

TREATIES: ACHPR(P), ICCPR

Gambia – NC, NP, LM

Gambia Const. art. 24(5):

> No person shall be charged with or held to be guilty of a criminal offence on account of any act or omission which did not at the time it took place constitute such an offence, and no penalty shall be imposed for any criminal offence which is more severe in degree or description than the maximum penalty which might have been imposed for that offence at the time when it was committed.

TREATIES: ACHPR(P), ICCPR(P)

Georgia – NC, NP, LM

Georgia Const. art. 42(5):

> No one shall be held responsible for an act which did not constitute a criminal offense at the time it was committed. The law shall have no retroactive effect, except insofar as it mitigates or extinguishes criminal responsibility.

TREATIES: ECHR, ICCPR(P)

Germany – NC, NP, LM, SJ

Germany Basic Law [Grundgesetz] art. 96(5):

> In the case of criminal proceedings in the following areas, a Federal law with the assent of the "Bundesrat" may provide that courts in the "Länder" exercise the jurisdiction of the Federal Government: 1. genocide; 2. crimes against humanity under international law; 3. war crimes; 4. other actions designed for the purpose of, and carried out with the intention of, disturbing peaceful cohabitation between peoples;. . . .

Germany Basic Law [Grundgesetz] art. 101:

> (1) Extraordinary courts are not allowed. No one may be removed from the jurisdiction of his lawful judge.
> (2) Courts for particular fields of law may be established only by a law.

Germany Basic Law [Grundgesetz] art. 103(2):

> (Hearing in accordance with law; prohibition of retroactive criminal laws and of a multiple punishment)
>
> . . .
>
> (2) An act may be punished only if it was defined by a law as a criminal offense before the act was committed.

STATUTE:

Germany §1, StGB:

> No Punishment Without a Law
>
> An act may only be punished if its punishability was determined by law before the act was committed.

Germany §2, StGB:

> Temporal Applicability
>
> (1) The punishment and its collateral consequences are determined by the law which is in force at the time of the act.

(2) If the threatened punishment is amended during the commission of the act, then the law shall be applicable which is in force at the time the act is completed.
(3) If the law in force upon the completion of the act is amended before judgment, then the most lenient law shall be applicable.
(4) A law, which was intended to be in force only for a determinate time, shall be applicable to acts committed while it was in force, even if it is no longer in force. This shall not apply to the extent a law provides otherwise.
(5) Subsections (1) through (4) shall apply, correspondingly, to forfeiture, confiscation and rendering unusable.
(6) Unless the law provides otherwise, decisions as to measures of reform and prevention shall be according to the law which is in force at the time of judgment.

Translation of Statute by German Federal Ministry of Justice.

TREATIES: ECHR, ICCPR(P)

Ghana – NC, NP, LM

Ghana Const. art. 19(5, 6 & 11):

(5) A person shall not be charged with or held to be guilty of a criminal offence which is founded on an act or omission that did not at the time it took place constitute an offence.
(6) No penalty shall be imposed for a criminal offence that is severer in degree or description than the maximum penalty that could have been imposed for that offence at the time when it was committed.
. . .
(11) No person shall be convicted of a criminal offence unless the offence is defined and the penalty for it is prescribed in a written law.

Ghana Const. art. 107:

Parliament shall have no power to pass any law – . . . (b) which operates retrospectively to impose any limitations on, or to adversely affect the personal rights and liberties of any person or to impose a burden, obligation or liability on any person except in the case of a law enacted under articles 178 to 182 of this Constitution.

TREATIES: ACHPR(P), ICCPR(P)

Greece – NC, NP, LM

Greece Const. art. 7(1):

There shall be no crime, nor shall punishment be inflicted unless specified by law in force prior to the perpetration of the act, defining the constitutive elements of the act. In no case shall punishment more severe than that specified at the time of the perpetration of the act be inflicted.

TREATIES: ECHR, ICCPR(P)

Grenada – NC, NP, LM

Grenada Const. Order art. 8(4):

> No person shall be held to be guilty of a criminal offence on account of any act or omission that did not, at the time it took place, constitute such an offence, and no penalty shall be imposed for any criminal offence that is severer in degree or description than the maximum penalty that might have been imposed for that offence at the time when it was committed.

TREATIES: ACHR (has not accepted jurisdiction of the IACtHR), ICCPR

Guatemala – NC, NP, LM

Guatemala Const. art. 5 (Freedom of Action):

> Any person has the right to do whatever the law does not prohibit; he is not obligated to obey orders not based on the law or issued according to it. Neither can he be harassed or persecuted for his opinions or for acts that do not involve violation of same.

Guatemala Const. art. 15:

> Non-Retroactivity of the Law. The law does not have retroactive effect, except in a criminal case when it favors the defendant.

Guatemala Const. art. 17:

> There is No Offense nor Penalty without an Earlier Law. Those actions or omissions that are not characterized as crimes or misdemeanors [*falta*] or sanctioned by a law preceding their perpetration are not punishable....

TREATIES: ACHR, ICCPR(P)

Guinea – NC, NP, LM

Guinea Fundamental Law art. 59:

> Subject to the provisions of Article 45, the National Assembly alone shall pass laws.
>
> The law shall only be prospective....

Guinea Fundamental Law art. 86:

> ... The Ministers shall be penally responsible for acts accomplished in the exercise of their functions and qualified as crimes or misdemeanors at the moment where they were committed.

. . .

> The High Court of Justice shall be bound by the definition of crimes and misdemeanors as well as the determination of penalties such that they result from the law in effect at the moment where the acts were committed.

TREATIES: ACHPR(P-signed), ICCPR(P)

Guinea-Bissau – NC, NP, LM

Guinea-Bissau Const. art. 33(2):

> No law may be retroactive, unless it would benefit the accused person.

TREATIES: ACHPR(P-signed), ICCPR&P-both signed

Guyana – NC, NP, LM

Guyana Const. art. 144(4):

> No person shall be held to be guilty of a criminal offence on account of any act or omission that did not, at the time it took place, constitute such an offence, and no penalty shall be imposed for any criminal offence that is more severe in degree or nature than the most severe penalty that might have been imposed for that offence at the time when it was committed.

TREATIES: ICCPR(P) – but Guyana reserved against the ability the Human Rights Committee to receive and consider communications from persons under sentence of death for murder or treason. It did not reserve against any of its substantive obligations under the ICCPR, including legality in criminal matters. A number of states objected to this reservation. See http://www.ohchr.org/english/countries/ratification/5.html, including list of reservations and declarations & n.2.

Haiti – NC, NP, LM, SJ

Haiti Const. art. 51:

> The law may not be made retroactive except in criminal cases when it favors the accused.

Haiti Const. art. 173–2:

> No court and no jurisdiction in disputed matters may be established except by law. No special court may be established under any name whatever.

TREATIES: ACHR, ICCPR

Honduras – NC, NP, LM

Honduras Const. art. 70:

> All Hondurans have the right to do that which is not harmful to others; likewise, no one shall be obliged to do that which is not legally prescribed nor shall be prevented from doing that which the Law does not prohibit. . . .

Honduras Const. art. 95:

> No person shall be punished with penalty not previously established by the Law. . . .

Honduras Const. art. 96:

> No law has retroactive effect, except in criminal matters when the new law favors the defendant.

TREATIES: ACHR, ICCPR(P)

Hungary – NC, NP, LM

Hungary [Magyar] Const. art. 57(4):

> No one may be declared guilty and subjected to punishment for an offense that was not a criminal offence under Hungarian law at the time such offense was committed.

STATUTE:

Hungary Criminal Code §2 confirms that *nulla poena* is part of Hungarian law:

> Section 2. A crime shall be adjudged in accordance with the law in force at the time of its perpetration. If, in accordance with the new Criminal Code in force at the time of the judgment of an act, the act is no longer a crime or it is to be adjudged more leniently, then the new law shall apply; otherwise, the new Criminal Code has no retroactive force.

Statute translation from OSCE Office of Democratic Institutions and Human Rights Web site, http://www.legislationline.org/upload/legislations/15/ef/84d98ff3242b74e606dcb1da83aa.pdf.

TREATIES: ECHR, ICCPR(P)

Iceland – NC, NP, LM

Iceland Const. art. 69:

> No one may be subjected to punishment unless found guilty of conduct that constituted a criminal offence according to the law at the time when

it was committed, or is totally analogous to such conduct. The sanctions may not be more severe than the law permitted at the time of commission.

. . .

STATUTE:

The Iceland General Penal Code, arts. 1, 2 & 2a confirms that the use of analogy is strictly limited, and that *nulla poena* is part of Icelandic law:

Art. 1 A person shall not be subjected to penalties unless found guilty of behaviour deemed punishable by Law, or totally analogous to such conduct.

[Penalties can only be imposed in accordance with Chapter VII of the present Act if provided for in the conditions referred to in para. 1.]

Art. 2 If a criminal statute has been amended from the time an act is committed until Judgment is rendered, the Judgment shall be based on the new statute, both regarding the criminality of the act and the penalty imposed. A penalty may, however, never be imposed unless provided for by Law at the time of commission and cannot be ordered heavier than it would have been under that Law. If a criminal provision has been invalidated for reasons unrelated to a change in the legislator's assessment of the criminality of an act, the Judgment shall be based on the Law in force at the time of commission.

If an act ceases to be punishable for reasons other than those stated above, the penalty ordered as a result of the act shall be cancelled to the extent it has not already been enforced. Any other results of an act's criminality under the older Law shall also be cancelled, except an order to pay legal costs. In such a case the question whether the penalty ordered shall be cancelled, or reduced if the Judgment has also been rendered with respect to other offences, may be referred to the Court that rendered the Judgment at the District level, or a Court in the home venue of the offender. Appeal can be lodged against the conclusion of the District Court.

[**Art. 2 a.** Penalties provided for on account of offences according to Chapter VII of this Act cannot be ordered unless provided for in the conditions referred to in Art. 1 at the time of commission and the principles provided for in Art. 2 shall be observed when determining those penalties.]

Official translation from Web site of Iceland Ministry of Justice and Ecclesiastical Affairs, http://eng.domsmalaraduneyti.is/laws-and-regulations/nr/1145 (footnotes omitted; materials in brackets added by Iceland Act 31 of 1961; Chapter VII concerns persons suffering from mental illness or defect as described in Iceland General Penal Code, arts. 15 & 16).

TREATIES: ECHR, ICCPR(P)

India – NC, NP, LM

India Const. art. 20(1):

> No person shall be convicted of any offence except for violation of a law in force at the time of the commission of the act charged as an offence, nor be subjected to a penalty greater than that which might have been inflicted under the law in force at the time of the commission of the offence.

TREATY: ICCPR

Indonesia – NC, NP, LM

Indonesia Const. art. 28I(1):

> The rights to life, freedom from torture, freedom of thought and conscience, freedom of religion, freedom from enslavement, recognition as a person before the law, and the right not to be tried under a law with retrospective effect are all human rights that cannot be limited under any circumstances. . . .

TREATY: ICCPR

Iran – NC, NP, LM

Iran Const. art. 169:

> No act or omission may be regarded as a crime with retrospective effect on the basis of a law framed subsequently.

TREATY: ICCPR

Iraq – NC, NP, LM, SJ

Iraq Const. art. 19(2, 8, 9 & 10):

> (2) There is no crime or punishment except by stipulation. The punishment shall only be for an act that the law considers a crime when perpetrated. A harsher sentence than the applicable sentence at the time of the offense may not be imposed.
>
> . . .
>
> (8) Punishment is personal.
>
> (9) A law does not have a retroactive effect unless the law stipulates otherwise. This prohibition shall not include laws relating to taxes and fees.
>
> (10) Criminal law does not have a retroactive effect, unless it is to the benefit of the accused.

Iraq Const. art. 92:

> Special or exceptional courts may not be established.

Iraq Const. art. 130 (Transitional provision):

> The Iraqi High Criminal Court shall continue its duties as an independent judicial body in examining the crimes of the defunct dictatorial regime and its symbols. The Council of Representatives shall have the right to dissolve, by law, the Iraqi High Criminal Court after the completion of its work.

TREATY: ICCPR

Ireland – NC, NP, LM, SJ

Ireland Const. art. 15(5)(1):

> The Oireachtas [Parliament] shall not declare acts to be infringements of the law which were not so at the date of their commission.

Ireland Const. art. 38(3)(1):

> Special courts may be established by law for the trial of offences in cases where it may be determined in accordance with such law that the ordinary courts are inadequate to secure the effective administration of justice, and the preservation of public peace and order.

TREATIES: ECHR, ICCPR(P)

Israel – NC, NP,[8] LM, SJ

STATUTES:

Israel Basic Law: The Judiciary art. 1(c):

> No court or court[s] (*beit din*) shall be established for a particular case.
>
> Translation of Basic Law: The Judiciary provision from CCW [bracketed and parenthetical material in CCW].

Israel Penal Law §§1-6 (headings included):

> Punishment only under Law
>
> 1. Nothing constitutes an offense and there is no penalty for it, unless it is so prescribed by law or under it.
>   Punishment under subsidiary legislation

[8] Except for "updating the amount of a fine."

2. (a) The power to make regulations for the implementation of a Law also includes the power to designate offences and to set penalties for their commission; however, a penalty of imprisonment prescribed by a regulation shall not exceed six months, and if the penalty prescribed is a fine, then it shall not exceed the amount of fine that can be imposed for an offense, for which the penalty is a fine the amount of which was not set.
(b) Regulations in which offenses are designated and penalties set require approval by a Knesset committee.

No retroactive penalty

3. (a) An enactment that creates an offence shall not apply to an act committed before the day on which it was lawfully published, or the day on which it went into effect, whichever is later.
(b) If an enactment sets a more severe penalty for an offense, than was set for it on the day on which it was committed, then it shall not apply to any act committed before the day on which it was lawfully published, or before the day on which it went into effect, whichever is later; however, updating the amount of a fine is not deemed setting a more severe penalty.

Chapter Two Applicability of Penal Laws According to Time of Commission

Cancellation of offense after its commission

4. If an offense was committed and its prohibition was canceled by an enactment – then the criminal liability for its commission shall be canceled; proceedings initiated shall be dropped; if the judgment was pronounced its implementation shall be halted; and there shall be no future results that derive from the conviction.

Change of enactment after offense was committed

5. (a) If an offense was committed and final judgment of it has not yet been pronounced, and if a change occurred in respect of its definition, of liability for it or of the penalty set therefor, then the less severe enactment shall apply to the matter; "liability therefor" – includes the applicability of restrictions on criminal liability for the act.
(b) If a person was convicted by final judgment of an offense, and if thereafter an enactment set a penalty, which – in respect of its degree or category – is lighter than the penalty imposed on him, then his penalty shall be the maximum penalty set by the enactment, as if it had been imposed originally.

Offenses caused by time

6. The provisions of sections 4 and 5 shall not apply to an offense under an enactment, in which or in respect of which it has been

> prescribed that it shall be in effect for a certain period of time, or which by its very nature is subject to changes from time to time.

Penal Law translation ed. by Aryeh Greenfield, Penal Law 5737–1977 Part One 5–6 (5th ed., Aryeh Greenfield–A.G. Publications, 2005) (through Amendment 63).

TREATY: ICCPR

Italy – NC, NP, LM, SJ

Italy Const. art. 25:

> No one may be removed from the regular judge pre-established by law.
>
> No one may be punished except on the basis of a law already in force before the offence was committed.
>
> . . .

Italy Const. art. 102:

> . . . Extraordinary or special judges may not be established. Only specialized sections for specific matters within the ordinary judicial bodies can be established, and with the participation of qualified citizens who are not members of the judiciary. . . .

STATUTE:

Italy Codice Penale §§1, 2:

> Art. 1 – Reati e pene: disposizione espressa di legge
>
> Nessuno può essere punito per un fatto che non sia espressamente preveduto come reato dalla legge, nè con pene che non siano da essa stabilite.
>
> Art. 2 – Successione di leggi penali
>
> Nessuno può essere punito per un fatto che, secondo la legge del tempo in cui fu commesso, non costituiva reato.
>
> Nessuno può essere punito per un fatto che, secondo una legge posteriore non costituisce reato; e, se vi è stata condanna, ne cessano la esecuzione e gli effetti penali.
>
> Se la legge del tempo in cui fu commesso il reato e le posteriori sono diverse, si applica quella le cui disposizioni sono più favorevoli al reo, salvo che sia stata pronunciata sentenza irrevocabile.
>
> Se si tratta di leggi eccezionali o temporanee, non si applicano le disposizioni dei capoversi precedenti.

> Le disposizioni di questo articolo si applicano altresì nei casi di decadenza e di mancata ratifica di un decreto-legge e nei casi di un decreto-legge convertito in legge con emendamenti.

Statute from http://www.usl4.toscana.it/dp/isll/lex/cp_l1.htm#L1t1.

TREATIES: ECHR, ICCPR(P)

Jamaica – NC, NP, LM

Jamaica Const. art. 20(7):

> No person shall be held to be guilty of a criminal offence on account of any act or omission which did not, at the time it took place, constitute such an offence, and no penalty shall be imposed for any criminal offence which is severer in degree or description than the maximum penalty which might have been imposed for that offence at the time when it was committed.

TREATIES: ACHR – has accepted right of other states parties to make complaints to IACtHR, ICCPR

Japan – NC, NP, LM, SJ

Japan Const. [Kenpō] art. 39:

> No person shall be held criminally liable for an act which was lawful at the time it was committed. . . .

Japan Const. [Kenpō] art. 76:

> The whole judicial power is vested in the Supreme Court and in the lower courts as are established by law.
>
> No extraordinary tribunals shall be established, nor shall any organ or agency of the executive be given final judicial power.
>
> All judges shall be independent in the exercise of their conscience and shall be bound only by this Constitution and the laws.

STATUTE:

Japan Crim. Code art. 6:

> In cases where a change of punishment takes place after the occurrence of a crime, the lesser punishment shall be applied.

Statute translation from LexisNexis subscription online research service source, Doing Business in Japan, Chapter 11, Appendix A (Japan Criminal Code).

TREATIES: ICCPR

Jordan – NC, NP, LM, SJ

Jordan Const. art. 110:

> Special Courts shall exercise jurisdiction in accordance with the provisions of the law constituting them.

TREATIES: ArCHR, ICCPR

Kazakhstan – NC, NP, LM, SJ

Kazakhstan Const. art. 77(3)(3, 5 & 10):

> In applying law, judges must be guided by the following principles:
>
> ...
>
> (3) no one can have his jurisdiction, as determined by law, changed without his consent;
>
> ...
>
> (5) the laws establishing or intensifying liability, imposing new responsibilities on the citizens have no retroactive force. If after the commitment of an offense accountability for it is canceled by law or reduced, the new law shall be applied;
>
> ...
>
> (10) the application of the criminal law by analogy is not allowed.

TREATY: ICCPR

Kenya – NC, NP, LM

Kenya Const. art. 77(4 & 8):

> (4) No person shall be held guilty of a criminal offence on account of an act or omission that did not, at the time it took place, constitute such an offence, and no penalty shall be imposed for a criminal offence that is severer in degree or description than the maximum penalty that might have been imposed for that offence at the time when it was committed.
>
> ...
>
> (8) No person shall be convicted of a criminal offence unless that offence is defined, and the penalty therefor is prescribed, in a written law:
>
> Provided that nothing in this subsection shall prevent a court from punishing a person for contempt notwithstanding that the act or omission constituting the contempt is not defined in a written law and the penalty therefor is not so prescribed.

TREATY: ACHPR(P), ICCPR

Kiribati – NC, NP

Kiribati Const. art. 10(4):

> No person shall be held to be guilty of a criminal offence on account of any act or omission that did not, at the time it took place, constitute such an offence, and no penalty shall be imposed for any criminal offence that is severer in degree or description than the maximum penalty that might have been imposed for that offence at the time when it was committed.

Korea, Democratic People's Republic of [North] – NC, NP, LM

TREATY: ICCPR

Korea, Republic of [South] – NC, NP, LM

Rep. of [South] Korea Const. art. 13(1):

> No citizen shall be prosecuted for an act which does not constitute a crime under the law in force at the time it was committed. . . .

TREATY: ICCPR(P)

Kosovo – X, NC, NP, LM

Kosovo Const., art. 33 [The Principle of Legality and Proportionality in Criminal Cases]:

> 1. No one shall be charged or punished for any act which did not constitute a penal offense under law at the time it was committed, except acts that at the time they were committed constituted genocide, war crimes or crimes against humanity according to international law.
> 2. No punishment for a criminal act shall exceed the penalty provided by law at the time the criminal act was committed.
> 3. The degree of punishment cannot be disproportional to the criminal offense.
> 4. Punishments shall be administered in accordance with the law in force at the time a criminal act was committed, unless the penalties in a subsequent applicable law are more favorable to the perpetrator

Presented to the President of Kosovo, 7 April 2008. From Kosovo Constitutional Commission web site, www.kosovoconstitution.info. Entered into force 15 June 2008, too late to be noted in the main text of this book. See AFP, *Newly independent Kosovo's constitution enters force* (15 June 2008) (also noting Serbian objection to Kosovo's Constitution).

Kuwait – NC, NP, LM

Kuwait Const. art. 32:

> No crime and no penalty may be established except by virtue of law, and no penalty may be imposed except for offences committed after the relevant law has come into force.

TREATY: ICCPR

Kyrgyzstan – NC, NP, LM

Kyrgyzstan Const. art. 41:

> The publication of laws and other normative legal acts concerning the rights, freedoms and duties of a person and a citizen is an obligatory condition for their application.

Kyrgyzstan Const. art. 85(10):

> A law establishing or aggravating the responsibility of a person does not have a retroactive force. No one may bear responsibility for actions which at the time when they were committed were not recognized as an offence. If after committing an offence the responsibility for it is removed or commuted, a new law is applied.

TREATY: ICCPR(P)

Laos – NC, NP, LM

TREATY: ICCPR

Latvia – NC, NP, LM

Latvia Const. art. 89:

> The State shall recognize and protect fundamental human rights in accordance with this Constitution, laws and international agreements binding upon Latvia.

TREATIES: ECHR, ICCPR(P)

Lebanon – NC, NP, LM

Lebanon Const. art. 8:

> Personal liberty is guaranteed and protected by the law. No one can be arrested or detained except in accordance with the provisions of law. No offense can be determined and no penalty can be imposed except according to the law.

STATUTE:

Lebanon Code Pénal arts. 1-3, 6-8, 12-14:

Art. 1:

Nulle infraction ne peut être sanctionnée par une peine, ou par une mesure de sûreté ou d'éducation, si elle n'était pas prévue par la loi au moment où elle fut commise.

Ne seront pas retenus à la charge de l'inculpé les faits constitutifs d'une infraction, les acts de participation principale ou accessoire, qu'il aura accomplis avant que cette infraction ait été prévue par la loi.

Art. 2:

Nulle infraction ne sera réprimée par une peine, ou par une mesure de sûreté ou d'éducation, si elle est supprimée par une loi nouvelle. Les condamnations pénales prononcées cesseront d'avoir effet.

Toutfois, l'infraction à une loi temporaire, commise pendant la période d'application de cette loi, ne cessera pas d'être poursuivie et réprimée après l'expiration de la dite période.

Art. 3:

Toute loi qui modifis les conditions de l'incrimination dans un sens favorable au prévenu, s'applique aux infractions commises antérieurment à sa mise en vigueur, sauf au cas où un condemnation definitive a été prononcée.

Art. 6:

Nulle peine ne peut être prononcée, si elle n'était pas prévue par la loi au moment où l'infraction fut commise.

L'infraction est reputée commise dès que les actes d'exécution ont été accomplish, indépendamment du moment où le résultat a eu lieu.

Art. 7:

Toute loi nouvelle, même plus rigoureuse, s'applique aux infractions continues, continuées, successives ou d'habitude dont l'exécution a été poursuive sous son empire.

Art. 8:

Toute loi nouvelle abolissant une peine ou en édictant une plus douce s'applique aux infractions antérieurment à sa mise en vigueur, sauf au cas où une condemnations definitive a été prononcée.

Art. 12:

Nulle mesure de sûreté, nulle mesure d'éducation ne peuvent être prononcées que sous les conditions et dans les cas prévus par la loi.

Art. 13:

Toute loi nouvelle établissant une mesure de sûreté ou une mesure d'éducation s'applique aux infractions sur lesquelles il n'a pas été statué par la dernière jurisdiction compétente sur le fait.

Les condamnations encourues antérieurement à la mise en vigueur de la nouvelle loi seront, lors de la répression du fait commis sous son empire, comptées en vue de l'application des dispositions relatives à la délinquence d'habitude.

Art. 14:

Toute mesure de sûreté, toute mesure d'éducation supprimées par la loi ou remplacées par une autre mesure cessent de recevoir effet.

Si une condemnation definitive est prononcée, elle sera soumise à révision pour l'application de la nouvelle mesure de sûreté ou d'éducation.

Decret legislative No. 340/ni du 1 Mars 1943, avec ses modifications, in CODE PENAL (Bureau des Documentations Libanaises et Arabes, 1976).

TREATY: ICCPR

Lesotho – NC, NP, LM

Lesotho Const. art. 12(4):

> No person shall be held to be guilty of a criminal offence on account of any act or omission that did not, at the time it took place, constitute such an offence, and no penalty shall be imposed for a criminal offence that is severer in degree or description than the maximum penalty that might have been imposed for that offence at the time when it was committed.

TREATIES: ACHPR(P), ICCPR(P)

Liberia – NC, NP, LM

Liberia Const. art. 21(a):

> No person shall be made subject to any law or punishment which was not in effect at the time of commission of an offense, nor shall the Legislature enact any bill of attainder or ex post facto law.

TREATIES: ACHPR(P-signed), ICCPR(P-signed)

Libya – NC, NP, LM, PP

Constitutional Proclamation (1969) of the Revolutionary Command Council of Libya art. 31(a, b):

> (a) Crime and penalty are only determined by law.
> (b) The penalty is personal.

Declaration on the Establishment of the Authority of the People, art. 2 (1977):

> The Holy Kuran is the constitution of the Socialist People's Libyan Arab Jamahiriya.

General People's Congress Law No 20 of 1991 on the Consolidation of Freedom has no direct reference to non-retroactivity of crimes and punishments, although it is otherwise like a bill of rights.

TREATIES: ACHPR(P), ArCHR, ICCPR(P)

Liechtenstein – NC, NP, LM, SJ

Liechtenstein Const. art. 33(2):

> Nobody may be threatened with or subjected to penalties other than those provided by law.

Liechtenstein Const. art. 33(1):

> Nobody may be deprived of his proper judge; special tribunals may not be instituted.

STATUTE:
Liechtenstein Strafgesetzbuch (StGB) §1:

> (1) Eine Strafe oder eine vorbeugende Massnahme darf nur wegen einer Tat verhängt werden, die unter eine ausdrückliche gesetzliche Strafdrohung fällt und schon zur Zeit ihrer Begehung mit Strafe bedroht war.
> (2) Eine schwerere als die zur Zeit der Begehung angedrohte Strafe darf nicht verhängt werden. Eine vorbeugende Massnahme darf nur angeordnet werden, wenn zur Zeit der Begehung diese vorbeugende Massnahme oder eine der Art nach vergleichbare Strafe oder vorbeugende Massnahme vorgesehen war. Durch die Anordnung einer bloss der Art nach vergleichbaren vorbeugenden Massnahme darf der Täter keiner ungünstigeren Behandlung unterworfen werden, als sie nach dem zur Zeit der Tat geltenden Gesetz zulässig war.

Statute text from private website offering Liechtenstein laws, http://www.recht.li.

TREATIES: ECHR, ICCPR(P)

Lithuania – NC, NP, LM, SJ

Lithuania Const. art. 31:

> Punishment may be imposed or implied only on the grounds established by law.

Lithuania Const. art. 111:

> For the consideration of administrative, labour, family and cases of other categories, specialised courts may be established according to law. Courts with extraordinary powers may not be established in the republic of Lithuania in a time of peace.

STATUTE:

Lithuania Penal Code, art. 3:

> 3. straipsnis. Baudžiamojo įstatymo galiojimo laikas
>
> 1. Veikos nusikalstamumą ir asmens baudžiamumą nustato tos veikos padarymo metu galiojęs baudžiamasis įstatymas. Nusikalstamos veikos padarymo laikas yra veikimo (neveikimo) laikas arba baudžiamojo įstatymo numatytų padarinių atsiradimo laikas, jeigu asmuo norėjo, kad padariniai atsirastų kitu laiku.
> 2. Veikos nusikalstamumą panaikinantis, bausmę švelninantis arba kitokiu būdu nusikalstamą veiką padariusio asmens teisinę padėtį palengvinantis baudžiamasis įstatymas turi grįžtamąją galią, t. y. taikomas iki tokio įstatymo įsigaliojimo nusikalstamą veiką padariusiems asmenims, taip pat atliekantiems bausmę bei turintiems teistumą asmenims.
> 3. Baudžiamasis įstatymas, nustatantis veikos nusikalstamumą, griežtinantis bausmę arba kitaip sunkinantis nusikalstamą veiką padariusio asmens teisinę padėtį, neturi grįžtamosios galios. Išimtį sudaro šio kodekso normos, nustatančios atsakomybę už genocidą (99 straipsnis), tarptautinės teisės draudžiamą elgesį su žmonėmis (100 straipsnis), tarptautinės humanitarinės teisės saugomų asmenų žudymą (101 straipsnis), okupuotos valstybės civilių trėmimą (102 straipsnis), tarptautinės humanitarinės teisės saugomų asmenų žalojimą, kankinimą ar kitokį nežmonišką elgesį su jais (103 straipsnis), civilių ar karo belaisvių prievartinį panaudojimą priešo ginkluotosiose pajėgose (105 straipsnis), draudžiamą karo ataką (111 straipsnis).
> 4. Skiriamos tos baudžiamojo ar auklėjamojo poveikio priemonės bei priverčiamosios medicinos priemonės, kurias numato teismo sprendimo priėmimo metu galiojantis baudžiamasis įstatymas.

Interpreted as belonging here by Maryna O. Jackson.

TREATIES: ECHR, ICCPR(P)

Luxembourg – NC, NP, LM, SJ
Luxembourg Const. art. 12:

> Individual freedom is guaranteed. – No one may be prosecuted otherwise than in cases and according to the procedure laid down by law. – No

one may be arrested or detained otherwise than in cases and according to the procedure laid down by law. – Except in cases of *flagrante delicto* no one may be arrested without a warrant of a judge served at the time of arrest or within twenty-four hours at the latest. – Every individual must be informed without delay about the legal means of recourse at his disposal to recover his freedom.

Luxembourg Const. art. 14:

No penalty may be fined or applied except in pursuance of the law.

Luxembourg Const. art. 13:

No one may be deprived against his will of the judge assigned to him by law.

Luxembourg Const. art. 86:

No court or jurisdiction in contentious matters may be set up, except by virtue of a law. No extraordinary commission or courts may be set up, under whatever name.

STATUTE:

Luxembourg Code Pénal art. 2:

Nulle infraction ne peut être punie de peines qui n'étaient pas portées par la loi avant que l'infraction fût commise.

Si la peine établie au temps du jugement diffère de celle qui était portée au temps de l'infraction, la peine la moins forte sera appliquée.

TREATIES: ECHR, ICCPR(P)

Macedonia – NC, NP, LM, SJ

Macedonia Const. art. 14:

No one may be punished for an act which had not been declared, prior to it being performed, a punishable offence under law, or other regulation, and for which no punishment had been prescribed.

. . .

Macedonia Const. art. 52:

Laws and other regulations may not have a retroactive effect, except in cases when this is more favourable for the citizens.

Macedonia Const. amend. XXV:

1. Judiciary power is exercised by courts.

   Courts are autonomous and independent. Courts judge on the basis of the Constitution and laws and international agreements ratified in accordance with the Constitution.

   Emergency courts are prohibited.

   The types of courts, their spheres of competence, their establishment, abrogation, organization and composition, as well as the procedure they follow are regulated by a law adopted by a of [*sic*] two-thirds majority vote of the total number of Representatives.
2. Clause 1 of this Amendment replaces Article 98 of the Constitution of the Republic of Macedonia.

TREATIES: ECHR, ICCPR(P)

Madagascar – NC, NP, LM

Madagascar Const. art. 13:

> . . .
>
> No one may be prosecuted, arrested or detained, except in cases determined by law and according to the forms that it has proscribed.
>
> No one may be punished except by virtue of a law promulgated and published prior to the commission of the punishable act.
>
> . . .

TREATIES: ACHPR(P-signed), ICCPR(P)

Malawi – NC, NP, LM

Malawi Const. art. 42(2)(f)(vi) (made non-derogable by Malawi Const. art. 44(f)):

> Every person arrested for, or accused of, the alleged commission of an offence shall, in addition to the rights which he or she has as a detained person, have the right –
>
> . . .
>
> (f) as an accused person, to a fair trial, which shall include the right –
>
> . . .
>
> (vi) not to be convicted of an offence in respect of any act or omission which was not an offence at the time when the act was committed or

omitted to be done, and not to be sentenced to a more severe punishment than that which was applicable when the offence was committed;

. . . .

TREATIES: ACHPR(P-signed), ICCPR(P)

Malaysia – NC, NP

Malaysia Const. art. 7(1):

No person shall be punished for an act or omission which was not punishable by law when it was done or made, and no person shall suffer greater punishment for an offence than was prescribed by law at the time it was committed.

Maldives – NC, NP, LM

Maldives Const. art. 17(1 & 2):

(1) No law shall authorise the punishment of a person for an act or omission that did not constitute a criminal offence at the time of the act or omission.
(2) No law shall authorise the punishment of a person for an offence by a penalty greater than, or of a kind different from the penalty prescribed by law for that offence at the time that offence was committed.
. . .

TREATY: ICCPR(P)

Mali – NC, NP, LM, PP

Mali Const. art. 9:

Punishment is personal.

No one may be pursued, arrested or accused except by virtue of a law promulgated anterior to the acts for which he is reproached.

. . .

Mali Const. art. 95:

The High court of Justice is competent to judge the President of the Republic and the Ministers accused before it by the National Assembly for high treason or for reason of facts qualified as crimes or misdemeanors committed in the exercise of their functions as well as their accomplices in the case of conspiracy against the security of the state.

> The Act of accusation is voted open to public scrutiny by a two-thirds majority of the Deputies composing the National Assembly.
>
> The High Court of Justice is constrained by the definition of crimes and misdemeanors and by the determination of penalties resulting from the penal laws in force at the time of the acts comprised in the pursuit.

TREATIES: ACHPR(P), ICCPR(P)

Malta – NC, NP, LM

Malta Const. art. 39(8):

> No person shall be held to be guilty of a criminal offence on account of any act or omission that did not, at the time it took place, constitute such an offence, and no penalty shall be imposed for any criminal offence which is severer in degree or description than the maximum penalty which might have been imposed for that offence at the time when it was committed.

TREATIES: ECHR, ICCPR(P)

Marshall Islands – NC, NP

Marshall Islands Const. art. II(8):

1. No person shall be subjected to ex post facto punishment – such as punishment in excess of that validly applicable at the time the act in question was committed, or punishment imposed by a procedure less favorable to the accused than that validly applicable at the time the act was committed.
2. No person shall be subjected to punishment under a bill of attainder – such as a law which singles out for penalty a named or readily identifiable individual or group of individuals.

Mauritania – NC, NP, LM

Mauritania Const. art. 13:

> . . .
>
> No one may be prosecuted, arrested, detained or punished except in cases determined by the law and according to the formalities which it prescribes . . .

STATUTE:

Mauritania Code Pénal art. 4:

> Nulle contravention, nul délit, nul crime, ne peuvent être punis de peines qui n'étaient pas prononcées par la loi avant qu'ils fussent commis.

Statute: Ordonnance n° 83.162 from Journal Officiel de la République Islamique de Mauritanie n° 608–609, pp. 112–49 (date de promulgation : 09.07.1983; date de publication : 29.02.1984).

TREATIES: ACHPR(P), ICCPR

Mauritius – NC, NP, LM

Mauritius Const., ch. II, art. 10(4):

> No person shall be held to be guilty of a criminal offence on account of any act or omission that did not, at the time it took place, constitute such an offence, and no penalty shall be imposed for any criminal offence that is severer in degree or description than the maximum penalty that might have been imposed for that offence at the time when it was committed.

TREATIES: ACHPR(P), ICCPR(P)

Mexico – NC, NP, LM, SJ

Mexico Const. art. 13:

> No one may be tried by private laws or special tribunals. No person or corporation can have privileges or enjoy emoluments other than those given in compensation for public services and which are set forth by law. Military jurisdiction is recognized for the trial of crimes against the violation of military discipline, but the military tribunals can in no case have jurisdiction over persons who do not belong to the armed forces. Whenever a civilian is implicated in a military crime or violation, the corresponding civil authority shall have jurisdiction over the case.

Mexico Const. art. 14:

> No law shall be given retroactive effect to the detriment of any person whatsoever.
>
> No one can be deprived of life, liberty, property, possessions or rights, except by means of a judicial proceeding before a duly created court in which the essential formalities of procedure are observed and in accordance with laws enacted prior to the act in question.
>
> No penalty may be imposed in criminal cases by mere analogy or even by preponderance of the evidence unless such penalty is pronounced in the law and is in every respect applicable to the crime in question. . . .

See Stephen Zamora, José Ramón Cossío, Leonel Pereznieto, José Roldán-Xopa & David Lopez, Mexican Law 360-61 (Oxford Univ. Press 2004) (explaining that this provision does not permit "extrapolating from a general principle, even when logic appears to support such a conviction; rather the court may only convict on the basis of a law that lists the precise elements found in the offence in question").

TREATIES: ACHR (ratified, but acceptance of the adjudicatory jurisdiction of the Inter-American Court of Human Rights shall only be applicable to facts or juridical acts subsequent to the date of deposit of this declaration, and shall not therefore apply retroactively), ICCPR(P)

Micronesia – NC, NP
Micronesia Const. art. IV(11):

> A bill of attainder or ex post facto law may not be passed.

Moldova – NC, NP, LM, SJ

Moldova Const. art. 22:

> No one may be sentenced for actions or omissions which did not constitute a crime at the time they were committed. Also, punishment more severe than that applicable at the time the crime was committed may not be applied.

Moldova Const. art. 115(3):

> The creation of extraordinary (*extraordinare*) courts is prohibited.

TREATIES: ECHR, ICCPR(P-signed)

Monaco – NC, NP, LM

Monaco Const. art. 20:

> No penalty shall be established nor applied, except in pursuance of the law.
>
> . . .
>
> Criminal laws cannot have a retroactive effect.

TREATIES: ECHR, ICCPR

Mongolia – NC, NP, LM

TREATIES: ICCPR

Montenegro – NC, NP, LM, SJ

Montenegro Const. art. 33 (made non-limitable by art. 25):

> No one may be punished for an act that, prior to being committed, was not stipulated by the law as punishable, nor may be pronounced a punishment which was not envisaged for that act.

Montenegro Const. art. 34:

> Criminal and other punishable acts are stipulated and the punishments for them are pronounced in accordance with the law in force at the time

> when the act was committed, unless the new law is more favorable for the perpetrator.

Montenegro Const. art. 118:

> . . .
>
> Establishment of court marshal [*sic*] and extraordinary courts shall be prohibited.

New Montenegro Constitution approved by "Constitutional parliament" on 19 October 2007, effective 22 October 2007. Text and translation from LegislatiOnline, OSCE Office for Democratic Institutions and Human Rights Web site at http://www.legislationline.org/upload/legislations/01/9c/b4b87026790c8b427942670691488.htm. For effective date, see legal academic Web site Jurist at http://jurist.law.pitt.edu/paperchase/2007/10/montenegro-lawmakers-adopt-new.php.

TREATIES: ICCPR, ECHR

Morocco – NC, NP, LM

Morocco Const. art. 4:

> The law is the supreme expression of the Nation's will. All must submit to it. Law can have no retroactive effect.

TREATIES: ArCHR(signed), ICCPR

Mozambique – NC, NP, LM, SJ

Mozambique Const. art. 99:

> 1. No one may be punished for an act that was not considered a crime at the time it was committed.
> 2. Penal laws may be applied retroactively only in favour of the accused.

Mozambique Const. art. 167(2):

> Other than courts specified in the Constitution, no other court may be established with jurisdiction over specific categories of crimes.

Mozambique Const. art. 201:

> In the Republic of Mozambique, law may only be retroactive when this is to the benefit of citizens and other legal persons.

TREATIES: ACHPR(P), ICCPR

Myanmar – NC, NP

Myanmar Const. art. 23:

> No penal law shall have retrospective effect.

Namibia – NC, NP, LM

Namibia Const. art. 12(3):

> No persons shall be tried or convicted for any criminal offence or on account of any act or omission which did not constitute a criminal offence at the time when it was committed, nor shall a penalty be imposed exceeding that which was applicable at the time when the offence was committed.

TREATIES: ACHPR(P-signed), ICCPR(P)

Nauru – NC, NP

Nauru Const. art. 10(1 & 4):

> (1) No person shall be convicted of an offence which is not defined by law.
>
> ...
>
> (4) No person shall be convicted of an offense on account of any act or omission that did not, at the time it took place, constitute such an offence and no penalty shall be imposed for an offence that is more severe in degree or description than the maximum penalty that might have been imposed for that offence at the time when it was committed.

Nauru Const. art. 81(6):

> Where a law is repealed, or is deemed to have been repealed, by, under or by reason of this Constitution, the repeal does not –
>
> (a) revive anything not in force or existing at the time at which the repeal takes effect;
> (b) affect the previous operation of the law or anything only done or suffered under the law;
> (c) affect any right, privilege, obligation or liability acquired, accrued or incurred under the law;
> (d) affect any penalty, forfeiture or punishment incurred in respect of any offence committed against the law; or
> (e) affect any investigation, legal proceeding or remedy in respect of any such right, privilege, obligation, liability, penalty, forfeiture or punishment,

> and any such investigation, legal proceeding or remedy may be instituted, continued or enforced, and any such penalty, forfeiture or punishment may be imposed, as if the law had not been repealed.

TREATIES: ICCPR&P-both signed

Nepal – NC, NP, LM, SJ

The Comprehensive Peace Agreement held between Government of Nepal and Communist Party of Nepal (Maoist), preamble (21 November 2006) states that Nepal is:

> Remaining committed towards Universal Declaration of Human rights, 2048, international humanitarian laws and basic principles and acceptance relating to human rights;. . . .

From http://www.reliefweb.int (unofficial English translation).

Nepal Interim Const. [2007], art. 24(4) (enacted as a result of Comprehensive Peace Agreement, pending enactment of a new permanent constitution):

> No person shall be punished for an act which was not punishable by law when the act was committed, nor shall any person be subjected to a punishment greater than that prescribed by the law in force at the time of the commission of the offence.

This provision is the same as Nepal Const. (1990) art. 14(1).

Nepal Interim Const. [2007] art. 101(2):

> In addition to the courts referred to in clause (1) above, the law may also constitute and establish special types of courts, judicial institutions or tribunals for the purpose of proceeding and hearing special types of cases. Provided that no court, judicial institution or tribunal shall be constituted for the purpose of hearing a particular case.

This provision is similar to Nepal Const (1990) art. 85(2).

TREATIES: ICCPR(P)

Netherlands – NC, NP, LM

Netherlands Const. art. 16:

> Any offense is punishable only if it was a punishable offense under the law at the time it was committed.

Netherlands Const. art. 89(2):

> Any regulations to which penalties are attached can be enacted only on the basis of law. The penalties to be imposed are determined by law.

STATUTE:

Netherlands Penal Code art. 1:

1. No act or omission is punishable which did not constitute a criminal offense under the law at the time it was committed.
2. Where a change has been made in the law subsequent to the time the offense was committed, the provisions of the law most favorable to the accused shall be applicable.

Statute from THE DUTCH PENAL CODE 35 (Louise Rayer & Stafford Wadsworth trans., Fred B. Rothman & Co. 1997).

TREATIES: ECHR, ICCPR(P)

New Zealand – NC, NP, LM

New Zealand Bill of Rights Act 1990 art. 25:

Everyone who is charged with an offence has, in relation to the determination of the charge, the following minimum rights:

. . .

(g) The right, if convicted of an offence in respect of which the penalty has been varied between the commission of the offence and sentencing, to the benefit of the lesser penalty:

. . .

New Zealand Bill of Rights Act 1990 art. 26(1) ("Retroactive penalties and double jeopardy"):

No one shall be liable to conviction of any offence on account of any act or omission which did not constitute an offence by such person under the law of New Zealand at the time it occurred.

TREATIES: ICCPR(P)

Nicaragua – NC, NP, LM

Nicaragua Const. art. 32:

No person is obligated to do what is not mandated by law or barred from doing what is not prohibited by it.

Nicaragua Const. art. 34 (made non-suspendable by art. 186):

Any accused has the right, under equal conditions, to the following minimal guarantees:

. . .

11. Not to be tried or sentenced for an act or omission which, at the time of committing it, had not been previously specified expressly

> or unequivocally in the law as punishment or sanctioned with a penalty not provided by law. Dictating proscriptive laws or applying demeaning penalties or treatment to the accused is prohibited. . . .

Nicaragua Const. art. 38 (made non-suspendable by art. 186):

> The law has no retroactive effect except in penal matters that favor the accused.

Nicaragua Const. art. 160:

> The administration of justice guarantees the principle of legality; it protects and safeguards human rights through the application of law in cases and proceedings falling within its jurisdiction.

TREATIES: ACHR, ICCPR(P)

Niger – NC, NP, LM

Niger Const. art. 15:

> No one shall not be arrested or charged except in pursuance of a law enacted previously to the facts complained.
>
> . . .

Niger Const. art. 16:

> The laws and regulations shall have a retroactive effect only with regards to the rights and benefits that they can confer to citizens.

Niger Const. art. 17:

> . . .
>
> No one shall be condemned for his actions or omissions if, at the time the actions or omissions were committed, they did not constitute an infraction according to the national law. Similarly, it shall not be possible to punish somebody more than the punishment that was applicable on the day the offence was committed.

Niger Const. art. 120:

> The Highest Court of Justice is bound by the definition of crimes and other major offenses and such determination of penalties as are laid down by the laws applicable at the time of the facts concerned by the proceedings.

TREATIES: ACHPR(P), ICCPR(P)

Nigeria – NC, NP, LM, SJ

Nigeria Const. art. 4(8, 9):

> ...
>
> (8) Save as otherwise provided by this constitution, the exercise of legislative powers by the National Assembly or by a House of Assembly shall be subject to the jurisdiction of courts of law and of judicial tribunals established by law, and accordingly, the National Assembly or a House of Assembly shall not enact any law, that ousts or purports to oust the jurisdiction of a court of law or of a judicial tribunal established by law.
>
> (9) Notwithstanding the foregoing provisions of this section, the National Assembly or a House of Assembly shall not, in relation to any criminal offence whatsoever, have power to make any law which shall have retrospective effect.

Nigeria Const. art. 36(8 & 12):

> ...
>
> (8) No person shall be held to be guilty of a criminal offence on account of any act or omission that did not, at the time it took place, constitute such an offence, and no penalty shall be imposed for any criminal offence heavier than the penalty in force at the time the offence was committed.
>
> ...
>
> (12) Subject as otherwise provided by this Constitution, a person shall not be convicted of a criminal offence unless that offence is defined and the penalty therefore is prescribed in a written law; and in this subsection, a written law refers to an Act of the National Assembly or a Law of a State, any subsidiary legislation or instrument under the provisions of a law.

TREATIES: ACHPR(P), ICCPR

Norway – NC, NP, LM

Norway Const. art. 96:

> No one may be convicted except according to law, or be punished except after a court judgment. Interrogation by torture must not take place.

Norway Const. art. 97:

> No law must be given retroactive effect.

TREATIES: ECHR, ICCPR(P)

Oman[9] – NC, NP

Oman Basic Statute of the State art. 21:

> No crime or penalty is cognisable as such except by virtue of a Law, and no punishment except for acts subsequent to coming into force of Law wherein such acts are provided for. Penalty is personal.

Oman Basic Statute of the State art. 75:

> The provisions of the Laws shall only apply to events subsequent to the date of their coming into force. They shall have no effect on events prior to that date unless otherwise stipulated therein. This exception shall not include penal, taxation and financial dues laws.

Pakistan – NC,[10] NP

Proclamation of emergency, declared by Pakistani President General Pervez Musharraf, 3 November 2007, available at http://news.bbc.co.uk/2/hi/south_asia/7077136.stm (visited 3 November 2007), placed the Constitution of Pakistan "in abeyance." The state of emergency was terminated and the constitution restored as of 15 December 2007.

Pakistan Const. art. 12 (Protection Against Retrospective Punishment):

> (1) No law shall authorize the punishment of a person –
> (a) for an act or omission that was not punishable by law at the time of the act or omission; or
> (b) for an offence by a penalty greater than, or of a kind of different from, the penalty prescribed by law for that offence at the time the offence was committed.
> (2) Nothing in clause (1) or in Article 270 shall apply to any law making acts of abrogation or subversion of a Constitution in force in Pakistan at any time since the twenty-third day of March, one thousand nine hundred and fifty-six, an offence.

Pakistan Constitution provision from CCW.

[9] The Basic Statute of the State of Oman, proclaimed by the Sultan, Sultani Decree No. 101/96 (1996) is treated here as serving the function of a Constitution.

[10] *Nullum crimen* and *nulla poena* provisions do not apply "to any law making acts of abrogation or subversion of a Constitution in force in Pakistan at any time since the twenty-third day of March, one thousand nine hundred and fifty-six, an offence." Const. of Pakistan art. 12(2).

Palau – NC, NP

Palau Const. art. IV §6

> . . . No person shall be held criminally liable for an act which was not a legally recognized crime at the time of its commission, nor shall the penalty for an act be increased after the act was committed. . . .

Palestinian Authority[11] – X, NC, NP, PP

Palestine Amended Basic Law art. 15:

> Punishment shall only be imposed upon individuals. Collective punishment is prohibited. Crime and punishment shall only be determined by law. Punishment shall be imposed only by judicial judgement, and shall apply only to actions committed after the promulgation of law.

Translated text from U.S. government Web site http://www.usaid.gov/wbg/misc/Amended_Basic_Law.pdf.

TREATY: ArCHR

Panama – NC, NP, LM

Panama Const. art. 31:

> Only those acts shall be punished which have been declared punishable by a law that predates their perpetration, and is exactly applicable to the act for which charges are brought.

Panama Const. art. 33:

> The following authorities may impose penalties without previous trial in the cases and under the conditions defined by law: 1. The heads of the security forces who may impose penalties on their subordinates in order to suppress insubordination, mutiny, or lack of discipline; 2. Captains of ships or aircraft outside the port or the airport or authorized to suppress insubordination or mutiny, or to maintain order on board, or to detain provisionally any actual or presumed offender.

Panama Const. art. 46:

> Laws have no retroactive effect, except those of public order or social interest when such is expressed. In criminal matters the law favorable to the accused always has preference and retroactivity, even though the judgment may have become final.

TREATIES: ACHR, ICCPR(P)

[11] At time of writing, not yet a state, but gaining international legal personality. Observer at United Nations. West Bank remains under occupation by Israel. Amended Basic Law of Palestine serves purpose of a Constitution. See Appendix C.

Papua New Guinea[12] – NC, NP, LM, SJ

Papua New Guinea Const. art 32(2):

> Every person has the right to freedom based on law, and accordingly has a legal right to do any thing that – (a) does not injure or interfere with the rights and freedoms of others; and (b) is not prohibited by law, And no person – (c) is obliged to do anything that is not required by law; and (d) may be prevented from doing anything that complies with the provisions of paragraphs (a) and (b).

Papua New Guinea Const. art. 37(2, 7, 21 & 22):

> ...
>
> (2) Except, subject to any Act of the Parliament to the contrary, in the case of the offence commonly known as contempt of court, nobody may be convicted of an offence that is not defined by, and the penalty for which is not prescribed by, a written law.
>
> ...
>
> (7) No person shall be convicted of an offence on account of any act that did not, at the time when it took place, constitute an offence, and no penalty shall be imposed for an offence that is more severe in degree or description than the maximum penalty that might have been imposed for the offence at the time when it was committed.
>
> ...
>
> (21) Nothing in this section –
> (a) derogates Division III.4 (*principles of natural justice*); or
> (b) affects the powers and procedures of village courts.
>
> (22) Notwithstanding Subsection 21(*b*) the powers and procedures of village courts shall be exercised in accordance with the principles of natural justice.

Papua New Guinea Const. art. 172(2), allows establishment of village courts "intended to deal with matters primarily by reference to custom or in accordance with customary procedures or both."

Papua New Guinea Const. art. 159:

> (1) Subject to Subsection (3), nothing in this Constitution prevents an Organic Law or a statute from conferring judicial authority on a person or body outside the National Judicial System, or the establishment by or in accordance with law, or by consent of the parties, of arbitral or conciliatory tribunals, whether ad hoc or other, outside the National Judicial System.

[12] Constitutional *nullum crimen nulla poena praevia lege scripta* provision does not apply to contempt of court, and may not apply in village courts applying traditional law. However, statutory provisions appear to have rejected any right of village courts to create retroactive crimes and punishments.

(2) Nothing in, or done in accordance with, Subsection (1) affects the operation of Section 155(4) or (5) (the *National Judicial System*)

(3) No person or body outside the National Judicial System has, or may be given, power to impose a sentence of death or imprisonment, or to impose any other penalty as for a criminal offence, but nothing in this subsection prevents –

  (a) the imposition, in accordance with law, of disciplinary detention or any other disciplinary punishment (other than death) by a disciplinary authority of a disciplined force on persons subject to the disciplinary law of the force; or

  (b) the imposition, in accordance with law, of disciplinary punishments (other than death or detention) on members of other State or provincial services; or

  (c) the imposition of reasonable penalties (other than death or detention) by an association on its members for breaches of its rules. . . .

STATUTES:

Papua New Guinea Criminal Code Act 1974 art. 11 (Effect of Changes in Law):

(1) A person cannot be punished for doing or omitting to do an act unless –

  (a) the act or omission constituted an offence under the law in force when it occurred; and

  (b) doing or omitting to do the act under the same circumstances would constitute an offence under the law in force at the time when he is charged with the offence.

(2) If the law in force when the act or omission occurred differs from that in force at the time of the conviction, the offender cannot be punished to any greater extent than was authorized by the former law, or to any greater extent than is authorized by the latter law.

The potential power of Village Courts to define new crimes and punishments by reference to customary criminal law under the Constitution appears to have been rejected by statute and regulation:

Papua New Guinea Village Courts Act 1989 pt. V (Jurisdiction), div. 3 (General Criminal Jurisdiction), arts. 41-42:

41. EXTENT OF JURISDICTION.

A Village Court has criminal jurisdiction –

  (a) in respect of offences that are prescribed offences for the purposes of this section; and

(b) in respect of contravention of, or failure to comply with –
 (i) a Local-level Government law; or
 (ii) a law made by or under an Act of a Provincial Legislature, if the rule or law, as the case may be, provides that an offence against it may be dealt with by a Village Court; and
(c) in accordance with Division 5 and Sections 29, 40 and 104.

42. PENALTIES.

(1) Subject to Subsections (2), in the exercise of the jurisdiction referred to in Section 41, a Village Court may –
 (a) in respect of Section 41(a) order an offender to pay, in cash or in goods, a fine not exceeding K200.00; or
 (b) in respect of Section 41(b) order an offender to pay, in cash or in goods, a fine not exceeding –
  (i) K200.00; or
  (ii) the amount fixed in the rule or in the law, whichever is the lesser.
(2) A Village Court may, instead of imposing a penalty under Subsection (1), order an offender to perform, for community purposes, specified work or work of a specified kind, for a period or periods not exceeding–
 (a) eight hours in any one day; and
 (b) six days in any one week; and
 (c) a total period of six months, in such manner, at such times and subject to such conditions as to supervision or otherwise as are specified in the order.

Papua New Guinea Village Court Regulation 1974 (as amended through 25 November 2006), art. 3:

3. PRESCRIBED OFFENCES.

The following are prescribed offences for the purposes of Section 22(a) of the Act: –

(a) taking or keeping, without the consent of the owner, the property of another to a value not exceeding K100.00;
(b) striking another person without reasonable cause;
(c) using insulting words or conduct;
(d) using threatening words or conduct;
(e) using offensive words or conduct;
(f) intentional damage to trees, plants or crops belonging to another person;
(g) intentional damage to trees, plants or crops belonging to the defendant and another person;

(h) intentional damage to any other property belonging to another person;
(i) making a false statement concerning another person that offends or upsets him;
(j) spreading false reports that are liable to cause alarm, fear or discontent in the village community;
(k) conduct that disturbs the peace, quiet and good order of the village, or of a resident of the village;
(l) drunkenness in the Village Court area;
(m) carrying weapons so as to cause alarm to others in the Village Court area;
(n) failure to perform customary duties or to meet customary obligations after having been informed of them by a Village Magistrate;
(o) failure to comply with the direction of a Village Magistrate with regard to hygiene or cleanliness within a Village Court area;
(p) sorcery, including –
  (i) practising or pretending to practise sorcery; or
  (ii) threatening any person with sorcery practised by another; or
  (iii) procuring or attempting to procure a person to practise or pretend to practise, or to assist in, sorcery; or
  (iv) the possession of implements or charms used in practising sorcery; or
  (v) paying or offering to pay a person to perform acts of sorcery.

Papua New Guinea statutes and regulations from Pacific Islands Legal Information Institute of the University of the South Pacific School of Law Web site http://www.paclii.org/pg/legis/consol_act/.

Note that failure to perform customary duties or meet customary obligations is only criminal "after having been informed of them by a Village Magistrate," Village Courts Regulation, art. 3(n) – i.e., after notice. The reference in the Regulation to Article 22 of the Village Courts Act appears to refer to the number of an earlier version of the Act than the one quoted here.

Paraguay – NC, NP, LM, SJ

Paraguay Const. art. 9:

> Everyone has the right to have his freedom and security protected.
>
> No one may be forced to do anything that is not mandated by law, and no one may be prevented from doing something that is not prohibited by law.

Paraguay Const. art. 14:

> No law will be retroactive, except those which benefit a defendant or convict.

Paraguay Const. art. 17:

> In a criminal process or in any other process in which a punishment or sanction could be handed down, everyone has the right:
>
> . . .
>
> (3) To be sentenced only at the end of a trial based on a law that was already enforced when the criminal offense was committed, and not to be tried by special tribunals;
>
> . . . .

TREATIES: ACHR, ICCPR(P)

Peru – NC, NP, LM, SJ

Peru Const. art. 2(24)(a, d):

> Every person has the right:
>
> . . .
>
> 24. To personal freedom and security. Consequently,
>
> . . .
>
> a. No one is obliged to do what the law does not mandate or be prevented from doing what the law does not prohibit.
>
> . . .
>
> d. No one may be tried or sentenced for an act or omission which, when committed, had not previously been prohibited by the law in express and unequivocal manner as a punishable offense. Nor may one be sanctioned by penalties not provided by law.
>
> . . .

Peru Const. art. 103:

> Special laws may be passed because they are required by the nature of things (*naturaleza de las cosas*) but not because of the differences between persons. With its entry into force, the law applies to the consequences of existing legal relationships and situations and does not have retroactive legal force or effects except in criminal law when it favors the accused. . . .

Peru Const. art. 139(3):

> The following are principles and rights of the judicial function:
>
> . . .

3. The observance of due process and judicial oversight.

No person may be turned away from a jurisdiction predetermined by the law, or be subjected to a procedure different from those previously established, or adjudicated by the [state of] exception judicial organs or by special commissions created for that purpose no matter how denominated.

. . .

TREATIES: ACHR, ICCPR(P)

Philippines – NC, NP, LM, SJ

Philippines Const. art. III(22):

> No *Ex Post Facto* Law or Bill of Attainder shall be enacted.

Philippines Const. art. VII(18):

> . . . A state of martial law does not suspend the operation of the Constitution, nor supplant the functioning of the civil courts or legislative assemblies, nor authorize the conferment of jurisdiction on military courts and agencies over civilians where civil courts are able to function, nor automatically suspend the privilege of the writ. . . .

TREATIES: ICCPR(P)

Poland – NC, NP, LM, SJ

Poland Const. art. 42(1) (made non-limitable by art. 233(1)):

> To criminal responsibility can be subjected only one who has committed an act prohibited by a law in force at the moment of its commission, and which is subject to a penalty. This principle shall not prevent punishment of any at which, at the moment of its commission, constituted an offense within the meaning of international law.

Poland Const. art. 175(2):

> Extraordinary courts or summary procedures may be established only during a time of war.

Poland Const. art. 228(6):

> During a period of introduction of extraordinary measures, the following shall not be subject to change: the Constitution, the Laws on Elections to the Sejm, the Senate and organs of territorial self-governments, the Law on Elections to the Presidency, as well as laws on extraordinary measures.

TREATIES: ECHR, ICCPR(P)

Portugal – NC, NP, LM, SJ

Portugal Const. art. 7(7):

> Portugal may, in view of the realization of an international justice that promotes respect for the rights of the human person, and of peoples, accept the jurisdiction of the International Criminal Court (*Tribunal Penal Internacional*), under conditions of complementarity and also under the terms established in the Treaty of Rome.

Portugal Const. art. 8:

> (1) The norms and principles of general or customary international law are an integral part of Portuguese law.
> (2) The rules provided for in international conventions that have been duly ratified or approved, apply in internal law, after their official publication, so long as they remain internationally binding with respect to the Portuguese State.
> (3) Rules made by the competent organs of international organizations to which Portugal belongs apply directly in internal law to the extent that the constitutive treaties provide.
> (4) The provisions of the treaties governing the European Union and the rules adopted by its institutions in the exercise of their respective powers are applicable in the domestic legal order in the terms defined by the law of the Union, with respect for the fundamental principles of a democratic state based on the rule of the law.

Portugal Const. art. 29(1 & 4) (made non-derogable by declaration of state of emergency or state of siege by art. 19(6)):

> (1) No one can be convicted under the criminal law except for an act or omission made punishable under existing law; and no one can be subjected to a security measure, except for reasons specified under existing law.
> ...
> (4) No one maybe subjected to a sentence or security measure that is more severe than those applicable at the time that the act was committed or the preparations for its commission were made. Criminal laws that are favorable to the offender apply retroactively.
> ...

Portugal Const. art. 205(3):

> The law regulates the terms for the enforcement of court decisions affecting other authorities, and determines the penalties.

Portugal Const. art. 209(4):

> Without prejudice to provisions concerning military tribunals, courts with exclusive jurisdiction to try specific categories of offense shall not be established.

TREATIES; ECHR, ICCPR(P)

Qatar – NC, NP, SJ, PP

Qatar Const. art. 40:

> No crime and no punishment except according to the law. No punishment except on acts occurring subsequent to its implementation. Punishment is personal.
>
> Laws are not applicable except on what happens subsequent to the date of putting them into force, and they have no impact on what occurs retroactively. However, in non-criminal articles, it may be otherwise specified by the majority of two-thirds (2/3) of the members of the Advisory Council.

Qatar Const. art. 132:

> The law regulates the courts with its different types and levels and defines their functions and jurisdictions. The jurisdiction of Military Courts is restricted, except in the case of martial law, to military crimes committed by members of the Armed Forces and Security Forces, within the limits specified by the law.

Romania – NC, NP, LM, SJ

Romania Const. art. 15(2):

> The law produces legal effects only for the future, with the exception of more favorable criminal or administrative laws.

Romania Const. art. 23(12):

> Punishment can be imposed or executed only on a legal basis and in the conditions defined by the law.

Romania Const. art. 126(5):

> It is prohibited to set up courts with special jurisdiction. Courts specialized in certain areas of law may be set up by an organic law which may provide, as the case may be, for the participation of persons from outside the judiciary.

Romania Const. art. 115(6):

> Emergency ordinances may not be adopted in the field of constitutional laws; they may not affect the status of fundamental institutions of the state, the rights, freedoms and duties stipulated in the Constitution, and the voting rights, and may not envisage measures for the forcible transfer of certain assets into public property.

TREATIES: ECHR, ICCPR(P)

Russia – NC, NP, LM, SJ

Russia Const. art. 15(3):

> The laws must be officially published. Unpublished laws shall not be applied. Any normative legal acts concerning human and civil rights, freedoms and obligations shall not be applied unless they have been officially published for the information of the general public.

Russia Const. art. 54 (made non-derogable by art. 56(3)):

> (1) A law, which introduces or increases liability, shall not have retroactive force.
> (2) Nobody shall be liable for an action which was not regarded as a crime when it was committed. If, after an offense has been committed, the extent of liability for it is lifted or mitigated, the new law shall be applied.

Russia Const. art. 118(3):

> The judicial system in the Russian Federation shall be established by the Constitution of the Russian Federation and federal constitutional law. The creation of extraordinary courts shall not be permitted.

TREATIES: ECHR, ICCPR(P)

Rwanda – NC, NP, LM, SJ

Rwanda Const., preamble ¶ 9:

> 9. Reaffirming our adherence to the principles of human rights enshrined in the United Nations Charter of June 26, 1945, the Convention on the Prevention and Punishment of the Crime of Genocide of December 9, 1948, the Universal Declaration of Human Rights of December 10, 1948, the International Convention on the Elimination of All Forms of Racial Discrimination of December 21, 1965, the International Covenant on Economic, Social and Cultural Rights of December 19, 1966, the International Covenant on Civil and Political Rights of December 19, 1966, the Convention on the

Elimination of All Forms of Discrimination Against Women of May 1, 1980, the African Charter of Human and Peoples' Rights of June 27, 1981 and the Convention on the Rights of the Child of November 20, 1989;

. . . .

Rwanda Const. art. 18 (made non-violable by art. 137):

. . .

No one shall be subjected to prosecution, arrest, detention or punishment on account of any act or omission which did not constitute a crime under the law in force at the time it was committed.

. . .

Rwanda Const. art. 20 (made non-violable by art. 137):

Nobody shall be punished for acts or omissions that did not constitute an offense under national or international law at the time of commission.

Neither shall any person be punished with a penalty which is heavier than the one that was applicable under the law at the time when the offense was committed.

Rwanda Const. art. 137:

. . . A declaration of a state of siege or of a state of emergency (urgence) cannot under any circumstances violate the right to life and physical integrity of the person, the rights accorded to people by law in relation to their status, capacity and nationality, the principle of non-retroactivity of criminal law, the right to legal defense and freedom of conscience and religion. . . .

Rwanda Const. art. 143:

. . .

However, no exceptional courts may be created.

. . .

Rwanda Const. art. 152:

There is hereby established Gacaca Courts charged with the trial and judgment of cases against persons accused of the crime of genocide and crimes against humanity which were committed between October 1, 1990 and December 31, 1994 with the exception of cases whose competence is vested in other courts.

An organic law determines the organization, competence and functioning of these jurisdictions.

. . .

TREATIES: ACHPR(P), ICCPR

Sahrawi Arab Democratic Republic (Western Sahara) – X

Sahrawi Arab Democratic Republic [Western Sahara] Const. art. 26:

> Article 26 : La liberté individuelle est garantie. Nul ne peut être privé de l'exercice de sa liberté que conformément à la loi.
>
> . . .
>
> Nul ne peut être arrêté ou détenu que conformément à la loi.
>
> Pas de crime ni de sanction hors du cadre de la loi.
>
> . . .

Text of Constitution in French from http://www.arso.org/03-const.99.htm. The Sahrawi Arab Democratic Republic is recognized by a substantial minority of states. It is not a member of the United Nations. It has been allowed to become part of the regime of the ACHPR.

TREATY: ACHPR

St. Kitts and Nevis – NC, NP

St. Kitts & Nevis Const. art. 10(4):

> A person shall not be held to be guilty of a criminal offence on account of any act or omission that did not, at the time it took place, constitute such an offence, and no penalty shall be imposed for any criminal offence that is severer in degree or description than the maximum penalty that might have been imposed for that offence at the time when it was committed.

St. Lucia – NC, NP

St. Lucia Const. art. 8(4):

> A person shall not be held to be guilty of a criminal offence on account of any act or omission that did not, at the time it took place, constitute such an offence, and no penalty shall be imposed for any criminal offence that is severer in degree or description than the maximum penalty that might have been imposed for that offence at the time when it was committed.

St. Vincent and the Grenadines – NC, NP, LM

St. Vincent & the Grenadines Const. art. 8(4):

> A person shall not be held to be guilty of a criminal offence on account of any act or omission that did not, at the time it took place, constitute such an offence, and no penalty shall be imposed for any criminal offence that is severer in degree or description than the maximum penalty that might have been imposed for that offence at the time when it was committed.

TREATIES: ICCPR(P)

Samoa – NC, NP

Samoa Const. art. 10(1 & 2):

> (1) No person shall be convicted of an offence other than an offence defined by law.
> (2) No person shall be held guilty of any offence on account of any act or omission which did not constitute an offence at the time when it was committed; nor shall a heavier penalty be imposed than the one that was applicable at the time that the offence was committed.

San Marino – NC, NP, LM

TREATIES: ECHR, ICCPR(P)

São Tomé and Príncipe – NC, NP, LM, SJ

São Tomé & Príncipe Const. art. 7 (Justice and Legality):

> The State of democratic Law implies the safeguard of justice and legality as fundamental values of collective life.

São Tomé & Príncipe Const. art. 36:

> 1. No one may be sentenced criminally except by virtue of prior law which declares punishable the action or omission nor suffer security measures whose purposes are not fixed in prior law.
> 2. However, penal laws are applied retroactively when their content is more favorable to the accused or to the sentenced.

São Tomé & Príncipe Const. art. 39(7):

> No case may be removed from the court whose competence has been established in prior law.

São Tomé & Príncipe Const. art. 110:

> 1. The existence is prohibited of courts meant exclusively for adjudication of certain categories of crimes.
> 2. Excepting themselves from the provisions of the prior number are the military courts, with whom resides the judgment of essentially military crimes defined by law.

TREATIES: ACHPR, ICCPR&P-both signed

Saudi Arabia – NC, NP

Saudi Arabia Basic System of the Consultative Council art. 1, Decree A/90, 1 March 1992, confirms, by decree of the King, the Holy Quran and the Prophet's Sunna as the Constitution of Saudi Arabia.

Saudi Arabia Basic System of the Consultative Council art. 36:

> The state provides security for all its citizens and all residents within its territory and no one shall be arrested, imprisoned, or have their actions restricted except in cases specified by statutes.

Saudi Arabia Basic System of the Consultative Council art. 38:

> Penalties shall be personal and there shall be no crime or penalty except in accordance with the Shari'ah or organizational law. There shall be no punishment except for acts committed subsequent to the coming into force of the organizational law.

Text translation from international constitutional law Web site at http://www.oefre.unibe.ch/law/icl/sa00000_.html.

Title of Document as stated in CCW.

TREATY: ArCHR-signed[13]

Senegal – NC, NP, LM

Senegal Const. art. 9:

> All attacks on freedoms, all interference with the exercise of freedom are punished by law. Nobody can be sentenced except by virtue of a law which entered into force before the act was committed. . . .

TREATIES: ACHPR(P), ICCPR(P)

Serbia – NC, NP, LM

Serbia Const. art. 34 (made non-derogable by Serbia Const. art. 202):

> Legal certainty in criminal law
>
> No person may be held guilty for any act which did not constitute a criminal offense under law or any other regulation based on the law at the time when it was committed, nor shall a penalty be imposed which was not prescribed for this act.
>
> The penalties shall be determined pursuant to a regulation in force at the time when the act was committed, save when subsequent regulation is more lenient for the perpetrator. Criminal offenses and penalties shall be laid down by the law.
>
> . . .

[13] Saudi Arabia has signed the Revised ArCHR, and has taken internal steps needed to ratify it. See *Shura Council ratifies Arab Charter on Human Rights*, at http://www.saudiembassy.net/2008News/News/RigDetail.asp?cIndex=7698 (Web site of the Royal Embassy of Saudi Arabia in the U.S., 24 February 2008).

Serbia Const. art. 196:

> Laws and all other general acts shall be published prior to coming into force.
>
> . . .

Serbia Const. art. 197:

> Laws and other general acts may not have a retroactive effect.
>
> Exceptionally, only some of the law provisions may have a retroactive effect, if so required by general public interest as established in the procedure of adopting the Law.
>
> A provision of the Penal Code may have a retroactive effect only if it shall be more favorable for the perpetrator.
>
> From Constitution of Serbia following 2006 separation from Montenegro.

TREATIES: ECHR, ICCPR

Seychelles – NC, NP,[14] LM

Seychelles Const. art. 19(4) (made non-derogable during public emergency by art. 43):

> Except for the offence of genocide or an offence against humanity, a person shall not be held to be guilty of an offence on account of any act or omission that did not, at the time it took place, constitute an offence, and a penalty shall not be imposed for any offence that is more severe in degree or description than the maximum penalty that might have been imposed for the offence at the time when it was committed.

Seychelles Const. art. 48:

> This chapter shall be interpreted in such a way so as not to be inconsistent with any international obligations of Seychelles relating to human rights and freedoms and a court shall, when interpreting the provision of this Chapter, take judicial notice of –
>
> (a) the international instruments containing these obligations;
> (b) the reports and expression of views of bodies administering or enforcing these instruments;

[14] Constitutional text excepts genocide and crimes against humanity from operation of *nullum crimen* and *nulla poena*. However, text shall be interpreted in accordance with treaty obligations relating to human rights and freedoms.

(c) the reports, decisions or opinions of international and regional institutions administering or enforcing Conventions on human rights and freedoms;
(d) the Constitutions of other democratic States or nations and decisions of the courts of the States or nations in respect of their Constitutions.

TREATIES: ACHPR(P-signed), ICCPR(P)

Sierra Leone – NC, NP, LM

Sierra Leone Const. art. 23(7, 8 & 10):

...

(7) No person shall be held to be guilty of a criminal offence on account of any act or omission which did not, at the time it took place, constitute such an offence.
(8) No penalty shall be imposed for any criminal offence which is severer in degree or description than the maximum penalty which might have been imposed for that offence at the time when it was committed.

...

(10) Nothing contained in or done under the authority of any law shall be held to be inconsistent with or in contravention of any provisions of this section, other than subsections (7) and (8), to the extent that the law in question authorises the taking during a period of public emergency of measures that are reasonably justifiable for the purpose of dealing with the situation that exists before or during that period of public emergency.

...

TREATIES: ACHPR(P-signed), ICCPR(P)

Singapore – NC,[15] NP

Singapore Const. art. 11(1):

No person shall be punished for an act or omission which was not punishable by law when it was done or made, and no person shall suffer greater punishment for an offence than was prescribed by law at the time it was committed.

[15] Constitutional text excepts several security and other measures from operation of *nullum crimen* and *nulla poena*, including acts by a "substantial body of persons, whether inside or outside Singapore... tending to excite disaffection against the President or the Government."

Singapore Const. art. 149(1):

> If an Act recites that action has been taken or threatened by any substantial body of persons, whether inside or outside Singapore –
>
> (a) to cause, or to cause a substantial number of citizens to fear, organised violence against persons or property;
> (b) to excite disaffection against the President or the Government;
> (c) to promote feelings of ill-will and hostility between different races or other classes of the population likely to cause violence;
> (d) to procure the alteration, otherwise than by lawful means, of anything by law established; or
> (e) which is prejudicial to the security of Singapore, any provision of that law designed to stop or prevent that action or any amendment to that law or any provision in any law enacted under clause (3) is valid notwithstanding that it is inconsistent with Article 9, 11, 12, 13 or 14, or would, apart from this Article, be outside the legislative power of Parliament.

TREATY: CRC only

Slovakia – NC, NP, LM, SJ

Slovakia Const. art. 48(1):

> No one may be taken out of the competence of his legal judge. The jurisdiction of courts shall be defined by law.

Slovakia Const. art. 49:

> The law shall define all offenses, the punishment or the measure restricting personal or property rights to be imposed on the offender in particular cases.

Slovakia Const. art. 50(6):

> Any criminal act shall be judged by, and punished under, the law effective at the time of the act. The law passed after the commission of the offense shall apply only if the law is more favorable to the offender.

TREATIES: ECHR, ICCPR(P)

Slovenia – NC, NP, LM

Slovenia Const. art. 28:

> No one may be punished for an act which had not been declared a criminal offence under law, or for which a penalty had not been prescribed, at the

> time the act was performed. Acts that are criminal shall be established and the resulting penalties pronounced according to the law that was in force at the time the act was performed, save where a more recent law adopted is more lenient on the offender.

Slovenia Const. art. 153:

> ...
>
> Laws must be in conformity with generally accepted principles of international law and with valid treaties ratified by the State Assembly, whereas regulations and other general legal acts must also be in conformity with other ratified treaties.
>
> ...

Slovenia Const. art. 155 (Prohibition of Retroactive Effect of Legal Acts):

> Laws and other regulations and general legal acts cannot have retroactive effect. Only a law may establish that certain of its provisions have retroactive effect, if this is required in the public interest and provided that no acquired rights are infringed thereby.

TREATIES: ECHR, ICCPR(P)

Solomon Islands – NC, NP

Solomon Is. Const. art. 10(4):

> No person shall be held to be guilty of a criminal offence on account of any act or omission that did not, at the time it took place, constitute such an offence, and no penalty shall be imposed for any criminal offence that is severer in degree or description than the maximum penalty that might have been imposed for that offence at the time when it was committed.

Somalia – NC, NP, LM

Somalia Const. art. 34:

> No person may be punished for an act which was not an offence under the law at the time when it was committed, nor may a punishment be imposed other than the one prescribed by the law enforced at the time such offence was committed.
>
> There has been no effective national government in Somalia for some years.

TREATIES: ACHPR(P-signed), ICCPR(P)

Somaliland – X, PP

A portion of Somalia that has claimed independence since 1991, and that has had a more stable government than Somalia since that time. Not generally recognized as an independent state.

Somaliland Revised Const. art. 26:

> 1. Crimes and [*their*] punishment shall be laid down by the law, and no punishment shall be administered in a manner which is contrary to the law.
> 2. The liability for the punishment of any crime shall be confined to the offender only.
> 3. An accused person is innocent until proven guilty in a court.

Translation by Ibrahim Hashi Jama from private Web site http://www.somalilandforum.com/somaliland/constitution/revised_constitution.htm.

South Africa – NC, NP, LM

South Africa Const. art. 35(3)(l & n):

> Every accused person has a right to a fair trial, which includes the right –
>
> . . .
>
> (l) not to be convicted for an act or omission that was not an offence under either national or international law at the time it was committed or omitted;
>
> . . .
>
> (n) to the benefit of the least severe of the prescribed punishments if the prescribed punishment for the offence has been changed between the time that the offence was committed and the time of sentencing;
>
> . . . .

TREATIES: ACHPR(P). ICCPR(P)

Spain – NC, NP, LM

Spain Const. art. 9(3):

> The Constitution guarantees the principle of legality, the hierarchy of legal provisions, the publicity of legal statutes, the non-retroactivity of punitive provisions that are not favourable to or restrictive of individual rights [*sic*[16]], the certainty that the rule of law shall prevail, the accountability of public authorities, and the prohibition of arbitrary action of public authorities.

[16] Phrase might be rendered "are not favorable to or *are* restrictive of."

Spain Const. art. 25(1):

> No one may be convicted or sentenced for actions or omissions which, when committed, did not constitute a criminal offense, misdemeanour or administrative offense under the law then in force.

TREATIES: ECHR, ICCPR(P)

Sri Lanka – NC,[17] NP

Sri Lanka Const. art. 13(Freedom from arbitrary arrest, detention and punishment, and prohibition of retroactive penal legislation)(6):

> No person shall be held guilty of an offense on account of any act or omission which did not, at the time of such act or omission, constitute such an offense, and no penalty shall be imposed for any offense more severe than the penalty in force at the time such offense was committed.
>
> Nothing in this Article shall prejudice the trial and punishment of any person for any act or omission which, at the time when it was committed, was criminal according to the general principles of law recognized by the community of nations.
>
> It shall not be a contravention of this Article to require the imposition of a minimum penalty for an offense provided that such penalty does not exceed the maximum penalty prescribed for such offense at the time such offense was committed.

The Sri Lanka Supreme Court has held that certain crimes set forth in international conventions to protect aircraft were crimes recognized by "general principles of law recognized by the community of nations." See Ekanayake v. The Attorney-General, C.A. 132/84 (Sri Lanka Ct. of App., 28 May 1986), aff'd, S.C. App. No. 68/86 (Sri Lanka S.Ct., 9 December 1987) [both available through official Sri Lanka government Web site, http://www.lawnet.lk], discussed without citation in RICHARD CLAYTON, HUGH TOMLINSON, ET AL., THE LAW OF HUMAN RIGHTS ¶ 11.511–12, at p. 769 (Oxford Univ. Press 2000).

TREATY: ICCPR(P)

Sudan – NC, NP, LM

Sudan Interim National Const. art. 34(4):

> No person shall be charged of any act or omission which did not constitute an offence at the time of its commission.

[17] Allows criminalization of act that was at the time "criminal according to the general principles of law recognized by the community of nations."

TREATIES: ACHPR(P-signed), ICCPR

Suriname – NC, NP, LM, SJ

Suriname Const. art. 11:

> No person may be withdrawn against his own will from the judge whom the law assigns to him.

Suriname Const. art. 131(2):

> No act shall be punishable other than by virtue of a previously determined legal rule.

TREATIES: ACHR, ICCPR(P)

Swaziland – NC, NP, LM

Swaziland Const. Act §21(5, 6) (made non-derogable by §38(b)):

> (5) A person shall not be charged with or held to be guilty of a criminal offence on account of any act or omission that did not, at the time the act or omission took place, constitute an offence.
> (6) A penalty shall not be imposed for any criminal offence that is severer in degree or description than the maximum penalty that might have been imposed for that offence at the time when it was committed.

TREATIES: ACHPR(P-signed), ICCPR

Sweden – NC, NP, LM, SJ

Sweden Instrument of Government, ch. 2, art. 10:

> No penalty or penal sanction may be imposed in respect of an act which was not subject to a penal sanction at the time it was committed. Nor may any penal sanction be imposed which is more severe than that which was in force when the act was committed. The provisions thus laid down with respect to penal sanctions apply in like manner to forfeiture and other special legal effects attaching to a criminal act.
>
> No taxes or charges due the State may be exacted except inasmuch as this follows from provisions which were in force when the circumstance arose which occasioned the liability for the tax or charge. Should the Riksdag find that special reasons so warrant, it may however provide under an act of law that taxes or charges due the State shall be exacted even although no such act had entered into force when the aforementioned circumstance arose, provided the Government, or a committee of the Riksdag, had submitted a proposal to this effect to the Riksdag at the time concerned. A written communication from the Government to the Riksdag announcing

the forthcoming introduction of such a proposal shall be equated with a formal proposal. The Riksdag may furthermore prescribe that exceptions shall be made to the provisions of sentence one if it considers this is warranted on special grounds connected with war, the danger of war, or grave economic crisis.

Sweden Instrument of Government, ch. 2, art. 11:

No court of law shall be established on account of an act already committed, or for a particular dispute or otherwise for a particular case.

. . .

Sweden Instrument of Government, ch. 2, art. 22:

A foreign national within the Realm is equated with a Swedish citizen in respect of:

. . .

5. protection against retroactive penal sanctions and other retroactive legal effects of criminal acts, and against retroactive taxes or charges due the State (Article 10);
6. protection against the establishment of a court of law for a particular case (Article 11, paragraph one);

. . .

TREATIES: ECHR, ICCPR(P)

Switzerland – NC, NP, LM, SJ

Switzerland Constitution [Constitution fédérale de la Confédération Suisse] [aBV] [] art. 30(1):

Every person whose case must be judged in judicial procedure has the right to have this done by a court established by law, has jurisdiction, is independent and impartial. Exceptional courts are prohibited.

STATUTE:

Code pénal Suisse arts. 1, 2:

Art. 1

Nul ne peut être puni s'il n'a commis un acte expressément réprimé par la loi.

Art. 2

1 Sera jugée d'après le présent code toute personne qui aura commis un crime ou un délit après l'entrée en vigueur de ce code.

2 Le présent code est aussi applicable aux crimes et aux délits commis avant la date de son entrée en vigueur, si l'auteur n'est mis en jugement qu'après cette date et si le présent code lui est plus favorable que la loi en vigueur au moment de l'infraction.

Statute text (French version) from OSCE Office of Democratic Institutions and Human Rights Web site, http://www.legislationline.org/upload/legislations/09/89/825a0444c0f270da1c21e01ae284.pdf. Note that this is the penal code of the Swiss Federation. The statutes of all of the Swiss cantons have not been searched.

TREATIES: ECHR, ICCPR

Syria – NC, NP, LM

Syria Const. art. 29:

> What constitutes a crime or penalty can only be determined by law.

Syria Const. art. 30:

> Laws are binding only following the date of their enactment and cannot be retroactive. In other than penal cases, the contrary may be stipulated.

TREATIES: ArCHR, ICCPR

Taiwan: *see China, Republic of*

Tajikistan – NC, NP, LM

Tajikistan Const. art. 20.

> . . .
>
> No one may be held responsible after the expiration of the criminal prosecution period as well for actions that were not considered a crime at the time they were committed. . . .
>
> A law adopted after a person has committed an illegal act that increases the punishment for it does not have retroactive force. If after committing of an illegal act the responsibility [for that act] is repealed or reduced, the new law applies.
>
> . . .

TREATY: ICCPR(P)

Tanzania – NC, NP, LM

Tanzania Const. art. 13(6):

> To ensure equality before the law, the state authority shall make procedures which are appropriate or which take into account the following principles, namely:
>
> . . .
>
> (c) no person shall be punished for any act which at the time of its commission was not an offence under the law, and also no penalty shall be imposed which is heavier than the penalty in force at the time the offence was committed;
>
> . . .

TREATIES: ACHPR(P), ICCPR

Thailand – NC, NP, LM, SJ

Thailand Const. §39:

> A person shall not be punished except for having committed an act or acts which the law at the time of commission forbade and for which the law prescribed punishment. The punishment shall not exceed what was allowed by the law in force at the time of commission of such act.

Thailand Const. §197:

> . . .
>
> A judge is free and independent to adjudicate correctly, justly, and quickly in accordance with the Constitution and law.

Thailand Const. §198:

> All Courts can only be established by Acts.
>
> A new Court for the trial and adjudication of any particular case or a case of any particular charge in place of an ordinary Court existing under the law and having jurisdiction over such case shall not be established.
>
> A law is prohibited if it would have the effect of changing or amending the law on the organization of Courts or on judicial procedure for the purpose of its application to a particular case.

Unofficial English translation by IFES Thailand and the Political Section and Public Diplomacy Office of the United States Embassy in Bangkok at http://www.ect.go.th/english/files/forum/Constitution2007byIFES.pdf, Web site of the Election Commission of Thailand (last visited 21 November 2007). This Constitution was approved by plebiscite 19 August 2007 and formally approved by the king on 24 August 2007. These provisions are similar to provisions in the now superseded Thailand Const. (1997) §§32, 234, 235.

TREATY: ICCPR

Timor-Leste: *see East Timor*

Togo – NC, NP, LM, PP

Togo Const. art. 19:

> ...
>
> No one may be sentenced for acts that did not constitute a breach of the law at the moment when they were committed.
>
> Besides the cases provided by the law, no one may be prosecuted or sentenced for acts reproached to others.
>
> ...

Togo Const. art. 20:

> No one shall be subjected to measures of control or security apart from cases envisaged by the law.

Togo Const. art. 129:

> The High Court of Justice is bound by the definition of crimes and offenses as well as by the determination of their penalties as provided by the criminal laws, which were applicable when the acts were committed.
>
> ...

TREATIES: ACHPR(P), ICCPR(P)

Tonga – NC, NP

Tonga Const. art. 20:

> It shall not be lawful to enact any retrospective laws in so far as they may curtail or take away or affect rights or privileges existing at the time of the passing of such laws.

Trinidad and Tobago – NC, NP, LM

Trinidad & Tobago Const. art. 5:

> (1) Except as is otherwise expressly provided in this Chapter and in section 54, no law may abrogate, abridge or infringe or authorise the abrogation, abridgement or infringement of any of the rights and freedoms hereinbefore recognised and declared.

(2) Without prejudice to subsection (1), but subject to this Chapter and to section 54, Parliament may not-
  (a) authorise or effect the arbitrary detention, imprisonment or exile of any person;
  (b) impose or authorise the imposition of cruel and unusual treatment or punishment;
  (c) deprive a person who has been arrested or detained-
    (i) of the right to be informed promptly and with sufficient particularity of the reason for his arrest or detention;
    (ii) of the right to retain and instruct without delay a legal adviser of his own choice and to hold communication with him;
    (iii) of the right to be brought promptly before an appropriate judicial authority;
    (iv) of the remedy by way of habeas corpus for the determination of the validity of his detention and for his release if the detention is not lawful;
  (d) authorise a court, or tribunal, commission, board or other authority to compel a person to give evidence unless he is afforded protection against self-incrimination and, where necessary to ensure such protection, the right to legal representation;
  (e) deprive a person of the right to a fair hearing in accordance with the principles of fundamental justice for the determination of his rights and obligations;
  (f) deprive a person charged with a criminal offense of the right-
    (i) to be presumed innocent until proved guilty according to law, but this shall not invalidate a law by reason only that the law imposes on any such person the burden of proving particular facts;
    (ii) to a fair and public hearing by an independent and impartial tribunal or;
    (iii) to reasonable bail without just cause;
  (g) deprive a person of the right to the assistance of an interpreter in any proceedings in which he is involved or in which he is a party or a witness, before a court, commission, board or other tribunal, if he does not understand or speak English; or
  (h) deprive a person of the right to such procedural provisions as are necessary for the purpose of giving effect and protection to the aforesaid rights and freedoms.

Trinidad & Tobago Const. art. 19 (criminal liability of Commonwealth citizens):

(1) A Commonwealth citizen who is not a citizen of Trinidad and Tobago, or a citizen of the Republic of Ireland who is not a citizen

of Trinidad and Tobago, shall not be guilty of any offence against any law in force in Trinidad and Tobago by reason of anything done or omitted in any part of the Commonwealth other than Trinidad and Tobago or in the Republic of Ireland or in any foreign country unless –

(a) the act or omission would be an offence if he were an alien; and

(b) in the case of an act or omission in any part of the Commonwealth or in the Republic of Ireland, it would be an offence if the country in which the act was done or the omission made were a foreign country.

(2) In this section "foreign country" means a country (other than the Republic of Ireland) that is not part of the Commonwealth.

TREATY: ICCPR

Tunisia – NC, NP, LM, PP

Tunisia Const. art. 13:

> The sentence is personal and cannot be pronounced except by virtue of a law existing prior to the punishable act.

TREATIES: ACHPR(P-signed), ICCPR

Turkey – NC, NP, LM

Turkey Const. art. 38:

> No one can be punished for any act which does not constitute a criminal offence under the law in force at the time committed; no one can be given a heavier penalty for an offence other than the penalty applicable at the time when the offence was committed.
>
> The provisions of the above paragraph also apply to the statute of limitations on offences and penalties and one the results of conviction.
>
> Penalties, and security measures in lieu of penalties, are prescribed only by law.
>
> ...

TREATIES: ECHR, ICCPR(P)

Turkmenistan – NC, NP, LM

Turkmenistan Const. art. 43:

> A law worsening the position of a citizen does not have retroactive force. No one may bear responsibility for actions, which were not recognized as a violation of the law at the time they were committed.

TREATY: ICCPR(P)

Tuvalu – NC, NP

Tuvalu Const. §22(6 & 7):

. . .

(6) No-one shall be convicted of an offence on account of an act that was not, at the time of the doing of the act, an offence or a legal element of an offence.

(7) No penalty shall be imposed for an offence that is more severe in amount or in kind than the maximum that might have been imposed for the offence at the time when it was committed.

. . .

Tuvalu Const. §36 (Restrictions on certain rights and freedoms during public emergencies):

Nothing in or done under a law shall be considered to be inconsistent with –

(a) section 16 (life); or
(b) section 17 (personal liberty); or
(c) section 21 (privacy of home and property); or
(d) section 23 (freedom of belief); or
(e) section 24 (freedom of expression); or
(f) section 25 (freedom of assembly and association); or
(g) section 26 (freedom of movement); or
(h) section 27 (freedom from discrimination), to the extent that the law –
(i) makes any provision, in relation to a period of public emergency; or
(j) authorizes the doing, during any such period, of any thing, that is reasonably justifiable for the purpose of dealing with any situation that arises or exists during that period.

Uganda – NC, NP, LM

Uganda Const. art. 28(7 & 8) (apparently made non-derogable by art. 44):

. . .

(7) No person shall be charged with or convicted of a criminal offence which is founded on an act or omission that did not at the time it took place constitute a criminal offence.

(8) No penalty shall be imposed for a criminal offence that is severer in degree or description than the maximum penalty that could have been imposed for that offence at the time when it was committed.

. . .

TREATIES: ACHPR(P), ICCPR(P)

Ukraine – NC, NP, LM, SJ

Ukraine Const. art. 58 (made non-restrictable by art. 64):

> Laws and other normative legal acts have no retroactive force, except in cases where they mitigate or annul the responsibility of a person.
>
> No one shall bear responsibility for acts that, at the time they were committed, were not deemed by law to be an offense.

Ukraine Const. art. 129:

> In the administration of justice, judges are independent and subject only to the law.
>
> Judicial proceedings are conducted by a single judge, by a panel of judges, or by a court of the jury.

The main principles of judicial proceedings are:

> (1) legality;
>
> . . . .

Ukraine Const. art. 125:

> In Ukraine, the system of courts of general jurisdiction is formed in accordance with the territorial principle and the principle of specialization.
>
> The Supreme Court of Ukraine is the highest judicial body in the system of courts of general jurisdiction.
>
> The respective high courts are the highest judicial bodies of specialized courts.
>
> Courts of appeal and local courts operate in accordance with the law.
>
> The creation of extraordinary and special courts shall not be permitted.

TREATIES: ECHR, ICCPR(P)

United Arab Emirates – NC, NP

United Arab Emirates Const. art. 27:

> Crimes and punishments shall be prescribed by the law. No punishment shall be imposed for any act of commission or act of omission which was completed before the issue of the law which provided for such punishment.

["Provisional" removed from title of United Arab Emirates Const. in 1996.]

TREATY: ArCHR

United Kingdom of Great Britain and Northern Ireland – NC, NP, LM

STATUTE:

United Kingdom Human Rights Act 1998 § 1(1–3) and Sched. 1 incorporates (among others) the ECHR, art. 7 provision on legality in criminal law into the domestic law of Britain.

United Kingdom Human Rights Act 1998, sched. 1, pt. 1, art. 7 (No punishment without law):

> 1. No one shall be held guilty of any criminal offence on account of any act or omission which did not constitute a criminal offence under national or international law at the time when it was committed. Nor shall a heavier penalty be imposed than the one that was applicable at the time the criminal offence was committed.
> 2. This Article shall not prejudice the trial and punishment of any person for any act or omission which, at the time when it was committed, was criminal according to the general principles of law recognised by civilised nations.

See also *Knuller (Publishing, Printing and Promotions), Ltd. v. DPP*, [1973] AC 435 (H.L.).

TREATIES: ECHR, ICCPR

United States of America – NC, NP

Const. art. I §9:

> ...
>
> No Bill of Attainder or ex post facto Law shall be passed.
>
> ...

US Const. art. I §10:

> ...
>
> No State shall... pass any Bill of Attainder, ex post facto Law, or Law impairing the Obligation of Contracts...

US Const. amend V:

> No person shall... be deprived of life, liberty or property, without due process of law....

US Const. amend XIV(1):

> No State shall make or enforce any law which shall abridge the privileges or immunities of citizens of the United States; or shall any State deprive any person of life, liberty, or property, without due process of law....

The ex post facto clauses were interpreted in the U.S. Supreme Court to prohibit retroactive legislative creation of crimes or increase of penalties in *Calder v. Bull*, 3 U.S. (3 Dallas) 386, 391, 396 (1798), and the due process clauses, U.S. Const., amends. V, XIV(1), were held to prohibit unforeseeable judicial expansion of criminal liability in *Bouie v. City of Columbia*, 378 U.S. 347 (1964), and *Rogers v. Tennessee*, 532 U.S. 451 (2001).

TREATY: ICCPR (but United States reserved against application of the *lex mitior* provision)

Uruguay – NC, NP, LM, SJ

Uruguay Const. art. 10:

> Private actions of persons which do not in any way affect the public order or prejudice others shall be outside the jurisdiction of the magistrates.
>
> No inhabitant of the Republic shall be obliged to do what the law does not require, or prevented from doing what it does not prohibit.

Uruguay Const. art. 12:

> No one may be punished or imprisoned without due process of law and a legal sentence.

Uruguay Const. art. 19:

> Trials by commission are prohibited.

STATUTE:

Uruguay, Código Penal art. 15:

> (De la ley penal en orden al tiempo)
>
> (Cuando las leyes penales configuran nuevos delitos, o establecen una pena más severa, no se aplican a los hechos cometidos con anterioridad a su vigencia. Cuando se suprimen, en cambio, delitos existentes o se disminuye la pena de los mismos, se aplican a los hechos anteriores a su vigencia, determinando la cesación del procedimiento o de la condena en el primer caso, y sólo la modificación de la pena, en el segundo, en cuanto no se hallare ésta fijada por sentencia ejecutoriada.)
>
> Text from Uruguay Parliament Web site, http://www.parlamento.gub.uy/Codigos/CodigoPenal/l1t1.htm.

TREATIES: ACHR, ICCPR(P)

Uzbekistan – NC, NP, LM

STATUTE:

Uzbekistan Crim. Code art. 4:

> Criminality, punishability of the act and other legal consequences of its commission shall be determined by the Criminal Code only.
>
> No one may be recognized guilty in commission of a crime other than by a sentence of the court and in accordance with the law. A person, who committed a crime, shall enjoy rights and bear responsibilities established by law.

Uzbekistan Crim. Code art. 13:

> Criminality and punishability of an act shall be established by a law being valid at the moment of commission of the act. As time of commission of an [*sic*] crime shall be recognized the time of commission of a socially dangerous act, if an Article of this Code determines a moment of completion of an crime as a moment of completion of action or inaction. As time of commission of an crime shall be recognized the time of emergence of criminal consequences of an crime, if an article of this Code determines a moment of completion of an crime as a moment of emergence thereof.
>
> A law decriminalizing an act, mitigating a penalty or otherwise improving the position of a person, shall be retroactive, that is, shall be applied to persons, who had committed the appropriate act before this law came into effect, as well as to persons, who are serving their penalty or have served it with non-cancelled conviction.
>
> A law criminalizing an act, severing [*sic*, probably should be "increasing the severity of" —*KSG*] a penalty or otherwise worsening position of a person, shall not be retroactive.

Statute translation from OSCE Office of Democratic Institutions and Human Rights Web site http://www.legislationline.org/upload/legislations/34/fc/a45cbf3cc66c17f04420786aa164.htm. Bracketed material added.

TREATY: ICCPR

Vanuatu – NC, NP

Vanuatu Const. art. 5(2)(f & g):

> Protection of the law shall include the following –
>
> ...
>
> (f) no-one shall be convicted in respect of an act or omission which did not constitute an offense known to written or custom law at the time it committed;

g) no-one shall be punished with a greater penalty than that which exists at the time of the commission of the offence;

. . . .

Vatican City – X

Vatican City Fundamental Law of the State (2001) art. 16:

> The Supreme Pontiff can, in any civil or criminal case and at whatever stage of the proceedings, transfer the examination and decision to a special body with the right to make a decision according to equity to the exclusion of any further appeal.

TREATIES: CRC, APII

Venezuela – NC, NP,[18] LM, SJ

Venezuela Const. art. 24:

> No legislative provision will have retroactive effect, except when it imposes a minor penalty. Procedural laws will be applied from the very moment they enter into force, even in those processes that should be in progress; but in penal processes, the evidence already concluded will be evaluated which benefit[s] the defendant, in conformity with the law in force on the date in which they were promoted.
>
> When there are doubts the norm that benefits the defendant will be applied.

Venezuela Const. art. 49(4, 6):

> Due Process will be applied to all the judicial and administrative actions, and in consequence:
>
> . . .
>
> 4. Any person has the right to be judged by his legitimate [*naturales*] judges in the ordinary, or special, jurisdictions with the guarantees established in this Constitution and the law. No person can be sentenced to judgment without cognizance of the identity of those who judge him, nor can [a person] be processed by tribunals of exception or by commissions created to this effect.
>
> . . .
>
> 6. No person can be sanctioned for acts or omissions that were not specified as crimes, misdemeanors [*faltas*] or infractions in pre-existing laws.

TREATIES: ACHR, ICCPR(P)

[18] Retroactive creation of "minor penalty" acceptable.

Vietnam – NC, NP, LM

Vietnam Const. art. 127:

> The Supreme People's Court, the local people's courts, the military tribunals, and other courts set up by law are adjudicating organs of the Socialist Republic of Vietnam.
>
> Under special circumstances, the National Assembly may decide to set up special tribunals.
>
> Appropriate people's organizations shall be formed at the grass roots to deal with minor breaches of law or disputes, as stipulated by law.

TREATIES: ICCPR

Yemen – NC, NP, LM, PP

Yemen Const. art. 46:

> Crime shall be the sole responsibility of the culprit. Crime and Punishment shall be determined by the provisions of Sharia'a and law. The accused shall remain innocent until proven guilty by a final decision of a court of law. No retroactive laws shall be promulgated.

Yemen Const. art. 103:

> No law shall have retrospective power except as may be in non-taxation and non-criminal provisions of law provided with the consent of two-thirds of the members of the House of Representatives.

TREATY: ICCPR

Zambia – NC, NP, LM

Zambia Const. Act art. 18(4 & 8):

> . . .
>
> (4) No person shall be held to be guilty of a criminal offence on account of any act or omission that did not, at the time it took place, constitute such an offence, and no penalty shall be imposed for any criminal offence that is severer in degree or description that the maximum penalty that might have been imposed for that offence at the time it was committed.
>
> . . .
>
> (8) No person shall be convicted of a criminal offence unless that offence is defined and the penalty is prescribed in a written law:
>
> Provided that nothing in this clause shall prevent a court of record from punishing any person for contempt of itself notwithstanding that the act

or omission constituting the contempt is not defined in written law and the penalty therefore is not so prescribed.

Zambia Const. Act art. 32(2):

> In relation to any person who is a member of a disciplined force raised under the law of Zambia, nothing contained in or done under the authority of the disciplinary law of that force shall be held to be inconsistent with or in contravention of any of the provisions of this Part other than Articles 12, 14, and 15.

Zambia Const. (Constitution Act 1991) art. 25 (Derogation from fundamental rights and freedoms):

> Nothing contained in or done under the authority of any law shall be held to be inconsistent with or in contravention of Articles 13, 16, 17, 19, 20, 21, 22, 23, or 24 to the extent that it is shown that the law in question authorises the taking, during any period when the Republic is at war or when a declaration under Article 30 is in force, of measures for the purpose of dealing with any situation existing or arising during that period; and nothing done by any person under the authority of any such law shall be held to be in contravention of any of the said provisions if it is shown that the measures taken were, having due regard to the circumstances prevailing at the time, reasonably required for the purpose of dealing with the situation in question.

Zambia Const. Act art. 78(7):

> No law made by Parliament shall come into operation until it is published in the *Gazette*, but Parliament may postpone the coming into operation of any such law and may make laws with retrospective effects.

TREATIES: ACHPR(P-signed), ICCPR(P)

Zimbabwe – NC, NP, LM, SJ

Zimbabwe Const. art. 18(5):

> No person shall be held to be guilty of a criminal offence on account of any act or omission that did not, at the time it took place, constitute such an offence, and no penalty shall be imposed for any criminal offence that is severer in degree or description than the maximum penalty that might have been imposed for that offence at the time when it was committed.

Zimbabwe Const. art. 81(4):

> No law, other than a disciplinary law, shall confer jurisdiction in criminal matters upon a court or other adjudicating authority, other than the

Supreme Court or the High Court, which did not have such jurisdiction before the appointed day: Provided that the provisions of this subsection shall not apply to a law which confers any such jurisdiction on a court in terms of which the only penalty that may be imposed by the court is a monetary one.

Zimbabwe Const. art. 92(4)(c):

(4) In this section, "special court" means –

. . .

(c) any court or other adjudicating authority established by law which is declared by that law to be a special court for the purposes of this section.

Zimbabwe Const. art. 25:

Notwithstanding the foregoing provisions of this Chapter, an Act of Parliament may in accordance with Schedule 2 derogate from certain provisions of the Declaration of Rights in respect of a period of public emergency or a period when a resolution under section 31J(6) is in effect.

Zimbabwe Const. art. 26(2, 5, 6, 7):

(2) Nothing contained in or done under the authority of any written law shall be held to be in contravention of the Declaration of Rights to the extent that the law in question –
   (a) is a law with respect to which the requirements of section 52 were applicable and were complied with;

. . .

(5) In relation to any person who is a member of a disciplined force of Zimbabwe, nothing contained in or done under the authority of the disciplinary law of that force shall be held to be in contravention of any of the provisions of the Declaration of Rights, other than sections 12, 14, 15, 16 and 23.

(6) In relation to any person who is a member of a disciplined force that is not a disciplined force of Zimbabwe and who is present in Zimbabwe under arrangements made between the Government and the government of some other country or an international organization, nothing contained in or done under the authority of the disciplinary law of that force shall be held to be in contravention of the Declaration of Rights.

(7) No measures taken in relation to a person who is a member of a disciplined force of a country with which Zimbabwe is at war or with which a state of hostilities exists and no law, to the extent that

it authorises the taking of such measures, shall be held to be in contravention of the Declaration of Rights.

Zimbabwe Const., sched. 2, §1:

(1) Nothing contained in any law shall be held to be in contravention of section 13, 17, 20, 21, 22 or 23 to the extent that the law in question provides for the taking, during a period of public emergency, of action for the purpose of dealing with any situation arising during that period, and nothing done by any person under the authority of any such law shall be held to be in contravention of any of the said provisions unless it is shown that the action taken exceeded anything which, having due regard to the circumstances prevailing at the time, could reasonably have been thought to be required for the purpose of dealing with the situation.

(2) Nothing contained in any law shall be held to be in contravention of section 13 to the extent that the law in question provides for preventive detention, during a period when a resolution under section 31J(6) is in effect, in the interests of defence, public safety or public order, and nothing done by any person under the authority of any such law shall be held to be in contravention of section 13 unless it is shown that the action taken exceeded anything which, having due regard to the circumstances prevailing at the time, could reasonably have been thought to be required for the purpose of dealing with the situation. [*Subparagraph (2) as amended by section 20 of Act No. 23 of 1987 (Amendment No. 7)*]

TREATIES: ACHPR(P-signed), ICCPR

Bibliography

Some bibliographic information may be missing where sources are listed solely because they were cited by other sources. Information on the authors of some of the post–World War II editorial material is incomplete in the originals.

BOOKS

Alvarez, José E. INTERNATIONAL ORGANIZATIONS AS LAW-MAKERS. Oxford: Oxford University Press, 2005.

American Law Institute. RESTATEMENT (THIRD) OF FOREIGN RELATIONS LAW OF THE UNITED STATES. St. Paul, MN: American Law Institute, 1987.

Americano, Jorge. NEW FOUNDATIONS OF INTERNATIONAL LAW. New York: MacMillan, 1947.

Ashworth, Andrew. PRINCIPLES OF CRIMINAL LAW. 5th ed. Oxford: Oxford University Press, 2006.

Ball, Howard. PROSECUTING WAR CRIMES AND GENOCIDE: THE TWENTIETH-CENTURY EXPERIENCE. Lawrence: University Press of Kansas, 1999.

Bantekas, Ilias, & Susan Nash. INTERNATIONAL CRIMINAL LAW. 2d ed. London: Cavendish Publishing, 2003.

Bassiouni, M. Cherif, & Ved P. Nanda, eds. A TREATISE ON INTERNATIONAL CRIMINAL LAW. 2 vols. Springfield, IL: Charles C. Thomas, 1973.

Bassiouni, M. Cherif. CRIMES AGAINST HUMANITY IN INTERNATIONAL CRIMINAL LAW. 2d rev. ed. The Hague: Kluwer Law International, 1999.

Bassiouni, M. Cherif. INTERNATIONAL EXTRADITION AND WORLD PUBLIC ORDER. Leyden: A.W. Sijthoff, 1974.

Bassiouni, M. Cherif, ed. INTERNATIONAL CRIMINAL LAW. 3 vols., 2d ed. Ardsley, NY: Transnational Publishers, 1999.

Bassiouni, M. Cherif, ed. THE ISLAMIC CRIMINAL JUSTICE SYSTEM. London: Oceana Publications, 1982.

Beccaria, Cesare. ON CRIMES AND PUNISHMENTS (DEI DELITTI E DELLE PENE). Trans. with introd. by Henry Paolucci. New York: Macmillan, 1963 (original in Italian, 1764).

Berman, Harold J. SOVIET CRIMINAL LAW AND PROCEDURE: THE RSFSR CODES. Trans. by Harold J. Berman and James W. Slindler, 2d ed. Cambridge, MA: Harvard University Press, 1972.

Biddle, Francis. IN BRIEF AUTHORITY. Westport, CT: Greenwood Press, 1962.

Blackstone, William. COMMENTARIES ON THE LAWS OF ENGLAND. 4 vols. Chicago: University of Chicago Press, 1979 (original, 1765).

Boisson de Chazournes, Laurence, & Vera Gowlland-Debbas, eds. THE INTERNATIONAL LEGAL SYSTEM IN QUEST OF EQUITY AND UNIVERSALITY: *L'ORDRE JURIDIQUE INTERNATIONAL, UN SYSTÈME EN QUÊTE D'ÉQUITÉ ET D'UNIVERSALITÉ:* Liber Amicorum *GEORGES ABI-SAAB*. The Hague: Martinus Nijhoff Publishers, 2001.

Boot, Machteld. GENOCIDE, CRIMES AGAINST HUMANITY, WAR CRIMES: NULLUM CRIMEN SINE LEGE AND THE SUBJECT MATTER JURISDICTION OF THE INTERNATIONAL CRIMINAL COURT. Antwerpen: Intersentia, 2002.

Bossuyt, Marc J. GUIDE TO THE "*TRAVAUX PRÉPARATOIRES*" OF THE INTERNATIONAL COVENANT ON CIVIL AND POLITICAL RIGHTS. Dordrecht: Martinus Nijhoff Publishers, 1987.

Brackman, Arnold C. THE OTHER NUREMBERG. New York: William Morrow, 1987.

Brownlie, Ian, & Guy S. Goodwin-Gill, eds. BASIC DOCUMENTS IN HUMAN RIGHTS. 5th ed. Oxford: Oxford University Press, 2006.

Cassese, Antonio. INTERNATIONAL CRIMINAL LAW. Trans. with an introd. by Henry Paolucci. Oxford: Oxford University Press, 2003.

Cassese, Antonio, Paola Gaeta, & John R.W.D. Jones, eds. THE ROME STATUTE OF THE INTERNATIONAL CRIMINAL COURT: A COMMENTARY. 2 vols. Oxford: Oxford University Press, 2002.

Clayton, Richard, Hugh Tomlinson, et al. THE LAW OF HUMAN RIGHTS. Oxford: Oxford University Press, 2000. (Also 2D ANNUAL SUPP. [2003]).

Commager, Henry Steele, ed. DOCUMENTS OF AMERICAN HISTORY. 4th ed., New York: Appleton-Century-Crofts, 1948.

Conot, Robert E. JUSTICE AT NUREMBERG. New York: Harper & Row, 1983.

Covarruvias, D. PRACTICORUM QUAESTIONUM (no publication information given).

Czarnota, Adam, Martin Krygier, & Wojciech Sadurski. RETHINKING THE RULE OF LAW AFTER COMMUNISM. Budapest: Central European University Press, 2005.

Donnedieu de Vabres, Henri Felix August. LES PRINCIPES MODERNES DE DROIT PÉNAL INTERNATIONAL. Paris: Librairie du Recueil Sirey, 1928.

Doswald-Beck, Louise, & Robert Kolb. JUDICIAL PROCESS AND HUMAN RIGHTS: UNITED NATIONS, EUROPEAN, AMERICAN AND AFRICAN SYSTEMS: TEXTS AND SUMMARIES OF INTERNATIONAL CASE-LAW. Kehl: N.P. Engel, 2004.

Dressler, Joshua. UNDERSTANDING CRIMINAL LAW. 4th ed., New York: LexisNexis, 2006.

Engel, Salo, ed. LAW, STATE, AND INTERNATIONAL LEGAL ORDER: ESSAYS IN HONOR OF HANS KELSEN. Knoxville: University of Tennessee Press, 1964.

Evans, Malcolm, & Rachel Murray, eds. THE AFRICAN CHARTER ON HUMAN AND PEOPLES' RIGHTS: THE SYSTEM IN PRACTICE, 1986–2000. Cambridge: Cambridge University Press, 2002.

Fehr, Hans. *RECHT UND WIRKLICHKEIT; EINBLICK IN WERDEN UND VERGEHEN DER RECHTSFORMEN*. 1927.

Ferdinandusse, Ward N. DIRECT APPLICATION OF INTERNATIONAL CRIMINAL LAW IN NATIONAL COURTS. The Hague: T.M.C. Asser Press, 2006.

Ferencz, Benjamin. AN INTERNATIONAL CRIMINAL COURT: A STEP TOWARDS WORLD PEACE: A DOCUMENTARY HISTORY AND ANALYSIS. 2 vols. London: Oceana, 1980.

Feuerbach, Paul Johann Anselm Ritter von. *LEHRBUCH DES GEMEINEN IN DEUTSCHLAND GELTENDEN PEINLICHEN RECHTS*. Giessen: Georg Friedrich Heyer, 1801.

Fletcher, George P. THE GRAMMAR OF CRIMINAL LAW: AMERICAN, COMPARATIVE, AND INTERNATIONAL (FOUNDATIONS). Vol. 1. Oxford: Oxford University Press, 2007.

Friedman, Leon, ed. THE LAW OF WAR: A DOCUMENTARY HISTORY. New York: Random House, 1972.

Fuller, Lon L. THE MORALITY OF LAW. Rev. ed. New Haven, CT: Yale University Press, 1969 (1st ed., 1964).

Glueck, Sheldon. THE NUREMBERG TRIAL AND AGGRESSIVE WAR. New York: Alfred A. Knopf, 1946; reprinted, Millwood, NY: Kraus Reprint Co., 1976.

Goodman, Carl F. THE RULE OF LAW IN JAPAN: A COMPARATIVE ANALYSIS. The Hague: Kluwer Law International, 2003.

Greenfield, Aryeh, trans. [Israel] PENAL LAW 5737–1977 PART ONE. 5th ed. Haifa: Aryeh Greenfield–A. G. Publications, 2005.

Grotius, Hugo. *DE JURE PACIS AC BELLI* (TREATING OF THE RIGHTS OF WAR AND PEACE). 1625 (orig. in Latin; various translations used, especially where citing to authorities who have used this classic work).

Gu, Sharron. THE BOUNDARIES OF MEANING AND THE FORMATION OF LAW: LEGAL CONCEPTS AND REASONING IN THE ENGLISH, ARABIC, AND CHINESE TRADITIONS. Montreal: McGill-Queen's University Press, 2006.

Hanski, Raija, & Martin Scheinin. LEADING CASES OF THE HUMAN RIGHTS COMMITTEE. Turku, Finland: Institute for Human Rights, Åbo Akademi University, 2003.

Hart, H. L. A. THE CONCEPT OF LAW. 2d ed. Oxford: Clarendon Press, 1994 (1961).

Haveman, R., & O. Olusanya, eds., SENTENCING AND SANCTIONING IN INTERNATIONAL CRIMINAL LAW (no publisher or date cited).

Hayek, Friedrich A. von. THE ROAD TO SERFDOM. Chicago: University of Chicago Press, 1975 (original 1944).

Hazard, John N., & Isaac Shapiro. THE SOVIET LEGAL SYSTEM: POST-STALIN DOCUMENTATION AND HISTORICAL COMMENTARY. Dobbs Ferry, NY: Published for the Parker School of Foreign and Comparative Law Columbia University in the City of New York by Oceana Publishers, 1962.

Hazard, John N., William E. Butler, & Peter B. Maggs. THE SOVIET LEGAL SYSTEM. 3d ed. Dobbs Ferry, NY: Published for the Parker School of Foreign and Comparative Law Columbia University in the City of New York by Oceana Publishers, 1977.

Henckaerts, Jean-Marie, & Louise Doswald-Beck, eds. CUSTOMARY INTERNATIONAL HUMANITARIAN LAW. Cambridge: Cambridge University Press, 2005 (Report of International Committee of the Red Cross).

Henkin, Louis, ed. THE INTERNATIONAL BILL OF RIGHTS: THE COVENANT ON CIVIL AND POLITICAL RIGHTS. New York: Columbia University Press, 1981.

Herik, L. J. van den. THE CONTRIBUTION OF THE RWANDA TRIBUNAL TO THE DEVELOPMENT OF INTERNATIONAL LAW. Leiden: Martinus Nijhoff Publishers, 2005.

Henzelin, Marc. *Le principe de l'universalité en droit pénal inernational: Droit et obligation pour les États de poursuivre et juger selon le principe de l'universalité*. Bâle, France: Helbing & Lichtenhahn, 2000.

The Holy Qu'ran. Various renderings into English from Arabic.

Humphrey, John P. Human Rights and the United Nations: A Great Adventure. Dobbs Ferry, NY: Transnational Publishers, 1984.

International Military Tribunal [Nuremberg Tribunal]. Trial of the Major War Criminals before the International Military Tribunal: Nuremberg 14 November 1945–1 October 1946. 24 vols. Nuremberg: International Military Tribunal, 1947.

International Military Tribunal for the Far East [Tokyo Tribunal]. The Tokyo Major War Crimes Trial. 124 vols., ed. by John R. Pritchard. Lewiston, NY: Robert M. W. Kemper Collegium and Edwin Mellen Press, 1998.

Jackson, Robert H. Report of Robert H. Jackson United States Representative to the International Conference on Military Trials: London, 1945. Washington: U.S. Government Printing Office, 1949 [submitted by Justice Jackson to the Secretary of State 15 December 1947] (rep., AMS Press, 1971).

Jareborg, Nils, ed. Double Criminality: Studies in International Criminal Law. Uppsala: Iustis Förlag AB, 1989.

Jayawickrame, Nihal. The Judicial Application of Human Rights Law: National, Regional and International Jurisprudence. Cambridge: Cambridge University Press, 2002.

Jones, William C., trans. The Great Qing Code. Oxford: Clarendon Press, 1994.

Jørgensen, Nina H.B. The Responsibility of States for International Crimes. Oxford: Oxford University Press, 2001.

Joseph, Sarah, Jenny Schultz, & Melissa Catan. The International Covenant on Civil and Political Rights: Cases, Materials and Commentary. 2d ed. Oxford: Oxford University Press, 2004.

Kim, Chin, trans. The Criminal Code of the People's Republic of China. Littleton, CO: Fred B. Rothman & Co., 1982.

Kissinger, Henry. Diplomacy. New York: Simon & Schuster, 1994.

Knoops, Geert-Jan G.J. Defenses in Contemporary International Criminal Law. Dobbs Ferry, NY: Transnational Publishers, 2001.

Kochavi, Arieh J. Prelude to Nuremberg: Allied War Crimes Policy and the Question of Punishment. Chapel Hill: University of North Carolina Press, 1998.

Kohler, J. *International Strafrecht*. Stuttgart, 1917.

Kramer, Matthew H. Objectivity and the Rule of Law. Cambridge: Cambridge University Press, 2007.

Krey, Volker. *Studien zum Gesetzesvorbehalt im Strafrecht: Eine Einführung in die Problematik des Analogieverbots*. Berlin: Duncker & Humblot, 1977.

Kucherov, Samuel. Courts, Lawyers and Trials under the Last Three Tsars. New York: Frederick A. Praeger, 1953; rep. Westport, CT: Greenwood Press, 1974.

Levy, Leonard. Judgments: Essays on American Constitutional History. Chicago: Quadrangle Books, 1972.

Locke, John. Two Treatises of Government. Special ed. New York: The Classics of Liberty Library Division of Gryphon Editions, 1992 (orig. 1689–90).

Malden, Henry Elliot, ed. Magna Carta Commemoration Essays. London: Royal Historical Society, 1917; rep. Clark, NJ: The Lawbook Exchange, 2005.

McGoldrick, Dominic, Peter Rowe, & Eric Donnelly, eds., The Permanent International Criminal Court: Legal and Policy Issues. Oxford: Hart Publishing, 2004.

Melikan, R. A., ed. Domestic and International Trials, 1700–2000: The Trial in History, Vol. II. Manchester, UK: Manchester University Press, 2003.

Mettraux, Guénaël. International Crimes and the *ad hoc* Tribunals. Oxford: Oxford University Press, 2005.

Minear, Richard H. Victor's Justice: The Tokyo War Crimes Trial. Princeton, NJ: Princeton University Press, 1971.

Montesquieu, Charles de S. De L'Esprit des Lois. 1748.

Oehler, Dietrich. *Internationales Strafrecht*. 2d ed. Cologne: Carl Heymanns Verlag, 1983.

Permanent Court of International Justice. Annual Report, 1922–1925. PCIJ Series E, No. 1, Leyden: Sijthoff, 1925.

Posner, Richard A. Law and Literature. Rev. and enlarged ed., Cambridge, MA: Harvard University Press, 1998.

Ramadan, Hisham M., ed. Understanding Islamic Law: From Classical to Contemporary. Lanham, MD: AltaMira Press, 2006.

Rawls, John. A Theory of Justice. Cambridge, MA: Belknap Press of Harvard University Press, 1971.

Raworth, Philip, ed. Constitutions of Dependencies and Territories. Oxford: Oxford University Press, various dates (formerly published by Oceana) (including both paper version and online subscription version available at www.oceanalaw.com).

Reydams, Luc. Universal Jurisdiction: International and Municipal Legal Perspectives. Oxford: Oxford University Press, 2003.

Rubin, Alfred P. The Law of Piracy. Newport, RI: Naval War College Press, 1988.

Sachleben, Mark. Human Rights Treaties: Considering Patterns of Participation, 1948–2000. New York: Routledge, 2006.

Sadat, Leila N. The International Criminal Court and the Transformation of International Law: Justice for the New Millenium. Ardsley, NY: Transnational Publishers, 2002.

Sampford, Charles. Retrospectivity and the Rule of Law. Oxford: Oxford University Press, 2006.

Sandoz, Yves, Christophe Swinarski, & Bruno Zimmerman, eds., Commentary on the Additional Protocols. Geneva: International Committee of the Red Cross, 1987.

Schabas, William A. The UN International Criminal Tribunals: The Former Yugoslavia, Rwanda and Sierra Leone. Cambridge: Cambridge University Press, 2006.

Schabas, William A. An Introduction to the International Criminal Court. 2d ed. Cambridge: Cambridge University Press, 2004.

Schachter, Oscar. INTERNATIONAL LAW IN THEORY AND PRACTICE. The Hague: Kluwer, 1991.

Schmitt, Carl. LEGALITY AND LEGITIMACY. Trans. and ed. by Jeffrey Seitzer; intro. by John P. McCormick. Durham, NC: Duke University Press, 2004 (orig. in German, 1932; afterword by Schmitt in 1958).

Schmitt, Carl. ON THE THREE TYPES OF JURISTIC THOUGHT. Trans. and intro. by Joseph W. Bendersky. Westport, CT: Praeger Publishers, 2004 (orig. in German, 1934).

Schreiber, H.-L. *GESETZ UND RICHTER: ZUR GESCHICHTLICHEN ENTWICKLUNG DES SATZES "NULLUM CRIMEN, NULLA POENA SINE LEGE."* Frankfurt: Metzner, 1976.

Smith, Bradley F. THE AMERICAN ROAD TO NUREMBERG: THE DOCUMENTARY RECORD 1944–1945. Stanford, CA: Hoover Institution Press, 1982.

Smith, Bradley F. REACHING JUDGMENT AT NUREMBERG. New York: Basic Books, 1977.

Solna, G. DAS WELTRECHTSPRINZIP IM INTERNATIONALEN STRAFRECHT. 1925.

Spiermann, Ole. INTERNATIONAL LEGAL ARGUMENT IN THE PERMANENT COURT OF INTERNATIONAL JUSTICE: THE RISE OF THE INTERNATIONAL JUDICIARY. Cambridge: Cambridge University Press, 2005.

Story, Joseph. COMMENTARIES ON THE CONSTITUTION OF THE UNITED STATES. 2d ed. Boston: Charles C. Little & James Brown, 1851; rep. Clark, NJ: The Lawbook Exchange, 2005 (1st ed., 1833).

Stuchka, P. I. SELECTED WRITINGS ON SOVIET LAW AND MARXISM. Trans. & ed. by Robert Sharlet, Peter B. Maggs, & Piers Beirne, Armonk, NY: M. E. Sharpe, 1988.

Tamanaha, Brian Z. ON THE RULE OF LAW: HISTORY, POLITICS, THEORY. Cambridge: Cambridge University Press, 2004.

Taylor, Telford. THE ANATOMY OF THE NUREMBERG TRIALS: A PERSONAL MEMOIR. New York: Alfred A. Knopf, 1992.

Travers, Maurice. *LE DROIT PÉNAL INTERNATIONAL ET SA MISE EN OEUVRE EN TEMPS DE PAIX ET EN TEMPS DE GUERRE.* 3 vols. Paris: Sirey, 1920–22.

Triffterer, Otto, ed. COMMENTARY ON THE ROME STATUTE OF THE INTERNATIONAL CRIMINAL COURT: OBSERVERS' NOTES, ARTICLE BY ARTICLE. Baden-Baden, Germany: Nomos Verlagsgesellschaft, 1999.

Tyler, Tom R. WHY PEOPLE OBEY THE LAW. Princeton, NJ: Princeton University Press, 2006.

Unger, Aryeh L. CONSTITUTIONAL DEVELOPMENT IN THE USSR. New York: Pica Press, 1981.

United Nations War Crimes Commission. HISTORY OF THE UNITED NATIONS WAR CRIMES COMMISSION AND THE DEVELOPMENT OF THE LAWS OF WAR. London: H. M. Stationery Office for the United Nations War Crimes Commission, 1948.

United Nations War Crimes Commission. LAW REPORTS OF TRIALS OF WAR CRIMINALS. 15 vols., London: Published for the United Nations War Crimes Commission by His Majesty's Stationery Office, 1947–49; rep. in 3 vols., Buffalo, NY: William S. Hein, 1997.

United Nations. YEAR BOOK ON HUMAN RIGHTS. Annual since 1946. (Rep. Buffalo: William S. Hein & Co., 1996). During the years studied, the Yearbooks generally came out about two years after the date of events covered. E.g., the YEAR BOOK for 1946 was originally published by the United Nations in 1948.

United States Military Tribunals. TRIALS OF WAR CRIMINALS BEFORE THE NUERNBERG MILITARY TRIBUNALS UNDER CONTROL COUNCIL LAW NO. 10. 15 vols., Nuernberg: Nuernberg Military Tribunals, 1949–53.

Vattel, Emerich de. THE LAW OF NATIONS: OR THE PRINCIPLES OF THE LAW OF NATURE, APPLIED TO THE CONDUCT AND AFFAIRS OF NATIONS AND SOVEREIGNS. Pomeroy trans., 1805 (orig. in French, 1758).

Verdoodt, Albert. *NAISSANCE ET SIGNIFICATION DE LA DÉCLARATION UNIVERSELLE DES DROITS DE L'HOMME*. Louvain: E. Warny/Université Catholique de Louvain, 1964.

Walker, Geoffrey De Q. THE RULE OF LAW: FOUNDATION OF CONSTITUTIONAL DEMOCRACY. Carlton, Victoria: Melbourne University Press, 1989.

Wang, Guiguo, & John Mo, eds. CHINESE LAW. The Hague: Kluwer Law International, 1999.

Watkins, John C., Jr., & John Paul Weber, eds. WAR CRIMES AND WAR CRIME TRIALS: FROM LEIPZIG TO THE ICC AND BEYOND: CASES, MATERIALS AND COMMENTS. Durham, NC: Carolina Academic Press, 2006.

Weissbrodt, David. THE RIGHT TO A FAIR TRIAL UNDER THE UNIVERSAL DECLARATION OF HUMAN RIGHTS AND THE INTERNATIONAL COVENANT ON CIVIL AND POLITICAL RIGHTS. The Hague: Martinus Nijhoff Publishers, 2001.

Werle, Gerhard, et al. PRINCIPLES OF INTERNATIONAL CRIMINAL LAW. The Hague: TMC Asser Press, 2005.

Weston, Burns H., et al. INTERNATIONAL LAW AND WORLD ORDER: A PROBLEM-ORIENTED COURSEBOOK. 3d ed. St. Paul, MN: West, 1997.

White, T. H. THE ONCE AND FUTURE KING. New York: G. P. Putnam's Sons, 1958.

Wolfrum, Rüdiger H., Rainer Grote, & Gisbert H. Flanz, eds. CONSTITUTIONS OF THE COUNTRIES OF THE WORLD. Oxford: Oxford University Press, various dates (formerly published by Oceana) (including both paper version and online subscription version available at www.oceanalaw.com).

Zamora, Stephen, José Ramón Cossío, Leonel Pereznieto, José Roldán-Xopa, & David Lopez. MEXICAN LAW. Oxford: Oxford University Press, 2004.

Zappalà, Salvatore. HUMAN RIGHTS IN INTERNATIONAL CRIMINAL PROCEEDINGS. Oxford: Oxford University Press, 2003.

Articles, Book Chapters, Papers, Lectures, and Other Writings

Muhammad Salim al-'Awwa, *The Basis of Islamic Penal Legislation*, in Bassiouni, ed. (1982), 127

Michael Akehurst, *Jurisdiction in International Law*, 46 Brit. Y.B. Int'l L. 145 (1972–73).

Ahmad Fathi Bahnassi, *Criminal Responsibility in Islamic Law*, in Bassiouni, ed. (1982), 171.

Ahmad Abd al-Aziz al-Alfi, *Punishment in Islamic Criminal Law*, in Bassiouni, ed. (1982), 227.

K. Ambos, *Nulla Poena Sine Lege in International Criminal Law*, in Haveman & Olusanya, eds., 17.

M. Cherif Bassiouni, *Quesas Crimes*, in Bassiouni, ed. (1982), 203.

BBC News, Mukhtar Mai – history of a rape case, at http://news.bbc.co.uk/2/hi/south_asia/4620065.stm (28 June 2005).
Ghaouti Benmelha, *Ta'azir Crimes*, in Bassiouni, ed. (1982), 211.
Paul Schiff Berman, *The Globalization of Jurisdiction*, 151 U. Pa. L. Rev. 311 (2002).
Christopher L. Blakesley, *Extraterritorial Jurisdiction*, in 2 Bassiouni, ed. (1999) 33.
British Law Concerning Trials of War Criminals by Military Courts, 1 UNWCC, Law Rep. 105.
Stéphane Bourgon, Jurisdiction *Ratione Temporis*, in 1 Cassese, Gaeta & Jones (2002), 543.
[George Brand], The Sources of International Criminal Law, 15 UNWCC, Law Rep., 5, 6–7 (1949).
[George Brand,] Punishment of Criminals, 15 UNWCC, Law Rep. 200-01 (1949).
Bruce Broomhall, *Nullum crimen sine lege*, in Triffterer, ed. (1999), 447.
Iain Cameron, Jurisdiction and Admissibility Issues under the ICC Statute, in McGoldrick, Rowe & Donnelly, eds. (2004), 65.
A. H. Campbell, *Fascism and Legality*, 62 L.Q. Rev. 141 (1946).
Choucri Cardahi, *Commentary on Lebanon*, in 1946 UNYBHR 177.
Antonio Cassese, *Crimes Against Humanity: Comments on Some Problematical Aspects*, in Boisson de Chazournes & Vera Gowlland-Debbas, eds. (2001), 429.
Chung-fu Chang, *Commentary on China*, 1946 UNYBHR at 61.
Luigi Condorelli & Santiago Villalpando, *Referral and Deferral by the Security Council*, in 1 Cassese, Gaeta, & Jones (2002), 627.
Raymond Dacey & Kenneth S. Gallant, *Crime Control and the Harassment of the Innocent*, 25 J. of Crim. Justice 325 (1997).
P. D., *Note on the Nuremberg Trials*, 62 L.Q. Rev. 229 (1946).
Vahakn N. Dadrian, *A Typology of Genocide*, 5 Int'l Rev. of Modern Sociology 201 (1975).
Shigemitsu Dando, *Basic Concepts in Temporal and Territorial Limits on the Applicability of the Penal Law of Japan*, 9 N.Y. L. Sch. J. Int'l Comp. L. 237 (1988).
Henri Felix August Donnedieu de Vabres, *Le procès de Nuremberg devant les principes modernes du droit pénal international*, 70(I) Recueil des Cours 477 (1947).
Henri Felix August Donnedieu de Vabres, *Le jugement de Nuremberg et le principe de légalité des délits et des peines*, 27 Revue de Droit Penal et de Criminologie 813 (1947).
Mark A. Drumbl, *Collective Violence and Individual Punishment: The Criminality of Mass Atrocity*, 99 Northwestern L. Rev. 539 (2005).
Mark A. Drumbl, *Punishment, Postgenocide: From Guilt to Shame to* Civis *in Rwanda*, 75 N.Y.U. L. REV. 1221 (2000).
George P. Fletcher, *Collective Guilt and Collective Punishment*, 5 THEORETICAL INQUIRIES IN LAW 163 (2004).
Hans Frank, *Statement of 14 September 1935*, translated and printed in Opinion and Judgment, *Justice Case*, 3 United States Military Tribunals, Trials of War Criminals before the Nuernberg Military Tribunals under Control Council Law No. 10, 979, 1022.
Kenneth S. Gallant, *Jurisdiction to Adjudicate and Jurisdiction to Prescribe in International Criminal Courts*, 48 Villanova L. Rev. 763 (2003).

Kenneth S. Gallant, *The International Criminal Court in the System of States and International Organizations*, 16 Leiden J.I.L. 553 (2003).
Andrés Garibello and Jhon Torres Martínez, *Corte Penal Internacional sigue pista a la parapolítica, asegura su fiscal jefe, Luis Moreno Ocampo*, ElTiempo.com, 21 October 2007, available at http://www.eltiempo.com/justicia/2007-10-22/ARTICULO-WEB-NOTA_INTERIOR-3776563.html (last visited 30 October 2007).
Stefan Glaser, *La méthode d'interpretation en droit international pénal*, 9 Rivista Italiana di Diritto e Procedura Penale, 757, 762–64 (1966).
Gu Minkang, Criminal Law, in Wang & Mo, eds. (1999), 591.
G. Guillaume, *La competence universelle, formes anciennes et nouvelles*, in *Melanges offerts à Georges Levasseur: Droit pénal, droit européen* 23 (Paris, 1992).
Jafar Habibzadeh, *The Legality Principle of Crimes and Punishments in the Iranian Legal System*, 5 Global Jurist Topics 1, Article 1, p. 9 (2005), available at http://www.bepress.com/gj.
Jerome Hall, *Nulla Poena Sine Lege*, 47 Yale L.J. 165 (1937).
Haidar Ala Hamoudi, *The Muezzin's Call and the Dow Jones Bell: On the Necessity of Realism in the Study of Islamic Law*, 56:2 Am. J. Comp. L. (forthcoming).
Louis Henkin, *International Law: Politics, Values, and Functions*, 216 Recueil de Cours 27 (1989).
Christof Heyns, *Civil and Political Rights in the African Charter*, in Evans & Murray, 137.
Institute de droit international, Session de Munich, Résolution 10 (23 September 1883), 7 *Annuaire de l'Institut de droit international* 157 (1885).
John Calvin Jeffries, Jr., *Legality, Vagueness, and the Construction of Penal Statutes*, 71 Va. L. Rev. 189 (1985).
Bushra Juhi, *Death Sentences Upheld in Iraq For 'Chemical Ali,' Two Others, Washington Post*, 5 September 2007, p. A-11.
Taymour Kamel, *The Principle of Legality and Its Application in Islamic Criminal Justice*, in Bassiouni, ed. (1982), 149.
Hans Kelsen, *Will the Judgment in the Nuremberg Trial Constitute a Precedent in International Law?*, 1 Int'l L.Q. 153 (1947).
Elizabeth S. Kopelman, *Ideology and International Law: The Dissent of the Indian Justice at the Tokyo War Crimes Trial*, 23 NYU J. Int'l L. & Politics 373 (1991).
Serge Krylov, *Les Notions Principales du Droit des Gens (La doctrine soviétique du droit international)*, 70-I Recuiel des Cours 407 (1947)
Susan Lamb, Nullum crimen, nulla poena sine lege *in International Criminal Law*, in 1 Cassese, Gaeta, & Jones, eds. (2002), 733.
Leonard Levy, *No Establishment of Religion: The Original Understanding*, in Levy (1972), 169.
Aly Aly Mansour, *Hudud Crimes*, in Bassiouni, ed. (1982), 195.
Myres S. McDougal, Harold D. Lasswell, & Lung-chu Chen, *Nationality and Human Rights: The Protection of the Individual in External Arenas*, 83 Yale L.J. 900 (1974).
R. A. Melikan, *Pains and Penalties Procedure: How the House of Lords 'Tried' Queen Caroline*, in Melikan (2003), 54.

A. Mercier, *Le conflit des lois pénales en matière de competence*, [1931] Annuaire l'Institute de Droit International, I, 87.
Theodore Meron, *The Role of Custom in the Formation of International Humanitarian Law*, 90 Am. J. Int'l L. 238 (1996).
Jürgen Meyer, *The Vicarious Administration of Justice: An Overlooked Basis of Jurisdiction*, 31 Harv. Int'l L.J. 108 (1990).
Madeline Morris, *High Crimes and Misconceptions: The ICC and Non-Party States*, 64 Law & Contemp. Probs. 13 (2001).
Haji N. A. Noor Muhammad, *Due Process of Law for Persons Accused of a Crime*, in Henkin, ed. (1981), 138
Raul C. Pangalangan, Article 24, *Non-retroactivity ratione personae*, in Triffterer, ed. (1999), 467.
Zdenek Peska, *Commentary on Czechoslovakia*, 1946 UNYBHR 86.
F. M. Powicke, *Per Iudicium Parium vel per Legem Terrae*, in Malden, ed. (1917), 96.
R. John Pritchard, *The International Military Tribunal for the Far East and the Allied National War Crimes Trials in Asia*, in 3 Bassiouni (1999), 109.
Pushtunwali: Honour among them, *The Economist*, Vol. 381, No. 8509, p. 36 (23 December 2006).
Hisham M. Ramadan, *On Islamic Punishment*, in Ramadan, ed. (2006), 43.
Kenneth C. Randall, *Universal Jurisdiction under International Law*, 66 Tex. L. Rev. 785 (1988).
Joseph Raz, *The Rule of Law and Its Virtue*, 93 L.Q. Rev. 195 (1977).
Paul H. Robinson, *Fair Notice and Fair Adjudication: Two Kinds of Legality*, 154 U. Pa. L. Rev. 335 (2005).
Hubert Rottleuthner & Matthias Mahlmann, *Models of Transition: Old Theories and Recent Developments*, in Czarnota, Krygier & Sadurski, eds. (2005), 191.
Alfred P. Rubin, *An International Criminal Tribunal for the Former Yugoslavia?*, 6 Pace Int'l L.J. 7 (1994).
Paul K. Ryu & Helen Silving, *International Criminal Law: A Search for Meaning*, in Bassiouni & Nanda, eds. (1973), 22.
William A. Schabas, Article 23: *Nulla poena sine lege*, in Triffterer, ed. (1999), 463.
Oscar Schachter, *Interpretation of the Charter in the Political Organs of the United Nations*, in Engel, ed. (1964), 270.
Franz Schlegelberger, *Speech, 10 March 1936*, University of Rostock, translated and printed in Opinion and Judgment, *Justice Case*, 3 United States Military Tribunals, TRIALS OF WAR CRIMINALS BEFORE THE NUERNBERG MILITARY TRIBUNALS UNDER CONTROL COUNCIL LAW NO. 10, 979, 1082.
F. R. Scott, *Commenary on Canada*, 1946 UNYBHR 56.
Shura Council ratifies Arab Charter on Human Rights, at the Web site of the Royal Embassy of Saudi Arabia in the U.S., http://www.saudiembassy.net/2008News/News/RigDetail.asp?cIndex=7698 (24 February 2008).
P. I. Stuchka, *Law*, in Stuchka (1988), 143.
Per Ole Träskman, *Should We Take the Condition of Double Criminality Seriously?*, in Jareborg, ed. (1989), 148.
UAE ratifies Arab charter on human rights, from Emirates News Agency at http://www.uaeinteract.com/docs/UAE_ratifies_Arab_charter_on_human_rights/28218.htm (UAE Interact, Web site of National Media Council, posted 16 January 2008).

Paul Vinogradoff, *Magna Carta*, in Malden, ed. (1917), 96.
Peter Westen, *Two Rules of Legality in Criminal Law*, 26 Law & Philosophy 229, 239 (2006).
Sharon A. Williams, *Article 11, Jurisdiction ratione temporis*, in Triffterer, ed. (1999), 323.
Wright, *War Crimes under International Law*, 62 L.Q. Rev. 40 (1946).
Christine van den Wyngaert, *Double Criminality as a Requirement to Jurisdiction*, in Jareborg, ed. (1989), 43.
L. Zegfeld, *The Bouterse Case*, 32 Netherlands YBIL 97 (2001).
[Zivkovic], *Notes on the Case [Trial of Greifelt]*, 13 UNWCC, Law Rep., Case No. 73, pp. 1, 36.
[Zivkovic,] *Notes on Trial of Rauter*, 14 UNWCC, Law Rep. at 111, 120.

Table of Authorities

CASES (BY JURISDICTION)

International (including international, joint national/international, internationalized, occupation and, following World War II, the International Military Tribunals and Control Council No. 10 courts, tribunals, arbitral panels, commissions and committees)

Ad hoc Arbitrations

Arbitration between Petroleum Development (Trucial Coast) Ltd. and the Sheikh of Abu Dhabi, 1 ICLQ 247, 250–51 (1952) (Lord Asquith of Bishopstone, Arbitrator)

African Commission on Human and Peoples' Rights

Communications 105/93, 128/94, 130/94 & 152/96, *Media Rights Agenda & Constitutional Rights Project v. Nigeria* (ACommHPR, Twelfth Activity Report 1998–99)

European Court of Human Rights and European Commission on Human Rights

Baskaya v. Turkey, Judgment of 8 July 1999, Eur. Ct. H.R., Application Nos. 23536/94 and 24408/94

Cantoni v. France, Judgment of 15 November 1996, Eur. Ct. H.R., Case No. 45/1995/551/637, Application No. 17862/91

C.R. v. United Kingdom, Judgment of 22 November 1995, Eur. Ct.H.R., Case No. 48/1994/495/577, Application No. 20190/92

G. v. France, Judgment of 27 September 1995, Eur. Ct. H.R., Case No. 29/1994/476/557, Application No. 15312/89

K.-H. W. v. Germany, Judgment of 22 March 2001, Eur. Ct. H.R., 2001-II, Applications Nos. 37201/97

Kokkinakis v. Greece, Judgment of 25 May 1993, Eur. Ct. H.R., Application No. 14307/88

Naletilic v. Croatia, Admissibility Decision, Eur. Ct. H.R., App no., 51891/99, 4 May 2000

Streletz, Kessler & Krenz v. Germany, Judgment of 22 March 2001, Eur. Ct. H.R., Applications Nos. 34044/96, 35532/97 & 44801/98
Sunday Times v. United Kingdom, Judgment of 26 April 1979, Eur. Ct. H.R., Ser. A, No. 30
S.W. v. United Kingdom, Judgment of 27 October 1995, Eur. Ct. H.R., Case No. 47/1994/494/576
X, Ltd. v. UK, 28 DR 77 (Eur. Comm.H.R., 1982)

Inter-American Court of Human Rights

Castillo-Petruzzi v. Peru, Judgement of 30 May 1999, Inter-Am. Ct. H.R., Petition No. 11,319

International Court of Justice

Arrest Warrant of 11 April 2000 (Dem. Rep. of Congo v. Belgium), ICJ (14 February 2002)
Military and Paramilitary Activities in and against Nicaragua (Nicaragua v. United States), Merits, 1986 ICJ Rep. 14
Northern Cameroons Case, 1963 ICJ Rep.
North Sea Continental Shelf Cases (Fed. Rep. of Germany v. Denmark, Fed. Rep. of Germany v. Netherlands, 1969 ICJ 3
Nottebaum Case (Leichtenstein v. Guatemala), 1955 ICJ 4
Nuclear Tests Case, 1974 ICJ Rep.

International Criminal Court

Procureur c. Dyilo, No. ICC-01/04-01/06, Décision sur la confirmation des charges (Version publique) (La Chamber Préliminaire I, 29 January 2007)

International Criminal Tribunal for Rwanda

Prosecutor v. Akayesu, Judgement, Case No. ICTR-96-4-T (ICTR Trial Ch., 2 September 1998)
Prosecutor v. Akayesu, Sentencing Judgment (ICTR Tr. Ch., 2 October 1998)
Prosecutor v. Kanyabashi, Decision on the Defence Motion on Jurisdiction of 18 June 1997, ICTR, Case No. ICTR-96–15-T (ICTR Tr. Ch., 18 June 1997)
Prosecutor v. Kayishema, Judgement (Reasons), Case No. 95–1-A (ICTR App. Ch., 1 June 2001)
Prosecutor v. Serushago, Case No. ICTR 98–39-A (ICTR App. Ch., 6 April 2000)

International Criminal Tribunal for the Former Yugoslavia

Prosecutor v. Aleksovski, Appeals Judgement Case No. IT-95–14/1 (ICTY App. Ch., 24 March 2000)
Prosecutor v. Aleksovski (Appeal of Nobilo), Judgment on Appeal by Anto Nobilo against Finding of Contempt, Case No. IT-95–14/1-AR77 (ICTY App. Ch., 30 May 2001)

Prosecutor v Blaskic, Case IT-95–14-AR108*bis*, Judgement on the Request of the Republic of Croatia for Review of the Decision of Trial Chamber II of 18 July 1997 (ICTY App. Ch., 29 October 1997) ("*Blaskic Subpoena Decision*")
Prosecutor v. Blaskic, Appeals Judgement, Case No. IT-95–14-A (ICTY App. Ch, 29 July 2004)
Prosecutor v. Delalic, Appeals Judgement, Case No. IT-96–21 (ICTY App. Ch., 20 February 2001), Case No. IT-95–14/1 (ICTY App. Ch., 24 March 2000)
Prosecutor v. Erdemovic, Sentencing Judgement, (ICTY Tr. Ch., 29 November 1996)
Prosecutor v. Furundzija, Judgement, Case No. IT-95–17/1-T (ICTY Tr. Ch., 10 December 1998), aff'd (ICTY App. Ch., 21 July 2000)
Prosecutor v. Galic, Judgement, Case No. IT-98–29 (ICTY Tr. Ch., 5 December 2003)
Prosecutor v. Hadzihasanovic, Decision on Interlocutory Appeal Challenging Jurisdiction in Relation to Command Responsibility, Case No. IT-01-47-AR72 (ICTY App. Ch., 16 July 2003)
Prosecutor v. Hadzihasanovic, Decision Pursuant to Rule 72(E) as to Validity of Appeal, Case No. IT-01–47-AR72, (ICTY App. Ch. Bench, 21 February 2003)
Prosecutor v. Marijacic, Case No. IT-95-14-R77.2 (ICTY App. Ch., 10 March 2006)
Prosecutor v. Milosevic, Indictment, ICTY No. IT-02–54 (24 May 1999)
Prosecutor v. Milutinovic, Decision on Dragojub Ojdanic's Motion Challenging Jurisdiction: Joint Criminal Enterprise, Case No. IT-99–37-AR72 (ICTY App. Ch., 21 May 2003)
Prosecutor v. Tadic, Decision on the Defence Motion for Interlocutory Appeal on Jurisdiction, Case No. IT-94–1[-A] (ICTY App. Ch., 2 October 1995)
Prosecutor v Tadic, Case No. IT-94–1-A, Appeals Judgement, (ICTY App. Ch., 15 July 1999)
Prosecutor v. Tadic (Appeal of Vujin), Judgement on Allegations of Contempt against Prior Counsel, Milan Vujin, Case No. IT-94–1-A-R77 (ICTY App. Ch., 27 February 2001)
Prosecutor v. Vasiljevic, Trial Judgement, Case No. IT-98–32-T (ICTY Trial Chamber, 29 November 2002)

Italian–United States Conciliation Commission

Flegenheimer Claim, 25 ILR 91 (Italian–United States Conciliation Comm'n, 1963)

Permanent Court of International Justice

Consistency of Certain Danzig Legislative Decrees with the Constitution of the Free City, Advisory Opinion of 4 December 1935, PCIJ, Series A/B, No. 65
S.S. Lotus (France v. Turkey), PCIJ, Ser. A, No. 10
Jurisdiction of the Courts of Danzig (Polish Railways), Advisory Opinion of 3 March 1928, PCIJ Series B, No. 15
Polish Postal Service in Danzig, Advisory Opinion of 16 May 1925, Series B, No. 11
Free City of Danzig and the International Labour Organization, Advisory Opinion of 26 August 1930, PCIJ Series B, No. 18
Treatment of Polish Nationals and Other Persons of Polish Origin or Speech in the Danzig Territory, Advisory Opinion of 4 February 1932, PCIJ Series A/B, No. 44

Post–World War II Cases (including the Major War Crimes trials, Control Council Law No. 10 cases and other occupation cases) (for post–World War II cases in fully national courts, see National table below)

Case against Bl., 1 ENTSCHEIDUNGEN DES OBERSTEN GERICHTSHOFES FÜR DIE BRITISCHE ZONE IN STRAFSACHEN 5 (Germany Supreme Court British Occupied Zone, 4 May 1948)

Trial of Bommer, 9 UNWCC, Law Rep. 62 ([French] Permanent Military Tribunal at Metz, 19 February 1947)

Case against M., 2 ENTSCHEIDUNGEN DES OBERSTEN GERICHTSHOFES FÜR DIE BRITISCHE ZONE IN STRAFSACHEN 378 (Germany Supreme Court British Occupied Zone, 21 March 1950)

Trial of Klein (Hadamar Trial), 1 UNWCC, Law Rep. 46 (United States Military Commission, 15 October 1945)

Trial of Krupp, 10 UNWCC, Law Rep. Case No. 58, pp. 69, 158 (USMT, 30 June 1948)

Trial of Tesch (The Zyklon B Case), 1 UNWCC, Law Rep. 93 (British Military Court, Hamburg, 8 March 1946)

United States v. Altstoetter ("Justice Case"), USMT, 3 TRIALS OF WAR CRIMINALS BEFORE THE NUERNBERG MILITARY TRIBUNALS UNDER CONTROL COUNCIL LAW NO. 10 (4 December 1947) (Washington, DC: U.S. Government Printing Office, October 1946–April 1949)

United States v. Araki, THE TOKYO MAJOR WAR CRIMES TRIAL: THE JUDGMENT, SEPARATE OPINIONS, PROCEEDINGS IN CHAMBERS, APPEALS AND REVIEWS OF THE INTERNATIONAL MILITARY TRIBUNAL FOR THE FAR EAST, Vols. 101–109 (1948) (R. John Pritchard ed., Published for Robert M. W. Kempner Collegium by Edwin Mellen Press, 1998)

United States v. Brandt ("Medical Case"), 2 T.W.C. 171 (USMT, October 25 1946)

United States v. Göring, TRIAL OF THE MAJOR WAR CRIMINALS BEFORE THE INTERNATIONAL MILITARY TRIBUNAL: NUREMBERG 14 NOVEMBER 1945–1 OCTOBER 1946 (Nuremberg: IMT, 1947)

United States v. Ohlendorf (Einsatzgruppen Case), 4 TRIALS OF WAR CRIMINALS BEFORE THE NUERNBERG MILITARY TRIBUNALS UNDER CONTROL COUNCIL LAW NO. 10 (1948) (Washington, DC: U.S. Government Printing Office, October 1946–April 1949)

United States v. Von Leeb ("The High Command Case"), Opinion and Judgment, 11 T.W.C. 462 (USMT V, 27 October 1948)

Trial of Max Weilen, 11 UNWCC, Law Rep. 31 (Brit. Mil. Ct., Hamburg, Germany, 3 September 1947)

Special Court for Sierra Leone

Prosecutor v. Norman, Decision on Preliminary Motion Based on Lack of Jurisdiction, Case No. SCSL 04-14-AR72(E) (SCSL App. Ch., 31 May 2004)

United Nations Human Rights Committee under the ICCPR

A.R.S.v. Canada, Comm. No. 91/81

General Comment No. 29 (72), UN Doc. CCPR/C/21/Rev.1/Add.11.

MacIsaac v. Canada, HRC Comm. No. 53/79 (1983)
Weinberger Weisz v. Uruguay, HRC Comm. No. 28/1978, UN Doc. CCPR/C/OP/1
Westerman v. Netherlands, HRC Comm. No. 682/1986, UN Doc. A/55/40, Annex IX (UNHRC, 3 November 1999)

Special Court for Sierra Leone

Prosecutor v. Norman, Judgment (SCSL App. Ch., 31 May 2004)

National

Australia

Polyukovich v. Commonwealth, 172 CLR 501 (Australia, High Ct., 1991)

Canada

Regina v. Finta, 104 ILR 285 (Canada, Sup. Ct., 24 March 1994)

China (incl. Hong Kong)

Shum Kwok Sher v. HKSAR, [2002] HKCEA 17 (Hong Kong)

East Timor

Prosecutor v. dos Santos, Applicable Subsidiary Law Decision, Case No. 16/2001 (Timor-Leste, Court of Appeal, 15 July 2003)
Public Prosecutor v. Sarmento, Decision on the defense (Domingos Mendonca) motion for the Court to order the Public Prosecutor to amend the indictment, Case No. 18a/2001 (Timor-Leste, Dili District Special Court for Serious Crimes, 24 July 2003)

France

Matter of Barbie (France, Cour de Cassation, 1983), 78 Int'l. L. Rep. 125 (1988)
Barbie Case No. 2, Bull. Crim. No. 34, 78 ILR 132 (France, Cour de Cassation, 26 January 1984)
Decision of the Constitutional Council of 16 July 1971 (Liberty of Association)
Trial of Wagner, 3 UNWCC, Law Rep. Case No. 13 (French Permanent Military Court, Strasbourg, 3 May 1946, aff'd, Cour de Cassation, 24 July 1946)

Germany

Kalkar Case 1, Judgment of 8 August 1988, 49 BVerfGE 89 (Germany, Federal Constitutional Court), published in Entscheidungen des Bundesverfassungsgerichts (from West Germany, 1951–1990)
Publication of Treaties Case, (Reichsgericht in Strafsachen, 25 September 1920), partial translation into English in Annual Digest 1919–1922, No. 234, p. 323

Hungary

On War Crimes and Crimes against Humanity, Decision No. 53/1993 (Hungary Const. Ct., 13 October 1993)

Iraq

Saddam Hussein, Lawsuit No.1/Criminal/2005, judgment delivered orally 5 November 2006 (Iraqi High Tribunal), aff'd 26 December 2006 (Iraqi High Tribunal Appeals Commission)

Al Anfal, Case No 1/ CSecond/2006, 24 June 2007 (Iraqi High Tribunal)

Israel

Eichmann v. Attorney-General, [1962] 16 Piske Din 2033 (Israel, Sup. Ct., 29 May 1962), reprinted in 36 Int'l L. Rep. 277 (1968), aff'g 45 Pesakim Mehoziim 3 (Jerusalem Dist. Ct., 11 December 1961), reprinted in 36 Int'l L. Rep. 18

Netherlands

Trial of Rauter, 14 UNWCC Law Reports of Trials of War Criminals, Case No. 88, 89 (Netherlands Special Ct. of Cass. 12 January 1949)

[*Wijngaarde v. Bouterse*,] Appeal in cassation in the interests of the law, (Hoge Raad der Nederlanden [Supreme Court of the Netherlands], 18 September 2001), translated into English at 32 Netherlands YBIL 282 (2001)

Norway

Trial of Klinge, 3 UNWCC, Law Rep., Case No. 11 (Supreme Court of Norway 27, February 1946)

Poland

Trial of Goeth, 7 UNWCC, Law Rep. 1, 4 (Sup. Nat. Trib. of Poland, 5 September 1946)

Trial of Greiser, 13 UNWCC, Law Rep., Case No. 74, pp. 70, 104 (Sup. Nat. Trib. of Poland, 7 July 1946)

Trial of Hoess, 7 UNWCC, Law Rep. 11, 17 (Sup. Nat. Trib. of Poland, 29 March 1947)

Rwanda

Ministère Public v. Karamira, 1 Recueil de jurisprudence contentieux du genocide et des massacres au Rwanda 75 (1st inst., Kigali, 14 February 1997)

Singapore

Public Prosecutor v. Manogaran, [1997] 2 LRC 288 (Ct. of App. of Singapore)

Slovenia

Case U-1–248/96 (Slovenia Const. Ct., 30 September 1998)

Sri Lanka

Ekanayake v. The Attorney-General, C.A. 132/84 (Sri Lanka Ct. of App., 28 May 1986), app. dis., S.C. App. No. 68/86 (Sri Lanka S.Ct., 9 December 1987) [both available through official Sri Lanka government Web site at http://www.lawnet.lk]

United Kingdom

R. v R., U.K. Crown Court, Judgment, 30 July 1990, [1991] 1 All E.R. 747, aff'd, Ct. App., Crim. Div., 14 March 1991, [1991] 2 All E.R. 257
Shaw v. DPP, [1962] AC 220 (H.L.)
The King v. Pear, 1 Leach 212, 168 Eng. Rep. 208 (Cent. Crim. Ct., 1779)
Knuller (Publishing, Printing and Promotions), Ltd v. DPP [1973] AC 435 (H.L.)
The Queen v. Hall, 169 Eng. Rep. 291 (1868)
Regina v. Bartle (Pinochet), U.K. House of Lords, 24 March 1999, reprinted in 38 ILM 581 (1999)
Rex v. Chisser, T. Raym. 275, 83 Eng. Rep. 142 (K.B. 1678)

United States

Bouie v. City of Columbia, 378 U.S. 347 (1964)
Calder v. Bull, 3 U.S. (3 Dall.) 386 (1798)
Commonwealth v. Mochan, 177 Pa. Super. 454, 110 A.2d 788 (1955)
Demanjuk v. Petrovsky, 776 F.2d 571 (6th Cir. 1985), cert. denied, 475 U.S. 1016 (1986)
Hamdan v. Rumsfeld, 548 U.S. 557 (2006)
Kansas v. Hendricks, 521 U.S. 346, 361 (1997)
Kring v. Missouri, 107 U.S. 221 (1883)
Lambert v. California, 355 U.S. 225 (1957)
Loucks v. Standard Oil Co. of New York, 224 N.Y. 99, 120 N.E. 198 (1918)
Papachristou v. City of Jacksonville, 405 U.S. 156 (1972)
Ex parte Quirin, 317 U.S. 1 (1942)
Rogers v. Tennessee, 532 U.S. 451 (2001)
United States v. Smith, 18 U.S. (5 Wheat.) 153 (1820)
United States v. Wiltberger, 18 U.S. (5 Wheat.) 76 (1820)
Ex parte Yamashita, 327 U.S. 1 (1946)

OTHER AUTHORITIES

International Sources

Treaties and Other International Agreements and Understandings (associated documents, protocols, etc., listed below main treaty, indented)

African Charter of Human and Peoples Rights arts. 2, 6, 7, 13, 45 (concluded [at Banjul], 26 June 1981. Entered into force 21 October 1986), OAU Doc. CAB/LEG/67/3/Rev. 5 (27 June 1981), reprinted in 21 ILM 59 (1982)

Protocol to the African Charter on Human and Peoples' Rights on the Establishment of an African Court on Human and Peoples' Rights (Ouagadougou, Burkina Faso, 9 June 1998; entered into force 25 January 2004)

Agreement Between the United Nations and the Royal Government of Cambodia Concerning the Prosecution under Cambodian Law of Crimes Committed During the Period of Democratic Kampuchea art. 32 (signed at Phnom Penh on 6 June 2003; entered into force on 29 April 2005)

Agreement between the United Nations and the Government of Sierra Leone on the Establishment of a Special Court for Sierra Leone (16 January 2002)

American Convention on Human Rights arts. 3, 5, 7–9, 27, 44, 45, 48–51, 57, 61, 62, 68, 69 (concluded [at San José, Costa Rica], 22 November 1969; entered into force 18 July 1978), OASTS No. 36, OAS Off. Rec. O.E.A./Ser. L/V/II.23 Doc. 21 Rev. 6 (1979), 1114 UNTS 123, reprinted in 9 ILM 673 (1970)

[Revised] Arab Charter on Human Rights arts. 3, 14, 15, 24 (concluded by the Summit of the Heads of State of the Arab League at Tunis, May 2004; entered into force 15 March 2008)

Arab Charter on Human Rights art. 6, adopted by the Council of the League of Arab States, Resolution 5437, 102d Reg. Sess., 15 September 1994 (never in force)

Convention for the Protection of Human Rights and Fundamental Freedoms, also known as the European Convention on Human Rights (ECHR), arts. 7, 9, 14, 15, 34–39, 46, 49 (concluded 4 November 1950; entered into force 3 September 1953), 213 UNTS 221 11th Protocol to the ECHR

Convention on the Rights of the Child art. 40, UNGA Res. 44/25 (Annex) (20 November 1989; entered into force 2 September 1990)

Crimea (Yalta) Declaration [UK, USA, USSR] (released in part 13 February 1945; released in full 24 March 1945)

Draft Agreement between the United Nations and the Royal Government of Cambodia concerning the Prosecution under Cambodian Law of Crimes Committed during the Period of Democratic Kampuchea art. 12(2), approved in and annexed to Khmer Rouge Trials, UNGA Res. 57/228 B, UN Doc. A/RES/57/228 B (22 May 2003)

European Union Charter of Fundamental Rights of the European Union art. 49, 2000/C 364/01 (7 December 2000; pub. date 18 December 2000; not yet in force)

Geneva Convention for the Amelioration of the Condition of the Wounded and Sick in Armies in the Field (27 July 1929; entered into force 19 June 1931), 118 LNTS 303

Geneva Convention Relative to Prisoners of War (27 July 1929; entered into force 19 June 1931), 118 LNTS 343)

Geneva Convention (No. IV) Relative to the Protection of Civilian Persons in Time of War arts. 4, 33, 34, 65, 147 (concluded, 12 Aug. 1949; entered into force, 21 October 1950), 75 UNTS 287

Geneva Convention (No. III) Relative to the Treatment of Prisoners of War arts. 3, 13, 26, 85, 87, 99 (concluded, 12 August 1949; entered into force 21 October 1950), 75 UNTS 135

Geneva Conventions (Nos. I & II) common art. 3 (concluded 12 August 1949; entered into force 21 October 1950)

Additional Protocol No. I to the Geneva Conventions of 1949 art. 75

Additional Protocol No. II to the Geneva Conventions of 1949 arts. 4, 6

Hague Convention (No. IV) Respecting the Laws and Customs of War on Land (18 October 1907, entered into force 26 January 1910), reprinted in 2 AM. J. INT'L L. Supp. 90

Hague Conventions (Nos. I-X) (18 October 1907)

International Covenant on Civil and Political Rights arts. 4, 9, 14, 15, 25 (concluded at New York, 16 December 1966; entered into force 23 March 1976), 999 UNTS 171, reprinted in 6 ILM 368 (1967)

First Optional Protocol to the International Covenant on Civil and Political Rights, 999 UNTS 171

Japanese Instrument of Surrender (2 September 1945)

London Agreement of 8 August 1945, 59 Stat. 1544, with annexed Charter of the International Military Tribunal [Nuremberg Charter] arts. 6, 8, 9

Protocol Rectifying Discrepancy in Text of [Nuremberg] Charter, 6 October 1945

Moscow Conference Agreement § 5 (26 December 1945)

Moscow Declaration (30 October 1943) (Concerning Responsibility of Hitlerites for Committed Atrocities)

Potsdam Declaration of United States, United Kingdom and China (26 July 1945)

Protocol for the Pacific Settlement of International Disputes (Geneva Protocol), Preamble, 1924 (never entered into force)

Rome Statute of the International Criminal Court [ICC Statute] arts. 2, 5, 7, 8, 10, 11–13, 17–19, 21–24, 38, 75, 77, 82, 121, 123, 124 (adopted 17 July 1998, entered into force 1 July 2002), UN Doc. A/CONF 183/9 (17 July [1998]), 37 ILM 999 (1998)

Relationship Agreement between the United Nations and the International Criminal Court

Statute of the Permanent Court of International Justice [PCIJ Statute] art. 38

Treaty Providing for the Renunciation of War as an Instrument of National Policy ["Pact of Paris" or "Kellogg-Briand Pact"] arts. 1 & 2 (concluded, 27 August 1928; entered into force 24 July 1929), 94 LNTS 57.

Treaty of Lausanne (24 July 1923), with associated Declaration of Amnesty (24 July 1923)

Treaty of Sèvres arts. 226–228, 230, (10 August 1920; never entered into force, superseded by Treaty of Lausanne)

Treaty of Versailles arts. 100–08, 227, 228, 229 (28 June 1919; entered into force 10 January 1920)

United Nations Charter, Chap. XII, art. 103

Statute of the International Court of Justice art. 38 (concluded at San Francisco, 26 June 1945; entered into force 24 October 1945)

Yugoslavia-Croatia Agreement of 27 November 1991

League of Nations and Permanent Court of International Justice Documents

League of Nations Council, Resolution, 17 May 1922
Permanent Court of International Justice. ANNUAL REPORT, 1922–1925. PCIJ Series E, No. 1

United Nations Documents

Economic and Social Council Resolutions and Documents:

Resolutions
ECOSOC Res. 1/5 (16 February 1946)
ECOSOC Res. 2/9 (21 June 1946)
ECOSOC Res. No. 46 (IV) (28 March 1947)
ECOSOC Res. No. 151 (VII) (26 August 1948)
ESCOR, 1st yr., 1st sess., p. 163
ESCOR, 5th year, 11th sess., Supp. No. 5 & Annex I at 15, 17 (Draft First International Covenant on Human Rights, art. 11)
ESCOR, 14th sess., Supp. 4, pp. 1, 33

Documents
E/38/Rev.1 (Report of the Commission on Human Rights to the Second Session of the Economic and Social Council) (May 21, 1946)
E/259 (Report to the Economic and Social Council on the First Session of the Commission) (27 January to 10 February 1947)
E/600 (17 December 1947)
E/800 (28 June 1948) (Report of the third session of the Commission on Human Rights)
E/1065
E/1371 and E/CN.4/350 (23 June 1949) (Report of the Fifth Session of the Commission on Human Rights to the Economic and Social Council)
E/1681 (Report to the Economic and Social Council on the Work of the sixth session of the Commission [on Human Rights]) (25 May 1950)
E/1992 (17 May 1951)
E/2256 (Report to the Economic and Social Council on the eighth session of the Commission, held in New York, from 14 April–14 June 1952)

ECOSOC Human Rights Commission Documents
E/CN.4/AC.1/1 (Drafting Committee: Draft Provisional Agenda) (May 28, 1947)
E/CN.4/AC.1/3 & Add.1 (Draft Outline of an International Bill of Rights & Annotated Draft Outline) (2–4 June 1947)
E/CN.4/21 (Report of the Drafting Committee to the Commission on Human Rights) (1 July 1947)
E/CN.4/37 (26 November 1947) (U.S. Proposal for a Human Rights Convention)
E/CN.4/56 (Report of the Working Party on and International Convention on Human Rights) (11 December 1947)

E/CN.4/57 (Report of the Working Group on the Declaration on Human Rights) (December 10, 1947)
E/CN.4/82/Adds. 7, 8, 11 (Comments From Governments on The Draft International Declaration on Human Rights, Draft International Covenant on Human Rights and the Question of Implementation) (4, 6, and 19 May 1948)
E/CN.4/85 (Collation of the Comments of Governments on the Draft International Declaration of Human Rights, Draft International Covenant on Human Rights, and the Question of Implementation) (1 May 1948)
E/CN.4/95 (Report of the Drafting Committee to the Commission on Human Rights) (21 May 1948)
E/CN.4/170 (United States: Proposals Relating to the Draft International Covenant on Human Rights) (6 May 1949)
E/CN.4/188 (United Kingdom: Proposals on Certain Articles) (16 May 1948)
E/CN.4/233 (23 May 1949)
Draft International Covenant on Human Rights, U.N. Doc E/CN.4/228 (23 May 1949)
E/CN.4/253 (Draft International Covenant on Human Rights: Recapitulation of amendments to Articles 13,14, and 15) (24 May 1949)
E/CN.4/350
E/CN.4/353/Add.10 (Comments of Governments of the Draft International Covenant on Human Rights and Measures of Implementation) (22 March 1950)
E/CN.4/365 Compilation of the Comments of Governments on the Draft International Covenant on Human Rights and on the Proposed Additional Articles: Memorandum by the Secretary-General (March 22, 1950)
E/CN.4/425 Draft International Covenant on Human Rights, UN Doc. E/CN.4/425 (14 April 1950)
E/CN.4/524 (Regional Activities in The Promotion of Human Rights: The Convention for the Protection of Human Rights and Fundamental Freedoms concluded by members of the Council of Europe) (April 1951)
E/CN.4/528 (Draft International Covenant on Human Rights and Measures of Implementation, The General Adequacy of the First Eighteen Articles (Parts I and II), Memorandum by the Secretary-General) (2 April 1951)
E/CN.4/528 /Add.1 (Draft International Covenant on Human Rights and Measures of Implementation: The General Adequacy of the Provisions Concerning Civil and Political Rights) (20 March 1952)
E/CN.4/552 (22 April 1951) (Compilation of the Observations of Governments of Member States on the Draft International Covenant on Human Rights and Measures of Implementation, as Drafted at the Sixth Session of the Commission on Human Rights)
E/CN.4/694/Add.7 (Draft International Covenants on Human Rights and Measures of Implementation: Observations of Governments received by the Secretary-General pursuant to Economic and Social Council Resolution 501 B (XVI)) (23 March 1954)
E/CN.4/L.3 (April 19, 1950) (Text of Articles 12, 14, and 15 as Adopted by the Commission in First Reading)
E/CN.4/L.10/Corr.1 (Draft International Covenant on Human Rights: Memorandum by the Secretary General) (15 May 1950)

E/CN.4/L.16 (22 May 1950) (Text of Articles 5,6 and 8–15 of the Draft Covenant on Human Rights as revised by the Style Committee during its meetings held on 16 May 1950)

Summary Records
E/AC.7/SR.148 (10 August 1950)
E/CN.4/SR.7 (31 January 1947)
E/CN.4/SR.12 (3 February 1947)
E/CN.4/AC.1/SR.25
E/CN.4/AC.1/SR.30
E/CN.4/AC.1/SR.31
E/CN.4/SR.54
E/CN.4/SR.56 (4 June 1948)
E/CN.4/SR.112 (7 June 1949, reporting session of 3 June 1949)
E/CN.4/SR.159 (27 April 1950)
E/CN.4/SR.199 (31 May 1950)
E/CN.4/SR.324 (27 June 1952)

Year Books on Human Rights
1946 UNYBHR
1947 UNYBHR
1948 UNYBHR
1949 UNYBHR
1951 UNYBHR
1952 UNYBHR
1957 UNYBHR
1958 UNYBHR
1960 UNYBHR
1961 UNYBHR
1962 UNYBHR
1968 UNYBHR
1975 UNYBHR

General Assembly Resolutions and Documents:

Resolutions
G.A. Res. 95 (I), Affirmation of the Principles of International Law Recognized by the Charter of the Nürnberg Tribunal, 1st sess., UN Doc. A/236 (11 December 1946)
GAOR, 3d sess., Plenary Meetings, pp. 852–934 (1948).
G.A. Res. 217 (III), Universal Declaration of Human Rights (UDHR), preamble & arts. 8, 11, 28, 30, 10 December 1948, GAOR 3d sess., pt. I, p. 71
G.A. Res. 217E (III) (1948)
G.A. Res. 2200A (XXI), International Covenant on Civil and Political Rights, 21 GAOR Supp. No. 16, p. 52, UN Doc. A/6316, 993 UNTS 171 (16 December 1966, entered into force 23 March 1976)
G.A. Res. 2200 A (XXI) (1966)
G.A. Res. 44/25 (Annex) (20 November 1989), UN Doc. A/RES/44/49 (Convention on the Rights of the Child)

G.A. Res. 57/228 B, Khmer Rouge Trials, UN Doc. A/RES/57/228 B (22 May 2003), with annexed Draft Agreement between the United Nations and the Royal Government of Cambodia concerning the Prosecution under Cambodian Law of Crimes Committed during the Period of Democratic Kampuchea
G.A. Res. 60/251 (3 April 2006)
GAOR, 3d sess., 1st pt., Third Committee, pp. 265–75, 849, 879–80 (1948)
GAOR, 3d sess., 1st pt., Third Committee, Annexes to the Summary Records of Meetings, pp. 124–25 (1948)
GAOR 10th sess., Annexes, p. 45 (1955)
GAOR, 15th sess., Third Committee, pp. 129ff. (1960)

Documents
A/777 (Report of the Third Committee) (1948)
A/2929 (Annotations on the text of the draft International Covenants on Human Rights (Prepared by the Secretary-General)) (1 July 1955)
A/4397 (1960)
A/4625 (Draft International Covenants on Human Rights: Report of the Third Committee) (8 December 1960)
A/C.3/220
A/C.3/223
A/C.3/230, p. 10 (6 October 1948)
A/C.3/400/Rev.1 (4 December 1948)
A/C.3/L.865 (31 October 1960)
A/CN.4/16 (3 March 1950) (Manley Hudson, Working Paper)
A/PV.1496 (16 December 1966)

Summary Records (General Assembly and Third Committee)
A/C.3/SR.111
A/C.3/SR.112
A/C.3/SR.113
A/C.3/SR.114
A/C.3/SR.115
A/C.3/SR.116
A/C.3/SR.1007
A/C.3/SR.1008
A/C.3/SR.1009
A/C.3/SR.1010
A/C.3/SR.1011
A/C.3/SR.1012
A/C.3/SR.1013
A/C.3/SR.1014

International Law Commission Documents
International Law Commission, Principles of International Law Recognized in the Charter of the Nürnberg Tribunal and in the Judgment of the Tribunal, UN Doc. A/1316, 2 YBILC 374-78 ¶¶ 95128 (2 August 1950).

Security Council Resolutions and Documents:

Resolutions

Security Council Resolution 541, UN Doc. S/RES/541 (18 November 1983)
Security Council Resolution 748, UN Doc. S/RES/748 (31 March 1992)
Security Council Resolution 827, UN Doc. S/RES/827, with appended Statute of the International Tribunal [for the Former Yugoslavia]
Security Council Resolution 1244, UN Doc. S/RES/1244 (10 June 1999)
Security Council Resolution 1267, UN Doc. S/RES/1267 (15 October 1999).
Security Council Resolution 1272, UN Doc. No. S/RES/1272 (25 October 1999)
Security Council Resolution 1373, UN Doc. S/RES/1373 (28 September 2001)
Security Council Resolution 1390, UN Doc. S/RES/1390 (16 January 2002)
Security Council Res. 1483, UN Doc. S/RES.1483 (22 May 2003)
Security Council Resolution 1593, UN Doc. S/RES/1593 (31 March 2005)
Security Council Resolution 1757, UN Doc. S/RES/1757 (30 May 2007), with appended agreement between the United Nations and Lebanon and Statute of the Special Tribunal for Lebanon

Documents

Provisional Verbatim Record, SCOR, 3217th Meeting., at 11, 15, 19, UN Doc. S/PV.3217 (25 May 1993)
Report of the Secretary-General pursuant to Paragraph 2 of Security Council Resolution 808, UN Doc. S/25704 (3 May 1993), available at http://www.un.org/icty/legaldoc-e/basic/statut/s25704.htm
Report of the Secretary-General on the establishment of a special tribunal for Lebanon, UN Doc. S/2006/893 (15 November 2006)

Tribunal Statutes and Documents Other Than Case Documents and Security Council Documents:

International Criminal Tribunal for the Former Yugoslavia Rules of Procedure and Evidence, R. 77
International Criminal Tribunal for Rwanda [ICTR] Statute art. 1
International Criminal Tribunal for the Former Yugoslavia [ICTY] Statute art. 8
Special Court for Sierra Leone [SCSL] Statute arts. 1, 5, 6, 19
Special Tribunal for Lebanon [STL] Statute art. 6

UN Mission in Kosovo [UNMIK] Documents

UNMIK Regulation. No. 1999/24 (10 Jun 1999)
UNMIK Regulation No. 2000/59, UN Doc. UNMIK/REG/2000/59, Amending UNMIK Regulation No. 1999/24 [10 June 1999] On the Law Applicable In Kosovo (27 October 2000), §§ 1.3, 1.4

UN Transitional Authority in East Timor [UNTAET] Documents

UNTAET Regulation No. 1999/1, UNTAET/REG/1999/1, On the Authority of the Transitional Administration in East Timor § 2 (27 November 1999)
UNTAET Regulation No. 2000/15, UNTAET/REG/2000/15, On the Establishment of Panels with Exclusive Jurisdiction over Serious Criminal Offenses §§ 3, 10, 12, 13 (6 June 2000)

Other Official International Sources

Post–World War I

Commission on the Responsibility of the Authors of the War and on Enforcement of Penalties, Report Presented to the Preliminary Peace Conference (Versailles, 29 March 1919), published at 14 AJIL 95 (1920)
Reservations by the Japanese Delegation [Annex I to the Report]
Robert Lansing & James Brown Scott, Memorandum of Reservations Presented by the Representatives of the United States to the Report of the Commission on Responsibilities (April 4, 1919) [Annex II to the Report]
Demand of Allied Powers to the Netherlands for Extradition of the Kaiser

Post–World War II (Occupation of Germany and Japan)

Germany Control Council Law (Proclamation) No. 3 (20 October 1945), and Military Order No. 1 (issued in pursuance thereof)
Germany Control Council Law No. 10, art. II (31 January 1946)
Germany Control Council Law No. 11, Official Gazette of the Control Council for Germany, No. 3 (31 January 1946)
Special Proclamation by the Supreme Commander of the Allied Powers, Establishment of an International Military Tribunal for the Far East (19 January 1946)
Charter of the International Military Tribunal for the Far East [IMTFE Charter or Tokyo Tribunal Charter] art. 5
Amendment to IMTFE Charter, 26 April 1946, 4 Bevans 20

Occupation of Iraq

Statute of the Iraqi Special Tribunal arts. 1, 4, 6, 8, 10, 17, 24, Statute No. 1, Iraqi Governing Council, 10 December 2003 (under authority of Coalition Provisional Authority for Iraq), later a statute of Iraq after restoration of sovereignty

National Sources

Constitutions and Constitutional Documents (alphabetical by jurisdiction) (dates given where referring to historic documents or otherwise of particular interest; where no dates are given, current as of autumn 2007)

Afghanistan Const. arts. 24, 26, 27 [alternately numbered ch. 2, arts. 3, 5, 6]
Afghanistan Fundamental Principles of the Government, art. 11 (as of 1947)
Albania Const. arts. 29, 135, 175
Albania Const. art. 19 (as of 1946)
Algeria Const. arts. 46, 140, 142
Andorra Const. arts. 3, 9, 85
Angola Const. Law art. 36, 52, 125, 126
Antigua and Barbuda Const. art. 15
Argentina Const. arts. 18, 19 (current and as of 1947)
Armenia Const. arts. 22, 42, 44, 92
Azerbaijan Const. arts. 71, 125

Bahamas Const. arts. 20, 29
Bahrain Const. art. 20
Bangladesh Const. arts. 35, 47, 47A
Barbados Const. art. 18
Belarus Const. arts. 104, 109
Belgium Coord. Const. arts. 12–14, 146
Belgium Const. art. 9 (as of 1947)
Belize Const. art. 6
Benin Const. arts. 7, 17
Bolivia Const. arts. 14, 16, 32, 33, 116
Bolivia Const. art. 13, 29, 31 (as of 1947)
Bosnia and Herzegovina Const. art. II, § 2
Bosnia and Herzegovina subnational entities:
Bosnia and Herzegovina (Fed. Of [entity within state of Bosnia and Herzegovina]) Const. part II(A), art. 2; Annex
Srpska (Rep. of [entity within state of Bosnia and Herzegovina]) Const. art. 20
Botswana Const. art. 10
Brazil Const. art. 5
Brazil Const. art. 14, 140, 141 (as of 1947)
Bulgaria Const. arts. 5, 119
Burkina Faso Const. arts. 5, 140
Burundi Const. arts. 19, 39, 40, 41
Burundi Const. (1 July 1962) art. 9
Cambodia Const. arts. 31, 38
Cameroun [Cameroon] Const., preamble
Canada Const. Act art. 11
Cape Verde Const. arts. 16, 30, 222
Central African Rep. Const. art. 3
Chad Const. art. 23
Chile Const. art. 19
Chile Const. arts. 11, 26, 28 (as of 1947)
Colombia Const. arts. 28, 29
Colombia Const. arts. 26, 28 (as of 1947)
Comoros Const. art. 48
Congo (Dem. Rep. of) Const. arts. 17, 19, 149
Costa Rica Const. arts. 28, 34, 35, 39
Costa Rica Const. arts. 26, 36, 38, 43 (as of 1947)
Cote d'Ivoire Const. arts. 21, 112
Croatia [Republike Hrvatske] Const. arts. 31, 87, 89
Cuba Const. arts. 59, 61
Cuba Const. arts. 21, 22 (as of 1947)
Cyprus (Rep. of) Const. art. 12
Cyprus (Turkish Rep. of Northern) Const. arts. 17, 18, 21
Czech Rep. Const. art. 3
Czech Rep. Charter of Fundamental Rights and Basic Freedoms arts. 2, 39, 40
Czechoslovakia Charter of Fundamental Rights and Freedoms art. 40 (1991)
Czechoslovak Rep. Const. Charter arts. 94, 111 (1920, as of 1946–47)

Danzig (Free City of) Const. arts. 71–75 (entity between World Wars I and II)
Denmark Const. Act, art. 61
Djibouti Const. art. 10
Dominica Const. arts. 8, 49
Dominican Rep. Const. arts. 8, 47
Dominican Rep. Const. art. 88 (as of 1947)
Ecuador Const. art. 24
Ecuador Const. art. 169 (as of 1947)
Egypt Const. arts. 66, 187
Egypt Royal Rescript No. 42 Establishing the Constitutional Regime art. 6 (1923, as of 1947)
El Salvador Const. arts. 8, 15
El Salvador Const. arts. 24, 25 (as of 1947)
England [now part of United Kingdom] Magna Carta art. 39 (1215)
Equatorial Guinea Fundamental Law art. 13
Eritrea Const. arts. 17, 27
Estonia Const. art. 23
Ethiopia Const. arts. 22, 78
Ethiopia Const. arts. 23, 24 (as of 1946–47)
Fiji Const. art. 28
Finland Const., ch. 2, § 8; ch. 9, § 98
Finland Const. art. 13 (1919, as of 1946)
France Const., preamble
France Const., preamble (27 October 1946)
France Const. (1791)
France Declaration of the Rights of Man and of the Citizen arts. 5, 8 (1789)
Gabon Const. arts. 47, 79
Gambia Const. art. 24
Georgia Const. art. 42
Germany (Dem. Rep. of [East]), Const. art. 135 (1949)
Germany (Fed. Rep. of [West and current unified state]), Basic Law [Grundgesetz], arts. 96, 101, 103 (1949)
Germany ("Weimar") Const. art. 116 (1919)
German States during Occupation:
- Baden (Germany, French Zone) Const. art. 116 (18 May 1947)
- Bavaria (Germany, American Zone) Const. art. 104(1) (1 December 1946)
- Brandenburg (Germany, Soviet Zone) Const. art. 41(2) (6 February 1947)
- Bremen (Germany, American Zone) Const. art. 7 (12 October 1947)
- Hesse (Germany, American Zone) Const. art. 22 (1 December 1946)
- Mecklenburg (Germany, Soviet Zone) Const. art. 66 (15 January 1946)
- Rhineland-Palatinate (Germany, French Zone) Const. art. 6 (18 May 1947)
- Saxony (Germany, Soviet Zone) Const. art. 9 (28 February 1947)
- Saxony-Anhalt (Germany, Soviet Zone) Const. art. 9(1) (10 January 1947)
- Thuringia (Germany, Soviet Zone) Const. art. 3(3) (20 December 1946)
- Wuerttemberg-Baden (Germany, American Zone, art. 4 (24 November 1946)
- Württemberg-Hohenzollern (Germany, French Zone) Const. art. 17(1) (18 May 1947)

Ghana Const. arts. 19, 107
Greece Const. art. 7 (current and as of 1947)
Grenada Const. Order art. 8
Guatemala Const. arts. 5, 15, 17
Guatemala Const. art. 23, 49 (as of 1947)
Guinea Fundamental Law arts. 59. 86
Guinea-Bissau Const. art. 33
Guyana Const. art. 144
Haiti Const. arts. 51, 173–2
Haiti Const. arts. 15 and "D" (22 November 1946)
Honduras Const, arts. 70, 95, 96
Honduras Const. arts. 43, 54 (as of 1947)
Hungary [Magyar] Const. art. 5
Hungary Const. art. 57 (1949)
Hungary Act I (On the State Form) (31 January 1946)
Ireland Const. arts. 15, 38
Ireland [Eire] Const. art. 40 (as of 1946)
Iceland Const. art. 69
India Const. art. 20
Indonesia Const. arts. 28I, 29
Iran Const. art. 169
Iran Supplementary Fundamental Laws of 8 October 1907 art. 12 (8 October 1907, as of 1947)
Iraq Const. arts. 19, 92, 130
Iraq Organic Law art. 7 (21 March 1925, as of 1946)
Iraq Interim Const. art. 21 (1970)
Ireland Const. arts. 15, 38
Ireland (Eire) Const. art. 40
Italy Const. arts. 25, 102
Jamaica Const, art. 20
Japan Const. [Kenpō], arts. 39, 76
Japan ("Meiji") Const.
Jordan Const. art. 110:
Kazakhstan Const. art. 77
Kenya Const. art. 77
Kiribati Const. art. 10
Korea (Rep. of [South]), art. 13
Kosovo Const. art. 33 (7 April 2008; entered into force, 15 June 2008)
Kuwait Const. art. 32
Kyrgyzstan Const. arts. 41, 85
Latvia Const. art. 89
Lebanon Const. art. 8 (current and as of 1947)
Lesotho Const. art. 12
Liechtenstein Const. art. 33
Liechtenstein Const. art. 33 (as of 1946)
Liberia Const. art. 21
Liberia Const. art.8 (as of 1947)
Libya Const. art. 17 (7 October 1951)

Libya Constitutional Proclamation of the Revolutionary Command Council art. 31 (1969)
Libya Declaration on the Establishment of the Authority of the People art. 2 (1977) declaring Holy Kuran as the Constitution of Libya
Libya General People's Congress Law No 20 (1991)
Liechtenstein Const. art. 33
Lithuania Const. arts. 31, 111
Luxembourg Const. arts. 12–14, 86
Luxembourg Const. arts. 12–14 (as of 1947)
Macedonia Const. arts. 14, 52, amend. XXV
Madagascar Const. art. 13
Malawi Const. arts. 42, 44
Malaysia Const. art. 7
Maldives Const. art. 17
Mali Const. arts. 9, 95
Malta Const. arts. 13, 32, 39
Marshall Islands Const. art. II, § 8
Mauritania Const., preamble, art. 13
Mauritius Const., ch. II, arts. 10, 12
Mexico Const. arts. 13, 14
Mexico Const. arts. 13, 14 (as of 1947)
Micronesia Const. art. IV, § 11
Moldova Const. arts. 22, 115
Monaco Const. art. 20
Monaco Const. art. 7 (as of 1946)
Mongol People's Republic Constitution (Fundamental Law) (30 June 1940; as amended 28 September 1944)
Montenegro Const. arts. 25, 33, 34, 118 (2007)
Morocco Const. art. 4
Mozambique Const. arts. 99, 167, 201
Myanmar [Burma] Const. art. 23
Namibia Const. art. 12
Nauru Const. arts. 10, 81
Nepal Comprehensive Peace Agreement held between Government of Nepal and Communist Party of Nepal (Maoist), preamble (21 November 2006)
Nepal Interim Const. arts. 24, 101 (2007)
Nepal Const. (1990), arts. 14, 85
Netherlands Const. arts. 16, 89, 93
Netherlands Const. art. 162 (as of 1947)
Nicaragua Const. arts. 32, 34, 38. 160, 186
Nicaragua Const. arts. 23, 41, 43, 44 (as of 1947)
Niger Const. arts. 15–17, 120
Nigeria Const. arts. 4, 36
Norway Const. arts. 96, 97 (current and as of 1947)
Oman Basic Statute of the State arts. 21, 75
Pakistan Const. art. 12 ("in abeyance" as of 3 November 2007; restored 15 December 2007)
Pakistan, Proclamation of emergency (3 November 2007)

Palau Const. art. IV, sec. 6
Palestine Amended Basic Law art. 15
Panama Const. arts. 31, 33, 43
Panama Const. arts. 31, 33, 44 (as of 1947)
Papua New Guinea Const. art. 32, 37, 159, 172
Paraguay Const. arts. 9, 14, 17
Paraguay Const. art. 26, 30 (as of 1947)
Peru Const. arts. 2, 103, 139
Peru Const. art. 24, 26, 30, 57, 64 (as of 1947)
Philippines Const. art. III, § 22; art. VII, sec. 18
Philippines Const. art. III, § 11 (as of 1947)
Poland Const. arts. 42, 157, 228, 233
Poland Const. art. 98 (17 March 1921; declared by Polish Comm. on Nat'l Liberation to be in force in its "basic provisions" on 22 July 1944, pending adoption of new const.)
Portugal Const. arts. 7, 8, 19, 29, 205, 209
Portugal Const. art. 8 (as of 1946)
Qatar Const. arts. 40, 132
Romania Const. art. 15, 23, 115, 126
Roumania Const. art. 14 (as of 1946)
Russia Const. art. 15, 52, 54, 118
Russian Socialist Federated Soviet Republic Fundamental Law (10 July 1918)
Rwanda Const., preamble, ¶ 9; arts. 18, 20, 137, 143, 152
Rwanda Const. (24 November 1962) art. 13
Sahrawi Arab Democratic Republic [Western Sahara] Const. art. 26
St. Kitts and Nevis Const. arts. 4, 10
St. Lucia Const. art. 8
St. Vincent and the Grenadines Const. art. 8
Samoa Const. art. 10
São Tomé & Príncipe Const. arts. 7, 36, 39, 110
Saudi Arabia Basic System of the Consultative Council, art. 1, Decree A-90 (1 March 1992) decreeing that Quran and Sunna of the Prophet are Saudi Constitution
Senegal Const. art. 9
Serbia Const. arts. 196, 197
Seychelles Const. art. 19, 43, 48
Sierra Leone Const. art. 23
Singapore Const. arts. 11, 149
Slovakia Const. arts. 48–50
Slovenia Const. arts. 28, 153, 155
Solomon Is. Const. art. 10
Somalia Const. art. 34
Somalia Const. (1961), art. 42
Somaliland Revised Const. article 26
South Africa Const. art. 35
Spain Const. arts. 9, 25
Sri Lanka Const. art. 13
Sudan Interim National Const. art. 34

Suriname Const. arts. 11, 131, 132:
Sweden Instrument of Government arts. 10, 11, 22
Sweden Const. art. 16 (as of 1946)
Switzerland Const. art. 30
Syria Const. arts. 29, 30
Syria Const. art. 9 (as of 1947)
Tajikistan Const. art. 20
Tanganyika [now part of Tanzania] Const. (9 December 1961)
Tanzania Const. art. 13
Thailand Const. §§ 39, 197, 198 (2007)
Thailand Const. (Interim), art. 18 (2006)
Thailand Const. art. 32 (1997)
Timor-Leste [East Timor] Const. arts. 24, 31, 123, 163
Togo Const. arts. 19, 20, 129
Tonga Const. art. 20
Trinidad and Tobago Const. arts. 5, 19
Tunisia Const. art. 13
Turkey Const. art. 38
Turkmenistan Const. art. 43
Tuvalu Const. arts. 22, 36
Uganda Const. arts. 28, 44
Ukraine Const. arts. 58, 64, 125, 129
United Arab Emirates Const. arts. 27, 36, 38
United States Const. art. I, §§ 9 & 10; amends. V & XIV (current and as of 1947)
United States, State Constitutions before 1787
  Delaware [state of United States] Declaration of Rights and Fundamental Rules art. 3 (1776)
  Massachusetts [state of United States] Bill of Rights art. XXIV (1780)
Union of Soviet Socialist Republics Fundamental Law (31 January 1924)
Uruguay Const. arts. 10, 12, 19
Uruguay Const. art. 10 (as of 1947)
Vanuatu Const. art. 5
Vatican City Fundamental Law of the State art. 16
Venezuela Const. arts. 24, 49
Venezuela Const. art. 17(II) (as of 1947)
Vietnam Const. art. 127
Western Samoa [now Samoa] Const. (1962) art. 10
Yemen Const. arts. 46, 103
Yugoslavia Const. art. 28 (as of 1947)
Zambia Const. Act art. 18, 25, 32, 78
Zimbabwe Const. art. 18, 25, 26, 81, 92; sched. 2, § 1

National Statutes, Regulations and other Law (alphabetical by jurisdiction; including colonial and Trust Territory Laws) (dates given where referring to historic documents or otherwise of particular interest)

Algeria:
Algeria Penal Code art. 2

Argentina:
Argentina, Law of War Manual §§ 3.30, 5.025, 5.026 (1969)
Australia:
Australia Code Amendment (Offenses Against Australians) Act (2002)
Austria (including Austro-Hungarian Empire):
Austria, StGB § 1, 65
Austria Penal Code § 40 (1852)
Austro-Hungarian Military Penal Code art. 158 (1855)
Bangladesh:
International Crimes (Tribunal) Act § 3 (1973)
Belgium:
Belgium Crim. Code art. 2
Bhutan:
Bhutan Penal Code art. 6
Brunei:
Brunei Penal Code § 2
Laws of Brunei, Ch. 4 (Interpretation and General Clauses), § 37 (Rev. 2001), at http://www.agc.gov.bn/pdf/Cap4.pdf.
Bulgaria:
Bulgaria Penal Code arts. 2, 6
Cambodia:
Cambodia Law on the Establishment of the Extraordinary Chambers (as amended through 27 October 2004), NS/RKM/1004/006
Cameroons [UN Trust Territory]:
Decree No. 57–501, setting forth the Statute of Cameroun, art. 15 (16 April 1957)
Canada:
Canada LOAC Manual § 49(a) (1999)
China:
Peoples' Republic of China Criminal Law art. 3, 12
Peoples' Republic of China Legislation Law art. 9, 84
Qing Code art. 44
Côte d'Ivoire:
Côte d'Ivoire Criminal Code arts. 19–21
Danzig, Free City of:
Danzig Senate of the Free City, Decree of August 29, 1935 to Amend Certain Provisions of the Penal Code, arts. 1 & 2, amending Penal Code of the Free City of Danzig, arts. 2 & 2a, original in German as Verordung zur Änderung einiger Bestimmungen des Strafgesetzbuches. Vom 29. August 1935, *Gesetzblatt für die Freie Stadt Danzig*, No. 91, 31 August 1935
Denmark:
Denmark Crim. Code §§ 3, 4, 8, 56–70
Finland:
Decree Regarding Restrictions of Personal Freedom, No. 899 (30 December 1946)
France:
France Penal Code (1810). Available at http://www.legifrance.gouv.fr/html/codes_traduits/code_penal_textan.htm.

Germany (including states existing before the German Empire; German Empire; Weimar Republic; Third Reich; Fed. Rep. of [West] Germany; Dem. Rep. of [East] Germany; and current unified Fed. Rep. of Germany; for post-World War II Occupation, see Other Official International Sources, above):
Germany Decree of 16 March 1939art. 1 (on Bohemia and Moravia)
Germany, §§ 1, 2, 7 StGB
Germany Criminal (Penal) Code (1871) art. 2
Law of 28 June 1935 Amending the German Criminal (Penal) Code, §I, published in 1935 Reichgesetzblatt, part I, p. 839 (Germany), amending German Penal Code [StGB] art. 2
Law of 28 June 1935 Code of Criminal Procedure and Judicature Act, §§I, II, published in 1935 Reichgesetzblatt, part I, p. 844 (Germany), adding Germany Code of Criminal Procedure, arts. 170a & 267a
Statute "*Lex van der Lubbe*," RGBl. I, 151 (Germany, 29 March 1933)
Germany and Former German States Military Codes:
Baden Military Penal Code (1870)
Bavarian Military Penal Code (1869)
German Military Penal Code art. 47 (1872; rev. 1940)
Prussian Military Code (1845)
Saxony Military Penal Code (1857)
Hungary:
Hungary Crim. Code § 2
Iceland:
Iceland Gen. Penal Code art. 2
Iraq (including Baghdadi government, Iraqi governments before 2003 occupation; and government under restored Iraqi sovereignty; for occupation Coalition Provisional Authority see also Other Official International Sources above):
Baghdadi Criminal Code of 1919, as amended through 17 July 1968
Iraqi Criminal Code, Law No. 111 of 1969 (as of 15 December 1969)
Iraqi Criminal Procedure Law, Law No. 23 of 1971
Statute of the Iraqi Special Tribunal, arts. 1, 4, 6, 8, 10, 17, 24, Statute No. 1, Iraqi Governing Council, 10 December 2003 (under authority of Coalition Provisional Authority for Iraq; later statute of Iraq after sovereignty restored)
Ireland:
Geneva Conventions Act as amended §§ 4(1&4) (1962)
Israel:
Israel Penal Law §§ 1–6, 14–17
Israel Basic Law: The Judiciary art. 1
Italy:
Italy Criminal Code arts. 1, 2
Italy Criminal Code arts. 1, 2 (1931)
Japan:
Japan Crim. Code arts.1, 6
Lebanon:
Lebanon Code Pénal arts. 1–3, 6–8, 12–14
Lebanon Penal Code arts. 1–14 (1943; as of 1946)

Liechtenstein:
Liechtenstein StGB § 1
Lithuania:
Lithuania, Penal Code art. 3
Luxembourg:
Luxembourg Penal Code art. 2
Mauritania:
Mauritania Code Pénal art. 4
Netherlands:
Netherlands Penal Code art. 1
New Zealand:
New Zealand Bill of Rights Act arts. 25, 26
New Zealand, Military Manual §§ 1327(1)(a), 1815(2)(c) (1993)
Norway:
Norway, Military Penal Code
Pacific Islands [UN Trust Territory]:
Trust Territory of the Pacific Islands Code (22 December 1952) art. 5
Papua New Guinea:
Papua New Guinea Criminal Code Act art. 11
Papua New Guinea Village Courts Act arts. 41, 42
Papua New Guinea Village Court Regulation art. 3
Poland:
Poland Criminal Code art. 113 (1932)
Russia (including former USSR, and Russia as a subunit of the USSR):
USSR (Russia) 1926 RSFSR Crim. Code arts. 7–16, Decree of 22 November 1926, [1926] I Sov. Uzak. RSFSR, No. 80, Item 600 (effective 1 January 1927)
1926 RSFSR Crim. Code art. 7
USSR (Russia) 1922 RSFSR Crim. Code, art. 10, [1922] 1 Sob. Uzak. RSFSR, No. 15, item 153 (effective 1 June 1922)
USSR *Osnovy ugolovnogozakonodatel'stva Soiuza SSR I soiuznykh respublik* (Fundamental Principles of Criminal Legislation of the USSR and the Union Republics), arts. 3, 6 &7, 25 December 1958, *Vedomosti SSSR* (1959), no. 1, item 6
USSR (Russia) 1960 RSFSR Crim. Code arts. 3, 6
Saudi Arabia:
Saudi Arabia Basic System of the Consultative Council arts. 1, 38, 83
Somalia:
Somalia Penal Code, arts. 1, 2, Legis. Decree No. 5 (16 December 1962)
Somaliland [UN Trust Territory]:
Judicial Regs. of Somaliland arts. 23, 24
Somaliland Ord. No. 14 (2 August 1954), Bulletino Officiale No. 8 (16 August 1954)
Sweden:
Sweden, International Humanitarian Law Manual § 2.2.3 (1991)
Switzerland:
Switzerland Code Pénal arts. 1, 2, 6bis
Togoland [UN Trust Territory]:
Decree No. 58–187, setting forth the Statute of Togoland art. 32 (22 February 1958)

Transjordan [British Mandate/UN Trust Territory]:
Transjordan Const. art. 8 (1947)
Union of Soviet Socialist Republics (see Russia)
United Kingdom:
Royal Warrant of 14 June 1945
Statute, 39 Geo. III., c. 85
United Kingdom Human Rights Act 1998, sched. 1, pt. 1, art. 7
United Kingdom Sexual Offenses Act 1956 § 1
United Kingdom Sexual Offenses (Amendment) Act 1976 § 1.1
United Kingdom Military Manual § 233 (1958)
United Kingdom, LOAC Manual (1981)
United States:
Code of Criminal Procedure, art. 1 and note (20 November 1864)
Detainee Treatment Act of 2005, 42 U.S.C. § 801
Military Commissions Act of 2006, 10 U.S.C. § 948a(1)(i).
Model Penal Code art. 223 (unofficial code proposal)
U.S. Army, Rules of Land Warfare, Field Manual 27–10, para. 357 (1 October 1940)
Uruguay:
Uruguay Código Penal art. 15
Uzbekistan:
Uzbekistan Crim. Code arts. 4, 13

Other Official Sources (National)

United Kingdom
War Cabinet shorthand notes W.M. (42)86th mtg., 6 July 1942
W.M. (45)43rd mtg., 12 April 1945, transcribed, summarized and released at http://www.nationalarchives.gov.uk/releases/2006/january/january1/war_crimes.htm (1 January 2006; last visited 2 January 2006)
War Cabinet notes, W.M. (45)57th mtg., 3 May 1945

United States
Jackson, Robert H. REPORT OF ROBERT H. JACKSON UNITED STATES REPRESENTATIVE TO THE INTERNATIONAL CONFERENCE ON MILITARY TRIALS: LONDON, 1945. Washington: U.S. Gov't Printing Off. 1949 [submitted by Justice Jackson to the Secretary of State 15 December 1947]

Index

Accessibility of law, 20–21, 363–364
Accomplices, 295, 307
Accountability, retribution and, 30
ACHR. *See* American Convention on Human Rights
African Charter of Human and Peoples' Rights, 205, 248–249, 293, 297, 395
African Commission on Human and Peoples' Rights, 227–228, 372, 397
African Court of Human and Peoples' Rights, 397
Aggressive war
  criminality of, 117
  customary international law, under, 115–116, 154–155
  ex post facto law, as, 93, 125–126
  ICC, in, 406–407
  League of Nations and, 128
  London Conference, at
    American position, 78–79
    French position, 82–83, 85
    Soviet position, 79–80
  Nuremberg Trial and
    defense arguments regarding, 102–104
    divisions within tribunal regarding, 127–128
    indictments, 91–92, 93
    judgments of, 115–116, 125
    prosecutorial arguments, 98–99
  Tokyo Tribunal and, 145–147, 152
  Versailles Treaty and, 128, 146
al Qaeda, 278
al-'Awwa, Muhammad Salim, 52–53
Alexander II (Czar), 64–65
American Convention on Human Rights (ACHR)
  collective punishment prohibited under, 205, 293, 297
  comparative law analysis, 233–234
  individual claims based on legality under, 226–227
  lex mitior under, 203–204
  non-retroactivity under, 204
  nulla poena under, 203–204
  nullum crimen under, 203–204, 355–356
  retroactive creation of courts under, 204–205, 394
  retroactive non-punishment, 392–393
Analogy
  application of, 37
  common law compared, 37–38, 49
  comparative law analysis, 276
  crimes against humanity and, 124
  critique of, 36–37
  ECHR and, 37
  foreseeability and, 360–362
  ICC and, 124
  limits on legality from, 223
  overview, 36
  retroactive re-characterization and, 322
  Third Reich, legality in compared, 61–62
Arab Charter on Human Rights, 205–206, 233–234
Arbitrariness, protection against
  purpose of legality, as, 21, 22–23
  rule of law and, 17
Arbitrary detention, 376–378
Australia
  dualist theory of international law in, 242
  retroactive expansion of jurisdiction in, 276–278

Austria
  Anschluss, 121–122
  Penal Code, 47–48, 285–286
Authoritarianism, 44–45

Bangladesh, non-retroactivity in, 262
Bassiouni, M. Cherif, 38, 124, 294–295, 316, 322, 383, 384, 388
Beccaria, Cesare, 47–48
Belgium, retroactive non-punishment in,
Bernard, Henri, 85–86, 143, 147–150, 151
Bhutan, non-acceptance of legality in, 241–242, 250–251, 379
Biddle, Francis, 111, 126
Bills of attainder, 17, 21, 25
Blackstone, William, 47–48
Boot, Machteld, 195–196
Border Guards cases, 220–222, 323, 375–376
Bossuyt, Marc, 195–196
Botswana, retroactive penalties in, 278–279
Bowie, J.M., 195–196
Bracton, Henry de, 51
Brunei Darussalam, non-acceptance of legality in, 241–242, 250–251, 302, 379

Cambodia. *See* Extraordinary Chambers for Cambodia
Canada
  Constitution Act, 262
  retroactive non-punishment in, 288
Cape Verde Islands, *ex post facto* laws in, 257
Case law
  comparative law analysis of legality
    overview, 233, 247
    statutory law contrasted, 247
  foreseeability and, 360–362
Cassese, Antonio, 95, 123, 135
Cassin, René, 156–157, 161, 165, 166, 167–169, 171, 180, 181–182, 183, 251–252
Castro, Fidel, 39, 199
Chang, P.C., 162–163
Chile, *lex certa* in, 274
China
  legality in, 45, 55
  Qing Dynasty, 55, 268–269, 270
  readoption of legality in, 246, 268–270, 401
Churchill, Winston, 73–75, 80–81
Cisneros, Pérez, 174
Civil law
  analogy (*See* Analogy)
  common law distinguished, 48
  comparative law analysis of legality in civil law nations, 237–238, 246
  courts, retroactive creation in civil law nations, 293
  lex mitior in civil law nations, 272
  representation jurisdiction in civil law nations, 283
  statutory enactment, necessity of, 48–49
Civil wars, 208, 212
Co-operative general universality principle. *See* Representation jurisdiction
Collective punishment
  accomplices and, 295
  ACHR, prohibited under, 205, 293, 297, 395
  African Charter of Human and Peoples' Rights, prohibited under, 293, 297, 395
  conspiracy and, 295
  constitutions, prohibited under, 293–294, 296–297
  corporations and, 298
  criminal organizations and, 295–296
  customary international law, prohibited under, 396
  extra-legal nature of, 396
  general principles of law, prohibition as, 297–298
  Geneva Conventions, prohibited under, 43, 207, 211–212, 293, 297
  hostage taking, 212, 396
  individuation of desert, 295
  international humanitarian law and, 211–213, 298
  Islamic law, under, 294–295
  national criminal law, under, 395–396
  non-retroactivity and, 43
  Nuremberg Trial, in, 137–138
  overview, 42–43
  Post–World War II cases, in, 136–138
  prohibition against, 44, 395
  purposes of, 43–44
  rule of law and, 17
  terrorism and, 295–296
  weakness of state authority and, 298
Commission on Human Rights. *See* United Nations
Commission on the Responsibility of the Authors of the War and on Enforcement of Penalties, 56–57
Common law
  civil law distinguished, 48

comparative law analysis of legality in common law nations, 253–254
crime creation, non-retroactivity of, 48
definitions of crimes, 49
felonies, 49–50
lex mitior in common law nations, 272
limits on legality from, 217–218, 220
marital rape example, 50–51
misdemeanors, 50
nulla poena, 14, 223–224
nullum crimen,
stability of, 51
UDHR, applicability to, 173
United Kingdom, in, 49–50
Communism. *See also specific nation*
comparative law analysis of legality, 239–240
lex mitior in Communist nations, 272
Marxist theory and legality, 64–65, 66
readoption of legality
Asian communist nations, in, 270
former Communist nations, in, 268
Comparative law analysis of legality
ACHR, in, 233–234
African Charter of Human and Peoples' Rights, in, 248–249
Arab Charter on Human Rights, in, 233–234
case law as source
overview, 233, 247
statutory law contrasted, 251–261
chart, 411–424
collective punishment (*See* Collective punishment)
common law nations, in, 253–254
constitutions as source
analogy, 276
civil law nations, in, 237–238
collective punishment, 293–294, 296–297
Communist nations, in, 239–240
domestic incorporation of other nations' laws, 259, 276–278
double non-retroactivity provisions, 257–258
ex post facto laws, 238–239
international human rights law, incorporation of, 258
international law requiring, 259
lack of provisions, 239–240
lex certa, 274–275
lex mitior,
libertarian principles, 239, 274
narrow interpretation, 275–276
overview, 232–233, 237, 240–241, 243–246
single non-retroactivity provisions, 258
strong legality, 238–239
treaties, non-signatories of, 250
weak legality, 237–238
Convention on the Rights of the Child, in, 234–235, 241–242, 250–251
courts, retroactive creation of (*See* Courts, retroactive creation of)
current acceptance of legality, 241–242
dualist theory of law and, 242
ECHR, in, 233–234, 264
ex post facto laws, 238–239, 256–257, 259
exceptions to non-retroactivity (*See* Exceptions to non-retroactivity)
general principles of law as source, 261–264
Geneva Conventions, in, 234–235, 241–242, 250–251
ICCPR, in, 233–234, 248–249, 252–253, 260, 262, 264
international criminal law as source, 261–264
legislative enactment requirement, 254–255
lex mitior (*See Lex mitior*)
non-retroactivity, lack of specific reference to, 249–250
nulla poena,
nullum crimen,
overview, 231–232, 235–236
proclamations as source, 255
punishment, what constitutes (*See* Punishment, what constitutes)
readoption of legality, 265–271
representation jurisdiction (*See* Representation jurisdiction)
shar'ia as source, 259–260
sources of law, 243–251
special tribunals, retroactive creation of, 291–293
statutory law as source
case law contrasted, 251–261
civil law nations, in, 246
criminal law statutes, 246, 247–248
human rights statutes, 246–247
lex mitior,
overview, 233
summary, 425–437, 438–539
traditional law as source, 259–260
transformation of legality since World War II, 301–302
translation, problems with, 236, 256
treaties, 233–235, 248–249
UDHR, in, 252–253, 260, 262

Competitors to legality
  analogy (*See* Analogy)
  authoritarianism, 44–45
  collective punishment (*See* Collective punishment)
  defenses
    culpability, 39–40
    insanity, 39
    justification, 40
  extraordinary or transitional times exception, 39
  impossibility of pure non-retroactivity (*See* Impossibility of pure non-retroactivity)
  jurisdiction, change of
    international courts, in, 41–42
    national courts, in, 42
    overview, 40–41
  limited or non-binding effect of legality, 38
  newly-established courts, 40
  offense, change of
    international courts, in, 41–42
    national courts, in, 42
    overview, 40–41
  optional principle of law, legality as, 38
  overview, 31
Complementarity, 337, 398–399
Compliance, legality and, 27–28
Conspiracy
  collective punishment and, 295
  Nuremberg Trial and
    defense arguments regarding, 102–104
    divisions within tribunal regarding, 126–127
    judgments of, 115–116
Constitutions. *See* Comparative law analysis of legality
Contempt of court
  constitutions, in, 278–279
  customary international law, in, 309
  general principles of law and, 310–311
  ICTY, in, 309–311, 350
  Nuremberg Trial, at, 309–310
Convention on the Rights of the Child
  comparative law analysis, 234–235, 241–242, 250–251
  incorporation of, 325–326
  Islamic law nations, acceptance in, 214–216, 400
  nulla poena under, 201–202
  nullum crimen under, 201, 202, 401
  reservations to, 213
  UDHR, impact of, 159
Core rules of legality
  ACHR, in, 352–353
  African Charter of Human Rights, in, 352–353
  ECHR, in, 352–353
  ICCPR, in, 352–353
  jurisdiction, as limitation on, 356–357
  national courts, in, 355
  nulla poena (See Nulla poena)
  nullum crimen (See Nullum crimen)
  overview, 352, 357
  reinforcement of, 354–355
  sovereignty, as limitation on, 356–357
  substantive law, as change in, 356–357
  UDHR, in, 352–353
Corporations, 298
Courts, retroactive creation of
  ACHR, under, 204–205
  civil law nations, in, 293
  constitutions, under, 290
  generally, 394
  overview, 290
  removal of persons from jurisdictions, 290–291
  Tokyo Tribunal, 150–152
Covarruvias, Diego, 283
Crimes against humanity
  analogy and, 124
  comparative law analysis, 262–263
  customary international law, under, 154
  general principles of law, based on, 122–123, 391–392
  ICC, in, 335–336, 339
  lack of explanation of, 120
  malum in se acts as, 123–124
  national criminal law, retroactive re-characterization of, 130–134
  Nuremberg Charter, under, 122
  Nuremberg Trial and
    defense arguments, 104–110
    indictments, 92–93
    judgments of, 119–124, 125
    prosecutorial arguments, 95
  overview, 72
  penalties, 382–383, 385–388
  retroactive expansion of jurisdiction over, 277
  sources of, 41–42
  war crimes and
    distinguished, 121–122

retroactive re-characterization of, 123, 130–134
Crimes against peace. *See* Aggressive war
Crimes, retroactive creation of
common law, under, 48
emotion, role of, 404–405
ICCPR, under, 192, 199
preclusion of, 355
Tokyo Tribunal, in, 150–152
treaties, under, 401
Criminal organizations, 295–296
Cuba, readoption of legality in, 268
Culpability defenses, 39–40
Customary international law
aggressive war under, 115–116, 154–155
collective punishment prohibited under, 396
contempt of court in, 309
crimes against humanity under, 154
definition of crimes under, 113–114
ECHR, in, 402–403
Geneva Conventions and, 70
ICC, in, 333, 339, 342, 343
ICTR, in, 306–307, 348–349, 402
ICTY, in, 305, 348–349, 365, 402
individual claims based on legality under, 397–398
International Court of Justice, in, 349
international criminal tribunals and, 314–316, 348, 349–350, 402–403
international organizations, role of, 10, 402–403
lex mitior as part of, 355–356
non-retroactivity as part of, 352, 353–354
nulla poena as part of, 14, 378–379, 404, 405–406
nullum crimen as part of, 14, 355–356, 357–358, 404, 405–406
Nuremberg Trial, in
divisions within tribunal regarding authority of, 126, 128
legitimation of, 152–153
SCSL, in, 306–307, 402
state practice adopted as, 299–300
Tokyo Tribunal, legitimation of, 152–153
treaties transformed into, 229
UDHR, applicability to, 173, 174
United Nations, role of, 402
war crimes under, 118–119

Danzig (Free City), legality in, 62–64, 362–363
de Menthon, François, 71, 94–96, 108, 122–123
de Vabres, Henri Donnedieu, 67–68, 117, 123, 126–129, 130–131, 283
Death penalty, 144, 147, 385–386, 387–388
Defenses
culpability, 39–40
insanity, 39
justification, 40
retroactive elimination of, 375–376
rule of law and, 18
Definition of crimes
customary international law, under, 113–114
ICC, amendments in, 334
ICCPR, in, 188
international criminal tribunals, in, 307–308, 315, 349–350
London Conference, at
French position, 83–84
overview, 77–78
national function, as, 114
Nuremberg Charter, in, 87–91, 112, 125
Nuremberg Trial, judgments of, 111–112, 113–114, 125
UDHR, in, 160–161, 172
Denmark, retroactive non-punishment in, 288
Deterrence, legality and, 26–27
Dili Special Court for Serious Crimes, 326–327
Domestic incorporation of other nations' laws, 259, 276–278
Dönitz, Karl, 107, 119
Drumbl, Mark, 44
Dualist theory of international law, 242
Dukes, Charles, 165–166, 167–169

East Germany, Border Guards cases, 220–222, 323, 375–376
East Timor Special Tribunal
customary international law in, 402
definition of crimes, 315
Dili Special Court for Serious Crimes, 326–327
individual claims based on legality, 346, 397
international organization, as, 345–346
new jurisdiction, retroactive creation of, 319–320
non-retroactivity in, 325, 326
opinio juris in, 347–348
overview, 303–304
practice in, 347–348

East Timor Special Tribunal (*cont.*)
retroactive creation, challenge based on, 316–317
ECHR. *See* European Convention on Human Rights
ECOSOC. *See* United Nations
Ecuador, narrow interpretation of statutes in, 275–276
Einsatzgruppen case, 131–132
England. *See* United Kingdom
Established by law requirement, 316–317, 395
European Charter of Fundamental Rights, 181–182, 206
European Convention on Human Rights (ECHR)
analogy and, 37
comparative law analysis, 233–234, 264
Convention on the Rights of the Child, incorporation by, 325–326
customary international law in, 402–403
general principles of law and, 188–189, 373–374
individual claims based on legality under, 226, 397
lex certa and, 363
nulla poena in, 379–380
overview, 176, 187–188
provisions of, 203
European Court of Human Rights, 50, 217–224, 226, 229, 286–287, 361–362, 372
Ex post facto laws
aggressive war as, 93, 125–126
comparative law analysis, 238–239, 256–257, 259
London Conference, at
British position, 86–87
French position, 82, 84
Nuremberg Charter, negotiation regarding, 68, 87–91
Nuremberg Trial and
defense arguments, 99–100
divisions within tribunal regarding, 126–127
judgments of, 125
Tokyo Tribunal and, 145, 147–148
Exceptions to non-retroactivity
contempt of court, 278–279
military forces, offenses by, 279
minor penalties, 279
overview, 278
retroactive non-punishment, 279
subversive acts, 279–281
traditional law, 279
Extraordinary Chambers for Cambodia
international organization, as, 346
new jurisdiction, retroactive creation of, 319–320
non-retroactivity in, 325, 327–328
nullum crimen in, 355–356
overview, 303–304
retroactive creation of court, as, 394
Extraordinary or transitional times exception to legality, 39

Fairness, 17
Fehr, Hans, 100–102
Ferdinandusse, Ward N., 221–222, 362
Feuerbach, Paul Anselm, 47–48, 82
Finland, legality in, 240
Fläschner, Hans, 108–109
Fletcher, George, 221
Flexible jurisdiction, 408
Foreseeability
accessibility of law and, 363–364
analogy and, 360–362
case law and, 360–362
dangers of, 364–366
indeterminacy of language and, 359–360
lex certa and, 362–363
limitations on, 364–366
overview, 354, 359
statutory interpretation and, 360–362
void for vagueness doctrine and, 362–363
France
Declaration of the Rights of Man and of the Citizen, 36, 47–49, 165, 239, 254–256, 258–259
international criminal law, incorporation of, 263
London Conference, at
aggressive war, position on, 82–83, 85
authority of tribunal, position on, 84–85
definition of crimes, position on, 83–84
ex post facto laws, position on, 82, 84
internal atrocities, position on, 85–86
jurisdiction of tribunal, position on, 83–84, 87
laws and customs of war, position on, 81–82
national court jurisdiction, retroactive expansion of, 135–136
Franco, Francisco, 39, 200

Frank, Hans, 60–62, 100–102, 105–106
Frick, Wilhelm, 100
Fritz, Heinz, 102
Fritzsche, Hans, 102
Fuller, Lon, 408
Fyfe, David Maxwell, 83, 86–87

General principles of law
  collective punishment, prohibition of, 297–298
  comparative law analysis, 261–264
  contempt of court and, 310–311
  crimes against humanity based on, 122–123, 391–392
  ECHR and, 188–189, 373–374
  ICC, in, 339–340
  ICCPR and (*See* International Covenant on Civil and Political Rights)
  ICTY, in, 222, 373, 391–392
  nulla poena and, 391–392
  Nuremberg Trial and
    legitimation of, 154
    prosecutorial arguments regarding, 94–95
  sources of law, as, 373–374
  Tokyo Tribunal, legitimation of, 154
Generality of enactments, 17
Geneva Conventions
  Additional Protocol I, 207–208, 212, 279, 377, 379–380
  Additional Protocol II, 207–210, 212, 297, 313, 322, 377, 379–380
  arbitrary detention under, 377
  civil wars, applicability to, 208, 212
  collective punishment prohibited, 43, 207, 211–212, 293, 297
  Common Article 3, 209–211, 322
  comparative law analysis, 234–235, 241–242, 250–251
  customary international law and, 70
  Fourth Convention, 207, 211–212, 379–380
  hostage taking prohibited, 212
  Islamic law nations, acceptance by, 216
  non-international conflicts, applicability to, 209–210, 212
  non-retroactivity under, 207–208, 210–211
  non-state actors under, 208
  nulla poena under, 207, 208, 378–380
  nullum crimen under, 207, 208
  prisoners of war under, 69–70, 207, 208–209
  punishment of individuals as guaranty of behavior prohibited, 212
  reservations, lack of, 213
  Third Convention, 207, 208–209, 211–212, 279
  UDHR, impact of, 159
  war crimes under, 77–78, 92, 343
Genocide, 262–263, 277, 339, 382–383, 387–388
Genocide Convention, 199
Germany
  Border Guards cases, 220–222, 323, 375–376
  Criminal Code of 1871, 59–60
  de-Nazification laws, 137–138
  international criminal law, incorporation of, 263
  Nuremberg Trial (*See* Nuremberg Trial)
  Penal Code, 94–95, 103–104, 122–123
  readoption of legality in, 265–266
  retroactive non-punishment, 288
  Third Reich, legality in
    abandonment of, 60–61
    analogy compared, 61–62
  Weimar Republic, legality in, 59–60
Gestapo,
Giraud, Emile, 163–164
Glaser, Stefan, 355–356
Globalization, 407–408
Göring, Hermann, 100, 103, 107–108
Great Britain. *See* United Kingdom
Gros, André, 81–89, 125–127, 149–150, 151, 314–315, 327–328
Grotius, 107
Grotius, Hugo, 283
Group criminality. *See* Collective punishment
Guantanamo Bay, 278

Habeas corpus, 318
Hague Conventions, 70, 77–78, 92, 108–110, 118, 343
Hague Regulations of Land Warfare, 105–106, 108–109, 118
Hall, Jerome, 31, 32, 33, 36, 143–144, 146–147, 355, 359, 360, 408
Hamoudi, Haider Ala, 270–271
Hariri, Rafiq, 319–320, 324
Hart, H.L.A., 7, 32–33
Hess, Rudolf, 98
High Command case, 133
Himmler, Heinrich, 75
Historical background of legality
  China, in, 55
  Czarist Russia, in, 64–65
  Czarist Russia, legality in, 64–65
  Danzig (Free City), legality in, 62–64

Historical background of legality (*cont.*)
  Enlightenment and, 47–48
  Germany, in (*See* Germany)
  Islamic law, in (*See* Islamic law)
  Italy, legality in, 66
  Japan, in, 54–55
  literacy, role of, 55–56
  overview, 46–47
  positivism and, 47–48
  pre–World War II, 56, 59
  Soviet Union, in (*See* Soviet Union)
  United Kingdom, in, 49–50
  Versailles Treaty, under (*See* Versailles, Treaty of)
Hitler, Adolf, 45, 60–61, 74–75, 103–104
Hoare, Samuel, 198
Holocaust, 120–121
Horn, Martin, 108
Hostage taking, 212, 396
Humanity, crimes against. *See* Crimes against humanity
Humphrey, John P., 163–164, 235
Hungary, incorporation of international criminal law in, 263
Hussein, Saddam, 319–320, 328, 329–330

ICC. *See* International Criminal Court
ICCPR. *See* International Covenant on Civil and Political Rights
Iceland, analogy in, 276
ICTR. *See* International Criminal Tribunal for Rwanda
ICTY. *See* International Criminal Tribunal for the Former Yugoslavia
Impossibility of pure non-retroactivity
  common law, in
    overview, 32–33
    statutory interpretation compared, 35–36
  critique of, 33
  language, indeterminacy of, 31–32, 33
  overview, 31
  statutory interpretation, necessity of
    common law compared, 35–36
    error regarding criminality, danger of, 34
    extensive interpretation, 33–34
    overdeterrence, danger of, 34–35
    overview, 32–33
    retroactive expansion, danger of, 34
IMTFE. *See* Tokyo Tribunal
Incapacitation, 28
Individuality of guilt, 17
Indonesia
  ex post facto laws in, 257
  readoption of legality in, 32–33
  Insanity defense, 39
  Institute of International Law, 285–286
  Inter-American Commission on Human Rights, 226–227
  Inter-American Court of Human Rights, 226–227, 372, 397
  International Committee of the Red Cross, 211, 212–213, 377, 380–381
  International Court of Justice, 94–95, 300, 349
  International Covenant on Civil and Political Rights (ICCPR)
    adoption of, 189
    amendments to, 188
    annotations, 189, 195, 196–198
    comments on, 184
    Commission on Human Rights, role of, 178, 179–180, 184, 186–188, 189–190, 192–193, 196–198
    comparative law analysis, 233–234, 252–253, 260, 262, 264
    Convention on the Rights of the Child, incorporation by, 325–326
    criminal law, limitation to, 185, 191
    debate regarding, 189–190
    definition of crimes in, 188
    democracy, promotion of, 25
    Drafting Committee, 178–179
    dualist theory of law and, 242
    ECOSOC, role of, 179–180, 187–188, 196–198
    general principles of law and
      amendments regarding, 188–189
      background, 154
      basic requirement, 192
      broader than international law, as, 195–198
      criticisms of, 192–193, 198
      economic crimes, 198–199
      overview, 176–178
      sources of law, as, 373–374
      subset of international law, as, 193–195
    Human Rights Committee, 227, 260, 288, 363, 372, 397
    ICC compared, 331–332, 334–335
    individual claims based on legality under, 227, 228
    individual rights, focus on, 180–181

international organizations, applicability to, 181–182
Islamic law nations, acceptance by, 214
legal force of, 176
lex certa in, 274–275
lex mitior in, 176, 184–186, 188, 190–191
negotiations regarding, 156–157, 178
non-derogability of legality, 178, 229, 401
non-retroactivity in, 10, 175, 180, 182, 183, 184
nulla poena in, 181, 182–185, 190–191, 378, 379–380
nullum crimen in, 179, 182, 190–191, 355–356
Nuremberg Trial, impact of, 154–155, 176, 179, 182, 183, 186, 191–192, 198, 199–200
provisions of, 176
repression and, 185
reservations, lack of, 213
retroactive creation of crimes under, 192, 199
sources of law, 177–178, 182, 183–184, 190
Tokyo Tribunal, impact of, 154–155, 176, 179, 182, 183, 186, 191–192, 198, 199–200
UDHR, impact of, 159
widespread acceptance of, 228–229
International Criminal Court (ICC)
aggressive war in, 406–407
analogy and, 124
complementarity, 337, 398–399
criticism as violating legality, 375
customary international law in, 333
defenses in, 323–324
Elements of Crimes, 351
establishment of, 154–155
human rights law in, 350–351
ICCPR compared, 331–332, 334–335
individual claims based on legality, 347
international organization, as, 347
jurisdictional issue, legality as, 343–344
lex certa in, 275
narrow interpretation of statutes in, 276, 362
national law legality stronger than, when, 399
non-party states
acceptance of jurisdiction, 337–338
adjudicative jurisdiction, 338–339
crimes against humanity, 339
customary international law in, 339, 342, 343
general principles of law in, 339–340
genocide, 339
no source of law, when, 340
nulla poena in, 341–342
nullum crimen in, 340–341, 343
prescriptive jurisdiction, 338–339
referrals, 337–338
retroactive re-characterization of crimes in, 340
treaties in, 340
war crimes, 339, 343
non-retroactivity in, 320, 365
nulla poena in, 379–380
nullum crimen in, 303, 355–356
overview, 331–333
penalties in, 383–384, 386–387, 388
Pre-Trial Chamber, 333, 335
referrals to, 333, 334, 336, 337–338, 342–343
retroactive creation of courts and, 293
retroactive re-characterization of crimes in, 340, 369, 406
Rules of Procedure and Evidence, 351
states parties
complementarity, 337
crimes against humanity, 335–336
decisions on legality, 335
definition of crimes, amendments to, 334
effective dates, 337
penalties, 334, 335
strength of legality, 335
temporal jurisdiction, 333–334, 336–337
UDHR compared, 331–332, 334–335
International criminal law
comparative law analysis, 261–264
criticism as violating legality, 374–375
direct application in national courts, 369–370
nulla poena, applicability of, 379–383, 388
underenforcement of, 350
universal jurisdiction over, 370–371, 390
weakness of, 350
International Criminal Tribunal for Rwanda (ICTR)
atrocities involved, 44, 323–324
customary international law in, 348–349, 402
individual claims based on legality
Geneva Conventions and, 313
overview, 311–312, 345
subject matter jurisdiction, issue of, 313
international organization, as, 344
legality in, 304
national law, incorporation of, 306–307

International Criminal Tribunal (*cont.*)
new jurisdiction, retroactive creation of, 319–320
nullum crimen in, 355–356
opinio juris in, 348, 349
overview, 303–304
penalties in, 383–384, 386–387, 388
practice in, 349
retroactive creation, challenges based on, 316–317
retroactive re-characterization of crimes, 322, 324, 390
sentencing, 308
International Criminal Tribunal for the Former Yugoslavia (ICTY)
Appeals Chamber, 306, 309–311, 317–318
arbitrary detention and, 377–378
contempt of court in, 309–311, 350
customary international law in, 305, 348–349, 365, 402
establishment of, 181–182
general principles of law in, 222, 373–374, 391–392
individual claims based on legality
overview, 311–312
subject matter jurisdiction, issue of, 312–313
international organization, as, 344
legality in, 304
new jurisdiction, retroactive creation of, 319–320
non-retroactivity in, 305
nullum crimen in, 305–306, 355–356
opinio juris in, 348, 349–350
overview, 303–304
penalties in, 383–384, 386–387, 388
practice in, 349–350
Report, 305–306, 318, 348
retroactive creation, challenges based on, 316–317
retroactive re-characterization of crimes, 320–321, 324, 390
Rules of Procedure and Evidence, 309, 310–311, 391–392
sentencing, 308
treaties and, 306
International criminal tribunals. *See also specific tribunal*
accomplices, 307
binding nature of non-retroactivity, 393–394
customary international law and, 314–316, 348, 349–350, 402–403
definition of crimes, 307–308, 315, 349–350
detention, challenging, 318
individual claims based on legality in, 397–398
jus cogens, 314
new jurisdictions, retroactive creation of, 318–320
nulla poena in, 303, 315, 380
nullum crimen in, 303, 315
opinio juris in, 349–350
organic documents, crimes named in, 314–316
practice in, 349–350
retroactive creation, challenge based on, 316–318
International humanitarian law
collective punishment and, 211–213, 298
non-retroactivity under, 207–211
SCSL, in, 308
state practice adopted as, 301
International Military Tribunal for the Far East. *See* Tokyo Tribunal
International organizations. *See also specific organization*
authority of, 351
binding nature of non-retroactivity, 393–394
customary international law, role in, 10, 402–403
ICCPR, applicability of, 181–182
individual claims based on legality, 345
opinio juris and, 230
source of law, as, 230
Iraq
High Criminal Tribunal, 328–330
Penal Code, 329
Special Tribunal, 303–304, 328, 346–347, 355–356, 394
Islamic law
application of legality, 53
codification of law and legality, 54
collective punishment under, 294–295
Convention on the Rights of the Child, acceptance of, 214–216, 400
diyya crimes, 52, 294–295
Geneva Conventions, acceptance of, 216
hudud crimes, 51–52
ICCPR, acceptance of, 214
international law, acceptance of, 53
judges, punishment by, 52–53

legalist aspects, 54
punishment, what constitutes, 289
Qu'ran, authority of, 51–52, 53–54
quesas crimes, 52, 294–295
shar'ia,
ta'azir crimes
legality and, 52–53, 270–271, 399–401
reservations in treaties for, 214–217
victims, punishment by, 52
Israel, retroactive expansion of national court jurisdiction, 136
Italy, legality in, 66, 240

Jackson, Robert H., 78–79, 87, 94, 98
Jahrreiss, Hermann, 100, 102–104, 106–107
Japan
Instrument of Surrender, 139–141
legality in, 54–55
Meiji Constitution, 124
readoption of legality in, 266
Tokyo Tribunal (*See* Tokyo Tribunal)
Jaranilla, Delfin, 143–144
Jevremovic, Branko, 186
Jews, extermination of, 120–121
Jodl, Alfred, 102–103
Joint criminal responsibility, 17–18
Jurisdiction
change of
international courts, in, 41–42
national courts, in, 42
overview, 40–41
exercise in violation of legality, 404, 407
flexible jurisdiction, 408
retroactive expansion of
crimes against humanity, over, 277
generally, 394
national criminal law, in, 135–136, 276–278
war crimes, over, 277
Jus cogens, 314, 399–402
Justice case, 129–130
Justification defenses, 40
Justinian, 46–47

Kazakhstan, analogy in, 276
Kellogg-Briand Pact, 115–116, 128, 144
Kelsen, Hans, 51, 115–116
Kenya, retroactive penalties in, 278–279
Kharkov Trial, 69–70
Khmer Rouge, 327
Kosovo Special Tribunal
Convention on the Rights of the Child, incorporation of, 325–326
customary international law in, 402
definition of crimes, 315
ECHR, incorporation of, 325–326
ICCPR, incorporation of, 325–326
individual claims based on legality, 346, 397
international organization, as, 345–346
new jurisdiction, retroactive creation of, 319–320
non-retroactivity in, 325
opinio juris in, 347–348
overview, 303–304
practice in, 347–348
retroactive creation, challenge based on, 316–317
UDHR, incorporation of, 325–326
Kramer, Matthew H., 33
Kranzbühler, Otto, 107

Language, indeterminacy of
foreseeability and, 359–360
impossibility of pure non-retroactivity and, 31–32, 33
Lausanne, Treaty of, 72
Laws and customs of war
Allies' position on prosecution under, 69
fighting out of uniform, 71
German atrocities, applicability to, 71
individual violations, 70
international criminal law *versus* national criminal law, 71–72
London Conference, French position at, 81–82
pre–World War II, 69
UNWCC, 70–71, 72
Versailles Treaty and, 69
League of Nations
aggressive war and, 128
Danzig (Free City) under, 62–63
Lebanon. *See* Special Tribunal for Lebanon
Legitimacy
compliance and, 27
deterrence and, 26–27
purpose of legality, as, 23–24
Lenin, V.I., 64–65
Lex certa, 274–275, 362–363
Lex mitior
ACHR, under, 203–204
Arab Charter on Human Rights, under, 205–206

Lex mitior, (*cont.*)
  comparative law analysis
    civil law nations, in, 272
    common law nations, in, 272
    Communist nations, in, 272
    constitutions as source, 271–272
    legality distinguished, 273–274
    limitations on, 272–273
    overview, 233, 271
    statutory law as source, 272
    temporary crimes, 273
  customary international law, as part of, 355–356
  ICCPR, under, 176, 184–186, 188, 190–191
Liberia, non-retroactivity in, 258
Liberty, protection of
  purpose of legality, as, 21–22, 25–26
  rule of law and, 18–19
Limitations of actions, 398
Limited or non-binding effect of legality, 38
Literacy, role of, 55–56
Lithuania
  non-retroactivity in, 263
  retroactive non-punishment in, 288
Locke, John, 15–16
London Conference
  aggressive war
    American position, 78–79
    French position, 82–83, 85
    Soviet position, 79–80
  authority of tribunal
    French position, 84–85
    overview, 77–78
  calling of, 75
  debate at, 76–77
  definition of crimes
    French position, 83–84
    negotiation regarding, 87–91
    overview, 77–78
  ex post facto laws
    British position, 86–87
    French position, 82, 84
    negotiation regarding, 87–91
  internal atrocities, French position, 85–86
  issues at, 76
  jurisdiction of tribunal, French position, 83–84, 87
  laws and customs of war, French position, 81–82
  non-retroactivity at, 9–10
  overview, 155
  punishment, Soviet position, 79
  Tokyo Tribunal compared, 149

MacArthur, Douglas, 139–141
Magna Carta, 46–47
Malik, Charles, 162–163
Malum in se acts, 123–124
Marital rape, 50–51, 218–220, 361–362, 375–376
Marshall Islands, *ex post facto* laws in, 257, 259
Marxism–Leninism, 64–65, 66
McDougal, Myres, 408
Mehta, Hansa, 186
Mercy doctrine. *See Lex mitior*
Meron, Theodore, 3, 315, 322–323, 349–350, 356–357, 365, 399, 401–402
Mexico, analogy in, 276
Meyer, Jürgen, 286
Micronesia, *ex post facto* laws in, 257
Military commissions, 15
Military forces, offenses by, 279
Montesquieu, Charles de S., 47–48
Moral wrongs, retroactive re-characterization of, 134–135
Morgenthau, Henry, Jr., 73
Morosov, P.D., 196–198
Moscow Declaration, 80–81
Mussolini, Benito, 74–75

Narrow interpretation of statutes, 275–276, 362
National criminal law
  collective punishment under, 395–396
  comparative law analysis (*See* Comparative law analysis of legality)
  crimes against humanity, retroactive recharacterization as, 130–134
  direct application of international criminal law, 369–370
  international criminal law *versus*,
  Nuremberg Trial, prosecutorial arguments regarding re-characterization of, 97–98
  retroactive expansion of jurisdiction, 135–136, 276–278
  retroactive re-characterization of, 323, 367–369, 389–390
  stronger legality than under international law, when, 398–399
  Versailles Treaty, incorporation in, 56–57
Natural law not retroactive, 147–150
Nazi Germany. *See* Germany
Neogi, K.C., 161
Netherlands

incorporation of international criminal law in, 264
retroactive expansion of jurisdiction in, 277–278
New Haven School, 408
New Zealand, 1990 Bill of Rights Act, 247
Newly-established courts, 40
Nietzsche, Friedrich, 45
Nikitchenko, I.T., 79–80, 88–89, 96, 126
Non-criminal violations, retroactive re-characterization of, 134–135
Non-derogability of legality, 178, 206–207, 229, 401
Non-international conflicts, 209–210, 212
Non-punishment, retroactive, 279, 289–290, 392–393
Non-retroactivity generally
American Convention on Human Rights, under, 204
crimes, creation of (*See* Crimes, retroactive creation of)
customary international law, as part of, 352, 353–354
exceptions to (*See* Exceptions to non-retroactivity)
Geneva Conventions, under, 207–208, 210–211
ICC, in, 320, 365
ICCPR, in (*See* International Covenant on Civil and Political Rights)
importance of, 408–409
impossibility of (*See* Impossibility of pure non-retroactivity)
international humanitarian law, under, 207–211
London Conference, at, 9–10
nulla poena (*See Nulla poena*)
nullum crimen (*See Nullum crimen*)
Nuremberg Trial, at, 9
overview, 8–9
re-characterization of crimes, retroactive (*See* Re-characterization of crimes, retroactive)
UDHR, in (*See* Universal Declaration of Human Rights)
Norway, retroactive expansion of national court jurisdiction in, 135–136
Nulla poena
ACHR, under, 203–204
African Charter of Human and Peoples' Rights, under, 205
Arab Charter on Human Rights, under, 205–206
common law, 14, 223–224
comparative law analysis, 243–246, 248
Convention on the Rights of the Child, under, 201–202
criticism of, 383–389
customary international law, as part of, 14, 378, 379, 404, 405–406
different meanings of, 383
ECHR, under, 379–380
evidentiary rules, 14
general principles of law and, 391–392
general rules, 11–12
Geneva Conventions, under, 207, 208, 379–380
ICC, in, 341–342, 379–380
ICCPR, in, 181, 182–185, 190–191, 378, 379–380
importance of, 388–389
incapacitation and, 28
individual rights and, 388
international criminal law, applicability to, 379–383, 388
international criminal tribunals, in, 303, 315, 380
international law, applicability to, 150
judicial decisions, 13–14
lack of sentencing schemes, effect of, 383–385, 386
procedural rules, 14
regional treaties, under, 202–203
representation jurisdiction and, 286, 391
retroactive non-punishment and, 392–393
statutory law, 13–14
treaties, in, 379
UDHR, in, 158, 160, 166, 169–170, 171–173, 379–380
variations, 12–13
Versailles Treaty, under, 56–57
Nullum crimen
ACHR, under, 203–204, 355–356
African Charter of Human and Peoples' Rights, under, 205
Arab Charter on Human Rights, under, 205–206
common law, 14
comparative law analysis, 233, 243–246, 258–259
Convention on the Rights of the Child, under, 201, 202, 401

Nullum crimen (*cont.*)
customary international law, as part of, 14, 355–356, 357–358, 404, 405–406
evidentiary rules, 14
Extraordinary Chambers for Cambodia, in, 355–356
general rules, 11–12
Geneva Conventions, under, 207, 208
human right, as, 3
ICC, in, 303, 340–341, 343, 355–356
ICCPR, in, 179, 182, 190–191, 355–356
ICTR, in, 355–356
ICTY, in, 305–306, 355–356
incapacitation and, 28
international criminal tribunals, in, 303, 315
international law, applicability to, 143–144, 150
judicial decisions, 13–14
Nuremberg Trial, at (*See* Nuremberg Trial)
optional principle of law, as, 1–3, 67–68
policy rule, as, 144–145, 146–147
procedural rules, 14
regional treaties, under, 202–203
representation jurisdiction and, 286
SCSL, in, 355–356
sovereignty, not limitation on, 67, 113, 125, 128–129
statutory law, 13–14
UDHR, in, 158, 160, 169–171
variations, 12–13
Nuremberg Charter
crimes against humanity under, 122
defense arguments regarding, 100–102
definition of crimes in, 87–91, 112, 125
divisions within tribunal regarding authority of, 126–127
ex post facto laws, negotiation regarding, 68, 87–91
IMTFE Charter compared, 141
London Conference (*See* London Conference)
prosecutors, arguments regarding, 93–94
war crimes under, 118–119
Nuremberg Trial
ambivalence toward legality, 125–126
authority of tribunal
challenging, 114, 317–318
French position, 84–85
overview, 77–78
collective punishment in, 137–138
contempt of court at, 309–310
customary international law, legitimation through, 152–153
defense arguments in
aggressive war, regarding, 102–104
Charter, regarding, 100–102
conspiracy, regarding, 102–104
crimes against humanity, regarding, 104–110
overview, 99–100
war crimes, regarding, 104–110
divisions within tribunal
aggressive war, regarding, 127–128
Charter, regarding authority of, 126–127
conspiracy, regarding, 126–127
customary international law, regarding authority of, 126, 128
ex post facto laws, regarding, 126–127
overview, 126
war crimes, regarding, 129
general principles of law, legitimation through, 154
indictments in
aggressive war, for, 91–92, 93
crimes against humanity, for, 92–93
overview, 91
war crimes, for, 92
international organization, tribunal as, 402
judgments of
aggressive war, regarding, 115–116, 125
authority of tribunal, regarding, 111–113
conspiracy, regarding, 115–116
crimes against humanity, regarding, 119–124, 125
definition of crimes, regarding, 111–112, 113–114, 125
dual focus of, 112
ex post facto laws, regarding, 125
overview, 110–111
summary, 125–126
Tokyo Tribunal majority judgment compared, 142–143
war crimes, regarding, 117–119
jurisdiction of tribunal, French position, 83–84, 87
London Conference (*See* London Conference)
new jurisdiction, retroactive creation of, 319–320
non-retroactivity at, 9
nullum crimen
compliance with, 68

optional principle of law, as, 67–68
sovereignty, not limitation on, 67, 113, 125, 128–129
overview, 91, 155
precedential value of, 153
prescriptive force of, 152
prosecutorial arguments in
aggressive war, regarding, 98–99
ambiguity regarding legality, 94
Charter, regarding, 96–97
crimes against humanity, regarding, 95
general principles of law, regarding, 94–95
national criminal law, re-characterization of, 97–98
overview, 93–94
retroactive creation of court, as, 394
summary executions, proposals for, 73–76
Tokyo Tribunal compared, 139
treaties, legitimation through, 152–154
violation of legality in, 156
war crimes at, 343

Ocampo, Moreno, 337–338
Offense, change of
international courts, in, 41–42
national courts, in, 42
overview, 40–41
Optional principle of law
legality as, 38
nullum crimen as, 1–3
Overview, 4–6

Pakistan, retroactive penalties in, 280
Pal, Radhabinod, 1–2, 150–154
Pannenbecker, Otto, 100–102, 115–116
Papua New Guinea, retroactive penalties in, 278–279
Paris, Pact of. *See* Kellogg-Briand Pact
Parker, John J., 111, 126
Peace, crimes against.*See* Aggressive war
Permanent Court of International Justice, 62–64, 94–95, 362–363
Personality of punishment. *See* Collective punishment
Philippines, *ex post facto* laws in, 257, 259
Plutarch, 107
Policy-based law, 19
Portugal, non-retroactivity in, 258
Positivism, 47–48, 374
Post–World War II cases
British Military Courts, 134
collective punishment in, 136–138
Control Council Law No. 10, 130, 131–132, 133–134, 136–137, 309–310, 386–387
Control Council Law No. 11, 133–134
Einsatzgruppen case, 131–132
High Command case, 133
Justice case, 129–130
legality in, 129–130
moral wrongs, retroactive re-characterization of, 134–135
national criminal law
crimes against humanity, retroactive recharacterization as, 130–134
jurisdiction, retroactive expansion of, 135–136
non-criminal violations, retroactive re-characterization of, 134–135
Nuremberg Trial (*See* Nuremberg Trial)
Tokyo Tribunal (*See* Tokyo Tribunal)
United States Military Court, 131–132, 138
war crimes, retroactive re-characterization as crimes against humanity, 130–134
Potsdam Declaration, 139–141, 144–145
Principles of law
defined, 7
rules of law distinguished, 6, 8
Prisoners of war, 69–70, 207, 208–209
Process-based law, 19
Prospectivity
criminal law, importance to, 16–17
property law, in, 15–16
Protocol for the Pacific Settlement of International Disputes, 115
Prussian Military Code of 1845, 131–132
Punishment, what constitutes
independent legal determination requirement, 287
Islamic law, in, 289
mental health treatment, 287–288
overview, 287
retroactive non-punishment, dangers of, 289–290
security and education measures, 288
statutory law, based in, 288–289
supervision of parolees, 288
Purposes of criminalization
accountability, 30
compliance, 27–28
deterrence, 26–27
incapacitation, 28
overview, 26, 29–30

Purposes of criminalization (*cont.*)
reconciliation, 30–31
restorative justice, 30–31
retribution, 28–29
Purposes of legality
human rights
accessibility of law, 20–21
arbitrariness, protection against, 21, 22–23
innocence, protection of, 22
liberty, protection of, 21–22
notice requirement, 20, 22
overview, 20
legitimacy, 23–24
overview, 19–20
separation of powers
bills of attainder, prohibition against, 25
common law, in, 25
democracy, promotion of, 25
jurisdiction, limitation on, 26
legislative action requirement, 24–25
liberty, protection of, 25–26
overview, 24
states, informing of duties, 26

Qu'ran, 51–52, 53–54

Raeder, Erich, 110
Ramadan, Hisham M., 52–53
Rawls, John, 16
Readoption of legality, 265–271
Re-characterization of crimes, retroactive
abuse, danger of, 369
analogy and, 322
applicable international law, 367–368
atrocities, 323–324
direct application of international criminal law in national courts and, 369–370
end of, 406
ICC, in, 340, 369, 406
ICTR, in, 322, 324, 390
ICTY, in, 320–321, 324, 390
infrequency of, 367
law binding actors, 368
legality and, 322
moral wrongs, of, 134–135
national criminal law, of, 130–134, 322–323, 367–369, 389–390
new crimes, limitation to, 368–369
non-criminal violations, of, 134–135
overview, 367
penalties, 322–323
preclusion of, 369
representation jurisdiction and, 371–372
SCSL, in, 320–321, 324
sentencing considerations, 368
universal jurisdiction over international criminal law and, 370–371
war crimes, of, 123, 130–134, 367
weakness of requirements, 321–322
Reconciliation, legality and, 30–31
Reismann, W. Michael, 408
Representation jurisdiction
application of, 284–286
civil law nations, in, 283
double criminality requirement, 372
infrequency of, 286–287
motivations for, 283–284
nulla poena and, 286, 391
nullum crimen and, 286
overview, 41, 42, 282–283
retroactive re-characterization of crimes and, 371–372
Restorative justice, legality and, 30–31
Retribution
accountability and, 30
legality and, 28–29
Reydams, Luc, 283
Right not to be prosecuted, 376–378
Röling, Bernard Victor Aloysius, 3, 143–147, 151, 152–153
Rome Statute. *See* International Criminal Court
Roosevelt, Eleanor, 161, 162–163, 167, 170–171, 173, 180, 186–187, 191, 251–252, 275
Roosevelt, Franklin D., 73–75, 80–81
Rosenberg, Alfred, 105
Rudenko, Roman Andreevich, 96–97
Rule of law
arbitrariness, protection against, 17
collective punishment, rejection of, 17
connection with legality, 15
defenses and, 18
fairness, 17
generality of enactments, 17
individual freedom, protection of, 18–19
individuality of guilt, 17
joint criminal responsibility and, 17–18
minimum requirements for, 15
overview, 14–15
personality of punishment, 17
policy-based law and, 19
process-based law and, 19

Rules of law
defined, 6–7
first order rules, 7
principles of law distinguished, 6, 8
second order rules, 7
Russia
Czarist Russia, legality in, 64–65
readoption of legality in, 267–268, 401
Soviet Union (*See* Soviet Union)
Rwanda. *See* International Criminal Tribunal for Rwanda

Sauckel, Fritz, 102, 109
Saudi Arabia, Basic System of the Consultative Council, 247
Sauter, Fritz, 110
Schabas, William A., 314, 316, 317, 342–343
SCSL. *See* Special Court for Sierra Leone
Security Council. *See* United Nations
Seidl, Alfred, 105–106
Servatius, Robert, 102, 109
Sèvres, Treaty of, 72
Seychelles, non-retroactivity in, 262–263
Shawcross, Hartley, 94, 97–99, 122–123, 134–135
Siemers, Walter, 110
Sierra Leone. *See* Special Court for Sierra Leone
Singapore, retroactive penalties in, 280–281
Slovenia
international criminal law, incorporation of, 263
non-retroactivity in, 258
Soviet Union
Fundamental Principles of Criminal Legislation, 266–267
German prisoners of war, prosecution of, 69–70
legality in
acceptance of, 64
Marxism–Leninism and, 64–65, 66
political instrumentality, law as, 66, 80–81
rejection of, 45, 64–66, 240, 266–267
London Conference, at
aggressive war, position on, 79–80
punishment, position on, 79
non-retroactivity in, 199–200
Spain, non-retroactivity in, 200
Special Court for Sierra Leone (SCSL)
arbitrary detention and, 377–378
customary international law in, 306–307, 402
individual claims based on legality
overview, 311–312
recruitment of child soldiers, 313
subject matter jurisdiction, issue of, 312–313
international humanitarian law in, 308
international organization, as, 344–345
legality in, 304
new jurisdiction, retroactive creation of, 319–320
nullum crimen in, 355–356
overview, 303–304
retroactive creation of court, as, 317, 394
retroactive re-characterization of crimes, 320–321, 324
sentencing, 308
Special Tribunal for Lebanon, 304, 319–320, 324–325
Special tribunals, retroactive creation of, 291–293
Speer, Albert, 108–109
Sri Lanka, general principles of law in, 261–262
SS *(Schutzstaffeln)*,
Stahmer, Otto, 100–102, 103, 107–108
Stalin, Josef, 73, 80–81, 266–267
Statutes of limitations, 398
Statutory interpretation
common law compared, 35–36
foreseeability and, 360–362
impossibility of pure non-retroactivity resulting from (*See* Impossibility of pure non-retroactivity)
limits on legality from, 217–218
Statutory law. *See* Comparative law analysis of legality
Streicher, Julius, 119–121
Subsidiary universal jurisdiction. *See* Representation jurisdiction
Subversive acts, 279–281
Suharto, 270–271
Summary executions, 73–76

Taiwan, legality in, 55, 270
Taleban, 278
Taylor, Telford, 122, 126–127
Terrorism, 295–296
Thailand, readoption of legality in, 271
Third Reich. *See* Germany
Thoma, Alfred, 105
Togo, accomplices and conspiracy in, 295

Tokyo Tribunal
aggressive war and, 145–147, 152
customary international law, legitimation through, 152–153
death penalty at, 144, 147
ex post facto laws and, 145, 147–148
general principles of law, legitimation through, 154
IMTFE Charter, 139–141, 144–145, 147–150, 151, 152–153
Instrument of Surrender, 139–141
judges at, 141
legality and, 142–143
London Conference compared, 149
majority judgment, 142–143
new jurisdiction, retroactive creation of, 319–320
Nuremberg Trial compared, 139, 142–143
overview, 139, 155
precedential value of, 153
prescriptive force of, 152
retroactive creation of court, as, 394
separate opinions
crimes, retroactive creation of, 150–152
natural law not retroactive, 147–150
overview, 141, 143
political disposition, retroactivity permissible as alternative to, 144–147
retroactivity is permissible, 143–144
retroactivity may be permissible, 144
tribunal, retroactive creation of, 150–152
summary executions, proposals for, 75–76
treaties, legitimation through, 152–154
violation of legality in, 156
war crimes and, 151–152
Torture Convention, 264, 370
Traditional law, 259–260, 279
Trainin, A.N., 79–80
Transformation of legality since World War II, 301–302
Treaties. *See also specific treaty*
comparative law analysis, 233–235
customary international law, transformed into, 229
detention, challenging, 318
ICC, in, 340
ICTY and, 306
individual claims based on legality
ACHR, under, 226
African Charter of Human and Peoples' Rights, under, 227–228
ECHR, under, 226
ICCPR, under, 227, 228
legality in, 156, 157
limits on legality
analogy, from, 223
common law, from, 217–218, 220
statutory interpretation, from, 217–218
non-derogability of legality, 206–207
non-participation in
internal rules of non-retroactivity in non-participating nations, 225
island nations, 224
overview, 224
small nations, 224–225
nulla poena in, 378, 379
Nuremberg Trial, legitimation of, 152–154
regional treaties, 202–203
retroactive creation of crimes under, 401
state claims based on legality, 225–226, 228
ta'azir crimes, reservations in treaties for, 214–217
Tokyo Tribunal, legitimation of, 152–154
widespread acceptance of, 228–229, 230
Trust Territories, 304, 330–331
Turkey, atrocities in, 72

UDHR. *See* Universal Declaration of Human Rights
United Kingdom
British Military Courts, 134
German nationals, prosecution of, 69–70
Human Rights Act, 247
legality in, 49–50
London Conference, position on *ex post facto* laws, 86–87
marital rape in, 218–220, 361–362, 375–376
retroactive expansion of jurisdiction, 277–278
United Nations
Charter, 300–301, 316–317, 355
Commission on Human Rights
ICCPR, role in, 178, 179–180, 184, 186–188, 189–190, 192–193, 196–198
opinio juris and, 229
UDHR, role in, 161–163, 167–170, 171–172
customary international law, role in, 402
Division of Human Rights, 163–164
Documented Outline, 232, 235, 237, 239
Economic and Social Council (ECOSOC)
ICCPR, role in, 179–180, 187–188, 196–198
UDHR, role in, 161–163, 169, 172

Human Rights Council, 225–226
Security Council
authority of, 316–317
challenges to, 317
ICC, referrals to, 333, 334, 336, 337–338, 342–343
international organization, as, 347
retroactive non-punishment, 393
Trust Territories, 304, 330–331
War Crimes Commission, 72
War Crimes Commission (UNWCC), 70–71
Yearbook of Human Rights, 232, 237, 240, 289, 330–331
United States
Constitution, 47–48
ex post facto laws in, 256–257
German saboteurs, prosecution of, 69–70
international criminal law, incorporation of, 263–264
London Conference, position on aggressive war, 78–79
Military Court, 131–132, 138
national court jurisdiction, retroactive expansion of, 135–136
retroactive expansion of jurisdiction, 278
retroactive non-punishment, 393
Universal Declaration of Human Rights (UDHR)
adoption of, 174–175
ambiguous nature of, 229–230
Commission on Human Rights, role of, 161–163, 167–170, 171–172
comparative law analysis, 252–253, 260, 262
Convention on the Rights of the Child, incorporation by, 325–326
criminal law, limitation to, 173–174
definition of crimes in, 160–161, 172
Division of Human Rights, role of, 163–164
Drafting Committee, 162–164, 166–167, 169–171
ECOSOC, role of, 161–163, 169, 172
ICC compared, 331–332, 334–335
impact of, 159
legal force of, 158–159, 160
lex certa in, 274–275
non-retroactivity in, 164–169, 171, 172
nulla poena in, 158, 160, 166, 169–170, 171–173, 379–380
nullum crimen in, 158, 160, 169–171
Nuremberg Trial, impact of, 154–155, 167–170, 174
opinio juris and, 229
outlines, 163–165
provisions of, 159–160
sources of law, 173, 174
Tokyo Tribunal, impact of, 154–155, 167–170, 174
unrestricted documents, 161–162
Working Groups, 167
Universal jurisdiction over international criminal law, 370–371, 390
UNMIK. *See* Kosovo Special Tribunal
UNTAET. *See* East Timor Special Tribunal
Uruguay, political parties in, 260
USSR. *See* Soviet Union

Vatican, non-acceptance of legality in, 241–242, 250–251, 281
Venezuela, retroactive penalties in, 279
Versailles, Treaty of
aggressive war and, 128, 146
Austrian *Anschluss* and, 122
Danzig (Free City) under, 62–63
Kaiser William II, lack of prosecution, 58–59, 115, 128, 146
legality under
international criminal law, resistance to, 57–58
national criminal law, incorporation of, 56–57
new jurisdiction, necessity of, 58
overview, 56
tribunal, lack of, 58
prosecutions under, 58
war crimes and, 118
war, laws and customs of, 69
Vicarious jurisdiction. *See* Representation jurisdiction
Void for vagueness doctrine, 362–363
von Lüdinghausen, Otto Freiherr, 103, 106–107, 109–110
von Neurath, Constantin, 103, 106–107, 109–110
von Ribbentrop, Joachim, 108
von Schirach, Baldur, 110, 119–120, 121–122

War crimes
crimes against humanity and
distinguished, 121–122
retroactive re-characterization as, 123, 130–134, 367
customary international law, under, 118–119
Geneva Conventions, under, 77–78, 92, 343

War crimes (*cont.*)
ICC, in, 339, 343
Nuremberg Charter, under, 118–119
Nuremberg Trial
defense arguments, 104–110
divisions within tribunal regarding, 129
indictments, 92
judgments of, 117–119
penalties, 382–383, 385–388
retroactive expansion of jurisdiction over, 277
sources of, 41–42
Tokyo Tribunal and, 151–152
Versailles Treaty and, 118
Warnotte, Daniel, 289
Webb, William, 142, 144, 147, 151
William II (Kaiser), 58–59, 115, 128, 146
Wilson, Geoffrey, 171–172
Wilson, Woodrow, 161–162
Wright, Lord, 1–2

Yugoslavia. *See* International Criminal Tribunal for the Former Yugoslavia

Zambia
military forces, discipline of, 279
retroactive penalties in,
Zappalà, Salvatore, 383, 387, 388
Zimbabwe, discipline of military forces in, 279

Afterword and Update

No book on current law is ever really finished. Any practicing lawyer who uses this book knows that its citations must always be checked for postpublication developments.

Several developments concerning legality in national constitutional law have occurred since the completion of the main text of this book. These have occurred in both generally recognized states (Senegal and Myanmar) and entities seeking recognition as states (Abkhazia, Kosovo, and South Ossetia). They generally conform to trends noted in the main text. They are organized next according to the sections of Chapter 5 (Modern Comparative Law Development: National Provisions Concerning Legality) in which the developments would have been noted. These developments generally confirm the conclusions reached in Chapter 5 and provide further evidence for the overall conclusions of the book discussed in Chapter 7 (Legality in Customary International Law Today).

5.c.i. *Sources of the Requirement of Non-Retroactivity of Crimes and Punishments in National Law*

The trend toward including non-retroactivity in criminal law as a national constitutional protection continues in entities seeking to be recognized as states, but which have not yet gained universal recognition or United Nations membership – specifically Kosovo, South Ossetia, and Abkhazia.

The Constitution of Kosovo, with non-retroactivity of crimes and punishments and a *lex mitior* provision, noted as a proposal in the main text, took effect 15 June 2008. The President of Serbia has stated that Serbia "does not accept the proclamation of Kosovo's constitution as a legal fact."[1]

[1] Kosovo Const. art. 33, at www.kosovoconstitution.info (text as proposal in Appendix C); for entry into force and Serbia's objection, see AFP, *Newly Independent Kosovo's Constitution Enters into Force* (15 June 2008).

Both South Ossetia and Abkhazia have constitutions that endorse non-retroactivity of crimes and punishments. The South Ossetian Constitution, in an article whose other sections deal only with criminal law, states, "Laws establishing or increasing liability shall not be retroactive."[2] The Abkhazian Constitution appears to have a similar provision, though the available translation is questionable: "A law which establishes or aggravates the responsibility may not be retroactive."[3]

These two constitutions are not new, but recent events have emphasized the position of South Ossetia and Abkhazia as entities claiming statehood. Both of these entities have claimed independence from Georgia since shortly after the breakup of the Soviet Union. As a result of the long-standing conflict between Russia and Georgia over these areas, which erupted into war in August 2008, Russia recognized the independence of South Ossetia and Abkhazia. At this writing, it is uncertain whether these two entities will seek permanent independence or seek union with Russia. It is also uncertain what Georgia will do concerning its claim to sovereignty in these areas.

5.c.ii. *Non-Retroactivity in the Constitutional Texts: Act Focus and Law Focus*

There have been new constitutional texts involving non-retroactivity of substantive criminal law both in a generally recognized state, Myanmar (Burma), and in other entities, Kosovo, South Ossetia, and Abkhazia. They follow three of the patterns discussed in the main text.

The first pattern focuses on whether the charged act was criminal or a given penalty applied to it at the time the act was committed, similar to the provisions of the International Covenant on Civil and Political Rights (ICCPR) and many national constitutions. Kosovo's constitutional non-retroactivity provisions prohibit punishing a given act if it was not a "penal

[2] South Ossetia Const. art. 38(4) (trans. Maryna O. Jackson), available in Russian through the Web site of the State Committee on Information and Press of the Republic of South Ossetia, cominf.org.

[3] Abkhazia Const. art. 25, as translated at http://en.wikisource.org/w/index.php?title=Constitution_of_Abkhazia&oldid=751353 (as of 3 September 2008). This immediately follows articles concerning rights in criminal cases. The translation cannot be considered definitive both because it is unidiomatic and because of the Wikisource policy of allowing almost anyone to change it. Nonetheless, I have no reason to believe that it is fundamentally misleading.

offense under law" at the time committed.[4] They also prohibit punishments that "exceed the penalty provided by law at the time the criminal act was committed.[5]

The second pattern prohibits the legislature from enacting retroactive criminal laws or retroactive laws generally. The constitutions of South Ossetia and Abkhazia, quoted as earlier, prohibit the retroactivity of criminal law,[6] rather than focus on the act.

The third pattern focuses on both the protection of the individual actor and the prohibition of legislative power, and those states that follow it generally have two non-retroactivity provisions in their constitutions. The development here comes from an extremely authoritarian state, Myanmar (Burma), which is not a party to the ICCPR. This emphasizes the universality of the non-retroactivity of crimes and punishments.

Myanmar held a constitutional referendum in May 2008 and declared a new constitution to be "ratified and promulgated."[7] I have not yet found a definitive postreferendum text of the new constitution or been able to obtain a translation. However, in 2007, Myanmar's National Convention adopted a document entitled "Fundamental Principles and Detailed General Principles," and published an English translation.[8] The 2008 Draft Constitution approved in the referendum was mostly based on this document.

"The Fundamental Principles and Detailed General Principles" contains two prohibitions of retroactivity in criminal law. One, in the chapter on state fundamental principles, prohibits retroactivity of laws directly.[9] Later, the

[4] Kosovo Const. art. 33(1).

[5] *Id.* art. 33(2).

[6] Abkhazia Const. art. 25; South Ossetia Const. art. 38(4).

[7] Myanmar State Peace and Development Council Announcement No. 7/2008 (29 May 2008), published in *The New Light of Myanmar*, Vol. 16, No. 42, p. 1 (30 May 2008) (daily English newspaper published by Myanmar Ministry of Information).

[8] Myanmar Fundamental Principles and Detailed General Principles (National Convention, adopted 3 September 2007, portions published on various dates from 27 August – 4 September 2007) in trans. in *The New Light of Myanmar*, Vol. 15, Nos. 134–41 (28 August – 4 September 2007), Burmese text and consolidation of the English text by Khin Kyaw Han available at www.burmalibrary.org/show.php?cat=1140&lo=d&sl=0 (along with Burmese text). Copies of the relevant issues of *The New Light of Myanmar* also available at www.burmalibrary.org (all Internet references as of 9 September 2008).

[9] Myanmar Fundamental Principles and Detailed General Principles, Chap. 1, art. 30(a) ("In connection with punishments, it is laid down that – (a) there is no right for any penal law to provide for retrospective effect; . . . ") (bold typeface and line break omitted), trans. in *The New Light of Myanmar*, Vol. 15, No. 134, pp. 4, 5 (28 August 2007).

chapter on fundamental rights and duties of citizens contains a provision that is focused on what is prohibited at the time of the act charged.[10] This double prohibition of retroactivity in criminal law follows the pattern of about a dozen states noted in the main text.

5.c.iii. *Crimes According to International Law and General Principles of Law in the Constitutional Non-Retroactivity Provisions and in National Judicial Practice*

Two newly effective constitutional provisions provide for prosecutions of core international crimes, so long as the acts were criminal under international law at the time committed. One is from a generally recognized state, Senegal, and the other from an entity recognized by many but not all states, Kosovo.

In July 2008, Senegal adopted a constitutional amendment allowing for prosecution of acts "which, when they were committed, were criminal according to the rules of international law relating to genocide, crimes against humanity and war crimes."[11]

Kosovo's new constitution permits prosecutions for "acts that at the time they were committed constituted genocide, war crimes or crimes against humanity according to international law."[12]

Neither of these texts refers specifically to crimes under "general principles of law." Neither, however, prohibits the use of already-existing general principles in the definition of these core international crimes.

[10] Myanmar Fundamental Principles and Detailed General Principles, Chap. 8, art. 32 ("No person shall be convicted of crime except for violation of a law in force at the time of the commission of the act charged as an offence. Moreover, he shall not be subject to a penalty greater than that is applicable."), trans. in *The New Light of Myanmar*, Vol. 15, No. 139, pp. 5, 16 (2 September 2007). This translation does not make the non-retroactivity of punishments crystal clear, though it is implied by the provision in Chap. 1, art. 30(a), as earlier.

[11] Senegal Const. art. 9 as amended through 7 August 2008, available at www.gouv.sn/texts/Constitution_sn.pdf (as of 10 September 2008), adds the following French text as the third unnumbered sentence of the following article: "Toutefois, les dispositions de l'alinéa précédent ne s'opposent pas à la poursuite, au jugement et à la condamnation de tout individu en raison d'actes ou omissions qui, au moment où ils ont été commis, étaient tenus pour criminels d'après les règles du droit international relatives aux faits de génocide, crimes contre l'humanité, crimes de guerre." The first two sentences appear in translation in Appendix C of the main text. The translation here is from Human Rights Watch, *Senegal: Government Amends Constitution to Pave Way for Hissène Habré Trial* (23 July 2008), at hrw.org/english/docs/2008/07/23/senega19438.htm.

[12] Kosovo Const. art. 33(1).

5.c.v.E. Retroactive Expansion of National Jurisdiction: Domestic Incorporation of Crimes under the Law of Another State or Crimes under International Law – A Current Version of Retroactive Re-Characterization?

In July 2008, Senegal joined the ranks of nations whose constitutions allow retrospective assertion of jurisdiction over acts "which, when they were committed, were criminal according to the rules of international law relating to genocide, crimes against humanity and war crimes."[13] This was done in order to allow for the trial of former Chadian dictator Hissène Habré, at the request of the African Union.[14] This appears to be consistent with the view that jurisdiction may be asserted retrospectively only over acts that were crimes under law applicable to the accused when they were committed.

10 September 2008

[13] Senegal Const. art. 9 (third unnumbered sentence), as amended.
[14] Human Rights Watch, *supra* note 11.

CAMBRIDGE STUDIES IN INTERNATIONAL AND COMPARATIVE LAW

Books in the series

International Courts and Environmental Protection
Tim Stephens

Legal Principles in WTO Dispute
Andrew D. Mitchell

War Crimes in Internal Armed Conflicts
Eve La Haye

Humanitarian Occupation
Gregory H . Fox

The International Law of Environmental Impact Assessment: Process, Substance and Integration
Neil Craik

The Law and Practice of International Territorial Administration: Versailles, Iraq and Beyond
Carsten Stahn

Cultural Products and the World Trade Organization
Tania Voon

United Nations Sanctions and the Rule of Law
Jeremy Farrall

National Law in WTO Law Effectiveness and Good Governance in the World Trading System
Sharif Bhuiyan

The Threat of Force in International Law
Nikolas Stürchler

Indigenous Rights and United Nations Standards
Alexandra Xanthaki

International Refugee Law and Socio-Economic Rights
Michelle Foster

The Protection of Cultural Property in Armed Conflict
Roger O'Keefe

Interpretation and Revision of International Boundary Decisions
Kaiyan Homi Kaikobad

Multinationals and Corporate Social Responsibility Limitations and Opportunities in International Law
Jennifer A. Zerk

Judiciaries within Europe: A Comparative Review
John Bell

Law in Times of Crisis Emergency Powers in Theory and Practice
Oren Gross and Fionnuala Ní Aoláin

Vessel-Source Marine Pollution: The Law and Politics of International Regulation
Alan Tan

Enforcing Obligations Erga Omnes in International Law
Christian J. Tams

Non-Governmental Organisations in International Law
Anna-Karin Lindblom

Democracy, Minorities and International Law
Steven Wheatley

Prosecuting International Crimes Selectivity and the International Law Regime
Robert Cryer

Compensation for Personal Injury in English, German and Italian Law: A Comparative Outline
Basil Markesinis, Michael Coester, Guido Alpa, Augustus Ullstein

Dispute Settlement in the UN Convention on the Law of the Sea
Natalie Klein

The International Protection of Internally Displaced Persons
Catherine Phuong

Imperialism, Sovereignty and the Making of International Law
Antony Anghie

Necessity, Proportionality and the Use of Force by States
Judith Gardam

International Legal Argument in the Permanent Court of International Justice: The Rise of the International Judiciary
Ole Spiermann

Great Powers and Outlaw States: Unequal Sovereigns in the International Legal Order
Gerry Simpson

Local Remedies in International Law
C. F. Amerasinghe

Reading Humanitarian Intervention Human Rights and the Use of Force in International Law
Anne Orford

Conflict of Norms in Public International Law: How WTO Law Relates to Other Rules of Law
Joost Pauwelyn

Transboundary Damage in International Law
Hanqin Xue

European Criminal Procedures
Edited by Mireille Delmas-Marty and John Spencer

The Accountability of Armed Opposition Groups in International Law
Liesbeth Zegveld

Sharing Transboundary Resources: International Law and Optimal Resource Use
Eyal Benvenisti

International Human Rights and Humanitarian Law
René Provost

Remedies Against International Organisations
Karel Wellens

Diversity and Self-Determination in International Law
Karen Knop

The Law of Internal Armed Conflict
Lindsay Moir

International Commercial Arbitration and African States Practice, Participation and Institutional Development
Amazu A. Asouzu

The Enforceability of Promises in European Contract Law
James Gordley

International Law in Antiquity
David J. Bederman

Money Laundering: A New International Law Enforcement Model
Guy Stessens

Good Faith in European Contract Law
Reinhard Zimmermann and Simon Whittaker

On Civil Procedure
J. A. Jolowicz

Trusts: A Comparative Study
Maurizio Lupoi

The Right to Property in Commonwealth Constitutions
Tom Allen

International Organizations Before National Courts
August Reinisch

The Changing International Law of High Seas Fisheries
Francisco Orrego Vicuña

Trade and the Environment: A Comparative Study of EC and US Law
Damien Geradin

Unjust Enrichment A Study of Private Law and Public Values
Hanoch Dagan

Religious Liberty and International Law in Europe
Malcolm D. Evans

Ethics and Authority in International Law
Alfred P. Rubin

Sovereignty Over Natural Resources: Balancing Rights and Duties
Nico Schrijver

The Polar Regions and the Development of International Law
Donald R. Rothwell

Fragmentation and the International Relations of Micro-States
Self-Determination and Statehood
Jorri Duursma

Principles of the Institutional Law of International Organizations
C. F. Amerasinghe